"America's leading source of self-help legal information." ★★★★

—YAHOO!

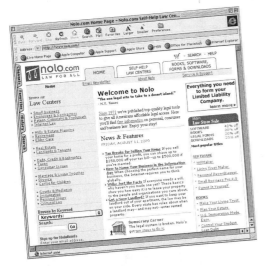

LEGAL INFORMATION ONLINE ANYTIME
24 hours a day

www.nolo.com

AT THE NOLO.COM SELF-HELP LAW CENTER, YOU'LL FIND

- **Nolo's comprehensive Legal Encyclopedia filled with plain-English information on a variety of legal topics**
- **Nolo's Law Dictionary—legal terms <u>without</u> the legalese**
- **Auntie Nolo—if you've got questions, Auntie's got answers**
- **The Law Store—over 200 self-help legal products including Downloadable Software, Books, Form Kits and eGuides**
- **Legal and product updates**
- **Frequently Asked Questions**
- **NoloBriefs, our free monthly email newsletter**
- **Legal Research Center, for access to state and federal statutes**
- **Our ever-popular lawyer jokes**

Quality LAW BOOKS & SOFTWARE FOR EVERYONE

Nolo's user-friendly products are consistently first-rate. Here's why:

- A dozen in-house legal editors, working with highly skilled authors, ensure that our products are accurate, up-to-date and easy to use

- We continually update every book and software program to keep up with changes in the law

- Our commitment to a more democratic legal system informs all of our work

- We appreciate & listen to your feedback. Please fill out and return the card at the back of this book.

OUR "NO-HASSLE" GUARANTEE

Return anything you buy directly from Nolo for any reason and we'll cheerfully refund your purchase price. No ifs, ands or buts.

Read This First

The information in this book is as up-to-date and accurate as we can make it. But it's important to realize that the law changes frequently, as do fees, forms, and other important legal details. If you handle your own legal matters, it's up to you to be sure that all information you use—including the information in this book—is accurate. Here are some suggestions to help you do this:

First, check the edition number on the book's spine to make sure you've got the most recent edition of this book. To learn whether a later edition is available, go to Nolo's online Law Store at www.nolo.com or call Nolo's Customer Service Department at 800-728-3555.

Next, because the law can change overnight, users of even a current edition need to be sure it's fully up-to-date. At www.nolo.com, we post notices of major legal and practical changes that affect a book's current edition only. To check for updates, go to the Law Store portion of Nolo's website and find the page devoted to the book (use the "A to Z Product List" and click on the book's title). If you see an "Updates" link on the left side of the page, click on it. If you don't see a link, there are no posted changes—but check back regularly.

Finally, while Nolo believes that accurate and current legal information in its books can help you solve many of your legal problems on a cost-effective basis, this book is not intended to be a substitute for personalized advice from a knowledgeable lawyer. If you want the help of a trained professional, consult an attorney licensed to practice in your state.

11th edition

U.S. Immigration Made Easy

by Attorneys Laurence A. Canter & Martha S. Siegel

edited and updated by Attorney Ilona Bray

Eleventh edition	APRIL 2004
Editor	ILONA M. BRAY
Illustrations	LINDA ALLISON
Book Design	TERRI HEARSH
Cover Design	TONI IHARA
Index	ELLEN DAVENPORT
Production	MARGARET LIVINGSTON
Proofreading	MU'AFRIDA BELL
Printing	CONSOLIDATED PRINTERS, INC.

International Standard Serial Number (ISSN) 1055-9647
ISBN 1-4133-0036-7

Quantity sales: For information on bulk purchases or corporate premium sales, please contact the Special Sales department. For academic sales or textbook adoptions, ask for Academic Sales, 800-955-4775. Nolo, 950 Parker St., Berkeley, CA, 94710.

Acknowledgments

This book represents a collaboration between the authors and the many people who have edited and updated it over the years that it has been in print. At Nolo, those who deserve particular thanks include Barbara Kate Repa, Robin Leonard, Spencer Sherman, and Ilona Bray for their eagle-eyed and thoughtful editing; and Stephanie Harolde, Jaleh Doane, Susan Putney, Lulu Cornell, and Toni Ihara for their excellent proofreading, layout, and design. In addition, Professor Richard A. Boswell, of the University of California's Hastings College of the Law, took on the challenge of incorporating major changes in the immigration laws into the Seventh Edition. Subsequent editions have been updated by Ilona Bray.

Table of Contents

16 Temporary Specialty Workers: H-1B Visas

17 Temporary Nonagricultural Workers: H-2B Visas

18 Temporary Trainees: H-3 Visas

19 Intracompany Transfers: L-1 Visas

How to Use This Book

U.S. Immigration Made Easy was developed to give you the help you need to live legally in the United States, either on a temporary or permanent basis. For example, you may be interested in working, joining family, studying, or retiring in the U.S. We will tell you about the different kinds of visas available and the qualifications you need to get each one. Then we will show you, step by step, how to prepare the paperwork for the visa you want. We will tell you how long it takes to get each visa and how to avoid common pitfalls. You will find out whether or not you have a realistic chance of immigrating to the U.S. We have also included some brief material on U.S. taxes for those with business interests or people who simply want to know the tax consequences of life in the U.S.

WATCH FOR CHANGES IN THE LAW

These days, Congress and the immigration authorities change the immigration laws and procedures so regularly that it hardly makes the news. But one of these changes could have a major impact on your life. You can rely on this book up to the date it was published. After that, check the Legal Updates section of Nolo's website at www.nolo.com. We'll do our best to let you know what's new. Also, check the U.S. Citizenship and Immigration Services (USCIS) website at www.uscis .gov and the U.S. State Department website at www .state.gov. *Fee changes are almost certain!*

A. Basic Strategy for Immigration

Not everyone can immigrate to the U.S., but you can improve your chances by knowing the inside information on immigration. U.S. immigration laws may not be what the immigrant expects. Often these laws were written as much to keep immigrants out as they were to provide orderly procedures for letting them in. Immigration policies are not always logical or sensible. Many people from other nations who wish to live in the U.S. and could make wonderful contributions to the country are the very people kept from getting green cards or visas.

More and more, U.S. immigration law is a controversial issue among Americans. Everyone agrees there must be some limits. No one agrees on how these limits should work. If you don't like the law the way it is, don't give up! Sooner or later, it may change.

⚠️ Information given out at U.S. consulates, embassies, and immigration offices isn't always complete or correct. Most immigration officials lack the time to fully review your case or share all their knowledge with you.

For the immigrant, a greater danger than having too little information is having information that is wrong. Common sources of confusion are well-meaning friends and relatives as well as general rumormongers, all of whom are only too happy to share their ignorance with you. Stories from those who claim to have gotten green cards or visas by ignoring the rules or using special influence are by far the most creative. Enjoy them for their entertainment value, but don't harm yourself by believing them.

In this book we have made the rules and procedures of immigration as clear and understandable as possible, but we have not stopped with the laws themselves. You must also know how things really work—often a matter of unannounced and frequently changing government policy.

1. Can You Cheat the System?

We've already mentioned briefly the stories in circulation about how some people have found shortcuts through the system, legal or illegal. Let's get it straight right now. If you know someone who insists he or she walked into a consulate and got a green card immediately just for the asking, or successfully bribed a U.S. immigration official, most likely that person has an overactive imagination. The hard fact is that shortcutting the American immigration system is close to impossible. And, if you're caught offering or giving a bribe, your chances of immigrating to the U.S. legally drop to zero. Any U.S. government employee found guilty of selling visas will be severely punished.

Another plan popular among those determined to bypass the system is asking for help from U.S. congressional representatives or senators. The offices of these officials are besieged with such requests. While a U.S. politician will always treat you courteously and may write a letter asking for a status report on your case, one thing he or she will not do is fight with the immigration services to get you a green card or visa. No matter how strong your political influence, no government official can get immigration benefits for someone who is not truly qualified, nor will he or she try to do so.

2. What Is the Best Way Through the System?

To prepare an immigration case, you must fit yourself into an eligibility category, gather evidence, make arguments, and complete paperwork. The finished product is then considered by a U.S. government officer. The officer looks at the case and makes a decision based on his or her knowledge of the law and evaluation of the evidence. Each case is different.

It helps to know who you'll be working with. The main government offices with which you'll be working include U.S. consulates, whose offices are overseas, and U.S. Citizenship and Immigration Services (USCIS), whose offices are primarily in the United States. If you come through a U.S. border, you'll also meet an officer of Customs and Border Protection (CBP). The consulates answer to the U.S. State Department; USCIS and CBP answer to the Department of Homeland Security (DHS). (Note: You may remember that the main U.S. agency to contact in the past was the Immigration and Naturalization Service, or INS. This was broken up into separate agencies under DHS in 2003.)

One of the most important concerns in successfully getting a U.S. visa or green card is simply to avoid potential legal or practical problems. For example, the immigration laws are written to punish people who have committed past immigration violations, and to keep out people considered undesirable—perhaps because they have criminal records, carry contagious diseases, will need government financial assistance, or might be a security threat to the United States. It's better to know about these issues in advance and be prepared to deal with them than to turn in an application that possibly gets you into bigger trouble than you were before.

You're also likely to face delays and confusion because of the size of the immigration bureaucracy—misplaced or lost files are not uncommon. That's why it's important to closely follow the advice in this book about not turning in original documents except when absolutely necessary, sending applications in as soon as possible before the time you'll need a decision, and making photocopies of everything you send.

3. Choosing a Category

Let's give away one of the biggest secrets of being successful at U.S. immigration right at the beginning. It's picking the visa category that's best for you. The cornerstone of the U.S. immigration system is a rigid group of visa categories. Each category carries with it a very specific list of requirements. Your job is to prove that you fit into one of the categories. Much of this book is devoted to describing the categories and explaining how you can prove to the U.S. government that you do in fact fit into one of them.

There are no exceptions to the rule that you must meet the qualifications of some immigration category. If you cannot do so, you cannot get a green card or visa. You may find as you read on that you already fit into one or more qualifying categories. If not, you have the option of trying to change your situation so you do. It is you and not the categories that will have to change. Keep in mind, however, that it is often perfectly possible to arrange your life or your business so you become qualified for a category, even if you are not right now.

4. The Visa System

The visa system can be divided into two major classes. The first is the permanent class, officially called permanent residence. Those who become permanent residents of the U.S. are given Alien Registration Receipt Cards, more popularly known as green cards. Because the term *green card* is familiar to so many, we will use it here most of the time.

There are many ways to get a green card, but once you get one, all green cards are exactly alike. Each one carries the same privileges: namely, the right to work and live in the U.S. permanently. Green cards are available mostly to those who have immediate family members in the U.S. or job skills in demand by a U.S. employer. Also, a large number of green cards are given to educated professionals, investors, and refugees, or on a lottery basis to those with few qualifications other than luck.

The second broad class of visas is temporary. People wanting to enter the U.S. on a temporary basis receive what are known as nonimmigrant visas. Unlike green cards, nonimmigrant visas come in a variety of types with different privileges attached to each. Generally, they are issued for specific purposes, such as vacation, study, or employment.

Besides the fact that green cards are permanent while nonimmigrant visas are temporary, the most significant difference between the two is that the number of green cards issued each year is limited by a quota in most categories, while the number of nonimmigrant visas issued in most categories is unrestricted. Green cards in certain categories can be obtained relatively quickly. In other categories, it can still take months or years to get one because of the quotas, and there is no way to speed up the wait. Nonimmigrant visas, however, can be obtained more quickly, usually within days or weeks of when you apply.

5. Timing

How long it takes to get a green card or visa is often affected by quotas—in other words, annual limits on how many are available. Most categories of green cards and a few nonimmigrant visa categories are affected by them. Sometimes quotas move quickly and are not a problem. At other times, quotas can mean waits of many years.

Quotas can slow down the process of getting green cards and visas, but they are not the only source of immigration delays. U.S. consulates and immigration offices, which are typically understaffed, often get behind on paperwork. Human error, yours or theirs, can also cause processing to drag on. Sometimes files become lost in the system and that means taking time to straighten out the confusion. For all these reasons it is impossible to say exactly how long any one case will take.

In this book, we give our best estimates of how long it takes to get an approval in each green card and visa category. As you go through the application process, use our estimates as guidelines. Check up if something seems overdue, but don't be disappointed if you must wait.

B. How to Use *U.S. Immigration Made Easy*

To use this book effectively, there are six steps you must follow:
1. Learn the types of visas available.
2. Choose the one right for your needs.
3. Decide if you have the proper qualifications for the visa you want.
4. If you do not qualify for the visa you want, think about what changes you can make to become qualified.
5. If you still cannot qualify for your first choice, consider what other visas are available and see if you can qualify for one of them.
6. Apply for the visa you choose, using the directions in this book, but always double-checking with your local consulate or U.S. immigration office to see whether there have been changes or additions to the procedures, forms, or fees.

Everyone should read this chapter and the following:

Chapter 2	Chapter 4	Chapter 25
Chapter 3	Chapter 14	

These chapters give you a basic knowledge of immigration. Until you have read these chapters through, you will not be able to understand the rest of the book.

Next, you should read the top portion and first section only of each of the following chapters:

Chapter 5	Chapter 10	Chapter 16	Chapter 21
Chapter 6	Chapter 11	Chapter 17	Chapter 22
Chapter 7	Chapter 12	Chapter 18	Chapter 23
Chapter 8	Chapter 13	Chapter 19	Chapter 24
Chapter 9	Chapter 15	Chapter 20	Chapter 26

Always double check with USCIS or the State Department about required forms and documents. Within this book, we give you instructions regarding which application forms and documents to submit. However, the procedures change frequently, and many USCIS and consular offices have developed alternate or additional forms for local use. So before you submit any application, check with your local office to make sure you have up-to-date and complete information about their requirements.

Each of these chapters discusses a different green card or visa. The beginning of each chapter describes the privileges and limitations of the green card or visa category covered in that chapter. It also tells you how long it takes and who qualifies for the visa. We strongly recommend that you read the first section in all the chapters listed, even if you think you aren't particularly interested in some of the green cards or visas discussed. This is the only way you can discover the full range of options available to you.

You will probably find that not all the green cards or visas described in this book are right for you. When you select the one you want and for which you are qualified, you need not read about the others. Each chapter devoted to a particular green card or visa is virtually complete within itself. You may notice that certain pieces of information are repeated over and over in each chapter. This has been done so you will not have to flip back and forth between pages.

Unfortunately, you may find you do not meet all the requirements for the green card or visa of your choice. If that is the case, keep in mind the possibility of changing conditions in your life so you can fulfill the requirements. For example, making an investment in or opening a U.S. business, increasing your education, or finding a job with a U.S. employer may help you qualify for certain types of immigration benefits.

C. Preliminary Strategies for Green Card or Visa Selection

Below are some examples of how certain groups might approach green card and visa selection. Perhaps you fall into one of these groups. If not, we strongly urge you to read about them anyway. Here you will get your first taste of the kinds of options available in the U.S. immigration system.

1. Visitors

If a short trip to the U.S. is all you need, you can act as a tourist and transact temporary business for a foreign employer on a visitor's visa (B-1/B-2). However, you cannot accept work. When someone enters the U.S. with a visitor's visa, he or she is normally given permission to stay for six months (indicated on Form I-94, which is a card tucked into your passport on entry to the U.S.). (Although USCIS has been threatening to take away this automatic six-months' permission, it seems to have backed down.)

Technically, you may leave the U.S. at the end of your permitted stay, return the next day, and be readmitted. Alternatively, when one I-94 date is up, you can apply for an extension of stay without even leaving. If the extension is approved, you may get to remain for another six months.

Some people, believing that they have found a loophole in the system, try to live permanently in the U.S. by taking short trips out of the country and then returning again. Unfortunately, this tactic doesn't work for long. A condition of being admitted to the U.S. as a visitor is that you truly plan to leave at a specific point in time. You must also keep a home abroad to which you can return. If a government officer sees from the stamps in your passport or hears from your answers to questions at a border checkpoint that you are spending most of your time in the U.S., he or she will conclude that you are an unauthorized resident. Then you will be stopped from entering the country.

On the bright side, if you can be content with dividing your time between the U.S. and some other country, you can continue that lifestyle indefinitely with a visitor's visa. As a visitor, you can engage in many activities. We've already mentioned that you may travel around as a tourist. You may also transact business for a foreign employer, or purchase real estate and make other investments. (USCIS is aware that many people own or rent retirement homes in the U.S., and tries not to interfere with their enjoyment of these homes.) Finally, you may normally remain for at least six months, and it is all perfectly legal.

2. Retirees

Residents of many nations find the U.S. a desirable place to retire. Many Canadians and Europeans want to trade their colder homelands for the warm climates of America's southern states. Unfortunately, there is no category specifically designed for those who simply want to retire in the U.S. The only realistic ways to get a green card as a retiree are by qualifying as a relative of a U.S. citizen or green card holder, a special immigrant, or through one of the lottery programs now available.

If you're still able and willing to work, one alternative is to get a green card through employment. To do so, you must find a job in the U.S. (See Chapter 8.) Although you must actually begin working in the U.S. in the job for which you were issued the green card, you will not lose your card if you retire only a year or so later.

After thinking it over, many retirees decide they don't need or even want green cards to meet their desired goals. Retirees are allowed to spend a long time each year in the U.S. as visitors. Holders of B-2 visitors' visas, or any Canadian visitor without a visa, can be admitted for a period of up to six months. The only restriction on your activities during this time is that you may not work. If you wish to buy and live in a winter residence, you may do so. In fact, many Canadians prefer this arrangement because it allows them to spend the winter months in the U.S. without losing government health benefits at home.

3. Families

The greatest number of green cards, by far, have historically gone to people with sponsoring relatives already in the U.S. Under current law, you may get a green card if you have a husband, wife, parent, child (who is over 21 years old), brother, or sister who is a U.S. citizen. U.S. citizen stepparents and stepchildren, adopted children, half-brothers, and half-sisters also count as sponsoring relatives. In addition, you may get a green card if you have a husband, wife, or parent who is not a U.S. citizen but who holds a green card.

It is important to understand that your American relative must invite you to come to the U.S. and be willing to cooperate in the immigration process, including acting as your financial sponsor. Also realize that some of the family categories, especially brothers and sisters of U.S. citizens, have very long waits under the green card quota system—in some cases, for many years. If you fall into a family category where there is a long wait, you may want to look at the possibilities in employment categories, or even the lottery, because those methods can take less time. It is okay to submit green card petitions in more than one category.

4. Employees and Owners of Small Businesses

Small U.S. businesses frequently want to hire foreign workers. Even more often, small business owners want U.S. immigration benefits for themselves. A small business can sponsor a worker for a green card, but a small business owner normally cannot use his or her business to sponsor himself or herself. Therefore, the small business owner may have to choose between working for someone else who can act as a green card sponsor or being satisfied with one of the nonimmigrant visas.

Nonimmigrant categories available to employees of smaller companies are the B-1, E-1, E-2, H-1B, H-2B, and L-1 visas. E-1 and E-2 (treaty trader and investor) visas are especially useful for providing immigration benefits to owners as well as their employees. Although we list L-1 visas, called intracompany transfers, as a possibility for smaller businesses, they are usually difficult to get for companies having only a very few employees. L-1 is, however, another category where owners stand a good chance.

With any kind of work-related visa, the smaller company must be prepared to show the U.S. government that it is financially stable and able to pay foreign workers reasonable wages. This is most likely to be an issue with companies having fewer than 100 employees.

5. Employees and Owners of Large Businesses

It is very common for large U.S. businesses to hire foreign workers. In fact there is probably no large business in existence that does not do so. The U.S. immigration system offers large businesses several options for bringing foreign workers to the U.S. Either green cards or nonimmigrant visas can be used. If a company wishes to hire the foreign worker on a permanent basis, the worker should try for a green card. The biggest consideration for the company in picking the best category is time. If the worker has the equivalent of an advanced university degree, or at least a bachelor's degree and some experience, it may take several months to a year to get a green card. When the worker has no college degree and little experience, the wait will be a minimum of several years, up to ten years or more.

A large U.S. business can more quickly bring in foreign workers on a temporary basis for periods ranging from several days to several years by getting them nonimmigrant visas. B-1, E-1, E-2, H-1B, H-2B, L-1, O, P, and R visas all serve the employment needs of U.S. businesses. Frequently the workers can then go on to apply for green cards while working in the U.S.

In many cases, these same visas are available to the large business owner. Although none of them are strictly available for the self-employed, many legal entities, such as corporations, are treated as separate from the individual who owns the company. Generally, only owners of larger businesses can be sponsored for green cards and visas as employees of their own companies.

6. Investors

Since 1990, anyone who invests $1,000,000 ($500,000 in an economically depressed region) in a new U.S. business that hires at least ten full-time American employees can get a green card. Obviously, this category is not for everyone. If you are among the fortunate few who can meet the qualifications, take a close look at Chapter 10. If you are not so fortunate, consider the nonimmigrant investor visa described in Chapter 21. You'll find the money requirements in this category much more reasonable. Furthermore, nonimmigrant investor visas last many years.

7. Registered Nurses

If the U.S. government has a special interest in those who practice a certain occupation, there will be special rules or categories just for them. Nursing is an example of such an occupation. Nurses who qualify for special green cards do not have to go through an individual labor certification process. The details of qualifying for a special green card as a registered nurse are discussed in Chapter 8.

8. Employees of the Entertainment and Sports Industries

Entertainment and sports employees are very interested in U.S. visas and green cards. If you wonder why, think about how many popular Broadway plays have British casts and crews, or how many non-U.S.-born players participate in tennis tournaments in the U.S. There are some special rules controlling green cards for those who are well known in the entertainment and sports industries.

Nonimmigrant visa category O is available for better-known individual athletes and entertainers and their support personnel. P visas are given to performers who are part of a well-known or unique troupe or entourage. These visas can supposedly be obtained quickly, though increased security checks have added some kinks to the process. The visas last for the period of time needed to complete a season or tour. Less well-known entertainers and athletes get H-2B visas. H-2B visas can be issued for only one year at a time and take several months or more to get.

Other business-oriented nonimmigrant visas may offer some solutions to people in the entertainment or sports industries that the O and P visas do not. Depending on the legal structure of the businesses involved, L-1, E-1, and E-2 visas are worth exploring.

D. Sponsorship

By now, you have probably noticed that you often need the cooperation of another person such as an employer or relative in order to get green cards and some nonimmigrant visas. Just exactly how much can another person do to help you with immigration? A question often asked is, "Can I get a green card by finding a sponsor?" The answer is "yes and no." The word *sponsor* does not appear anywhere in the U.S. immigration laws. Years ago, a willing U.S. citizen could bring any foreigner into the U.S. simply by vouching for his or her character and guaranteeing financial support. Under present law, this type of sponsorship is no longer possible.

When relatives or employers participate in an immigration application, they are called not sponsors, but *petitioners*. You will learn later the details of the role of the petitioner in each green card and visa application.

E. Inadmissibility

A darker side to the immigration hopes of some people comes in the form of a problem called *inadmissibility* (formerly called excludability). Inadmissibility keeps certain otherwise qualified individuals from getting green cards. Generally, it affects those who have committed crimes or fraud, are mentally ill, have a communicable disease, or are likely to need government assistance. Inadmissibility is also a factor in cases of former U.S. citizens who either deserted the U.S. Army or evaded the military draft. We say more about inadmissibility in Chapter 25.

⚠ **There are severe penalties for persons who, when attempting to enter the U.S., use fraudulent documents, make misrepresentations, or don't have proper documentation.** Individuals who commit one of these acts can be quickly deported from the U.S. without the right to a hearing. If this happens, you will not be able to request entry

for five years. Accordingly, it is extremely important to understand the requirements of the visa classification you are requesting, and not make any misrepresentations of your intent or qualifications for a particular visa.

F. U.S. Citizenship

Becoming a U.S. citizen is the highest form of immigration benefit a foreign national can get. However, there is considerable confusion about how green cards compare to U.S. citizenship. Many people believe the only difference is that U.S. citizens can vote, while those who have green cards cannot. Of equal importance, however, is the fact that even if you live outside the U.S. indefinitely or commit a crime, you can keep your U.S. citizenship once you get it. Under the same circumstances, you might lose a green card.

In all but a very few special cases, no one can apply directly for U.S. citizenship. You must first get a green card and live in the U.S. as a permanent resident for a certain length of time. Then you must go through an application process called *naturalization*.

Occasionally, a person born or raised in another nation is already a U.S. citizen but doesn't know it. This happens most often when a foreign national has an American parent or grandparent who was taken from the U.S. at an early age. Usually, the parent or grandparent is also unaware of a claim to U.S. citizenship. This is especially true where the U.S. citizen is a grandparent who passes U.S. citizenship to a parent, who in turn passes it to the foreign national. The skipping of a generation adds to the confusion.

U.S. citizenship is not an easy thing to lose. If there is anyone in your direct line of ancestry who you think might ever have been a U.S. citizen, you should explore that possibility by reading Chapter 27.

G. Should You Use a Lawyer?

Many people can handle their own immigration work without professional help. We hope this book will get you the results you want without spending money on legal fees. However, each immigration case is different. Some cases are more legally complex than others. Sometimes human error or plain bad luck make things go wrong. If things get really tough, it is often foolish as well as dangerous to go it alone.

If you do feel a need for help, we can't emphasize too strongly that you should check thoroughly the credentials of the person you hire. How many years has the attorney been practicing immigration law? How many immigration cases has he or she handled? Does the attorney practice in many areas of law, or is the practice devoted exclusively to immigration work? Get some answers to these questions before choosing the person in whose hands you will place your future in America.

If you are successful in reaching your immigration goals, it means that we have succeeded, too. Over the years, we have had the great pleasure of seeing thousands who have been able to begin new careers and new lives in the U.S. We hope you will soon be joining them.

ICONS USED IN THIS BOOK

 The caution icon warns you of potential problems.

 This icon indicates that the information is a useful tip.

 This icon refers you to helpful books or other resources.

 This icon indicates when you should consider consulting an attorney or other expert.

 This icon refers you to a further discussion of the topic somewhere else in the book.

Basic Immigration Terms

Knowing the terms defined below is essential to understanding the other chapters of this book. These terms are the foundation of immigration procedure.

Accompanying relative. In most cases, a person who is eligible to receive some type of visa or green card can also obtain green cards or similar visas for immediate members of his or her family. These family members are called accompanying relatives, and may include only your spouse and unmarried children under the age of 21 who will be traveling with you.

Alien Registration Receipt Card. An Alien Registration Receipt Card is the official name used in immigration law for a green card.

Applicant. When you make a formal request for a green card or nonimmigrant visa, you are an applicant. In cases where the green card or visa requires the filing of a petition, you may not become an applicant until your petitioner has successfully completed a petition on your behalf.

Application. An application is a formal request for a green card or visa. In the case of most green cards and many nonimmigrant visas, an application cannot be made until you obtain proof that you are qualified. This is done by submitting a petition or, most commonly, by having a family member or employer submit one for you. In a few cases, a petition is not required and only an application is required to get immigration privileges.

Asylum status. See **Refugee and political asylee.** Those seeking political asylum status are in a different situation from refugees, even though the basis for eligibility is very similar. Those applying for refugee status are outside the U.S., while potential political asylees must have already gotten to America. They apply for asylee status at USCIS Service Centers in the U.S.

Attestation. Attestations are sworn statements that employers must make to the U.S. Department of Labor before being able to bring foreign workers to the U.S. Attestations may include statements that the employer is trying to hire more Americans, or may simply be statements that foreign workers will be paid the same as U.S. workers. Attestations are required only for certain types of employment-based visas.

Beneficiary. If your relative or employer is filing a petition on your behalf, you are a beneficiary. Almost all green cards as well as certain types of nonimmigrant visas require petitioners, and whenever there is a petitioner there is also a beneficiary. The word "beneficiary" comes from the fact that you benefit from the petition by becoming qualified to apply for a green card or visa.

Border Patrol. The Border Patrol is the informal name for an agency called Customs and Border Protection (CBP), which, like USCIS, is part of the Department of Homeland Security (DHS). Its primary functions include keeping the borders secure from illegal crossers, and meeting legal entrants at airports and border posts to check their visas and decide whether they should be allowed into the United States.

Customs and Border Protection (CBP). See Border Patrol, above.

Department of Homeland Security (DHS). A government agency created in 2003 to handle immigration and other security-related issues.

Department of Labor. The Department of Labor (DOL) is a U.S. government agency involved with many types of visas that are job related. It is the DOL that receives applications for Labor Certifications and decides whether or not there is a shortage of American citizens available to fill a particular position in a U.S. company.

Department of State. U.S. embassies and consulates are operated by the branch of the U.S. government called the Department of State (DOS). Generally, it is the DOS that determines who is entitled to a visa or green card when the application is filed outside the U.S. at a U.S. embassy or consulate, but it is USCIS, under the Department of Homeland Security, that regulates immigration processing inside the U.S.

Diversity visa (the Lottery). A green card lottery program is held for persons born in certain countries. Every year (more or less), the Department of State determines which countries have sent the fewest number of immigrants to the U.S., relative to the size of the country's population. A certain number of persons from those countries are then permitted to apply for green cards. People who receive this opportunity are selected at random from qualifying persons who register for that year's lottery. To qualify, you must meet certain minimum educational and other requirements.

Employee. Employee is a term used to describe a foreign person seeking U.S. immigration privileges through a job offer from a U.S. company. Both a green card in the preference categories and several nonimmigrant visas can be obtained if you have such a job offer.

Employer. An employer, for immigration purposes, is a U.S. company or individual who has made a firm job offer to a foreign person and is acting with that person in an attempt to acquire a preference category green card or nonimmigrant visa.

Green card. The well-known term *green card* is actually a popular name for an Alien Registration Receipt Card. We use the term green card throughout this book because it is familiar to most people. At one time, the card was actually green in color. It was changed to pink, but it is still called a green card the world over.

This plastic photo identification card is given to individuals who successfully become legal permanent residents of the U.S. It serves as a U.S. entry document in place of a visa, enabling permanent residents to return to the U.S. after temporary absences. The key characteristic of a green card is its permanence. Unless you abandon your U.S. residence or commit certain types of crimes or immigration violations, your green card can never be taken away. Possession of a green card also allows you to work in the U.S. legally.

You can apply for a green card while you are in the U.S. or while you are elsewhere, but you can actually receive the green card only inside American borders. If you apply for your green card outside the U.S., you will first be issued an immigrant visa. Only after you use the immigrant visa to enter the U.S. can you get a green card.

Those who hold green cards for a certain length of time may apply to become U.S. citizens. Green cards have an expiration date of ten years from issuance. This does not mean that the permanent resident status itself expires, only that a new, updated green card must be applied for.

I-94 card. The I-94 card is a small green or white card given to all nonimmigrants when they enter the U.S. The I-94 card serves as evidence that a nonimmigrant has entered the country legally. Before the I-94 card is handed out, it is stamped with a date indicating how long the nonimmigrant may stay for that particular trip. It is this date and not the expiration date of the visa that controls how long a nonimmigrant can remain in the U.S. A new I-94 card with a new date is issued each time the nonimmigrant legally enters the United States. Canadian visitors are not normally issued I-94 cards.

Immediate relative. If you are an immediate relative of a U.S. citizen, you are eligible to receive a green card. The number of immediate relatives who may receive green cards is not limited by a quota. The list of those who are considered immediate relatives is as follows:

- Spouses of U.S. citizens. This also includes widows and widowers who apply for green cards within two years of the U.S. citizen spouse's death.
- Unmarried people under the age of 21 who have at least one U.S. citizen parent.
- Parents of U.S. citizens, if the U.S. citizen child is over the age of 21.

Immigrant visa. If you are approved for a green card at a U.S. consulate or U.S. embassy, you will not receive your green card until after you enter the U.S. In order to enter the U.S., you must have a visa. Therefore, when you are granted the right to a green card, you are issued an immigrant visa. An immigrant visa enables you to enter the U.S., take up permanent residence, and receive a green card.

Immigration and Customs Enforcement (ICE). This agency of the Department of Homeland Security handles enforcement of the immigration laws within the U.S. borders.

Immigration and Naturalization Service. The Immigration and Naturalization Service (INS) is the name of the former U.S. government agency having primary responsibility for most immigration matters. However, in 2003, the INS was absorbed into the Department of Homeland Security, and its functions divided between U.S. Citizenship and Immigration Services (USCIS), Customs and Border Protection (CBP), and Immigration and Customs Enforcement (ICE).

Inadmissible. Potential immigrants who are disqualified from obtaining visas or green cards because they are judged by the U.S. government to be in some way undesirable are called *inadmissible* (formerly "excludable"). Green card holders who leave the United States can also be found inadmissible upon attempting to return. In general, most of these people are considered inadmissible because they have criminal records, have certain health problems, commit certain criminal acts, are thought to be subversives or terrorists, or are unable to support themselves financially. In some cases, there are legal ways to overcome inadmissibility.

Labor Certification. To get a green card through a job offer from a U.S. employer, you must first prove that there are no qualified U.S. workers available and willing to take the job. The U.S. agency to which you must prove this is the U.S. Department of Labor and the procedure for proving it is called *Labor Certification*. People who fall under the employment second and third preferences usually need Labor Certifications in order to get green cards.

National Visa Center. The National Visa Center (NVC), located in Portsmouth, New Hampshire, is run by a private company under contract with the DOS for the purpose of carrying out certain immigration functions. The NVC receives approved green card petitions directly from USCIS or the DOS. In some cases, the NVC may hold onto these files for years, while the immigrant is on the waiting list for a visa. The NVC initiates the final green card application process by sending forms and instructions to the applicant and forwarding the file to the appropriate U.S. consulate abroad.

Naturalization. When a foreign person takes legal action to become a U.S. citizen, the process is called naturalization. Almost everyone who goes through naturalization must first have held a green card for several years before becoming eligible for U.S. citizenship. They must then submit an application and pass an exam. A naturalized U.S. citizen has virtually the same rights as a native-born American citizen.

Nonimmigrant. Nonimmigrants are those who come to the U.S. temporarily for some particular purpose but do not remain permanently. The main difference between a permanent resident who holds a green card and a nonimmigrant is that all nonimmigrants must intend to be in the U.S. only on a temporary basis. There are many types of nonimmigrants. Students, temporary workers, and visitors are some of the most common.

Nonimmigrant visa. Nonimmigrants enter the U.S. by obtaining nonimmigrant visas. Each nonimmigrant visa comes with a different set of privileges, such as the right to work or study. In addition to a descriptive name, each type of nonimmigrant visa is identified by a letter of the alphabet and a number. Student visas, for example, are F-1, and treaty investors are E-2. Nonimmigrant visas also vary according to how long they enable you to stay in the U.S. For example, on an investor visa, you can remain for many years, but on a visitor's visa, you can stay for only up to six months at a time.

Parole. The term "parole" has a special meaning in immigration law. It allows a person to enter the U.S. for humanitarian purposes, even when he or she does not meet the technical visa requirements. Those who are allowed to come to the U.S. without a visa in this manner are known as parolees. "Advance Parole" may be granted to a person who is already in the U.S., but needs to leave temporarily and return without a visa. This is most common when someone has a green card application in process and wants to leave the U.S. for a trip.

Permanent resident. A permanent resident is a non-U.S. citizen who has been given permission to live permanently in the U.S. If you acquire permanent residence, you will be issued a green card to prove it. The terms permanent resident and green card holder refer to exactly the same thing. Both words in the phrase permanent resident are important. As a permanent resident, you may travel as much as you like, but your place of residence must be the U.S., and you must keep that residence on a permanent basis.

Petition. A petition is a formal request that you be legally recognized as qualified for a green card or some types of nonimmigrant visas. Paper proof that you do indeed qualify must always be submitted with the petition.

Petitioner. The petitioner is a U.S. person or business who makes the formal request that you be legally recognized as qualified for a green card or nonimmigrant visa. The petitioner must be your U.S. citizen relative, green card holder relative, or U.S. employer. No one else may act as your petitioner. Almost all green card categories and some types of nonimmigrant visa categories require you to have a petitioner.

Preference categories. Certain groups of people who fall into categories known as *preferences* are only eligible for green cards as they become available under the annual quota. The preferences are broken into two broad groups: family preferences and employment preferences. The number of green cards available each year to the family preferences is around 480,000 and the number available in the employment preferences is 140,000. The categories are:

- **Family First Preference.** Unmarried children (including divorced), any age, of U.S. citizens.
- **Family Second Preference. 2A:** Spouses and unmarried children under 21 years, of green card holders; and **2B:** unmarried sons and daughters (over 21 years) of green card holders.
- **Family Third Preference.** Married children, any age, of U.S. citizens.
- **Family Fourth Preference.** Brothers and sisters of U.S. citizens where the U.S. citizen is at least 21 years old.
- **Employment First Preference.** Priority workers, including persons of extraordinary ability, outstanding professors and researchers, and multinational executives and managers.
- **Employment Second Preference.** Persons with advanced degrees and persons of exceptional ability, coming to the U.S. to accept jobs with U.S. employers for which U.S. workers are in short supply or where it would serve the national interest.
- **Employment Third Preference.** Skilled and unskilled workers coming to the U.S. to accept jobs with U.S. employers for which U.S. workers are in short supply.
- **Employment Fourth Preference.** Religious workers and various miscellaneous categories of workers and other individuals.
- **Employment Fifth Preference.** Individual investors willing to invest $1,000,000 in a U.S. business (or $500,000 if the business is in an economically depressed area).

Preference relatives. Preference relative is a general term for a foreign relative of a U.S. citizen or green card holder as defined in the preference categories listed above. Preference relatives and immediate relatives are the only foreign family members of U.S. citizens or green card holders who are eligible for green cards on the basis of their family relationships.

Priority Date. If you are applying for a green card in a preference category, your application is controlled by a quota. Since only a limited number of green cards are issued each year, you must wait your turn behind the others who have filed before you. The date on which you first entered the immigration application process is called the Priority Date. Your Priority Date marks your place in the waiting line. Each month the U.S. Department of State makes green cards available to all those who applied on or before a certain Priority Date. You can get a green card only when your date comes up on the DOS list.

Qualifying relative. Qualifying relative is a general term for either an immediate relative or a preference relative. A qualifying relative is any U.S. citizen or green card holder family member legally close enough to qualify an applicant for a green card or other immigrant benefit, such as a waiver.

Quota. Certain categories of qualified green card applicants are allowed into the U.S. in unlimited numbers. Certain other categories are restricted by a quota.

If there are more green card applicants than there are green cards allocated under the quota each year, a backlog is created and applicants must wait their turns. It is because of the quota that it can often take years to get a green card.

Refugee and political asylee. Refugees and political asylees are persons who have been allowed to live in the U.S. indefinitely to protect them from persecution in their home countries. Refugees get their status before coming to the U.S. Political asylees apply for their status after they arrive in the U.S. by some other means. Both may eventually get green cards.

Removal proceeding. Removal (formerly "deportation") proceedings are carried on before an immigration judge to decide whether or not an immigrant will be allowed to enter or remain in the country. While, generally speaking, a person cannot be expelled without first going through a removal hearing, someone arriving at the border or a port of entry can be forced to leave without a hearing or ever seeing a judge. If an immigrant is found removable, he or she can be "deported," or forced to leave the U.S.

Special immigrant. Laws are occasionally passed directing that green cards be given to special groups of people. When it comes to visa allocation, special immigrants are considered a subcategory of employment-based visas, and receive 7.1% of the yearly allotment of 140,000 such visas. Common categories of special immigrants are workers for recognized religions, former U.S. government workers, and foreign doctors who have been practicing medicine in the U.S. for many years.

Special U.S. entry documents for refugees. Political refugees are granted refugee status when they apply for American protection while still outside the U.S. Applications for refugee status must be filed at one of the few USCIS offices located overseas. On approval, the refugee receives a special U.S. entry document, but no visa. This document is good for only one entry. After spending one year in the U.S., refugees can apply for green cards. Although refugees have the privilege of living and working anywhere in the U.S., they must apply for what's called a refugee travel document if they want to leave the country and return again before getting a green card.

Sponsor. The word sponsor does not appear anywhere in the U.S. immigration laws. When people refer to a sponsor for immigration purposes, they usually mean a **Petitioner**. See definition above.

Status. Status is the name for the group of privileges you are given when you receive immigration benefits, either as a permanent resident or a nonimmigrant. Nonimmigrant statuses have exactly the same names and privileges as the corresponding nonimmigrant visas. A green card holder has the status of permanent resident. Visas and green cards are things you can see. A status is not.

While you must be given a status with each visa, the reverse is not true. If you want nonimmigrant privileges, you can get a nonimmigrant status by applying in the U.S. and you can keep that status for as long as you remain on U.S. soil. You will not, however, get a physical visa at the same time because visas can be issued only outside the U.S. The theory is that since a visa is an entry document, persons already in America do not need them. This is important for nonimmigrants, because they can travel in and out of the U.S. on visas, but not with a status. Those with permanent resident status do not have the same problem, of course, because they have green cards.

If you have nonimmigrant status, but not a corresponding visa, you will lose it as soon as you leave the U.S. You can regain your privileges only by getting a proper nonimmigrant visa from a U.S. consulate before returning.

Temporary Protected Status (TPS). A temporary status for persons already in the U.S. who came from certain countries experiencing conditions of war or natural disasters. Temporary Protected Status (TPS) allows someone to live and work in the U.S. for a specific time period, but it does not lead to a green card. At present, TPS is available to persons from Burundi, El Salvador, Honduras, Montserrat, Nicaragua, Sierra Leone, Somalia, and Sudan.

U.S. consulates. U.S. consulates are simply branch offices of U.S. embassies. They, too, are located all over the world. The U.S. government frequently operates both consulates and embassies in a single foreign country. Many consulates accept and process green card and visa applications.

U.S. embassies. U.S. embassies are agencies that represent the U.S. government in other countries. The U.S. has embassies located in many countries around the world. Most U.S. embassies accept and process green card and visa applications.

Visa. A visa is a stamp placed in your passport by a U.S. consulate outside of the U.S. All visas serve as U.S. entry documents. Visas can be designated as either immigrant or nonimmigrant. Immigrant visas are issued to those who will live in the U.S. permanently and get green cards. Everyone else gets nonimmigrant visas. Except for a few types of visa renewals, visas cannot be issued inside American borders, and so you must be outside the U.S. to get a visa.

Visa Waiver Program. Nationals from certain countries may come to the U.S. without a visa as tourists for 90 days. They can do so under what is known as the Visa Waiver Program. These countries currently include Andorra, Australia, Austria, Belgium, Brunei, Denmark, Finland, France, Germany, Iceland, Ireland, Italy, Japan, Liechtenstein, Luxembourg, Monaco, the Netherlands, New Zealand, Norway, Portugal, San Marino, Singapore, Slovenia, Spain, Sweden, Switzerland, and the United Kingdom. Persons coming to the U.S. on this program receive green-colored I-94 cards. They are not permitted to extend their stay or change their statuses, with very limited exceptions. The Visa Waiver Program is covered in more detail in Chapter 15. ■

Government Immigration Agencies: How They Work

Getting your green card or nonimmigrant visa may require dealing with between one and four different U.S. government agencies. They are:

- The U.S. Department of State (DOS), through U.S. embassies and U.S. consulates located around the world
- U.S. Citizenship and Immigration Services (USCIS) (formerly called the INS), an agency of the Department of Homeland Security (DHS)
- Customs and Border Protection (CBP), also under DHS, and
- The U.S. Department of Labor (DOL).

As you go on to our explanations of how to get your green card or nonimmigrant visa, we'll tell you exactly where to file the appropriate paperwork. In this chapter, however, we will give you a general idea of what to expect when you do file.

A. Department of State, U.S. Embassies, and U.S. Consulates

Embassies and consulates are part of the U.S. Department of State. Virtually every U.S. embassy and many U.S. consulates located in major cities worldwide have visa sections. However, not every consulate issues every type of visa. When you are ready to apply, you will have to locate the consulate nearest you that is authorized to issue the visa you want. Visa sections are subdivided into immigrant and nonimmigrant departments. Some consulates handle only one type or the other. To find an embassy or consulate near you, check the State Department's website at www.state.gov.

When you apply for a green card at a U.S. embassy or consulate, you must usually do so in the country where you live. Embassies and consulates located in nations other than your home country will normally refuse to accept your case. Occasionally, a consulate in a country other than your present homeland may be persuaded to process your application, but those are exceptions and require advance approval. Furthermore, to get the right to apply in some other country, you must show a compelling reason why you are unable to apply at home. Usually, you will be allowed to apply for a green card outside your home country only if the U.S. has no diplomatic relationship with the government of your homeland.

Unlike green cards, you may apply for nonimmigrant visas at certain U.S. embassies or consulates outside your home country. They must be authorized to issue the type of visa you seek, and accept nonimmigrant visa applications from third country nationals, that is, nationals of neither the U.S. nor the country where the consulate is located. You must be physically present within its geographic jurisdiction.

Furthermore, if you have been present in the U.S. unlawfully, in general you cannot apply as a third country national. Even if you overstayed your status in the U.S. by just one day, your visa will be automatically cancelled, and you must return to your home country and apply for the visa from that consulate. There is an exception. If you were admitted to the U.S. for the duration of your status (indicated by a "D/S" on your I-94 form) and you remained in the U.S. beyond the appropriate length of time, you may still be able to apply as a third country national. The State Department's current regulations imply that you will be barred from third country national processing only if USCIS (or the former INS) or an immigration judge has determined that you were unlawfully present.

If at all possible, it is thus usually best to apply in your country of residence, because your case will receive greatest consideration there.

Virtually all applications for green cards, as well as those for certain nonimmigrant visas, require a first step called the *petition*. Most petitions are filed at USCIS Service Centers (see Section B, below) in the U.S. and not at embassies or consulates. However, if the petitioner is a U.S. citizen living abroad, the petition may be filed at the U.S. embassy or consulate in his or her country of residence.

In addition to operating the green card and visa sections of U.S. embassies and consulates, the DOS is responsible for running the green card lottery that takes place each year. (See Chapter 9.)

NATIONAL VISA CENTER

The National Visa Center, or NVC, is run by a private company under contract to the DOS for the purpose of handling final green card applications. After USCIS approves a green card petition, the NVC sends the first set of forms and instructions to applicants and forwards their files to the appropriate U.S. consulates abroad.

B. U.S. Citizenship and Immigration Services

Most U.S. Citizenship and Immigration Services (USCIS) offices are located inside the U.S. USCIS is part of the U.S. Department of Justice. Various types of petitions and applications are filed with USCIS.

1. Local Offices

There are about 60 USCIS local offices placed all over the U.S., and several located within U.S. territories. USCIS local offices are classified as district or suboffices. Suboffices are primarily intake offices. They receive petitions and applications, but send the paperwork elsewhere for much of the actual processing. While interviews and some limited visa functions do take place at suboffices, the district offices perform more of the work on-site. For this reason, you can often get faster results at a district office. A complete list of USCIS district offices and suboffices is in Appendix I; also check their website at www.uscis.gov.

Filing procedures vary somewhat from one USCIS office to another. Most offices permit paperwork to be filed either by mail or in person, but some allow only one method or the other. If the type of benefit for which you are applying requires an interview, most offices will conduct the interview after the papers are processed. It is a good idea either to call or visit your nearest USCIS local office to find out about procedures at that particular location. If you try to call, be prepared for the fact that many USCIS local offices are poorly staffed and the telephones are always busy.

Most people who apply for green cards or visas want them as soon as possible. While nothing can be done to shorten waits due to quotas, the district offices and suboffices of the USCIS do have the power to speed up the paperwork on cases not involving quotas or where the Priority Date has already come up. This special attention is reserved for those who can show a genuine and pressing need for quick action, such as a medical emergency. Simple convenience of the applicant is not a good enough reason and, even when the need is truly urgent, requests for faster processing may be turned down. Still, such requests are given consideration and are often granted. Again, different offices have different policies. Call or visit your local USCIS office if you wish to ask whether expedited processing is available in your locale.

2. Regional Service Centers

Four special USCIS offices, known as regional service centers, have full responsibility for certain types of cases. Virtually all applications that do not automatically require interviews must be submitted by mail directly to a regional service center. It is anticipated that in the future, all immigration petitions and applications may initially be filed at the service centers. A complete list of the regional service centers is in Appendix I. More specific addresses, including the post office box numbers to which you must send particular types of applications, can be obtained by calling the main USCIS information line at 800-375-5283 or visiting the USCIS website at www.uscis.gov.

Dealing with the regional service centers may be frustrating because public telephone access is limited and the possibility of a one-on-one discussion with an immigration examiner is almost nonexistent. This makes it difficult to get information on pending cases. The regional service centers have an automated phone inquiry system whereby punching in your file number provides limited information. Of course, to use this system, you must first have your file number—which you won't have if the service center has failed to send you any response to your application. This inquiry service has recently become available online at http://egov.immigration.gov/graphics/cris/jsps/index.jsp.

3. Customs and Border Protection

If you obtain a visa from an overseas U.S. embassy or consulate, you're almost cleared for entry to the United States—but not quite. When you arrive at a U.S. border, airport, or seaport, there is one more government agency that has a say in whether you'll be allowed in—Customs and Border Protection, or CBP (a sister agency to USCIS. Formerly, border patrol functions were handled by the INS, but this was changed with the 2003 restructuring.)

A CBP officer will request all your visa paperwork, check to see that it's in order, and ask you questions to make sure that you didn't get the visa through fraud or by providing false information. The officer will also ask questions to make sure that you intend to use your visa for the proper purposes—for example, that you aren't using a tourist visa as a way to come to the U.S. to work or get married. If the officer finds a problem, you can be "summarily excluded," that is, forced to return home, and barred from returning for five years. (For more on summary exclusion, see Chapter 25, Section C.) If, on the other hand, everything is in order, your passport will be stamped for entry to the United States, and if you're a nonimmigrant, you'll be given Form I-94.

C. Department of Labor

If your visa or green card application is based on a job with a U.S. employer, certain parts of the paperwork may have to be filed with and ruled on by the U.S. Department of Labor (DOL). Have a look at their website, at www.workforcesecurity.doleta.gov. Applications filed with USCIS or a consulate for most green cards based on the employment-related preferences must be accompanied by an approved Labor Certification. The exceptions are first preference employment-sponsored green cards and Schedule A occupations, which do not require Labor Certifications. These are described in detail in Chapter 8. Other

applications for green cards through employment, and for H-2 nonimmigrant visas, must be accompanied by an approved Labor Certification. If you read Chapter 2, Basic Immigration Terms, you will remember that a Labor Certification is an official recognition by the DOL that no Americans are available and willing to take the U.S. job that has been offered to you. In certain types of cases, a Labor Certification must be obtained before a petition can be filed with USCIS.

In carrying out its duties to process Labor Certifications, the DOL makes use of the services of the labor departments operated by each U.S. state. State employment offices perform certain parts of the Labor Certification procedure. It is at a state employment office where an application for Labor Certification is first filed. In some states, this is done at the local state employment office nearest the U.S. employer's place of business. In others, the state is divided geographically into regions, and the application goes to the nearest regional office. Still other states have a central filing, usually with a state job service office in the capital city. To find out where your Labor Certification should be filed, contact the office of the state labor department, division of employment, training and administration, nearest your prospective employer.

Labor Certification applications can sometimes take as long as two years or more to complete. As with USCIS offices, waiting periods due to quotas cannot be speeded up, but delays due to paperwork backlogs can sometimes be overcome in an emergency. If you are applying for a nonimmigrant visa where quotas are not involved, and the need to get your visa quickly is truly urgent, or if your Priority Date for a green card has come up so that the quota is no longer a factor, you or your U.S. employer can explain the problem to the state labor department office and it may be willing to handle the case right away. Like USCIS, however, the DOL grants requests for expedited processing only in the most unusual and compelling circumstances. ■

Green Cards: An Overview

People all over the world have heard of green cards. It is the unofficial term for what is properly known as an Alien Registration Receipt Card. Years ago, these cards were green in color. Then, for a while they were red, white, and blue. Today they are pink.

A lot of people mistakenly believe that green cards are nothing more than work permits. While a green card does give you the right to work legally in the U.S. where and when you wish, that is just one of its features. Identifying the holder as a permanent resident of the U.S. is its main function.

When you have a green card, you are required to make the U.S. your permanent home. If you don't, you risk losing your card. This does not mean your ability to travel in and out of the U.S. is limited. Freedom to travel as you choose is an important benefit of a green card. However, no matter how much you travel, your permanent home must be in the U.S., or your card will be revoked. It's wise not to spend more than six months at a time outside the United States.

All green cards issued since 1989 carry expiration dates of ten years from the date of issue. This does not mean that the residency itself expires in ten years, just that the card must be replaced.

A. Categories of Green Card Applicants

There are nine categories of green card applicants, some of whom are immediately eligible for green cards, others of whom must wait until one is available.

1. Immediate Relatives

There is no quota limit on the number of green cards that can be issued to immigrants who are immediate relatives of U.S. citizens. Immediate relatives are defined as:

- spouses of U.S. citizens, including recent widows and widowers
- unmarried people under the age of 21 who have at least one U.S. citizen parent
- parents of U.S. citizens, if the U.S. citizen child is over the age of 21

- stepchildren and stepparents, if the marriage creating the stepparent/stepchild relationship took place before the child's 18th birthday, or
- parents and children related through adoption, if the adoption took place before the child reached the age of 16—all immigration rules governing natural parents and children apply to adoptive relatives but there are some additional procedures. (See Chapter 6.)

Immediate relatives (other than adopted relatives) are discussed in Chapter 5.

2. Preferences

Only a limited number of green cards are available to applicants in the "preference" categories. The preference categories cover only two general types of people: certain family members of U.S. citizens or permanent residents, and those with job skills wanted by U.S. employers, as outlined below.

a. Group I: Family Preference Green Cards

- **Family First Preference.** Unmarried people, any age, who have at least one U.S. citizen parent.
- **Family Second Preference. 2A:** Spouses of green card holders and unmarried children under 21.
  2B: unmarried sons and daughters (who are over 21) of green card holders.
- **Family Third Preference.** Married people, any age, who have at least one U.S. citizen parent.
- **Family Fourth Preference.** Sisters and brothers of U.S. citizens where the citizen is over 21 years old.

b. Group II: Employment Preference Based Green Cards

- **Employment First Preference.** Priority workers, including the following three groups:
  - persons of extraordinary ability in the arts, sciences, education, business, or athletics
  - outstanding professors and researchers, and
  - managers and executives of multinational companies.
- **Employment Second Preference.** Professionals with advanced degrees or exceptional ability.

- **Employment Third Preference.** Professionals and skilled or unskilled workers.
- **Employment Fourth Preference.** Religious workers, various miscellaneous categories of workers, and so-called "Special Immigrants."
- **Employment Fifth Preference.** Individual investors willing to invest $1,000,000 in a U.S. business (or $500,000 if the business is in an economically depressed area).

Preference green cards are discussed in Chapters 5 and 8.

3. How the Quota System Affects Your Wait for a Green Card

If a family member or employer petitions for you in a preference category, your wait could be several years long. Although we will give you an estimate of the likely wait in the chapter, this will be only an estimate. To get a better idea of your actual wait, you will need to learn to track it, month by month, based on the *Visa Bulletin* published by the U.S. State Department. This system can be confusing at first. You might want to read this explanation now, to get an idea of how it works, then refer back to it after you are deeper into the application process.

Every government fiscal year (which starts October 1), a fresh supply of "visa numbers" is made available. These visa numbers correspond to the numbers of people that Con-

gress has said can get green cards in the preference categories in a single year. (For purposes of this explanation, a visa means the same thing as green card.) There's just one problem. Thousands of people who applied in previous years are probably still waiting for their visa. So you won't be able to make use of this fresh crop of visas right away.

Instead, the State Department (DOS) has devised a system where the people who have been waiting longest have the first right to a visa. DOS keeps track of your place on the waiting list using the date that your family member or employer first submitted a "visa petition" indicating that they'd like to help you immigrate. That date is called your Priority Date.

You will need to know your Priority Date, because the whole system of figuring out where you are in your wait for a green card depends on it. The DOS's *Visa Bulletin* gives you one and only one clue about the length of your wait: a list of the Priority Dates of other people who are now getting visas and green cards. By comparing your Priority Date to theirs, you'll be able to track your progress.

Let's take a closer look at how this works, by examining the sample charts from the *Visa Bulletin*, below. (One chart is for family-based applicants, the other is for employment-based applicants.) This chart is from January 2004. To access a current *Visa Bulletin*, go to www.state.gov. Under "Travel and Living Abroad," click "more," then look for "Visa Bulletin" under the heading "Visas."

JANUARY 2004 PRIORITY DATES FOR FAMILY-BASED IMMIGRANT VISAS

	All Chargeability Areas Except Those Listed	India	Mexico	Philippines
Family				
1st	01AUG00	01AUG00	15OCT94	22DEC89
2A	01JAN99	01JAN99	01JUN96	01JAN99
2B	08MAY95	08MAY95	08DEC91	08MAY95
3rd	22AUG97	22AUG97	22NOV94	01SEP89
4th	22FEB92	22NOV90	22FEB92	22DEC81

PRIORITY DATES FOR EMPLOYMENT-BASED IMMIGRANT VISAS

	All Chargeability Areas Except Those Listed	China—Mainland-Born	India	Mexico	Philippines
Employment-Based					
1st	C	C	C	C	C
2nd	C	C	C	C	C
3rd	C	C	C	C	C
Other Workers	C	C	C	C	C
4th	C	C	C	C	C
Certain Religious Workers	C	C	C	C	C
5th	C	C	C	C	C
Targeted Employment Areas/Regional Centers	C	C	C	C	C

You can ask to have the *Visa Bulletin* sent to you monthly, by email. This is a great way to make sure you don't forget to check how your Priority Date is advancing. Complete instructions for how to subscribe to this service can be found toward the bottom of any *Visa Bulletin.*

You'll see on the chart that the preference categories are listed in the column on the left and the countries of origin are listed in the row across the top. The rest of the squares contain the "current" Priority Dates—also called the visa cutoff dates. Anyone whose date shows up on this chart has finished their wait and is eligible for a green card. Let's say you were the brother of a U.S. citizen and you're from the Philippines. Let's also imagine that your brother filed a petition for you to immigrate in January 2004. You would need to locate your Preference Category in the left column (4th Preference, on the bottom line), and your country on the top row, then find the square that corresponds to both—it's the square at the bottom right. The Priority Date listed in that square is 22DEC81 (December 22, 1981). That tells you that brothers of U.S. citizens who started this process on December 22, 1981, became eligible for green cards in the month this *Visa Bulletin* came out (January 2004). To estimate your wait, figure out how long they waited—about 22 years. That's how long you can expect to wait starting from your January 2004 Priority Date.

The waiting periods for people from the Philippines tend to be longer than from other countries, because there are so many applicants and a limit on how many can come from any one country. Most people will wait less time. For example, if you were from Brazil and were the spouse of a lawful permanent resident, you would look at the row for category "2A," under the first box saying "All Chargeability Areas Except Those Listed." The corresponding current Priority Date there is January 1, 1999—meaning you could expect a wait of about five years if you applied in 2004 (the date this *Visa Bulletin* was published).

These waits are frustrating, but there is truly nothing you can do to move them along (unless your family petitioner can become a U.S. citizen, which will often put you into a higher preference category or make you an immediate relative).

As you track these dates over the years, you'll notice they don't advance smoothly. Sometimes they get stuck on one date for months at a time. Other times your square will just say "U" for unavailable, meaning no one is eligible for a green card in that category until further notice. But if you're really lucky, you may see a "C," meaning that everyone who has a visa petition on file is immediately eligible for a green card, regardless of Priority Date. Most likely you will eventually see your own Priority Date (or a later date) on the *Visa Bulletin* chart. Then you'll know you're ready for the next step in obtaining your green card, as discussed in the relevant chapter of this book.

4. Diversity Visa: Green Card Lotteries

A certain number of green cards are offered each year to people from countries that in recent years have sent the fewest immigrants to the U.S. The purpose of this program is to ensure a varied ethnic mix among those who immigrate to America. Therefore, green cards in this category are said to be based on ethnic diversity. The method used for choosing people who can apply for these green cards is a random selection by computer, so the program is popularly known as the *green card lottery.* The future of these lotteries is uncertain. If you are interested, do not procrastinate—the opportunities may disappear. Green card lotteries are discussed in Chapter 9.

5. Investors

Ten thousand green cards are now available each year to people who make large business investments in the U.S. The investment must be in a new business that will hire at least ten full-time American workers. A minimum investment of $500,000 is required if the business is located in a rural or economically depressed area of the U.S. Otherwise, the minimum is $1 million. Green cards through investment are discussed in Chapter 10.

6. Special Immigrants

Occasionally, laws are passed making green cards available to people in special situations. Groups singled out for these green cards are not included in the preference system and are referred to as special immigrants. The current special immigrant categories include:

- ministers and other religious workers for legitimate religious organizations
- foreign medical graduates who have been in the U.S. since 1978
- foreign workers who were formerly longtime employees of the U.S. government or the American Institute in Taiwan
- retired officers or employees of certain international organizations who have lived in the U.S. for a certain time
- foreign workers who have been employees of the U.S. consulate in Hong Kong for at least three years
- foreign children who have been declared dependent in juvenile courts in the U.S.
- Panama Canal Treaty employees

• service people with 12 years' honorable service outside the United States

• NATO civilian employees, and

• broadcasters working for the International Broadcasting Board of Governors or Broadcasting Bureau.

Applying for special immigrant status is discussed in Chapter 11.

7. Refugees and Political Asylees

Every year, many people seek political asylum in America or try to get green cards as refugees. The two are often thought of as the same category, but there are some technical differences. A refugee receives permission to come to the U.S. in refugee status *before* actually arriving. Political asylum is granted only *after* someone has physically entered the U.S., usually either as a nonimmigrant or an undocumented alien, and then submitted an application.

The qualifications for refugee status and political asylum are similar. You must have either been persecuted or fear future persecution in your home country, on account of your race, religion, nationality, membership in a particular social group, or political opinion. If you are only fleeing poverty, you do not qualify in either category. Both refugees and political asylees can apply for green cards after one year. (See Chapter 12 for details.)

8. Temporary Protected Status

The U.S. Congress may decide to give citizens of certain countries temporary safe haven in the U.S. when conditions in their homeland become dangerous. This is called Temporary Protected Status (TPS). TPS is similar to political asylum except that it is always temporary, and will never turn directly into a green card. (See Chapter 12 for more details.)

9. Amnesty

Congress added an amnesty for Nicaraguan and Cuban nationals in a 1997 bill called the Nicaraguan Adjustment and Central American Relief Act (NACARA). Some provisions, discussed in Chapter 13, also benefit Salvadorans, Guatemalans, and Eastern Europeans.

The Immigration Reform and Control Act of 1986 (IRCA) gave amnesty to aliens who had been living in the U.S. illegally since January 1, 1982, by making green cards available to them. The deadline for filing temporary residency applications as amnesty candidates was May 4, 1988. However, certain people may still benefit from this law. Chapter 13 contains the details.

10. Special Agricultural Workers (SAWs)

The Immigration Reform and Control Act of 1986 also contained an amnesty green card opportunity for agricultural laborers who worked in the fields for at least 90 days between May 1, 1985, and May 1, 1986. The filing deadline for these applications was November 30, 1988. However, certain people may still benefit from this law. Once again, check with an immigration attorney if you think you are eligible in this category. Chapter 13 contains additional details.

11. Long-Term Residents and Other Special Cases

The law also allows certain people who have lived illegally in the U.S. for more than ten years to obtain permanent legal residence. They must show that their spouse or children—who must be U.S. citizens—would face "extraordinary and exceptionally unusual hardship" if the undocumented alien were forced to leave the country.

Anyone who believes that they meet this requirement should consult with a lawyer before going to the immigration service. They might be causing their own deportation by making themselves known to the authorities. Even if you are within this category, applying is difficult, because there is no regular process unless you are in deportation proceedings. For this reason, we do not cover the application procedures in this book.

Individual members of Congress have, on occasion, intervened for humanitarian reasons in extraordinary cases, helping an individual obtain permanent residence even if the law would not allow it. However, this is a last resort, and you should explore all other possible options first.

B. How Many Green Cards Are Available?

There are no limits on the number of green cards that can be issued to immediate relatives of U.S. citizens. For those who qualify in any other category, there are annual quotas. Both family and employment preference-based green cards are affected by quotas.

Green cards allocated annually to employment-based categories, including investors and Special Immigrants, number 140,000 worldwide. Approximately 480,000 green cards worldwide can be issued each year in the family categories.

Only 7% of all worldwide preference totals added together can be given to persons born in any one country. There are, therefore, two separate quotas: one for each country and one that is worldwide. This produces an odd result, because when you multiply the number of countries in the world by seven (the percentage allowed to each country) you get a much larger total than 100. What this means from a practical standpoint is that the 7% allotment to each country is an allowable maximum, not a guaranteed number. Applicants from a single country that has not used up its 7% green card allotment can still be prevented from getting green cards if the worldwide quota has been exhausted. Right now, there are in fact waiting periods in most preference categories, caused by the limits of the worldwide quota.

In addition to the fixed worldwide totals, 50,000 extra green cards are given each year through the ethnic diversity or lottery category. Qualifying countries and the number of green cards available to each are determined each year according to a formula. Chapter 9 gives the details of the lottery program.

C. How to Keep a Green Card Once You Get It

When you successfully complete an application for permanent residence at a U.S. consulate abroad, you do not get a green card immediately. First you are issued an immigrant visa. You must then use the immigrant visa within six months to enter the U.S. and claim your green card. If you do not act in time, the immigrant visa will expire and your right to a green card will be lost. (If you are already in the U.S. when you apply for a green card you will not get an immigrant visa, and so will not have to deal with this deadline.)

Once you receive a green card, there are several conditions required to keep it for life. You must not become removable or inadmissible. The most common way of doing so is to be convicted of a serious crime. Another way to become removable is to violate the immigration laws. For example, if you change your address, you're obligated to report this to USCIS within ten days of your move. In the past, failing to do this was almost never used as a ground to deport someone—but with increased security concerns, there have been reports of USCIS using this section to try to deport people about whom it had other, unproven suspicions.

NOTIFYING USCIS OF CHANGES OF ADDRESS

Use Form AR-11 to tell USCIS when you've moved. It's available in Appendix II to this book and on the USCIS website at www.uscis.gov. There is no filing fee. Instructions on where to send it are contained on the form itself.

Another requirement to keep your green card is that you not abandon the U.S. as your permanent residence. Residence, for immigration purposes, depends on your intent when you depart the country. When you leave, if you do not plan to make your home somewhere else, then legally you are still a U.S. resident. Problems come up, however, because the immigration authorities will try to judge what is in your mind by the way you act.

As a general rule, if you have a green card and leave the U.S. for more than one year, you may have a difficult time reentering the U.S. USCIS feels that an absence of longer than one year indicates a possible abandonment of U.S. residence. Even if you do return before one year is up, that may not be enough. It is best to come back within six months. That way, you will not be subject to a full-scale inspection, unless you have been convicted of a crime or done other serious acts. It is a common misconception that to keep your green card all you need to do is enter the U.S. at least once a year. The fact is that if you ever leave with the intention of making some other country your permanent home, you give up your U.S. residency when you go.

On the other hand, remaining outside the U.S. for more than one year does not mean you have automatically given up your green card. If your absence was intended from the start to be only temporary, you may still keep your permanent resident status. Staying away for more than one year does mean, however, that you may no longer use your green card as a U.S. entry document. Under these circumstances, you must either apply at a U.S. consulate for a special immigrant visa as a returning resident or you must plan ahead and get what is known as a *reentry permit.*

1. Reentry Permits

Reentry permits are for people who hold green cards and know in advance that they must be outside the U.S. for more than one year. USCIS can allow you to stay away for up to two years. You should apply for this privilege *before* leaving. If the application is approved, a reentry permit will be issued. The permit will help you prove that your absence from the U.S. is not an abandonment of residence. It also serves as an entry document when you are ready to return. Reentry permits cannot be renewed and can be applied for only inside the U.S. Therefore, if you want to stay away for more than two years, you must return briefly and apply for another reentry permit. You can apply for reentry permits by filling out Form I-131 and submitting it to the USCIS Nebraska Service Center.

If you stay outside the U.S. for more than one year and do not get a reentry permit before leaving, then in order to come back again, you must apply at a U.S. consulate abroad for a special immigrant visa as a returning resident. To get this visa you will have to convince the consular officer that your absence from the U.S. has been temporary and you never planned to abandon your U.S. residence. You will have to show evidence that you were kept away longer than one year due to unforeseen circumstances. Such evidence might be a letter from a doctor showing that you or a family member had a medical problem. If you do not have a very good reason for failing to return within one year, there is a strong chance you will lose your green card.

THE COMMUTER EXCEPTION

Green card holders who commute to work in the U.S. from Canada or Mexico on a daily or seasonal basis may keep their cards even while actually living outside the country. USCIS will grant you commuter status if, when you get a green card, you advise them of your intention to live in Canada or Mexico. If you live in the U.S. with a green card but later move to the other side of the border, you will be given commuter status when you notify USCIS of your new address.

2. Renewing Your Green Card

Your green card contains an expiration date, usually ten years from the date it was issued. That doesn't mean your permanent residency expires—you remain a permanent resident whether or not you renew the green card—but the law requires that you carry a valid green card at all times, so renewal is a good idea.

Use Form I-90 (available on the USCIS website (www.uscis.gov) or by calling 800-870-3676) to apply for renewal. You'll need to submit it to your local office. Contact that office, or check its home page via the USCIS website, for more information and procedures.

D. Green Cards and U.S. Citizenship

Green card holders can, after a certain time, apply for U.S. citizenship. Except in rare cases, no one can become a U.S. citizen without first receiving a green card. It is frequently said that green cards give all the benefits of U.S. citizenship except the rights to vote and hold public office. The differences between the two are actually greater. The most important distinction is that if you violate certain laws or abandon your U.S. residence, you can lose your green card. U.S. citizenship cannot be taken away, unless you acquired it fraudulently or voluntarily give it up.

E. Green Cards and U.S. Taxes

Once you get a green card, you automatically become a U.S. tax resident. U.S. tax residents must declare their entire incomes to the U.S. government, even if part or all of that income has been earned from investments or business activities carried on outside American borders. This does not necessarily mean that the U.S. government will tax all of your worldwide income. International treaties often regulate whether or not you must pay U.S. taxes on income earned elsewhere. However, green card holders do have to at least report all income they have earned worldwide.

You may believe that the number of days you spend in the U.S. each year has some effect on whether or not you are a U.S. tax resident. This is true for people who have nonimmigrant visas. It is not true for green card holders. If you have a green card, your worldwide income must be reported to the U.S. government, even if you remain outside the U.S. for an entire year.

As a green card holder, you must file U.S. tax return Form 1040 each year by April 15th. Failure to follow U.S. tax laws may be considered a crime. If you are found guilty of a tax crime, your green card can be revoked and you may be deported. To find out exactly how to follow U.S. tax laws, consult an accountant, a tax attorney, or the nearest office of the U.S. Internal Revenue Service (or see its website at www.irs.gov). ■

Getting a Green Card Through Relatives

Privileges

- You may live anywhere in the U.S. and stay as long as you want.

- You may work at any job, for any company, anywhere in the U.S., or you may choose not to work at all.

- You may travel in and out of the U.S. whenever you wish.

- You may apply to become a U.S. citizen after you have held your green card for a certain length of time.

- In some types of cases, your spouse and unmarried children under the age of 21 may also be eligible for green cards as accompanying relatives.

Limitations

- Your place of actual residence must be in the U.S. You cannot use a green card just for work and travel purposes. (The only exception to this is commuters, discussed in Chapter 4.)

- You must pay U.S. taxes on your worldwide income.

- You cannot remain outside the U.S. for more than one year at a time without special permission or you risk losing your green card. (It is recommended that you return within six months.)

- If you violate certain immigration or criminal laws, your green card can be taken away and you can be deported.

This chapter will explain who is eligible for a green card through their family members and how to apply for it.

A. Who Qualifies for a Green Card Through a Relative?

You qualify for a green card if you have a close family member who is a U.S. citizen or green card holder. You may qualify for a green card through relatives if you fall into one of the following categories:

- immediate relative of a U.S. citizen
- preference relative of a U.S. citizen or green card holder, or
- accompanying relative of someone in a preference category.

1. Immediate Relatives

These people qualify as immediate relatives:

- Spouses of U.S. citizens. This includes widows and widowers of U.S. citizens if they were married to the U.S. citizen for at least two years and are applying for a green card within two years of the U.S. citizen's death.

- Unmarried people under the age of 21 who have at least one U.S. citizen parent.
- Parents of U.S. citizens, if the U.S. citizen child is over the age of 21.

Immediate relatives may immigrate to the U.S. in unlimited numbers. They are not controlled by a quota.

Stepparents and stepchildren qualify as immediate relatives if the marriage creating the parent/child relationship took place before the child's 18th birthday. Parents and children related through adoption also qualify as immediate relatives, if the adoption took place before the child reached the age of 16. In addition, the adopted child must have been in the legal custody of the adoptive parent or parents for at least two years prior to filing the petition for a green card.

2. Preference Relatives

In Chapter 4, we listed a number of preference categories under which you can qualify for a green card. Four of them require family relationships with Americans. Here is a review of the qualifications needed for the four preferences based on relatives:

- **Family First Preference.** Unmarried people, any age, who have at least one U.S. citizen parent.

- **Family Second Preference.** 2A: Spouses and children under 21 years old, of green card holders; and **2B:** unmarried sons and daughters of green card holders who are at least 21 years old.
- **Family Third Preference.** Married people, any age, who have at least one U.S. citizen parent.
- **Family Fourth Preference.** Sisters and brothers of U.S. citizens, where the U.S. citizen is at least 21 years old.

MOVING BETWEEN VISA CATEGORIES

During the long wait for a green card, people's life circumstances change. This may mean they move from one preference category to another, or even lose eligibility for a green card altogether. Here's a summary of the changes that most commonly affect applicants:

- **Immediate relatives:** If the spouse of a U.S. citizen divorces before being approved for a green card, she loses her eligibility (except in cases where the U.S. citizen was abusive). If the child of a U.S. citizen marries, she drops from immediate relative to Family Third Preference. If the unmarried child of a U.S. citizen turns 21 after the visa petition is filed, she is protected, under the 2002 Child Status Protection Act (CSPA), from changing visa categories ("aging out")—she will remain an immediate relative.
- **Family First Preference:** If the child of a U.S. citizen gets married, she drops to Family Third Preference, but keeps the same Priority Date.
- **Family Second Preference:** If the child of a permanent resident marries, he completely loses his green card eligibility under this petition. If a child in category 2A turns 21 before her Priority Date is current, she drops into category 2B and faces a longer wait (but if she turns 21 after her Priority Date is current, she can retain 2A status by filing for a green card within one year, under the CSPA). In cases where the petitioning spouse or parent of a Second Preference beneficiary becomes a U.S. citizen, the immigrant spouse or children in category 2A become immediate relatives and the children in category 2B move up to Family First Preference, keeping the same Priority Date.
- **Family Third Preference:** If the child of a U.S. citizen divorces (for real reasons, not just to get a green card), he moves up to Family First Preference and retains the same Priority Date.

3. Accompanying Relatives

If you are getting a green card as a preference relative and you are married or have unmarried children below the age of 21, your spouse and children can get green cards as accompanying relatives by proving their family relationship to you and filling out some applications of their own. If, however, you qualify as an immediate relative, they *cannot.* Ordinarily, this doesn't cause problems—for example, a U.S. citizen petitioning his spouse can simply file separate visa petitions for each child so that they don't have to ride on their parent's visa application. This difference may create some real problems in cases involving parents immigrating through their adult children or stepparents and stepchildren who wish to immigrate as a family, however, as illustrated in the examples below. This is probably one of the most difficult areas in immigration to understand. It may take several readings before you grasp it completely. If you don't have adult children or stepchildren involved in your immigration plans, skip these examples.

> **EXAMPLE 1:** Suppose your child is over age 21 and is a U.S. citizen. You are applying for a green card as an immediate relative, with your U.S.-citizen child acting as petitioner. If you are married to someone other than your U.S.-citizen child's other parent, your spouse can't get a green card automatically as an accompanying relative because *accompanying relatives are included only with preference relatives, not immediate relatives.* Any children you may have, even if they are minors, cannot be accompanying relatives either, for the same reason.
>
> If your U.S.-citizen child is the offspring of your spouse as well, your child may file petitions for each parent at the same time, but the two filings will be completely separate. The marriage between you and your spouse will not be relevant when the USCIS considers your cases.
>
> Likewise, your U.S-citizen child may also sponsor his or her brothers and sisters under the Family Fourth Preference, but again, the fact that you qualify for a green card will not help your children. There is a long wait under the quota for Family Fourth Preference applicants, while there is no wait at all for immediate relatives. In this manner, members of the same family may be forced to immigrate on different time schedules.

> **EXAMPLE 2:** Again, suppose you are the parent of a U.S.-citizen child who is over age 21. You are applying for a green card as an immediate relative, with your U.S.-citizen child acting as petitioner. You are married, but your spouse is not the other parent of your U.S.-citizen child. Clearly, you have a problem. Your spouse can't get a green card automatically as an accompanying relative

because *accompanying relatives are included only with preference relatives, not immediate relatives.* Neither can your spouse be sponsored separately by your U.S.-citizen child, because your spouse is not the child's parent.

If your present marriage took place before your U.S. son or daughter reached the age of 18, your problem is solved, because your spouse is, according to immigration law, a stepparent. Likewise, if your spouse adopted your child before the child's 16th birthday, your spouse qualifies as an adopting parent. Stepparent and adopting parents can qualify as the immediate relatives of a U.S. citizen, and your child can petition for a stepparent or adopting parent just as if he or she were a natural parent.

What if your marriage took place after the petitioning child's 18th birthday? Now your spouse is not considered a stepparent for immigration purposes. You will have to wait until you get your own green card before anything can be done for your spouse. Once you get your own green card, you will be able to act as petitioner for your spouse, who will then qualify under the Family Second Preference as the relative of a green card holder. Unfortunately, this category is currently subject to a quota wait of several years, so your spouse will have to wait even longer before getting a green card.

The same sort of problem also comes up when the U.S.-citizen petitioner is the stepparent. The U.S. stepparent may petition for the alien husband or wife, but if the alien spouse has children by a previous marriage and those children were over the age of 18 when the present marriage took place, they will have no one to petition for them until their natural parent gets a green card and they qualify under the Family Second Preference.

EXAMPLE 3: Suppose you are unmarried and under age 21. Your parent is a U.S. citizen and you are applying for a green card with your parent acting as petitioner. You are in the unique situation of being able to choose between classifications. You qualify either as an immediate relative or in the Family First Preference category. It would seem logical for you to choose the immediate relative category because preference relatives are limited by quota while immediate relatives are not.

Let us further suppose that you have a child of your own. It now seems logical to place yourself in the preference rather than the immediate relative category because then your child could automatically be eligible for a green card as an accompanying relative. On the other hand, preference relatives, limited by quotas, usually wait longer for green cards than immediate relatives. At present, the Family First Preference has waiting lists of from 18 months to two years for most countries, and waiting periods of seven and more than 12 years, respec-

tively, for people born in Mexico and the Philippines. The First Preference waiting period moves abruptly back and forth, so you are well advised to consult the *Visa Bulletin* closely before making a choice between a preference category and immediate relative status.

4. Marriage to a U.S. Citizen

Almost everyone knows that there are immigration advantages to marrying a U.S. citizen. It is also no secret that many who are not fortunate enough to have U.S. citizen relatives try to acquire one through a marriage of convenience.

 For a fuller discussion of all aspects of applying for a green card through marriage to a U.S. citizen or permanent resident, see *Fiancé & Marriage Visas: A Couple's Guide to U.S. Immigration*, by Ilona Bray (Nolo).

SHAM MARRIAGES AND THE LAW

By law, green cards are not available to those people who marry only for immigration purposes. Such marriages, even though they may be legal in every other way, are regarded by immigration officials as shams. Of course, it is very difficult for U.S. government officers to tell which marriages are shams and which are not. However, USCIS and the Department of State assert that more than half of all the marriage applications they process are based on shams. It is not surprising, then, that they are especially careful about investigating marriage cases.

It is a criminal offense to file a green card application based on a sham marriage. If you attempt to qualify for a green card in this way, you will risk money penalties and a long jail sentence as well as deportation. In addition, you will almost certainly be permanently barred from getting a green card. The U.S. citizen also risks being charged a fine and/or going to jail.

a. Conditions on Green Cards Through Marriage

Because suspicions are so high regarding foreign nationals who marry U.S. citizens, there are some special restrictions on immigration benefits available to them. If you apply for a green card through marriage and the USCIS believes the marriage is valid, and you are otherwise eligible, you will get a green card. However, if you have been married for less than two years when your application is approved, the card will be issued only conditionally. These conditional green cards last for two years.

When that time is up, you must apply to the USCIS to have the condition removed and your green card made permanent. If you are still married, you and your U.S. spouse should file an application together. Then, if the USCIS continues to believe your marriage was for real, not just for immigration purposes, you will receive a permanent green card.

If, however, your marriage has ended or your U.S. spouse simply refuses to cooperate, you must file for removal of the condition yourself. Under these circumstances you can still keep your green card if you can show one of the following things:

- your spouse has died, but you entered into the marriage in good faith
- you are now divorced, but you originally entered into the marriage in good faith, or, in other words, your marriage was not a sham
- your eventual deportation will cause you extreme hardship, greater than that suffered by most people who are deported, or
- you were abused or subjected to extreme cruelty by your U.S. citizen or green card holder spouse.

If you have been married for close to two years, and have a green card marriage interview scheduled shortly before your anniversary, you may want to consider postponing the interview until afterward. If your interview is overseas, there is no need to delay it if you will reach your two-year anniversary before you actually use your visa to enter the United States. A green card approved after two years of marriage is permanent, with no condition attached.

Even when you stay married for two years or more and get your permanent green card, if you divorce at a later time, your immigration benefits are still restricted. Although you can keep the green card, should you remarry within five years and petition for your next husband or wife to get a green card, the USCIS will assume that your first marriage was one of convenience, unless and until you prove through convincing documentation that it was not. If you can make such a showing, you may sponsor your new spouse within five years of the first marriage. Otherwise you have to wait until the five years has passed.

b. Shaky Marriages Heading for Divorce

What happens if you got married in good faith, are still married, but the marriage is failing—perhaps divorce proceedings are now being considered or have already begun? The courts have long held that the present strength of a marriage is not a factor in judging eligibility for a green card. All that matters is the intent of the parties at the time of the marriage, and whether or not you are still legally married now. Therefore, if the marriage was legitimate from the beginning, and your American spouse is willing to file a petition, you can still get a green card. Just be absolutely certain that a divorce decree does not become final until the green card is issued. Remember, though, if you have been married for less than

two years, your green card will be issued only conditionally, subject to the rules discussed above. It is important that your divorce lawyer have a thorough understanding of these rules.

c. Battered Spouses and Children

If you are the battered or abused spouse or child of a U.S. citizen and he or she refuses to petition on your behalf, then you can petition for yourself. You are required to be physically inside the U.S. to take advantage of this opportunity.

You must also establish with credible evidence all of the following:

- that you were either battered or subjected to extreme cruelty
- that you have good moral character
- that you resided with the spouse or parent inside the U.S., and
- if you're a spouse, that the marriage was entered into in good faith—that is, not just to get a green card.

d. Marriage During Deportation Proceedings

If you marry a U.S. citizen or green card holder while you are in the middle of deportation proceedings, you may still apply for a green card. However, an even stricter standard will be applied when your motives for marriage are examined. You will be required to produce clear and convincing evidence that your marriage is not a sham. Expect a very detailed marriage interview. Hire an immigration attorney in such a situation.

e. Widows and Widowers

Special rules apply to foreign nationals who wish to get green cards as widows or widowers of U.S. citizens. They may do so, but only if they were married for at least two years before the U.S. spouse's death occurred. Then, the surviving foreign national may file his or her own petition (on Form I-360). This petition must be filed no more than two years after the death of the U.S. citizen. If the surviving foreign national remarries, then he or she loses the right to apply for a green card as a widow or widower. However, if the widow or widower remarries after getting a green card, it will not be taken away for that reason.

These rules apply only to the surviving spouses of U.S. citizens. Husbands and wives of green card holders may get green cards themselves only if the petitioner remains alive until the permanent residence is actually approved. In extraordinarily sympathetic circumstances, however, you can ask USCIS to grant the green card even though the petitioner died. You will probably need a lawyer's help for this.

3. Inadmissibility

If you have ever been arrested for a crime, were unlawfully in the U.S. for more than six months, lied on an immigration application, lied to an immigration officer, or you suffer certain physical or mental illnesses, among other circumstances, you may be inadmissible from receiving a green card unless you can qualify for what is known as a *Waiver of Inadmissibility*. (See Chapter 25, to find out exactly who is inadmissible and how or whether these obstacles can be overcome.)

B. Quota Restrictions

The preference relative categories (see Section A2) are limited by quotas. The immediate relative category (see Section A1) is not.

The estimated forecasts for the Preference Relative categories quotas as of January 2004 are:

- **Family First Preference**. Waiting periods of three years for natives of all countries except the Philippines and Mexico. Filipinos can expect waiting periods of at least 14 years. Mexicans can expect to wait at least nine years.
- **Family Second Preference**. Waiting periods of four years can be expected for natives of all countries except Mexico for family-based 2As (spouses and children of permanent residents). Mexican 2As can expect to wait seven years. The expected wait is nine years for all family-based 2Bs (unmarried sons and daughters over 21 years old) other than Mexicans, for whom the wait is at least 12 years.
- **Family Third Preference**. Waiting periods of at least six years can be expected for natives of all countries except Mexico, where the wait is about nine years and the Philippines, where the wait is at least 14 years.
- **Family Fourth Preference**. Natives of all countries may expect waiting periods of at least 11 years. Filipinos will have to wait at least 22 years.

The initial petitions are normally approved within six months to three years, depending on USCIS backlogs. Green card applications take several months to a year after the waiting period is over and the quota becomes current. See Chapter 4, Section A3, for information on how to track your wait for your quota category to become current.

C. Applying for a Green Card Through a Relative

Getting a green card through a relative is a two-step process. Certain parts of this process are technically the responsibility of your sponsoring relative. Other parts are meant to be done by you. As we give you step-by-step instructions for getting a green card, we will discuss each task according to who has the legal responsibility for carrying it out. However, even if the

law presumes your relative is performing a particular task, there is nothing to stop you from helping your relative with the paperwork. In fact, we recommend that you do so. For example, you can fill out forms intended to be completed by your relative and simply ask him or her to check them over, fill in whatever is left, and sign them.

1. Overview of Step One: The Visa Petition

The petition that starts the process is filed in most cases by your sponsoring relative (Form I-130). In the case of widows or abused spouses, however, the petition, called a self-petition, is filed by you (Form I-360). Unless the petitioner is living outside the U.S., all petitions are submitted to USCIS regional service centers. The object of the petition is to establish that you are what you say you are: namely, the qualifying relative of a qualifying sponsor.

If you are a preference relative and therefore subject to a quota, the date on which you file the petition is called your Priority Date. The Priority Date is important because it marks the legally recognized moment when your waiting period for a green card starts. (See Chapter 4, Section A3 for a full explanation of Priority Dates.) If all goes well, your petition will eventually be approved.

Be aware, however, that an approved petition does not by itself give you any right to be present, enter, or work in the U.S. It is only a prerequisite to Step Two, submitting the application for a green card. Your petition must be approved and your Priority Date must be current before you are eligible for Step Two.

However, if you file Step Two papers in the U.S. on the basis of a marriage to a U.S. citizen, you will usually submit them at the same time and in the same place as the Step One visa petition.

 The new V visa may allow spouses and children of permanent residents to live in the U.S. while waiting. In December 2000, Congress created the new "V" visa. This gives a break to a limited group of husbands, wives, and minor unmarried children of lawful permanent residents, allowing them to live and work in the United States until they get their green card. To be eligible, their initial visa petition must have been submitted to the former INS before this law was enacted (December 21, 2000), and the person must have since waited at least three years for either approval of the visa petition or for an immigrant visa or green card to become available. People who have already lived in the United States illegally will still be eligible for V visas.

To apply from overseas, contact your local U.S. consulate. To apply in the U.S., submit Form I-539 with accompanying documents and fees to a USCIS Service Center. For more information, see Supplement A, Form I-539, in the

MARRIED BENEFICIARIES WHO LIVE OVERSEAS CAN USE FIANCÉ VISAS (K-3)

Before December 2000, there was a clear split between the types of visas available to foreign-born persons living overseas but intending to immigrate through their U.S. citizen fiancé or spouse. Those who were engaged to U.S. citizens could use a fiancé visa to enter the United States (after which they could marry and apply for their green card), while the already-married persons had to go through the whole green card application process overseas and use a marriage-based visa to enter the United States. The problem was, the fiancé visa application process was simpler, and therefore unmarried couples were being reunited in the United States faster than the already-married ones.

To address this unfairness, in December 2000, Congress passed legislation providing a new visa option to immigrating spouses of U.S. citizens. These spouses are now able to use a variety of the fiancé visa to enter the United States, even though they are already married. Like the fiancé visa, their visa is coded with the letter "K"—the new spouse visa is called a K-3 visa (and accompanying children receive "K-4" visas), while the regular fiancé visa is still called a K-1 (and the children receive K-2s).

The reason that this new visa should be faster is that the immigrant spouse doesn't have to wait overseas through the entire green card application process. It's sort of like cutting the process into two halves, the second of which will be conducted in the United States. Although this allows the couple to be together sooner than they otherwise would have, the new visa is no savings on overall paperwork. The married immigrant using a fiancé visa will still have to go through the full application process for a green card ("Adjustment of Status") once he or she is in the United States. (The immigrant also has the option of returning to the U.S. consulate overseas for final green card processing.)

To apply, the petitioning U.S. spouse should file a single Form I-129F (the fiancé visa petition, covered in Chapter 7; include the proper fee and proof of having submitted Form I-130 as well) and a separate Form I-130 for the immigrating spouse. Forms I-130 should also be submitted for each accompanying child, unless the child is between age 18 and 21, in which case filing an I-130 would destroy their eligibility to enter the U.S.

using a fiancé visa. (Form I-130 is covered in this chapter). (Form I-129F is usually used for regular fiancés—the USCIS will design a new form for K-3/K-4 visas as soon as possible.) On Question 22 of Form I-130, the petitioner should find a place to write "applicant plans to obtain a K-3/K-4 visa abroad and [*adjust status in the United States or return overseas for consular processing, whichever is applicable*]." The applications must be filed with USCIS Service Centers in the United States—the Form I-130 goes to your regular regional service center, while Form I-129F must be sent to a special address: P.O. Box 7218, Chicago, IL 60680-7218.

You can submit these two applications almost simultaneously, but start with the Form I-130 application—you'll need to make a copy of it and get proof of its mailing (such as a delivery service receipt) to include with the Form I-129F fiancé visa application. (Eventually USCIS may start insisting that you wait for the USCIS notice indicating its receipt of your Form I-130 application to include with your Form I-129F application, but so far USCIS has been willing to accept lesser forms of proof that you filed Form I-130.)

After your Form I-129F application is approved, the case will be transferred to a U.S. consulate. The consulate will follow up with the applicant, but the procedures should return to the normal steps for fiancé visas as described in Chapter 7. You won't need to wait for approval of the Form I-130 to enter the U.S.—but you will need to wait for its approval to submit the green card (Adjustment of Status) application at a USCIS office. Apparently to cover this waiting period, the K-3/K-4 visas will cover a two-year stay in the U.S. (Children who will turn 21 within those two years, however, will be issued K-4 visas that are only good until their 21st birthday. To make sure that the green card application can be submitted and approved before that date, keep writing to the USCIS service center handling the Form I-130 and ask it to "expedite," or speed up its decision.)

Holders of K-3 and K-4 visas are eligible to apply for work authorization. Use Form I-765 (available in Appendix II or on the USCIS website). Send it, along with two photos and the proper fee (currently $120), to the USCIS service center that handled the fiancé visa application (in Chicago).

Appendix to this book. Although overseas U.S. consulates can process V visas, you should not leave the U.S. to get one, not even if they send you a letter with an appointment—USCIS says that not even a V visa will protect you from the three- and ten-year bars on returning to the U.S. if you've lived here illegally for six months or more. (See Chapter 25 for more on this ground of inadmissibility.) Also be careful about leaving the U.S. on short trips if you've been in the U.S. illegally for more than 180 days—even though you'll be let back in (assuming you've gotten an actual V visa from a U.S. consulate), you may be unable to adjust status after your return. Consult an attorney for more information.

2. Overview of Step Two: The Application

The second application is filed by you and your accompanying relatives, if any. It is your formal request for a green card. Step Two may be carried out in the U.S. at a USCIS office or in your home country at a U.S. consulate there.

The majority of family-based Step Two applications are filed at consulates. Those filed in the U.S. are mainly marriage cases. If you are in the U.S. legally on a nonimmigrant visa and you are an immediate relative or a preference relative with a current Priority Date (you filed a petition earlier and your wait under the quota is over or the preference category under which you filed is up to date and there is no wait), you may apply for your green card either inside or outside the U.S., whichever you prefer. There are exceptions to this rule. If you've worked without authorization or have stayed past the date you were supposed to leave the U.S. (usually shown on your I-94 card), and you're not the immediate relative of a U.S. citizen (parent, spouse, or unmarried child), then you lose the right to submit your application in the United States. If you entered the U.S. illegally, or entered legally but without a visa, using the Visa Waiver Program (unless you are the immediate relative of a U.S. citizen), you may be barred from a U.S. filing.

If you have an approved I-130 petition (Step One) but your Priority Date is not yet current, you must wait until it is current to file your Step Two application. If you wait in the U.S., you are technically here illegally if you don't have a visa or some other immigration status. (See below, "Staying in the U.S. to Apply: Risks and Benefits.")

The consulate will advise you by mail when your Priority Date finally comes up. However, it's also good to keep track yourself, in case they lose your file during the many years you're waiting. If you want to check quota progress from time to time, you may do so by calling the U.S. State Department in Washington, D.C., at 202-663-1541 for the latest quota information or check the *Visa Bulletin* online at www.travel.state.gov/visa_bulletin.html.

STAYING IN THE U.S. TO APPLY: RISKS AND BENEFITS

The rules concerning getting a green card in the U.S. are complicated. If you entered the U.S. properly and your visa or status hasn't expired, you can probably get your green card without leaving the U.S. Other people are expected to apply for their green card at an overseas U.S. consulate. Most people who marry U.S. citizens can get a green card in the U.S. even if they have fallen out of status or worked without authorization, as long as they did not enter without being properly inspected, such as crossing the border illegally.

Other people may be barred from getting a green card in the U.S., even though they have an approved petition and their Priority Date is current. For example, you cannot apply for adjustment of status (green card within the U.S.) as a preference relative unless your stay is still covered by an unexpired visa or other lawful status, and you have not worked illegally. Many family members of petitioners are out of status for a long time waiting for their Priority Date to come up.

The exception is that you can use an old provision called § 245(i) if you had a visa petition or labor certification on file by January 14, 1998, or, under recent laws, by April 30, 2001, so long as you were living in the United States on the date the laws were signed, December 21, 2000. This exception allows an otherwise ineligible applicant to get their green card without leaving the U.S., upon paying a $1,000 penalty. Section 245(i) doesn't make your stay in the U.S. legal while you're waiting for your Priority Date to come up—but it does mean that USCIS won't take any interest in looking for you, and that if you make it to when your Priority Date is current without getting caught, you can apply at a local USCIS office without fear.

If you're already living in the U.S. illegally, look very hard for a way to stay in the U.S. to apply. The reason is that once you leave, you become subject to a bar on returning. People who have lived in the U.S. unlawfully for between six and 12 continuous months after April 1, 1997, and who then leave the U.S., will not be allowed to return for three years, even if they have a family member petitioning them. The consulate will simply refuse the visa, even if all the rest of the paperwork is in order. People who have lived in the U.S. unlawfully for 12 months or more will not be allowed back for ten years.

A waiver is available for the spouse, son, or daughter of a U.S. citizen or permanent resident, if it would cause that spouse or child "extreme hardship." But you'll need a lawyer's help—the waiver is hard to get. (See Chapter 25 for more details.)

3. Who's Who in Getting Your Green Card

Getting a green card will be easier if you familiarize yourself with the technical names used for each participant in the process. During Step One, the petition, you are known as the *beneficiary* and your sponsoring relative is called the *petitioner*. In Step Two, the application, you are referred to as *applicant*, but your relative remains the petitioner. If you are applying in a preference category, and bringing your spouse and children with you as accompanying relatives, they are known as *derivative beneficiaries* and later as applicants.

4. Tips on Preparing the Paperwork

Steps One and Two involve two types of paperwork. The first consists of official government forms completed by you or your relative. The second is personal documents such as birth and marriage certificates.

It is vital that forms are properly filled out and all necessary documents are supplied. You or your U.S. relative may resent the intrusion into your privacy and the sizable effort it takes to prepare immigration applications, but you should realize the process is an impersonal matter to immigration officials. Your getting a green card is more important to you than it is to the U.S. government.

The documents you or your U.S. relative supply to USCIS or the consulate should not be originals. Ignore the instructions on some of the USCIS forms to send originals—if you send them you may never get them back. Photocopies of all documents are acceptable as long as you have the originals in your possession and are willing to produce them upon request. But add the following language to the photocopy, with your signature and the date:

> *Copies of documents submitted are exact photocopies of unaltered original documents and I understand that I may be required to submit original documents to an immigration or consular official at a later date.*
> *Signature* _____
> *Typed or Printed Name* _____
> *Date* _____

Documents will be accepted if they are in either English, or, with papers filed at most U.S. consulates abroad, the language of the country where the documents are being filed. An exception exists for papers filed at the U.S. consulates in Japan, where all documents must be translated into English. If the documents are not in an acceptable language as just explained, they must be accompanied by a full, word for word, written English translation. Any capable person may act as translator. It is not necessary to hire a professional. At the end of each translation, the following statement must appear:

> *I hereby certify that I translated this document from [language] to English. This translation is accurate and complete. I further certify that I am fully competent to translate from [language] to English.*
> *Signature* _____
> *Typed or Printed Name* _____
> *Date* _____

The translator should sign this statement, but it does not have to be witnessed or notarized.

Later in this chapter we describe the forms and documents needed to get your green card through a relative. A summary checklist of forms and documents appears at the end of the chapter.

D. Carrying Out Step One: The Petition

This section includes the information you need to submit the visa petition that starts your immigration process.

1. General Procedures

Normally, your sponsoring relative submits the visa petition (Form I-130 and documents), to the USCIS regional service center that has been designated for your sponsoring relative's place of residence (see the USCIS website for the address). However, if both Steps One and Two will be carried out in the U.S. and the person being petitioned for will have a current Priority Date or is an immediate relative not subject to quota, the petition will be filed, together with Step Two paperwork, at the USCIS local office nearest your place of residence. (See Appendix I for a complete list.) But don't assume that you can do all the steps in the U.S. just because you're living here now. See "Staying in the U.S. to Apply: Risks and Benefits," above.

If your sponsoring relative lives abroad and USCIS has an office in the country where he or she lives, the visa petition should be filed there. In all other countries, the visa petition should be filed with the U.S. consulate in the country where your sponsoring relative resides.

If the petition is to be filed at a USCIS regional service center, it must be sent by mail. Certified mail, return receipt requested, is recommended so you will have proof that the petition arrived.

The filing fee for each petition is currently $130. Checks, money orders, and cash are accepted. When filing by mail, do not send cash. If you file in person, you will be given a written receipt for the filing fee.

When your relative files by mail and USCIS finds defects or omissions such as unsigned forms or missing payment, all petition papers, forms, and documents will be returned. The returned package will contain either a note or a form (I-797) telling your relative what corrections, additional pieces of information, or additional documents are expected. If the papers are properly filed but missing some evidence needed to approve the case, USCIS will keep the papers but issue a request for evidence (RFE). Your relative should make the corrections or supply the extra data and mail the whole package back to USCIS. When all materials have been received, the USCIS service center will send you a written receipt notice. If you're a preference relative, the receipt notice will show the date on which the petition was filed, which will be your eventual Priority Date. All receipt notices also contain an estimate of how many days the USCIS will take to make a decision.

Keep all USCIS receipts in a safe place, together with a complete copy of everything submitted. Then you can confirm on what date your petition was filed. The number on the receipt will help locate your papers should they get lost or delayed in processing. Also, remember that your Priority Date is established on the day your petition is filed, so it is important to have proof of exactly when this took place.

Once your petition is approved, a Notice of Action (Form I-797) will be sent to your petitioning relative, indicating the approval. If you plan to execute Step Two at a U.S. consulate abroad, USCIS will forward the file to the National Visa Center (NVC), located in Portsmouth, New Hampshire. The NVC will then send a packet of forms and instructions to you so that you may proceed with Step Two, your application for a visa.

2. Petition Forms

Copies of all the required USCIS forms can be found in Appendix II and on the USCIS website.

Form I-130

The basic form for Step One, the petition, is immigration Form I-130. It is used for nearly all family-based cases. Section B of the form (the left column) asks only about your petitioning relative. Section C (the right column) asks about you. Section D is relevant only if the petitioner has petitioned for other relatives before.

If a particular question does not apply, it should be answered "None" or "N/A." Do not leave any spaces blank or USCIS will return the form.

Note: If you are petitioning for yourself as a battered spouse or a widow(er) use Form I-360 instead. You will sign the form instead of your U.S. spouse.

It is essential to answer each question truthfully, even if it means disclosing that you are in the U.S. illegally. Failure to reveal requested information may result in your being permanently barred from the U.S.

Box at the Top of the Form. Do not fill in this boldfaced box.

Section A. These questions are self-explanatory.

Section B. These questions are self-explanatory. Include your full middle name, not just your initial.

Section C, Questions 1–21. These questions are self-explanatory.

Section C, Question 22. If you are currently in the U.S. but are planning to process Step Two, the application, at a U.S. consulate, fill in the location of the nearest consulate in your country of residence. The U.S. consulate in your country of residence is the only one legally required to accept your case. If there is an overwhelming need to file elsewhere, you can contact a consulate in some other country and ask if it will agree to process your application. That consulate is under no obligation to grant your request and is very likely to turn you down, but there is no harm in asking. Unless

you have received permission in advance, don't write down the name of any consulate other than the one in your country of residence. This brings about unnecessary delays and increases the chances of your paperwork being lost.

If you are sure you are eligible to process Step Two in the U.S. and wish to do so, put down the location of the USCIS local office nearest your home in the U.S. Also, name a consulate where you wish your petition sent in the event that USCIS decides you really aren't qualified for U.S. filing.

Section D. These questions are self-explanatory.

Form I-360

Remember, use this form only as a substitute for Form I-130 if you are petitioning for yourself as a battered spouse or widow(er).

Part 1. Fill in this section only if you want to give USCIS an alternate mailing address.

Part 2. Check box "i" if you're a battered spouse; if your children are also applying, they should fill out a separate form and check box "j." If you're the widow(er) or a U.S. citizen, check box "b."

Part 3. Fill in information about yourself.

Part 4. Fill in information about yourself.

Part 5. Skip this section.

Part 6. Skip this section.

Part 7. The questions for Sections A and B are self-explanatory.

Part 8. This section is self-explanatory.

Part 9. This section is self-explanatory.

Part 10. Skip this section.

The fee for an I-360 petition is $130.

Form G-325A

In most types of relative cases, the G-325A Biographic Data Form is a part of Step Two, not Step One. If, however, your petition is based on marriage to a U.S. citizen and it is being filed separately from the application, Form G-325A must be filled out in Step One as well. In marriage cases, G-325A forms must be completed for both you and your U.S. spouse. This is the only type of case where full biographic data is requested on someone who is already a U.S. citizen. Form G-325A is meant to gather personal background information. The questions are self-explanatory.

3. Petition Documents

All relative petitions must be filed with evidence that the petitioner is a U.S. citizen or green card holder. (Send copies, not originals.) If the petitioner is a U.S. citizen by birth, a birth certificate is the best proof. Only birth certificates issued by a U.S. state government are acceptable. Hospital birth certificates cannot be used. When the petitioner is a U.S. citizen born outside U.S. territory, a certificate of citizenship, naturalization certificate, U.S. consular record of birth abroad, or unexpired U.S. passport will serve as proof. If the petitioner is a U.S. citizen but does not have any of these documents, read Chapter 27 to learn how to obtain them.

If the petitioner is not a U.S. citizen but is a permanent resident, this can be proven with the petitioner's green card (copy both sides), unexpired reentry permit, or passport with an unexpired stamp indicating admission to the U.S. as a permanent resident. (The unexpired stamp in a foreign passport is used only in the few cases where the petitioner has just been approved for a green card but is still waiting to receive the card itself. The card typically arrives by mail several months later.) When green card holders act as petitioners, USCIS will not check its own records to establish the existence of the green card. Your petitioning relative is responsible for supplying this evidence.

The above-described documents proving the eligibility of the petitioner to act as a sponsor must be included in every Step One petition. The next documents we will describe are not the same in all cases but differ according to which of your relatives will act as your petitioner. But don't forget, there must be proof in every case that the petitioner is a U.S. citizen or green card holder.

a.   Your Sponsoring Relative Is Your Spouse

When the basis of the petition is marriage to a U.S. citizen or green card holder, you must establish that you are lawfully married to the petitioner. Do this by showing a valid civil marriage certificate. Church certificates are generally insufficient. (There are a few exceptions, depending on the laws of your particular country. Canadians, for example, may use church marriage certificates if the marriage took place in Quebec Province, but not elsewhere. If a civil certificate is available, however, you should always use it.) You may have married in a country where marriages are not customarily recorded. Tribal areas of Africa are an example. In such situations, call the nearest consulate or embassy of your home country for help with finding acceptable proof of marriage.

If either you or your spouse has been married before, you must prove that all prior marriages were legally terminated. This requires presenting either a divorce decree or death certificate ending every prior marriage. Where a death certificate is needed, it must be an official document issued by a government. Certificates from funeral homes are not acceptable. Divorce papers must be official court or government documents. If the death or divorce occurred in one of those few countries where such records are not kept, call the nearest consulate or embassy of your home country for advice on getting acceptable proof of death or divorce.

It is also necessary to present one photograph each of you and your spouse. The photos should meet certain exact specifications, detailed in Appendix II on Form M-378.

b. Your Sponsoring Relative Is Your Child

Usually, you may verify a parent/child relationship simply by presenting the child's birth certificate. Many countries, including Canada and England, issue both short- and long-form birth certificates. Where both are available, the long form is needed because it contains the names of the parents, while the short form does not.

c. Your Sponsoring Relative Is Your Stepchild

U.S. stepchildren may petition for the green cards of step-parents where the marriage creating the family relationship took place before the child's 18th birthday. However, for a stepchild to act as petitioner for a stepparent, the marriage that created the stepchild/stepparent relationship must still exist. If the marriage ends, the stepchild/stepparent relationship also legally ends. Accordingly, you must prove you are currently married to the stepchild's natural parent.

Do this by showing your present marriage certificate as well as divorce decrees or death certificates indicating that all prior marriages of you and your current spouse were legally terminated. Where a death certificate is needed, it must be an official document issued by the government. Certificates from funeral homes are not acceptable. You must also present your stepchild's long-form birth certificate to show the names of his or her natural parents.

d. Your Sponsoring Relative Is Your Illegitimate Child

U.S. illegitimate children (children of unmarried parents) may petition for the green cards of their parents. If you are the mother, legitimacy is irrelevant for immigration purposes. The documents needed are exactly the same as those for a petition by a legitimate child. If you are the father, however, something more is required. You must present documents proving two additional elements—paternity and either legitimation or the existence of a genuine parent/child relationship.

i. Documents Proving Paternity

Paternity (biological fatherhood) can be documented by presenting your child's birth certificate with your name on it, although it is common to find that the father's name is not registered on the birth certificate of an illegitimate child. If you want to prove paternity, go to the government office that issued your illegitimate child's original birth certificate and try to get it amended to include your name.

When your name does not appear on your child's birth certificate and amending is not possible, USCIS may require a blood test to establish paternity. If USCIS deems this necessary, it will tell you so after you have submitted your visa petition (Step One), and give you instructions on how to proceed. USCIS may allow you to substitute a sworn affidavit from the child's mother identifying you as the father. USCIS has the discretion to demand whatever proof it wants.

ii. Documents Proving Legitimation

Legitimation is a legal procedure where a father of an illegitimate child acknowledges before a court or government body that he is the parent of the child. Laws establishing legitimation procedures exist in many countries. Illegitimate children may petition for the green cards of their fathers if they were legitimated before their 18th birthday.

In matters of legitimation, USCIS recognizes the procedures and documents called for by the law of the country where the child was born. Some nations have abolished the legal difference between legitimate and illegitimate children. In Jamaica, for example, a father need only sign an acknowledgment of paternity and the legal distinction of illegitimacy is erased. In any country where legitimation laws are in effect, provided the law was enacted before the child's 18th birthday, USCIS will ask for the same legitimation documents required by the law in the child's home country.

iii. Documents Proving a Genuine Parent/Child Relationship

If the child was not legally legitimated prior to his or her 18th birthday, there is an alternative. Fathers may then choose to prove that before the child's 21st (not 18th) birthday and while the child was unmarried, a real father/child relationship existed, involving personal contact and financial support. Evidence of this might include documents showing that the father and child resided in the same house. Also valuable are affidavits from people who know your family, stating that you have acted as a father, or copies of the child's school records with your name registered as a parent. Proof that you contributed money to the child's support is considered particularly strong evidence of a paternal relationship. U.S. income tax returns declaring the child as a dependent, canceled checks, or other financial records can be used to show this.

e.   You Are a Battered or Abused Spouse or Child

If you will be petitioning for yourself as a battered or abused spouse or child, you must supply credible evidence of having been battered or subjected to extreme cruelty. Police reports or arrest records reflecting the abuse would be the strongest evidence. Medical and psychiatric reports if you sought treatment for the abuse would also be helpful. If no complaints were filed with the police and you never sought medical attention, you will probably have to obtain affidavits from other knowledgeable people, such as friends, landlords, or employers. Statements from any shelters you stayed in or friends or neighbors who were aware of the situation would all be useful. Your own statements without any substantiating evidence will probably not be sufficient.

f.   Your Sponsoring Relative Is Your Adopted Child

Adopted children petitioning for adoptive parents must submit all the same documents as do natural children who petition for their parents. There are, however, some additional requirements that have been established in cases where adopted children are the petitioners or beneficiaries. (See Chapter 6 for a full explanation.)

g.   Your Sponsoring Relative Is Your Parent

Usually, you can show that you are the child of a U.S. citizen or green card holder simply by submitting your long-form birth certificate with your parents' names listed. When the petitioner is your father, you must also submit your parents' marriage certificate. It is, therefore, easier to choose your mother over your father as a petitioner if you have a choice, because you will then need one less document. If you are subject to the quota system, however, you might want to have both of them submit petitions, in case one passes away during the waiting period.

h.   Your Sponsoring Relative Is Your Parent and You Are an Illegitimate Child

U.S. parents may petition for their illegitimate children. If your parents were not married at your birth, you will be treated as illegitimate. In that case, you must present the same documents required of a parent whose petitioner is an illegitimate child. (See Subsection d, above, to see what documents you need.)

i.   Your Sponsoring Relative Is Your Stepparent and You Are a Stepchild

If you are a stepchild, your U.S. stepparent may petition for you if the marriage creating the family relationship took place before your 18th birthday. The marriage must still exist—if it has ended, the stepchild/stepparent relationship ceases to exist in the eyes of USCIS. If you are a stepchild, you must present all the same documents required of a parent utilizing a stepchild as petitioner. Therefore, you must prove that your parent and stepparent are currently married. Do this by showing their marriage certificate as well as divorce decrees or death certificates indicating that all prior marriages of each were legally terminated. You also must present your long-form birth certificate to show the names of your natural parents.

j.   Your Sponsoring Relative Is Your Parent and You Are an Adopted Child

Parents petitioning for adopted children must submit all the same documents as do parents who petition for their natural children. There are, however, some additional requirements for cases where adopted children are the petitioners or beneficiaries. (See Chapter 6 for a full explanation.)

k.   Your Sponsoring Relative Is Your Brother or Sister (Includes Half-Brothers and Half-Sisters)

To petition for your green card, your brother or sister must be at least 21 years of age. You must also demonstrate that the two of you have at least one common parent. To achieve this, submit both of your birth certificates, which will have your parents' names listed. If the only common parent is your father, you must prove that your father was married to your mother at the time of your birth, and to your sibling's mother at the time of his or her birth. This means verifying the existence of both marriages. You may accomplish this by producing all the same documents called for in the case of a U.S. spouse petition. (See Subsection a, above.)

l.   Name Tracing Documents

If you've ever changed your name and your old name appears on documents you're submitting to USCIS, be careful not to create confusion. For example, a married woman participating in an immigration matter, whether as petitioner, beneficiary, or accompanying relative applicant, should submit all marriage and divorce certificates so USCIS can follow the chain of all her name changes up to the present. It is routinely necessary to show that a woman whose name appears on a birth certificate is the same woman listed on an immigration form or marriage certificate, though the names are different. This is equally true of a man who has ever used more than one name.

m. You Are a Widow(er)

If you will be petitioning for yourself as the widow or widower of a U.S. citizen who died within the last two years, add copies of the following to your I-360 petition:

- your marriage certificate (showing that the two of you were married for at least two years before your spouse died)
- proof that any prior marriages (yours or your spouse's) were legally ended, such as divorce, annulment, or death certificates, and
- your deceased spouse's death certificate, showing that the death occurred within the last two years.

4. Petition Interviews

USCIS may require a personal interview after submission of the I-130 if the existence of the family relationship between you and the petitioner is in doubt. Most of the time, the facts are clear from the documents presented, so petition interviews are rarely held, except in cases where the petition is based on marriage. See below, "Marriage Interviews After Filing I-130."

MARRIAGE INTERVIEWS AFTER FILING I-130

The USCIS sometimes requires petition interviews in marriage cases, especially if the marriage recently took place or if there are great age or cultural differences between the spouses. Interviews are less common if the application is being filed at a U.S. consulate.

Marriage interview procedures vary with the individual personality of the examining officer, and you should be prepared to adjust to that officer's interviewing style. You and your U.S. spouse may be brought into the interviewing room separately. Each of you may then be questioned about your life together, how you met, what sorts of things you do as a couple, daily routines, common friends, favorite places to go, what the inside of your home looks like, and so on. These questions are intended to reveal whether or not you and your U.S. spouse actually share a life—or whether you're just committing immigration fraud. You may refuse to answer some or all questions, but doing so could result in the petition being denied.

Many couples wonder if they will be asked about the more intimate details of their relationship. USCIS policy states that the interviewers should not ask embarrassingly personal questions, but sometimes USCIS officials believe it is necessary to ask intimate questions in an attempt to uncover a fraudulent case. Most USCIS offices now videotape all interviews, so the likelihood of abuse has been diminished. The best advice we can offer is be prepared for anything and cooperate as much as possible.

5. Petition Appeals

When the family relationship between you and your U.S. relative has been poorly documented, or if your marriage to a U.S. citizen looks suspicious, the petition will probably be denied. Your sponsoring relative will then receive written notice of the USCIS's unfavorable decision, a written statement of the reasons for the negative outcome, and an explanation of how to make a formal appeal.

The best way to handle an appeal is to try avoiding it altogether. Filing an appeal means making an argument to USCIS that its judgment was wrong. If you think you can eliminate the reason why your petition failed by improving your paperwork, it makes sense to forget about the appeals process and simply file a new petition, being careful to see that it is better prepared than the first.

If the petition was denied because the petitioner left out necessary documents that have since been located, the new documents should be sent, together with a written request that the case be reopened, to the same USCIS office that issued the denial. This is technically called a *Motion to Reopen*. There is a $110 fee for filing this motion. Appeals often take a long time. A Motion to Reopen can be concluded faster than an appeal.

If your sponsoring relative does choose to appeal, he or she must do so within 30 days of the date on the Notice of Denial. USCIS will then forward the papers for consideration to the Board of Immigration Appeals (BIA) in Washington, DC. The appeals decision, which can take many months, will be sent to your relative by mail. The vast majority of appeals fail.

When an appeal to USCIS has been denied, the next step is an appeal through the U.S. judicial system. Your relative may not file an action in court without first going through the appeals process available from USCIS. If the case has reached this stage and you are living illegally in the U.S., we strongly recommend seeking representation from a qualified immigration attorney, as you are now in danger of being deported.

E. Carrying Out Step Two: The Application (Consular Filing)

After the I-130 visa petition that your relative submitted for you has been approved, and (if you're a preference relative) you've waited some years for your Priority Date to become current, you'll move to the next step of the process—your application for an immigrant visa or green card. Whether you're currently living in the U.S. or overseas, the normal procedure is for you to apply for the green card at a U.S. consulate in your home country or last country of residence. (You must be physically present in order to apply there.)

However, if you have been or are now working or living illegally in the U.S., read Chapter 25 to make sure you are not subject to the three- and ten-year overstay bars or other laws punishing individuals who were out of status and then departed and/or reentered the U.S. If you are subject to these bars, don't leave the United States without talking to a lawyer, even if you've received an appointment letter from the consulate. Without applying for and being granted a "waiver," you may not be allowed back to the U.S. for three or ten years.

CITIZENS OF COUNTRIES WITHOUT U.S. EMBASSIES

Citizens of countries not having formal diplomatic relations with the U.S. are faced with the problem of where to apply for immigrant visas.

Persons from such countries who are physically present in the U.S. may have Step Two papers processed at the U.S. consulate in Ciudad Juárez, Mexico. For those who are not physically in the U.S., contact the U.S. State Department or the nearest U.S. consulate in an adjoining country for information.

---

1. Benefits and Drawbacks of Consular Filing

Anyone with an approved petition and a current Priority Date can apply for a green card at the appropriate consulate. (That is not the case with U.S. applications since you must be physically inside the U.S. and be eligible to use a procedure called "adjustment of status" to apply there. See above, "Staying in the U.S. to Apply: Risks and Benefits.") In fact, most applicants have no choice but to apply at a consulate, either because they live overseas or because they aren't eligible for adjustment of status. However, if you are now in the U.S. illegally, but you elect to or must file at a consulate, you may run into other difficulties due to the three- and ten-year waiting periods imposed on individuals who have lived in the U.S. illegally. Be sure to understand these issues, discussed in Chapter 25, before proceeding.

A plus to consular filing is that some consulate offices work more quickly to issue green cards than do some USCIS offices. You may save several months. (Remember, however, that the difference in waiting time between the USCIS and consulate offices applies only to processing paperwork. Quotas move at the same rate of speed no matter where your application is filed.)

One drawback to consular filing is the travel expense and inconvenience you will experience in returning to your home country if you are already in the U.S. Another problem is that should your consular application fail, you will have fewer ways to appeal than a U.S. filing would offer.

The new "K-3" visa may allow spouses of U.S. citizens to enter the United States more quickly. See "Married Beneficiaries Who Live Overseas Can Use Fiancé Visas (K-3)," above.

2. Application General Procedures: Consular Filing

The law states that only a U.S. consulate or embassy where you live is required to accept your green card application. This is true for all individuals except persons from countries without U.S. embassies, discussed in Citizens of Countries Without U.S. Embassies, above. You can ask a consulate located elsewhere (*not* where you reside) to accept your application, but most consulates turn down such requests unless you show extremely compelling reasons. If you plan to ask for this privilege, contact the consulate of your choice before your relative files the Step One petition.

You may not file an application for a green card at a consulate until after your petition has been approved. At that time, the USCIS office where your petition was originally submitted will forward your file to the National Visa Center (NVC) in Portsmouth, New Hampshire. At the same time, a Notice of Approval will be sent directly to your relative.

The NVC will then forward your file to the U.S. consulate you have named on Form I-130 in Step One. The NVC will send instructions and application forms to you within a month or two after petition approval. If, after waiting a reasonable time, you have not heard from the NVC, you should phone or write them and look into the matter.

Complete and send Forms DS-230 Part I and DS-2001 as soon as possible. This will allow the consulate to begin a required security check into your background.

The application for your green card is made in person, by appointment. Once your quota number is current and the consulate is ready for your final processing, it will send another group of papers, including an interview appointment letter, instructions for obtaining your medical examination, and still more forms to be completed. Do not mail this paperwork to the consulate. Instead, bring the rest of your forms and all documents with you at the time of your appointment. The exception is that some applicants will be asked to send the Form I-864 Affidavit of Support (that their petitioner fills out to show that the applicant will be supported financially) to the NVC. Only after the NVC confirms that the Form I-864 is adequate will the applicant be allowed to continue with the rest of the Step Two paperwork. Other applicants, however, will simply be told to include Form I-864 with the remainder of the paperwork when they take it to their consular appointment.

The fee for filing an application is $335 per person in U.S. currency or local currency subject to the exchange rate.

3. Application Forms: Consular Filing

When you file at a U.S. consulate abroad, the consulate officials will provide you with certain forms designated by a "DS" preceding a number. Instructions for completing DS forms and what to do with them once they are filled out will come with the forms. We do not include copies of these forms in the Appendix, because local consulates sometimes use their own versions. Copies of all non-"DS" forms can be found in Appendix II.

Affidavit of Support: Form I-864

You may be required to submit Form I-864 either to the NVC before you receive your Step Two paperwork or as part of the package that you take to your interview.

There are two exceptions to the I-864 requirement. First, if the immigrant beneficiary has already worked in the U.S. for a total of 40 "quarters" (as defined by the Social Security Administration—it's about ten years), no I-864 needs to be submitted on his or her behalf. Second, if the immigrant beneficiary is a child who will become a U.S. citizen immediately upon entering the U.S. for a green card (as discussed in Chapter 27) no I-864 needs to be submitted on his or her behalf.

Form I-864 helps an immigrant show she is not likely to become a public charge (receive public assistance or welfare). The sponsor must show that he or she earns at least 125% of the income levels shown in the federal Poverty Guidelines.

Form I-864 is legally enforceable by the government for most public benefits utilized by the sponsored immigrant. It is also enforceable by the immigrant family member against the sponsor for support.

All family-based immigrants who file immigrant visa applications are required to have Form I-864 filed by the person who is sponsoring their immigrant petition, whether or not the sponsor's income is high enough to meet the Poverty Guidelines minimum. Applicants filing from overseas must also pay a $65 fee with this form. If the main sponsor's income is too low, another person (a joint sponsor) may add her income if the joint sponsor:

- is willing to be jointly liable
- is a legal permanent resident or U.S. citizen
- is over 18 years old, and
- resides in the U.S.,

as long as she meets the 125% income requirement when counting her own household. The joint sponsor files a separate I-864 affidavit of support.

In addition, the main sponsor's household members may add their income to help reach the 125% level, but only if they have been living with the sponsor for six months and they agree to be jointly liable by filing a shorter form called Form I-864A.

Personal assets of the sponsor or the immigrant, such as property, bank account deposits, and personal property such as automobiles, may also be used to supplement the sponsor's income (minus any debts or liens). However, the assets will have to add up to at least five times the difference between the 125% Poverty Guidelines income level for an equivalent family and the sponsors' actual income.

The sponsors take on certain long-term responsibilities. They must notify the USCIS within 30 days of a change of address, using Form I-865. Failure to do so is punishable by fines of $250-$2,000, or $2,000-$5,000 if the sponsor fails to notify knowing that the sponsored alien received a public benefit. The requirements and paperwork burden of Form I-864 are complicated and substantial; most of the requirements are spelled out on the form. If you have questions about meeting the eligibility requirements or the scope of the sponsor's legal responsibility—which may last ten or more years, or until the immigrant permanently leaves the country, dies, or naturalizes—consult an immigration attorney.

4. Application Documents: Consular Filing

You'll also be required to include a number of documents in your green card application.

Notice of Action. The most important document in your application is the Notice of Action showing approval of your petition. It is sent directly from the NVC in the U.S. to the consulate that will be conducting your interview. This is the only document you will not have to submit yourself.

Originals. When you go to your interview, you must show the consulate originals of virtually all of the documents first filed as photocopies in Step One. Only the proof of U.S. citizenship or the green card of your petitioning relative need not be resubmitted. If not included in Step One, you must have your long-form birth certificate and birth certificates of any unmarried minor children who are not immigrating with you.

Passport. You'll need a valid passport from your home country. Check the expiration date on the passport—it must remain valid at least six months beyond the date of your interview.

Police Certificates. Unlike applications made in the U.S., you personally must collect police clearance certificates from each country you have lived in for one year or more since your 16th birthday (unless they're unavailable). Get working on this as soon as you can, so you'll have them ready for your interview. Additionally, you must have a police certificate from your home country and your country of residence at the time of your visa application, if you lived there for at least six months since the age of 16. You do not need to obtain police certificates from the U.S. Additionally, a consular officer can request that you obtain a police certificate from any country—regardless of how long you lived there—if he or she believes you have a criminal record there.

Contact the local police department in your home country for instructions on how to get police certificates. To obtain police certificates from nations other than your home country, it is best to contact the nearest consulate representing that country for instructions. Some nations refuse to supply police certificates, or their certificates are not considered reliable, and so you will not be required to obtain them from those locations. The U.S. consulate will give you a list of countries from which police certificates are not required.

Photos. You and each accompanying relative must bring to the interview three photographs taken in compliance with the consulate's instructions. Often you will also receive a list of local photographers who take this type of picture.

Fingerprints. Some consulates require you to submit fingerprints. Consulates wanting fingerprints will send you instructions. The current fingerprinting fee is $85.

5. Application Interviews: Consular Filing

Consulates hold interviews on all green card applications. You'll get written notice of your interview appointment. Immediately before the interview you and your accompanying relatives will be required to have medical examinations. Some consulates conduct the medical exams up to several days before the interview. Others schedule the medical exam and the interview on the same day. You will be told where to go and what to do in your appointment letter.

a. The Medical Exam

The medical examinations are conducted by private doctors and you are required to pay the doctor a fee. The fees vary from as little as $50 to more than $150 per exam, depending on the country. The amount of the medical exam fee will be stated in your appointment letter. The exam itself involves the taking of a medical history, blood test, and chest X-ray. You will also need to present documentation that you have received vaccination against vaccine-preventable diseases, unless USCIS regulations state that vaccination is inappropriate for you or you are granted a waiver based on your moral or religious beliefs. Pregnant women can refuse to be X-rayed if they have no symptoms of tuberculosis, but will have to be X-rayed after the child's birth.

The main purpose of the medical exam is to verify that you are not medically inadmissible. The primary medical grounds of inadmissibility are tuberculosis and HIV (AIDS). Some medical conditions that would make you inadmissible can be overcome with treatment. (See Chapter 25 for more details.) If not, and you need a medical waiver, you will be given complete instructions by the consulate at the time of your interview.

b.   What Happens at the Interview

After the medical exam, you and your accompanying relatives will report to the consulate for the interview. At that time, you must pay one more fee: $335 per person. (This fee and procedure changed in 2002. If you already paid $260 to the NVC under the old procedures, then you'll only be asked to pay $65 per person at the the interview.) Some consulates accept payment only by certified check, money order, or traveler's check. Others accept cash. You will be told the proper method of payment.

Bring with you to the interview the completed forms, photographs, your passports, and all of the required documents discussed here. The interviewing officer will verify your application's accuracy and inspect your documents. If all is in order, you will be asked to return later, when you will be issued an immigrant visa. You are not yet a permanent resident. In fact, the process often gets held up at this point, waiting for security checks to be completed.

c.   Using Your Immigrant Visa

The immigrant visa allows you to enter the U.S. within six months. You acquire the full status of green card holder at the moment of making entry into the U.S. with your immigrant visa. At that time, your passport is stamped and you are immediately authorized to work. If you are bringing any accompanying relatives, they must enter at either the same time or after you do in order to become permanent residents. Green cards for you and your accompanying relatives are then ordered. They will come to you by mail several months later.

MARRIAGE INTERVIEW OVERSEAS

Some consulates, including the consulate in Ciudad Juárez, Mexico, routinely request the American spouse to appear at the interview in cases based on a marriage. Even though USCIS may have already conducted a marriage interview during Step One, these consulates feel they have the right to conduct another. When your U.S. spouse's appearance is specifically requested, but he or she is unable to attend, tell this to the consulate in advance. If the consulate continues to insist that your American spouse must travel abroad to attend your interview, it may be wise to hire an immigration lawyer to deal with the consulate. Interviews of this kind must be handled with special care. Otherwise, the consulate could send the entire file back to USCIS in the U.S. with a request for a formal investigation of your marriage. This could delay the issuance of a green card by months or even years. During that time, you might be forced to remain outside the U.S.

6.   Application Appeals: Consular Filing

When a consulate denies a green card application, there is no formal appeal available, although you are normally free to reapply as often as you like. (Check with your local consulate to be sure, however—some place limits on the number of repeat applications, or require you to wait a certain number of months before reapplying.) If the denial was caused by a lack of evidence, this will be explained in a written notice. The most common reason for denial is failure to supply all the required documents. Sometimes presenting more evidence on an unclear fact can bring about a better result.

Another common reason for denial of a green card is that the consular officer believes you are inadmissible. If you are found to be inadmissible, you will be given an opportunity to apply for a Waiver of Inadmissibility, if one is applicable. (See Chapter 25.)

When all these possibilities are exhausted, if the consulate still refuses you a green card, your opportunities for further appeals are severely limited. Contact a lawyer for more information.

Or, you can simply to wait a while, try to change whatever sunk your earlier application, reapply, and hope for better luck next time. The fact that you have been turned down once does not stop you from trying again.

F. Carrying Out Step Two: The Application (U.S. Filing)

If you are physically present in the U.S., you may be able to apply for a green card without leaving the country, on the conditions described in Section C2, above.

1. Benefits and Drawbacks of U.S. Filing

If you're one of the few people who is allowed to submit Step Two of your application in the U.S.—in other words, apply to "adjust status" and get your green card approval from a local USCIS office—it's probably best to take advantage of this. For one thing, if you are already in the country, you avoid the expense and inconvenience of overseas travel. For another, if you have already lived in the U.S. illegally for six months or more, you avoid the double inconvenience of having the consulate find that you are inadmissible and cannot return to the U.S. for three or ten years. When you file in the U.S., should problems arise in your case, you will at least be able to wait for a decision in America, a circumstance most green card applicants prefer. And in most cases, you will also be able to renew your application in deportation proceedings, in case your application is denied by the USCIS.

Another important benefit of U.S. filing is that you will receive permission to work while you wait for the results of your case. To obtain this benefit, you must make a separate application at the local USCIS office where your Step Two application has been filed. Some USCIS offices allow you to apply for work authorization in person, soon after filing your green card application. However, more and more offices are now requiring you to send in the application by mail, together with the rest of your green card application materials. Ask your local USCIS office about its procedures. If you do not need to work right away, you should probably still get your work authorization as soon as possible, since many states require you to have it to apply for other benefits such as Social Security cards and driver licenses.

There is also a paperwork benefit to applying in the U.S. You will not have to obtain required police certificates and submit them yourself to the USCIS. Instead, the USCIS will take your fingerprints (for a $50 fee) and order all necessary police certificates directly.

There are some disadvantages to applying in the U.S. It may take longer to get results. Processing times at USCIS offices average 12 months, but at some offices may even be longer, even on cases not affected by quotas or those where quotas are current.

While your case is pending at a USCIS office, you may not leave the U.S. without getting special permission. If you do leave without the USCIS's permission, even for a genuine emergency, this will be regarded as a withdrawal of your application and you will have to start Step Two all over again when you return. The exception is if you have an unexpired K-3 or K-4 visa.

PROCEDURES FOR WORK AUTHORIZATION

If you want to work before your application for a green card is approved, you must file a separate application for employment authorization. This can be done by completing Form I-765 and filing it with the same local USCIS office where you filed the Step Two papers. Together with Form I-765, you must submit a copy of your filing receipts and photos, and pay a filing fee of $120. It is very important to keep the fee receipt USCIS gives you so you can prove that the I-765 was filed. Normally you will want to file the application for employment authorization on the same day, but right after your application papers.

USCIS will either mail you the card or it will give you an appointment to return for your work authorization card.

USCIS does not have to make a decision on your employment authorization application for up to 90 days. If for some reason you are not given a decision within 90 days, you will, at your request, be granted an interim employment authorization that will last 240 days. To receive an interim card, you must return in person to the USCIS local office and show your fee receipt. Then your interim work authorization card should be issued.

If 240 days pass and you still have not received a final decision on the I-765, you must stop working. Interim work authorization cards cannot be renewed. However, if you reach this point, you have the option to file a new I-765 application and, if you do not get a decision on the new application within 90 days, ask for another interim work authorization card.

2. Application General Procedures: U.S. Filing

The application, consisting of both forms and documents, is submitted either by mail or in person to the local USCIS office nearest the place you are living. Ask your local office about its procedures. (Appendix I contains a list of all USCIS offices with telephone numbers and addresses.)

For U.S. filings, the basic form used for the green card application is Form I-485, Application for Permanent Residence. Form I-485 is filed to adjust your status in the U.S. "Adjusting status" is a technical term used only in U.S. filings. It simply means that you are presently in the U.S. and are in the process of "adjusting" your current status (nonimmigrant) to the status of a permanent resident.

SOME IMMIGRANTS CAN COMBINE STEPS ONE AND TWO

A few applicants are allowed to submit the application and the petition at the same time, to a local USCIS office, without involving the service centers. However, this option is only available to immigrants who won't be subject to a wait under the quota system—immediate relatives, for the most part. Concurrent filing of Steps One and Two requires coordination with your sponsoring relative who, you will remember, has full legal responsibility for Step One. If the petition was filed separately, you must wait to submit the application until after the petition has been approved. (Or resubmit the petition to your local USCIS office with a new fee.)

a. Filing Fees

The filing fee for each application is $255 for applicants age 14 and over, and $160 for applicants under age 14. Also include $50 for fingerprinting of every applicant age 14 or over. A separate application must be filed for you and each accompanying relative. In addition, if your visa has expired and you're not the immediate relative of a U.S. citizen, or if you entered without being inspected, you may also be subject to a $1,000 penalty fee. Checks and money orders are accepted. It is not advisable to send cash through the mail but cash is satisfactory if you file in person. Cash is accepted only in the exact amount. USCIS offices will not make change.

b. Filing in Person or by Mail

We recommend filing your papers in person if at all possible, as you will be given a written receipt from USCIS and your papers are likely to be processed faster. Even if you submit the petition and application together, each has a separate filing fee that must be paid. If you mail in your application, you should do so by certified mail, return receipt requested. In either case, keep a complete copy of everything you submit.

c. Trips Outside the U.S. While You Wait

Once your application has been filed, you should not leave the U.S. before your application has been approved without first requesting advance permission to come back. Any unauthorized absence will be viewed as a termination of your application for a green card (unless you have an unexpired K-3 or K-4 visa). If you want to leave the U.S. for any legitimate business or personal reason, go in person to the USCIS office processing your application, bringing three passport-type photographs. Ask for Advance Parole, by filing Form I-131 and paying a $110 filing fee. You may also file Form I-131 with your green card application if you already know you want to travel—many people do this now, almost automatically. If approved, you will be allowed to leave the U.S. and return again with no break in the processing of your application. However, you should not use Advance Parole if you have lived in the U.S. illegally for six months or more—you won't be allowed back in for three or ten years.

d. Fingerprints and Interview Notice

Generally, after filing your application, you will not hear anything from USCIS for several months. Then you should receive a notice of your fingerprint appointment, and a few months later, of your interview appointment. The interview notice will also contain instructions for getting the required medical exam, and will tell you if any further documentation is needed. For what happens at the interview, see Subsection 5, below.

3. Application Forms: U.S. Filing

Copies of all required USCIS forms can be found in Appendix II and on the USCIS website.

Form I-485

While most of the form is self-explanatory, a few items typically raise concerns. If a particular question does not apply to you, answer it with "None" or "N/A." The questions on this form requiring explanation are as follows:

Part 1. This asks for general information about when and where you were born, your present address, and immigration status. It also asks for an "A" number. Normally, you will not have an "A" number unless you previously applied for a green card or have been in deportation proceedings (in which case you should see a lawyer). It also asks for your I-94 number. This is the number on the little white or green card that was tucked into your passport when you entered the U.S. If you entered illegally, write "none" here (but double check whether you're allowed to adjust your status in the U.S.—see Section C2, above). Under "Current INS Status," write the type of visa you're on, such as F-1 student or H-1B worker—or if your visa has expired, write "OOS," which stands for "out of status."

Part 2. Mark Box "A" if you are the principal applicant. Box "B" is marked if your spouse or parent is the principal applicant. Choose Box "C" if you entered the U.S. on a K-1 fiancé(e) or a K-2 child of fiancé(e) visa. Do not mark any other box.

Part 3. Under "Place of Last Entry into the US," be sure to name the city through which you most recently entered—even if it was after a short trip and you'd spent time in the U.S. before. The question about whether you were "inspected" by an immigration officer simply asks whether you entered legally, with the approval of a CBP officer. The nonimmigrant visa number is the number that appears on the very top of the visa stamp. It is not the same as your visa classification.

The questions in Section C are meant to identify people who are inadmissible. With the exception of certain memberships in terrorist, Communist Party, or similar organizations, you will not be deemed inadmissible simply because you joined an organization. However, if your answer to any of the other questions is "yes," you may be inadmissible. Chapter 25 is intended to help you remove such obstacles. Don't lie on your answers, because you will probably be found out, especially if you have engaged in criminal activity. Many grounds of inadmissibility can be legally overcome, but once a lie is detected, you will lose the legal right to correct the problem. In addition, a false answer is grounds for denying your application in itself and may result in your being permanently barred from getting a green card.

Form I-485A

This form is required only if you are subject to the $1,000 penalty fee for residing in the U.S. illegally and are eligible to file for adjustment of status. You would only be eligible if you had a visa petition or labor certification on file before January 14, 1998, or before April 30, 2001, so long as you were in the United States on December 21, 2000. The form is self-explanatory, and is intended only to determine if you are subject to the penalty.

Form G-325A

G-325A Biographic Data Forms must be filled out for you and each accompanying relative. You need not file a G-325A for any child under the age of 14 or any adult over the age of 79. If the basis of your immigration case is marriage to a U.S. citizen, a G-325A must be completed for both you and your U.S. spouse. This is the only type of case

where full biographic data is requested on someone who is already a U.S. citizen. Please note that if yours is a marriage case and you are filing Step Two in the U.S., but at a separate time from Step One, you must include the G-325A forms in Step One as well as Step Two. Form G-325A is meant to gather personal background information. The questions are self-explanatory.

Affidavit of Support: Form I-864

Most family-based immigrants must have this form filed by the petitioner in order to apply for permanent residence. It helps the immigrant show that he or she is not likely to become a public charge (receive government assistance). The sponsor must prove that she earns at least 125% of the income levels shown in the federal Poverty Guidelines.

However, there are two exceptions to the Form I-864 requirement. First, if the immigrant beneficiary has already worked in the U.S. for a total of 40 "quarters" (as defined by the Social Security Administration—it's about ten years), no I-864 needs to be submitted on his or her behalf. Second, if the immigrant beneficiary is a child who will become a U.S. citizen immediately upon approval for a green card (as discussed in Chapter 27) no I-864 needs to be submitted on his or her behalf.

Form I-864 is legally enforceable by the government for most public benefits utilized by the sponsored immigrant. It is also enforceable by the immigrant family member against the sponsor for support.

All family-based immigrants who file adjustment of status applications are required to have the I-864 filed by the person who is sponsoring their immigrant petition, whether or not the sponsor's income is high enough to meet the Poverty Guidelines minimum. However, if the sponsor's income is too low, another person (a joint sponsor) may add his or her income if the joint sponsor:

- is willing to be jointly liable
- is a legal permanent resident or U.S. citizen
- is over 18 years old, and
- resides in the U.S.,

as long as she meets the 125% income requirement when counting her own household as well. The joint sponsor must file a separate Form I-864 affidavit of support.

In addition, the main sponsor's household members may join their income with that of the primary sponsor to help reach the 125% level, but only if they have been living with the sponsor for six months and they agree to be jointly liable by filing a shorter form called Form I-864A.

Personal assets of the sponsor or the immigrant, such as property, bank account deposits, and personal property such as automobiles (minus debts or liens), may also be used to supplement the sponsor's income. However, the assets will have to add up to five times the difference between the 125% Poverty Guidelines income level for an equivalent family, and the sponsors' actual income.

The sponsors take on certain long-term responsibilities. They must notify USCIS within 30 days of a change of address, using Form I-865. Failure to do so is punishable by fines of $250-$2,000, or $2,000-$5,000 if the sponsor fails to notify with knowledge that the sponsored alien received a public benefit. The requirements and paperwork burden of the I-864 affidavit are complicated and substantial; most of the requirements are spelled out on the forms. If you have questions about meeting the eligibility or the scope of the sponsor's legal responsibility—which may last ten or more years for sponsors, or until the immigrant permanently leaves the country, dies, or naturalizes—you may want to consult an immigration attorney.

Form I-765

Block above Question 1. Mark the first box, "Permission to accept employment."

Questions 1–8. These questions are self-explanatory.

Question 9. This asks for your Social Security number, including all numbers you have ever used. If you have never used a Social Security number, answer "None." If you have a nonworking Social Security number, write down the number followed by the words "nonworking, for tax purposes only." If you have ever used a false number, give that number, followed by the words: "Not my valid number." However, be aware that if you have used false documents for employment or other purposes, you may be inadmissible. (See Chapter 25.)

Question 10. If you've already submitted your adjustment of status forms and gotten a receipt from USCIS, that receipt will show your new A number. If not, you will not usually have an Alien Registration Number unless you previously applied for a green card, were in deportation proceedings, or have had certain types of immigration applications denied. All Alien Registration Numbers begin with the letter "A." If you have no "A" number but you entered the U.S. with a valid visa, or without a visa under the Visa Waiver Program, you should have an I-94 card. In this case, answer Question 10 by putting down the admission number from the I-94 card.

If you are from Mexico, you may have entered the U.S. with a border crossing card, in which case you should put down the number on the entry document you received at the border, if any. Otherwise simply put down the number of the border crossing card itself, followed with "BCC." If you are Canadian and you entered the U.S. as a visitor, you will not usually have any of the documents described here, in which case you should put down "None."

Questions 11–14. These questions are self-explanatory.

Question 15. Answer this question "Adjustment of Status applicant."

Question 16. Answer this question "(c)(9)."

The fee for this application is $120.

4. Application Documents: U.S. Filing

In addition to the forms, you'll need to submit copies of various documents.

Notice of Action. An application filed in the U.S. for the spouse of a U.S. citizen is usually submitted at the same time as the petition, so you won't have—or need to submit—a Notice of Action. In cases when the petition was filed earlier, like for a family member of a permanent resident, you must submit the Notice of Action showing petition approval with the application.

Financial Documents. Your family member-sponsor must submit financial documents to prove the statements in the I-864 Affidavit of Support. (See Section 3, above.) These include proof of employment and your sponsor's last three years' federal tax returns (with W-2s).

Photos. You and each of your accompanying relatives are required to submit two photographs. These photos should meet the specifications on the photo instruction sheet found in Appendix II (Form M-378).

Birth Certificate. You must submit a copy of your birth certificate, with a certified translation. This is primarily for identification purposes.

Medical Exam. You must also submit a Medical Examination Report for each applicant, including proof of vaccinations. This is done on Form I-693, which must be taken to a USCIS authorized physician or medical clinic. The USCIS local office will provide you with this form and a list of approved physicians in your area. After completion of the medical exam, and upon obtaining the test results, the doctor will give you the results in a sealed envelope. *Do not open the envelope.*

Proof of Legal Entry. Each applicant must submit an I-94 card if one was issued. Failure to do so may result in a conclusion that you entered the U.S illegally and are inadmissible or subject to the $1,000 penalty described earlier. This is the small white or green card you received on entering the U.S. If you are a Canadian citizen and entered the U.S. as a tourist, you will not need to present the I-94 card. If you are from Mexico and entered the U.S. with a border crossing card instead of a visa, you must submit your original border crossing card, which will be canceled.

5. Application Interviews: U.S. Filing

Whenever a green card application is based on a marital relationship, a personal interview is required. Interviews can be waived in other types of cases, at the discretion of the local USCIS office. Assume both you and your petitioning relative will be interviewed unless you hear otherwise.

The USCIS officer will go over your application to make sure that everything is correct. He or she will also ask questions to see whether or not you are inadmissible. (See Chapter 25.) Your index fingerprints will then be taken and you will be asked to sign your application under oath. Accompanying relatives, all of whom must attend the interview with you, will go through the same procedure.

The interview normally takes about 30 minutes. If all goes well your case should be approved on the spot, although recently USCIS has been postponing the final decision on many cases because they have not yet received the FBI clearance. You may be expected to wait for the results if this is the case.

When you are approved, most USCIS offices will place a temporary stamp in your passport showing that you have become a permanent U.S. resident. With this stamp you acquire all the rights of a green card holder, including the right to work and freedom to travel in and out of the U.S., as long as your passport remains valid. The stamp is not your green card. You will receive your green card by mail several months later.

If your fingerprints have not been cleared yet, your application will be approved only provisionally, pending clearance. In those cases, no stamp will be placed in your passport at the interview. Instead, you will receive a written notice of approval within a few months. That notice serves as your proof of U.S. residency until you receive your green card, which takes yet another six or so months. If you need to travel outside the U.S. before your green card arrives, however, you must go back to the USCIS office with your passport and the written notice of approval. A temporary stamp will then be placed in your passport, enabling you to return after your trip. Never leave the U.S. without either your green card or a temporary stamp in your passport.

6. Application Appeals: U.S. Filing

If your application is denied, you will receive a written decision by mail explaining the reasons for the denial. There is no way of making a formal appeal to USCIS when your application to adjust status is turned down. If the problem is too little evidence, you may be able to overcome this obstacle by adding more documents and resubmitting the entire application to the same USCIS office you have been dealing with, together with a written request that the case be reopened. The written request does not have to be in any special form. This is technically called a Motion to Reopen. There is a $110 fee to file this motion. Alternatively, you may wait until USCIS begins deportation proceedings, in which case you may refile your application with the immigration judge (with a lawyer's help).

If your application is denied because you are ruled inadmissible, you may be given the opportunity to apply for what is known as a Waiver of Inadmissibility, if a waiver is available for your situation. (See Chapter 25.)

Although there is no appeal to USCIS for the denial of a green card application as there is for the denial of a petition, you have the right to file an appeal in a U.S. district court. This requires employing an attorney at considerable expense. Such appeals are usually unsuccessful.

G. Removing Conditional Residence in Marriage Cases

As we've already mentioned, green cards based on recent marriage to a U.S. citizen (within the last two years) are issued only conditionally, meaning they will expire after two years. This is true of cards issued both to spouses and stepchildren of U.S. citizens.

After holding your conditional green card for two years, if you are still married, you and your U.S. spouse must file a joint petition (Form I-751) to remove the condition, allowing you to receive permanent residence. The condition should be removed not only from your green card but from those of any children who came with you. If you are divorced, or your spouse has died or refuses to join in the petition, you must file for a waiver of the requirement.

1. Filing a Joint Petition With Your Spouse

You may file the joint petition even if you are separated or a divorce is in progress, as long as you remain legally married and your U.S.-citizen spouse agrees to sign the I-751 petition. You may also file the petition on your own if your U.S.-citizen spouse died no more than two years ago.

You must file the petition 90 days or fewer before the expiration of the two-year conditional period. If you fail to meet this deadline, be prepared to show an extremely good reason why you could not file on time. Otherwise you will lose your U.S. residence and could be deported.

The petition to remove the conditional status of your green card is made by filling out Form I-751. A copy of this form is in Appendix II. The form is self-explanatory. Where stepchildren are involved, one form may be used for the entire family. It must be signed by both you and your U.S. spouse, unless, of course, you are filing on your own because your spouse has died, you are divorced, or your spouse is abusive.

Together with your form, you must also supply documents to show that your marriage was not entered into only for immigration purposes. Look for documents that prove that you and your spouse have been living together and sharing your financial and other matters, such as joint bank accounts, credit card statements, automobile and insurance policies in both names, and leases or contracts showing you rent or purchased your home in both names. Sworn affidavits from people who know both you and your U.S. spouse, stating that they observed you living together during a particular period are also helpful. If you wish, you may bring witnesses to the interview (if you are called in for one) who can testify to observing that you and your U.S. spouse are truly married.

Forms and documents should be mailed together with a $145 filing fee to the USCIS regional service center nearest your home. A list of the USCIS regional service centers with their addresses is in Appendix I. However, check the USCIS website for the appropriate P.O. box.

Within a few weeks of mailing your petition to the regional service center, you will receive a written receipt (Form I-797) by return mail. The receipt is very important—it will be your only proof of legal status in the U.S. until your application is approved. Make a copy for your files, and use the original, together with your expired card, to prove your status to employers. Carefully note the expiration date on the receipt. It normally expires one year after USCIS received your application.

If you plan to travel in and out of the U.S. for that one year, you'll need to take your conditional green card, and this receipt. Be careful not to leave the U.S. after your receipt has expired if you haven't yet received a USCIS decision. Unfortunately, the USCIS often takes more than a year to make its decision. If you need to take a trip outside the U.S., or if your employer is asking for proof that you're allowed to work, visit your local USCIS office. Under a policy begun in 2003, USCIS can give you either a temporary "I-551" stamp in your passport or an I-94 card, either of which will extend the expiration date of your conditional residence by another year.

Eventually, you will either get a decision approving your petition or be asked to come to the USCIS local office for an interview. The interview is at the USCIS's discretion and does not necessarily indicate a problem. If your interview is successful, you will usually be approved at that time. After approval, your permanent green card will be sent to you by mail (months later).

2. Getting a Waiver of the Requirement to File a Joint Petition

If you are unable to file a joint petition with your U.S. spouse to remove the condition on your residency, either because of divorce or because he or she died or refuses to cooperate, you must then file for a waiver of the requirement to file the joint petition. This waiver will be granted in only three circumstances:

- you entered into a good faith marriage but the marriage is legally terminated (death or divorce)
- your deportation will result in an extreme hardship (one greater than that normally experienced by someone who is deported), and the marriage was originally entered into in good faith, or
- you were battered or subjected to extreme cruelty by your U.S. spouse and the marriage was originally entered into in good faith.

Like the joint petition, an application for a waiver must ordinarily be filed before your two-year conditional residency expires. However, if you are forced to file late because you were abused, or for another good reason—especially a reason connected to your waiver request—USCIS may excuse the delay.

Waiver applications, like joint petitions, are filed on Form I-751. Where stepchildren are involved, one form may be used for the entire family.

Together with your form, you must also supply documents showing that your marriage was not entered into only for immigration purposes. Proving that a marriage lasting less than two years was not a sham can be very difficult. First, you are not likely to have the cooperation of your ex-spouse, who in fact may even testify against you. In this situation, any other proof you can present to show that you married for love and not to get a green card can help.

This is best accomplished by submitting records that you and your spouse held joint bank accounts and credit cards, had automobile and insurance policies in both names, and rented or purchased your home in both names. Sworn affidavits from people who know both you and your U.S. spouse, stating that they observed you living together during a particular period of time, are also helpful. If you had children together, this too is excellent evidence that your marriage was not a sham—include their birth certificates or your hospital records.

If you are divorced, you should also provide a copy of your divorce decree. If divorce proceedings have been started but aren't yet finished, your waiver will be denied, and you will be placed in removal proceedings. Don't panic, however—the immigration judge should be willing to postpone your case until the divorce proceedings are done. If your spouse died, provide a copy of the death certificate.

Proving extreme hardship is more difficult. Situations that might qualify include serious illness, other close family members living in the U.S., financial loss such as vested pension benefits or lost career opportunities, and serious political or economic problems in your home country. You should submit a detailed, written statement in your own words explaining the circumstances of your marriage, what you gave up to come to the U.S, and what you will lose by returning to your home country. The statement should be supported by written documentation.

If the basis of your waiver is that you were abused by your U.S. spouse, you must supply evidence such as police reports, medical or psychiatric reports, photographs, or affidavits from witnesses. If you are in divorce proceedings, court records including pleadings and depositions may be used. Your own personal written statement explaining the details of the abuse should also be submitted.

Your forms and documents must be mailed, together with a $145 filing fee, to the USCIS regional service center nearest your home. A list of the USCIS regional service centers is in Appendix I, but see the USCIS website for the correct P.O. box. Within a few weeks, you will receive a written receipt by return mail. The receipt is very important—it will be your only proof of legal status in the U.S. until your application is approved. Make a copy for your files, and use the original, together with your expired card, to prove your status to employers. Carefully note the expiration date on the receipt. It normally expires one year after USCIS received your application.

If you plan to travel in and out of the U.S. during that one year, you'll need to present your conditional green card and this receipt at a local USCIS office and get a temporary "I-551" stamp in your passport.

Many applications for waivers will require a personal interview before being approved. If an interview is required in your case, you will be notified by mail. The interview will be held at the USCIS local office nearest your home.

Due to the complexity of this type of application and the severe consequences of its failure, we strongly recommend that you hire an experienced immigration lawyer to assist you.

FORMS AND DOCUMENTS CHECKLIST

STEP ONE: VISA PETITION

Forms

- ☐ Form I-130 (needed in all family cases except those involving widows and widowers or battered spouses).
- ☐ Form I-360 (needed for widows and widowers or battered spouses only).
- ☐ Form G-325A (needed only in marriage cases; one form is required for each spouse).

Documents

- ☐ Petitioner's proof of U.S. citizenship or green card status.
- ☐ Foreign national's long-form birth certificate.
- ☐ Long-form birth or marriage certificate to show family relationship.
- ☐ If either the petitioner or beneficiary have ever been married before, copies of all divorce and death certificates showing termination of all previous marriages.
- ☐ If you are applying as a battered spouse, evidence of physical abuse, such as police reports, medical reports, or affidavits from people familiar with the situation.
- ☐ If you are a father petitioning for a child, certificate showing marriage to child's mother.
- ☐ If your are a father petitioning for an illegitimate child, documents proving both paternity and either legitimation or a genuine parent/child relationship.
- ☐ If the petition is for an adopted child:
  - ☐ adoption decree, or child's new birth certificate showing you are the parent
  - ☐ evidence you and the child have lived together for at least two years, and
  - ☐ evidence you have had legal custody of the child for at least two years.
- ☐ If the petition is for a brother or sister, a copy of the parents' marriage certificate and the brother or sister's birth certificate.
- ☐ In marriage cases, one photograph of each spouse.
- ☐ If you are filing a petition as a widow(er), your marriage certificate, proof that any previous marriages were legally ended, and your spouse's death certificate.

STEP TWO: GREEN CARD APPLICATION

Forms

- ☐ DS Forms (available from U.S. consulate abroad for consular filing only).
- ☐ Form I-485 (U.S. filing only).
- ☐ Form I-485A (U.S. filing only, if you need to pay the penalty fee).
- ☐ Form G-325A (U.S. filing only).
- ☐ Form I-864 (consular and U.S. filing).
- ☐ Form I-765, if permission to work is desired (U.S. filing only).

Documents

- ☐ Notice of approval of the visa petition.
- ☐ Originals of all documents originally filed with the petition, except the petitioner's proof of U.S. citizenship or green card (bring to interview).
- ☐ Passports for the applicant and each accompanying relative, valid for at least six months beyond the date of the final interview.
- ☐ I-94 card or other proof of legal entry for the applicant and each accompanying relative (U.S. filing only).
- ☐ Police certificates from every country in which the applicant and each accompanying relative have lived for at least six months since age 16 (consular filing only).
- ☐ Military records for the applicant and each accompanying relative (consular filing only).
- ☐ Three photographs of the applicant and each accompanying relative.
- ☐ Financial documents to accompany Form I-864, Affidavit of Support, for the applicant and each accompanying relative.
- ☐ Medical exam report for the applicant and each accompanying relative.

CHAPTER

6

Getting a Green Card Through an Adoption

Privileges

- The adopted child may live anywhere in the U.S.
- The adopted child may work at any job, for any company, anywhere in the U.S., or may choose not to work at all.
- The adopted child may travel in and out of the U.S. nearly whenever he or she wishes.
- The adopted child may become a U.S. citizen immediately after obtaining his or her green card.

Limitations

- The adopted child's place of actual residence must be in the U.S. He or she cannot use a green card just for work or travel purposes.
- The adopted child will *never* be able to confer U.S. immigration benefits on his or her natural (biological) parents.
- The adopted child cannot remain outside the U.S. for more than one year at a time without special permission, or the child will risk losing his or her green card. We recommend that he or she return before being gone for six months.
- If the adopted child commits a crime or participates in politically subversive or other proscribed activities, his or her green card can be taken away and removal proceedings begun.

Adopted children have many of the same rights as biological children when it comes to U.S. immigration. However, qualifying for a green card through adoption has some limitations.

A. Who Qualifies for a Green Card Through Adoption?

In Chapter 5 we explained that children can get green cards through their American parents, and likewise, parents may get green cards through U.S. children. Both possibilities are available to adopted children and parents if certain requirements are met. The most significant requirements for non-orphans are that the adoption must have been finalized before the child's 16th birthday and that the child has lived in the parent's legal custody for two years before applying for the green card. If the child is an orphan, then the main requirements are that the visa petition be submitted before the child turns 16 and that the parents be U.S. citizens. Also, in situations where an adopted U.S. citizen child wants to petition for his or her parents, note that the child will have to turn 21 before submitting the visa petition. For more on children petitioning for parents, see Chapter 5.

The remainder of this chapter will focus on U.S. citizen parents adopting foreign-born children.

Often our adult clients ask us if having themselves legally adopted by a U.S. citizen is an effective way of becoming eligible for a green card. Clearly, if you are more than 16 years of age, the answer is "no."

In Chapter 5 we explained that there are several categories of relatives eligible for green cards. Foreign children who are adopted by a U.S. citizen parent or parents are considered immediate relatives of U.S. citizens. No quota applies to this category and so immediate relatives may immigrate to the U.S. in unlimited numbers. (There are even more benefits in cases of adoptions by U.S. citizens if the adopted child is an orphan; see Subsection 1, below.) Adopted children of green card holders are in the preference relative category. This category is subject to quotas.

1. Orphans

A child under 16 may obtain a green card as an orphan, but only if he or she is being adopted by a U.S. citizen rather than a permanent resident (green card holder). A child is an orphan if both natural parents are either deceased, have disappeared, or have permanently and legally deserted or abandoned the child. A child can also be an orphan if only one parent is deceased but the other parent has not remarried and is incapable of providing childcare that meets the standard of living in their country.

Be careful: some parents may put a child into an orphanage temporarily, without necessarily abandoning the child—however, the parents need to give up all of their parental rights for the child to be eligible to immigrate. In the case of an illegitimate birth, if the law of the native country confers equal benefits to illegitimate children as it does to legitimate, both parents must relinquish their rights.

In addition, to be classified as an orphan, the child must be living outside the U.S. and, if not already adopted by the U.S. parents, must either be in the U.S. parents' custody or in the custody of an agent acting on their behalf in accordance with local law. You cannot get a green card for a child you've adopted while the child was already in the U.S., whether the child is here on a visa or is undocumented. Finally, the child must be under 16 years of age when the petition is filed.

If the adopting parent is single, he or she must be at least 25 years of age in order to act as petitioner in an orphan green card application. There are no age restrictions if the petitioner is married.

Orphans may have green card petitions filed on their behalf either before or after the legal adoption by U.S. parents is completed. It is not essential that the adopting U.S. parents have met the orphan. In fact, it is not necessary that a particular child be identified before paperwork begins. There is a special procedure for those parents who know they will be adopting a child from a certain country but have not yet selected the particular child. To take advantage of this procedure, it is necessary that the adopting parents have satisfied any pre-adoption requirements existing in the laws of the U.S. state where they live, including a home study by the state government or an approved agency.

 Your application to immigrate an orphan will be denied if USCIS thinks you "bought" the child. Any sign that you paid money to the child's parents or other guardian or agent, or that someone bargained them into giving the child up, may be looked upon as "child buying." This has caused delays and denials in Central America and Cambodia, among other places.

2. Non-Orphans

A non-orphan is any person already adopted, whose adoption was finalized prior to his or her 16th birthday. It does not matter how old the child is when the petition is filed. In addition to being legally adopted, the child must have been in the legal custody of and physically residing with the adopting parents for at least two years before applying for a green card. It doesn't matter whether those two years were before or after the adoption took place. However, as a practical matter, the residency requirement usually means that at least one of the parents must live overseas with the child for two years. USCIS doesn't offer any temporary visas allowing the child to come to the U.S. to fulfill the two-year requirement before applying for the green card. (Though in rare cases usually amounting to emergencies, it might allow something called humanitarian parole.) Most U.S. parents who don't already have a particular child in mind find it easier to locate an orphan to adopt.

Unfortunately, the combination of the quotas and the two-year residency requirement can make it impossible for a permanent resident parent or parents to be united with a newly adopted child. Here's why: the child won't be able to legally enter the U.S. until he or she has a green card. (As an "intending immigrant," the child is not going to be allowed a tourist visa.) But the child can't get a green card unless he or she has already lived in the U.S. parent's legal custody for two years. If the child had been adopted before his or her parent(s) came to the U.S., and they had lived together overseas for two years, this would not be a problem. But if the child has recently been adopted, the family is stuck in an impossible situation. The permanent resident parent can't even choose to live overseas for the two years, since by doing so he or she will be considered to have "abandoned," or given up his or her U.S. residence and green card.

For a non-orphan to get a green card, it is also necessary that the adopting parents meet certain requirements. They must be investigated by a U.S. state public or government-licensed private adoption agency. Such an investigation is usually part of standard adoption procedure in most U.S. states and so this qualification may have already been met prior to the adoption. If, however, the adoption takes place outside the U.S., or an investigation is not compulsory in the particular American state where the adoption occurs, this study must now be satisfactorily completed. The age of the petitioning parent is irrelevant in filing a non-orphan petition, even if the parent is unmarried.

IMMEDIATE CITIZENSHIP FOR SOME ADOPTEES

If you or your spouse is a U.S. citizen and your adopted child is under age 18, the child may be able to obtain U.S. citizenship immediately after getting his or her green card—or even before, depending on whether you live in the U.S. or overseas. (This is based on the Child Citizenship Act of 2000.) There are two possible scenarios.

If you live in the U.S.: You will need to start by applying for your adopted child to enter the U.S. as a permanent resident. But the child's citizenship will follow soon after entry to the U.S. As soon as your child is living in your legal and physical custody, your child will become a citizen automatically. You don't even need to submit an application. Beginning in 2004, USCIS will send newly adopted children a certificate of citizenship within 45 days of their entry into the United States. No fee or application form need be submitted. The USCIS district office in Buffalo, New York, will be handling this function. You may also want to apply for the child's U.S. passport for proof purposes.

If you are living overseas with your adopted child: Your child may be able to become a citizen by taking a quick trip to the U.S. The child could enter the U.S. on a tourist visa and submit an application for a certificate of citizenship on Form N-643 ("Application for Certificate of Citizenship on Behalf of Adopted Child"). You'll have to prove that:

- whichever parent is a U.S. citizen has, in the past, been physically present in the U.S. or outlying possessions for a total of five years, two of which were after the age of 14
- the child is under age 18
- the child lives in your legal and physical custody while outside the U.S.
- the child is temporarily in the U.S. after entering lawfully (most likely with a visa), and
- the child is maintaining his or her lawful status (in other words, the visa or other permission hasn't expired and the child hasn't violated its terms).

For planning purposes, note that the child will have to wait in the U.S. until the application has been processed (which could take several months) and until the child is sworn in as a citizen. For application instructions, see the USCIS website at www.uscis.gov. Click on the "Forms and Fees" links until you get to the instructional screen for Form N-643.

NEW ADOPTION OPPORTUNITIES ON THE WAY

In October 2000, President Clinton signed into law the "Intercountry Adoption Act of 2000," which implements the Hague Convention on International Adoption. This is expected to streamline and broaden opportunities for adoption of children from overseas. It will offer a third category of eligibility for adoption, open only to adoptees from countries that are party to the Hague Convention. However, it will probably be a few years before this law is actually implemented, since the government must first set up a Central Adoption Authority and issue regulations.

3.   Orphan or Non-Orphan: Benefits and Drawbacks

It is not unusual for a child to meet all the requirements of both the orphan and non-orphan categories. The U.S. parents can then choose which category will result in a simpler application. For example, the major benefits to an orphan filing are that the two-year cohabitation and legal custody requirements of the non-orphan category need not be met, and the petition can be filed before the adoption is completed.

On the other hand, if a child is already adopted and physically residing in the U.S., the current age of the child is not important in a non-orphan filing. In an orphan filing, the child must be under the age of 16 when the visa petition is submitted. Remember that only U.S citizens may petition for the green cards of orphans, whereas non-orphans may have either U.S. citizens or green card holders as their petitioners.

Parents who are planning to adopt a foreign-born child but have not yet located or identified a specific child, may nonetheless proceed with applying for a green card through advance processing in the orphan category. The parents are investigated in advance and the orphan petition pre-approved. Then, when the child is identified, the final processing goes much faster.

4. Inadmissibility

Like all green card applicants, children are subject to the grounds of inadmissibility. If they have been arrested for certain crimes or suffered certain physical or mental illness, they may be inadmissible from receiving a green card unless they are able to qualify for a "Waiver of Inadmissibility." For example, medical grounds of inadmissibility for conditions such as HIV and tuberculosis are not uncommon in orphan cases from certain parts of the world. (See Chapter 25 to find out exactly who is inadmissible and how these obstacles can be overcome.)

B. Quota Restrictions

Some adopted children will fall into preference relative categories, which are limited by quotas. Others, including orphans, will be considered immediate relatives.

The forecasts for the Preference Relative category quotas are (as of January 2004):

- **Family First Preference.** Three-year waiting periods for natives of all countries except the Philippines and Mexico. Filipinos can expect quota waiting periods of at least 14 years. Mexicans can expect to wait about nine years.
- **Family Second Preference.** Waiting periods of four years can be expected for natives of all countries for spouses and minor children unless they're from Mexico, where the wait is seven years. Unmarried adult children (over 21) can expect to wait nine years or more, 12 if they're from Mexico.
- **Family Third Preference.** Waiting periods of at least six years can be expected for natives of all countries except Mexico, where the wait is about nine years, and the Philippines, where the wait is at least 14 years.

Petition approval usually takes at least six months. After petition approval and once a green card becomes available under the quota, it will take an additional three to 12 months for visa application approval. See Chapter 4, Section A3 for information on how to track the wait for your quota category until the child's Priority Date comes up and a visa number becomes available.

C. Applying for a Green Card for a Non-Orphan

If a child adopted by a U.S. citizen parent or green card holder falls into the category of non-orphan, the procedures for obtaining a green card are exactly the same as those described in Chapter 5 for blood-related children of parents who are U.S. citizens or green card holders. See Chapter 5 for further instructions; this chapter's discussion of non-orphans ends here. Note that for an adopted child, either a consular or U.S. filing is possible, depending on the physical location of the child when the application is submitted.

D. Applying for a Green Card for an Orphan

Getting a green card for an orphan is a two-step process. Step One is called the petition. Step Two is called the application. The application is a formal request for a green card.

1. Overview of Step One: The Petition

The first step in the process is for the U.S.-citizen adopting parent to file what's called an "Orphan Petition." All petitions are submitted to USCIS offices in the U.S. The object of the petition is to establish that the parent is a U.S. citizen and is qualified to adopt a foreign child, and that the child is legally available for adoption. If all goes well, the petition will eventually be approved, but be aware that an approved petition does not, by itself, give the child the right to come in to the U.S. It is only a prerequisite to Step Two, submitting the application. The petition must be approved before the child is eligible for Step Two.

Sometimes prospective U.S. parents looking for a foreign child to adopt wish to begin paperwork before they have actually identified the specific child. Although it is necessary, eventually, to go through all of the Step One procedures, prospective adopting parents may begin some of the paperwork before having identified the child by filing a preliminary application with a USCIS office. Once it is approved, and the parent has actually identified the child to be adopted, the rest of Step One may be completed. Since the USCIS has by that time already finished its mandatory investigation of the prospective parents, the remainder of the petition procedures can usually be approved immediately.

⚠ Also look into adoption laws in the child's country. Some countries have stricter adoption laws than the U.S., for example requiring that only married couples, not single people adopt; or that the parents be of the same nationality as the child. Others may add requirements to the process, such as that you live with the child overseas for a certain length of time.

2. Overview of Step Two: The Application

The application for an orphan-based visa is technically filed by the child, although normally an adult, either the adopting parents, private attorneys, or foreign adoption officials, will actually do all of the paperwork on the child's behalf. Step Two must be carried out in the child's home country at a U.S. consulate there. Step Two may not begin until the Step One petition is first approved.

3. Who's Who in Getting an Adopted Orphan's Green Card

Getting a green card will be easier if you familiarize yourself with the technical names used for each participant in the process. For an orphan, during Step One, the petition, the adopting parent is known as the *petitioner* and the orphan is called the *beneficiary*. In Step Two, the application, the orphan is referred to as the *applicant* but the petitioning parent remains the petitioner. (For non-orphans, see Chapter 5.)

4. Tips on Handling the Paperwork

There are two types of paperwork you must submit to get a green card for an adopted orphan. The first consists of official government forms completed by you. The second is personal documents such as birth, adoption and marriage certificates.

It is vital that forms are properly filled out and all necessary documents are supplied. You may resent the intrusion into your privacy and the sizable effort it takes to prepare the immigration applications, but realize the process is an impersonal matter to immigration officials. Your getting a green card for an adopted child is more important to you than it is to the U.S. government.

The documents you supply to USCIS or the consulate do not have to be originals. (If you send originals, you are unlikely to get them back.) Photocopies of all documents are acceptable as long as you have the original in your possession and are willing to produce the originals at the request of the immigration authorities. But add the following language to the photocopy, with your signature and the date:

Copies of documents submitted are exact photocopies of unaltered original documents and I understand that I may be required to submit original documents to an immigration or consular official at a later date.
Signature _____
Typed or Printed Name _____
Date_____

Documents will be accepted if they are in either English, or, with papers filed at U.S. consulates abroad, the language of the country where the documents are being filed (except in Japan, where all documents must be translated into English). If the documents are not in an acceptable language as just explained, they must be accompanied by a full, word for word, written English translation. Any capable person may act as translator. It is not necessary to hire a professional. At the end of each translation, the following statement must appear:

I hereby certify that I translated this document from [language] to English. This translation is accurate and complete. I further certify that I am fully competent to translate from [language] to English.
Signature _____
Typed or Printed Name _____
Date_____

The translator should sign this statement, but it does not have to be witnessed or notarized.

Later in this chapter we describe in detail the forms and documents needed to get a green card through an adoption. A summary checklist of forms and documents appears at the end of the chapter.

E. Carrying Out Step One: The Orphan Petition

This section includes the information you need to submit the orphan petition.

1. General Procedures When the Child Has Been Identified

The parents will need to meet the child in person before or during the adoption proceedings. A U.S.-citizen adopting parent submits the petition, consisting of forms and documents, to the USCIS local office nearest the place where he or she lives. Appendix I contains a complete list of all U.S. immigration offices.

a. Where to Submit the Petition

USCIS offices differ in their procedures. Some want the paperwork sent in by mail while others require that the file be delivered in person. A visit to the office will tell parents how and where to file Step One papers. If possible, file in person to ensure that the receipt of the petition is recorded. When the papers are brought in in person, they will be checked and any defects or omissions pointed out so that you can fix them. When filing is done by mail and defects or omissions are found, all petition papers, forms, and documents, will be returned. The returned package will contain either a handwritten note or a form known as an I-797 (Request for Evidence), describing what corrections or additional pieces of information and documents are expected. The petitioner should make the corrections or supply the extra data and mail the whole package back to USCIS.

b. Filing Fees

The filing fee for each petition is currently $460. In addition, each parent and other household member over the age of 18 must include a $50 fingerprinting fee (you'll be called in later for your fingerprinting appointment). Don't include this fingerprinting fee if your family lives outside the U.S. In that case, you'll need to submit a fingerprint card instead, which you can have done at a U.S. consulate or military office. Checks, money orders and cash are accepted.

c. Safety Measures

When filing by mail, don't send cash. If the petitioner files in person, he or she will be given a written receipt for the filing fee. Keep it in a safe place, together with a complete copy of everything submitted. Then the date the petition was filed can be confirmed and the number on the receipt will help locate the papers should they get lost or delayed in processing. When filing by mail, send the papers by certified mail, return receipt requested, and, again, keep a complete copy as a record.

d. Awaiting Approval

The length of time it takes to obtain an approved petition varies from one USCIS office to another, but expect a minimum of 90 days. You will be called in for fingerprinting during this time.

Once the orphan petition is approved, a Notice of Action Form I-797, indicating approval, will be sent to the adopting parent. USCIS will also notify the consulate having jurisdiction over the child's residence, sending it a complete copy of the file.

2. General Procedures When the Orphan Child Has Not Been Identified

If a U.S. citizen knows he or she will be adopting a foreign child but has not yet identified the particular child, he or she may still begin processing the paperwork. A preliminary application consisting of forms and documents is sent to the USCIS regional service center having jurisdiction over the parent's residence. (See the USCIS website, www.uscis.gov,

for the address.) This has the effect of asking USCIS to begin the investigation of the parents at once. The purpose of the preliminary application is to save processing time once the child to be adopted is identified. Approval will take a minimum of 90 days. The 90-day minimum is due to the time it takes the USCIS to fingerprint and receive FBI clearance on the prospective parents. Once the USCIS completes its investigation, a Notice of Action form is sent to the petitioning adopting parent.

When the child finally has been identified, the parent may then proceed with Step One, the petition, as already outlined, but the filing fee is not required, so long as 18 months have not passed since the approval of the advance processing petition. Since the USCIS investigation has already been completed, Step One can usually be approved promptly.

3. Petition Forms

Copies of both forms can be found in Appendix II and on the USCIS website. The fee for Form I-600 as well as for Form I-600A is $460.

Form I-600

(USCIS has been considering eliminating this form, and combining all orphan/adoption petitions on a new I-130 relative petition form. It is not known if or when the new form will come into use and be available.)

Questions 1–27. These questions are self-explanatory. Remember that all questions are being answered by the petitioner, and therefore "You" on this form refers to the adopting parents. Only one adopting parent needs to answer the questions, but if the petitioning adopting parent is married, both parents will have to sign the form.

Question 28. The petitioner must designate a U.S. consulate outside the U.S. to process the orphan's visa. Normally this should be at a U.S. embassy or consulate in the country where the child is living.

Form I-600A (Used for Advance Processing Only)

This form is completely self-explanatory.

4. Petition Documents When the Orphan Child Has Been Identified

Only U.S. citizens may petition for orphans. Therefore, it is necessary for the petitioner to provide proof of U.S. citizenship. If the petitioner is a U.S. citizen by birth, a birth certificate is the best proof. Only birth certificates issued by a U.S. state government are acceptable. Hospital birth certificates cannot be used. A certificate of citizenship, naturalization certificate, U.S. consular record of birth abroad, or an unexpired U.S. passport will serve as proof of U.S. citizenship if the petitioner was born in another country. If the petitioner is a U.S. citizen but does not have any of these documents, read Chapter 27 to learn how to obtain one of them.

If the petitioner's spouse is not a U.S. citizen, then you must include proof of his or her legal immigration status with the petition.

The petitioning U.S. parent must also submit evidence that the child is under age 16, that the natural parents are deceased or have legally abandoned the child, and that the adopting parents either have already obtained legal custody of the child in his or her home country, or the child is in the legal custody of an approved agency acting on their behalf. This will require presenting the orphan's birth certificate and either the natural parents' death certificates or the legal papers terminating their parental rights. If a birth certificate is unavailable, other evidence of the child's age must be submitted, such as a letter or affidavit from a doctor or anyone who knows when the child was born. Also required is a court or government order or acknowledgment showing that the petitioners, or someone acting on their behalf, have legal custody of the child. Remember to translate these documents into English if necessary.

The marital status of the petitioner is relevant because if the petitioner is married, the fitness of both adopting parents will be evaluated. Therefore, if the petitioner is married, it is necessary to prove this by showing a valid civil marriage certificate. Church certificates are generally unacceptable. (There are a few exceptions, depending on the laws of the particular country where the marriage took place. Canadians, for example, may use church marriage certificates from Quebec Province, but not elsewhere. If a civil certificate is available, however, it should always be used.)

If either parental spouse has been married before, it must be proven that all prior marriages were legally terminated. Use a divorce decree or death certificate. Where a death certificate is needed, it must be an official document issued by the government, not a funeral home. Divorce papers must be official court or government documents. If the death or divorce occurred in one of those few countries where such records are not kept, call the nearest consulate

or embassy of that country for help with getting acceptable proof of death or divorce.

It is necessary to present a home study done either by the U.S. state government agency handling adoptions in the particular state where the petitioner lives, or any private agency licensed in that state to do home studies. Some U.S. states have additional pre-adoption requirements, such as that the parents must have met the child prior to adoption. If that is the case in the petitioner's state, he or she must present a letter or certificate from the state agency regulating adoptions, verifying that the petitioner has satisfied all pre-adoption requirements. Home studies must include statements that there is no history of abuse or violence within the household. All Step One orphan petition documents must be resubmitted to the consulate later during Step Two.

5. Petition Documents When the Orphan Child Has Not Been Identified

If the orphan has not yet been identified, but the prospective parents wish to apply for advance processing to speed up immigration once the child is chosen, the documentation needed to accompany the advance processing Form I-600A is identical to that required for a standard orphan petition as already described above, with only the following exceptions. It will not be necessary at the time of completing the Step One procedure to include the child's birth certificate or other proof of the child's age, nor will it be necessary to provide evidence that the natural parents are dead or have legally abandoned the child. Also, the petition may be filed without the home study in order to get things moving right away. The home study may be submitted up to one year later, but USCIS cannot approve the petition before receiving the home study.

Once the advance processing petition is approved and the child has been identified, the petitioner must submit the remainder of Step One forms and documents, together with the Notice of Action from the advance processing. It is also not necessary to submit the $460 fee with the Form I-600 since it was already paid at the time of advance processing. This action must be taken within 18 months after approval of the advance processing application.

6. Petition Interviews

Personal interviews on orphan petitions are held only in cases where there is a question about the likelihood that a legal adoption will actually take place. Most of the time, the facts are clear from the documents presented, so petition interviews are rarely necessary.

7. Petition Appeals

When the status of the child as an orphan has been poorly documented, the petition will probably be denied. The petitioning parent will then receive a Notice of Action including a written statement of the reasons for the negative outcome and an explanation of how to make a formal appeal.

The best way to handle an appeal is to try avoiding it altogether. Filing an appeal means making an argument to USCIS that its reasoning was wrong. This is not something USCIS likes to hear. If the reason why the petition failed can be eliminated by improving the paperwork, it makes sense to disregard the appeals process and simply file a new petition, being careful to see that it is better prepared than the first.

If the petition was denied because the petitioner left out necessary documents that have since been located, the new documents may be sent, together with a written request that the case be reopened, to the same USCIS office that issued the denial. This is technically called a *Motion to Reopen*, for which there is a $110 filing fee. Appeals often take a long time. A Motion to Reopen can be concluded faster than an appeal.

If the petitioning adopting parent does choose to appeal, it must be done within 30 days of the date on the Notice of Denial. The appeal should be filed at the same USCIS office that issued the decision. USCIS will then forward the papers for consideration by the Board of Immigration Appeals (BIA) in Falls Church, Virginia. As orphan cases frequently involve questions of foreign law, it may take many months before the petitioner will get back a decision by mail. In immigration matters generally, fewer than 5% of all appeals are successful.

When an appeal to USCIS has been denied, the next step is an appeal through the U.S. judicial system. The adopting parent may not file an action in court without first going through the appeals process available from USCIS. If the case has reached this stage, seek representation from a qualified immigration attorney.

F. Carrying Out Step Two: The Application for Orphans

This section includes the information you need to submit the application.

1. Application General Procedures

Only a U.S. consulate or embassy in the child's home country is required to accept his or her green card application (unless the country has no U.S. embassy, discussed below).

You can ask a consulate located elsewhere to accept your adopted child's application, but it has the option to say "no," and probably will. If you do wish to ask for this privilege, approach the consulate of your choice before filing the Step One petition. That is because Form I-600 asks where you will file your application and you must be prepared with an answer.

You may not file your child's application for a green card at a consulate until after your petition has been approved. At that time, the USCIS office where your petition was originally submitted will forward your file to the National Visa Center in Portsmouth, New Hampshire (NVC).

The NVC will next forward your file to the U.S. consulate you named on Form I-600 in Step One. The NVC will send instructions and application forms to you within a month or two after petition approval. You will then communicate directly with the consulate. If, after waiting a reasonable time, you have not heard from the NVC, call and look into the matter.

The NVC will send you a packet containing forms and instructions. Complete and send Forms DS-230 Part I and DS-2001 to the consulate as soon as possible. Failure to return these forms promptly can significantly delay your adopted child's green card.

Once the consulate is ready for final processing, it will send another group of papers, including an interview appointment letter, instructions for obtaining a medical examination, and still more forms to be completed. Do not mail this final paperwork to the consulate. Instead, whoever will be taking the child to the consular interview should bring the rest of the forms and all documents along at the time of the appointment. Young children, under age 14, will normally be exempted from having a personal interview.

CHILDREN FROM COUNTRIES WITHOUT U.S. EMBASSIES

Citizens of countries not having formal diplomatic relations with the U.S. are faced with the problem of where to apply for immigrant visas. If you are adopting a child who is living in one of those countries, how his or her immigrant visa will be processed depends on whether he or she resides in his or her home country or a third country.

Persons from these countries who are still residing in their home countries will apply at a designated foreign consulate. Persons who are outside of their home country in a third country which conducts visa processing will do visa processing in that country as if they were residents of the third country.

2. Application Forms

When you file at a U.S. consulate abroad, the consulate officials will provide you with certain forms designated by a "DS" preceding a number. Instructions for completing DS forms and what to do with them once they are filled out will come with the forms. We do not include copies of these forms in this book, since different consulates have different versions. (Copies of all non-"DS" forms are in Appendix II and on the USCIS website.)

Form I-864

It will be necessary for you to convince USCIS that once the child comes to the U.S., she will be supported financially. The sponsor must show that she earns at least 125% of the level of income shown in the federal Poverty Guidelines. To show this, you must submit a completed Form I-864, Affidavit of Support (available in Appendix II or on the USCIS website). Applicants filing from overseas must also pay a $65 fee with this form.

Form I-864 is legally enforceable by the government for most public benefits utilized by the sponsored immigrant. It is also enforceable by the immigrant family member against the sponsor for support.

The petitioner must file Form I-864 regardless of whether their income is high enough. However, another person (a joint sponsor) may add her income to the sponsor's if the joint sponsor:

- is willing to be jointly liable
- is a legal permanent resident or citizen
- is over 18 years old, and
- resides in the U.S.,

as long as she meets the 125% income requirement when counting her own household as well. The joint sponsor files a separate Form I-864 affidavit of support.

Household members of the primary sponsor may also join their income to help reach the 125% level, but only if they have been living with the sponsor for six months or are dependents on their tax return and they agree to be jointly liable by filing form I-864A.

Personal assets of the sponsor or the immigrant, such as property, bank account deposits, and personal property such as automobiles (minus debts or liens), may also be used to supplement the sponsor's income. However, the assets are calculated at one-fifth their value.

Sponsors must notify USCIS within 30 days of their change of address, using Form I-865. Failure to do so is punishable by fines of $250-$2,000 or $2,000-$5,000 if the sponsor fails to notify with knowledge that the sponsored alien received a public benefit. The requirements and paperwork burden of the affidavit are complicated and substantial; most of the requirements are spelled out on the forms. If you have questions about meeting the eligibility requirements or the scope of your legal responsibility—which may be ten or more years for sponsors, or until the immigrant permanently leaves the country, dies or naturalizes—you may want to consult an immigration attorney.

3. Application Documents

Except for the proof that the petitioning adopting parents are U.S. citizens, copies of all of the documents first filed in Step One should be resubmitted to the consulate. Copies of these documents will not be forwarded by USCIS to the consulate.

It is also necessary that the child have in his possession a valid passport from his or her home country. The expiration date on the passport must extend at least six months beyond the date of the final application interview.

Since a child must be under age 16 to qualify as an orphan, it is not necessary to collect police certificates, as is required in all other types of green card applications.

The child must bring to the interview three photographs taken in compliance with the consulate's instructions.

4. Application Interviews

Consulates hold interviews on all green card applications, although a formal interview is frequently waived for children under the age of 14. A written notice of the interview appointment is included with the final packet.

a. The Medical Exam

Immediately prior to the interview, the orphan, regardless of age, will be required to have a medical examination. The child will be told where to go and what to do in the appointment letter.

The medical examinations are conducted by private doctors and a fee must be paid. The fees vary from $50 to more than $150 per exam, depending on the country. The amount of the fee will be stated in the appointment letter. The exam itself involves taking a medical history, blood test, and chest X-ray ,and verifying or administering vaccinations, if applicable. The requirement to have an X-ray taken cannot be waived, though for a very young child, some of the blood tests may not be required.

The primary purpose of the medical exam is to verify that your adopted child is not medically inadmissible. The primary medical grounds of inadmissibility are tuberculosis and HIV (AIDS). Some medical grounds of inadmissibility can be overcome with treatment. (See Chapter 25 for more details.) If a medical waiver is needed, you will be given complete instructions by the consulate at the time of your child's interview or final processing.

b.   What Happens at the Interview

After the medical exam, the child will report to the consulate for the interview. At that time, one more fee must be paid: $335. Some consulates accept payment only by certified check, money order, or traveler's check. Others accept cash. The proper method of payment will be explained in your appointment packet.

The completed forms, photographs, the child's passport, and all of the required documents discussed here should be brought to the interview. The interview process involves verification of the application's accuracy and an inspection of the documents. If all is in order, the child will be asked to return at a later time, when he or she will be issued an immigrant visa. The child is not yet a permanent resident.

c.   Using the Immigrant Visa

After you pick up the child's immigrant visa, it allows the child to travel to and request entry to the U.S. as a resident within six months. He or she will acquire the full status of green card holder at the moment of being inspected and admitted into the U.S. At that time, the child's passport will be stamped with an indication of permanent residence. A green card will then be ordered for the child. It will come in the mail several months later. By the time the green card comes, however, your child should no longer need it. Assuming that one of the parents is a U.S. citizen and the child is now living in the parent's legal and physical custody, the child is already a citizen, automatically. You can apply for a U.S. passport for the child.

It is important to note that the child's immigration status will not be affected if the legal adoption never takes place. The child may keep the green card anyway. It is certainly possible that circumstances might arise which would stop an adoption from being finalized. However, it is illegal for a U.S. citizen to file an orphan petition simply to help the child but with no genuine intent to complete the adoption. Although the child will be allowed to keep the green card, the U.S. petitioner will risk criminal prosecution for filing a fraudulent petition.

5.   Application Appeals

When a consulate denies a green card application, there is no formal appeal available, although the child is free to reapply. (Check with your local consulate, however—some place limits on the number of repeat applications, or require you to wait a certain number of months before reapplying.) When a green card is refused, the consulate will explain why. The most common ground for denial is failure to present all required documents. Sometimes presenting more evidence on an unclear fact can bring a better result. If a lack of evidence is the problem, the child or his custodian will be so advised in writing.

Another common reason for denial of a green card is that the consular officer believes the child is inadmissible. If ruled inadmissible, the child will be given an opportunity to apply for a waiver of inadmissibility, if one exists (see Chapter 25).

FORMS AND DOCUMENTS CHECKLIST

ORPHANS

STEP ONE: PETITION

Forms

☐ Form I-600.

☐ Form I-600A (advance processing only).

Documents

☐ Child's long-form birth certificate or other proof of age.

☐ Proof that the child is available for adoption:

    ☐ natural parents' death certificates

    ☐ proof that the child has been abandoned, or

    ☐ legal papers terminating parental rights.

☐ Proof that the child is in the legal custody of either the adopting parents or an approved agency acting on the parents' behalf.

☐ Petitioning parent's birth certificate, or other proof of U.S. citizenship.

☐ If petitioner is married, marriage certificate.

☐ If petitioner is married to a non-U.S. citizen, proof that the non-citizen has lawful U.S. immigration status.

☐ If either or both petitioners have ever been married, copies of all divorce and death certificates showing termination of each previous marriage.

☐ Documents showing completion of adoption agency home investigation.

☐ Documents showing the adopting parents have satisfied any pre-adoption requirements of the state where they live.

STEP TWO: APPLICATION

Forms

☐ DS forms (available at U.S. consulate only).

☐ Form I-864.

Documents

☐ Notice showing approval of orphan petition.

☐ All documents originally filed with the orphan petition, except the petitioning parent's proof of U.S. citizenship and fingerprint cards.

☐ Financial documents to accompany Form I-864, including proof of the sponsor's income and assets and tax returns from the last three years.

☐ Passport from the orphan's home country, valid for at least six months beyond the date of the final interview.

☐ Three photographs of the orphan.

NON-ORPHANS

(See checklists for relatives in Chapter 5.)

Getting a Green Card Through Your Fiancé: K-1 Visas

Privileges

- You may come to the U.S. in order to marry a U.S. citizen.
- You may apply for permission to work immediately upon arriving in the U.S.
- If your U.S.-citizen fiancé is unable to travel to your home country to marry you, the K-1 visa may be the only solution.
- Your unmarried children under age 21 may come with you as accompanying relatives.
- You can use the K-1 visa to enter the U.S. more than once.

Limitations

- You must marry your U.S.-citizen petitioner within 90 days after you enter the U.S.
- You must still apply for a green card after you get married if you want to stay in the U.S.
- A K-1 visa lasts only 90 days. It cannot be extended beyond that period under any circumstances.
- If you fail to get married within the 90-day period, you may be forced to leave the U.S.

This chapter covers who is eligible for a K-1 visa and how to apply. Fiancés are fortunate in that there are no quota restrictions for K-1 visas, and thus no long waiting periods. The first step, visa petition approval, normally takes at least four months. After the petition has been approved, it will take an additional two to five months for the U.S. consulate overseas to issue a visa.

Note: Although the accurate way to generally refer to both male and female fiancés is "fiancé(e)," we are using the term "fiancé" for simplicity's sake.

A. Who Qualifies for a K-1 Visa?

If you intend to marry a U.S. citizen, your fiancé may bring you to America for the wedding with a K-1 visa. Although it is a nonimmigrant visa, we have included it with the chapters on green cards because after you get married, it can easily be converted into a green card.

To get a K-1 visa, both members of the couple must be legally able to marry. That is to say, both must be single and of legal age. If either party is already married, a K-1 visa cannot be granted—but you can either apply for an immigrant visa or, to save time, special fiancé visa for already-married couples (the K-3) discussed in Chapter 5, Section C.

Not only must the couple actually intend to marry, but, with limited exception, they must have met and seen each

other in person within the past two years. Under the right circumstances this requirement may be waived for people who practice religions in which marriages are customarily arranged by families and premarital meetings are prohibited. Generally, to be released from the requirement of having met your fiancé, you must show that both parties will be following all the customs of marriage and weddings that are part of the religion.

It is also possible to get a waiver of the personal meeting requirement if such a meeting would cause an extreme hardship to the U.S. citizen member of the couple. Only the most extreme situations involving medical problems are likely to be regarded as a good enough reason for the waiver to be granted. Economic problems alone are not usually acceptable.

In summary, there are four conditions to getting a K-1 visa:

- the petitioner must be a U.S. citizen
- both members of the couple must be legally able to marry
- the foreign national must have a genuine intention to marry the petitioner after arriving in the U.S., and
- the couple must have met and seen each other within the past two years, unless they practice a religion that forbids couples to meet before marriage, or if their meeting would cause an extreme hardship to the petitioner.

ACCOMPANYING CHILDREN

When you get a K-1 visa, any of your unmarried children under the age of 21 can be issued K visas. This will enable them to accompany you to the U.S. They, too, will be able to apply for green cards once you get married.

⚠️ **You'll need to separately apply for a green card after the marriage.** Once you marry, if the 90-day validity period of the K-1 visa has not yet expired, you may file for a green card without leaving the U.S. Simply follow the directions in Chapter 5 starting with Step Two. Because you have already gotten a K-1 visa, you are excused from Step One (the I-130 visa petition). You will, however, be subject to the two-year conditional residency placed on green cards obtained through marriage to an American. This, too, is covered in Chapter 5. Read it carefully before applying for a fiancé visa.

B. Applying for a K-1 Visa

Getting a K-1 visa is a two-step process. Step One is called the petition. Step Two is called the application. (Note: "Step One" and "Step Two" are not technical terms, so if you're talking to USCIS or the consulate, you'll need to refer instead to the "petition" and "application.")

1. Overview of Step One: The Petition

The petition is filed by your U.S.-citizen fiancé. All K-1 visa petitions are submitted to USCIS regional service centers in the U.S. The object of the petition is to prove three things:
- you have a bona fide intention of marrying a U.S. citizen within 90 days after you arrive in the U.S.
- both parties are legally able to marry, and
- you have physically met each other within the past two years—or can prove that this requirement should be waived based on religion or extreme hardship.

An approved petition does not by itself give you any immigration benefits. It is only a prerequisite to Step Two, submitting your application. The petition must be approved before you are eligible for Step Two. See Section D, below, for instructions on preparing the petition.

2. Overview of Step Two: The Application

Step Two must be carried out at a U.S. consulate in your country of residence. See Section E, below, for instructions. You must wait to file the application until Step One, the petition, is first approved.

You may not, under any circumstances, complete Step Two while you are in the U.S. The whole objective of the K-1 visa is to allow your entry into the U.S. for the purpose of marrying. If you are already in the U.S., or if your fiancé lives overseas with you, getting a K-1 visa is unnecessary. Instead, you should get married and then apply for a green card as outlined in Chapter 5.

3. Who's Who in Getting Your K-1 Visa

Getting a K-1 visa will be easier if you familiarize yourself with the technical names used for each participant in the process. During Step One, the petition, you are known as the *beneficiary* and your U.S. fiancé is known as the *petitioner*. In Step Two, the application, you are referred to as *applicant* but your U.S.-citizen fiancé is still known as the *petitioner*. Your accompanying children will also be known as *beneficiaries* in Step One and *applicants* in Step Two.

4. Tips on Preparing the Paperwork

There are two types of paperwork you must submit to get a fiancé visa. The first consists of USCIS and consular forms completed by you or your fiancé. The second is personal documents such as birth and marriage certificates.

It is vital that the forms are properly filled out and all necessary documents are supplied. You or your fiancé may resent the intrusion into your privacy and the sizable effort it takes to prepare immigration applications but you should realize the process is an impersonal matter to immigration officials. Your getting a visa is more important to you than it is to the U.S. government. There is no shortage of visa applicants.

The documents you or your fiancé supply to USCIS or the consulate do not have to be originals. In fact, if you send originals, you're unlikely to get them back. Photocopies of all documents are acceptable as long as you have the original in your possession and are willing to produce the originals at the request of USCIS or the consulate. But add the following language to the photocopy, with your signature and the date:

> *Copies of documents submitted are exact photocopies of unaltered original documents and I understand that I may be required to submit original documents to an immigration or consular official at a later date.*
> *Signature _____*
> *Typed or Printed Name _____*
> *Date_____*

Documents will be accepted if they are in either English, or, with papers filed at U.S. consulates abroad, the language of the country where the documents are being filed (except in Japan, where all documents must be translated into English). If the documents are not in an acceptable language as just explained, they must be accompanied by a full, word for word, written English translation. Any capable person may act as translator. It is not necessary to hire a professional. At the end of each translation, the following statement must appear:

> *I hereby certify that I translated this document from [language] to English. This translation is accurate and complete. I further certify that I am fully competent to translate from [language] to English.*
> *Signature _____*
> *Typed or Printed Name _____*
> *Date_____*

The translator must sign this statement, but it does not have to be witnessed or notarized.

Later in this chapter we describe in detail the forms and documents needed to get your fiancé visa. A summary checklist of forms and documents appears at the end of the chapter.

C. Carrying Out Step One: The Petition

This section includes the information you need to submit the petition.

1. General Procedures

The fiancé petition, consisting of forms and documents, is filed by mail at the USCIS regional service center nearest the home of your U.S.-citizen fiancé. USCIS service centers are not the same as local offices—for one thing, you cannot visit service centers in person. There are many USCIS local offices but only four USCIS regional service centers spread across the country. Appendix I contains complete lists of all U.S. immigration offices and regional service centers, but you should check the USCIS website to get their appropriate P.O. box for this application: www.uscis.gov. Look for "Field Offices."

As mentioned earlier, petitions filed at regional service centers are submitted by mail. The filing fee for the petition is $110. Checks or money orders are accepted. It is not advisable to send cash. We recommend sending your papers by certified mail, return receipt requested, and making a copy of everything sent in to keep with your records.

Within a few weeks after mailing your petition, your fiancé should get back written confirmation that the papers are being processed, together with a receipt for the fees. This notice will also give your immigration file number and tell approximately when you should expect to have a decision.

If USCIS wants further information before acting on your case, the petition papers, forms, and documents may be returned to your fiancé, together with another form known as an I-797. The I-797 tells your fiancé what additional pieces of information or documents are expected. Your fiancé should supply the extra data and mail the whole package back to the service center.

Once your petition is approved, a Notice of Action Form I-797 will be sent to your fiancé, indicating the approval, and the file will be forwarded to the appropriate U.S. consulate abroad. The consulate will then contact you directly with instructions on how to move on to Step Two and complete the visa processing.

2. Petition Forms

Copies of all the required USCIS forms can be found in Appendix II and are available on the USCIS website.

Form I-129F

Section A, Questions 1–13. These questions, which pertain to your U.S.-citizen petitioner, are all self-explanatory.

Section B, Questions 1–8. These questions, which pertain to the K-1 visa applicant, are all self-explanatory. Be sure to write your full middle name, not just your initial, or USCIS will send the form back to you. (It needs your middle name to do a security check.)

Section B, Question 9. Alien Registration Numbers, which all begin with the letter "A," are given only to people who have applied for green cards, have applied for political asylum, or have been placed in deportation proceedings. If you have an "A" number, put that number down and explain how you got it, such as "number issued from previous green card petition filed by my brother." (USCIS will then check your file to see if it contains any negative information about you.) If you do not have an "A" number, write down "None."

Section B, Questions 10–12. These questions are self-explanatory.

Section B, Question 13. If you are in the U.S. when your fiancé mails this petition, you will need to fill in this section—but return to your home country before turning in your K-1 visa application. Hopefully your current visa is still valid. If it's not, USCIS won't come after you, but you could have problems when you go to the U.S. consulate to collect your visa. If the consulate sees that you stayed in the U.S. illegally for between six and 12 months, you could be prevented from returning for three years. If you stayed in the U.S. illegally for more than 12 months, you could be prevented from returning for ten years. See Chapter 25 for more information.

Section B, Questions 14–19. These questions are self-explanatory.

Section B, Question 20. Your fiancé must designate a U.S. consulate outside of the U.S. where you will apply for your K-1 visa. Normally this should be in the fiancé's home country. Other consulates can also be designated if necessary, but they are often reluctant to take K-1 cases from persons who are not residents or nationals of that country. It is better not to press the issue.

Section C. The first question applies only to petitioners who are in the U.S. armed forces overseas. This section is self-explanatory. If it does not apply to you put down "N/A." Your fiancé must sign the form. Ignore the section asking for "Signature of Person Preparing Form, If Other Than Above."

G-325A

You and your U.S. fiancé must each complete a Form G-325A, which is meant to gather personal background information. The questions are all self-explanatory.

3. Petition Documents

You must provide several documents with the petition.

a. Proof That the Petitioner Is a U.S. Citizen

The first document that must be filed with the petition is evidence that the petitioner is a U.S. citizen. If the petitioner is a U.S. citizen by birth, a copy of the birth certificate is the best proof. Only birth certificates issued by U.S. state governments are acceptable. Hospital birth certificates cannot be used. When the petitioner is a U.S. citizen born outside U.S. territory, a copy of a certificate of citizenship, naturalization certificate, U.S. consular record of birth abroad, or unexpired U.S. passport will serve as proof.

If the petitioner is a U.S. citizen but does not have one of these documents, read Chapter 27 to learn how to obtain one of them. A fiancé petition cannot be filed without this proof.

b. Proof That You and Your Fiancé Can Legally Marry

You and your fiancé will have to prove you are both over the legal age of consent (usually 18) in the U.S. state where you plan to marry. Birth certificate copies for each of you will serve to prove this.

If either of you has been married before, you must also prove that all prior marriages were legally terminated. This requires presenting a divorce decree or death certificate for every prior marriage. Divorce papers must be official court or government documents. Likewise, when a death certificate is needed, it must be an official document issued by the government. Certificates from funeral homes are not acceptable. If either of you comes from a country where divorces and deaths are not officially recorded, contact the nearest embassy or consulate representing that country in the U.S. to find out what other types of proof are acceptable.

c. Proof of Intent to Marry

If a wedding ceremony is planned, which is strongly recommended in K-1 visa cases, your fiancé should provide evidence that a wedding will take place, such as copies of wedding announcements, catering contracts, etc. A letter or affidavit from your pastor or justice of the peace stating that he has been contacted about performing your marriage ceremony is helpful.

Your fiancé petitioner should also prepare and submit a statement explaining how you met each other, why he or she cannot travel to your home country to marry you there, and describing your wedding plans. This statement does not have to be in any special form, but simply in the petitioner's own words.

d.   Proof That You Have Met Each Other

Your fiancé must prove that you and he or she have met each other in person and have seen each other within the past two years. This is best shown by submitting photographs of the two of you together and letters you have written to each other indicating that there has been a meeting. Copies of plane tickets, credit card receipts, and hotel receipts are also helpful.

e.   If You Haven't Met Each Other

It is virtually impossible to get an approval of a K-1 petition without a personal meeting unless both you and your fiancé practice a religion that prohibits spouses from meeting each other before the wedding. If that is your situation, you must present evidence of your membership in such a religion. This is usually done with two documents: a letter from an official in your religious organization verifying that you and your fiancé are members, and a detailed statement from a clergyperson explaining the religious laws concerning marriage. A letter from your parents is also helpful.

If you are asking for a waiver of the requirement of having met, based upon a showing of extreme hardship, you must submit a written statement explaining in detail why you cannot meet. If there is a medical reason why your U.S.-citizen fiancé can't travel to meet you, include a letter from a medical doctor explaining the condition.

f.   Identification Photographs

It is necessary to submit one photograph each of you and your U.S.-citizen fiancé. This is in addition to photographs that may have been provided showing you had previously met each other. These identification photographs must meet certain exact specifications, as described on Form M-378, found in Appendix II.

4.   Petition Interviews

Sometimes USCIS will request a personal interview with the petitioner prior to approving a fiancé petition. The purpose of the interview is to make sure a marriage will really take place after you arrive in the U.S. and to confirm that you have previously met each other. All interviews are held at USCIS local offices. The regional service center will forward the file to the USCIS local office nearest the petitioner's home, before the interview. The USCIS local office will send the petitioner a notice of when and where to appear for the interview, and instructions to bring additional documentation, if any is required.

5.   Petition Appeals

Usually a fiancé petition is turned down either because you and your fiancé haven't met each other or your fiancé hasn't convinced USCIS that you really intend to marry upon your arrival in the U.S. When the petition is denied, USCIS will send your fiancé a written statement of the reasons, and an explanation of how to appeal.

The best way to handle an appeal is to avoid it altogether. Filing an appeal means making an argument to USCIS that its reasoning was wrong. This is not something USCIS likes to hear. If you think you can eliminate the reason why your petition failed by improving your paperwork, it makes sense to disregard the appeals process and simply file a new petition, being careful to see that it is better prepared than the first time.

If the petition was denied because your U.S.-citizen fiancé left out necessary documents that have since been located, the new documents should be sent together with a written request that the case be reopened to the same USCIS office that issued the denial. This is technically called a Motion to Reopen, for which there is a $110 filing fee. A Motion to Reopen can usually be concluded faster than an appeal.

An alternative solution is for your U.S.-citizen fiancé to travel to your country, marry you there, and then petition for you as an immediate relative of a U.S. citizen, as discussed in Chapter 5.

If your fiancé does choose to appeal, it must be done within 30 days of the date on the Notice of Denial. The appeal should be filed at the same USCIS office that issued the denial. There is a $110 filing fee. USCIS will then forward the papers for consideration by the Administrative Appeals Unit in Washington, DC. In six to 18 months or more, your fiancé will get back a decision by mail. Less than 5% of all appeals are successful.

When an appeal to USCIS has been denied, the next step is to make an appeal through the U.S. judicial system. Your fiancé may not file an action in court without first going through the appeals process available from USCIS. If the case has reached this stage, we strongly recommend seeking representation from a qualified immigration attorney.

D. Carrying Out Step Two: The Application

This section includes the information you need to submit your visa application to a U.S. consulate.

1. Who Is Eligible?

Anyone with an approved K-1 petition can apply for a K-1 visa at a U.S. consulate in his or her home country. You must be physically present in order to apply there. Remember, unlike most other visas, a K-1 visa cannot be obtained in the U.S.

2. General Procedures

The law states that any consulate will accept nonimmigrant cases, regardless of the residence of the applicant. However, in the case of K-1 visas, the attitude of the consulates is usually different. Because K-1 visas are so closely related to green cards, all but the consulate in your home country are usually reluctant to accept your application. You can ask a consulate located elsewhere to accept your application, but it has the option to say "no" and will probably do so. Therefore, you should attempt to process your K-1 application in some other country only if it is absolutely essential. Approach the consulate of your choice before filing the Step One petition. This is because Form I-129F in Step One asks where you will file your application, and your fiancé must be prepared with an answer to this question.

You may not file an application for a fiancé visa at a consulate before your petition has been approved. After its approval, the USCIS service center where your petition was originally submitted will forward a complete copy of your file to the U.S. consulate you designated on Form I-129F in Step One. At the same time a Notice of Action from Step One will be sent directly to your U.S. fiancé. It typically takes a month or longer for the approved petition and file to arrive at the consulate. The consulate will in turn contact you by mail, sending the necessary forms and detailed instructions for your application. If, after waiting a reasonable time, you have not heard from the consulate, call and look into the matter. Files do get lost, so check up.

Once the consulate has received your file from USCIS, you will receive a letter containing the needed forms and instructions, including the requirements for obtaining a medical exam. One important item it will contain is Biographical Information Form DS-2001 (formerly numbered OF-169). Complete and return this form to the consulate as soon as possible. This will initiate a security check. The consulate may also ask you to send other forms in, such as Form DS-230I.

The application for your fiancé visa is made in person, by appointment. When the consulate is ready, it will send you an appointment letter and still more forms to be completed. Do not mail this paperwork to the consulate. Instead, bring it with you at the time of your appointment. The filing fee for the K-1 visa application is $100.

3. Application Forms

When you file at a U.S. consulate abroad, the consulate officials will provide you with certain forms designated by a "DS" preceding a number. Instructions for completing DS forms and what to do with them once they are filled out will come with the forms. We do not include copies of these forms in this book, because different consulates sometimes use different versions. Copies of non-"DS" forms are in Appendix II and available from the USCIS website.

Affidavit of Support

Your fiancé will have to fill out an Affidavit of Support to prove that you will not become a "public charge" (go on welfare) in the U.S. You actually have a choice between two forms: Form I-864 and a shorter one, Form I-134. But bear in mind that K visa applicants will eventually have no choice but to submit the lengthier Affidavit of Support, Form I-864, with their green card application in the U.S. They are allowed to use the less burdensome and older I-134 for the K visa, since the K visa is a nonimmigrant visa. In cases where the level of financial support is clearly not a problem, you could submit the I-864 in support of the K visa to avoid duplicating your efforts. On the other hand, there are advantages to using the old I-134 initially, and then using the I-864 during the U.S. application. The main advantage is that Form I-134 is not considered legally enforceable. In other words, the U.S. government is very unlikely to go after whoever signs the I-134 for reimbursement if the immigrant ends up needing public benefits. That's a particular advantage if your U.S. citizen fiancé can't satisfy the financial requirements to be a sponsor and you need to convince a friend or family member to sign an additional affidavit of support on your behalf.

Form I-864 is legally enforceable by the government for most public benefits utilized by the sponsored immigrant. It is also enforceable by the immigrant family member against the sponsor for support. It also requires that the sponsor show that she has at least 125% of income for a similar family size, according to the federal Poverty Guidelines level.

When you file for adjustment of status in the U.S. or if you choose to use Form I-864 now, you are required to have the I-864 filed by the person who is sponsoring you, whether or not that person's income is high enough to meet the minimum. However, another person (a joint sponsor) may add her income to the sponsor's if the joint sponsor:

- is willing to be jointly liable
- is a legal permanent resident or citizen of the U.S.
- is over 18 years old, and
- resides in the U.S.,

as long as she meets the 125% income requirement when counting her own household as well. The joint sponsor files a separate Form I-864 Affidavit of Support.

A sponsor's other household members may combine their income to help reach the 125% level, but only if they have been living with the sponsor for six months and they agree to be jointly liable by filing Form I-864A.

Personal assets of the sponsor or the immigrant, such as property, bank account deposits, and personal property such as automobiles, may also be used to supplement the sponsor's income on Form I-864. To use assets, however, the assets, minus debts and liens, will have to add up to five times the difference between the 125% Poverty Guidelines income level for an equivalent family and the sponsors' actual income.

The sponsors must also notify USCIS within 30 days of the sponsor's change of address, using Form I-865. Failure to do so is punishable by fines of $250-$2,000, or $2,000-$5,000 if the sponsor fails to notify with knowledge that the sponsored alien received a public benefit.

The requirements and paperwork burden of the I-864 affidavit are complicated and substantial; most of the requirements are spelled out on the forms. If you have questions about meeting the eligibility or the scope of the sponsor(s)' legal responsibility—which may last ten or more years, or until the immigrant permanently leaves the country, dies, or naturalizes—you may want to consult an immigration attorney.

4. Application Documents

The most important document in your application is the Notice of Action indicating approval of your fiancé visa petition. It is sent directly from the USCIS office in the U.S. to the consulate you designated on Form I-129F in Step One. This is the only document you will not have to submit yourself. Do not mail in your other documents, unless specifically requested to do so. Bring them with you to your interview.

You must resubmit to the consulate all of the documents first filed in Step One. Copies of these documents will probably not be forwarded by USCIS to the consulate for you. Bring originals of documents such as birth or divorce certificates to the consulate for them to compare with the copies.

It is also necessary that you have in your possession a valid passport from your home country. The expiration date on the passport must be at least six months beyond the date of your interview.

Police clearance certificates are required from each country you have lived in for one year or more since your 16th birthday, unless the country does not make them available. Additionally, you must have a police certificate from your home country or country of last residence, if you lived there for at least six months since the age of 16. You do not need to obtain police certificates from the U.S. If you go to your interview without the required certificates, you will be refused a visa and told to return after you get them.

Contact the local police department in your home country for instructions on how to get police certificates. To obtain police certificates from nations other than your home country, it is best to contact the nearest consulate representing that country for instructions. Some nations refuse to supply police certificates, or their certificates are not considered reliable, and so you will not be required to obtain them from those locations. The U.S. consulate will give you a list of countries from which police certificates are not required.

Some countries will send certificates directly to U.S. consulates but not to you personally. Before they send the certificates out, however, you must request that it be done. Usually this requires filing some type of request form together with a set of your fingerprints.

You and each accompanying child must bring to the interview three photographs taken in compliance with the instructions provided in your appointment letter. The instructions may also contain a list of local photographers who take this type of picture.

A few consulates require you to submit fingerprints, though most do not. Consulates wanting fingerprints will send you blank fingerprint cards with instructions. The current fingerprinting fee is $85.

5. Application Interviews

Consulates hold interviews on all fiancé visa applications. You will receive written notice of your interview appointment. Immediately prior to the interview, you and your accompanying children will need to have medical examinations. Some consulates conduct the medical exams the day before the interview. Others schedule the medical exam and the interview on the same day. You will be told where to go and what to do in your appointment letter.

a. The Medical Exam

The medical examinations are conducted by private doctors and you are required to pay the doctor a fee. The fees vary from $50 to more than $150 per exam, depending on the country. The amount of the medical exam fee will be stated in your appointment letter. The exam itself involves taking a medical history, blood test, and chest X-ray, and verifying or administering vaccinations, if applicable. Pregnant women may refuse to be X-rayed (although they will have to have an X-ray after the pregnancy).

The main purpose of the medical exam is to verify that you are not medically inadmissible. The primary medical grounds of inadmissibility are tuberculosis and HIV (AIDS). Some of the medical grounds of inadmissibility can be overcome with treatment. (See Chapter 25 for more details.) If you need a medical waiver, you will be given complete instructions by the consulate at the time of your interview.

b. What Happens at the Interview

After the medical exam, you and your accompanying children will report to the consulate for the interview. Bring with you to the interview the completed forms, photographs, your passports, and all of the required documents discussed in this chapter and a visa application fee (currently $100). The interview process involves verification of your application's accuracy and an inspection of your documents.

Because of new security requirements, you are unlikely to be approved for your visa on the same day as your consular interview. Your name will first need to be checked against various FBI and CIA databases of people with a history of criminal activity, violations of U.S. immigration laws, or terrorist affiliations. This can add weeks or months

to the processing of your visa, particularly if you come from a country that the U.S. suspects of supporting terrorism. Once your visa has been approved, however, the consulate will contact you to pick it up.

c. Using the Fiancé Visa

Normally, you must use the visa to enter the U.S. within six months, though the consulate can extend this period if necessary. Upon entering the U.S. with that visa, your passport is stamped and you will be authorized to remain in the U.S. for 90 days. If you are bringing accompanying children, they must enter the U.S. at either the same time or after you do. You can apply for a work permit once you're in the U.S.—see below, "Employment Authorization."

6. Application Appeals

When a consulate denies a fiancé visa application, there is no formal appeal available, although you are normally free to reapply as often as you like. (Check with your local consulate to be sure, however—some place limits on repeat applications, or require you to wait a certain number of months before reapplying.) When your visa is refused, you will be told the reasons. The most common reason for denial is failure to supply all the required documents. Sometimes presenting more evidence on an unclear fact can bring about a better result. If the denial was caused by a lack of evidence, this will be explained in a written notice sent to you by mail.

Another common reason for denial of a visa is that the consular officer believes you are inadmissible. If you are found to be inadmissible, you will be given an opportunity to apply for a Waiver of Inadmissibility, if one is applicable. (See Chapter 25 for more information.)

When all these possibilities are exhausted, if the consulate still refuses you a visa, your opportunities for further appeals are severely limited. Consult an experienced immigration attorney for more information.

EMPLOYMENT AUTHORIZATION

To file an application for employment authorization for the 90 days you're on a Fiancé visa, complete Form I-765 and file it with a USCIS Service Center (though a few local district offices accept these; check first). Together with Form I-765, you must submit a copy of your I-94 card. The filing fee is $120.

You can also apply for a work permit when you submit your green card application. This may be worth waiting for—you're likely to get the work permit a lot faster, since it's handled by the local district office, not a service center. This work permit will also last a lot longer.

Instructions for Completing Form I-765

Block above Question 1. Mark the first box, "Permission to accept employment."

Questions 1–8. These questions are self-explanatory. In filling out your name, include your full middle name, not just an initial.

Question 9. This asks for your Social Security number, including all numbers you have ever used. If you have never used a Social Security number, answer "None." If you have a nonworking Social Security number, write down the number followed by the words "nonworking, for tax purposes only." If you have ever used a false number, give that number, followed by the words: "Not my valid number." (Before submitting information about any use of false documents or false information, be sure to read Chapter 25.)

Question 10. You will not usually have an Alien Registration Number unless you previously applied for a green card, were in deportation proceedings, or have had certain types of immigration applications denied. All Alien Registration Numbers begin with the letter "A." If you have no "A" number, answer Question 10 by putting down the admission number from the I-94 card.

Questions 11–14. These questions are self-explanatory.

Question 15. Your current immigration status is Fiancé Visa Holder.

Question 16. Answer this question "(a)(6)."

For a fuller discussion of all aspects of applying for a fiancé visa and for your green card after you've arrived in the U.S. and gotten married, see *Fiancé and Marriage Visas: A Couple's Guide to U.S. Immigration*, by Ilona Bray (Nolo).

FORMS AND DOCUMENTS CHECKLIST

STEP ONE: PETITION

Forms

☐ Form I-129F.

☐ Form G-325A (one form is required for each person).

Documents

☐ One identification photograph each of the petitioner and the beneficiary.

☐ Documents proving the petitioner is a U.S. citizen.

☐ Documents proving that both parties are legally free to marry, including:

  ☐ copies of all divorce and death certificates, if either party was previously married, and

  ☐ if either party is under the age of legal consent in the U.S. state where the marriage will take place, appropriate documents to overcome this, such as written consent from a parent or guardian.

☐ Documents showing that the foreign national has a real intent to marry the petitioner, including:

  ☐ copies of wedding announcements

  ☐ letter or affidavit from a pastor or justice of the peace stating that he or she has been contacted about performing the marriage ceremony, and

  ☐ detailed letter from the petitioner explaining how the couple met, why the petitioner cannot travel to the beneficiary's home country and marry there, and what plans have been made for the wedding ceremony.

☐ Documents proving that the couple has physically met within the past two years.

☐ If the couple has not met and their religion does not allow meeting before marriage:

  ☐ letter from an authority in the religious organization verifying that both parties are members of that religion

  ☐ detailed statement by a clergyperson explaining the religious laws concerning marriage, and

  ☐ detailed letter from the petitioner explaining how the couple will comply with all customs of the religion concerning marriage and weddings.

☐ If the couple has not personally met but to do so would cause extreme hardship:

  ☐ letter explaining the extreme hardship preventing the petitioner from traveling to meet the beneficiary, and

  ☐ if the hardship is medical, a letter from a licensed physician explaining the condition.

STEP TWO: APPLICATION

Forms

☐ DS forms (available from U.S. consulate).

☐ Form I-134 or Form I-864, Affidavit of Support.

Documents

☐ Notice showing approval of the fiancé(e) visa petition.

☐ All documents originally filed with the petition.

☐ Long-form birth certificate for the applicant and each accompanying child.

☐ Passports for the applicant and each accompanying child, valid for at least six months beyond the date of the final interview.

☐ Police certificates from every country in which the applicant and each accompanying child has lived for at least six months since age 16.

☐ Three photographs each of the applicant and each accompanying child.

☐ Financial documents to accompany Affidavit of Support for the applicant and each accompanying child.

In the United States:

☐ Form I-765 (for work authorization only).

Getting a Green Card Through Employment

Privileges

- You may live anywhere in the U.S. and stay as long as you want.

- As long as you start out working for the company through which you obtained the green card, you may later work at any job, for any company, anywhere in the U.S., or you may choose not to work at all.

- You may travel in and out of the U.S. whenever you wish.

- You may apply to become a U.S. citizen after you have held your green card for a certain length of time.

- In some types of cases, your spouse and unmarried children under the age of 21 may also be eligible for green cards as accompanying relatives.

Limitations

- Your place of actual residence must be in the U.S. You cannot use a green card just for work and travel purposes. (The only exception to this is Alien Commuters, discussed in Chapter 4.)

- You must pay U.S. taxes on your worldwide income, because you are regarded as a U.S. resident.

- You cannot remain outside the U.S. for more than one year at a time without special permission, or you risk losing your green card. (It is highly recommended that you return to the U.S. before you have been gone six months.)

- If you commit certain crimes, participate in politically subversive activities, or engage in other prohibited activities, your green card can be taken away and you can be deported.

- Under most categories, you must work full time, and not be self-employed.

This chapter will explain who is eligible for a green card through employment and how to apply for it.

A. Who Qualifies for a Green Card Through Employment?

In order to qualify for a green card through employment:
- you must have a job offer from a U.S. employer
- you must have the correct background in terms of education and work experience for the job you have been offered, and
- there must be no qualified American willing or able to take the job—except in categories of green cards where Labor Certification is not required.

1. Job Offer From a U.S. Employer

You need a specific job offer from a U.S. employer to get a green card through employment. There are two main exceptions to this rule. The first is for those who can qualify as people of extraordinary ability. This is a small subgroup of the green card through employment category called *priority workers.* The second exception is for persons who have exceptional ability under the employment-based Second Preference. This exception usually applies when it is deemed in the national interest to do so. Both categories are described later in this chapter.

Labor Certification is one of the steps often necessary for getting a green card through employment. Labor Certification is a procedure required by the U.S. Labor Department to prove that there are no qualified Americans available to take the job being offered to a foreign national green card applicant. In all cases requiring Labor Certification, the employer acts as the petitioner in obtaining the green card.

Many people are surprised to learn that they need a job offer *before* filing a green card application. The idea behind it is that you are getting a green card only because your services are essential to an American employer. Put another way, the U.S. government is issuing a green card not for your benefit, but to help a U.S. company or institution.

It may be hard for you to find such an employer, for the employer must not only offer you a job, but also be willing to take part in the procedure of getting you a green card. The paperwork can include producing company financial records and tax returns for review by USCIS. Your prospective employer should also have the patience to wait because, although you need a job offer to apply, unless you already have a nonimmigrant work visa, you cannot legally start on the job until your green card application is approved. This can take anywhere from several months to several years, depending on your qualifications and nationality. However, when a potential employer badly needs your skills, it will usually cooperate with the various requirements.

The employer who offers you a job may be a company, institution, organization, or individual. If you, yourself, have a U.S. business, normally you cannot act as the petitioning employer for your own green card. The only situation in which you may be able to hire yourself is where the business is a corporation employing many others as well.

An agent who books your talents for a variety of jobs, as is common in the entertainment industry, may also be the source of your job offer. For an agent to act as petitioner, you must receive your salary directly from the agent.

WHAT TO TELL AN EMPLOYER

When you are trying to find a U.S. job, it may help if you can assure the employer that he or she is taking limited legal risks by participating in your green card application. The employer assumes absolutely no financial responsibility for you during the application process or after you enter the U.S. except that it guarantees to pay you the market wage for the position during the time you are actually employed. The employer also has the right to withdraw the petition for any reason and at any time. Once you receive a green card and begin working, your employer is free to fire you at will.

Prospective employers will be asked to supply business financial records to USCIS. Many are afraid to do this. You can reassure them by explaining that USCIS checks these records for the purpose of proving the business has enough money to pay your salary.

---

2. Correct Background

You must have the correct background in terms of experience, training, and education for the job you have been offered. For example, if you are a qualified nuclear scientist, but are asked to take employment managing a U.S. bakery, you cannot use that job offer to get a green card, because you have no background in bakery management. It is irrelevant that your native intelligence and general knowledge of business may make you quite capable of handling the bakery job. Likewise, reliability, honesty, or willingness to work hard, characteristics that are much in demand by real-world employers, are not a USCIS consideration. A match between your background and the job is the main concern.

c. No Qualified Americans

Labor Certification may or may not be a requirement for you. It depends on your background and the kind of job you have been offered in the U.S. Later, we will explain which types of applications need Labor Certifications and which do not. Where a Labor Certification is required, there must be no qualified Americans available and willing to take the job you have been offered in the region where the job is offered. This is not an abstract requirement. Your prospective employer will have to advertise the job and conduct interviews. If someone is found who fits the job requirements even if that person isn't given the job, you won't receive certification.

Usually, to fulfill the requirement of no qualified Americans, there must be no American workers who meet the *minimum* qualifications. In the case of college professors or persons of exceptional ability in the arts and sciences, however, the standard is less difficult to meet. In these subcategories it is necessary to show that you are *more* qualified than any suitable U.S. workers, but you do not have to be the only one available. This difference may seem small, but it really does make getting Labor Certifications much easier for college and university faculty.

Even in the majority of categories, where the requirement is that there be no minimally qualified American workers to fill the job, the standard may not always be hard to meet. It all depends on the occupation involved and where the job is located. And more jobs than you would think go begging for want of either qualified or willing U.S. applicants. Jobs that typically make successful opportunities for green card applications are those requiring workers with a college education, special knowledge, or unusual skills. Unskilled jobs that have odd working hours or other undesirable factors are also good possibilities for green card applicants.

B. Employment Categories

Various eligibility rules and application procedures, including whether or not you need a Labor Certification to get a green card, depend on the work category in which you apply. Green cards through employment are divided into five preference categories. The first one has no Labor Certification requirements. The rest do.

All employment preference categories are subject to quotas (annual limits). The quotas for the first two employment preferences move more quickly than the third. In certain categories, you require a specific job offer from a U.S. employer. In others you do not. The five employment preference categories are:

- **Employment First Preference ("EB-1").** Priority workers.
- **Employment Second Preference ("EB-2").** Workers with advanced degrees or exceptional ability.
- **Employment Third Preference ("EB-3").** Skilled or unskilled workers without advanced degrees.
- **Employment Fourth Preference ("EB-4").** Religious workers and various miscellaneous categories of workers and other individuals. Also called "Special Immigrants."
- **Employment Fifth Preference ("EB-5").** Individual investors willing to invest $1,000,000 in a U.S. business (or $500,000 in economically depressed areas).

1. Employment First Preference (EB-1)

Priority workers are divided into three subcategories: persons of extraordinary ability, outstanding university professors or researchers, and transferring executives or managers of multinational companies. No Labor Certification is required for any of these subcategories. To apply for a green card as a professor or researcher, you first need a job offer from a U.S. employer. If you are a person of extraordinary ability, you do not even require that. Transferring executives or managers must, of course, already be employed by the company that is transferring them.

a. Workers of Extraordinary Ability

You qualify for a green card as a priority worker if you have extraordinary ability in the sciences, arts, education, business, or athletics. Your achievements must have been publicly recognized, and resulted in a period of sustained national or international acclaim. A further condition of this subcategory is that your entry into the U.S. will substantially benefit America in the future—you must still be at the top of your field when you apply, not in a decline, or retiring. You do not need a specific job offer as long you will continue working in your field of expertise once you arrive in the U.S. (though if you have a job offer, the employer can petition for you).

b. Outstanding Professors and Researchers

You qualify for a green card as a priority worker under the outstanding professors and researchers subcategory if you have an international reputation for being outstanding in a particular academic field. You need three year's minimum of either teaching or research experience in that field. You must also be entering the U.S. to accept a specific tenured or tenure-track teaching or research position at a university or institution of higher learning. Alternatively, you may accept a job conducting research in industry or with a research organization. The U.S. company or institution employing you should have a history of making significant achievements in research and must employ at least three other full-time research workers. Research positions must not be temporary, but rather be expected to last for an unlimited or indefinite duration.

c. Multinational Executives and Managers

You qualify for a green card as a priority worker under the multinational executives and managers subcategory if you have been employed as an executive or manager by a qualified company outside the U.S. for at least one out of the past three years, or, if you're already in the U.S. on a temporary visa, one of the three years before you arrived here. You must now be going to take a similar position with a U.S. branch, affiliate, or subsidiary of the same company. The U.S. company must have been in business for at least one year. The qualifications needed are similar to those for L-1 intracompany transfer visas, discussed in Chapter 19.

For U.S. and foreign companies to act as petitioners in this subcategory, they should fit one of the following four descriptions:

- different branches of the same company
- a joint venture where the parent company owns half or has equal control and veto power
- one company is a majority-controlled subsidiary of the other, or
- the foreign and U.S. companies are affiliated in a way such that both companies are under the control of the same person, persons, company, or group of companies.

Since the positions held by the green card applicant both in and out of the U.S. are required to be executive or managerial in nature, the exact meaning of these terms is important. A manager is defined as a person who has all four of the following characteristics:

- he or she manages the organization or a department, subdivision, function, or component of the organization

- he or she supervises and controls the work of other supervisory, professional, or managerial employees, or manages an essential function of the organization
- he or she has the authority to hire and fire those persons supervised, or if none are supervised, works at a senior level within the organization, and
- he or she has the authority to make decisions concerning the day-to-day operations of the activities or function of the organization over which he or she has authority.

A supervisor below the level of middle management is often called a first-line supervisor. First-line supervisors are not normally considered managers for green card qualifying purposes unless the employees they supervise are professionals. The word "professional" here means a worker holding a university degree.

An executive is defined as a person who has all four of the following characteristics:

- he or she directs the management of the organization or a major part or function of the organization
- he or she sets the goals and policies of the organization or a part or function of the organization
- he or she has extensive decision-making authority, and
- he or she receives only general supervision or direction from higher level executives, a board of directors, or the stockholders of the organization.

2. Employment Second Preference (EB-2)

The Employment Second Preference category of green cards through employment is for professionals holding advanced university degrees, and for persons of exceptional ability in the sciences, arts, or business. To qualify in this category, you must be coming to the U.S. specifically to work full-time in your field of expertise. With limited exceptions, you must have a definite job offer from a U.S. employer. Your entry must substantially benefit the U.S. economy, cultural, or educational interests or welfare. Labor Certifications are normally required for this category. (For exceptions, see Subsection c, below.) This is another preference category that is divided into subcategories.

a. Advanced Degree Professionals

The plain term "professional" is defined under the immigration laws to mean a person in an occupation that requires, at a minimum, a baccalaureate degree or its equivalent from a college or university. Therefore, to qualify as an "advanced degree professional" takes something more. Specifically, you must hold a graduate level degree, or a professional degree requiring postgraduate education, such as is standard in U.S. law or medicine. You

must also be internationally recognized or outstanding in your field.

Many who qualify for temporary, H-1 visas in professions like nursing and engineering do not qualify for green cards in this subcategory unless they have completed postgraduate degrees.

There is a substitute for having an advanced degree. You can also qualify if you have a baccalaureate degree plus five years of work experience in a professional position. Your work experience can be either in the U.S. or abroad. In addition, the level of responsibility you exerted and knowledge you gained in that position must have increased progressively over the course of the five years.

ACADEMIC CREDENTIAL EVALUATIONS

Not every country in the world operates on the same academic degree and grade level system found in the U.S. If you were educated in some other country, USCIS, as part of judging your eligibility, will usually ask for an academic credential evaluation from an approved consulting service to determine the American equivalent of your educational level.

Evaluations from accredited credential evaluation services are not binding on USCIS, but they are very persuasive. When the results are favorable, they strengthen your case. If, however, the evaluation shows that your credentials do not equal those required for advanced degree professionals, you will not qualify in this subcategory.

A list of these accreditation services can be found at www.naces.org/members.htm.

We recommend getting a credential evaluation in every case where non-U.S. education is a factor. In addition, we advise getting the evaluation before USCIS asks for it. When the evaluation is favorable, you can automatically include it with your petition. This strengthens your case and saves time if USCIS decides to request it later. If your evaluation is unfavorable, submit the results only if USCIS insists you do. You may also wish to consider applying in a different category because your application in this one is likely to fail.

b. Persons of Exceptional Ability

The priority worker category described in Section 1a, above, covers the subcategory of persons of "extraordinary ability" in the sciences, arts, education, business, or athletics. Do not confuse this with the exceptional ability subcategory of the Employment Second Preference, which includes only those in the sciences, arts, and business. Something less than the international acclaim required for extraordinary workers is enough for the exceptional ability subcategory. Proven sustained national acclaim in your field will meet the required standard. You must, however, still be considered significantly more accomplished than the average person in that profession.

c.   Waiver of the Labor Certificate Requirement

If you're applying in the Second Preference category and your presence will benefit the U.S. in the future, you may be exempted from having a job offer or Labor Certification. By "benefit," USCIS means that your coming to the U.S. will have a favorable impact on the economic, employment, educational, housing, environmental, cultural, or other important aspect of the country. The impact must be *national* in scope. You must also show that the field in which you'll be working has "substantial intrinsic merit." In addition, you'll need to demonstrate that forcing you to go through the labor certification process would actually have an adverse impact on the U.S. national interest. A local labor shortage is not considered to be an adverse impact.

Because the combination of the above criteria is difficult to satisfy, obtaining a national interest waiver is very rare.

3.   Employment Third Preference (EB-3)

This is the third broad category of green cards through employment. You'll need a job offer and a Labor Certification. (No national interest waiver is available for the Third Preference.) Employment Third Preference is also divided into subcategories—professional workers, skilled workers, and unskilled workers. The work cannot be temporary or seasonal.

You may wonder what difference it makes whether you are classified as a professional worker, skilled worker, or unskilled worker, since all three categories require Labor Certifications and draw green cards from the same 40,000 quota allocation. The answer is that of those 40,000 green cards available each year, only 10,000 are for unskilled workers. Accordingly, those classified as unskilled often have to wait much longer for green cards than workers in the other subcategories, depending on how many other people apply. The wait has been as long as ten years.

a.   Professional Workers (No Advanced Degree)

Immigration law is always vague about the definition of the term "professional," stating only that the meaning includes such occupations as architects, lawyers, physicians, engineers, and teachers. Other occupations that have routinely been approved as professional include accountants, computer systems analysts, physical therapists, chemists, pharmacists, medical technologists, hotel managers (large hotels only), fashion designers, certain upper-level business managers, and commercial airline pilots of 747s or other large aircraft. The professional workers subcategory of Employment Third Preference is for members of professions who hold only bachelor's degrees and have fewer than five years of work experience. The bachelor's degree must be the normal requirement for entry into the field of work. As long as you have the necessary degree, proving eligibility in this category is simple.

b.   Skilled Workers

Workers engaged in occupations that normally do not require college degrees, but do need at least two years of training or experience, qualify in the subcategory of skilled workers. Relevant post-secondary training can be counted as training. How much experience or training may be necessary for a specific job is not always clear. Your local state labor department office can tell you the exact number of years of education and experience they consider a minimum for the particular job you have been offered. Or you can look it up in the Department of Labor's publication *Dictionary of Occupational Titles*, available at a library or the local Government Printing Office bookstore, and being converted to a web-based form on http://online.onetcenter.org.

c.   Unskilled Workers

Any job not falling into one of the subcategories we've already described goes into the subcategory of unskilled workers. Generally, this includes occupations requiring less than two years training or experience. Whatever requirements the job does have must be met by your own qualifications or you will not be able to apply successfully for a green card in this subcategory. For example, if a job requires a one-year vocational training program, you must have completed such a program before you can begin applying for a green card on the basis of that job.

4.   Employment Fourth Preference (EB-4)

This is the fourth category of employment-based workers, also called "Special Immigrants." It encompasses religious workers, which include ministers and religious professionals. The Fourth Preference also includes various miscellaneous categories of workers. (See Chapter 11 for a full discussion of this category.)

5. Employment Fifth Preference (EB-5)

This employment category is for investors willing to invest a minimum of $500,000 to $1,000,000 in a new U.S. business that will create jobs. The minimum amount depends on the location of the enterprise. (See Chapter 10 for a full discussion of this category.)

6. Schedule A Labor Certification

In addition to the specific categories that do not require Labor Certification, there are other alternatives to meeting the condition that there be no qualified Americans available to take the job. One alternative is called a Schedule A Labor Certification. It allows some people (usually those in the Second Preference category) to get green cards through employment without first testing the market for the availability of U.S. workers.

Schedule A is not a separate green card category, like the ones we just described above. Schedule A is a special list of occupations that would fall into categories normally requiring Labor Certification except that shortages of such workers are already a recognized fact.

The Schedule A list is not permanent. It changes as U.S. labor needs change. Below are the occupations presently on the Schedule A list. To check the latest version of Schedule A yourself, see the Code of Federal Regulations, at 20 C.F.R. § 656.10 (available via Nolo's website at www.nolo .com; go to "U.S. Laws and Regulations" and enter the appropriate numbers).

a. Group I: Certain Medical Occupations

Physical therapists. You must be qualified for a license in the state where you intend to practice, but you need not be licensed already.

Professional nurses. This includes only registered nurses. Licensed practical nurses do not qualify. You must have passed the Commission on Graduates of Foreign Nursing Schools (CGFNS) examination. Alternatively, you qualify for Schedule A if you are licensed by the U.S. state in which you intend to practice. Although you still need to fill out the labor certification form, instead of filing it with the Department of Labor, you file it directly with the USCIS service center for your area.

b. Group II: People With Exceptional Ability in Arts or Sciences

It is difficult to qualify in this category. First, you must prove you are internationally recognized for your outstanding, well-above standard, performance in the arts or sciences. The likely candidates under this category are internationally famous scientists, writers, or fine artists such as painters and sculptors. Performing artists are excluded. You may, however, quality as a college or university teacher in one of the above fields.

Second, you must show that you have been practicing your science or art for at least the year prior to your application and intend to continue practicing it in the U.S.

If you try to avoid Labor Certification by using this category, your employer must submit extensive supporting documentation. See Section E5, below.

7. Schedule B: Low-Level Jobs

USCIS has predetermined that in a number of unskilled occupations, there are generally no worker shortages. These are called Schedule B occupations. Usually Labor Certifications will be denied for any job listed on Schedule B. An employer is allowed to file a Labor Certification application for a Schedule B worker if he or she wishes, but he or she must overcome USCIS's presumption that there are adequate workers for these occupations. Here is the current Schedule B occupation list (or double check it at 20 C.F.R. § 656.11):

- Assemblers
- Attendants (such as personal, amusement, and recreation service workers)
- Attendants (automobile service station)
- Attendants (parking lot)
- Bartenders
- Bookkeepers II (maintain one set of books for an establishment)
- Caretakers (of private homes)
- Cashiers
- Charworkers and cleaners
- Chauffeurs and taxicab drivers
- Cleaners (hotel and motel)
- Clerk typists
- Clerks and checkers (grocery)

- Clerks (general)
- Clerks (hotel)
- Cooks (short order)
- Counter and fountain workers
- Dining room attendants
- Electric truck operators
- Elevator operators
- Floorworkers
- Groundskeepers
- Guards
- Helpers (any industry)
- Household domestic service workers, or housekeepers (unless you have at least one year of prior paid experience)
- Janitors
- Keypunch operators
- Kitchen workers
- Laborers (common, farm, and mine)
- Loopers and toppers
- Material handlers
- Nurses' aides and orderlies
- Packers, markers and bottlers
- Porters
- Receptionists
- Sailors and deckhands
- Sales clerks (general)
- Sewing machine operators and handstitchers
- Stock room and warehouse workers
- Streetcar and bus conductors
- Telephone operators
- Truck drivers and tractor drivers
- Typists (lesser skilled only)
- Ushers, recreation and amusement
- Yard workers

8. Accompanying Relatives

If you are married or have children below the age of 21 and you acquire a green card through employment, your spouse and children can get green cards as accompanying relatives by providing proof of their family relationship to you. They must also prove that they are not inadmissible.

9. Inadmissibility

If you have ever committed a crime, lied on an immigration application, lied to an immigration officer, been a member of a terrorist organization, or been afflicted with certain physical or mental defects, you may be barred from receiving a green card unless you can qualify for what is known as a Waiver of Inadmissibility. (See Chapter 25 to identify and find out how you may be able to overcome these problems.)

C. Current Waiting Periods

There are currently no waiting periods other than the normal time that it takes to process visa applications. In general, waiting periods, due to excessive demand for the limited annual supply of visas, tend to be longer for people from China, India, Mexico, and the Philippines, especially for nonskilled workers.

The Department of State has a recorded message with information regarding quotas at 202-663-1541, or check their website at www.travel.state.gov for the most recent *Visa Bulletin.* (See detailed instructions in Chapter 4.)

In addition to waiting for a visa number to become available, applying for permanent residency under certain preference categories also requires certification that the alien worker is not taking a position that a U.S. worker could fill. This process is called Labor Certification. After a Labor Certification is issued, it will take about three months for visa petition approval. Once the petition is approved and the quota becomes current (a visa number becomes available), it will take an additional eight to 12 months for green card application approval.

D. Steps to Obtaining a Green Card

Once you have a suitable job offer, if one is required, getting a green card through employment is a three-step process for categories requiring Labor Certification, and a two-step process for categories that do not.

Often, applicants expect their employers to handle the entire procedure for them and, indeed, many large companies have experienced workers who will do this for highly desirable employees. Even smaller companies may be prepared to do whatever is necessary, including paying an immigration attorney's fees, to attract a key staff member. However, it is often the employee who is most interested in having the green card issued, and to U.S. employers, the red tape of hiring a foreign employee can be an unfamiliar nuisance.

1. Overview of Step One: Labor Certification

Labor Certification is filed by your U.S. employer. Employment First Preference priority workers and those with occupations appearing on Schedule A do not have to go through the full Step One procedures. They may move directly to Step Two, though during Step Two they do have to present the Step One forms and documents to show that they qualify as either priority workers or for Schedule A.

The object of Labor Certification is to satisfy the U.S. government that there are no qualified U.S. workers available and willing to take the specific job that has been offered to you. This must be proven to the U.S. Department of Labor (DOL), not USCIS. Therefore, your employer will file Labor Certification papers with the DOL.

Since you are applying for a green card under a preference category, you are subject to a quota. The date on which your employer files the Labor Certification is called your Priority Date. The Priority Date is important because it marks the legally recognized moment when your waiting period for a green card starts to elapse. (Where formal Labor Certification is not required, your Priority Date is the date your application is filed at USCIS.)

If all goes well, the Labor Certification will eventually be approved, but be aware that an approved Labor Certification does not, by itself, give you any right to live or work in the U.S. It is only a prerequisite to Steps Two and Three, submitting the petition and application for a green card. Where Labor Certification is required, it must be approved before you are eligible for Steps Two and Three.

2. Overview of Step Two: The Petition

The petition is filed by your U.S. employer. All petitions are submitted to the USCIS regional service centers in the U.S. With the successful completion of Step One, your employer has proven that no qualified Americans are available for the job. The object of the petition is to prove that you do, in fact, qualify. In the case of priority workers (First Preference), you must also prove as part of Step Two that you qualify in one of that category's three subgroups. In addition, it must be shown that your future employer truly needs someone with your skills and has the financial ability to pay your salary. Like the Labor Certification, an approved petition does not by itself give you any immigration privileges. It is only a prerequisite to Step Three, submitting your application. The petition must be approved before you are eligible for Step Three.

STEPS FOR SCHEDULE A

Step One procedures for Schedule A cases differ in many respects from those for standard Labor Certification. The principal difference is that it is not necessary to prove there are no U.S. workers available for the job. Instead, your employer will prove that you do in fact qualify for one of the groups on Schedule A. Another difference is that the Step One procedures in Schedule A cases are carried out simultaneously with, instead of before, those of Step Two, the petition. The differences in Schedule A procedures are explained where necessary throughout this chapter.

---

3. Step Three: The Green Card Application

The green card application is filed by you and your accompanying relatives, if any. This application is your formal request for a green card. Step Three may be carried out in the U.S. at a USCIS Service Center (as long as you're already in the U.S. legally) or in your home country at a U.S. consulate there.

The majority of work-related green card applications are filed at USCIS Service Centers inside the U.S., since usually the worker is already in the country. If you are in the U.S. legally on a nonimmigrant visa, and you have a current Priority Date, you may qualify to apply for your green card either inside or outside the U.S., whichever you prefer.

If you are in the U.S. out of status, or you entered legally without a visa under the Visa Waiver Program, you are barred from filing your green card application inside the U.S. The only exception is if you had a visa petition or Labor Certification filed before January 14, 1998; or before April 30, 2001, if you can also show that you were in the U.S. on December 21, 2000, in which case you must pay a penalty fee, (currently $1,000). The penalty fee is in addition to the regular filing fee for such applications. Children under the age of 16 are not subject to paying this penalty. If you are subject to these penalties and want to avoid them, you may instead elect to apply for your green card at a U.S. consulate abroad, but if you were in the U.S. out of legal status before leaving, be sure you are not inadmissible or subject to the three- or ten-year waiting periods before proceeding. (See Chapter 25.)

If you have an approved petition but your Priority Date is not yet current, you must wait until it is current to file your green card application. The consulate will advise you by mail when your Priority Date finally comes up, but if you want to check progress from time to time, you may do so by calling the U.S. State Department in Washington, DC at 202-663-1541 for the latest quota information, or checking their website at www.state.gov. (See Chapter 4, Section A3 for more information.)

4. Who's Who in Getting Your Green Card

Getting a green card will be easier if you familiarize yourself with the technical names used for each participant in the process. During Steps One and Two (the Labor Certification and the petition), you are known either as the *beneficiary* or the *employee* and your prospective U.S. employer is known either as the *petitioner* or the *employer*. The petitioner may be either a business or an individual, but usually it is a business. In Step Three, the application, you are referred to as *applicant*, but your U.S. employer remains the *petitioner* or *employer*. If you are bringing your spouse and children with you as accompanying relatives, they are known as *applicants* as well.

5. Tips on Preparing the Paperwork

There are two types of paperwork you must submit to get a green card through employment. The first consists of official government forms completed by you or your U.S. employer. The second consists of personal and business documents such as birth and marriage certificates, school transcripts and diplomas and company financial statements and tax returns. We will tell you exactly what forms and documents you need. It is vital that forms are properly filled out and all necessary documents are supplied. The documents you or your U.S. employer supply do not have to be originals. Photocopies of all documents are acceptable as long as you have the original in your possession and are willing to produce the originals at the request of the consulate or USCIS. But add the following language to the photocopy, with your signature and the date:

> *Copies of documents submitted are exact photocopies of unaltered original documents and I understand that I may be required to submit original documents to an immigration or consular official at a later date.*
> *Signature _____*
> *Typed or Printed Name _____*
> *Date_____*

Documents will be accepted if they are in either English, or, with papers filed at U.S. consulates abroad, the language of the country where the documents are being filed (except in Japan, where all documents must be translated into English). If the documents are not in an acceptable language as just explained, they must be accompanied by a full, word for word, written English translation. Any capable person may act as translator. It is not necessary to hire a professional. At the end of each translation, the following statement must appear:

> *I hereby certify that I translated this document from [language] to English. This translation is accurate and complete. I further certify that I am fully competent to translate from [language] to English.*
> *Signature _____*
> *Typed or Printed Name _____*
> *Date_____*

The translator should sign this statement but it does not have to be witnessed or notarized.

Later in this chapter we describe in detail the forms and documents needed to get your green card through employment. A summary checklist of forms and documents appears at the end of this chapter.

E. Carrying Out Step One: Labor Certification

➡️ If you are seeking a green card through an employment category that does not require Labor Certification, or practice an occupation listed in Schedule A, skip ahead to Section F.

1. General Procedures

Labor Certifications, consisting of forms and documents, are filed in the U.S. at the appropriate state labor department office in the state of the employer's place of business. We emphasize that this is an office of the state government, not the U.S. DOL. State labor department offices assist the DOL in the Labor Certification process by monitoring employers' efforts to locate U.S. workers. However, a regional office of the U.S. DOL, where the file is forwarded after the state office finishes its work, makes the final decision on your employer's Labor Certification.

States differ as to the exact place and procedure for filing Labor Certifications. Most states have centralized filing at the labor department headquarters in the state capital. A call to the state labor department office in the state capital will tell you where and how to file Step One papers. Different states give different names to these offices, including labor department, job service, department of economic security, and employment commission.

There is no filing fee for a Labor Certification. If possible, it is better for the employer to file in person so you can be sure that the arrival of the papers is recorded. When the papers are presented in person, a dated written receipt should be requested. The receipt should be kept in a safe place, together with a complete copy of everything submitted. Then your employer can confirm on what date your Labor Certification was filed and help to locate the papers should they get lost or delayed in processing.

When filing by mail, we recommend sending the papers by certified mail, return receipt requested, and again keeping a complete copy for your records. Also, remember that your Priority Date for quota purposes is established on the day the Labor Certification is filed, so it is important to have proof of exactly when this took place.

Because there is no uniformity in operating procedures among the various state labor departments, the length of time it takes to get a Labor Certification approved varies from one state to another. A delay of as much as a year and a half to two years is not unusual in some places, even for the strongest cases.

However, the time it takes for Labor Certification approval sometimes runs concurrently with the wait caused by the preference quotas. You will remember that you cannot begin Step Three of the green card process until your Priority Date is current. Since you may have to wait for your Priority Date to come up under the quota anyway, the processing time for a Labor Certification usually doesn't add anything to the total time it takes to get a green card. Because the Second Preference quota is often current, it is advantageous to qualify under that preference if possible. The Labor Certification may be completed long before your number under the quota is current. For this reason, even if the DOL could process and approve your Labor Certification more quickly, you still would not get your green card any faster. However, if you are in a nonimmigrant status that may expire before the Labor Certification is approved, then you need to be concerned about the time it takes to process your application. (See Chapter 25 on inadmissibility and penalties for being out of status.)

2. Advertising Procedures

The Labor Certification process starts with the U.S. employer trying to recruit American workers for the position that has been offered to a foreign national. It is crucial to the success of the green card application for the employer to fail at this attempt. To demonstrate that U.S. workers are in fact unavailable, the job must be publicly advertised. The employer must then wait to see if any qualified U.S. candidates come forward. The DOL has established a specific procedure for this advertising.

The procedure begins when the employer files Form ETA-750 with the state labor department. Once this form is submitted, the state labor department will send back a letter to the employer acknowledging receipt of the form and assigning an identification number known as a "job order number" to the case. The letter will also give instructions on how to advertise.

It is mandatory that the employer carry out the advertising procedures exactly as required. There are specific guidelines on how and where the advertisements must be placed. Three separate types of advertisements are necessary.

a. Government-Assisted Recruiting

First, the state labor department will enter a description of the position, identified by the job order number, in its statewide computer bank. For 30 days, anyone throughout the state who contacts the state labor department will have an opportunity to apply for the job. The state will collect the applications and resumes and forward them to the employer.

b. Public Advertising

Second, the petitioning employer must prepare a written advertisement for placement in the medium most likely to attract potential applicants—usually the classified section of a newspaper of general circulation, professional journal, or ethnic publication. The ad must state the job title, salary, and working hours of the position, as well as describe the duties and qualifications. It is important that the job descriptions in the ad match the one that appears in the ETA-750 form. The employer can only reject an American job applicant for lacking qualifications that are listed on both the ad and the form.

Normally, the employer should place the advertisement in the classified section of a standard newspaper circulated in the city where the employer's place of business is located. They're not allowed to bury it in the wrong section or under a misleading heading. If the city has only one daily newspaper, the ad should be placed there. If there are two or more daily newspapers in the area, the employer may choose whichever one he or she prefers. The same ad must be run for three consecutive days. In some states, one of those days must be a Sunday.

Sometimes the letter from the state labor department will suggest that the employer advertise in a professional journal, trade journal, or national publication, instead of a local newspaper. The employer is not required to follow this suggestion, but unless there is a good business reason for not doing so, it is generally best to comply. When the ad is placed in a national newspaper or journal, it need appear only once instead of three times.

c. On-Site Advertising

The third type of advertising required for Labor Certification is an official job notice posted at the employer's place of business. The notice must contain the identical language used in the newspaper or journal advertisement, but instead of giving the job order number, prospective candidates should be asked to contact a specific person in the company. The notice must be posted for at least ten business days on an employee bulletin board or other suitable location on the company premises.

If the job being offered is one represented by a labor union or collective bargaining group, that union or group must also be sent a notice that a Labor Certification application has been filed. This gives the union an opportunity to refer union members for the job.

FASTER PROCESSING DURING LABOR SHORTAGES

The DOL will process cases on an expedited "reduction in recruitment" basis if the employer and the position meet certain criteria. The employer must have made good faith efforts at recruitment for the position for the six months preceding the filing of the application. The DOL prefers to see at least one newspaper advertisement per month for the position during that period, although it may accept less. Other types of recruitment evidence should be submitted, as long as they are normal to the industry. There must be a documented labor shortage for the position in the region where the employer resides, and the employer must be offering the prevailing market wage for the position. The employer may not require experience or education for the position which are not within the normal parameters as defined in the DOL's *Dictionary of Occupational Titles.* Usually the employer requests RIR processing in the initial filing, but they can also request a conversion to RIR later if the initial petition was filed before August 3, 2001. Although these are the principal requirements, there are myriad procedural requirements involved, and you should probably retain or at least consult an experienced immigration attorney.

3. Handling Job Applications

If anyone applies for the job, the employer must then review the resumes. If the candidates do not meet the minimum qualifications for the job as described in the advertisement and on Form ETA-750, the employer must be prepared to state in writing why not. Even if a single requested qualification is missing from the resume, that is enough reason for the employer to reject an American job candidate in favor of you, if he wishes to do so.

However, when some acceptable resumes do turn up, the employer must interview those people within a reasonable time (it's best to contact them within ten days of their application being submitted). After the interview, if the employer is unsatisfied and still wishes to employ you, he should again put in writing why the U.S. job candidates were not suitable.

Once an interview has been held, the employer is no longer limited to rejecting candidates only because they do not meet the job description as stated in the ad or the ETA-750 form. Poor health or work habits, lack of job stability, questionable character, and similar business considerations, if legitimate, are also satisfactory reasons. In addition, it sometimes comes out in an interview that the prospective worker's qualifications are not in fact what they appeared to be on the resume, or that the worker is not willing to relocate or is not otherwise willing to accept the job. This provides still another reason to turn down the U.S. candidate.

With the exception of college and university teachers, the DOL does not consider the fact that you may be more qualified than any other candidate to be a valid reason for rejecting a U.S. worker. Being the most qualified is not enough. You must be the only one who is minimally qualified. The employer cannot be forced to hire a U.S. worker who happens to apply for the job as a result of the required advertising, but if a qualified U.S. worker does turn up and your prospective employer cannot find a solid business reason to reject him or her, the Labor Certification application filed on your behalf will fail. At the end of the interview process, the employer must prepare a written report on what occurred. See Section 5, below, for details.

If no minimally qualified American job candidates presented themselves, the Labor Certification will be approved. Then the stamped certification will be sent to your U.S. employer. Only the employer receives communications from the DOL, because technically it is the company that is seeking Labor Certification, in order to fill a staff need.

4. Labor Certification Forms

A copy of these forms can be found in Appendix II.

Form ETA-750

Forms ETA-750 A and B are the only forms used in Step One, Labor Certification. They must be submitted in duplicate. Each of the two sets of forms must have an original signature, although the forms themselves may be photocopies.

All questions on the ETA-750 should be answered truthfully, as is the case on all government forms. Giving false information on a government form is a criminal offense and could lead to your deportation from the U.S. There is a small risk that if the ETA-750 form discloses that you are presently in the U.S. illegally, the DOL will notify USCIS. Policies vary around the country. Even if the DOL does notify USCIS, it may take months before removal proceedings are initiated. Unfortunately, if you are in the U.S. illegally, it is a risk that you will have to take if you ever wish to get a legal green card (but see Chapter 25 regarding whether the three- and ten-year bars will block you in any case).

Form ETA-750 is divided into Parts A and B. In Part A, the U.S. employer is asked to give a very detailed description of the job. Part B requires a great deal of information about your (the employee's) qualifications and experience. If, in Part B, it is indicated that you have fewer qualifications than your prospective employer has asked for in the job description as written in Part A, that means the company has not accurately written down its expectations. Therefore, the job requirements should be reduced and the job description in Part A changed before it is filed with the state labor department. There should be no qualifications listed in Part A that you, as the potential employee, cannot meet, or you will not qualify for the position.

One of the questions asked in Part A is the number of years of work experience the job requires. Eventually you must prove that you have at least that much experience. When you count up how many years of relevant experience you have to offer, you cannot include experience gained from working for your petitioning employer in exactly the same job that is described in the ETA-750. Many people seeking green cards through employment have already begun to work illegally for their petitioning employers before they receive green cards. Others take U.S. jobs legally on temporary work visas and then begin green card processing using the same employer as petitioner. If some or all of the required experience comes from years of working for the petitioning employer in exactly the same job used for the Labor Certification, or if considered to be a training position for that job, absent unusual circumstances, neither the DOL nor USCIS will give you credit for these credentials.

Therefore, you must be prepared to prove that you met the minimum experience and education requirements as stated in Part A of the ETA-750 before you started working for the petitioner in the particular position described on the ETA-750, even if you have been employed in that job for some time. If, however, you have spent time working for your petitioning employer in a different job than the one described on the ETA-750, you may count that time toward your "related experience" requirement.

Suppose you had no experience when hired, but if your employer had to hire an inexperienced worker to replace you and then train that person, the business might fall apart. Your employer didn't need an experienced person when he first hired you, but now he must have an experienced person performing your job due to changes in technology, a loss of on-staff trainers or other major change in how the business operates. Under these circumstances, you can include your experience with the petitioning employer. To do so, your employer must convince the DOL there would be a substantial disruption of the business if he had to train a new person. The term "substantial disruption" is not well defined. For this reason, it is best to avoid relying on experience that you gained through your work for the petitioning employer unless absolutely necessary.

You will remember that the purpose of Step One is to convince the DOL that there are no qualified Americans available for the job in question. Although Part B of Form ETA-750 does ask for your work and education background, the DOL does not normally evaluate your job qualifications during this step. Nonetheless, the DOL will sometimes send the ETA-750 forms back to your employer and ask for such proof. This is not a proper request for the DOL to make. Still, when their demands are not too difficult to meet, giving them what they ask for is the easiest and quickest way to keep your case moving.

Although your job qualifications need not be verified in Step One, don't lose sight of the fact that this will eventually have to be done in Step Two. In Step Two, it must be proven to USCIS that you meet every requirement stated by the employer in Part A of Form ETA-750. A Labor Certification will be approved if no qualified American job candidates come forward, but that alone doesn't guarantee you a green card. If you can't meet the job qualifications either, the approved Labor Certification will turn out to be wasted effort. The discussion of documents under Step Two will explain how to prove your qualifications.

Now we will look at Form ETA-750 question by question.

Part A, Questions 1–11. These questions are self-explanatory.

Part A, Question 12. The DOL is concerned that a petitioning employer may offer a very low salary in order to discourage Americans from applying for the job. To ensure this tactic won't work, the DOL has salary guidelines that must be followed. The salary offer listed in Part A, Question 12, can be no more than 5% below the average salary paid to workers in the same type of job in the same geographical area where the employer's company is located. The DOL calls this average salary range the *prevailing wage.*

To find out the prevailing wage for your job, the state labor department conducts a wage survey of similar jobs in the area, or relies on wage data and surveys to do so. You can find out what the state labor department believes the prevailing wage is by filing a "prevailing wage request" with the local unit in charge of this. In many states, a publication is available listing by city or county the industry average wages for most occupations.

Before submitting the ETA-750 form, the employer should research these sources to determine the prevailing wage. The employer may want to list the lowest wage possible, although he is required by law to pay the higher of either the prevailing market wage or the actual wage paid to workers who occupy the same position. If your employer wants to pay you an even higher salary, that's just fine.

When an ETA-750 contains a salary offer that is too low and the Labor Certification is questioned ("assessed") for that reason alone, your employer has the option of raising the salary and resubmitting an amendment to the form. Then all advertising procedures will have to be repeated, adding more time and expense to the case. You will, however, be allowed to keep your original Priority Date. It is easier to find out in advance the amount of the prevailing wage. Then, if the petitioning employer is not willing to offer that much, at least everyone will be saved the effort of submitting a Labor Certification application that is guaranteed to fail. (Wage surveys are not required for Schedule A applicants.)

Part A, Question 13. This asks the employer to describe the job being offered and should be answered in as much detail as possible. Daily duties, typical projects, supervisory responsibilities, the kinds and uses of any machinery or equipment, foreign language skills needed, and so forth should all be thoroughly explained. If there are special job conditions, such as the requirement to live on the work premises or unusual physical demands, these too must be described. The employer should not fail to put down any reasonably necessary skill or activity the job requires, as long as it is a normal requirement for the occupation. The ability to reject U.S. workers will depend completely on how well the American job candidates match up to the job description in Part A, Question 13. The more detailed the job description, the more possible reasons for rejecting American candidates.

While the employer should do his best to describe the position and its demands fully, he should not invent requirements that don't exist or seem excessive for the industry, simply to discourage American job applicants. For example, suppose the job opening is for a bakery manager but in the job description the employer states that all applicants must have a background in nuclear science. This sort of unreasonable demand makes it clear to the state labor department reviewer that the job description is not legitimate. When the job description lacks real-world credibility, the ETA-750 will be sent back and the employer will be asked to justify the more unusual requirements. If it can't, the Labor Certification will be denied.

The employer should also guard against asking for such a variety of requirements that the job seems more appropriate for two separate workers instead of one. For example, if the job is that of bakery manager and the job description requires the applicant not only to manage the shop but to do the baking as well, the reviewer might say the business really needs two people, a baker and a store manager. Once again, this will result in the Labor Certification being denied. This approach will work only if the employer can convincingly explain that the business will be unable to function unless a single individual is hired to perform these combined duties. On the other hand, if the bakery manager is required to know accounting so he can handle the books, baking techniques so he can supervise the bakers, retailing so he can effectively promote the bake shop and sales techniques so he can deal with customers, all of these tasks can be classified as management activities. Therefore, this job description is reasonable.

Part A, Question 14. Question 14, Part A, asks for the minimum experience, training, and education the job requires. The answer to this question should describe the demands of the job, not the personal qualifications of the green card applicant. For example, you personally may have a bachelor's degree representing four years of music education or several years of work experience as an artist, but if the position you have been offered is for a live-in housekeeper, music education or experience in art usually has nothing to do with being a housekeeper and therefore should not be mentioned in the answer to this question.

As with salary levels, the DOL also has specific guidelines on what the minimum number of years of experience and education should be for a certain kind of job. If your employer references the DOL's *Dictionary of Occupational Titles*, he or she will be able to determine this. The number of years listed for each job in the *Dictionary of Occupational Titles* controls what you may put down in the answer to Part A, Question 14.

The number of years of experience and education listed in the *Dictionary of Occupational Titles* for each job is the total allowable years of experience and education combined. (If you wish to learn more about the *Dictionary of Occupational Titles*, it can be found in most U.S. public libraries or ordered from the U.S. Government Printing Office. Also, the DOL is moving to using a Web-based database with the same information, called O*NET. See http://online.onetcenter.org.

U.S. company personnel staff or others reading this book who work with Labor Certifications on a regular basis may find it useful to familiarize themselves with the *Dictionary of Occupational Titles* and its *Specific Vocational Preparation* (SVP) classifications which dictate the number of years of background presumed necessary for each job.)

The employer may divide the years up between experience and education in any way he sees fit, as long as he does not exceed the overall total. For example, if the *Dictionary of Occupational Titles* says there should be a minimum of two years of background for the job you have been offered, your employer has a choice of requiring two years of education, two years of experience, or one of each. He or she may even divide it by months, requiring, say, six months of training or education and 18 months of experience.

Suppose the employer truly believes he needs a person with more total years of education and experience than the *Dictionary of Occupational Titles* indicates? Then a letter from the employer should be submitted with the ETA-750 forms, giving the reason why the employer feels additional years are justified. The DOL will normally respect the employer's judgment if reasonable. This letter does not have to be in any special form. A simple explanation in your employer's own words will do. If you receive notice that this requirement is considered overly restrictive, contact an immigration attorney or other expert to advise you.

If possible, the employer should submit as supporting documentation evidence that other employers with similar positions also require the additional years of education or experience.

(Schedule A applicants are not subject to the limitation on experience set in the *Dictionary of Occupational Titles*. Therefore, an employer of a Schedule A applicant may answer this question in any manner he wishes without being concerned that the chances for the green card application's success will be harmed.)

When a certain number of years appears in the box marked "experience," it is understood that this means experience in the same occupation as the job being offered. If the experience is in a different but relevant field, or in the same field but at a lower level, it should go in the box marked "related occupations."

Once again, if, in Part A, Question 14, the employer asks for a background of specific education or experience, make sure you, yourself, can meet these requirements. In Step Two, the petition, your employer will be asked to prove that you can fulfill the job criteria established in Part A of the ETA-750.

Part A, Question 15. This question asks the employer to state any essential requirements for the job over and above years of formal education or work experience. Any special knowledge or skills detailed in Part A, Question 13, such as foreign language ability, familiarity with certain types of machinery, or special physical capabilities (strength to do heavy lifting, for example) should be repeated here. When you reach Step Two, you will have to prove in some way that you can perform the skills listed in Part A, Question 15, but you will not have to show an exact number of years of education or on-the-job experience, as you will for the qualifications listed in Part A, Question 14.

Part A, Question 21. Part A, Question 21, asks your employer to describe past attempts to hire U.S. workers for the position being offered to you. At this stage, it is not essential that such efforts have already been made. If the U.S. employer has not yet tried to hire a worker for the job, he should write the following statement in Part A, Question 21:

"Advertisements and job posting to begin upon receipt of job order number."

If, however, your employer has already made some attempt to hire a U.S. worker, the nature of these efforts (newspaper ads, use of employment agencies, etc.) and the results should be described here. Of course, we assume any prior efforts to fill the job have failed, or the employer would not be trying to hire you.

Remember, if your employer has already conducted six months of recruitment efforts that are similar to those required for the Labor Certification process, he or she may be able to get an expedited "reduction in recruitment" application approved.

If you are applying under Schedule A, this question should be answered as follows:

"Occupation is listed under Schedule A Group (number). No recruitment is required."

ETA-750 Part B, Questions 1–14. These questions are self-explanatory.

Part B, Question 15. You are asked to list any job experience you have had in your lifetime that is relevant to the job presently being offered. All your work activities for the past three years, relevant or not, must also be listed. Give full information on both these subjects. Don't explain one but not the other. Make sure your employer does not leave any gaps in accounting for your time during the past three years. If you were unemployed during these years, write this down. If an extra sheet of paper is needed to cover all your experience, note in this question that an extra sheet is attached.

5. Labor Certification Documents

Most of the documents your petitioning employer will submit to the DOL with the Labor Certification application are the written results of the mandatory advertising procedure that are not submitted with the forms but rather after completion of recruitment efforts. Be sure to read all communications from the state labor department, taking special note of the deadlines for filing various documents. Once the job order number is received from the state labor department, the job will remain open in the state labor department computer banks for only 30 days. Then the job order will be closed out. All documents are due in the state labor department office no more than 45 days from this closeout date.

The submission of all the documents described below normally completes the Labor Certification procedure. Once your employer has submitted them, the forms and documents are eventually sent from the state labor department office to the regional certifying office of the DOL, where a decision on the Labor Certification is made. If no qualified Americans applied for the job and the paperwork has been carefully prepared, the Labor Certification should be approved on the first try.

Sometimes, papers are returned to the employer with a request for additional information or instructions to remedy a defect in the advertising. After mistakes and deficiencies have been corrected, the papers should be returned to the DOL. When papers are sent back for additions or corrections, the employer is given a limited time, usually 45 days, to respond. If deadlines for returning corrected papers are not met, the entire advertising procedure will have to be repeated and you will lose your Priority Date.

When your employer has finally gotten the paperwork the way the DOL wants it, he or she will receive a written notice from the DOL either granting or denying the Labor Certification.

a.   Recruitment Report

A key document is the employer's report explaining why each American who applied for the job is unqualified. This report should include:

- the total number of applicants
- the source from which each applicant was recruited (in-house posting, newspaper ad, etc.)
- the name, address, and resume of each applicant as well as the job title of the person who interviewed them
- specific reasons for rejecting each applicant, and
- in some states, copies of the rejection letters sent to applicants.

By far the most acceptable reason for turning down a U.S. applicant is failure to meet the requirements as stated on Form ETA-750, Part A, and in the newspaper or journal advertisement. Other reasons are also considered adequate, as long as they reflect valid business concerns. If no U.S. applicants responded to the various advertisements, the employer should supply a written statement to that effect.

b.   Publication Pages Containing the Advertisement

The pages from the publications where the advertisements appeared must be torn out and submitted. If the ad ran in a newspaper for three days, three pages must be presented, one for each day, even if the exact same ad was published on all three days. Photocopies of the ads are not acceptable. Your employer must obtain a copy of the publication each time the ad appeared and tear out the entire page, showing each date the ad appeared.

c.   Job Notice

A copy of the job notice that was posted inside the employer's place of business and sent to the appropriate labor union must also be turned in. A statement from the employer giving the dates when the job notice was posted, and the results, should accompany the copy of the notice.

d.   Special Documents for Special Cases

There are certain types of jobs for which the DOL expects some special, additional documents. (Except in the case of Schedule A applications, where the special documents are submitted in place of, rather than in addition to, the standard documents for Step One. See Section F4, below, for Schedule A documents.) Unlike the advertising documents, credentials for special cases should be submitted together with the ETA-750.

i.   Documents for Restrictive Job Requirements

Any job requirements that exceed the normal minimum in terms of education or experience, or that combine two or more different occupations into one, are considered to be restrictive. The employer must then convince the DOL that it is a "business necessity" to have these particular requirements because the business would be substantially disrupted if the person taking the position did not meet them.

The best document for this purpose is a detailed letter from the employer explaining why the business is dependent on those requirements and how the business would be affected if someone with less education or experience were hired. Again, if you receive a notice that your requirements are unduly restrictive, consult an immigration attorney who specializes in this subject.

ii. Documents for Live-In Domestics

One occupation needing special documents for Labor Certification approval is that of a live-in domestic: a worker engaged in performing routine domestic chores, such as cooking and cleaning, or who cares for children while living in the home of the employer.

The first requirement is two copies of your employment contract, showing:

- wages, hourly and weekly, plus overtime rate
- hours of employment
- your right to leave the household during nonworking times
- special terms of live-in employment, such as free room and board
- any money advanced to you before starting work
- the rights of you and/or your employer to terminate the relationship with two weeks' notice, and
- indication that you've been given a copy of this agreement.

You and your employer must each sign and date the agreement.

If you have been offered a job as a live-in, you must produce documents proving that you already have at least one full year of paid domestic (though not necessarily live-in) experience. Up to nine months of this experience may come from working for the petitioning employer, but at least three months must come from another employer. Strangely, however, if you have been working in the U.S. as a live-in domestic for someone other than the present petitioner, all of that experience can be counted toward your one-year total, even if you were working illegally at the time.

To meet the one-year experience requirement, you need not have worked as a live-in for one consecutive year. The work periods may be at various times and include part-time work as long as they all add up to at least 12 months of full-time work. To document your experience, you will need letters signed by your previous employers stating that you have worked for them as a domestic and for how long. If possible, the letters should be notarized.

The DOL must be convinced that live-in services are a business necessity of your petitioning employer. The employer must provide the DOL with a signed statement explaining why his or her household cannot function without a live-in. To pass the DOL test, the household must usually contain small children or invalids, and the able-bodied adults must have erratic or difficult work schedules where they may be called away at any time or for long stretches, leaving the dependents unattended. A family where both parents are physicians is a good example. The fact that your prospective employer simply prefers to have live-in help is

not sufficient. The DOL must believe there is an actual need and that no alternative arrangement will meet that need.

Finally, be aware that the waiting period for Third Preference unskilled workers usually averages many years long. If you have fallen out of status or are subject to any of the many bars to admissibility or adjustment of status, you may be wasting your time by applying for a Labor Certification. Read Chapter 25 carefully before starting, or consult an attorney, to be sure you qualify for permanent residence.

iii. Documents Proving a Foreign Language Requirement

According to the DOL, foreign language capability is not a valid requirement for most jobs, except perhaps the occupations of foreign language teacher or translator. By foreign language capability we mean the ability to speak English plus one other language. Some Labor Certification job descriptions contain unnecessary foreign language requirements because petitioning employers know it is a good way to decrease the chances that qualified Americans will apply for the job.

If your employer wants a foreign language capability in his job description, he must prove his need is real, by preparing and submitting a signed statement explaining the business reasons; for example, if the job involves transacting business overseas or dealing with large numbers of clients, customers, or coworkers in that language. The statement does not have to be in any particular form but it should answer obvious questions, like: What is it about the employer's business that makes knowledge of a foreign language necessary? Why does this position require knowledge of a foreign language if someone else in the company already speaks that language? Why couldn't the company simply hire a translator as a separate employee or use a translator on a part-time basis when the need arises? The employer must show that the need for the employee to speak a foreign language is very great and that no alternative arrangement will be adequate.

Imagine an employer who owns a restaurant and is trying to justify a foreign language requirement for a waiter. The employer can explain in his statement that a large percentage of the restaurant's customers speak the particular foreign language in question and expect to be addressed in that language when they come in to eat. If the restaurant's clientele demands it, it is reasonable that all employees of this restaurant who have contact with them be able to speak their language.

The DOL doesn't like foreign language requirements because it is well aware that most people who apply for green cards can speak a language other than English. The DOL regards this as a poor excuse to keep an American worker from taking a job. Therefore, it is usually best not to include a language requirement, especially if the Labor Certification is likely to be approved anyway. If, however, the occupation being certified is relatively unskilled, as is the case with the job of a waiter, a language requirement supported by strong documents showing a real business need (and prior business transactions) may mean the difference between success and failure.

iv. Documents for Physicians

If you are a physician and will be caring for patients, your U.S. employer must show documents to the DOL proving that you have passed Parts I and II of the National Board of Medical Examiners examination, commonly known in immigration circles as the visa qualifying examination or VQE. The exception is if you are of "international renown," in which case you should look into doing a Schedule A Labor Certification as described in Section B6, above. The VQE test is administered by the Educational Commission for Foreign Medical Graduates. All foreign physicians are required to pass, unless they are graduates of approved medical schools in the U.S. or Canada. However, in the case of most foreign physicians, successfully passing a standardized exam such as FLEX (used for licensing by many U.S. states), or other state licensing exams, is not sufficient. Passing the VQE is also necessary.

EXAM INFORMATION

For information on the VQE, contact:
Educational Commission for Foreign Medical Graduates
3624 Market Street
Philadelphia, PA 19104-2685
Telephone: 215-386-5900
Fax: 215-386-9196
Website: www.ecfmg.org

The exam is offered continuously throughout the year. Most graduate residency programs in the U.S. also require foreign medical graduates to have passed this exam for acceptance in the program.

v. Documents for College and University Teachers

College and university teachers applying based on their exceptional ability in the sciences or arts can get Labor Certification if they are the most qualified applicant. This is the only occupation where a Labor Certification can be approved even though there are suitable U.S. workers available in the field.

The employer may also be exempted from the standard Labor Certification advertising procedures, provided a competitive recruitment process was used for selecting the foreign worker, at least one advertisement was placed in a national professional journal, and the recruitment was done within 18 months of filing the Labor Certification application.

Even if new advertising is required, instead of having to show why each of the other applicants is unqualified, the employer will simply prepare a written statement explaining why you are the best of the choices available. This statement does not have to be in any particular form, but must simply state your qualifications and achievements and why you are superior to any of the other candidates. If available, include a copy of the minutes of faculty search committee meetings or board of directors' meetings, where discussions were held on the merits of the various job candidates. Those minutes should, of course, reflect the reasons why you are considered to be the best choice.

6. Labor Certification Appeals

If the DOL thinks the Labor Certification application is unsatisfactory, it will issue a form called Notice of Findings (NOF). This notice will state that the DOL intends to deny the application and will give the reasons why the DOL has reached this decision. Labor Certification applications cannot actually be denied without first giving the employer an opportunity to present new evidence or answer the criticisms contained in the notice. The employer will be given 35 days to respond. If the employer does not answer, when the deadline passes, the Notice of Findings automatically becomes a denial of the Labor Certification. Labor Certifications are frequently approved in spite of the issuance of a Notice of Findings. If a Notice of Findings is issued in your case, do not give up.

If the petitioning employer fails to respond in time to the Notice of Findings, he or she loses all other rights of appeal as well. Under these circumstances, if the employer still wishes to pursue a Labor Certification on your behalf, the only alternative is to wait at least six months and then file again, starting the procedure from the beginning.

If the employer does respond on time but the case is denied anyway, the DOL will send a written decision and an explanation of what further rights of appeal are available. The employer will then have 35 days to file what is known as a Notice of Appeal. This is filed with the DOL and represents still another effort to make the DOL change its mind about your case. The decision will be made by three panel members from a national appeals board known as the Board of Alien Labor Certification Appeals (BALCA), which sits in Washington, D.C. If the employer loses the appeal to BALCA, he or she can take the case to U.S. district court for review.

A full explanation of the appeals process itself is beyond the scope of this book. Most appeals are unsuccessful. If the case has reached this point, it is highly advisable to employ an immigration attorney. However, sometimes it is faster and cheaper to start over and try to avoid making the same mistakes twice. You must wait six months from the date of the denial before filing again, but appeals are likely to take much longer than that.

F. Carrying Out Step Two: The Petition

Once your employer has obtained an approved Labor Certification on your behalf, or if you are not required to have a Labor Certification because you are in the priority worker category or practice a Schedule A occupation, it is time to file the petition.

EB-1s, EB-2s, AND EB-3s CAN FILE STEPS TWO AND THREE CONCURRENTLY

In 2002, USCIS restored an important option for applicants in categories EB-1 (priority workers, including outstanding professors and researchers, multinational managers and executives, and people with extraordinary ability); EB-2 (people with advanced degrees); and EB-3 (people with a bachelor's degree, as well as skilled and unskilled workers). If they have a current Priority Date, these applicants no longer need to wait for approval of the Step Two petition before moving on to Step Three, the adjustment of status application for a green card. They can simply combine Steps Two and Three and send the entire application package to the appropriate USCIS Service Center. To prevent confusion at the service center, it's best to label the outside of the package "I-140/I-485 concurrent filing," and explain it in a cover letter, as well.

Alternately, if your I-140 is already pending at a service center, you can send in the adjustment of status application to be joined with it, by including a copy of your I-140 receipt notice and explaining your request in a cover letter.

Concurrent filing offers many advantages, including giving applicants the right to stay in the U.S. while the application is pending (useful if their temporary visas have expired or were due to expire soon) and the right to apply for work permits for themselves and their immediate family members.

1. General Procedures

Your employer mails the petition, consisting of forms and documents, to the USCIS regional service center in the U.S. having jurisdiction over your employer's place of business. USCIS regional service centers are not the same as the USCIS local offices—for one thing, you cannot visit regional service centers in person. There are four USCIS regional service centers spread across the U.S.

When your employer files at a regional service center, within a few weeks after mailing the petition, he or she should receive a written confirmation that the papers are being processed, together with a receipt for the fees. This notice will also give your immigration case file number and tell approximately when to expect a decision. If USCIS wants further information before acting on your case, it will send you a request for evidence ("RFE") Form I-797. The I-797 tells your employer what corrections, additional pieces of information, or additional documents are expected. Your employer should make the corrections or supply the extra data and mail them back to USCIS regional service center with the request form on top.

The filing fee for each petition is currently $135. Checks or money orders are accepted. Regional service centers will not accept cash. When filing by mail, we recommend sending the papers by certified mail, return receipt requested, and keeping a complete copy of everything sent for your records. To find the right address and P.O. box, check www.uscis.gov.

The filing procedure is the same for all work-based green card petitions, but your employer must indicate which Employment Preference and subcategory is being requested. If you are turned down for one category, the petition will not automatically be considered for a lower category. However, your employer may always submit a new petition under a different Employment Preference or subcategory. For example, if you have a job offer that might fall under the skilled worker subcategory of the Employment Third Preference, but you are not sure, consider filing two petitions, one as a skilled worker and another as an unskilled worker. This will save some time if the petition under the higher level subcategory is turned down.

It generally takes between three and 14 months to get a decision on the petition. Once your petition is approved, a Notice of Action, Form I-797, will be sent to your employer, indicating the approval. If you plan to execute Step Three (the visa interview) at a U.S. consulate abroad, USCIS will forward the file to the National Visa Center (NVC) located in Portsmouth, New Hampshire. The NVC will then send a packet of forms and instructions to you so that you may proceed with Step Three, described later in this chapter.

2. Procedures for Schedule A and Priority Workers

If you qualify as a priority worker or Schedule A applicant, your employer must prove to USCIS that you do in fact qualify as a priority worker or for Schedule A. To do this, Step One forms and documents must be filed together with the Step Two forms and documents. The employer should not, however, follow the cumbersome Step One procedures. Only the paperwork is required. All papers are filed at the USCIS regional service center having jurisdiction over your employer's place of business. Although your employer must still fill out the same Step One form, the ETA-750, there will be an entirely different set of documents. A description of these documents is in Section 4d, below. When completing Form ETA-750, your employer may disregard any of the directions concerning how to meet and deal with certain standards set by the DOL for the minimum number of years of job experience and the minimum salary. Instead, the employer may set his or her own standards, provided any minimum requirements for the priority worker or Schedule A categories are not listed. This is explained in more detail in the instructions on how to fill out Form ETA-750.

3. Petition Forms

Copies of all forms can be found in Appendix II and on the USCIS website at www.uscis.gov. Persons applying under the Fourth Preference (special immigrant) or Fifth Preference (entrepreneur) categories should refer to their separate chapters (Chapters 11 and 10, respectively), as the required forms may differ.

Form I-140

The basic form for Step Two, the petition, is Form I-140. It is used for almost all green card through employment petitions. The form has one section asking for information about your petitioning employer and another section asking for information about you. If a particular question does not apply, it should be answered "None" or "N/A."

It is absolutely essential to answer each question truthfully, even if it means disclosing that you are in the U.S. illegally. Failure to reveal requested information may result in your being permanently barred from the U.S. (See Chapter 25.)

Part 1. Part 1 asks for basic information about the employer and is self-explanatory.

Part 2. Part 2 asks you to check the box indicating the classification you are seeking. Categories "a," "b" and "c" are priority worker categories. Category "d" is for the employment-based Second Preference. Category "e" is for skilled or professional workers applying under the employment third preference. Category "g" is for unskilled workers applying under the employment third preference.

Part 3. Part 3 asks questions about you. "A" numbers are usually issued only to people who previously held green cards or have made previous green card applications. Your current immigration ("nonimmigrant") status must be disclosed, even if you are in the U.S. illegally. If any of the boxes do not apply to you, answer "N/A."

Put down the address where you really live, even if it means revealing that you are in the U.S. without status. The DOL and USCIS offices during Steps One and Two and USCIS offices or consulates during Step Three will send correspondence to the address you put down in Part 3, so be sure it is correct.

Part 4. Part 4 asks where you intend to apply for your green card, and also requests your last foreign address, if you are currently living in the U.S. If you'll be applying at an overseas U.S. consulate, keep in mind that U.S. consulates in your last country of residence are the only ones legally required to accept your application. If there is an overwhelming need to file elsewhere, you can approach a consulate in some other country and ask if it will process your application there. It is under no obligation to grant your request and is likely to turn you down, but there is no harm in asking. Unless you have gotten permission in advance, your employer should not write down the name of any consulate other than the one in your last country of residence.

If you plan to apply for Adjustment of Status in the U.S., make sure that you are, or will be, eligible to do so. This usually requires having a valid nonimmigrant visa at the time you apply. See Chapter 25 for more information.

Part 5. Part 5 asks for additional information about the employer, including type of business, date established, gross and net annual income, and number of employees.

In priority worker petitions for persons of extraordinary ability, no offer of employment is required. If that is the case, under type of petitioner the box "Self" should be marked. The remaining questions about the employer may be answered "N/A."

Parts 6. Part 6 asks for basic information about your proposed employment. It also asks for a nontechnical description of the job, which should match the description put on Part A of the Form ETA-750 Labor Certification application.

Parts 7–9. These parts request information on family members, and require signatures. They are self-explanatory.

Form ETA-750

If you are applying under Schedule A, you must still fill out this form and submit it in duplicate as part of Step Two. See Section E4, above.

4. Petition Documents

Your employer must file a number of documents with the petition. These are intended to prove three things:

- you have an approved Labor Certification, are a priority worker, or qualify under Schedule A
- you are qualified for the job that you have been offered, and
- your petitioning employer has sufficient income to pay you the wage stated on the Labor Certification or petition.

a. Approved Labor Certification

The first and most important document your employer must submit with the petition forms is the approved Labor Certification. This is actually the ETA-750, Part A, which has been returned to your employer with a red and blue approval stamp. The original, approved form must be submitted. A copy is not acceptable.

If you are applying as a priority worker or under Schedule A, instead of with an approved Labor Certification, the documents you will need are listed in Section 4d, below.

b. Documents Proving Your Job Qualifications

Documents to prove your own qualifications for the job also go with the petition. There must be evidence that you have the minimum education and experience called for in the job description on Form ETA-750. If special requirements were written in Part A, Question 15, of the form, there must be proof that you have those skills as well.

Diplomas and transcripts from schools you attended must be shown to verify your education. USCIS insists on both a diploma and a transcript from each school where you graduated. If you attended a school but did not graduate, the transcript is required. If you were educated outside of the U.S., USCIS may request a credential evaluation from an approved evaluation service as explained in Section B2, above. Remember that an unfavorable evaluation should not be sent in unless requested. A bad evaluation should also give you reason to consider applying under a lesser preference or subcategory.

Evidence of your job experience should include letters or notarized affidavits from previous employers. These do not have to be in any special form, but simply in your former employer's own words. The letters or affidavits should clearly indicate what your position was with the company, your specific job duties, and the length of time you were employed. If letters from previous employers are unavailable, you may be able to prove your work experience with your personal tax returns or by affidavits from former co-workers. Proof of special knowledge or skills can be supplied through notarized affidavits, either from you or someone else who can swear you have the special ability (such as skill to use a particular machine or speak a foreign language) required. These, too, need not be in any special form.

c. Salary Level Documents

Your employer must also supply documents to prove the business can afford to pay you. Many petitions filed by smaller businesses are turned down because the employer cannot show sufficient income to pay the required salary. To prove the ability to pay, your employer should present the company's U.S. tax returns for the past two years or, if tax returns are unavailable, bank statements showing capital in the company and balance sheets, plus profit and loss statements. If your employer cannot produce tax returns, he should be prepared to explain why not. Usually the only excuse USCIS will accept is that the company is too new to have filed them.

Publicly held companies do not have to produce tax returns. For them, the annual reports of the corporation for the past two years are the accepted documents for proving ability to pay wages. As a general rule, the larger the company, the less evidence USCIS demands of its ability to pay additional salaries. When a company is nationally known, USCIS may require no proof at all.

d. Special Documents for EB-1 and EB-2 Workers and Schedule A Occupations

For priority workers and Schedule A occupations, all Step One Labor Certification forms and documents are submitted directly to USCIS at the same time as the forms and documents for Step Two, the petition. The documents required depend upon the priority worker subcategory or Schedule A group under which you are applying.

i. Employment First Preference: Workers of Extraordinary Ability

This category is reserved for only the most accomplished persons in the arts, sciences, education, business, or athletics. Extensive documentation must include either evidence that you have received a major, internationally recognized award or achievement (such as a Nobel Prize), or, alternatively, at least three of the following types of proof or other comparable evidence:

- Documentation of the receipt of several lesser nationally or internationally recognized prizes or awards for excellence. (If the award is major, as described above, only one is necessary.)
- Documentation of membership in associations which require outstanding achievements of their members, as judged by recognized national or international experts.
- Published material about you in professional or major trade publications or other major media outlets relating to your work.
- Evidence of your participation as a judge of the work of others in your field.
- Evidence of your original scientific, scholarly, artistic, athletic, or business-related contributions of major significance.
- Evidence of your authorship of scholarly articles in professional or major trade publications or other major media outlets.
- Evidence of the display of your work at artistic exhibitions or showcases.
- Evidence that you have performed in a leading or critical role for distinguished organizations.
- Evidence that you have commanded a high salary or other compensation as compared to others in your field, within your country.
- Evidence that you have achieved commercial successes in the performing arts as shown by box office receipts or sales of records, cassettes, compact discs, or videos.

ii. Employment First Preference: Outstanding Professors and Researchers

You must produce evidence that you are internationally recognized as outstanding in a specific academic area and have at least three years of teaching or research experience. This is best shown by letters from former employers. If you are coming to the U.S. as a university professor, the position must be a tenured or tenure-track position. A letter from the employing university should clearly state this. If the em-

ployer is a private industry, it must submit evidence that it has a history of significant achievements in research and employs at least three other full-time research workers and that the position will last indefinitely.

Additional documentation must include at least two of the following:

- Evidence that you have received major prizes or awards for outstanding achievement in your academic field.
- Evidence of your membership in associations in your academic field which require outstanding achievements for membership.
- Published material in professional publications written by others about your work. Mere citations to your work in bibliographies are not sufficient.
- Evidence of your participation as the judge of the work of others.
- Evidence of your original scientific or scholarly research contributions to the academic field.
- Evidence of your authorship of scholarly books or articles in scholarly journals having international circulation.

iii. Employment First Preference: Multinational Executives and Managers

An applicant claiming priority worker status as a multinational executive or manager must document eligibility in exactly the same way as he or she would do for Step One, the petition, of an L-1 visa application. Please refer to Chapter 19. Follow the instructions just as they are written there. We have, however, included a complete review of all the necessary forms and documents for this subcategory of priority workers in the summary checklist of forms and documents contained at the end of this chapter.

There are three categories of L-1 visa holders: managers, executives, and those with specialized knowledge. The only L-1 visa holders who qualify as priority workers are managers and executives. *If you qualify for an L-1 visa only under the specialized knowledge category, you must go through standard Labor Certification procedures to get a green card through employment, unless you qualify as an executive or manager.*

iv. Employment Second Preference: Workers of Exceptional Ability in the Sciences, Arts, Athletics, or Business

To successfully document your qualifications as a person of exceptional ability for purposes of the Second Preference category, your employer is required to provide evidence from at least three of the following categories of documents or other relevant documents:

- Evidence that you have an academic degree or certificate relating to your area of exceptional ability.

- Evidence that you have had at least ten years of full-time experience in the field (letters from current and former employers).
- A license to practice your profession.
- Evidence that you have at some time commanded a salary that indicates exceptional ability.
- Evidence of your membership in professional associations.
- Evidence of recognition for achievements and significant contributions to your industry or field.

If you are applying for a waiver of the job offer requirement and Labor Certification, you must also submit as a document Form ETA-750, Part B only, and a written statement explaining why an exemption from the job requirement is in the U.S. national interest.

v. Schedule A Group I: Physical Therapists

To qualify as a physical therapist, you must either be licensed in the U.S. state where you will work, or be qualified to take the state licensing exam. If you are already licensed in some U.S. state, a copy of your license should be submitted. If you are not licensed, a letter from the state physical therapy licensing agency in the state where you will work must be submitted, stating that you meet all of the qualifications of that state to take the licensing exam.

vi. Schedule A Group I: Registered Nurses

To receive a green card as a registered nurse, you must submit a copy of your full and unrestricted nursing license issued by the U.S. state where you plan to work. A license from any other U.S. state is not sufficient. If you are not yet licensed, you must provide evidence that you have passed the Commission on Graduates of Foreign Nursing Schools (CGFNS) exam. You can get information on how to take this exam from:

CGFNS
3600 Market Street, Suite 400
Philadelphia, PA 19104
Telephone: 215-349-8767
Website: www.cgfns.org

vii. Schedule A Group II: Persons of Exceptional Ability

To prove that you're a worker of exceptional ability for purposes of Schedule A and to avoid Labor Certification, you'll need to gather the following:

- Evidence of your current widespread acclaim and international recognition
- Documents showing that exceptional ability was required for your work over the past year and will be required in your new job, and
- Evidence showing at least two of the following:

- you've received international prizes or awards for excellence in your field
- you're a member of an international organization that requires outstanding achievement of its members
- people have written articles about your work in professional publications
- you've participated as a judge of others' work in your field or a similar one
- you've contributed original scientific or scholarly research to your field
- you've authored scientific or scholarly articles in your field in professional journals with international circulation, or
- your work has been displayed at artistic exhibitions in more than one country.

viii. Religious Occupations

Evidence is needed to show that you are recognized by your religion as qualified for the particular occupation in which you engage. To prove this, you should present your official certificates or licenses, if any. You should also obtain a letter from the governing body of your religion certifying the nature of your occupation and how long you have worked in that capacity and have been a member of that denomination. You must have been engaged in your occupation for at least two years before you begin the paperwork for a green card.

USCIS INVESTIGATION OF QUALIFICATIONS

Sometimes in Step Two, USCIS will go beyond the documents your employer submits and attempt to verify, through an investigation of its own, that you've got the work experience you claimed in Part B of the ETA-750 form. This is particularly true with live-in housekeepers and specialty chefs such as Chinese cooks.

If such an investigation is undertaken, you and your employer won't be told about it, but it could cause long delays in your case. When you find it is taking an unusually long time to get an approval on the petition, an investigation in progress could be the reason. Waits in excess of a year are typical under these circumstances.

If USCIS, through its own investigation, comes up with evidence showing you are not really qualified for the job, it must notify your employer of its intent to deny the petition and explain the nature of the evidence on which it is basing the denial. Your employer will then have ten days to argue against these findings.

5. Petition Interviews

Before approving a petition, USCIS occasionally requests an interview with the petitioning employer. This is fairly unusual. If the employer is a new company or an individual rather than a company (as is normally the case with employers of live-in housekeepers), an interview may be held concerning the employer's ability to pay wages. Interviews can best be avoided by providing good documentation from the beginning on both your job qualifications and the employer's ability to pay your salary.

6. Petition Appeals

When your job qualifications or the ability of your employer to pay your salary have been poorly documented, the petition will probably be denied. Your employer will then receive written notice of USCIS's unfavorable decision, a written statement of the reasons for the negative outcome, and an explanation of how to make a formal appeal.

The best way to handle an appeal is to try avoiding it altogether. Filing an appeal means arguing to USCIS that its reasoning was wrong. If your employer thinks it's possible to eliminate the reason why the petition failed by improving the paperwork, it makes sense to disregard the appeals process and simply file a new and better petition.

If the petition was denied because your U.S. employer left out necessary documents that have since been located, the new documents should be sent, together with a written request that the case be reopened, to the same USCIS office that issued the denial. This is technically called a *Motion to Reopen*. There is a $110 fee for filing this motion. Appeals often take a long time. A Motion to Reopen can be concluded faster.

If your U.S. employer does choose to file an appeal, it must be done within 30 days of the date on the Notice of Denial. The appeal should be filed at the same USCIS service center with which your employer has been dealing. There is a $110 filing fee. USCIS will then forward the papers for consideration to the Administrative Appeals Unit in Washington, DC. In six months or more, your employer will get back a decision by mail. Few appeals are successful.

When an appeal to USCIS has been denied, the next step is to make an appeal through the U.S. judicial system. Your employer may not file an action in court without first going through the appeals process available from USCIS. If your case has reached this stage, we strongly recommend seeking representation from a qualified immigration attorney, as you may now be in danger of being deported.

G. Carrying Out Step Three: The Application (Consular Filing)

Once you have an approved petition and a current Priority Date, you will probably need to apply for your green card at a U.S. consulate in your home country or last country of residence.

CITIZENS OF COUNTRIES WITHOUT U.S. EMBASSIES

Citizens of countries not having formal diplomatic relations with the U.S. are faced with the problem of where to apply for immigrant visas.

Persons from these countries who are still residing in their home countries will apply at a designated foreign consulate. Persons who are outside of their home country in a third country which conducts visa processing will do visa processing in that country as if they were residents of the third country.

1. Benefits and Drawbacks of Consular Filing

Anyone with an approved petition and a current Priority Date can apply for a green card at the appropriate consulate. That is not the case with U.S. applications, since you must be physically inside the U.S. to apply there. If you entered the U.S. legally and have spent 180 days or more out of status or working illegally, you may be ineligible to file in the U.S. (see I.N.A. § 245(k)). The exception would be if you had a certain visa petition or Labor Certification on file by January 14, 1998; or by April 30, 2001, if you can also prove that you were physically present in the U.S. on and around December 21, 2000.

If you plan to file at a consulate, but have spent any time in the U.S. illegally, however, be sure to understand the bars to admission discussed in Chapter 25 before proceeding.

A plus to consular filing is that some consulate offices may work more quickly to issue immigrant visas than do some USCIS offices. Your waiting time for the paperwork to be finished may be months shorter at a U.S. consulate abroad than at USCIS offices. Remember, however, that the difference in waiting time between the USCIS and consulate offices applies only to processing paperwork. Quotas move at the same rate of speed no matter where your application is filed.

One of two drawbacks to consular filing is the travel expense and inconvenience you will experience in returning to your home country if you are already in the U.S. The other problem is that should your consular application fail, not only will you be outside the U.S. but you will also have fewer ways to appeal than a U.S. filing would offer.

2.   Application Forms: Consular Filing

When you file at a U.S. consulate abroad, the consulate officials will provide you with certain forms designated by a "DS" preceding a number. Instructions for completing DS forms and what to do with them once they are filled out will come with the forms. We do not include copies of these forms in Appendix II, because some consulates use their own versions. Copies of all non-"DS" forms are in Appendix II and on the USCIS website.

Form I-134

It is necessary to convince the consulate that once you receive a green card you are not likely to go on public welfare. Since you have a job offer, that proves you have a way to support yourself, and an I-134 need not be filed for you, unless a relative owns 5% or more of the business that is petitioning for you. (In that case, you would need to file Form I-864, another version of an Affidavit of Support. A copy is in Appendix II and instructions for completing it are in Chapter 7.) You should still, however, fill out Form I-134, the Affidavit of Support, for any accompanying relatives. Because the consulate knows you will have an income, you must sign the I-134 forms and take financial responsibility for each family member.

If you are in the subcategory of priority workers that does not require you to have a specific job offer in order to get a green card, you have already submitted the documents in Step Two, showing your intent to continue working. These documents are a sufficient substitute for Form I-134.

In signing the Affidavit of Support, you are not actually promising to support your accompanying relatives. What you do promise is to reimburse the U.S. government for the sum total of any government support payments they might receive should they go on welfare. The Affidavit of Support binds you to this obligation for three years.

3.   Application Documents: Consular Filing

You'll also need to gather various documents in support of your immigrant visa application, as follows:

Notice of Action. The most important document in your application is the Notice of Action showing approval of your petition. This is the only document you will not have to submit yourself. It is sent directly from the USCIS office in the U.S. to the consulate you named on Form I-140 in Step Two. Do not mail in your other documents. Instead, bring them to your interview.

Copy of the petition. You must resubmit to the consulate all the documents first filed in Step Two.

Birth certificates. Additionally, you must have your long-form birth certificate and birth certificates of any unmarried minor children who are not immigrating with you.

Passports. It is also necessary to have in your possession a valid passport from your home country. The expiration date on the passport must leave enough time for the passport to remain valid at least six months beyond the date of your final application interview.

Police clearance. Unlike applications made in the U.S., you personally must collect police clearance certificates from each country you have lived in for one year or more since your 16th birthday. Additionally, you must have a police certificate from your home country or country of last residence, if you lived there for at least six months since the age of 16. You do not need to obtain police certificates from the U.S.

Contact the local police department in your home country for instructions on how to get police certificates. To obtain police certificates from nations other than your home country, contact the nearest consulate representing that country for instructions. Some nations refuse to supply police certificates, or their certificates are not considered reliable, and so you will not be required to obtain them from those locations. The U.S. consulate will tell you which countries police certificates are not required from.

Some countries will send certificates directly to U.S. consulates but not to you personally. Before they send the certificates out, however, you must request that it be done. Usually this requires filing some type of request form, together with a set of your fingerprints.

Photos. You and each accompanying relative must bring to the interview three photographs taken in compliance with the consulate's instructions. If your religious beliefs require wearing a head covering, you should be able to keep it on

for the photo, even if your right ear is covered up (it normally must be shown in the photo). However, your eyes and face must still be visible, and you must submit a written statement explaining why you can't submit a standard photograph that shows your hair and your right ear. Often this packet will also contain a list of local photographers who take this type of picture.

Fingerprints. A few consulates require you to submit fingerprints, though most do not. Consulates wanting fingerprints will send you blank fingerprint cards with instructions. The current fingerprinting fee is $85.

4. Application Interviews: Consular Filing

Consulates hold interviews on all green card applications. A written notice of your interview appointment is included when you receive the final packet.

Medical exam. Immediately before the interview, you and your accompanying relatives will be required to have medical examinations. Some consulates conduct the medical exams up to several days before the interview. Others schedule the medical exam and the interview on the same day. You will be told where to go and what to do in your appointment letter.

The medical examinations are conducted by private doctors. The fees vary from $50 to more than $150 per exam, depending on the country. The fee will be stated in your appointment letter. The exam itself involves taking a medical history, blood test, and chest X-ray, and vaccinations, if required. Although pregnant women can refuse to be X-rayed until after the pregnancy, the requirement to have an X-ray taken cannot be waived entirely. The vaccination requirement may be waived for religious, moral, or medical reasons.

The main purpose of the medical exam is to verify that you are not medically inadmissible. The primary medical grounds of inadmissibility are tuberculosis and HIV (AIDS). Some medical grounds of inadmissibility can be overcome with treatment or by applying for a waiver. (See Chapter 25 for more details.) If you need a medical waiver, you will be given complete instructions by the consulate at the time of your interview.

Interview fees. After the medical exam, you and your accompanying relatives will report to the consulate for the interview. At that time, you must pay $335 per person when your papers are submitted. Some consulates accept payment only by certified check, money order, or traveler's check. Others accept cash. You will be told the proper method of payment in your appointment packet.

At the interview. Bring with you to the interview the completed forms, photographs, your passports, and all of the required documents discussed here. The interview process involves verification of your application's accuracy and an inspection of your documents. Your name will also be checked against various security databases to see whether you have a history of criminal or terrorist behavior. This can add many weeks to the approval of your application, particularly if you come from a country that the U.S. government has identified as sponsoring terrorism. As of this book's printing, those countries included North Korea, Cuba, Syria, Sudan, Iran, Iraq, and Libya. If all is in order, you will be asked to return later, when you will be issued an immigrant visa. You are not yet a permanent resident.

Entering the U.S. The immigrant visa allows you to request entry to the U.S. You acquire the full status of green card holder at the moment of being inspected and admitted into the U.S. At that time, your passport is stamped and you are immediately authorized to work. If you are bringing any accompanying relatives, they must enter at either the same time or after you do in order to become permanent residents. Permanent green cards for you and your accompanying relatives are then ordered. They will come to you by mail several months later.

5. Application Appeals: Consular Filing

When a consulate denies a green card application, there is no formal appeal available, although you are normally free to reapply as often as you like. (Check with your local consulate to be sure, however—some place limits on the number of repeat applications, or require you to wait a certain number of months before reapplying.) When your green card is refused, you will be told the reasons why. The most common reason is failure to supply all the required documents. Sometimes presenting more evidence on an unclear fact can bring about a better result.

Another common reason for denial of a green card is that the consular officer believes you are inadmissible. If you are found to be inadmissible, you will be given an opportunity to apply for a Waiver of Inadmissibility, if one is applicable. (See Chapter 25 for directions on how to apply.)

When all these possibilities are exhausted, if the consulate still refuses you a green card, your opportunities for further appeals are severely limited. Historically, the courts have held that there is no right to judicial review and there is no formal appeal procedure through any U.S. government agency. See an experienced immigration attorney for more information and suggestions.

Overall, the best way to handle an application that has been turned down is simply to wait awhile, reapply on a different basis, and hope for better luck next time.

H. Carrying Out Step Three: The Application (U.S. Filing)

If you are presently in legal status in the U.S., (with an un-expired visa or status), you may apply for a green card with-out leaving the country on the following conditions:

- you have an approved Labor Certification or are exempt from Labor Certification
- you have already received an approved petition
- a green card number is currently available to you be-cause your waiting period under the quota is up, and
- you are admissible and none of the bars to adjustment apply to you; see Chapter 25.

Alternately, if your visa has expired and/or you have no legal right to be in the U.S., you can apply to adjust status if you entered the United States legally, and have not spent more than 180 days either out of status (for example, be-cause your visa expired), working without authorization, or otherwise violating the terms of your visa. This special pro-vision applies only to applicants in the first three employ-ment preference categories. See I.N.A. § 245(k).

If this provision doesn't work for you, you can still apply to adjust status if you had either a visa petition or a labor certification on file by January 1, 1998; or by April 30, 2001, if you can also prove that you were in the U.S. (legally or not) on December 21, 2000.

Unless you can meet the terms above, you may not be eligible to file an application (Step Three) for a green card in the U.S., and could cause your own deportation by try-ing.

1. Benefits and Drawbacks of U.S. Filing

The obvious benefit to applying for a green card in the U.S. is that if you are already in the country, you avoid the expense and inconvenience of overseas travel. Should prob-lems arise in your case, you will at least be able to wait for a decision in the U.S., a circumstance most green card appli-cants prefer.

Another important benefit of U.S. filing is that you may receive permission to work while you wait for the results of your case. See sidebar below, "Procedures for Advance Work Authorization." If you do not need to work right away, but can wait until after getting your green card, you do not need to file this separate application.

If your application for a green card is turned down, you have greater rights of appeal inside the U.S. than you do at a U.S. consulate. USCIS offices have different procedures from consular offices because they are controlled by a dif-ferent branch of the U.S. government.

There are some disadvantages to applying in the U.S. It may take much longer to get results. Processing times at several USCIS offices average around one year, even on cases where quotas are current. While your case is pending at a USCIS office, you may not leave the U.S. without get-ting special permission ("Advance Parole"). If you do leave without USCIS's permission, even for a genuine emergency, this will be regarded as withdrawal of your application and you will have to start your application over again when you return.

PROCEDURES FOR ADVANCE WORK AUTHORIZATION

If you want to work before your application for a green card is approved, you must file a separate application for employment authorization. This can be done by completing Form I-765 and filing it with the same USCIS service center where you filed the Step Three papers. Together with Form I-765, you must submit a copy of your I-94 card and pay a filing fee of $120. It is very important to keep the fee receipt that USCIS gives you so you can prove that the I-765 was filed. Normally, you will want to file the applica-tion for employment authorization at the same time as your Step Two application papers.

Legally, USCIS does not have to make a decision on your employment authorization application for up to 90 days. If for some reason you are not given a decision within 90 days, you will, at your request, be granted an interim employment authorization which will last 240 days. To receive an interim card, file a request for interim work authorization at the USCIS service center.

If 240 days pass and you still have not received a final decision on the I-765, you must stop working. Interim work authorization cards cannot be renewed. However, if you reach this point, you have the option to file a new I-765 application and, if you do not get a decision on the new application within 90 days, you will then be entitled to another interim work authori-zation card.

---

2. Application General Procedures: U.S. Filing

You may not begin Step Three until you have an approved Labor Certification, if one is required, and an approved visa petition. The application, consisting of both forms and documents, is submitted by mail to the USCIS service cen-ter nearest the place you are living. Check for the appropri-ate address and P.O. box at www.uscis.gov.

For U.S. filings, the basic form used in Step Three, the application, is Form I-485, Application for Permanent Residence. Form I-485 is filed to adjust your status in the U.S. "Adjusting status" is a technical term used only in U.S. filings. It simply means that you are presently in the U.S. and are in the process of acquiring a green card.

Fees. The filing fee for each application is $255 for applicants age 14 and over, and $160 for applicants under age 14. A separate application must be filed for you and each accompanying relative. In addition, if you are in the U.S. illegally, but are allowed to adjust status under old laws, you must pay a $1,000 penalty. Checks and money orders are accepted. Do not send cash through the mail.

Safety tips. You should send your papers by certified mail, return receipt requested. Keep a complete copy of everything you send in. USCIS is famous for losing paperwork.

PROCEDURES FOR ADVANCE PAROLE

Once your application has been filed, do not leave the U.S. for any reason before you have applied for and received advance permission to reenter the U.S. (Advance Parole). Any absence without this permission will be viewed as a termination of your application for a green card.

If you want to leave the U.S., file Form I-131 at the service center, together with three passport-type photographs and a short explanation for why you want to leave—you will need a bona fide personal or business reason. There is a $110 filing fee.

If approved, you will be allowed to leave the U.S. and return again with no break in the processing of your application. However, if you were out of status for six or more months after April 1, 1997, you should not depart the U.S. even on the basis of an Advance Parole, as this may subject you to the three- or ten-year bars to permanent residence.

Generally, after filing your application, you will receive a receipt which estimates the processing time for your application. If USCIS requires additional evidence or information, they will send you a Request for Evidence (I-797).

USCIS has the discretion to waive a personal interview in applications for green cards through employment, and in practice they do so unless there is a problem or issue in your case. Policies differ among the USCIS service centers. If an interview is not required, you will receive an approval letter in the mail, usually several months after the application is filed. Your approval notice will instruct you where to go to a local USCIS office for your green card or so-called "ADIT" processing.

The interview, if required, would be held at a local USCIS office near you. If everything is in order, your application will be approved at the conclusion of the interview. Your passport will be stamped to show that you have been admitted to the U.S. as a permanent resident, and your permanent green card will be ordered. The green card will come to you in the mail several months after your approval.

3. Application Forms: U.S. Filing

Copies of all USCIS forms needed for your Adjustment of Status application can be found in Appendix II and on the USCIS website.

Form I-485

While most of Form I-485 is self-explanatory, a few items typically raise concerns. If a particular question does not apply to you, answer it with "None" or "N/A."

Part 1. Part 1 asks for general information about when and where you were born, your present address and your immigration status. It also asks for an "A" number. Normally, you will not have an "A" number unless you previously applied for a green card or have been in deportation proceedings. Your I-94 is the small green or white card put in your passport when you entered the U.S.

Part 2. In Part 2, you will mark Box "a," saying that you have an approved immigrant petition, if you are the principal applicant. Although Box "a" won't seem like an exact match for your situation if you're filing your Form I-140 at the same time—because your immigrant petition won't have been approved yet—it's still okay to check this box. However, you should, in this situation, also write in, "concurrent filing," or "I-140 pending." Box "b" is marked if your spouse or parent is the principal applicant.

Part 3. The questions in Sections A through C are self-explanatory. The nonimmigrant visa number is the number that appears on the very top of the visa stamp. It is not the same as your visa classification. The questions in Section C are meant to identify people who are inadmissible. With the exception of certain memberships in the Communist Party or similar organizations, you will not be deemed inadmissible simply because you joined an organization. However, if your answer to any of the other questions is "yes," you may be inadmissible. See Chapter 25, which is intended to help you remove such obstacles. Don't lie on your answers, because you will probably be found out, especially if you have engaged in criminal activity. Many inadmissible conditions can be legally overcome, but once a lie is detected, you will probably lose the legal right to correct the problem. In addition, a false answer is grounds to deny your application and may result in your being permanently barred from getting a green card.

Form I-485 Supplement A

This form is required only if you are eligible to adjust status in the U.S. but subject to a $1,000 penalty for being in the U.S. illegally. The form is self-explanatory and is intended to determine only whether you are subject to the penalty.

Form G-325A

G-325A biographic data forms must be filled out for you and each accompanying relative. You need not file a G-325A for any child under the age of 14 or any adult over the age of 79. The G-325A form is meant to gather personal background information. The questions are self-explanatory.

Form I-134 Affidavit of Support

It is necessary to convince USCIS that once you receive a green card, you are not likely to go on public welfare. Since you have a job offer, this proves you have a way to support yourself. An Affidavit of Support need not be filed for you, unless a relative is a 5% or more owner of the petitioning business. (In that case, you would need to file Form I-864, a lengthier version of the Affidavit of Support.) You should still, however, fill out Form I-134, the Affidavit of Support, for any accompanying relative. Because USCIS knows you will have an income, you must sign the I-134 forms and take financial responsibility for each of them.

In signing the Affidavit of Support, you are promising to support your accompanying relatives and to reimburse the U.S. government for the sum total of any government support payments they might receive should they go on certain kinds of public assistance. The Affidavit of Support purportedly binds you to this obligation for three years.

Form I-765

This form is used to apply for work authorization.

Block above Question 1. Mark the first box, "Permission to accept employment."

Questions 1–8. These questions are self-explanatory.

Question 9. This asks for your Social Security number, including all numbers you have ever used. If you have never used a Social Security number, answer "None." If you have a nonworking Social Security number, write down the number followed by the words "nonworking, for tax purposes only." If you have ever used a false number, give that number, followed by the words: "Not my valid number." Be sure to read Chapter 25, however, before filing an application with such information; use of false documents can make you inadmissible.

Question 10. You will not usually have an Alien Registration ("A") Number unless you previously applied for a green card, were in deportation proceedings, or have had certain types of immigration applications denied. If you have no "A" number but you entered the U.S. with a valid visa, or without a visa under the Visa Waiver Program, you should have an I-94 card. In this case, answer Question 10 by putting down the admission number from the I-94 card.

If you are from Mexico, you may have entered the U.S. with a border crossing card, in which case you should put down the number on the entry document you received at the border, if any. Otherwise simply put down the number of the border crossing card itself, followed with "BCC." If you are Canadian and you entered the U.S. as a visitor, you will not usually have any of the documents described here, in which case you should put down "None."

Questions 11–15. These questions are self-explanatory.

Question 16. Answer this question "(c)(9)."

4. Application Documents: U.S. Filing

You'll also need to gather several documents in support of your green card application, as follows:

Notice of Action. You must submit the Notice of Action showing your petition approval.

Job offer. As a person applying for a green card through employment, you must show that the original job offer on which the Labor Certification was based is still open to you. Submit a current letter from your employer stating again his or her intent to hire you. This letter will also prove your ability to support yourself and any accompanying relatives once you get a green card. If you are in a category that does not require a specific job offer, submit your Step Two documents proving your intent to work.

Photos. You and each of your accompanying relatives are required to submit two photographs that meet the specifications on Form M-378, found in Appendix II. Additionally, you must submit your birth certificate or other record of birth; if married, a marriage certificate and your spouse's birth certificate; and birth certificates for all your children under age 21, even if they are not immigrating with you.

Medical exam. You must also submit a Medical Examination Report for each applicant. This is done on USCIS Form I-693, which must be taken to a USCIS-authorized physician. The USCIS local office will provide you with the form as well as a list of approved physicians. The doctor will interview you as to your medical history and vaccinations, take a blood test and chest X-ray, and give you the results in a sealed envelope. You will be charged a fee of around $150. Do not open the envelope.

Proof of legal entry. Each applicant must submit a copy of his or her I-94 card if one was issued. This is the small white or green card you received on entering the U.S. Failure to do so may result in a conclusion that you entered or remained in the U.S. illegally and either are not eligible to adjust your status or are subject to the $1,000 penalty described earlier.

Fingerprints. All fingerprinting now takes place at a USCIS-run fingerprinting center. You will be notified where and when to appear after submitting your application forms. The fee is $50 (submitted with your application).

5. Application Interviews: U.S. Filing

Personal interviews are usually waived in green card through employment applications. If an interview is not waived, you and your accompanying relatives will be asked to come in to the USCIS local office for final processing. The USCIS officer will go over your application to make sure that everything is correct. The officer will also ask questions to find out whether you are inadmissible. (See Chapter 25.) Try to find out the reason for the interview prior to appearing at USCIS. If you have an issue or problem, consult an attorney before the interview.

At USCIS, a single fingerprint will be taken and you will be asked to sign your application under oath. Accompanying relatives, all of whom must attend the interview with you, will go through the same procedure.

The interview normally takes about 30 minutes. If all goes well, your case should be approved on the spot. Most USCIS offices will place a temporary stamp in your passport (as long as it is still valid) showing that you have become a U.S. permanent resident. With this stamp, you acquire all the rights of a green card holder, including the right to work, and freedom to travel in and out of the U.S. You will receive your permanent green card by mail several months later.

If your fingerprints have not been cleared yet, your application will be approved only provisionally, pending FBI clearance. In those cases, no stamp will be placed in your passport at the interview. Instead, you should receive a written notice of approval within a month or two. That notice serves as your proof of U.S. residency until you receive your green card, which takes yet another two or three months. If you need to travel outside the U.S. before your green card arrives, however, you must go back to the USCIS office, with your passport and the written notice of approval, and a temporary stamp will be placed in your passport, enabling you to return after your trip. Never leave the U.S. without either your green card or a temporary stamp in your passport.

6. Application Appeals: U.S. Filing

If your application is denied, you will receive a written decision by mail explaining the reasons. There is no way of making a formal appeal to USCIS. If the problem is too little evidence, you may be able to overcome this obstacle by adding more documents and resubmitting the entire application to the same USCIS office you have been dealing with, together with a written request that the case be reopened. The written request does not have to be in any special form. This is technically called a *Motion to Reopen*. There is a $110 fee. Alternatively, you may wait until USCIS begins deportation proceedings, in which case you may refile your application with the immigration judge.

If your application is denied because you are ruled inadmissible, you will be given the opportunity to apply for what is known as a *Waiver of Inadmissibility*, provided a waiver is available for your ground of inadmissibility. (See Chapter 25.)

You also have the right to file an appeal in a U.S. district court. This requires employing an immigration attorney at considerable expense. Such appeals are usually unsuccessful.

FORMS AND DOCUMENTS CHECKLIST

STEP ONE: LABOR CERTIFICATION

Forms

- ☐ ETA-750 A & B.

Documents

- ☐ Statement from the employer justifying any unusual or restrictive job requirements.
- ☐ Tear sheets from all advertisements.
- ☐ Posted job notice with signed statement by the employer of the dates posted and the results.
- ☐ Statements from the employer of advertising results saying why each U.S. job candidate was turned down.

Additional Documents for Special Cases

LIVE-IN DOMESTICS

- ☐ Employment contract.
- ☐ Evidence that the domestic has at least one full year of paid domestic experience.
- ☐ Statement of the employer explaining the need for a live-in.

PHYSICIANS

- ☐ Evidence that the physician has passed Parts I and II of the National Board of Medical Examiners exam.

COLLEGE AND UNIVERSITY TEACHERS

- ☐ Statement of a university official explaining you are the best job candidate.
- ☐ Minutes of faculty search committee meetings.
- ☐ Evidence of previous advertising and the results.

STEP TWO: PETITION

Forms

- ☐ Form I-140.
- ☐ Form ETA-750 (if applying under Schedule A).

Documents

- ☐ Approved Labor Certification or evidence of qualifying as a priority worker of extraordinary ability, Schedule A, or as a Second Preference worker of exceptional ability.
- ☐ All forms and documents listed under Step One.
- ☐ Diplomas and transcripts from colleges or universities.
- ☐ Professional certificates.
- ☐ Documents proving previous job experience.
- ☐ Documents proving special skills.
- ☐ Tax returns of the employer's company for the past two years, if available.
- ☐ Financial statements, including profit and loss statements and balance sheets of the employer's company for the past two years, if available.

PRIORITY WORKERS

Persons of Extraordinary Ability

- ☐ Evidence you have received a major, internationally recognized award, or at least three of the following:
  - ☐ Evidence you have received several lesser nationally or internationally recognized prizes or awards for excellence.
  - ☐ Documentation of membership in associations that require outstanding achievements of their members.
  - ☐ Published material about you in professional or major trade publications or other major media relating to your work.
  - ☐ Evidence of your participation as a judge of the work of others.
  - ☐ Evidence of your original scientific, scholarly, artistic, athletic or business-related contributions of major significance.
  - ☐ Evidence of your authorship of scholarly articles in professional or major trade publications.
  - ☐ Evidence of the display of your work at artistic exhibitions.
  - ☐ Evidence you have performed in leading or critical roles for distinguished organizations.
  - ☐ Evidence you have commanded a comparatively high salary.
  - ☐ Evidence you have achieved commercial successes in the performing arts.
  - ☐ Copy of the U.S. employment contract, or a written statement explaining how you will continue your extraordinary work in the U.S.

FORMS AND DOCUMENTS CHECKLIST

Outstanding Professors and Researchers

☐ Letters from former employers verifying that you have at least three years of teaching or research experience.

☐ If it is a university position, a letter or contract from the university stating that the U.S. position is either a tenured or tenure-track position.

☐ If the employer is in a private industry, evidence that it has a history of significant achievements in research, and employs at least three other full-time research workers.

☐ At least two of the following:

   ☐ Evidence that you have received major prizes or awards for outstanding achievement in your academic field.

   ☐ Evidence of your membership in associations in your academic field which require outstanding achievements for membership.

   ☐ Published material in professional publications written by others about your work. Mere citations to your work in bibliographies are not sufficient.

   ☐ Evidence of your participation as the judge of the work of others.

   ☐ Evidence of your original scientific or scholarly research contributions to the academic field.

   ☐ Evidence of your authorship of scholarly books or articles in scholarly journals having international circulation.

Multinational Managers and Executives

☐ Notice of approval of an L-1 visa petition, if any.

☐ Documents proving employment with the parent company for one of the past three years outside of the U.S. as an executive or manager.

☐ Articles of incorporation or other legal charter or business license of the foreign business.

☐ Articles of incorporation or other legal charter or business license of the U.S. business.

☐ Legal business registration certificate of the foreign business.

☐ Legal business registration certificate of the U.S. business.

☐ Tax returns of the foreign business for the past two years, if available.

☐ Tax returns of the U.S. business for the past two years, if available.

☐ If the company is publicly held, annual shareholder reports of both the U.S. and foreign companies.

☐ Accountant's financial statements, including profit and loss statements, and balance sheets of both the U.S. and foreign company for the past two years.

☐ Payroll records of the foreign company for the past two years, if available.

☐ Promotional literature describing the nature of the employer's business, both U.S. and foreign.

☐ Copy of the business lease or deed for the premises of the U.S. business.

☐ If either company is publicly held, statements from the secretary of the corporation attesting to how the companies are related.

☐ For private companies, copies of all outstanding stock certificates.

☐ For private companies, a notarized affidavit from the corporations' secretaries verifying the names of the officers and directors.

☐ For private companies, copies of the minutes of shareholder meetings appointing the officers and directors.

☐ If a joint venture, copy of the joint venture agreement.

Persons of Exceptional Ability in the Sciences, Arts or Business

☐ At least three of the following:

   ☐ Evidence that you have an academic degree relating to your area of exceptional ability.

   ☐ Evidence that you have had at least ten years of full-time experience in the field.

   ☐ A license to practice your profession.

   ☐ Evidence that you have commanded a comparatively high salary.

   ☐ Evidence of your membership in professional associations.

   ☐ Evidence of recognition for achievements and significant contribution to your industry or field.

☐ If you are applying for a waiver of the job offer requirement and Labor Certification:

   ☐ Form ETA-750, Part B only, and

   ☐ Written statement, support letters, and other documentation explaining why an exemption from the job requirement is in the U.S. national interest.

FORMS AND DOCUMENTS CHECKLIST

GROUP I: MEDICAL OCCUPATIONS

Physical Therapists

- ☐ Copy of the U.S. state physical therapist license, or
- ☐ Letter from the state physical therapy licensing agency stating that you meet all the qualifications to sit for the state exam.

Registered Nurses

- ☐ Copy of a full and unrestricted state nursing license, or
- ☐ Evidence of having passed the Commission on Graduates of Foreign Nursing Schools exam.

GROUP II: EXCEPTIONAL ABILITY IN THE ARTS OR SCIENCES

- ☐ At least two of the following:
  - ☐ Documents proving that you have won internationally recognized prizes or awards.
  - ☐ Documents showing membership in selective international associations.
  - ☐ Articles about your work appearing in professional publications.
  - ☐ Documents proving that you have acted as a judge in international competitions.
  - ☐ Documents describing your original scientific or academic research.
  - ☐ Copies of scientific or academic articles by you that have been published in international journals.
  - ☐ Documents proving that your work has been exhibited in at least two different countries.

STEP THREE: APPLICATION

Forms

- ☐ DS forms (available from U.S. consulates abroad for consular filing only).
- ☐ Form I-485 (U.S. filing only).
- ☐ Form I-485A (U.S. filing only).
- ☐ Form G-325A (U.S. filing only).
- ☐ Form I-765 (U.S. filing only).
- ☐ Form I-134 (consular and U.S. filings).
- ☐ Form I-864 (If a relative owns 5% or more of the business).

Documents

- ☐ Notice of approval of the visa petition.
- ☐ Long-form birth certificate for you and each accompanying relative.
- ☐ Passport for you and each accompanying relative, valid for at least six months beyond the date of the final interview.
- ☐ Copy of I-94 card for you and each accompanying relative (U.S. filing only).
- ☐ Police certificates from every country in which you and each accompanying relative has lived for at least six months since age 16 (consular filing only).
- ☐ Military records for you and each accompanying relative (consular filing only).
- ☐ Three photographs each of you and each accompanying relative.
- ☐ Letter from the petitioning employer verifying the job is still open.
- ☐ Medical exam report for you and each accompanying relative.

CHAPTER

9

Getting a Green Card Through the Lottery

Privileges

- You may live anywhere in the U.S. and stay as long as you want.

- You may work at any job, for any company, anywhere in the U.S.

- You may travel in or out of the U.S. whenever you wish.

- You may apply to become a U.S. citizen after you have held your green card for at least five years.

- Your spouse and unmarried children under the age of 21 may also get green cards as accompanying relatives.

Limitations

- Your place of actual residence must be in the U.S. You cannot use a green card just for work and travel purposes. (The only exception to this rule is for Alien Commuters, discussed in Chapter 4.)

- You must pay U.S. taxes on your worldwide income, because you are regarded as a U.S. resident.

- You cannot remain outside the U.S. for more than one year at a time without special permission or you risk losing your green card. (It is recommended that you return from your trip abroad before you have been gone six months.)

- If you commit a crime or participate in politically subversive or other proscribed activities, your green card can be taken away and you can be deported.

This chapter will explain who can become eligible for a green card based on the diversity visa "lottery," and how to apply. Because the rules change annually, you should also check the State Department website at www.state.gov.

A. Who Qualifies for a Green Card Through the Lottery?

The Immigration Act of 1990 created a new green card category to benefit persons from countries that in recent years have sent the fewest numbers of immigrants to the U.S. You can enter the lottery only if you are a native of one of these countries. Because the method used to select those who receive green cards through the lottery is that of random drawing, the program is popularly known as the *green card lottery*.

U.S. job offers are not a requirement. The only other qualification to enter is that the applicant have either a high school diploma or a minimum of two years' experience in a job that normally requires at least two years of training or experience. Whether your work experience qualifies will be determined based on a U.S. Department of Labor database.

However, you will have to meet other qualifications to claim your green card, including showing that you can support yourself financially in the U.S.

There is a new application period every year, usually occurring in late winter or early spring. The most recent deadline was December 30, 2003. Registrations submitted one year are not held over to the next, so if you are not selected one year you need to reapply the next year to be considered. For the 2003 lottery (technically called DV-2005), the only countries not qualified were:

Canada
China (mainland)
Colombia
Dominican Republic
El Salvador
Haiti
India
Jamaica
Mexico
Pakistan
Philippines
Russia
South Korea

United Kingdom (except Northern Ireland) and its dependent territories, and
Vietnam.

If you are from a country not named on the list above, you could have applied for the lottery that took place in 2003. Winners were notified by mail between May and July of 2004.

⚠️ **A winning ticket won't help you if you're inadmissible.** As in all green card applications, if you have committed certain crimes, been involved in terrorist or subversive activities, or are afflicted with certain physical or mental defects, you may be inadmissible, and therefore barred from receiving a green card through the lottery. Also, if you are living in the United States illegally, it may be impossible for you to collect your green card anytime soon. Procedurally, you would (unless you fall into an exceptional category) have to leave the U.S. for an interview at an overseas consulate. At that point, however, you could be barred from reentering the U.S. for three or ten years, depending on the length of your illegal U.S. stay. (See Chapter 25 on inadmissibility.)

B. Numerical Limits

There are 55,000 green cards made available per year under the lottery program (although 5,000 of these are reserved for applicants under the "NACARA" program; see Chapter 13, Section A). They are distributed by dividing up the world into regions and allocating varying percentages of the total green cards to each region. Additionally, each qualifying country within any region is limited to no more than 7% of the available lottery green cards per year (or 3,850).

Different qualifying countries are selected each year, based on which ones, and which areas of the world, sent the fewest numbers of immigrants to the U.S. during the previous five years, in proportion to the size of their populations.

C. Applying for a Green Card Through the Lottery

Getting a green card through the lottery is a two-step process.

1. Overview of Step One: Registration

The object of registration is simply to place your name among those who may be selected through the lottery drawing system to receive green cards. Acceptance of your registration does not mean you are eligible for a green card. It means only that you appear to come from a qualifying country. You can only enter once (if you submit more than one application you'll be disqualified). However, husbands and wives can each submit a separate application. One of the latest registration requirements is purely technological—as of 2003, applicants must submit their applications via the Internet and attach a digital photo.

2. Overview of Step Two: The Application

The "winners" will be notified within approximately eight months. If you don't win, you will receive no further communications. If you do win, you can proceed to Step Two: the application. This is filed by you and your accompanying relatives, if any. It is your formal request for a green card.

If the green card cannot be issued by the end of the lottery (fiscal) year (September 30), your application becomes invalid and you lose your chances at a green card. This happens to thousands of people every year. It may not be within your control.

If you are in the U.S. legally on a nonimmigrant visa, you apply for your green card either inside or outside the U.S., whichever you prefer. The vast majority of lottery green card applications will be filed at consulates.

If you are in the U.S. illegally, or entered legally without a visa under the Visa Waiver Program, refer to Chapter 25 to see if you may still file your green card application inside the U.S.—it's highly unlikely. Therefore it's entirely possible that you'll be subject to the three- or ten-year waiting periods to getting a green card, which result from being in the U.S. out of status and then departing the U.S. (See Chapter 25.)

3. Tips on Handling the Paperwork

There are two types of paperwork you must submit to get a green card through the lottery. The first consists of official government forms. The second is personal documents such as birth and marriage certificates. We will tell you what forms and documents you need. A summary checklist appears at the end of this chapter.

It is vital that forms are properly filled out and all necessary documents are supplied. You may resent the intrusion into your privacy and the sizable effort it takes to prepare immigration applications, but you should realize the process is an impersonal matter to immigration officials. Your getting a green card is more important to you than it is to the U.S. government. There is no shortage of applicants.

The documents you supply to USCIS or the consulate do not have to be originals. Photocopies of all documents are acceptable as long as you have the originals in your possession and are willing to produce the originals upon request. But add the following language to the photocopy, with your signature and the date:

> *Copies of documents submitted are exact photocopies of unaltered original documents and I understand that I may be required to submit original documents to an immigration or consular official at a later date.*
>
> *Signature* _____
>
> *Typed or Printed Name* _____
>
> *Date* _____

Documents will be accepted if they are in either English, or, with papers filed at U.S. consulates abroad, the language of the country where the documents are being filed (except at the U.S. consulates in Japan, where all documents must be translated into English). Other documents must be accompanied by a full, word for word, written English translation. Any capable person may act as translator. It is not necessary to hire a professional. At the end of each translation, the following statement must appear:

> *I hereby certify that I translated this document from [language] to English. This translation is accurate and complete. I further certify that I am fully competent to translate from [language] to English.*
>
> *Signature* _____
>
> *Typed or Printed Name* _____
>
> *Date* _____

The translator should sign this statement but it does not have to be witnessed or notarized.

D. Carrying Out Step One: Registration

The registration rules change every year, so you should check the State Department website at www.state.gov. There is no fee to register.

For the 2003 deadline (DV-2005) applicants were asked to fill out an application form online, and to attach digital photographs meeting certain specifications. The information requested in the online form included the following:

---

1. **FULL NAME** - Last/Family Name, First Name, Middle Name
2. **DATE OF BIRTH** - Day, Month, Year
3. **GENDER** - Male or Female
4. **CITY/TOWN OF BIRTH**
5. **COUNTRY OF BIRTH** - The name of the country should be that which is currently in use for the place where the applicant was born (for example, Slovenia rather than Yugoslavia, or Kazakhstan rather than Soviet Union).
6. **APPLICANT PHOTOGRAPH** – (according to photo specifications).
7. **MAILING ADDRESS** - Address, City/Town, District/Country/Province/State, Postal Code/Zip Code, Country
8. **PHONE NUMBER** (optional)
9. **EMAIL ADDRESS** (optional)
10. **COUNTRY OF ELIGIBILITY IF THE APPLICANT'S NATIVE COUNTRY IS DIFFERENT FROM COUNTRY OF BIRTH** - If the applicant is claiming nativity in a country other than his/her place of birth, this information must be submitted on the entry. If an applicant is claiming nativity through spouse or parent, please indicate this on the entry.
11. **MARRIAGE STATUS** - Yes or No
12. **NUMBER OF CHILDREN THAT ARE UNMARRIED AND UNDER 21 YEARS OF AGE**
13. **SPOUSE INFORMATION** - Name, Date of Birth, Gender, City/Town of Birth, Country of Birth, Photograph
14. **CHILDREN INFORMATION** - Name, Date of Birth, Gender, City/Town of Birth, Country of Birth, Photograph

---

Applicants must state the name, birthday, and place of birth of their spouse and all natural children, as well as all legally-adopted and stepchildren, who are unmarried and under the age of 21, other than those children who are already U.S. citizens or green card holders. This is required even if you are no longer legally married to the child's parent, and even if the spouse or child does not currently live with you and/or does not plan to immigrate with you. Failure to list all children will result in disqualification for the visa.

Send only one registration per person. Do not send separate registrations for children unless they qualify on their own and are willing to immigrate without you. Although unmarried children under 21 automatically qualify to immigrate with their parents, if selected, the opposite is not true. If a child is selected, the parents will not get green cards unless they are selected separately.

⚠ **Paying someone won't help your application.** Some immigration consultants claim they can get special attention for your lottery registration if you pay them to handle it. Such claims are false. There's nothing wrong with paying a lawyer or qualified paralegal to help you complete the registration according to the instructions, but recognize that that's the only type of help you'll be getting.

E. Carrying Out Step Two: The Application (Consular Filing)

Anyone whose registration is selected for green card processing can apply for a green card at a U.S. consulate in his or her home country. If you have been or are now working and living illegally in the U.S., or you entered the U.S. improperly, read Chapter 25. This chapter discusses grounds of inadmissibility and bars to getting a green card, which you'll need to analyze before you depart the U.S. or apply for a visa or green card. You'll probably need to consult an attorney.

1. Benefits and Drawbacks of Consular Filing

Your waiting time for the paperwork to be finished may be shorter at a U.S. consulate abroad than at a USCIS office. This is particularly important with lottery green card cases because if your immigrant visa isn't issued before the end of the fiscal year for which you were selected, your registration becomes void and you lose your chance for the card. The deadline is the end of the fiscal year *for*, and not *in*, the year you were picked. The government fiscal years begin on October 1 and end on September 30. This means that if you were selected in the 2005 registration period (which was November 1 to December 30, 2003), your deadline for receiving a green card would be September 30, 2005. Successful registrants would be notified between May and July of 2004. Remember September 30, 2005 is the deadline for receiving your green card, not filing the green card application. You

must, therefore, file much earlier—as soon as you possibly can—to be sure the processing is completed in time.

Another reason for speed is that the U.S. government notifies twice as many people as there are green cards available. It assumes some of these people either will not qualify or will change their minds about immigrating. If the assumption is wrong and everyone selected does mail in applications, the green cards will be given on a first come, first served basis. It is therefore possible that even though you win the lottery, if that year's green card allotment is used up before your own interview is scheduled, you will not get a green card. Once again, the speedier consular filing offers some protection against this happening.

One drawback to consular filing is the travel expense and inconvenience you will experience in returning to your home country if you are already in the U.S. And, if you are living in the U.S. illegally, you may be subject to the three- or ten-year waiting periods if you have been out of status over six or 12 months. Be sure to read Chapter 25 before making your decision on whether to use the consular process or apply in the U.S. Another problem is that should your consular application fail, you will have fewer ways to appeal than a U.S. filing would offer.

USING A FAMILY MEMBER'S BIRTHPLACE AS YOUR NATIVE COUNTRY

To enter the lottery, an applicant must be able to claim what the law describes as "nativity" in an eligible country. "Nativity" in most cases is determined by the applicant's place of birth. However, if you were born in an ineligible country but your spouse was born in an eligible country, you can claim your spouse's country of birth rather than your own (if your spouse will be immigrating with you). Also, if you were born in an ineligible country, but neither of your parents was born there or resided there at the time of your birth, you may be able to claim nativity in one of your parents' country of birth.

2. Application General Procedures: Consular Filing

Only a U.S. consulate or embassy in your home country is required to accept your lottery green card application. You can ask a consulate located elsewhere to accept your application, but it has the option to say "no," and in fact will turn down most such requests.

If you are selected, your notification will include a packet containing forms and instructions. Biographical Information Form DS-230 Part I will be included and should be completed and returned together with Form DS-2001 (formerly called OF-169).

The application for your green card is made in person, by appointment. When the consulate is ready for your final processing, it will send you another group of papers. This packet includes an interview appointment letter, instructions for obtaining your medical examination and still more forms to be completed. Do not mail your paperwork to the consulate. Instead, bring the rest of your forms and all documents listed on Form DS-2001 or Form OF-169 or requested by the consulate with you at the time of your appointment. The fee for filing an application is $335 per person and there is a surcharge for diversity visa applicants of $100.

3.   Application Forms: Consular Filing

The consulate officials will provide you with certain forms, designated by a "DS" preceding a number. Instructions for completing DS forms and what to do with them once they are filled out will come with the forms. We do not include copies of these forms in this book because some consulates use their own version. Copies of all non-"DS" forms are in Appendix II and on the USCIS website.

Form I-134

You must convince the consulate that once you receive a green card you are not likely to go on public welfare. A job is not required, but if you do not have a written offer of employment in the U.S., you must show that you are independently wealthy, or that someone is filing an Affidavit of Support on your behalf. Form I-134, the Affidavit of Support, guarantees that someone is willing to take financial responsibility for you. It's most convincing if the person signing the Form I-134 is both your close relative and a U.S. resident, but consulates may allow more distant relatives or even friends to sign these forms, and the signer's country of residence may not be a factor.

If you can show that you are financially independent or have a job offer in the U.S., an I-134 need not be filed for you. You should still, however, fill out Form I-134 for any accompanying relatives. Because you will have an income, you should be the one to sign the Form I-134, taking financial responsibility for each of them.

When you request a family member or friend to sign an Affidavit of Support on your behalf, he or she will doubtless wish to know the legal extent of the financial obligation. In signing the Affidavit of Support, the signer does not promise to support you. What he or she does promise is to reimburse the U.S. government for the sum total of any government support payments you might receive should you go on welfare. The Affidavit of Support binds the person signing it to this obligation for three years. After that, his or her responsibility to both you and the U.S. government comes to an end.

4.   Application Documents: Consular Filing

All green card applicants must supply birth records, marriage records (if married), birth certificates of all children under age 21 (even those not immigrating with you), education records, photographs, police clearances, and evidence of financial support. Bring the originals and a set of copies with you to your interview.

Financial Support. In all cases, you must demonstrate the ability to support yourself once you get a green card. A source of support must be shown for your accompanying relatives as well. You have three alternatives. You can submit as a document a written job offer from a U.S. employer. As an alternative you can submit your own personal current financial documents showing you have sufficient savings and investment income to support yourself. The third possibility is to have a U.S. friend or relative sign Form I-134, Affidavit of Support, on your behalf. If this form is filed, then no further documentation is required from you, though the signer should attach documents to prove his or her statements regarding income and assets, such as a letter from his or her employer, pay stubs, recent tax returns, and a letter from his or her bank showing the balance. Each of your accompanying relatives must also submit proof of a job offer, evidence of independent financial assets, or an I-134 signed on his or her behalf. When you have a job offer or sufficient financial means, you can sign Affidavits of Support for your accompanying relatives.

Passport. You must have a valid passport from your home country. The expiration date on the passport must leave enough time for the passport to remain valid at least six months beyond the date of your final application interview.

Police Clearances. Unlike applications made in the U.S., you personally must collect police clearance certificates from each country you have lived in for one year or more since your 16th birthday. Additionally, you must have a police certificate from your home country or country of last residence, if you lived there for at least six months since the age of 16. You do not need to obtain police certificates from the U.S., even if you have lived there.

Contact the local police department in your home country for instructions on how to get police certificates. To obtain police certificates from nations other than your home country, it is best to contact the nearest consulate representing that country for instructions. Some nations refuse to supply police certificates, or their certificates are not considered reliable, and so you will not be required to obtain them from those locations. The U.S. consulate will give you a list of countries for which police certificates are not required.

For applicants who once lived in Japan but do not reside there at the time their green card applications are filed, the Department of State recognizes that police certificates are available from Japan only as far back as five years from the date of the green card application.

Other countries will send certificates directly to U.S. consulates but not to you personally. Before they send the certificates out, however, you must request that it be done. Usually this requires filing some type of request form together with a set of your fingerprints.

Photos. You and each accompanying relative must bring to the interview three photographs taken in compliance with the consulate's instructions. The final packet often gives you a list of local photographers, as well.

Fingerprints. A few consulates require you to submit fingerprints, though most do not. Consulates wanting fingerprints will send you blank fingerprint cards with instructions. The fingerprinting fee is currently $85.

Proof of Education. The lottery green card program requires applicants to have either a high school diploma or the equivalent, or job skills needing at least two years of experience or training to learn. Appropriate evidence would be either a copy of your high school diploma or proof of job skill training, such as a vocational school certificate, and proof of at least two years of skilled employment verified by letters from past employers. A specific job offer in the U.S. is not required.

5. Application Interviews: Consular Filing

Consulates hold interviews on all green card applications. A written notice of your interview appointment will be included when you receive your final packet. Immediately before the interview, you and your accompanying relatives will be required to have medical examinations. You will be told where to go and what to do in your appointment letter.

a. The Medical Exam

The medical examinations are conducted by private doctors and you are required to pay the doctor a fee. The fees vary from $50 to more than $150 per exam, depending on the country. The exam itself involves taking a medical history, blood test, chest X-ray, and administering vaccinations if applicable and/or recommended for you. Pregnant women may refuse to be X-rayed until after the baby is born.

The main purpose of the medical exam is to verify that you are not medically inadmissible. The primary medical grounds of inadmissibility are tuberculosis and HIV (AIDS). Some of the medical grounds of inadmissibility can be overcome with treatment. (See Chapter 25 for more details.) If you need a medical waiver, you will be given complete instructions by the consulate at the time of your interview.

b. What Happens at the Interview

At your interview, you must pay more fees: $335 per person when your papers are submitted, and a $100 visa lottery surcharge. Some consulates accept payment only by certified check, money order, or travelers check. Others accept cash. You will be told the proper method of payment in your final packet.

Bring with you to the interview the completed forms, photographs, your passports, and all of the required documents discussed here. The interview process involves verification of your application's accuracy and an inspection of your documents. Your name will also be checked against various security databases to see whether you have a history of criminal or terrorist behavior. This can add many weeks to the approval of your application, particularly if you come from a country that the U.S. government believes sponsors terrorism. As of this book's printing, those countries included North Korea, Cuba, Syria, Sudan, Iran, Iraq, and Libya.

If all is in order, you will be asked to return later, when you will be issued an immigrant visa. You are not yet a permanent resident.

c. Using Your Immigrant Visa

The immigrant visa allows you to travel to a U.S. port or border to request entry to the U.S. You acquire the full status of green card holder at the moment of making entry (being inspected and admitted) into the U.S. At that time, your passport is stamped to show you are now a permanent resident and authorized to work. If you are bringing any accompanying relatives, they must enter at either the same time or after you do. Permanent green cards for you and your accompanying relatives are then ordered. They will come to you by mail several months later.

6. Application Appeals: Consular Filing

When a consulate denies a green card application, there is no formal appeal available, although you are free to reapply. (Check with your local consulate, however—some place limits on the number of repeat applications, or require you to wait a certain number of months before reapplying.) When your visa is refused, the reasons will be explained. The most common reason for denial is failure to supply all the required documents. Sometimes, presenting more evidence on an unclear fact can bring about a better result. If the denial was caused by a lack of evidence, this will be explained in a written notice sent to you by mail.

Another common reason for denial is that the consular officer believes you are inadmissible. If you are found to be inadmissible, you will be given an opportunity to apply for a Waiver of Inadmissibility if one is applicable (see Chapter 25).

If the consulate still refuses you a visa, your opportunities for further appeals are severely limited. The courts have held that there is no right to judicial review and there is no formal appeal procedure through any U.S. government agency. For more information or suggestions, consult with an experienced immigration attorney.

F. Carrying Out Step Two: The Application (U.S. Filing)

If you are physically present in the U.S., you may apply for a green card without leaving the country if all of the following are true:

- you have been notified that your registration has been selected for a green card
- your lottery registration number is available under the quota, and
- you are not subject to any grounds of inadmissibility or bars to adjustment of status (see Chapter 25). For most people, this means they must be lawfully in the U.S. with an unexpired visa.

Unless you can meet these terms, you may not file an application (Step Two) for a green card in the U.S.

1. Benefits and Drawbacks of U.S. Filing

The obvious benefit to applying for a green card in the U.S. is that if you are already in the country, you avoid the expense and inconvenience of overseas travel. When you file in the U.S., should problems arise in your case, you will at least be able to wait for a decision in America, a circumstance most green card applicants prefer.

Another important benefit of U.S. filing is that you may receive permission to work while you wait for the results of your case. To obtain this benefit, see "Procedures for Advance Work Authorization," below. If you do not need to work right away, but can wait until after getting your green card, you do not need to file this separate application. However, you may need to get benefits such as a Social Security card and a driver's license, so you may want to apply for the work permit even if you do not intend to work.

If your application for a green card is turned down, you have greater rights of appeal inside the U.S. than you do at a U.S. consulate. USCIS offices have different procedures from consular offices because they are controlled by a different branch of the U.S. government.

There are some disadvantages to applying in the U.S. It usually takes much longer to get results. Processing times at USCIS offices average 12 months. We already discussed in Section E1, above, why speed is particularly important in lottery cases. Because lottery green cards must be issued by a specific date, USCIS delays could cause you to lose this opportunity.

While your case is pending at a USCIS office, you may not leave the U.S. without getting special permission. If you do leave without USCIS's permission, even for a genuine emergency, this will be regarded as a withdrawal of your application, and you will have to start your application all over again when you return.

PROCEDURES FOR ADVANCE WORK AUTHORIZATION

If you want to work before your application for a green card is approved, you must file a separate application for employment authorization. This can be done by completing Form I-765 and filing it at the time you file your green card application or later at the same USCIS local office where you filed the application. Together with Form I-765, you must submit a copy of your I-94 card and pay a filing fee of $120. It is very important to keep the fee receipt USCIS gives you so you can prove that the I-765 was filed. Normally, you will want to file the application for employment authorization at the same time as your Step Two application papers.

Most USCIS offices will give you an appointment to return within a few weeks and you will receive your work authorization card at that time.

Legally, USCIS does not have to make a decision on your employment authorization application for up to 90 days. If for some reason you are not given a decision within 90 days, you will, at your request, be granted an interim employment authorization which will last 240 days. To receive an interim card, you must return in person to the USCIS local office where you filed your I-765 and show your fee receipt. Then your interim work authorization card will be issued.

If 240 days pass and you still have not received a final decision on the I-765, you must stop working. Interim work authorization cards cannot be renewed. However, if you reach this point, you have the option to file a new I-765 application and, if you do not get a decision on the new application within 90 days, you will then be entitled to another interim work authorization card.

2. Application General Procedures: U.S. Filing

The green card application, consisting of both forms and documents, is submitted either by mail or in person to the USCIS local office nearest the place you are living. Appendix I contains a complete list of all local U.S. immigration offices with their telephone numbers and addresses. The procedure is now undergoing a change. It is expected that eventually all applications will be filed only by mail to the regional service centers.

For U.S. filings, the basic form used in Step Two, the application, is Form I-485, Application for Permanent Resi-

dence. The filing fee for each application is $255 for applicants age 14 and over, and $160 for applicants under age 14. In addition, you must pay $50 for fingerprinting. A separate application must be filed for you and each accompanying relative.

In addition, if you are in the U.S. illegally but fall into one of the exceptional categories of people allowed to file their paperwork in the U.S., you may have to pay a $1,000 penalty fee. But see Chapter 25 before departing the U.S. or filing any forms with USCIS.

Checks and money orders are accepted. It is not advisable to send cash through the mail but cash is satisfactory at some offices if you file in person. Cash is accepted only in the exact amount; USCIS offices will not make change.

We recommend filing your papers in person if at all possible, as you will be given a written receipt from USCIS and your papers are likely to be processed right away. If you must mail in your application, you should do so by certified mail, return receipt requested. In either case, keep a complete copy of everything you send, in case it gets lost.

Once your application has been filed, do not leave the U.S. for any reason before your application has been approved. Any absence will be viewed as a termination of your application for a green card. If you must leave the U.S., request Advance Parole by filing Form I-131 together with three passport-style photos and a $110 filing fee. (Many people simply file this at the same time as their adjustment of status application.) Be sure you are not inadmissible and that you have not been out of status for 180 days or more after April 1, 1997 (before filing your adjustment application), or you may be prevented from returning to the U.S. (See Chapter 25.) If approved, you will be allowed to leave the U.S. and return again with no break in the processing of your application.

Generally, after filing your application, you will not hear anything from USCIS for several months. Then you should receive notices of your fingerprint and interview appointments. The interview notice will tell you if any further documentation is needed.

Security checks are the most likely cause of delays. As part of your adjustment of status application, the FBI must run both a fingerprint check and a name check on you, and the CIA must run a separate name check. These name checks tend to take several weeks, especially because many applicants have similar names. If you've been informed that your case is stalled due to security checks, get the name of a person you can keep in touch with for updates, or hire a lawyer to help with this task.

3. Application Forms: U.S. Filing

Copies of all the required USCIS forms can be found in Appendix II and on the USCIS website.

Form I-485

While most of the form is self-explanatory, a few items typically raise concerns, as addressed below. If a particular question does not apply to you, answer it with "None" or "N/A."

Part 1. Part 1 asks for general information about when and where you were born, your present address and immigration status. It also asks for an "A" number. Normally, you will not have an "A" number unless you previously applied for a green card or have been in deportation proceedings. (If you have one, see a lawyer before going further.)

Part 2. You will mark Box "a" if you are the principal applicant. Also mark Box "h," "other," and write in "Diversity Lottery Winner." Leave the other boxes blank.

Part 3. The questions in Sections A through C are self-explanatory. The nonimmigrant visa number is the number that appears on the very top of the visa stamp. It is not the same as your visa classification. The questions in Section C are meant to identify people who are inadmissible. With the exception of certain memberships in the Communist Party or terrorist organizations, you will not be deemed inadmissible simply because you joined an organization. However, if your answer to any of the other questions is "yes," you may be inadmissible. (See Chapter 25, which is intended to help you remove such obstacles.) Don't lie on your answers, because you will probably be found out, especially if you have engaged in criminal activity. Many inadmissibility conditions can be legally overcome, but once a lie is detected, you will lose the legal right to correct the problem. In addition, a false answer is grounds to deny your application and may result in your being permanently barred from getting a green card.

Form I-485 Supplement A

This form is required only if you are subject to a $1,000 penalty for being in the U.S. illegally. You are only eligible to apply under this provision if you had a Labor Certification or visa petition on file by January 14, 1998; or by April 30, 2001, if you can prove that you were physically present in the U.S. on December 21, 2000. (See Chapter 25.) The form is intended only to determine if you are subject to the penalty.

Form G-325A

G-325A biographic data forms must be filled out for you and each accompanying relative. You need not file a G-325A for any child under the age of 14 or any adult over the age of 79. The G-325A form is meant to gather personal background information. The questions are self-explanatory.

Form I-134

You must convince USCIS that once you receive a green card you are not likely to go on public assistance or welfare. A job is not required, but if you do not have a written offer of employment in the U.S., you must show that you are independently wealthy or that someone is filing an Affidavit of Support on your behalf. Form I-134, the Affidavit of Support, guarantees that someone is willing to take financial responsibility for you. USCIS offices normally insist that the person signing the Form I-134 be both your close relative and a U.S. resident.

If you can show that you are financially independent or have a job offer in the U.S., an I-134 need not be filed for you. You should still, however, fill out Form I-134 for any accompanying relatives. Because you will have an income, you should be the one to sign the Form I-134, taking financial responsibility for each of them.

When you request a family member or friend to sign an Affidavit of Support on your behalf, he or she will doubtless wish to know the legal extent of the financial obligation. In signing the Affidavit of Support, the signer does not promise to support you. What he or she does promise to do is reimburse the U.S. government for the sum total of any government support payments you receive if you go on welfare. The Affidavit of Support purportedly binds the person signing it to this obligation for three years. After that, his or her responsibility to both you and the U.S. government comes to an end.

Form I-765

You need to fill out this form only if you wish to apply for a work permit.

Block above Question 1. Mark the first box, "Permission to accept employment."

Questions 1–8. These questions are self-explanatory.

Question 9. This asks for your Social Security number, including all numbers you have ever used. If you have never used a Social Security number, answer "None." If you have a nonworking Social Security number, write down the number followed by the words "nonworking, for tax purposes only." If you have ever used a false number, give that number, followed by the words: "Not my valid number." (Also read Chapter 25 before filing any applications with USCIS; use of false documents is a ground of inadmissibility.)

Question 10. You will not usually have an Alien Registration Number unless you previously applied for a green card, were in deportation proceedings, or had certain types of immigration applications denied. All Alien Registration Numbers begin with the letter "A." If you have no "A" number but you entered the U.S. either with a valid visa, or without a visa under the Visa Waiver Program, you should have an I-94 card. In this case, answer Question 10 by putting down the admission number from the I-94 card.

If you are from Mexico, you may have entered the U.S. with a border crossing card, in which case you should put down the number on the entry document you received at the border, if any. Otherwise simply put down the number of the border crossing card itself, followed with "BCC." If you are Canadian and you entered the U.S. as a visitor, you will not usually have any of the documents described here, in which case you should put down "None."

Questions 11–15. These questions are self-explanatory.

Question 16. Answer this question "(c)(9)."

4. Application Documents: U.S. Filing

You must also gather a number of documents to support your adjustment of status application, as follows:

Financial Support. You must demonstrate the ability to support yourself once you get a green card. A source of support must be shown for your accompanying relatives as well. You have three alternatives. You can submit a written job offer from a U.S. employer. You can also submit your own personal current financial documents showing you have sufficient savings and investment income to support yourself. The third possibility is to have a U.S. friend or relative sign an I-134 Affidavit of Support on your behalf. If this form is filed, then no further documentation is required.

Each of your accompanying relatives must also submit proof of a job offer, evidence of independent financial assets, or an I-134 signed on his or her behalf. When you have a job offer or sufficient financial means, you can sign Affidavits of Support for your accompanying relatives.

Medical Exam. You must also submit a medical examination report for each applicant. This is done on Form I-693, which must be taken to a USCIS authorized physician or medical clinic. The USCIS local office will provide you with the form as well as a list of approved physicians in your area. After completion of the medical exam, and upon obtaining the test results, the doctor will give you the results in a sealed envelope. Do not open the envelope.

Photos. You and each of your accompanying relatives are required to submit two photographs. These photos should meet the specifications on the photo instruction sheet found in Appendix II, Form M-378.

Birth and Marriage Certificates. Additionally, you must submit a copy of your birth certificate or other record of birth. If you are married, submit copies of a marriage certificate, your spouse's birth certificate, and birth certificates for all your children, even those not immigrating with you.

Proof of Legal Entry. Each applicant must submit a copy of his or her I-94 card if one was issued. Failure to do so may result in a conclusion that you entered or remained in the U.S. illegally and either are not eligible or are subject to the $1,000 penalty described earlier. This is the small white card you received on entering the U.S.

Proof of Education. The lottery green card program requires applicants to have either a high school diploma or the equivalent, or job skills needing at least two years of experience or training to learn. Appropriate evidence would be either a copy of your high school diploma or proof of job skill training, such as a vocational school certificate, and proof of at least two years of skilled employment verified by letters from past employers.

Fingerprints. All fingerprinting now takes place at a USCIS-run fingerprinting center. You will be notified where and when to appear after submitting your application forms. You will be required to pay $50 (when you file your application papers) to cover the fingerprinting costs.

5. Application Interviews: U.S. Filing

All lottery green card applications require personal interviews. These are scheduled by appointment. You will receive written notice of the interview time a few weeks in advance. Although you must arrive on time for the interview and even early to get through the security lines at the front door—expect to wait a long time before you're actually called in.

The USCIS officer who interviews you will go over your application to make sure that everything is correct. He will also ask questions to find out whether you are inadmissible. (See Chapter 25.) A single fingerprint will then be taken and you will be asked to sign your application under oath. Accompanying relatives, all of whom must attend the interview with you, will go through the same procedure.

The interview normally takes about 30 minutes. If all goes well, your case may approved on the spot.

Most USCIS offices will place a temporary stamp in your passport showing that you have become a permanent U.S. resident. With this stamp you acquire all the rights of a green card holder, including the right to work and freedom to travel in and out of the U.S. The stamp is not your green card. You will receive your green card by mail several months later.

If your fingerprints have not been cleared by the time of your interview, your application will be approved only provisionally, pending clearance. In those cases, no stamp will be placed in your passport at the interview. Instead, you will be mailed a written Notice of Approval within a month or two. That notice serves as your proof of U.S. residency until you receive your green card, which takes yet another several months.

If you need to travel outside the U.S. before you receive your green card, you must go back to the USCIS office with your passport and the written Notice of Approval, and a temporary stamp will be placed in your passport to enable you to return to the U.S. after your trip. Never leave the U.S. without either your green card or a temporary stamp in your passport.

6. Application Appeals: U.S. Filing

If your application is denied, you will receive a written decision by mail explaining the reasons for the denial. There is no way of making a formal appeal to USCIS when your application is turned down. If the problem is too little evidence, you may be able to overcome this obstacle by adding more documents and resubmitting the entire application to the same USCIS office you have been dealing with, together with a written request that the case be reopened. The written request does not have to be in any special form. This is technically called a *Motion to Reopen*. There is a $110 fee to file this motion. Alternatively, you may wait until USCIS begins deportation proceedings, in which case you may refile your application with the immigration judge.

If your application is denied because you are ruled inadmissible, you will be given the opportunity to apply for what is known as a *Waiver of Inadmissibility*. (See Chapter 25 for more information.)

Although there is no appeal to USCIS for the denial of a green card application, you have the right to file an appeal in a U.S. district court. This requires employing an immigration attorney at considerable expense. Such appeals are usually unsuccessful.

FORMS AND DOCUMENTS CHECKLIST

STEP ONE: REGISTRATION

Form

☐ Registration application, available at www.state.gov, for filing online.

Photographs

Digital (jpg) photo in accordance with State Department instructions. One photo is required for each family member.

Documents

None.

STEP TWO: APPLICATION

Forms

☐ DS forms (available from U.S. consulate abroad for consular filing only).

☐ Form I-134 (U.S. and consular filings).

☐ Form I-485 (U.S. filing only).

☐ Form I-485A (U.S. filing only).

☐ Form G-325A (U.S. filing only).

☐ Form I-765, if permission to work is desired (U.S. filing only).

Documents

☐ Evidence of registration selection.

☐ Long-form birth certificate for you and each accompanying relative.

☐ Passports for you and each accompanying relative, valid for at least six months beyond the date of the final consular interview.

☐ Police certificates from every country in which you and each accompanying relative have lived for at least one year since age 16 (consular filing only).

☐ Military records for you and each accompanying relative (consular filing only).

☐ Three photographs each of you and each accompanying relative.

☐ Proof of education or work background:

  ☐ Copy of high school diploma, or

  ☐ Letters from past employers verifying skills and experience.

☐ Copy of I-94 card or other proof of legal entry for you and each accompanying relative (U.S. filing only).

☐ Marriage certificate if you are married and bringing your spouse.

☐ If either you or your spouse have been previously married, copies of divorce and death certificates showing termination of all previous marriages.

☐ Medical exam report for you and each accompanying relative.

Getting a Green Card Through Investment

Privileges

- You may live anywhere in the U.S. and stay as long as you want.

- When you first receive your green card through investment, you may work in your own company. After a certain length of time, you may work anywhere you wish or not work at all.

- You may travel in or out of the U.S. whenever you wish.

- You may apply to become a U.S. citizen after you have held your green card for at least five years.

- If you qualify for a green card through investment, your spouse and unmarried children under the age of 21 may get green cards as accompanying relatives.

Limitations

- You must maintain a large business investment in the U.S. for at least three years.

- Your place of actual residence must be in the U.S. You cannot use a green card only for work and travel purposes.

- You must pay U.S. taxes on your worldwide income, because you are regarded as a U.S. resident.

- You cannot remain outside the U.S. for more than one year at a time without special permission, or you risk losing your green card. (It is recommended that you return from any trips abroad before you have been gone for six (6) months.)

- If you commit a crime or participate in politically subversive activities or commit other proscribed activities, your green card can be taken away and you can be removed from the U.S. (deported).

This chapter will discuss who is eligible for a green card through investment ("Employment Fifth Preference" or "EB-5") and how to apply.

A. Who Qualifies for a Green Card Through Investment?

Green cards through investment are available to anyone who invests a minimum of $1 million in creating a new U.S. business or restructuring or expanding one that already exists. The business must employ at least ten full-time workers and benefit the U.S. economy. Full-time employment is defined as requiring at least 35 hours of service per week.

The investor, his or her spouse, and their children may not be counted among the ten employees. Other family members may be counted, however. Also, the investor must be active in the management of the company. The ten workers don't necessarily have to be U.S. citizens, but they must have more than a temporary (nonimmigrant) visa—

U.S. green card holders, conditional residents, temporary residents, asylees, refugees, and recipients of suspension of deportation can all be counted.

The required dollar amount of the investment may be reduced to $500,000 if the business is located in a rural area or in an urban area with an unemployment rate certified by the state government to be at least 150% of the national average. Rural areas are defined as any location not part of an official metropolitan statistical area or not within the outer boundaries of any city having a population of 20,000 or more. State governments will identify the parts of the particular state that are high in unemployment, and will notify USCIS of which locations qualify. Even if you know that the area of your intended investment has extremely high unemployment, it will not qualify for the lesser dollar amount unless the state government has specifically designated it as a high unemployment area for green card through investment purposes.

Under a temporary pilot program (currently set to expire in 2008), 3,000 of the visas for high-unemployment areas are set aside for immigrants who invest in "designated regional centers." Regional centers are designed by USCIS, and work to promote economic growth through increased export sales, improved regional productivity, creation of new jobs, and increased domestic capital investment. Investors in regional centers need not prove that they themselves provided new jobs for ten U.S. workers, only that that regional center created ten or more jobs, directly or indirectly, or increased regional productivity.

USCIS also has the authority to require a greater amount of investment than $1 million. This may occur when the investor chooses to locate the business in an area of low unemployment. At present, USCIS has adopted the policy of not raising dollar investment requirements on this basis.

The entire investment does not have to be made in cash. Cash equivalents such as certificates of deposits, loans, and notes can count in the total. So can the value of equipment or inventory. Borrowed funds may be used as long as the investor is personally liable in the event of a default, and the loan is adequately secured, and not by assets of the business being purchased. This means that mortgages on the business assets disqualify the amount borrowed from being calculated into the total investment figure.

A number of investors may join together in creating or expanding a U.S. business and each may qualify for a green card through the single company. However, the individual investment of each person must still be for the minimum qualifying amount, and each investor must be separately responsible for the creation of ten new jobs. For example, if five individuals each invest $1 million in a new business that will employ at least 50 American workers, all five investors qualify for green cards.

Although it is expected that the investment will be well under way when the green card application is made, the law does require the investment to be in a new commercial enterprise. However, as of 2002, the enterprise does not need to have been established by the applicant. And "new" means only that the business was established after November 29, 1990.

There is also an exception to the "new enterprise" rule. The investor can purchase an existing business if he or she increases either its net worth or the number of employees by at least 40%. The rules requiring a $1 million investment and ten employees still apply, however. Therefore, the existing business must be large enough so that a 40% increase will amount to the fixed required dollar and employment minimums in the category.

If the existing business purchased is in financial trouble, an investment designed to save that business will qualify the investor for a green card in this category. Purchasing a troubled business releases the investor from having to increase the net worth or the number of employees. It does not, however, excuse the $1 million minimum investment requirement. To qualify as a troubled business, the company must have been in operation for at least two years, and have had an annual loss during those two years equal to at least 20% of the company's net worth. An investor buying a troubled business is prohibited from laying off any employees. And, if the business fails within the first two years, the investor may not be approved for the permanent green card.

A green card for an investor is first issued only conditionally. The conditional green card is granted for two years. When the two years are over, the investor will have to file a request with USCIS to remove the condition.

In deciding if the condition should be removed, USCIS will investigate whether or not the proposed investment has actually been made, whether ten full-time American workers have been hired, whether or not the business is still operating, and whether the business is still owned by the investor who got the green card. When any of the required factors cannot be established to the satisfaction of USCIS; or if the petition for removal of the condition is not filed within the final 90 days of the two-year conditional period, the investor will lose his or her green card and be subject to removal from the U.S. (deportation). If, on the other hand, USCIS is satisfied that the investment still meets all requirements, the condition will be removed and a permanent green card issued.

1. Accompanying Relatives

If you are married or have unmarried children below the age of 21 and you acquire a green card through investment, your spouse and children can get green cards as accompanying relatives by providing proof of their family relationship to you and submitting other required paperwork and documents. Their green cards will also be issued conditionally and will become permanent when yours does.

2. Inadmissibility

If you have ever committed a crime, been involved in a terrorist organization, lied on an immigration application, lied to an immigration officer, suffered certain physical or mental illness, or are otherwise inadmissible, you may be unable to receive a green card unless you can qualify for what is known as a *Waiver of Inadmissibility*. (See Chapter 25 to find out exactly who is inadmissible and how you can overcome these problems.) Your family members will also have to show that they are not inadmissible.

B. Numerical Limits

Green cards for investors are limited to 10,000 per year, with 3,000 of those reserved for persons investing in rural areas or areas of high unemployment. Only principal applicants are counted in the quota. Accompanying relatives are not. Therefore, in reality, many more than 10,000 per year can be admitted with green cards through investment.

At present, green cards are available to all qualified applicants. However, USCIS regards the majority of applicants as unqualified, and denies far more of these green cards than it grants. It appears unlikely that waiting periods will develop in the near future. Petition approval normally takes from four to six months. After petition approval, application approval should take an additional three to eight months.

C. Applying for a Green Card Through Investment

Getting a green card through investment is a two-step process. There is no sponsoring relative or employer involved in this type of green card. Therefore, the completion of both steps will be carried out by you alone.

1. Overview of Step One: The Petition

You file the petition on your own behalf. All petitions are submitted to USCIS regional service centers in the U.S. File in the office closest to where the business in which you are investing is located. The object of the petition is to prove that you either have made or are in the process of making a qualifying business investment in the U.S.

An approved petition does not by itself give you any immigration privileges. It is only a prerequisite to Step Two, submitting your application. The petition must be approved before you are eligible for Step Two.

2. Overview of Step Two: The Application

A separate application must be filed by you and your accompanying relatives, if any. The application is your formal request for a green card. Step Two may be carried out in the U.S. (assuming you're in the U.S. legally) at a USCIS office or in your home country at a U.S. consulate there. In either case, you may not file Step Two papers until Step One has been approved.

The majority of green card applications are filed at USCIS offices inside the U.S., since usually the applicant is already in the country. If you are in the U.S. legally on a nonimmigrant visa with a current Priority Date, you can probably apply for your green card either inside or outside the U.S., whichever you prefer.

If you are in the U.S. illegally, or entered legally without a visa under the Visa Waiver Program, whether you may still file your green card application inside the U.S. depends on whether you had a visa petition or Labor Certification application on file by January 14, 1998; or by April 30, 2001, if you can prove you were physically present in the U.S. on December 21, 2000. If you did, you may be able to get your green card in the U.S. by paying the $1,000 penalty fee. This is in addition to the regular filing fee for such applications.

If you are subject to these penalties and want to avoid them, you may instead elect to apply for your green card at a U.S. consulate abroad, but in that case, you must be sure that you are not subject to any grounds of inadmissibility or bars to re-entry, before you leave. (See Chapter 25.) If you've been in the U.S. illegally for more than six months, you could be barred from returning for three or ten years.

3. Who's Who in Getting Your Green Card

Getting a green card will be easier if you familiarize yourself with the technical names used for each participant in the process. During Step One, the petition, you are the *petitioner*. In Step Two, the application, you are referred to as *applicant*. If you are bringing your spouse and children with you as accompanying relatives, they are known as *applicants* as well.

4. Tips on Handling the Paperwork

There are two types of paperwork you must submit to get a green card through investment. The first consists of official government forms. The second is personal and business documents such as birth and marriage certificates, financial records, and legal papers showing your business investment.

It is vital that forms are properly filled out and all necessary documents are supplied. You may resent the intrusion into your privacy and the sizable effort it takes to prepare immigration applications, but the process is an impersonal matter to immigration officials. Your getting a green card is more important to you than it is to the U.S. government. Take the time and trouble to prepare your papers properly.

The documents you supply to USCIS or the consulate do not have to be originals. In fact, regardless of what the application instructions say, it's best not to submit original documents—you might never get them back. Photocopies of all documents are acceptable as long as you have the originals in your possession and are willing to produce the originals at the request of USCIS. But add the following language to the photocopy, with your signature and the date:

Copies of documents submitted are exact photo-copies of unaltered original documents and I understand that I may be required to submit original documents to an immigration or consular official at a later date.

Signature _____

Typed or Printed Name _____

Date _____

Documents will be accepted if they are in either English, or, with papers filed at U.S. consulates abroad, the language of the country where the documents are being filed (except in Japan, where all documents must be translated into English). If the documents are not in an acceptable language as just explained, they must be accompanied by a full, word for word, written English translation. Any capable person may act as translator. It is not necessary to hire a professional. At the end of each translation, the following statement must appear:

I hereby certify that I translated this document from [language] to English. This translation is accurate and complete. I further certify that I am fully competent to translate from [language] to English.

Signature _____

Typed or Printed Name _____

Date _____

The translator should sign this statement but it does not have to be witnessed or notarized.

Later in this chapter we describe in detail the forms and documents needed to get your green card through investment. A summary checklist of forms and documents appears at the end of this chapter.

D. Carrying Out Step One: The Petition

This section includes the information you need to submit the petition.

1. General Procedures

The Step One petition is mailed to one of two USCIS regional service centers in the U.S. having jurisdiction over your place of business. USCIS regional service centers are not the same as USCIS local offices. There are four USCIS regional service centers spread across the U.S. Send the petition to the Texas Service Center if the business is in an area normally served by the Texas or Vermont Service Centers; otherwise, send it to the California Service Center. The Texas Service Center's address (for use with I-140 applications only) is: USCIS TSC, P.O. Box 852135, Mesquite, TX

75185-2135. The California Service Center's address for this application is: USCIS California Service Center, P.O. Box 10526, Laguna Niguel, CA 92607-1052.

Within a few weeks after mailing the petition, you should receive a written confirmation that the papers are being processed, together with a receipt for the fees. This notice will also give your immigration case file number and tell approximately when to expect a decision. If USCIS wants further information before acting on your case, all petition papers, forms and documents will be returned to you, together with another form known as an I-797. The I-797 "Request for Evidence" tells you what corrections, additional pieces of information or additional documents are expected. You should make the corrections or supply the extra data and mail the whole package back to the regional service center.

The filing fee for each petition is currently $400. Checks or money orders are accepted. Regional service centers will not accept cash. To protect against loss, send the papers by certified mail, return receipt requested, and keep a complete copy of everything sent for your records.

It generally takes four to six months to get a decision on the petition. Once your petition is approved, a Notice of Action Form I-797 will be sent to you, indicating the approval. If you plan to execute Step Two at a U.S. consulate abroad, USCIS will forward the file to the National Visa Center (NVC) located in Portsmouth, New Hampshire. The NVC will then send a packet of forms and instructions to you so that you may proceed with Step Two, described later in this chapter.

2. Petition Forms

The petition includes only one form, found in Appendix II or on the USCIS website at www.uscis.gov.

Form I-526

This form, called Immigrant Petition by Alien Entrepreneur, is the only Step One form you need to complete.

Part 1 asks questions about you. Your current immigration status must be disclosed, even if you are in the U.S. illegally. "A" numbers are usually issued only to people who previously held green cards or have made previous green card applications. If any of the boxes do not apply to you, answer "N/A."

In listing your address, you will have to put down the address where you really live, even if it means revealing an illegal U.S. residence. If you are in the U.S. illegally, however, see an attorney. You may be ineligible to receive a change of status (from nonimmigrant to permanent resident) or even to get an immigrant visa. Again, be sure to understand if any grounds of inadmissibility or bars to permanent residence apply to you before you depart the U.S. or file your application. (See Chapter 25.)

Part 2 asks you to check off the box indicating the classification you are seeking. Box "b" applies only if you are investing in an area of high employment for which the law requires more than a $1 million investment. To date, USCIS has not utilized this provision, so box "b" will be checked only when USCIS policy changes. Check box "a" or "c."

Part 3 asks basic questions about your business investment in the U.S. and is self-explanatory.

Part 4 asks for financial information about your business investment. This should be self-explanatory.

Part 5 asks questions about the jobs your investment will create. Remember that you must create at least ten new jobs to qualify, but you have up to two years to actually create them.

Part 6 asks about your nationality and residence, in order to determine at which consulate you will apply for your green card. It also asks whether you're in exclusion or deportation proceedings, or have worked in the United States without permission. If your answer to either of these is yes, see an attorney.

Parts 7 and 8. These parts are merely for signatures and are self-explanatory.

3. Petition Documents

You must prove that you either have made or are actively in the process of making a qualifying business investment in the U.S. Generally, the amount invested must be at least $1 million. If your investment is in a targeted area of high unemployment or in a rural area, you should submit evidence of this. You must also show that the business will employ at least ten full-time American workers (which includes U.S. citizens, permanent residents, conditional residents, temporary residents, recipients of suspension of deportation, and asylees/refugees) not including you or your immediate family. Finally, you must show that the investment was made *after* November 29, 1990.

Documents to prove your eligibility should include:

- bank wire-transfer memos showing the amount of money sent to the U.S. from abroad
- contracts and bills of sale for purchase of capital goods and inventory showing the amount spent
- leases, deeds, or contracts for purchase of business premises
- construction contracts and blueprints for building business premises
- comprehensive business plans with cash flow projections for the next three years
- U.S. employment tax returns showing the number of employees on the qualifying company's payroll, and

- accountant's financial statements for the business, including balance sheets.

If you are in the process of starting up the business, you may be unable to produce all of the items listed above. In that case, at a minimum you will have to present evidence that you have sufficient funds to invest, such as bank statements or lines of credit sufficient to purchase the business, and a written contract legally committing you to make the investment. You must also include a detailed written explanation of the nature of the business, containing statements of how much will be invested, where the funds for investment will come from, how the funds will be used, and a list of the specific job openings you expect to have over the first two years of the business, including job title, job description, salary, and when these jobs will become available. Finally, you should submit a comprehensive business plan supporting all of these documents.

In addition to the above, you should submit as many documents as possible to show that your investment is being made in a real, ongoing business that requires daily supervision. Passive investments such as land speculation do not qualify you for a green card in this category. Evidence of an active business should include:

- articles of incorporation or other business charter of the qualifying company
- bank statements for the qualifying company
- credit agreements with suppliers
- letters of credit issued
- leases or deeds for business premises and warehouse space
- income and payroll tax returns filed, if any, and
- promotional literature or advertising.

If the qualifying business is not incorporated, instead of copies of stock certificates you will need to present legal papers proving the existence and ownership of the company, such as partnership agreements, business registration certificates, or business licenses, together with a notarized affidavit from an official of the company certifying who owns the business and in what percentages.

4. Petition Interviews

Personal interviews on the petition are very rare. There may be an interview only if the legitimacy of the paperwork in your case is questionable. If an interview is held, it will be at the USCIS local office nearest the place where your investment is located. You will be asked to explain all documents and to convince the USCIS officer that you intend to carry out your plans of investment and hiring American workers. The USCIS permits you to be represented by an immigration attorney if you wish (at your expense).

5. Petition Appeals

When the investment has been poorly documented, or if you have not been able to convince USCIS that you will be employing at least ten full-time American workers, the petition will probably be denied. You will then receive written notice of the unfavorable decision, a written statement of the reasons for the negative outcome, and an explanation of how to make a formal appeal.

The best way to handle an appeal is to try avoiding it altogether. Filing an appeal means making an argument to USCIS that its reasoning was wrong. If you think you can eliminate the reason why your petition failed by improving your paperwork, it makes sense to forget about the appeals process and simply file a new petition, being careful to see that it is better prepared than the first.

If the petition was denied because you left out necessary documents that have since been located, the new documents should be sent, together with a written request that the case be reopened, to the same USCIS office that issued the denial. This is technically called a *Motion to Reopen*. There is a $110 fee for filing this motion. Appeals often take a long time. A Motion to Reopen can be concluded faster than an appeal.

If you do choose to appeal, it must be done within 30 days of the date on the Notice of Denial. The appeal should be filed at the same USCIS office with which you have been dealing. There is a $110 filing fee. USCIS will then forward the papers for consideration by the Board of Immigration Appeals in Washington, DC. The appeals decision, which can take many months, will be sent to you by mail. The vast majority of appeals fail.

When an appeal to USCIS has been denied, the next step is an appeal through the U.S. judicial system. You may not file in court without first going through the appeals process available from USCIS. If the case has reached this stage and you are living illegally in the U.S., seek representation from a qualified immigration attorney, as you are now in danger of being removed (deported).

E. Carrying Out Step Two: The Application (Consular Filing)

Anyone with an approved petition can apply for a green card at a U.S. consulate in his or her home country or last country of residence. You must be physically present in order to apply there. However, if you have been or are now living illegally in the U.S., see Chapter 25 to be sure you will not be subjected to time bars before re-entry into the U.S.

CITIZENS OF COUNTRIES WITHOUT U.S. EMBASSIES

Citizens of countries not having formal diplomatic relations with the U.S. are faced with the problem of where to apply for immigrant visas.

Persons from these countries who are physically present in the U.S. may have Step Two papers processed at the U.S. consulate in Ciudad Juárez, Mexico.

Persons from these countries who are still residing in their home countries will apply at a designated foreign consulate. Persons who are outside of their home country, in a third country which conducts visa processing, will do visa processing in that country as if they were residents of the third country.

1. Benefits and Drawbacks of Consular Filing

Anyone with an approved petition can apply for a green card at the appropriate consulate. (Again, see Chapter 25 to make sure you are not inadmissible.) If you instead want to apply at a USCIS office in the U.S., by contrast, you must already be physically inside the U.S., and in legal status (unless you fall into one of the few exceptions described below). However, if you qualify for one of these exceptions, and if you've lived illegally in the U.S. for six months or more since April 1, 1997, don't even think of leaving the U.S. to apply through a consulate. Staying in the U.S. to apply will protect you from the three- and ten-year "time bars" to reentry that the consulates can impose on you.

Now for the exceptions: If you are in the U.S. illegally, you may be able to apply in the U.S. if you had a visa petition or Labor Certification on file by April 14, 1998; or by April 30, 2001, if you can prove you were physically present in the U.S. on December 21, 2000. You would also need to pay the $1,000 penalty fee.

If you are in the U.S. legally, and can keep your stay legal long enough to submit your green card application, then you do have a meaningful choice: you can either process at an overseas consulate or choose to submit your application at a USCIS office in the United States.

A further plus to consular filing is that consulate offices may work more quickly to issue green cards than do some USCIS offices. Your waiting time for the paperwork to be finished may be months shorter at a U.S. consulate abroad than at a USCIS office in the United States.

One drawback to consular filing is the travel expense and inconvenience you will experience in returning to your home country if you are already in the U.S. Another problem is that should your consular application fail, you will have fewer ways to appeal than a U.S. filing would offer.

2.   Application General Procedures: Consular Filing

The law states that only a U.S. consulate or embassy in your home country is required to accept your green card application. This is true for all except persons from countries without U.S. embassies. You can ask a consulate located elsewhere to accept your application, but it has the option to say no, and in fact consulates turn down most such requests.

You may not file an application for a green card at a consulate until after your petition has been approved. At that time, the USCIS office where your petition was originally submitted will forward your file to the National Visa Center (NVC) in Portsmouth, New Hampshire. The NVC will then forward your file to the appropriate U.S. consulate. At the same time, a Notice of Approval of your petition will be sent directly to you. The NVC will send instructions and application forms to you within a month or two after petition approval. You will return all paperwork, however, directly to the consulate. If, after waiting a reasonable time, you have not heard from the NVC, you should call and look into the matter.

The NVC will send you a packet containing forms and instructions. Complete and send Forms DS-230 I and DS-2001 to the consulate as soon as possible. This will allow the consulate to begin a required security check into your background. Failure to return these forms promptly can significantly delay your green card.

The application for your green card is made in person by appointment. Once the consulate is ready for your final processing, it will then send another group of papers, including an interview appointment letter, instructions for obtaining your medical examination and still more forms to be completed. Do not mail your forms to the consulate. Instead, bring your forms and all documents with you at the time of your appointment. The fee for filing an application is $335 per person.

3.   Application Forms: Consular Filing

When you file at a U.S. consulate abroad, the consulate officials will provide you with certain forms, designated by a "DS" preceding a number. Instructions for completing DS forms and what to do with them once they are filled out will come with the forms. We do not include copies of these forms in this book, because some consulates create their own versions. Copies of all non-"DS" forms are in Appendix II and on the USCIS website.

Form I-134

It is necessary to convince the consulate that once you receive a green card you are not likely to go on public welfare. Since your application is based on a large business investment, that alone should be sufficient proof that you have a way to support yourself and an I-134 need not be filed for you. You should still, however, fill out Form-134, the Affidavit of Support, for any accompanying relatives. Because the consulate knows you will have an income, you must sign the I-134 Forms and take financial responsibility for each of them.

In signing the Affidavit of Support, you are not actually promising to support your accompanying relatives. What you do promise is to reimburse the U.S. government for the sum total of any government support payments they might receive should they go on welfare. The Affidavit of Support supposedly binds you to this obligation for three years. Your responsibility to the government then comes to an end.

4.   Application Documents: Consular Filing

The most important document in your application is the Notice of Action showing approval of your petition. It is sent directly from the USCIS office in the U.S. to the U.S. consulate. This is the only document you will not have to submit yourself. Do not mail in your other documents. Instead, bring them to your interview.

You must resubmit to the consulate all the documents first filed in Step One. If not included in Step One, you must have your long-form birth certificate and birth certificates of any unmarried minor children who are not immigrating with you. Copies of these documents will not be forwarded by USCIS to the consulate for you.

You must also bring a valid passport from your home country. The expiration date on the passport must leave enough time for the passport to remain valid at least six months beyond the date of your final application interview.

You personally must collect police clearance certificates from each country you have lived in for one year or more since your 16th birthday. Additionally, you must have a police certificate from your home country or country of last residence, if you lived there for at least six months since the age of 16. You do not need to obtain police certificates from the U.S, or from countries that have no reliable procedure for supplying them. Ask your local U.S. consulate for more information.

Some countries will send certificates directly to U.S. consulates but not to you personally. Before they send the certificates out, however, you must request that it be done. Usually this requires filing some type of request form together with a set of your fingerprints.

You and each accompanying relative must bring to the interview three photographs taken in compliance with the instructions provided in your appointment packet. Often your appointment packet will also contain a list of local photographers.

A few consulates require you to submit fingerprints, though most do not. Consulates wanting fingerprints will send you instructions. The fee for such fingerprints is $85.

5. Application Interviews: Consular Filing

Consulates hold interviews on all green card applications. A written notice of your interview appointment is included when you receive the appointment packet. Immediately before the interview, you and your accompanying relatives will be required to have medical examinations. You will be told where to go and what to do in your appointment letter.

a. The Medical Exam

The medical examinations are conducted by private doctors and you are required to pay the doctor a fee. The fees vary from $50 to more than $150 per exam, depending on the country. The amount of the medical exam fee will be stated in your appointment letter. The exam itself involves taking a medical history, blood test, and chest X-ray, and verification or administering of vaccinations, if applicable. Pregnant women may refuse to be X-rayed until after the pregnancy.

The main purpose of the medical exam is to verify that you are not medically inadmissible. The primary medical grounds of inadmissibility are tuberculosis and HIV (AIDS). Some medical grounds of inadmissibility can be overcome with treatment. (See Chapter 25 for more details.) If you need a medical waiver, you will be given complete instructions by the consulate at the time of your interview.

b. What Happens at the Interview

After the medical exam, you and your accompanying relatives will report to the consulate for the interview. At that time, you must pay $335 per person when your papers are submitted. Some consulates accept payment only by certified check, money order or travelers check. Others accept cash. You will be told the proper method of payment in your appointment packet.

Bring with you to the interview the completed forms, photographs, your passports, and all of the required documents discussed here. The interview process involves verification of your application's accuracy and an inspection of

your documents. If all is in order, you will be asked to return later, when you should be issued an immigrant visa. Recently, however, increased security checks have added weeks and sometimes months to the time that applicants must wait for the final visa decision. You are not yet a U.S. resident.

c. Using Your Immigrant Visa

The immigrant visa allows you to travel to the U.S. and request entry. You acquire the full status of green card holder at the moment of being inspected and admitted into the U.S. with your immigrant visa. At that time, your passport is stamped to show that you are a conditional resident and authorized to work. If you are bringing any accompanying relatives, they must enter at either the same time or after you do in order to become conditional residents. Green cards for you and your accompanying relatives are then ordered. They will come to you by mail several months later, and will show a two-year expiration date. (See below, "Removing Conditional Residence" for how to become a permanent resident after two years.)

6. Application Appeals: Consular Filing

When a consulate denies a green card application, there is no formal appeal available, although you are free to reapply. (Check with your local consulate, however—some place limits on the number of repeat applications, or require you to wait a certain number of months before reapplying.) When your green card is refused, the consulate will tell you the reasons why. The most common reason for denial is failure to supply all the required documents. Sometimes presenting more evidence on an unclear fact can change the consulate's mind. If the denial was caused by a lack of evidence, this will be explained in a written notice sent to you by mail.

Another common reason for denial of a green card is that the consular officer believes you are inadmissible. If you are found to be inadmissible, you will be given an opportunity to apply for a Waiver of Inadmissibility, if one is available. (See Chapter 25.)

When all these possibilities are exhausted, if the consulate still refuses you a green card, your opportunities for further appeals are severely limited. See a competent immigration attorney for more information. Even with representation by an attorney, most appeals fail.

You may ask the consular office for a written notice of denial or an explanation to see if there is any way to fix the problem, such as providing additional documentation. Depending on the reason for the denial you may be able to apply again, although if the problem was a serious one, like inadmissibility, you will probably be denied again.

You may also simply wait awhile, reapply on a different basis, and hope for better luck next time. The fact that you have been turned down once does not stop you from trying again, although if the problem was a serious one, like inadmissibility, you will probably be denied again.

F. Carrying Out Step Two: The Application (U.S. Filing)

If you are physically present in the U.S., you may apply for a green card without leaving the country on the following conditions:

- you have received approval of your I-526 petition
- a green card is currently available to you because your waiting period under the quota is up, and
- you are in status (that is, you have an unexpired visa or other right to stay in the U.S.), and/or are otherwise eligible to adjust status based on one of the exceptions described in Section E1, above, and in Chapter 25.

Unless you can meet these terms, you may not file an application for a green card in the U.S.

1. Benefits and Drawbacks of U.S. Filing

The obvious benefit to applying for a green card in the U.S. is that if you are already in the country, you avoid the expense and inconvenience of overseas travel. Should problems arise in your case, you will at least be able to wait for a decision in the U.S., a circumstance most green card applicants prefer.

Another important benefit of U.S. filing is that you may receive permission to work while you wait for the results of your case. To obtain this benefit, see "Procedures for Work Authorization," below. If you do not need to work right away, but can wait until after getting your green card, you do not need to file this separate application.

If your application for a green card is turned down, you have greater rights of appeal inside the U.S. than you do at a U.S. consulate.

There are some disadvantages to applying in the U.S. It may take longer to get results. Processing times at USCIS offices can be one year or more. While your case is pending at a USCIS office, you may not leave the U.S. without getting special permission (Advance Parole). If you do leave without the USCIS's permission, even for a genuine emergency, this will be regarded as withdrawal of your application. You will have to start your application over again when you return.

PROCEDURES FOR WORK AUTHORIZATION

If you want to work before your application for a green card is approved, you must apply for employment authorization. Complete Form I-765 and file it with the same USCIS service center where you file the Step Two papers (preferably at the same time). Together with Form I-765, you must submit a copy of your I-94 card and pay a filing fee of $120. Keep the fee receipt so you can prove that the I-765 was filed in case it's lost.

Legally, USCIS does not have to make a decision on your employment authorization application for up to 90 days. If for some reason you are not given a decision within 90 days, you will, at your request, be granted an interim employment authorization, which will last 240 days.

If 240 days pass and you still have not received a final decision on the I-765, you must stop working. Interim work authorization cards cannot be renewed. However, if you reach this point, you have the option to file a new I-765 application and, if you do not get a decision on the new application within 90 days, you will then be entitled to another interim work authorization card.

2. Application General Procedures: U.S. Filing

The application, consisting of both forms and documents, is submitted by mail to the USCIS service center with responsibility over the place you are living. See the USCIS website for the appropriate address and P.O. box.

For U.S. filings, the basic form used in Step Two, the application, is Form I-485, Application for Permanent Residence. The filing fee for each application is $255 for applicants age 14 and over, and $160 for applicants under age 14. Fingerprints are an added $50. A separate application must be filed for you and each accompanying relative.

If you are in the U.S. illegally, or entered improperly, your ability to stay in the U.S. and get your green card may depend on whether you had a visa petition or Labor Certification on file by January 14, 1998; or by April 30, 2001, if you can prove that you were physically present in the U.S. on December 21, 2000. See Chapter 25 to be sure you qualify. If so, you'll still probably have to pay a $1,000 penalty fee, and file Form I-485A.

Checks and money orders are accepted. It is not advisable to send cash through the mail, but cash is satisfactory if you file in person. Cash is accepted only in the exact amount. USCIS offices will not make change.

File your papers in person if possible, as you will be given a written receipt from USCIS and your papers are likely to be processed right away. If you choose to mail in your application, do so by certified mail, return receipt requested. In either case, keep a complete copy of everything you send in.

Once your application has been filed, you should not leave the U.S. for any reason before your application has been approved, or until you apply for and receive Advance Parole. Any other absence will be viewed as a termination of your application for a green card. Apply for Advance Parole (Form I-131) by mail to the appropriate service center, sending three passport-type photographs and proof of the reason (any legitimate personal or business reason). There is a $110 filing fee. If approved, you will be allowed to leave the U.S. with no break in the processing of your application. However, if you have spent more than six months in the U.S. illegally, not even Advance Parole will protect you from the time bars on reentry (see Chapter 25).

Generally, after filing your green card application, you will not hear anything from USCIS for several months. Then you should receive notices of your fingerprint and interview appointments. The interview notice will also contain instructions for getting the required medical exam, and will tell you if any further documentation is needed.

If everything is in order, your application will be approved at the conclusion of the interview, or soon after. Your passport will be stamped to show that you have been admitted to the U.S. as a permanent resident, and your permanent green card will be ordered. The green card will come to you in the mail several months after the interview.

3. Application Forms: U.S. Filing

Copies of all the required forms can be found in Appendix II and on the USCIS website.

Form I-485

Form I-485 must be filled out for you and each accompanying relative. While most of the form is self-explanatory, a few items typically raise concerns. If a particular question does not apply to you, answer it with "None" or "N/A."

Part 1. Part 1 asks for general information about when and where you were born, your present address and immigration status. It also asks for an "A" number. Normally, you will not have an "A" number unless you previously applied for a green card or have been in deportation proceedings.

Part 2. In Part 2, mark Box "a" if you are the principal applicant. Box "b" is marked if your spouse or parent is the principal applicant.

Part 3. The questions in Sections A through C are self-explanatory. The nonimmigrant visa number is the number that appears on the very top of the visa stamp. It is not the same as your visa classification. The questions in Section C are meant to identify people who are inadmissible. With the exception of certain memberships in the Communist Party or terrorist organizations, you will not be deemed inadmissible simply because you joined an organization. However, if your answer to any of the other questions is "yes," you may be inadmissible. (See Chapter 25.) Don't lie on your answers because you will probably be found out, especially if you have engaged in criminal activity. Many grounds of inadmissibility can be legally overcome, but once a lie is detected, you will lose the legal right to correct the problem. In addition, a false answer is grounds to deny your application and may result in your being permanently barred from getting a green card.

Form I-485A

This form is required only if you are subject to the $1,000 penalty for entering, working in, or living in the U.S. illegally. The form is self-explanatory, and is intended only to determine if you are subject to the penalty. (See Chapter 25 for an explanation of when it is required.)

Form G-325A

G-325A biographic data forms must be filled out for you and each accompanying relative. You need not file a G-325A for any child under the age of 14 or any adult over the age of 79. The G-325A form is meant to gather personal background information. The questions are self-explanatory.

Form I-134

It is necessary to convince the USCIS that once you receive a green card you are not likely to go on public welfare. Since you have made a large business investment already, which proves you have a way to support yourself, an I-134 need not be filed for you. You should still, however, fill out Form I-134, the Affidavit of Support, for any accompanying relative. Because USCIS knows you will have an income, you must sign the I-134 forms and take financial responsibility for each of them.

In signing the Affidavit of Support, you are not actually promising to support your accompanying relatives. What you do promise is to reimburse the U.S. government for the sum total of any government support payments they might receive should they go on welfare. The Affidavit of Support supposedly binds you to this obligation for three years (though many lawyers say the contract would never hold up in court). Your responsibility to the government then comes to an end.

Form I-765

Fill out this form if you want a work permit card.

Block above Question 1. Mark the first box, "Permission to accept employment."

Questions 1–8. These questions are self-explanatory.

Question 9. This asks for your Social Security number, including all numbers you have ever used. If you have never used a Social Security number, answer "None." If you have a nonworking Social Security number, write down the number followed by the words "nonworking, for tax purposes only." If you have ever used a false number, give that number, followed by the words: "Not my valid number." Before submitting the form, read Chapter 25 as it relates to grounds of inadmissibility for document fraud, to be sure you are not barred from getting a green card.

Question 10. You will not usually have an Alien Registration Number unless you previously applied for a green card, were in deportation proceedings or have had certain types of immigration applications denied. All Alien Registration

Numbers begin with the letter "A." If you have no "A" number, but you entered the U.S. with a valid visa or without a visa under the Visa Waiver Program, you should have an I-94 card. In this case, answer Question 10 by putting down the admission number from the I-94 card.

If you are from Mexico, you may have entered the U.S. with a border crossing card, in which case you should put down the number on the entry document you received at the border, if any. Otherwise simply put down the number of the border crossing card itself, followed with "BCC." If you are Canadian and you entered the U.S. as a visitor, you will not usually have any of the documents described here, in which case you should put down "None."

Questions 11–15. These questions are self-explanatory.
Question 16. Answer this question "(c)(9)."

4. Application Documents: U.S. Filing

You must submit the Notice of Action showing petition approval with the application. You and each of your accompanying relatives are required to submit two photographs. These photos should meet the specifications on the photo instruction sheet found in Appendix II (Form M-378). Additionally, you must submit copies of your birth certificate or other record of birth; if married, a marriage certificate and your spouse's birth certificate; and birth certificates for all your children under age 21, even if they are not immigrating with you.

You must also submit a Medical Examination Report for each applicant. This is done on Form I-693, which must be taken to an USCIS authorized physician or medical clinic. You'll have to pay a fee. The USCIS local office will provide you with the form as well as a list of approved physicians in your area. After completion of the medical exam, and upon obtaining the test results, the doctor will give you the results in a sealed envelope. Do not open the envelope.

Each applicant must submit a copy of his or her I-94 card if one was issued or other proof of legal entry. Failure to do so may result in a conclusion that you entered or remained in the U.S. illegally and are not able to get your green card in the U.S. unless you qualify under the penalty provision. (See Chapter 25.) The I-94 is the small white or green card you received on entering the U.S.

The only other paperwork required is your fingerprints. All fingerprinting now takes place at a USCIS-run fingerprinting center. You will be notified where and when to appear after submitting your application forms.

5. Application Interviews: U.S. Filing

As previously explained, personal interviews may be waived in green-card-through-investment applications. If an interview is not waived, you and your accompanying relatives will be asked to come in to the USCIS local office for final processing. The USCIS officer will go over your application to make sure that everything is correct. He will also ask questions to convince himself that you are not inadmissible. (See Chapter 25.) A single fingerprint will then be taken and you will be asked to sign your application under oath. Accompanying relatives, all of whom must attend the interview with you, will go through the same procedure.

The interview normally takes about 30 minutes. If all goes well, your case may be approved on the spot. Most USCIS offices will place a temporary stamp in your passport showing that you have become a U.S. conditional resident (see below, "Removing Conditional Residence" for how to become a permanent resident). With this stamp, you acquire all the rights of a green card holder, including the right to work, and freedom to travel in and out of the U.S. The stamp is not your green card. You will receive your green card by mail several months later.

If your fingerprints have not cleared yet, your application will be approved only provisionally. No stamp will be placed in your passport at the interview. Instead, you will receive a written notice of approval within a month or two. That notice serves as your proof of U.S. conditional residency until you receive your green card, which takes yet another several months.

If you need to travel outside the U.S. before your green card arrives, however, you must go back to the USCIS office with your passport and the written notice of approval, and a temporary stamp will be placed in your passport, enabling you to return after your trip. Never leave the U.S. without either your green card or a temporary stamp in your passport.

6. Application Appeals: U.S. Filing

If your application is denied, you will receive a written decision by mail explaining the reasons for the denial. There is no way of making a formal appeal to USCIS. If the problem is too little evidence, you may be able to overcome this by adding more documents and resubmitting the entire application to the same USCIS office you have been dealing with, together with a written request that the case be reopened. The written request does not have to be in any special form. This is technically called a *Motion to Reopen*. There is a $110 fee. Alternatively, you may wait until USCIS begins deportation proceedings, in which case you may refile your application with the immigration judge.

If your application is denied because you are found inadmissible, you will be given the opportunity to apply for what is known as a Waiver of Inadmissibility, provided a waiver is available for your ground of inadmissibility. (See Chapter 25.)

Although there is no appeal to USCIS for the denial of a green card application, you have the right to file an appeal in a U.S. district court. This requires employing an immigration attorney at considerable expense. Such appeals are usually unsuccessful.

REMOVING CONDITIONAL RESIDENCE

As we've already stated, green cards through investment are first issued conditionally for two years. After the two years are up, in order to make the green cards permanent, you must then go through a procedure for removing the conditions on your residence.

File Form I-829 with the USCIS Service Center with jurisdiction over the area where your company is located. You can file this application up to 90 days prior to the second anniversary of your admission to the U.S. Your spouse and children should be included on the form. In addition to the $395 filing fee, include copies of your and your family members' green cards and the following documentation:

- evidence that you actually established the commercial enterprise (such as federal income tax returns)
- evidence that you actively invested the required capital (such as articles of incorporation, a business license, and financial statements)
- evidence that you have substantially met and maintained the capital investment requirement throughout your conditional residence (such as bank statements, invoices, receipts, contracts, tax returns, etc.)
- evidence that the enterprise has generated employment (or will soon do so) for ten U.S. workers, such as payroll records, tax documents, Forms I-9. (If the investment was in a "troubled business," submit evidence that the pre-investment level of employees was maintained during the two-year conditional residence period.)

Failure to submit the I-829 and documentation within the 90-day window period will, under USCIS regulations, result in termination of your resident status, and USCIS may start deportation proceedings against you and your family members. If you miss the deadline you can still file the removal petition for "good cause and extenuating circumstances" up to the time USCIS commences deportation proceedings. After your case arrives at the immigration court, the judge may only terminate proceedings and restore permanent resident status if the USCIS agrees to this. It is very important to get your I-829 in on time.

USCIS may waive the interview (in connection with the I-829 filing), if the accompanying documentation makes it clear you have fulfilled the requirements for the green card.

If USCIS requires an interview, it will be held at a local USCIS office near where your commercial enterprise is located. If you fail to appear for the interview, USCIS regulations specify that USCIS should put you, the petitioner-entrepreneur, into deportation proceedings. If that happens, you can still write USCIS and request that the interview be rescheduled or waived. If it is rescheduled or waived, your conditional resident status is restored. Otherwise, the petition has to be considered in deportation court as discussed above.

The primary purpose of the request to remove conditional status is to show all of the following:

- that you did actually make the investment
- that you did actually hire at least ten full-time American workers
- that the business in which you invested is still operating, and
- that you still own the business.

After USCIS receives your I-829 application, it will send you a receipt notice. Guard this notice carefully—it is also proof that your status has been extended for the six months that USCIS will take to approve your permanent residence. If you leave the U.S., you'll need to take both this notice and your expired green card to your local USCIS office and get what's called an "I-551" stamp in your passport in order to be allowed back in. If the extension expires before you've gotten an answer from USCIS, go to your local USCIS office with your passport for a stamp further extending your status.

On approval of your request to remove the conditions on your residence, your green card will become permanent. If you fail to file the request, or you are unable to prove that you still meet all the requirements for a green card through investment, your green card will be canceled. Your accompanying relatives will also lose their green cards. You and your family members will then have to leave the U.S.

FORMS AND DOCUMENTS CHECKLIST

STEP ONE: PETITION

Form

☐ Form I-526.

Documents

☐ Copies of all outstanding stock certificates, if the business is a corporation.

☐ Notarized affidavit from the secretary of the corporation, or, if the business is not a corporation, from the official record keeper of the business, stating the names of each owner and percentages of the company owned.

☐ Articles of incorporation or other legal charter or business license of the company.

☐ Letter from the state government certifying that the business is located in a rural or high unemployment area, if applicable.

☐ Tax returns of the company for the past two years, if available.

☐ Accountant's financial statements, including profit and loss statements and balance sheets of the company for the past two years, if available.

☐ Payroll records of the company for the past two years, if available.

☐ Promotional literature describing the nature of the business.

☐ Letters from banks or bank statements indicating the average account balance of the business.

☐ Evidence of deposits of funds in the business's bank account, and proof of sources of funds.

☐ Contracts for purchase and bills of sale for the purchase of capital goods and inventory.

☐ Lease agreements for the business premises, contracts to purchase, or deeds for business real estate or construction contracts and blueprints for building the business premises.

☐ Comprehensive business plan with cash flow projections for the next three years.

☐ Detailed written statement describing the business, where the investment is coming from, how the investment will be used, and an itemization of full-time positions that will be filled with qualifying workers, including duties, salaries, and when each job will become available.

STEP TWO: APPLICATION

Forms

☐ DS forms (available at U.S. consulate abroad for consular filing only).

☐ Form I-134 (U.S. and consular filings).

☐ Form I-485 (U.S. filing only).

☐ Form I-485A (U.S. filing only).

☐ Form G-325A (U.S. filing only).

☐ Form I-765, if work authorization is needed (U.S. filing only).

Documents

☐ Notice showing approval of your petition.

☐ I-94 card for you and each accompanying relative (U.S. filing only).

☐ Three photographs of you and each accompanying relative.

☐ Long-form birth certificates for you and each accompanying relative.

☐ Marriage certificate if you are bringing your spouse.

☐ If either you or your spouse has ever been married previously, copies of divorce and death certificates showing termination of all previous marriages.

☐ Passports for you and each accompanying relative, valid for at least six months beyond the date of the final interview.

☐ Police certificates from every country in which you and each accompanying relative has lived for at least one year since age 16 (consular filing only).

☐ Military records for you and each accompanying relative (consular filing only).

☐ Medical exam report for you and each accompanying relative.

STEP THREE: REMOVING THE CONDITIONS ON RESIDENCE

Form

☐ Form I-829.

Documents

☐ Articles of incorporation.

☐ Business license.

☐ Federal income tax return.

☐ Financial statements (profit and loss, balance sheet).

☐ Bank statements, invoices.

☐ Receipts, contracts.

☐ Payroll records, other tax documents, Forms I-9.

Getting a Green Card As a Special Immigrant

Privileges

- You may live anywhere in the U.S. and stay as long as you want.

- You may work at any job for any company, anywhere in the U.S., or you may choose not to work at all.

- You may travel in and out of the U.S. whenever you wish.

- You may apply to become a U.S. citizen after you have held your green card for a certain length of time.

- If you qualify as a special immigrant, your spouse and unmarried children under the age of 21 may get green cards as accompanying relatives.

Limitations

- Your place of actual residence must be in the U.S. You cannot use a green card just for work and travel purposes. (The only exception is for Alien Commuters, discussed in Chapter 4.)

- You must pay U.S. taxes on your worldwide income, because you are regarded as a U.S. resident.

- You cannot remain outside the U.S. for more than one year at a time without special permission or you risk losing your green card. (It is recommended that you limit your trips abroad to under six months.)

- If you commit a crime or participate in politically subversive or other proscribed activities, your green card can be taken away and you can be deported.

This chapter covers six categories of special immigrants ("Employment Fourth Preference"): religious workers, foreign medical graduates, employees of the U.S. consulate in Hong Kong, former overseas U.S. government workers, retired employees of international organizations, and juveniles declared dependent on a U.S. juvenile court. There are other categories of special immigrants that we don't cover in this book because they apply to so few people, such as veterans of the U.S. armed forces, former employees of the Panama Canal Zone, and international broadcasting employees.

For the categories we cover in this chapter, we'll discuss who is eligible for a green card and how to apply.

A. Who Qualifies for a Green Card As a Special Immigrant?

Occasionally, laws are passed making green cards available to people in special situations. Special immigrant green cards are available to the following people:

- workers for recognized religious organizations
- foreign medical graduates who have been in the U.S. a long time

- foreign workers who were formerly longtime employees of the U.S. government
- retired officers or employees of certain international organizations who have lived in the U.S. for a certain time
- foreign workers who have been employees of the U.S. consulate in Hong Kong for at least three years, and
- foreign nationals who have been declared dependent on juvenile courts in the U.S.
- persons who served honorably for 12 years on active U.S. military duty after October 15, 1978
- Panama Canal Treaty employees (a little-used category that is not discussed further in this chapter)
- NATO civilian employees (a little-used category that is not discussed further in this chapter), and
- a person coming to work as a broadcaster for the International Broadcasting Bureau of the Broadcasting Board of Governors, or for its grantee (a little-used category that is not discussed further in this chapter).

If you think you might fit into one of the more obscure categories that we don't cover in this chapter, you'll probably want to seek an immigration lawyer's help.

1. Religious Workers

There are two subcategories of religious workers: clergy and other religious workers. Clergy is defined as persons authorized by a recognized religious denomination to conduct religious activities. This includes not only ministers, priests, and rabbis, but also salaried Buddhist monks, commissioned officers of the Salvation Army, practitioners and nurses of the Christian Science Church, and ordained deacons. Usually, to be considered a member of the clergy, you must have formal recognition from the religion in question, such as a license, certificate of ordination, or other qualification to conduct religious worship.

The subcategory of "other religious workers" covers those who are authorized to perform normal religious duties but are not considered part of the clergy. This includes anyone performing a traditional religious function in a professional capacity, such as liturgical workers, religious instructors, religious counselors, cantors, catechists, workers in religious hospitals or religious health care facilities, missionaries, religious translators, or religious broadcasters. It does not cover workers involved in purely nonreligious functions such as janitors, maintenance workers, clerical staff, or fundraisers. It also does not cover volunteers.

To qualify for a green card in either of the two religious subcategories, you must have been a member for at least the past two years of a recognized religion that has a bona fide nonprofit organization in the U.S. During those two years, you must have been employed continuously (though not necessarily full-time) by that same religious group. Your sole purpose in coming to the U.S. must be to work as a minister of that religion (and your denomination must *need* additional ministers), or, at the request of the organization, to work in some other capacity related to the religion's activities in the U.S. Spouses and children may apply with you.

This provision of the law has been the subject of some controversy and there have been efforts in Congress to eliminate it as a way of getting permanent residency. In the year 2003, Congress extended the law to September 30, 2008.

2. Foreign Medical Graduates

If you are a graduate of a foreign medical school who came to the U.S. before January 10, 1978, on either an H or J visa, you qualify as a special immigrant if you can meet all of the following conditions:

- you were permanently licensed to practice medicine in some U.S. state on or before January 9, 1978
- you were physically in the U.S. and practicing medicine on January 9, 1978
- you have lived continuously in the U.S. and practiced medicine since January 9, 1978, and

- if you came to the U.S. on a J-1 visa and were subject to the two-year home residency requirement, you got a waiver of the home residency requirement, or you have a "no objection letter" from your home government (see Chapter 23).

3. Former Overseas U.S. Government Workers

If you have been employed abroad by the U.S. government for at least 15 years, you may apply for a green card as a special immigrant. Your spouse and children may apply with you. To qualify, you must have the recommendation of the principal officer-in-charge of the U.S. government foreign office in which you were employed. The U.S. Secretary of State must also approve the recommendation. In addition, certain employees of the American Institute in Taiwan can qualify under this category. The director of the Institute must recommend you.

4. Retired Employees of International Organizations

If you are a retired employee of an international organization, you qualify for a green card under the following conditions:

- you have resided in the U.S. for at least 15 years prior to your retirement, on a G-4 or N visa
- you lived and were physically present in the U.S. for at least half of the seven years immediately before applying for a green card, and
- you apply to receive a green card within six months after your retirement.

If you are the unmarried child of an officer, employee, former officer, or former employee of an international organization, you qualify for a green card if all of the following are true:

- you have a G-4 or N visa
- you lived and were physically present in the U.S. for at least half of the seven-year period before applying for a green card
- you lived in the U.S. for at least a total of seven years while you were between the ages of five and 21, and
- you apply for a green card before your 25th birthday.

If you are the spouse of an officer or employee in this special immigrant class, you qualify for a green card as an accompanying relative. However, if you were married to a qualifying officer or employee who has died, you can still get a green card if you lived in the U.S. for at least 15 years on a G-4 or N visa before the death of your spouse, you have lived in the U.S. for at least one half of the seven years before your application, and you apply within six months after your spouse's death.

5. Persons Employed at the United States Consulate in Hong Kong

If you have been employed at the U.S. consulate in Hong Kong for at least three years, you may qualify for a green card as a special immigrant. Your spouse and unmarried children under age 21 may accompany you if they were living with you on November 29, 1990. To do this, you will need to get the recommendation of the U.S. consul general in Hong Kong. The U.S. Secretary of State must also approve the recommendation. In addition, your welfare in Hong Kong must be threatened as a result of your consular employment. Green cards in this class had to have been applied for no later than January 1, 2002.

6. Persons Declared Dependent on a Juvenile Court

A foreign national child can qualify for a green card as a special immigrant if:

- he or she is under age 21 and unmarried
- he or she has been declared dependent on a juvenile court located in the U.S.
- that court says the child is eligible for long-term foster care, or has committed the child to the care of a state agency due to abuse, neglect, or abandonment, and
- the court has determined that it is in the minor's best interest to remain in the U.S.

If the child is already in USCIS custody, USCIS must consent to the court proceedings. Even if the child is not in custody, USCIS consent to the dependency order must be obtained. A minor who gets a green card in this class will never be allowed to act as a green card sponsor for either natural or prior adoptive parents.

7. Servicepeople with 12 Years' Duty

If you have served a total of 12 years of active duty with the U.S. armed services after October 12, 1978, you may qualify for special immigrant status. You need to have enlisted outside the U.S. under the terms of a treaty between the U.S. and your country. If you've served six years and have reenlisted for another six, you also qualify. Your spouse and child are eligible to apply with you.

8. Accompanying Relatives

If you are married or have children below the age of 21 and you get a green card as a special immigrant, your spouse and children can get green cards as accompanying relatives simply by providing proof of their family relationship to you. In a few special immigrant categories, they must additionally prove other factors, such as how long they lived with you.

 Anyone can be refused a green card based on inadmissibility. If you have ever been arrested for a crime, lied on an immigration application, lied to an immigration officer or suffer certain physical or mental illness, you may be inadmissible from receiving a green card. In some cases, a Waiver of Inadmissibility may be available. (See Chapter 25.)

B. Numerical Limits

A total of 10,000 green cards are available each year for all special immigrant categories taken together. No more than 5,000 of that total can go to nonclergy religious workers.

At present, green cards are available on a current basis for all special immigrants. However, if the demand increases, a waiting list could develop. Petitions are normally approved within six months. Green card applications take at least six months to a year or more after the quota becomes current and the application turned in.

C. Applying for a Green Card As a Special Immigrant

Getting a green card as a special immigrant is a two-step process. Each step will be briefly explained below.

1. Overview of Step One: The Petition

The petition is filed by you. Most petitions are submitted to USCIS regional service centers in the U.S. An exception is made for persons qualifying as special immigrants through employment at the U.S. consulate in Hong Kong. In those cases, the Step One petition must be filed directly with that consulate.

The object of the petition is to show that you meet the legal requirements of some special immigrant category as described above in Section A.

Special immigrants are subject to annual quotas. The date on which you file the petition is called your Priority Date. The Priority Date is important because it marks the legally recognized moment when your waiting period for a green card under the quota (if any) starts to elapse.

If all goes well, your petition will eventually be approved, but be aware that an approved petition does not by itself give you any right to live or work in the U.S. It is only a prerequisite to Step Two, submitting the application for a green card. Your petition must be approved before you can submit the application. An exception is made for juvenile court dependents, who can submit their petition together with their adjustment of status application, described under Step Two, below.

2. Overview of Step Two: The Application

The application is filed by you and your accompanying relatives, if any. The application is your formal request for a green card. Step Two may be carried out in the U.S. at a USCIS service center or in your home country at a U.S. consulate there. You may not proceed with Step Two until after your Step One petition has been approved.

The majority of green card applications are filed at USCIS service centers inside the U.S., since usually the applicant is already in the country. If you are in the U.S. legally on a nonimmigrant visa, with a current Priority Date, you may apply for your green card either inside or outside the U.S., whichever you prefer.

If you are in the U.S. illegally, overstayed prior visas, worked without authorization, or entered illegally or without a visa under the Visa Waiver Program, you may be barred from getting your green card application inside the U.S., unless you had a visa petition or Labor Certification on file by January 14, 1998; or by April 30, 2001, if you can prove that you were in the U.S. on December 21, 2000, and you pay a penalty fee (currently $1,000). This is in addition to the regular filing fee for such applications.

If you are subject to these penalties and want to avoid them, you may instead elect to apply for your green card at a U.S. consulate abroad, but in that case, you must make sure you are not ineligible to get a visa due to the three- or ten-year bars or other grounds of inadmissibility. (See Chapter 25.)

If you have an approved petition but your Priority Date is not yet current, you must wait until it is current to file your application. The consulate will advise you by mail when your Priority Date finally comes up, but if you want to check progress from time to time, you may do so by calling the U.S. State Department in Washington, DC, at 202-663-1541 for the latest quota information or see its website at www.travel.state.gov. Look for "Visa Bulletin."

3. Who's Who in Getting Your Green Card

Getting a green card will be easier if you familiarize yourself with the technical names used for each participant in the process. During Step One, you are the *beneficiary* and if there is a U.S. sponsor required (only in the case of non-clergy religious workers) that sponsor is called the *petitioner*. In Step Two, the application, you are called *applicant*. If you are bringing your spouse and children with you as accompanying relatives, they are known as *applicants* as well.

4. Tips on Handling the Paperwork

There are two types of paperwork you must submit to get a green card as a special immigrant. The first consists of official government forms completed by you or your U.S. employer. The second is personal documents such as birth and marriage certificates.

It is vital that forms are properly filled out and all necessary documents are supplied. You may resent the intrusion into your privacy and the sizable effort it takes to prepare immigration applications, but you should realize the process is an impersonal matter to immigration officials. Your getting a green card is more important to you than it is to the U.S. government. There is no shortage of applicants.

The documents you supply to USCIS or the consulate do not have to be originals. Photocopies of all documents are acceptable as long as you have the original in your possession and are willing to produce the originals upon request. But add the following language to the photocopy, with your signature and the date:

> *Copies of documents submitted are exact photocopies of unaltered original documents and I understand that I may be required to submit original documents to an immigration or consular official at a later date.*
> *Signature _____*
> *Typed or Printed Name _____*
> *Date_____*

Documents will be accepted if they are in either English, or, with papers filed at U.S. consulates abroad, the language of the country where the documents are being filed (except at the U.S. consulates in Japan, where all documents must be translated into English). If the documents are not in an acceptable language as just explained, they must be accompanied by a full, word for word, written English translation. Any capable person may act as translator. It is not necessary to hire a professional. At the end of each translation, the following statement must appear:

> *I hereby certify that I translated this document from [language] to English. This translation is accurate and complete. I further certify that I am fully competent to translate from [language] to English.*
> *Signature _____*
> *Typed or Printed Name _____*
> *Date_____*

The translator should sign this statement but it does not have to be witnessed or notarized.

Later in this chapter we describe in detail the forms and documents needed to get your green card as a special immigrant. A summary checklist of forms and documents appears at the end of the chapter.

D. Carrying Out Step One: The Petition

This section includes the information you need to submit the visa petition.

1. General Procedures

You mail the petition, consisting of forms and documents, to the USCIS regional service center in the U.S. having jurisdiction over the place you will be living or working. USCIS regional service centers are not the same as USCIS local offices—for one thing, you cannot visit regional service centers in person. There are four USCIS regional service centers spread across the U.S. All retired international organization applicants must use the Nebraska Service Center.

Within a few weeks after mailing the petition, you should receive a written confirmation that the papers are being processed, together with a receipt for the fees. This notice will also give your immigration case file number and tell you approximately when to expect a decision. If USCIS wants further information before acting on your case, all petition papers, forms, and documents may be returned to you, together with another form known as an I-797. The I-797 tells you what corrections, additional pieces of information, or additional documents are expected. You should

make the corrections or supply the extra data and mail the whole package back to the USCIS regional service center.

The filing fee for each petition is currently $130. Checks or money orders are accepted. Regional service centers will not accept cash. We recommend sending the papers by certified mail, return receipt requested, and keeping a complete copy of everything sent for your records. See the USCIS website (www.uscis.gov) for the appropriate address and P.O. box.

It generally takes at least three to six months to get a decision on the petition. Once your petition is approved, a Notice of Action Form I-797 will be sent to you. If you plan to execute Step Two at a U.S. consulate abroad, USCIS will forward the file to the National Visa Center (NVC) located in Portsmouth, New Hampshire. The NVC will then send a packet of forms and instructions to you so that you may proceed with Step Two.

Form I-360

The basic form for Step One, the petition, is immigration Form I-360. If a particular question on the form does not apply, it should be answered "None" or "N/A."

It is absolutely essential to answer each question truthfully, even if it means disclosing that you are in the U.S. illegally. (If you are in the U.S. out of status or have violated U.S. immigration or other laws, be sure to thoroughly understand the material in the chapter on inadmissibility (Chapter 25) before proceeding with your application.) Failure to reveal requested information may result in your being permanently barred from the U.S.

Part 1. The items under this part are self-explanatory. "A" numbers are usually issued only to people who previously held green cards or have made previous green card applications.

Part 2. Part 2 asks you to mark the category under which you are applying for special immigrant status, and is self-explanatory.

Part 3. Part 3 is self-explanatory, asking questions about your current address and immigration status. If any of the boxes do not apply to you, answer "N/A."

In listing your address, you must put down the address where you really live, even if it means revealing an illegal U.S. residence. USCIS offices during Steps One and Two and consular offices during Step Two will send correspondence to the address you put down in Part 3, so make sure it is correct.

Part 4. This part is self-explanatory.

Part 5. This part applies only to Amerasians (not a special immigrant category). Leave this blank.

Part 6. This part is filled in only if you are applying for special immigrant status for a juvenile declared dependent by a court. These questions are self-explanatory.

Part 7. This part only applies to widows or widowers of U.S. citizens, not a special immigrant category, and will therefore be left blank.

Part 8. This part asks for biographical information for your spouse and children and is self-explanatory.

2. Petition Documents

The documents you must submit in support of your petition depend on the category of special immigrant.

a. Religious Workers

To prove you qualify as a special immigrant religious worker, you should submit all diplomas and certificates showing your academic and professional qualifications (the minimum requirement is a bachelor's degree). If you are a minister, include proof of your ordination. In addition, submit a detailed letter from the religious organization in the U.S. explaining its organization, number of followers in both your home country and the U.S., and the details of your job offer in the U.S., including job title, duties, salary, and qualification requirements. If you are a minister, include proof that your services are needed, such as a letter from your employer detailing the current number of ministers, the congregation size, your duties, and what they've done before to meet the need. They should also supply proof of their nonprofit $(501(c)(3))$ status and their ability to pay you. Finally, you should include written verification from an authorized official of the religious organization that you have been a member and a paid employee of that organization for at least two years.

b. Foreign Medical Graduates

To prove you qualify as a special immigrant foreign medical graduate, you should submit a copy of your original I-94 card, even if it has expired, or passport with visa stamp showing you were admitted to the U.S. with a J or H visa prior to January 9, 1978. You will need to show your medical license issued by some U.S. state before January 9, 1978, or a letter from a medical board of a U.S. state verifying that you were licensed. You will also need evidence that you have been continuously employed as a physician since January 9, 1978. A letter from the employer or your personal income tax returns, including W-2 forms, for all years beginning with 1977 to the present, will provide such proof.

You must show that you have maintained continuous residence in the U.S. since your entry. Proof of this can include your personal income tax returns for each year, your children's school records, your utility bills, bank records, letters from employers, and the like.

If you came to the U.S. on a J-1 visa, you should also submit a copy of the pink form, IAP-66 certificate, given to you so you could get your J visa. If the IAP-66 certificate indicated you were subject to the two-year foreign residence requirement, you will also need a No Objection Letter from the embassy of your home country. No Objection Letters are discussed more fully in Chapter 23.

c. Former U.S. Government Workers

To prove that you qualify as a special immigrant former U.S. government worker, you must be able to verify at least 15 years of employment with the U.S. government outside of the U.S. or with the American Institute in Taiwan. You can do this by submitting copies of personal tax returns or a letter of verification from the U.S. government agency that employed you.

The same agency will also need to provide you with a letter of recommendation for a green card from the principal officer-in-charge of the agency in which you were employed. Finally, you will need a letter of recommendation from the U.S. Secretary of State or director of the American Institute in Taiwan. The agency you worked for should be able to assist you in getting this.

d. Retired Employees of International Organizations and Their Families

To prove your eligibility for this special immigrant category, you must have written documentation to show that you resided in the U.S. for at least 15 years on either a G-4 or N visa. Copies of your passports or I-94 cards covering the past 15 years, together with copies of U.S. income tax returns filed during that time, would be the best proof. If any of these are not available, then a detailed letter from the international organization in the U.S. stating your periods of employment and visa status should be acceptable.

You must also prove that you were physically present in the U.S. for at least half of the seven-year period immediately prior to applying for a green card. Copies of your passport and I-94 cards during the past seven years would again be the best proof. You need to make a complete copy of your passport to show your entries and departures. If unavailable, other acceptable proofs of your physical presence in the U.S. are a letter from your employer stating the number of days you worked in the U.S. and bank statements showing regular deposits and withdrawals during this time.

You must also present a letter from your employer stating your official retirement date. Remember that you must apply for your green card within six months after your retirement.

e. Children of Retired Employees

If you are the unmarried child of an officer, employee, former officer, or former employee of an international organization in the U.S., you must provide evidence that your parent was employed by an international organization in the U.S., through a letter from the organization verifying the position and dates of employment. Next you must prove you are his or her child. Normally, this will be shown on your birth certificate.

You must also provide evidence that you were physically present in the U.S. for at least half of the seven-year period immediately before applying for the green card. This can be shown with a complete copy of your passport and all I-94 cards issued to you during that period, letters from employers, if any, stating the number of days you worked in the U.S., or school records.

f. Persons Employed at the U.S. Consulate in Hong Kong

To qualify as a special immigrant in this category, the consul general in Hong Kong must recommend your approval based on a belief that your welfare will be threatened if you remain in Hong Kong. Since a petition in this category may be filed only with the U.S. consulate in Hong Kong, it is possible that specific documentation of your employment there and of the consul general's recommendation will not be needed. You should, however, expect to provide a written letter from the consul general recommending the approval of your special immigrant petition, a written statement from you explaining how your welfare in Hong Kong will be threatened because you worked for the U.S. government there, and evidence that you were employed at the Hong Kong consulate for at least three years. Evidence of the three-year employment period could be in the form of tax returns or a letter from the consulate itself.

g. Persons Declared Dependent on a Juvenile Court

The documents required for this category are the formal findings and recommendations from a U.S. juvenile court judge. Ideally, the qualifying elements of this category should be stated in the judge's written order declaring the child dependent. Included in the order should be statements that the child is eligible for long-term foster care, and that it would not be in the child's best interest to be returned to his or her home country. If these findings are not specifically stated in the court decree, try to have the decree amended to include them. If that isn't possible, you will need a letter from the judge who heard the child's dependency case in which the judge does state these facts.

h. Servicepeople

The special documents required for servicepeople include certified proof of your active duty status for 12 years, or of six years' duty plus reenlistment as well as your birth certificate showing that you are a native of a country that has a treaty with the U.S. covering military service.

3. Petition Interviews

Interviews are rarely held on Step One petitions.

4. Petition Appeals

If you have poorly documented your eligibility for a special immigrant classification, the petition will probably be denied. You will then receive written notice of the USCIS's unfavorable decision, a written statement of the reasons for the negative outcome, and an explanation of how to make a formal appeal.

The best way to handle an appeal is to avoid it altogether. Filing an appeal means making an argument to USCIS that its reasoning was wrong. If you think you can eliminate the reason why the petition failed by improving the paperwork, disregard the appeals process and simply file a new petition, being careful to see that it is better prepared than the first.

If the petition was denied because you left out necessary documents that have since been located, the new documents may be sent together with a written request that the case be reopened to the same USCIS office that issued the denial. This is technically called a *Motion to Reopen*. There is a $110 fee for filing this motion. Appeals often take a long time. A Motion to Reopen can be concluded faster than an appeal.

If you do file an appeal, it must be done within 30 days of the date on the Notice of Denial. The appeal should be filed at the same USCIS office with which you have been dealing. There is a $110 filing fee. USCIS will then forward the papers for consideration to the Administrative Appeals Unit in Washington, DC. In six months or more you will get back a decision by mail. Few appeals are successful.

When an appeal to USCIS has been denied, the next step is to make an appeal through the U.S. judicial system. You may not file an action in court without first going through the appeals process available from USCIS. If your case has reached this stage and you are living illegally in the U.S., seek representation from a qualified immigration attorney, as you are now in danger of being deported.

E. Carrying Out Step Two: The Application (Consular Filing)

Anyone with an approved petition and a current Priority Date can apply for a green card at a U.S. consulate in his or her home country or last country of residence. You must be physically present in order to apply there. If you have been or are now working and living illegally in the U.S., you may be barred from getting a green card from a U.S. consulate for three or ten years if you have been out of status for over six months in the U.S. Be sure to read Chapter 25 to understand whether you are at risk.

CITIZENS OF COUNTRIES WITHOUT U.S. EMBASSIES

Citizens of countries not having formal diplomatic relations with the U.S. are faced with the problem of where to apply for immigrant visas.

Persons from these countries who are physically present in the U.S. may have Step Two papers processed at the U.S. consulate in Ciudad Juárez, Mexico. Persons from these countries who are still residing in their home countries will apply at a designated foreign consulate. Persons who are ouside of their home country in a third country that conducts visa processing will do visa processing in that country as if they were residents of the third country.

1. Benefits and Drawbacks of Consular Filing

Anyone with an approved petition and a current Priority Date can apply for a green card at the appropriate consulate. That is not the case with U.S. applications, since you must be physically inside the U.S. to apply there. If you are in the U.S. illegally, you may not be able to stay in the U.S. and get your green card. On the other hand, you may subject yourself to a three- or ten-year waiting period if you leave after being out of status for six or ten months, even if you're going for a consular appointment. (See Chapter 25 for a full discussion.)

A further plus to consular filing is that consulate offices may work more quickly to issue green cards than do some USCIS offices. Your waiting time for the paperwork to be finished may be months shorter at a U.S. consulate abroad than at USCIS offices in the U.S. Remember, however, that the difference in waiting time between USCIS and consulate offices applies only to processing paperwork. Quotas move at the same rate of speed no matter where your application is filed.

One of two drawbacks to consular filing is the travel expense and inconvenience of returning to your home country if you are already in the U.S. The other problem is that should your consular application fail, you will have fewer ways to appeal than a U.S. filing would offer.

2. Application General Procedures: Consular Filing

Only a U.S. consulate or embassy in your home country is required to accept your green card application (unless your country has no U.S. embassy). You can ask a consulate located elsewhere to accept your application, but it has the option to say no, and in fact, many turn down most such requests. Approach the consulate of your choice before filing the Step One petition. That is because Form I-360 in Step One asks where you will file your application and you must be prepared with an answer to this question.

You may not file an application for a green card at a consulate until after your petition has been approved. At that time, the USCIS office where your petition was originally submitted will forward your file to the National Visa Center in Portsmouth, New Hampshire. The NVC will then forward your file to the U.S. consulate you named on Form I-360 in Step One. At the same time, a Notice of Approval from Step One will be sent directly to you. The NVC will send instructions and application forms to you within a month or two after petition approval. You will now communicate, however, directly with the consulate. If, after waiting a reasonable time, you have not heard from the NVC, you should call and look into the matter.

The NVC will send you an instruction packet containing forms and information. Complete and send Forms DS-230 Part I and DS-2001 to the consulate as soon as possible. This will allow the consulate to begin a required security check into your background.

The application for your green card is made in person by appointment. Once your quota number is current and the consulate is ready for your final processing, it will then send an interview appointment letter, instructions for obtaining your medical examination, and still more forms to be completed. Do not mail these forms to the consulate. Instead, bring the rest of your forms and all documents with you at the time of your appointment.

3. Application Forms: Consular Filing

When you file at a U.S. consulate abroad, the consulate officials will provide you with certain forms, designated by a "DS" preceding a number. Instructions for completing DS forms and what to do with them once they are filled will come with the forms. We do not include copies of these forms in this book, because some consulates create their own versions. Copies of all non-"DS" forms are in Appendix II and on the USCIS website.

Form I-134

You must convince the consulate that once you receive a green card you are not likely to go on public welfare. If your application is based on employment, that alone should be sufficient proof that you have a way to support yourself, and an I-134 need not be filed for you. You should still, however, fill out Form-134, the Affidavit of Support, for any accompanying relatives. Because the consulate knows you will have an income, you must sign the I-134 forms and take financial responsibility for each of them.

In signing the Affidavit of Support, you are not actually promising to support your accompanying relatives. What you do promise is to reimburse the U.S. government for the sum total of any government support payments your relatives might receive should they go on welfare. The Affidavit of Support supposedly binds you to this obligation for three years. Your responsibility to the government then comes to an end.

4. Application Documents: Consular Filing

The most important document in your application is the Notice of Action showing approval of your petition. It is sent directly from the USCIS office in the U.S. to the consulate you named on Form I-360 in Step One. This is the only document you will not have to submit yourself. Do not mail in your other documents. Instead, bring them to your interview.

At your interview, you must resubmit to the consulate copies of all the documents first filed in Step One. Additionally, you must have your long-form birth certificate and birth certificates of any unmarried minor children who are not immigrating with you.

It is also necessary to bring a valid passport from your home country. The expiration date on the passport must extend at least six months beyond the date of your final application interview.

You personally must collect police clearance certificates from each country you have lived in for one year or more since your 16th birthday. Additionally, you must have a police certificate from your home country or country of last residence, if you lived there for at least six months since the age of 16. You do not need to obtain police certificates from the U.S. Like all other documents, present the necessary police clearance certificates at your interview.

Contact the local police department in your home country for instructions on how to get police certificates. To obtain police certificates from nations other than your home

country, it is best to contact the nearest consulate representing that country for instructions. Some nations refuse to supply police certificates, or their certificates are not considered reliable, and so you will not be required to obtain them from those locations. The U.S. consulate will give you a list of those countries from which police certificates are not required.

Some countries will send certificates directly to U.S. consulates but not to you personally. Before they send the certificates out, however, you must request that it be done. Usually this requires filing some type of request form together with a set of your fingerprints.

You and each accompanying relative must bring to the interview three photographs taken in compliance with the consulate's instructions.

A few consulates require you to submit fingerprints, though most do not. Consulates wanting fingerprints will send you instructions and charge $85.

5. Application Interviews: Consular Filing

Consulates hold interviews on all green card applications. A written notice of your interview appointment is included when you receive your appointment packet. Immediately before the interview, you and your accompanying relatives will be required to have medical examinations. You will be told where to go and what to do in your appointment letter.

a. The Medical Exam

The medical examinations are conducted by private doctors and you are required to pay the doctor a fee. The fees vary from $50 to more than $150 per exam, depending on the country. The amount of the medical exam fee will be stated in your appointment letter. The exam itself involves taking a medical history, blood test, and chest X-ray, and verifying or administering vaccinations, if needed. Pregnant women may refuse to be X-rayed until after the pregnancy.

The main purpose of the medical exam is to verify that you are not medically inadmissible. The primary grounds of inadmissibility are tuberculosis and HIV (AIDS). Some medical grounds of inadmissibility can be overcome with treatment. (See Chapter 25 for more details.) If you need a medical waiver, you will be given complete instructions by the consulate at the time of your interview.

b. What Happens at the Interview

After the medical exam, you and your accompanying relatives will report to the consulate for the interview. At that time, you must pay $335 per person. Some consulates accept payment only by certified check, money order, or traveler's check. Others accept cash. You will be told the proper method of payment in your appointment packet.

Bring with you to the interview the completed forms, photographs, your passports, and all of the required documents discussed here. The interview process involves verification of your application's accuracy and an inspection of your documents. Your name will also be checked against various security databases to see whether you have a history of criminal or terrorist behavior. This can add many weeks to the approval of your application, particularly if you come from a country that the U.S. government believes sponsors terrorism. As of this book's printing, those countries included North Korea, Cuba, Syria, Sudan, Iran, Iraq, and Libya. If all is in order, you will be asked to return later when you will be issued an immigrant visa. You are not yet a permanent resident.

c.   Using Your Immigrant Visa

The immigrant visa allows you to request entry to the U.S. You acquire the full status of green card holder at the moment of being inspected and admitted into the U.S. with your immigrant visa. At that time, your passport is stamped and you are immediately authorized to work. If you are bringing any accompanying relatives, they must enter at either the same time or after you do in order to become permanent residents. Permanent green cards for you and your accompanying relatives are then ordered. They will come to you by mail several months later.

6.   Application Appeals: Consular Filing

When a consulate denies a green card application, there is no formal appeal available, although you are free to reapply as often as you like. (Check with your local consulate to be sure, however—some place limits on the number of repeat applications, or require you to wait a certain number of months before reapplying.) When your green card is refused, the reasons will be explained. The most common reason for denial is failure to supply all the required documents. Sometimes presenting more evidence on an unclear fact can bring about a better result. If the denial was caused by a lack of evidence, this will be explained in a written notice sent to you by mail.

Another common reason for denial of a green card is that the consular officer believes you are inadmissible. If you are found to be inadmissible, you will be given an opportunity to apply for a Waiver of Inadmissibility, if one is applicable. (See Chapter 25.)

If the consulate still refuses you a green card, your opportunities for further appeals are severely limited. Appeals of any kind are very technical and should be handled by a competent immigration attorney. Even with representation by an attorney, most appeals fail.

Overall, the best way to handle an application that has been turned down is simply to wait awhile, reapply on a different basis, and hope for better luck next time. The fact that you have been turned down once does not stop you from trying again.

F.   Carrying Out Step Two: The Application (U.S. Filing)

If you are physically present in the U.S., you may apply for a green card without leaving the country on the following conditions:

- you have already received an approved petition
- a green card is currently available to you because any waiting period under the quota is up
- none of the grounds of inadmissibility apply to you. (See Chapter 25. Pay particular attention to the explanation of the three- and ten-year bars on reentering the U.S.—you could face these if you've lived in the U.S. illegally for six months or more after April 1, 1997), and
- you are in the U.S. legally and/or are eligible otherwise to "adjust status" (see Chapter 25).

Unless you can meet these terms, you may not file an application (Step Two) for a green card in the U.S. (technically called "adjusting status").

1.   Benefits and Drawbacks of U.S. Filing

The obvious benefit to applying for a green card in the U.S. is that if you are already in the country, you avoid the expense and inconvenience of overseas travel. When you file in the U.S., should problems arise in your case, you will at least be able to wait for a decision in America, a circumstance most green card applicants prefer.

Another important benefit of U.S. filing is that you may receive permission to work while you wait for the results of your case. See below, "Procedures for Advance Work Authorization." If you do not need to work right away, but can wait until after getting your green card, you do not need to file this separate application, although states are increasingly requiring a work permit to apply for benefits such as driver's licenses.

If your application for a green card is turned down, you have greater rights of appeal inside the U.S. than you do at a U.S. consulate. USCIS offices have different procedures from consular offices because they are controlled by a different branch of the U.S. government.

There are some disadvantages to applying in the U.S. It may take longer to get results. Processing times at USCIS service centers may approach as long as one year in the future, even on cases where quotas are current. While your case is pending at a USCIS service center, you may not leave the U.S. without getting special permission (called Advance Parole). If you do leave without USCIS's permission, even for a genuine emergency, this will be regarded as a withdrawal of your application and you will have to start your application over again when you return.

PROCEDURES FOR ADVANCE WORK AUTHORIZATION

If you want to work before your application for a green card is approved, file an application for employment authorization. This can be done by completing Form I-765 and filing it with the same USCIS service center where you file the Step Two papers (preferably at the same time). Together with Form I-765, you must submit your I-94 card and pay a filing fee of $120. It is very important to keep the fee receipt USCIS gives you, so you can prove that the I-765 was filed.

Legally, USCIS does not have to make a decision on your employment authorization application for up to 90 days. If for some reason you are not given a decision within 90 days, you will, at your request, be granted an interim employment authorization which will last 240 days.

If 240 days pass and you still have not received a final decision on the I-765, you must stop working. Interim work authorization cards cannot be renewed. However, if you reach this point, you have the option to file a new I-765 application and, if you do not get a decision on the new application within 90 days, you will then be entitled to another interim work authorization card.

---

2. Application General Procedures: U.S. Filing

You may not begin Step Two, the green card application, until you have an approved Step One petition. The application is submitted by mail to the USCIS service center designated for the place you are living. See the USCIS website (www.uscis.gov) for the address and correct P.O. box. All retired international organization applicants must use the Nebraska Service Center.

For U.S. filings, the basic form used in Step Two, the application, is Form I-485, Application for Permanent Residence. Several other forms and documents and the results of your medical exam on Form I-693 must be combined with Form I-485.

The filing fee for each application is $255 for applicants age 14 and over, and $160 for applicants under age 14. Fingerprints are required, and cost an added $50. A separate application must be filed for you and each accompanying relative. (See the Chapter 25 section on the penalty provision to determine whether you are eligible or required to file the $1,000 penalty.)

Checks and money orders are accepted. It is not advisable to send cash through the mail.

Mail your application by certified mail, return receipt requested. Keep a complete copy of everything you send in.

Once your application has been filed, do not leave the U.S. for any reason before your application has been approved. Any absence will be viewed as a termination of your application for a green card. If you must leave the U.S. (for any legitimate personal or business reason), file an "Advance Parole" application with USCIS, submitting three passport-type photographs and Form I-131 with a $110 filing fee. If approved, you will be allowed to leave the U.S. and return again with no break in the processing of your application.

Generally, after filing your Application for Permanent Residence, you will not hear anything from USCIS for several months. Then you should receive notices of your fingerprint and interview appointments.

Your interview will be held at a local USCIS office. If everything is in order at the end of your interview, your application will be approved. Your passport will be stamped to show that you have been admitted to the U.S. as a permanent resident, and your permanent green card will be ordered. The green card will come to you in the mail several months after the interview.

3. Application Forms: U.S. Filing

Copies of all USCIS forms can be found in Appendix II and on the USCIS website.

Form I-485

While most of the form is self-explanatory, a few items typically raise concerns. If a particular question does not apply to you, answer it with "None" or "N/A." The questions on this form requiring explanation are as follows:

Part 1. Part 1 asks for general information about when and where you were born, your present address and immigration status. It also asks for an "A" number. Normally, you will not have an "A" number unless you previously applied for a green card or have been in deportation proceedings (in which case you should consult an attorney before applying).

Part 2. In Part 2, you will mark Box a if you are the principal applicant. Box b is marked if your spouse or parent is the principal applicant.

Part 3. The questions in Sections A through C are self-explanatory. The nonimmigrant visa number is the number that appears on the very top of the visa stamp. It is not the same as your visa classification. The questions in Section C are meant to identify people who are inadmissible. With the exception of certain memberships in the Communist Party or terrorist organizations, you will not be deemed inadmissible simply because you joined an organization. However, if your answer to any of the other questions is "yes," you may be inadmissible. Read Chapter 25, which is intended to help you remove such obstacles.

Don't lie on your answers, because you will probably be found out, especially if you have engaged in criminal activity. Many grounds of inad-missibility can be legally overcome, but once a lie is detected, you will lose the legal right to correct the problem. In addition, a false answer is grounds to deny your application and may result in your being permanently barred from getting a green card.

Form I-485A

This form is required only if you are subject to a $1,000 penalty fee. The form is self-explanatory, and is intended only to determine if you are subject to the penalty. (You are only eligible to file it, and your adjustment of status Application as a whole, if you had a visa petition or Labor Certification on file either by January 14, 1998; or by April 30, 2001, if you were also physically present in the United States on December 21, 2000. See Chapter 25.)

Form G-325A

G-325A biographic data forms must be filled out for you and each accompanying relative. You need not file a G-325A for any child under the age of 14 or any adult over the age of 79. The G-325A form is meant to gather personal background information. The questions are self-explanatory.

Form I-134

You must convince USCIS that once you receive a green card, you are not likely to go on public welfare. If your application is based on employment, that alone should be sufficient proof that you have a way to support yourself, and an I-134 need not be filed for you. You should still, however, fill out Form I-134, the Affidavit of Support, for any accompanying relative. Because you will have an income, you must sign the I-134 forms and take financial responsibility for each of your family members.

In signing the Affidavit of Support, you are not actually promising to support your accompanying relatives. What you do promise is to reimburse the U.S. government for the sum total of any government support payments they might receive should they go on welfare. The I-134 Affidavit of Support binds you to this obligation for three years. Your responsibility to the government then comes to an end.

Form I-765

Block above Question 1. Mark the first box, "Permission to accept employment."

Questions 1–8. These questions are self-explanatory.

Question 9. This asks for your Social Security number, including all numbers you have ever used. If you have never used a Social Security number, answer "None." If you have a nonworking Social Security number, write down the number followed by the words "nonworking, for tax purposes only." If you have ever used a false number, give that number, followed by the words: "Not my valid number." (See Chapter 25 regarding the penalties for document fraud, before filing an application with any information about false Social Security cards.)

Question 10. You will not usually have an Alien Registration Number unless you previously applied for a green card, were in deportation proceedings or have had certain types of immigration applications denied. All Alien Registration Numbers begin with the letter "A." If you have no "A" number but you entered the U.S. with a valid visa, or without a visa under the Visa Waiver Program, you should have an I-94 card. In this case, answer Question 10 by putting down the admission number from the I-94 card.

If you are from Mexico, you may have entered the U.S. with a border crossing card, in which case you should put down the number on the entry document you received at the border, if any. Otherwise simply put down the number of the border crossing card itself, followed with "BCC." If you are Canadian and you entered the U.S. as a visitor, you will not usually have any of the documents described here, in which case you should put down "None."

Questions 11–15. These questions are self-explanatory.

Question 16. Answer this question "(c)(9)."

4. Application Documents: U.S. Filing

You must submit the Notice of Action showing your petition approval with the application. You and each of your accompanying relatives are required to submit two photographs that meet the specifications on the photo instruction sheet found in Appendix II (Form M-378). Additionally, you must submit copies of your birth certificate or other record of birth, if married, a marriage certificate and your spouse's birth certificate, and birth certificates for all your children under age 21, even if they are not immigrating with you.

You must also submit a Medical Examination Report for each applicant. This is done on Form I-693, which must be taken to a USCIS-authorized physician or medical clinic. The USCIS local office will provide you with a list of approved physicians in your area. After completion of the medical exam and upon obtaining the test results, the doctor will give you the results in a sealed envelope. Do not open the envelope.

Each applicant must submit a copy of his or her I-94 card if one was issued. Failure to do so may result in a conclusion that you are not eligible to apply for adjustment of status. The I-94 is the small white card you received on entering the U.S.

5. Application Interviews: U.S. Filing

Personal interviews are sometimes waived for special immigrant applications. If an interview is not waived, you and your accompanying relatives will be asked to come in to the USCIS local office for final processing. The USCIS officer will go over your application to make sure that everything is correct. He will also ask questions to find out whether you are inadmissible. (See Chapter 25.) A single fingerprint will then be taken and you will be asked to sign your application under oath. Accompanying relatives, all of whom must attend the interview with you, will go through the same procedure.

The interview normally takes about 30 minutes. If all goes well, your case should be approved on the spot. Most USCIS offices will place a temporary stamp in your passport showing that you have become a U.S. permanent resident. With this stamp, you acquire all the rights of a green card holder, including the right to work, and freedom to travel in and out of the U.S. The stamp is not your green card. You will receive your permanent green card by mail several months later.

If, on the other hand, your fingerprints have not been cleared by the time of your interview, your application will be approved only provisionally, pending clearance. In those cases, no stamp will be placed in your passport at the interview. Instead, you will receive a written notice of approval within a month or two. That notice serves as your proof of U.S. residency until you receive your green card, which takes another several months. If you need to travel outside the U.S. before your green card arrives, however, you must go back to the USCIS office with your passport and the written notice of approval, and a temporary stamp will be placed in your passport, enabling you to return after your trip. Never leave the U.S. without either your green card or a temporary stamp in your passport.

6. Application Appeals: U.S. Filing

If your application is denied, you will receive a written decision by mail explaining the reasons for the denial. There is no way of making a formal appeal to USCIS when your application is turned down. If the problem is too little evidence, you may be able to overcome this obstacle by adding more documents and resubmitting the entire application to the same USCIS office you have been dealing with, together with a written request that the case be reopened. The written request does not have to be in any special form. This is technically called a *Motion to Reopen*. There is a $110 fee to file this motion. Alternatively, you may wait until USCIS begins deportation proceedings, in which case you may refile your application with the immigration judge.

If your application is denied because you are found inadmissible, you will be given the opportunity to apply for what is known as a *Waiver of Inadmissibility*, provided a waiver is available for your ground of inadmissibility. (See Chapter 25.)

Although there is no appeal to USCIS for the denial of a green card application, you have the right to file an appeal in a U.S. district court. This requires employing an attorney at considerable expense. Such appeals are usually unsuccessful.

FORMS AND DOCUMENTS CHECKLIST

STEP ONE: PETITION

Form

☐ Form I-360.

Documents

RELIGIOUS WORKERS

☐ Diplomas and certificates showing your academic and professional qualifications.

☐ Detailed letter from the U.S. religious organization, fully describing the operation of the organization both in and out of the U.S., and their need for you if you are a minister.

☐ Letter from the U.S. organization giving details of your U.S. job offer, including title, duties, qualifications, and how you will be paid.

☐ Written verification that you have been a member of and worked outside the U.S. for that same organization for at least two years.

☐ Evidence that the religious organization in the U.S. is eligible for tax-exempt (§501(c)(3)) status under the Internal Revenue Code.

FOREIGN MEDICAL GRADUATES

☐ A copy of your original I-94 card (even if it has expired) or your passport with a visa stamp showing you were admitted to the U.S. with a J or H visa prior to January 9, 1978.

☐ Copy of your medical license issued by some U.S. state prior to January 9, 1978, or a letter from the medical board of a state verifying you were licensed.

☐ Evidence that you have been employed as a physician since January 9, 1978.

☐ Evidence of your continuous residence in the U.S. since entry.

☐ If you had a J-1 visa, a copy of the IAP-66 and, if it indicated you were subject to the foreign residence requirement, a No Objection Letter from the embassy of your home country.

FORMER U.S. GOVERNMENT WORKERS

☐ Verification of at least 15 years of U.S. government employment outside the U.S. or with the American Institute in Taiwan.

☐ Letter of recommendation for a green card from the principal officer-in-charge of the agency where you worked.

☐ Letter of recommendation from the U.S. Secretary of State.

RETIRED EMPLOYEES OF INTERNATIONAL ORGANIZATIONS

☐ Evidence you have lived in the U.S. on a G-4 or N visa for the past 15 years (such as copies of passports, I-94 cards, or U.S. tax returns).

☐ Evidence that you lived in the U.S. for at least half of the seven-year period prior to filing for a green card.

☐ Complete copy of your passport.

☐ Copies of all I-94 cards issued.

☐ Income tax returns or W-2 forms for the past 15 years.

☐ If any of the above are unavailable, a detailed letter from the international organization in the U.S. stating your periods of employment, visa status, and period of actual physical presence in the U.S.

☐ A letter from the U.S. employer or other written verification of your retirement date.

CHILDREN OF INTERNATIONAL ORGANIZATION RETIREES

☐ Letter from the international organization in the U.S. employing your parent, verifying his or her position and period of employment.

☐ Your long-form birth certificate showing the names of your parents.

☐ A complete copy of your passport and all I-94 cards issued.

☐ If your passport and I-94 cards are unavailable or do not show your entries and departures for at least the past seven years, other evidence of your presence in the U.S. for one half of the past seven years.

PERSONS EMPLOYED AT THE U.S. CONSULATE IN HONG KONG

☐ Written recommendation to grant you a green card from the consul general of the U.S. consulate in Hong Kong.

☐ Written statement by the consul general explaining how your welfare in Hong Kong will be threatened because you are working for the U.S. government.

☐ Written evidence that you were employed at the U.S. consulate in Hong Kong for at least three years.

FORMS AND DOCUMENTS CHECKLIST

PERSONS DECLARED DEPENDENT ON A JUVENILE COURT

☐ Copy of a juvenile court decree declaring the child's dependency on the court.

☐ If it is not specifically stated in the court decree, a letter from the juvenile court judge stating the following:

    ☐ that the child is eligible for long-term foster care, and

    ☐ that it would not be in the child's best interest to return him or her to the home country.

STEP TWO: APPLICATION

Forms

☐ DS forms (available from U.S. consulate abroad for consular filings only).

☐ Form I-134 (U.S. and consular filings).

☐ Form I-485 for you and each accompanying relative (U.S. filing only).

☐ Form I-485A (U.S. filing only).

☐ Form G-325A for you and each accompanying relative between the ages of 14 and 79 (U.S. filing only).

☐ Form I-765, if work authorization is needed (U.S. filing only).

Documents

☐ Copy of the petition approval notice.

☐ Long-form birth certificate for you and each accompanying relative.

☐ Marriage certificate, if you are married and bringing your spouse.

☐ If either you or your spouse have been married before, copies of divorce and death certificates showing termination of all previous marriages.

☐ Passports for you and each accompanying relative, valid for at least six months beyond the date of the final consular interview.

☐ I-94 card for you and each accompanying relative (U.S. filing only).

☐ Police certificates from every country in which you and each accompanying relative have lived for at least six months since age 16 (consular filing only).

☐ Military records for you and each accompanying relative (consular filing only).

☐ Two photographs each of you and each accompanying relative.

☐ Proof of financial support:

    ☐ Form I-134, Affidavit of Support, for you and each accompanying relative

    ☐ written offer of employment from a U.S. employer, or

    ☐ financial documents showing sufficient funds and investments to support the principal applicant and accompanying relatives without employment.

☐ Medical exam report for you and each accompanying relative.

Refugees, Political Asylees, and Temporary Protected Status

Privileges

- You may come to the U.S. as a refugee to escape political, religious, or racial persecution by the government or groups in your home country.

- If you are already in the U.S, you may be granted political asylum so you will not have to return to face political, religious, or racial persecution.

- After one year as a refugee or political asylee, you may be eligible to apply for a green card.

- You may live anywhere in the U.S. until you either get a green card or it is safe to go home.

- You may work at any job for any company anywhere in the U.S. or you may choose not to work at all.

- Your spouse or unmarried children under the age of 21 may receive refugee or asylee status as accompanying relatives and, like you, they may receive permission to work and travel.

- If you are in the U.S. and don't qualify for asylum, but come from a country that is experiencing war or a natural disaster and so has been designated for special treatment, you may be granted Temporary Protected Status (TPS) or Deferred Enforced Departure (DED) with permission to work.

Limitations

- You may not travel in and out of the U.S. without making a special request to do so by getting a special travel document, or you will lose your special status. Refugees and asylees cannot return to their home country until they get a green card.

- You must wait five months after filing an application for political asylum before you can apply for a work permit; and if your case is denied before the five months, you won't get one at all (until and unless you later win your case).

- Political asylees (but not refugees) are subject to annual quotas on green cards, which may result in delays of months or years before a green card is issued. If you are an asylee and the persecution in your home country ends before your wait for a green card under the quota is up, you may lose your political asylee status and you may have to leave the U.S.

- TPS status must be renewed each year.

- Temporary Protected Status never leads to a green card. If you are under TPS and want a green card, you must additionally fulfill the qualifications of one of the standard green card categories. Otherwise, when the temporary period is over, you must leave the U.S. or risk deportation.

This chapter covers a variety of types of green cards or temporary rights to take shelter in the U.S. based on humanitarian reasons, including refugee status, political asylum, and Temporary Protected Status (TPS).

This chapter will give you an outline of how to apply for refugee, asylee, or TPS status. However, given the risks you'll face if your application is denied, it's worth trying to get additional help. An experienced lawyer can show you how to highlight the important parts of your story in a way that turns your case from a loser into a winner. Within the U.S., a number of organizations offer free or low-cost help to refugees and asylees. See, for example, the searchable directory on www.asylumlaw.org.

A. Who Qualifies as a Refugee or Asylee?

To qualify as a refugee or asylee, you must have experienced persecution in the past or have a well-founded fear of persecution in the future in your home country. The fact that you are suffering economically is not considered a reason for granting refugee or asylee status. Persecution is defined generally as a serious threat to your life or freedom.

To apply for refugee status, you must be physically outside the U.S. And even though you may have been designated as a refugee by the United Nations High Commissioner for Refugees (UNHCR), you will still need to apply separately to the U.S. government, which will make its own decision about whether to accept you.

As a refugee applicant, you must have a financial sponsor inside the U.S. before your application can be approved.

You must also show that you have not already been permanently resettled in another country.

You cannot apply as an asylee until you have reached U.S. soil. Asylees do not need financial sponsors to be granted asylum.

The other major difference between qualifications for refugees and asylees is that there is no annual quota limiting the number of people granted asylum. Beyond these differences, the qualifying requirements for refugees and asylees are the same.

1. Persecution or Well-Founded Fear of Persecution

You may establish eligibility for asylum or refugee status by proving you are the victim of either past persecution or have a fear of future persecution. In the case of past persecution, you must prove that you were persecuted in your home country or last country of residence. The persecution must be based on race, religion, nationality, political opinion, or membership in a particular social group. In addition, Congress amended the law in 1996 to state that refugees and asylees can include people who have undergone or fear a "coercive population control program" (such as forced abortion or sterilization—this provision was directed primarily at Mainland China). However, only 1,000 people can qualify under this category every year.

Persecution may also be based on your gender, including cultural practices such as female "circumcision." The persecution can be by the government, or by groups that the government is unable to control, such as guerrillas or organized vigilantes. However, remember that the persecution must have some political or social basis—a member of a criminal network who comes after you just because you haven't paid him off is not persecuting you according to refugee law.

Once you have proven past persecution, your eligibility for asylum or refugee status will be approved unless USCIS can show that, since you filed your application, there has been a fundamental change in the circumstances surrounding your fear of persecution. For example, USCIS could show that your personal circumstances have changed, or that the conditions in your home country or last country of residence have changed since you were persecuted, so that there is no reasonable likelihood it will happen again. USCIS might alternately show that you do not deserve asylum for another reason.

You will not be granted asylum or refugee status if you have persecuted others. For example, if a policeman committed abuses in tracking down guerrillas, his claim that the guerrillas were in turn sending him death threats will not be sufficient to qualify him for asylum.

If you have not actually suffered persecution in the past, you can still qualify for political asylum or refugee status if you have a genuine fear of future persecution in your home country or last country of residence. Again, that persecution must be based on race, religion, nationality, membership in a particular social group, or political opinion. You do not have to prove that you are likely to be singled out for persecution from the members of a generally persecuted group. You need only show a pattern or practice, where groups of persons who are similar to you are being persecuted. Then, you must show that you either belong to or would be identified with the persecuted group.

2. No Firm Resettlement in Another Country and Unavailability of Safe Haven Elsewhere

Though you may clearly be fleeing persecution, you generally cannot come to the U.S. as a refugee or asylee if you have already been granted or offered a permanent status in another country. You may prefer coming to the U.S., but that makes no difference. The availability of permanent status in another country is known as *firm resettlement.*

If you've lived in another country before coming to the U.S., however, you can still qualify for refugee or political asylum status in the U.S. if you entered the other country while fleeing persecution, stayed there only as long as was necessary to arrange your continued travel, and did not establish significant ties to that country. In addition, if your rights there with respect to living conditions, employment, holding of property, and travel were significantly less than those of actual citizens or full residents, you may still apply for refugee status or political asylum in the U.S.

3. One-Year Time Limit for Asylum Application

You must file an asylum application within one year after you arrive in the U.S. to be eligible for asylum.

There are a few exceptions. If you did not file your asylum application within the one-year filing deadline, you can still apply for asylum if you can show either changed circumstances that have a major effect on your eligibility for asylum or extraordinary circumstances for why your application wasn't filed on time. Changed circumstances can include changes in conditions in your country; extraordinary circumstances can include events or factors beyond your control that caused the late filing. Also, informal USCIS policy is to not consider the time you spend on a valid visa (as a student, for example) to count toward the one year. However, you must apply within a "reasonable time" of the visa's expiration—don't wait a whole year!

4. Financial Sponsorship—Refugees

Your refugee application will not be approved unless you can show that you have a way to pay for your transportation to the U.S. and a means of support once you arrive. This is usually done by finding a financial sponsor. Typically, promises of financial sponsorship come from relatives already in the U.S. or from private charitable groups such as churches and refugee-assistance organizations. Occasionally, the U.S. government itself allocates money for refugee assistance. Proof of financial sponsorship is not required for political asylum applications.

5. Parolees

If you qualify for refugee status but the quota has been exhausted for the year, you may be permitted to come to the U.S. as a parolee without a visa. Parolees are permitted to work and live indefinitely in the U.S., but their futures are less certain than those of refugees. Parolee status can be revoked at any time and does not lead to a green card. A parolee may apply for political asylum after arriving in the U.S., but there is no guarantee asylum will be granted.

6. Accompanying Relatives

If you are married or have children under the age of 21 and you get either refugee or political asylee status, your spouse and children can also be granted refugee or asylee status by providing proof of their family relationship to you. Accompanying relative status allows your family not only to stay with you in the U.S., but also to work.

If you're a refugee traveling with your family, or an asylee whose family is already in the U.S. with you, simply including your family's names and information on your application will be enough to get them granted refugee or asylee status along with you. If you are traveling separately from your spouse and children when you are granted refugee status, or they are outside the U.S. when you are granted asylum, you will need to submit a separate application to the USCIS Nebraska Service Center asking that they be allowed to join you. This is done on Form I-730; see the Appendix or the USCIS website at www.uscis.gov for the form and more information.

Accompanying relatives are not recognized under TPS or DED. Instead, each family member must qualify for TPS or DED on his or her own.

B. Numerical Limits

Refugees have an annual quota set each year by the president of the United States. The quota may vary by country.

The president also decides how the total will be divided among the various regions of the world such as Latin America, Southeast Asia, Eastern Europe, and Africa. Recently, the annual quota has gone down to 70,000. However, even after setting the quota, the U.S. government makes no guarantees that it will allow this many people in—in fact, due to security checks, it admitted only around 25,000 refugees in the year 2003. Top priority was given to people who could prove that they feared individual (as opposed to generalized, group-based) persecution, and to people from Vietnam, Cuba, the former Soviet Union, Iran, and Somalia. In 2003, President Bush also signed legislation giving refugee status to anyone who personally delivers a U.S. Persian Gulf War prisoner into U.S. government custody. Applications are approved on a first-come first-served basis. It is not unusual for qualified refugees to end up on a waiting list.

The refugee quota cannot be accurately forecast, because the number of slots available each year changes. Some countries get many refugee numbers in a given year while others receive practically none. Both refugee and political asylum applications can take from several months to a year or more for approval.

There are no quota restrictions on the number of individuals who may be granted asylum, TPS, or DED. TPS and DED are generally approved within a few weeks.

C. Who Qualifies for Temporary Protected Status (TPS)?

Temporary Protected Status (TPS) is granted to people from selected countries that the U.S. government has recognized as currently in turmoil and therefore unsafe. You must be in the U.S. when TPS is established for your country in order to qualify. TPS is very limited in time (though the government may allow renewals) and does not lead to a green card. TPS is currently available for citizens of Burundi, El Salvador, Honduras, Liberia, Montserrat, Nicaragua, Sierra Leone, Somalia, and Sudan.

Whenever a new country is named, a notice will be published in the *Federal Register*, stating the time period for which the protection is granted, and the dates and procedures for registering. Also see the Legal Updates section of Nolo's website at www.nolo.com, or the USCIS website.

Similar to TPS, Deferred Enforced Departure (DED) offers people temporary rights to remain in the U.S. while conditions in their home country are unsafe. However, only the U.S. president can designate countries under this program. At this time, no countries are designated for DED protection (Liberia's designation expired on September 29,

2002, and it was switched to TPS designation). See the USCIS website (www.uscis.gov) for more information.

⚠️ **Any inadmissible person may be denied U.S. entry or status.** If you have ever committed a serious crime, been involved in a terrorist group, lied on an immigration application, lied to an immigration officer, or suffered certain physical or mental illnesses, you may be inadmissible. That can cause a denial of your initial application, and is even more likely to cause a denial of your application for permanent resident status after being given refugee status or political asylum. However, most grounds of inadmissibility can be waived (forgiven) for refugees, political asylees, and persons seeking TPS or DED, except those grounds concerning the commission of serious crimes, persecution of others, or participation in subversive or terrorist activities such that you are considered a possible threat to U.S. security. (Unlike the normal waiver of inadmissibility, this waiver does not require you to have a family member who is already a permanent resident or U.S. citizen.)

D. Getting a Green Card

Refugees who get their statuses before entering the U.S. are entitled to apply for green cards one year or more after arriving in America.

Political asylees are also eligible to apply for green cards one year or more after their asylee status is granted. You will not receive a notice to come in for a green card interview. You will have to keep track on your own of when you are eligible to apply.

⚠️ **The sooner you get your green card, the sooner you can apply for U.S. citizenship.** Since citizenship is the most secure status the U.S. can offer, it's worth applying as soon as you're eligible.

After filing your green card application as an asylee, you may have to wait. Although there is no quota on the number of qualified applicants granted asylum, the number of asylees who may receive green cards each year is limited to 10,000. The small quota causes backlogs, leading to waits of several years before political asylum applicants actually receive green cards. This creates potentially serious problems for asylees. If the persecution conditions in the asylee's home country end before the wait for a green card is over under the quota, the asylee status may be revoked and the person could be forced to leave the U.S. However, the U.S. government rarely takes this step.

Uncertainty and long waits for green cards cause many asylees to try to obtain green cards in other ways, such as through employment or marriage to a U.S. citizen. Using your asylum status to get a green card is only one of your options. You may also try to qualify in any of the other green card categories. If you have the right qualifications, an alternative to applying for a green card as an asylee may be faster. If, however, you do manage to wait out the asylee quota, a green card application based on asylee status will almost certainly be successful, as long as the home country conditions on which your fear of persecution is based have not significantly improved and you are otherwise eligible.

As we have already stated, there is no specific method for those with TPS to get green cards. However, as one with TPS, all the standard ways to qualify for a green card, such as through family or a job with a U.S. employer, are open to you.

1. The Application

In terms of paperwork, getting status as a refugee, political asylee, or person with TPS or DED is a one-step process. The main step is called the *application* (but you may have to attend an interview later). The object of the application is to show that you meet all the qualifications of a refugee, asylee, or person entitled to TPS or DED. You alone must file the application. If you're applying for refugee or asylee status, your accompanying relatives do not need separate applications, though additional copies of your own application must be filed for each relative. However, if your relatives suffered separate forms of persecution, they may want to apply separately, to increase their chances of approval.

The application for political asylum is filed in the U.S., either at the USCIS regional service center or with an immigration judge. The application for status as a refugee must be filed outside the U.S. at a USCIS overseas office. USCIS overseas offices are not the same as U.S. embassies or consulates. There are only a few USCIS overseas offices. The cities in which these offices are located are listed in Section E, below.

2. Tips on Handling the Paperwork

There are two types of paperwork you must submit. The first consists of official government forms. The second is personal documents, such as birth and marriage certificates.

The documents you supply to USCIS do not have to be originals. In fact, if you submit originals, you're unlikely to get them back. Photocopies of all documents are acceptable as long as you have the original in your possession and are willing to produce them at the request of USCIS. But add the following language to the photocopy, with your signature and the date:

Copies of documents submitted are exact photo-copies of unaltered original documents and I understand that I may be required to submit original documents to an immigration or consular official at a later date.
Signature _____
Typed or Printed Name _____
Date _____

Documents will be accepted if they are in either English, or, with papers filed at an overseas USCIS office, the language of the country where the documents are being filed. If the documents are not in an acceptable language as just explained, they must be accompanied by a full, word for word, written English translation. Any capable person may act as translator. It is not necessary to hire a professional. At the end of each translation, the following statement must appear:

> *I hereby certify that I translated this document from [language] to English. This translation is accurate and complete. I further certify that I am fully competent to translate from [language] to English.*
> *Signature* _____
> *Typed or Printed Name* _____
> *Date* _____

The translator should sign this statement, but it does not have to be witnessed or notarized.

Later in this chapter we describe in detail the forms and documents needed. A summary checklist of forms and documents appears at the end of this chapter.

E. Application for Refugee Status: (Overseas Filing)

Anyone physically outside the U.S. who qualifies as a refugee may apply for refugee status at a USCIS overseas office. USCIS overseas offices are not the same as U.S. embassies or consulates, although most are located within consulate or embassy buildings. It is important that you be aware there are very few USCIS overseas offices. Not every foreign country has one.

You cannot apply for refugee status by mail. You must do so in person. In fact, USCIS will not accept your application for refugee status (on Form 1-590) until you have first been found eligible for a refugee interview. If you can make contact with the nearest UNHCR representative, this organization can help link you up with the USCIS. Any U.S.

consulate can help guide you to a USCIS office or contact person as well. At present, the main overseas USCIS offices handling refugee applications are:

- Bangkok, Thailand
- Mexico City, Mexico
- Rome, Italy.

However, these offices oversee numerous suboffices worldwide and can send USCIS officers to more remote locations.

1. Benefits and Drawbacks of Filing for Refugee Status

If you are outside the U.S. and have no U.S. visa, there is no alternative to filing an application as a refugee with the USCIS overseas. (But see "Summary Exclusion and Credible Fear," below.) A major benefit of a refugee application is that if it is approved, you qualify for a green card one year after arriving in the U.S.

There are two major drawbacks to applying overseas. First, there is a quota for getting refugee status. Each year, the president of the United States decides the maximum number of refugees to be allowed into the U.S. for the next year, distributing specific portions of the total to various parts of the world. If the quota is filled, once you apply, you may have to wait a year or more for a refugee number to become available. The other disadvantage is that you must remain outside the U.S. while your refugee paperwork is being processed. This is taking longer and longer, especially with the recent increases in the security and background checks done on refugee applicants. It is possible that you can overcome this disadvantage. The USCIS has the power to admit you as a parolee for a year at a time, even though your refugee status has not yet been approved. Section 2, below, includes information on obtaining admission to the U.S. as a parolee.

SUMMARY EXCLUSION AND CREDIBLE FEAR

If you can get a U.S. visa, such as a tourist visa, you can apply for political asylum when you arrive. However, the immigration law changes of 1996 made it much easier for people arriving at the U.S. to be turned back at the border or airport. In fact, someone requesting entry to the U.S. can now be quickly found inadmissible and deported for five years. This can happen if an inspector believes that you are making a misrepresentation (committing fraud), or misrepresented the truth when you got your visa, or if you do not have the proper travel or visa documents at the time you request entry. This quick deportation procedure is known as "summary exclusion." It can be applied to everyone except those entering the United States under the Visa Waiver Program (according to a 1999 decision by the Board of Immigration Appeals).

There is an exception to the summary exclusion process for people who fear persecution and request asylum. So, even if you do not have the proper documents or you have made a misrepresentation, you could still be allowed to enter the U.S. if you make clear that your reason is to apply for asylum and you can convince the immigration officer that you would be likely to win asylum.

After you have said you want to apply for asylum, you will be given a "credible fear" interview by an asylum officer. The purpose of this interview is to make sure you have a significant possibility of winning your case. Most importantly, the officer will want to be sure that your request for asylum protection is based on a fear of persecution as described earlier in this section. This interview is supposed to be scheduled quickly, within one or two days, but it has been taking longer. If you fail the test, you must request a hearing before an immigration judge, or you will be deported for five years. The judge may hold the hearing in person or by telephone. The hearing must be held within seven days.

If the judge finds that you have a credible fear of persecution, you will be scheduled for a full hearing. At that point, the proceeding will be a normal asylum proceeding as described in this chapter. Most asylum applicants are held in detention at this point, although you can and should request release. If you fail the credible fear test before the immigration judge, you will then be deported. USCIS may allow individuals to withdraw their application for entry without being subject to the five-year deportation bar.

2.   General Procedures in Filing for Refugee Status

You may apply for refugee status at any USCIS overseas office, provided you are physically able to remain in that location while your case is being processed. Since many refugees do not have passports, it is sometimes difficult to gain entry into a country where a USCIS office is located. Depending on what country you're in, you may need to start with an office of the U.S. Refugee Program (USRP) or the U.N. High Commissioner for Refugees (UNHCR). These offices may put you through an initial screening before you're allowed to file your application with USCIS.

In most USCIS overseas offices, you can simply walk in and begin the application process. At some, you may be given a specific appointment to come back later. You will also have to have a medical exam done by a doctor designated by USCIS. Procedures among USCIS overseas offices vary, so you should call in advance to find out the policies of the office where you intend to apply. However, be prepared for a long wait—getting through all the bureaucratic requirements can take anywhere from two months to two years. The U.S.'s increased attention to security checks has meant that for some refugees, the wait becomes seemingly endless.

If your application for refugee status has been approved but receiving status is delayed because the quota is back-logged, you may, under certain conditions, be admitted to the U.S. immediately as a parolee. A request for parole status must be made in writing to the USCIS central office in Washington, D.C. Such applications are most likely to be approved if you will be joining family already in the U.S., or if you cannot remain temporarily in the country where you filed your refugee application. There is no special form to file in requesting parole status. The USCIS overseas office that handles your refugee application can help you with the exact procedures.

On entering the U.S. as a refugee, you will be given an I-94 card. This is the small white card you are asked to fill out when you arrive. It will be stamped with a date showing for how long your refugee status has been approved. It will also state that you are authorized to work in the U.S. Normally, you are granted refugee status for one year, after which you can apply for a green card.

3.   Forms Needed for Filing for Refugee Status

Copies of all the required USCIS forms can be found in Appendix II.

Form I-590

This form is self-explanatory. Question 18 asks for the name and address of your U.S. sponsor. You must have a financial sponsor in the U.S. or you will not qualify as a refugee.

Form G-325C

This form collects biographical information. The questions are self-explanatory.

4. Documents Needed for Filing for Refugee Status

It is common for refugee applicants to have fled their home countries hurriedly, without time to gather many personal documents. Frequently, refugees also have been denied passports by their home countries. Therefore, USCIS does not insist on any specific documentation to support a refugee application. Some type of personal identification should be provided, however.

For each accompanying relative, you should bring documents proving their family relationship to you. You may verify a parent/child relationship using the child's long-form birth certificate. Many countries issue both short- and long-form birth certificates. Where both are available, the long-form is needed because it contains the names of the parents while the short form does not.

If you are accompanied by your spouse, you must show that you are lawfully married. This is best shown by a civil marriage certificate. If any of these documents are unavailable, the USCIS overseas office may, at its own discretion, accept other kinds of proof, including notarized affidavits from you or other people familiar with your family situation.

Additionally, you must provide documents to support your claim of persecution in your home country. Again, due to the varied circumstances under which refugees flee persecution, USCIS requires no specific types of documents to prove this qualification. However, the burden is on you to show your eligibility. One important document proving persecution is your detailed sworn statement describing your fear and any past persecution. This statement should be in your own words and need not be in any special form.

Additional documents may include:

- newspaper articles describing the type of persecution you would encounter if you returned to your home country
- affidavits from people who know of or have personally experienced similar persecution in your home country, and
- written human-rights reports about your country supplied by organizations such as Amnesty International, Human Rights Watch, or the U.S. State Department's *Country Reports.*

If the persecution is based on your membership in a particular social group, you must supply evidence that the group is experiencing persecution. You must also prove that you are a member of that group.

Finally, you must present documents showing you have a financial sponsor. If a relative is sponsoring you, the relative should fill out an Affidavit of Support, Form I-134. A copy of this self-explanatory form may be found in Appendix II. If you are being sponsored by an organization, the organization will supply you with a written sponsorship agreement.

Documenting your eligibility for refugee status can be extremely difficult. If, after reading this chapter, you believe you have a realistic chance of qualifying for refugee status, you may want to consider getting help with preparing your documents from one of the many refugee-assistance organizations that exist both in the U.S. and abroad. Many of these organizations will help you without charge. Your church, mosque or synagogue can show you how to find such an organization, or see www.asylumlaw.org.

5. Interviews Needed for Filing for Refugee Status

All refugee applications require personal interviews. Procedures vary from one USCIS overseas office to the next, but usually you will be told the time and place of your interview through an appointment letter sent by mail. Immediately before the interview, you and your accompanying relatives must have medical examinations. The procedures for these examinations will be explained in your appointment letter.

The exam itself involves the taking of a medical history, blood test, and chest X-ray, and if applicable, proof of vaccination. Pregnant women may refuse to be X-rayed until after the pregnancy.

The main purpose of the medical exam is to verify that you are not medically inadmissible. The primary medical exclusions are HIV (AIDS) and tuberculosis. Some medical grounds of inadmissibility can be overcome with treatment. (See Chapter 25 for more details.) If you need a medical waiver, you will be given complete instructions by USCIS at the time of your interview.

After the medical exam, you and your accompanying relatives will report to the USCIS overseas office for the interview. Your application will be reviewed, information verified and you will be questioned in detail about your claim of persecution in your home country.

If your application is approved, you will be issued what is known as a travel document. This document will allow you to enter the U.S. as a refugee. You must enter the U.S. within four months after the date your application was approved, or you will lose your refugee status.

6. Appeals When Refugee Status Denied

When a USCIS overseas office denies a refugee application, there is no formal appeal available, although you are free to reapply as often as you like. When your application is denied, the reasons will be explained. The most common reason is failure to show that you have been either subject to persecution or have a reasonable fear of being persecuted if you remain in your home country. Sometimes presenting more evidence on an unclear fact can bring about a better result.

Another common reason for denial of a refugee application is that the USCIS officer believes you are inadmissible. If you are found to be inadmissible, you will be given the opportunity to apply for a waiver of inadmissibility, if one exists. (See Chapter 25.)

When all these possibilities are exhausted, if the USCIS overseas office still refuses to approve your refugee application, your chances for further appeals are severely limited. There is no right to appeal through the U.S. courts and there is no formal appeal procedure through any U.S. government agency.

F. Application for Political Asylum: U.S. Filing

If you are physically present in the U.S. in either legal or undocumented status, and you are otherwise qualified, you may apply for political asylum. If you are not presently in removal proceedings, applications must be filed by mail to a USCIS regional service center. (See Section 2, below.) If you are in proceedings, the application must be filed with the court and immigration judge presiding over your case; but you should seek a lawyer's help.

1. Benefits and Drawbacks of Filing for Asylum

You rarely have a choice about whether to apply in the U.S. or overseas, since you must apply wherever you are physically located. However, there are several benefits to applying in the U.S. First, the number of possible approved political asylum applications is not limited by an annual quota. In addition, you are allowed to remain inside the U.S. while your asylum application is being considered. If your application is turned down, there are more avenues of appeal open in a U.S. filing. Also, even if you don't qualify for asylum, your deportation may be prevented if you qualify for either "withholding of removal" (if your life or freedom would be threatened if you were returned to your home country) or for "convention against torture withholding and deferral of removal" (if you are likely to suffer torture at the hands of your government if you are deported). However, since these are "last-chance" remedies

that usually arise when a lawyer is helping you present your case in immigration court, we will not discuss them further here. Finally, your application will be considered by a specialized asylum officer, trained in political asylum applications. This may result in a fairer decision than is sometimes made on refugee applications.

The biggest drawback to applying for political asylum inside the U.S. is that you cannot apply for work authorization until either the asylum application has been approved or it has been pending for five months without a decision. Also, if your case is denied, you will end up in removal proceedings, unless you are in a valid status at the time your application is denied (in technical terms, "referred" to an immigration judge). Furthermore, if you file an asylum application that USCIS decides is "frivolous" (has no basis), you will be permanently ineligible for any benefits under U.S. immigration law. That means that you will never be given any U.S. visa or green card, even if you were to marry a U.S. citizen, get a U.S. job offer, or the like. Don't worry that your application will be deemed frivolous if it is denied for any reason—USCIS will only find your application frivolous if you had no business even considering political asylum as an option.

Although there is no quota on the number of people granted asylum, there is a quota when an asylee applies for a green card. If you are a political asylee, you may apply for a green card one year after your application is approved, but due to annual quotas, you may have to wait months or years after that before a green card becomes available. If the situation causing the fear of persecution in your home country should end, your asylee status may be revoked (though this is rare). If the conditions supporting your claim to asylee status end before your wait for a green card under the quota is over, you may never receive a green card and you may have to leave the U.S.

2. General Procedures in Filing for Asylum

The application, consisting of Form I-589 and documents, is filed in triplicate, only by mail, at one of the four USCIS regional service centers. There is no filing fee. The proper regional service center jurisdiction for filing asylum cases is given on the I-589 form instructions.

The regional service center will initially review your application to determine if there is a legal prohibition to your application being approved, such as a serious criminal conviction, or if you have persecuted others. If that is the case, your application will be denied quickly and you will be placed in deportation proceedings.

Later you will receive an appointment to have your fingerprints taken. These will be used to check your police and immigration record.

If your application is not summarily denied, you will be asked to come to an asylum office for a personal interview. Asylum interviews are conducted at only a few locations, so you may be required to travel for the interview. You will receive notice of the time of your interview in the mail. Some applications for political asylum are sent by USCIS for review to the U.S. Department of State, which makes a recommendation on the application.

A few weeks after the interview, you'll have to return to the Asylum Office to get your decision. A clerk at the front desk will tell you the decision on your application in person and give you a written document confirming it. If your case is not approved, you will be referred to removal proceedings where you can again apply for political asylum before a judge. If your case is approved, you will be given documentation to show that you have the status of an asylee.

SPECIAL CONCERNS IF YOU ARE IN REMOVAL PROCEEDINGS

If you wish to apply for political asylum but removal proceedings have already been started against you, you must file your asylum application with the immigration judge who is presiding over your removal hearing. Hire a competent immigration lawyer to assist you. Not only are the paperwork requirements complicated, but if your application for asylum is turned down, you may be deported.

---

3. Forms Needed for Filing for Asylum

Copies of all the required forms can be found in Appendix II and on the USCIS website at www.uscis.gov.

Form I-589 (two copies plus the original)

Be sure to answer all questions as fully as possible. The USCIS or an immigration judge will closely review your answers for inconsistencies and will be doubtful about new information that arises during an interview or hearing unless you can show good reasons why such information was not initially included in your written application. If there isn't enough space to answer a question on the form, write "see attached sheet." Then prepare your own statement—as lengthy as you want.

The statement should be in your own words and be as detailed as you can make it. For example, USCIS will not be convinced if you say only "I was persecuted by the government and am afraid to go back." But an applicant who explains that "I was tortured by the local security forces after I joined the union and am terrified that if I go back they'll kill me in the same way they killed many other union members" has a much better chance. (And this is only the beginning—this applicant, for example, should include a history of his union involvement, a description of the torture, and an account of what happened to other union members.)

Part A Section I.

Question 1. Question 1 asks for your "A" number. Normally, you will not have an A number unless you have previously applied for a green card, were paroled into the U.S., or are already in deportation proceedings. If you do not have one, leave this question blank.

Questions 2–12. These questions are self-explanatory.

Question 13. This question asks for your nationality. If you are stateless, say how you became stateless. You are not stateless unless your nationality has been taken away from you and you have no legal right to live in any country. The fact that you might be arrested if you return to your home country does not make you stateless.

Questions 14-16. These are self-explanatory. Be sure that this information is consistent with your asylum claim; if you are claiming persecution based on your religion, race, or nationality, this section should reflect that fact.

Question 17. Check the box ("a," "b," or "c") to indicate whether you have ever been in immigration court proceedings.

Question 18. Box "b" asks for your I-94 number, which is the number on the white or green entry card you received if you entered the U.S. legally, at a border, airport, or seaport.

Questions 19-24. Self-explanatory.

Part A Section II.

This section is self-explanatory. It asks for information about your family members. Mention all of them, whether or not they are applying for asylum. Be aware that you must be legally married to your current spouse for him or her to be granted asylum under your application. Your children will be given asylum along with you only if they are unmarried and under 21 years old at the time of the asylum grant.

Part A Section III.

If your prior address was in a third country (not your home country) for an extended period of time, you will be required to show that you were not firmly resettled—that is, you were not granted permanent residence or otherwise entitled to substantial benefits and privileges in that country.

Part B.

Question 1. This question asks why you are seeking asylum. In the top part of question 1, you can check more than one box. Try to avoid checking nothing but the Torture Convention box—this means that you won't actually be applying for political asylum, but only to be spared from deportation for awhile. For questions A and B, your answers should be "yes," otherwise you don't qualify for asylum. If your answer cannot fit in the spaces on the form, it is best to put down "see attached" and write your entire response on a separate sheet of paper (with your name at the top to avoid the possibility of part of your answer getting misplaced).

Question B is intended to find out what you think will happen to you if you return to your home country. Be as specific as you can, explaining how you will be arrested, tried by the military, sentenced to jail, put to death, or whatever consequence you might suffer. You should also put down "See my affidavit and supporting documentation accompanying this application" (and then give more details in your affidavit).

Question 2. This question asks whether you have been accused, charged, arrested, detained, interrogated, convicted, sentenced, or imprisoned in any country. Your answer to this question can help your case if the action against you was a violation of your human rights, for example if you were arrested and beaten for taking part in a lawful, nonviolent protest march. However, your answer can hurt your case if it shows that you are a criminal and the government was merely taking appropriate, lawful action against you.

Question 3. This question asks about your and your family's involvement in organizations and groups, such as political parties, guerrilla groups, labor unions, and paramilitary organizations. It is very helpful to your claim if you can identify some group to which you belong. To succeed in your claim for asylum, you must have been persecuted for a reason—and that reason must be your connection with some identifiable group. However, if you identify yourself with a group that is known to commit acts of terrorism or persecute others, then your asylum application will likely be denied.

You must identify a group of which you are a member. If your persecution wasn't because of your race, religion, nationality, or political opinion, you must define a "particular social group" of which you are a member. Describe the group as specifically as possible, such as "women who refuse to wear the veil," "people who have the HIV virus," "people with olive-colored skin," or "people who live on the poor side of town." It should be a group whose history of experiencing discrimination or persecution you can explain and document.

Question 4. This question asks whether you fear being tortured in your home country. The answer may be based on what happened to you in the past or what is happening to persons who are in similar circumstances.

Part C.

Questions 1-2. These questions request information about any prior asylum applications and whether you were firmly resettled in another country before coming to the U.S. If you answer "yes" to any of these questions, consult with an asylum expert or attorney before filing your Form I-589.

Questions 3-6. If you answer "yes," consult with an asylum expert or attorney before filing your Form I-589, as one or more of your family members may be ineligible for asylum.

With regard to question 5, see the discussion of the time limits that apply to application for asylum, above. If you answer "yes" to this question, you are ineligible for asylum unless you fall under one of the exceptions discussed above. In that case, see an attorney or asylum expert before filing your application.

Parts D-E. This section requests your signature and information about the person who prepared the application. Keep in mind that a person who files a fraudulent application may be subject to criminal penalties and barred from getting any applications or benefits approved by USCIS and will probably be deported. There are also criminal penalties for failure to disclose one's role in helping to prepare and/or submit an application which contains false information. Finally, USCIS may use the information on the application to deport a person, if the person is not granted asylum.

Part F. Leave this blank for now.

4. Form I-765 (Application for Employment Authorization)

You can't submit Form I-765 with your asylum application. Until you're approved for asylum, you are eligible to apply for a work permit only if you receive no decision on your case within five months of applying for asylum—but USCIS works very hard to make sure you don't wait this long. If you are lucky enough to be able to apply for a work permit, follow the instructions below. There will be no fee for your first one.

Block above Question 1. Mark the first box, "Permission to accept employment."

Questions 1–8. These questions are self-explanatory.

Question 9. This asks for your Social Security number, including all numbers you have ever used. If you have never used a Social Security number, answer "None." If you have a nonworking Social Security number, write down the number followed by the words "Nonworking, for tax purposes only." If you have ever used a false number, give that number followed by the words "Not my valid number." (Be aware that use of false documents for work authorization is a ground of inadmissibility. See Chapter 25.)

Question 10. You will not usually have an Alien Registration Number unless you previously applied for a green card, were in deportation proceedings, or have had certain types of immigration applications denied. All Alien Registration Numbers begin with the letter "A." If you have no "A" number but you entered the U.S. with a valid visa, you should have an I-94 card. In this case, answer Question 10 by putting down the admission number from the I-94 card. If you entered the U.S. without a visa, put down "None."

Questions 11–15. These questions are self-explanatory.

Question 16. Answer this question "(c)(8)" if you've waited five months with no decision and "(a)(5)" if you've been approved.

With your I-765 form, you'll need to enclose evidence that your asylum application was filed with USCIS (its receipt notice is best) and evidence that USCIS has made no decision on your application yet. Also send a copy of the front and back of your I-94 card and two photos (the usual USCIS style, described on Form M-378 in Appendix II). On the back of the photos, write your name and A number in pencil.

Send your work permit application to the USCIS service center indicated in the instructions to Form I-765, available on the USCIS website (www.uscis.gov).

5. Documents Needed for Filing for Asylum

It is common for asylum applicants to have fled their home countries hurriedly without time to gather many personal documents. Frequently, asylees also have been denied passports. Therefore, USCIS does not insist upon any specific documentation to support asylum applications. Some type of personal identification should be provided, however. If you entered the U.S. legally, you should present copies of your I-94 card and passport.

For each accompanying relative (spouse or unmarried children under age 21), provide copies of documents showing their family relationship to you. You may prove a parent/child relationship by presenting the child's long-form birth certificate. Many countries issue both short- and long-form birth certificates. Where both are available, the long-form is needed, because it contains the names of the parents while the short-form does not. If you are accompanied by your spouse, you must prove that you are lawfully married. This is best shown by a civil marriage certificate. If any of these documents are unavailable, the USCIS office may, at its discretion, accept other kinds of proof, including notarized affidavits from you or other people familiar with your family situation.

Additionally, you must provide documents to support your claim of persecution by the government of your home country. Again, due to the varied circumstances under which asylees flee persecution, USCIS requires no specific documents to prove this qualification; however, the burden is on you to prove your eligibility. One document proving fear of persecution is your own sworn statement explaining your persecution or fear of persecution. The statement should be in your own words and need not be in any special form. Additional documents may include:

- newspaper articles describing the type of persecution you would encounter if you returned to your home country
- affidavits from other people who know of or have personally experienced similar persecution in your home country, and
- written human-rights reports about your country supplied by organizations such as Amnesty International, Human Rights Watch, or the U.S. State Department's *Country Reports.*

If the persecution is based on your membership in a particular social group, you must not only supply evidence that the group is experiencing persecution, but also you must offer proof that you are a member of that group.

Your application must include two photos of the main applicant and two each of your spouse and each child. The photos must be a certain size—see the instructions on Form M-378 in Appendix II. Write each person's name on the back of his or her photo in pencil and attach them to the application.

USCIS will notify you where and when to report to have your fingerprints taken. Fingerprints must be taken before your application can be considered; failure to report for a fingerprinting appointment may lead to dismissal of your application or referral to an immigration judge.

6. Interviews Needed for Filing for Asylum

All political asylum applications require personal interviews before they can be approved. You will receive a written notice from the appropriate USCIS office telling you the time and place of the interview and suggesting additional documentation you should bring. The interview itself will be long (about half an hour) and detailed. Your application will be reviewed carefully and you will be questioned at great length concerning your fear of persecution in your home country. You will be asked to return at a later date to be given the decision in person.

PROVING YOUR RIGHT TO WORK AFTER ASYLUM IS APPROVED

Once you've been granted asylum, whether by the USCIS Asylum Office or by an immigration judge, you'll be given a small card, called an "I-94," that proves your status and should be kept with your passport. (Make a copy for your records, too, and keep it in a safe place.) With your I-94, you can obtain a Social Security number and driver's license, which is more than enough to show an employer that you have a right to work. If you wish, however, you can also apply for a new employment authorization card, by filing a new Form I-765 at the USCIS Nebraska Service Center. Follow the instructions in Section D3, above, with two exceptions. Mark the first box "Renewal." Answer Question 16 by putting down "(a)(5)." There is no fee for your first work permit, but a $100 fee for renewals.

7. Appeals When Asylum Is Denied

If your asylum application is not going to be approved, you may, in rare cases, be sent a written notice by mail explaining the reasons why the officer intends to deny your request. In that case, you have an opportunity to send the Asylum Officer additional materials or a personal statement to try to overcome his doubts.

If he is still not convinced, you will later be given a Notice to Appear ("NTA"), which is the start of a removal proceeding. Such proceedings take place in immigration court, where your application may be reconsidered by an immigration judge. If your application is then turned down by the immigration judge, you may file an appeal with the Board of Immigration Appeals in Washington, DC. If that appeal is unsuccessful, you may have your case reviewed in a U.S. Circuit Court of Appeals. You should not attempt such appeals without the assistance of an experienced immigration lawyer, because you are in serious danger of being deported.

G. Application for Temporary Protected Status

Applying for Temporary Protective Status (described in C, above) is a one-step process usually performed at the USCIS local office nearest your home in the U.S., although some nationalities must mail their applications to a USCIS Service Center. Two forms, I-765 and I-821, are required.

Copies of these forms may be found in Appendix II or on the USCIS website at www.uscis.gov. The forms are simple and self-explanatory. The I-821 asks for your name, address, birth date, nationality, and the date you began living in the U.S. The I-765 is an application for a work permit. You will mark box (a)(11) in Question 16.

In addition to the above forms, you must also submit four 1½" x 1½" photographs, and documents showing you really come from the country that you say you do (such as a copy of your passport or birth certificate) and that you have lived in the U.S. for the time required under the TPS rules for your particular country. Evidence of your stay in the U.S. could include copies of your passport and I-94 card, employment records, and school records. Applicants must pay a $50 fee, plus $50 for fingerprinting, and $120 for work authorization. TPS applicants are subject to the grounds of inadmissibility (see Chapter 25), though certain ones can be waived.

You will be called for an interview before an immigration officer, who will approve or deny your application.

H. Deferred Enforced Departure

Another possible basis for remaining in the U.S. if you're from a country in the midst of political or civil conflict is called Deferred Enforced Departure (DED). This temporary form of relief allows you to work and stay in the U.S. for a certain period of time.

Under present policy, no countries are designated for DED, but this could change at any time.

DED protection does not extend to anyone:
- who has been convicted of an aggravated felony
- who is a persecutor of others
- whose removal, in the opinion of the Attorney General, is in the interest of the U.S.
- whose presence or activities in the U.S. are found by the Secretary of State to have potentially serious adverse foreign policy consequences for the U.S.
- who voluntarily returned or returns to Haiti or his or her country of last habitual residence outside the U.S.
- who was deported, excluded, or removed before December 23, 1997, or
- who is subject to extradition.

If you qualify for DED and are in removal proceedings, ask the immigration judge to defer action on your case. If your case is on appeal to the Board of Immigration Appeals, you should receive notice of the temporary suspension of your proceeding.

I. Application for Green Cards

If you are a political asylee or refugee, you may apply for a green card after one year of approval as an asylee or entry to the U.S. as a refugee. The application, consisting of both forms and documents, is submitted by mail to the Nebraska Service Center. The address for refugees is USCIS Nebraska Service Center, P.O. Box 87209, Lincoln, NE 68501-7209. The address for asylees is USCIS Nebraska Service Center, P.O. Box 87485, Lincoln, NE 68501-7485.

The basic form for a green card application is Form I-485, Application for Permanent Residence. The filing fee for each application is $255 if you are age 14 or over, and $160 if you are under age 14. A separate application must be filed by each family member. In addition, each applicant over age 14 must include $50 for fingerprinting costs. Checks and money orders are accepted. It is not advisable to send cash through the mail. Mail your application by certified mail, return receipt requested. Keep a complete copy of everything you send in.

Once your application has been filed, you should not leave the U.S. for any reason before your application has been approved. Any absence will be viewed as a termination of your application for a green card. If you must leave the U.S., you should go in person to your local USCIS office, processing your application, bringing three passport-type photographs and complete Form I-131, asking for Advance Parole. There is a filing fee of $110. If approved, you will be allowed to leave the U.S. and return again with no break in the processing of your application.

⚠ If you return to your home country—even with Advance Parole—USCIS will assume you no longer fear persecution. It may deny you permanent residence and take away your asylum status.

Generally, after filing your application, you will not hear anything from USCIS for several months. Then you should receive notices of your fingerprint and interview appointments. Applications cannot be approved without an interview. At the interview, your application will be reviewed, you will be fingerprinted (for the green card), and asked to sign the application in front of an Immigration Officer. If everything is in order, your application should be provisionally approved at the conclusion of the interview. However, because of the quotas, your permanent residency may not be granted until many months later.

1. Forms

Copies of all the required forms can be found in Appendix II and on the USCIS website at www.uscis.gov.

Form I-485

While most of the form is self-explanatory, a few items typically raise concerns. If a particular question does not apply to you, answer it with "None" or "N/A" for "not applicable." The questions on this form requiring explanation are as follows:

Part 1. Part 1 asks for general information about when and where you were born, your present address, and your immigration status. It also asks for an "A" number. Everyone who enters the U.S. as a refugee or has applied for political asylum is given an "A" number.

Part 2. Mark box "d."

Part 3. The questions in Sections A through C are self-explanatory. If you didn't use a visa to enter the U.S., write "N/A" for the related questions. The questions in Section C are meant to identify people who are inadmissible. With the exception of certain memberships in the Communist Party or terrorist organizations, you will not be deemed inadmissible simply because you joined an organization. However, if your answer to any of the other questions is "yes," you may be inadmissible. (See Chapter 25, which is intended to help you identify and overcome such obstacles.)

Don't lie on your answers, because you will probably be found out, especially if you have engaged in criminal activity. Many inadmissible conditions can be legally overcome, but once a lie is detected, you will lose the legal right to correct the problem. In addition, a false answer is grounds to deny your application and may result in your being permanently barred from getting a green card.

Form G-325A

G-325A Biographic Data forms must be filled out for you and each accompanying relative. You need not file a G-325A for any child under the age of 14 or any adult over the age of 79. The G-325A form is meant to gather personal background information. The questions are self-explanatory.

2. Documents

Each applicant must submit a copy of his or her I-94 card or other immigration document showing status as an asylee or parolee. You should also file, if available, birth certificates for each applicant, and if married, marriage certificates and proof that any previous marriages were terminated by death or divorce. You will also need two photographs for each applicant, taken in compliance with the special photograph instructions contained in Appendix II (Form M-378).

You must also submit a medical examination report for each applicant. This is done on Form I-693, which must be taken to a USCIS-authorized physician or medical clinic. The USCIS local office will give you the form, together with a list of approved physicians in your area. After completion of the medical exam and upon obtaining the test results, the doctor will give you the results in a sealed envelope. Do not open the envelope.

3.   Interviews

Personal interviews are normally held for green card applications. You and your accompanying relatives will be asked to come to the USCIS local office to verify your eligibility, and may be asked questions about the conditions in your home country that are relevant to your persecution claim. The USCIS officer will want to see that you still fear persecution if returned there.

4.   Appeals

If your application is denied, you will receive a written decision by mail explaining the reasons for the denial. There is no way of making a formal appeal to USCIS when your application is turned down. If the problem is too little evidence, you may be able to overcome this obstacle by adding more documents and resubmitting the entire application to the same USCIS office you have been dealing with, together with a written request that the case be reopened. The written request does not have to be in any special form. This is technically called a *Motion to Reopen*. If you believe USCIS made a mistake, it is called a *Motion to Reconsider*. There is a $110 fee to file this motion.

Alternatively, you may wait until the USCIS begins removal proceedings, in which case you may refile your application with the immigration judge.

If your application is denied because you are ruled inadmissible, you may be given the opportunity to apply for what is known as a Waiver of Inadmissibility, if a waiver is available for your ground of inadmissibility. (See Chapter 25 for more on inadmissibility.)

Although there is no appeal to USCIS for the denial of a green card application, you have the right to file an appeal in a U.S. district court. This requires employing an immigration attorney at considerable expense. Such appeals are usually unsuccessful.

FORMS AND DOCUMENTS CHECKLIST

REFUGEE APPLICATION

Forms

- ☐ Form I-590.
- ☐ Form G-325C.

Documents

- ☐ Personal identification for each applicant.
- ☐ Long-form birth certificate for you and each accompanying relative.
- ☐ Marriage certificate if you are married and bringing your spouse.
- ☐ If either you or your spouse have ever been married, copies of divorce and death certificates showing termination of all previous marriages.
- ☐ Personal sworn affidavit describing in detail your reasons for seeking refugee status.
- ☐ Newspaper articles describing the conditions of persecution in your home country.
- ☐ Affidavits from knowledgeable people describing the conditions of persecution in your home country.
- ☐ Written human-rights reports about your country supplied by organizations such as Amnesty International, Central American Resource Center, the Americas Watch Committee or the U.S. State Department's *Country Reports*.
- ☐ Documents showing you have a financial sponsor in the U.S., such as a completed Form I-134.
- ☐ Three photographs each of you and each accompanying relative.
- ☐ Medical Examination report for each applicant.

ASLYUM APPLICATION

Forms (original and two copies)

- ☐ Form I-589.
- ☐ Form G-325A for you and each accompanying relative between the ages of 14 and 79.
- ☐ Form I-765, (file later) if permission to work is needed and your case has either been approved or has been undecided after five months.

Documents (three copies)

- ☐ Personal identification for you and each accompanying relative.
- ☐ Long-form birth certificate for you and each accompanying relative.
- ☐ Marriage certificate if you are bringing your spouse.

- ☐ If either you or your spouse have ever been married, copies of divorce and death certificates showing termination of all previous marriages.
- ☐ Personal sworn affidavit describing in detail your reasons for seeking political asylum.
- ☐ Newspaper articles describing the conditions of persecution in your home country.
- ☐ Affidavits from knowledgeable people describing the conditions of persecution in your home country.
- ☐ Written human-rights reports about your country supplied by organizations such as Amnesty International, Human Rights Watch, or the U.S. State Department's *Country Reports*.
- ☐ Two 1½" square photos of the main applicant and of each spouse or child.

TEMPORARY PROTECTED STATUS

Forms

- ☐ Form I-821.
- ☐ Form I-765.

Documents

- ☐ Four 1½" x 1½" photographs of each applicant.
- ☐ Evidence of your presence during the necessary time period in the U.S.
- ☐ Evidence of your identity and nationality (birth certificate, passport, etc.).

GREEN CARD APPLICATION (REFUGEES AND ASYLEES)

Forms

- ☐ Form I-485.
- ☐ Form G-325A.

Documents

- ☐ I-94 card.
- ☐ Birth certificates for each applicant.
- ☐ Marriage certificates.
- ☐ Two 1½" x 1½" photographs of each applicant.
- ☐ Medical examination report for each applicant.

Amnesty and Special Agricultural Workers

This chapter covers certain special and limited time opportunities for green cards including:
- "NACARA," an amnesty-like program for natives of Central America, Cuba, and the former Soviet Union (Section A)
- the Haitian Immigrant Relief Act of 1998 (Section B)
- the Amnesty program of 1986 (Section C)
- the Farmworker Amnesty Program of 1986 (Section D), and
- the Family Unity program offering temporary U.S. residence rights to spouses and children of people awaiting amnesty (Section E).

Most of the deadlines for these programs have passed. This chapter provides a brief overview of what was available and points out remaining opportunities.

A. Special Suspension of Deportation Rules

Congress passed legislation in late 1997 that wasn't exactly an amnesty, but afforded relief to people from various countries. The law, called the Nicaraguan Adjustment and Central American Relief Act (NACARA), grants different relief depending on whether you are from Central America, Cuba, or a former Soviet bloc country. The application deadline has passed, but USCIS is still making decisions on previously submitted applications.

1. Applicants From Nicaragua or Cuba

An individual from Cuba or Nicaragua who had been continually present in the U.S. since December 1, 1995 (total absences cannot amount to more than 180 days) became eligible for permanent residence. So did the individual's spouse or unmarried child under age 21, even if that person would not qualify on his or her own.

An unmarried son or daughter over 21 years old could also qualify for permanent residence if the parent was granted a green card under this part of the law, but only if the son or daughter shows continuous physical presence in the U.S. since December 1, 1995.

A NACARA applicant must also show that he or she is admissible to the U.S.—that is, that none of the grounds of inadmissibility apply (or if one applies, that a waiver is available). Certain grounds of inadmissibility that apply to most green card applicants do not apply to NACARA applicants: public charge, the need for labor certification, illegal entry, failure to comply with certain documentary requirements, and being unlawfully present. (These grounds are more fully discussed in Chapter 25.)

If an applicant must leave the United States for a family emergency or some other reason, he or she will have to get permission by requesting Advance Parole on Form I-131. It may be necessary to consult with an immigration attorney.

a. Deadline for Applying

Cuban and Nicaraguan nationals had until March 31, 2000 to apply, although some may be eligible to have their cases reopened—consult a lawyer if you missed the deadline.

b. Applicants in Removal Proceedings

An immigration judge cannot order an eligible applicant deported while he or she has a pending NACARA application on file.

c. Proving Continuous Presence

The law requires the principal applicant to have been in the U.S. continuously since December 1, 1995. To prove this, the applicant will have to show evidence such as:
- an earlier application to the former INS for asylum, dated before December 2, 1995
- an INS order to appear for a deportation hearing, and proof that at that hearing the dates of entry were accepted by the immigration court, or that the applicant was issued a Notice to Appear at immigration court dated anytime before December 2, 1995
- an application for adjustment of status or employment authorization dated before December 2, 1995
- U.S. business or employment records from before December 2, 1995, including Social Security tax informa-

tion, W-2 forms, wage statements, rental agreements, or utility bills
- an earlier application for immigration benefits
- rent receipts or utility bills
- school or college transcripts
- a passport, or
- any other evidence that can support the claim.

The law does not require proof that an applicant was in the United States every single day since December 1, 1995, only that there are no significant chronological gaps in the documentation. Generally, a gap of three months or less will not be considered significant. If a person is relying on documents in the USCIS (or former INS) files, then all that is needed is to list the documents.

2. Applicants From Guatemala, El Salvador, or Certain Eastern European Nations

NACARA allowed certain Guatemalans, Salvadorans, and nationals of former Soviet bloc countries to apply for remedies called "suspension of deportation" or "cancellation of removal" under the rules that existed before the enactment of the 1996 immigration law changes.

a. Cancellation of Removal

Cancellation of removal is the granting of a green card based on ten years' presence in the U.S., provided that the removal (deportation) of the applicant would result in extreme and unusual hardship to a qualifying family member (not the applicant) who is a permanent resident or U.S. citizen. An applicant must also not be inadmissible under the criminal or security grounds of inadmissibility, or deportable under the criminal or security grounds of deportability. Applicants who have persecuted others or are deportable under certain document fraud grounds are not eligible, unless USCIS grants a waiver. (See Chapter 25.)

A similar form of relief available before the 1996 immigration law changes was called "suspension of deportation." That benefit required only seven years' presence, and allowed an applicant to qualify upon showing extreme hardship to himself or herself, or to a qualifying family member. The applicant must have had good moral character.

The old rules for suspension of deportation are clearly more flexible than the new ones; many asylum applicants from Central America and Eastern Europe do not have qualifying family members or ten years' presence. For that reason, NACARA allowed some people to apply under the old rules, including:

Salvadoran ABC or TPS registrants present since 1990. Salvadoran nationals who entered the U.S. on or before September 19, 1990, and who registered for ABC (American Baptist Church) benefits under that class action lawsuit on or before October 31, 1991, or registered for temporary protected status (TPS) on or before October 1, 1990.

Guatemalan ABC registrants. Guatemalan nationals who entered the U.S. on or before October 1, 1990, and who registered for ABC benefits on or before December 31, 1991.

Salvadoran or Guatemalan asylum applicants. Guatemalans or Salvadorans who applied for asylum on or before April 1, 1990.

Asylum applicants who are nationals of Eastern Bloc countries. Nationals of the Soviet Union, Russia, any republic of the former Soviet Union, Estonia, Latvia, Lithuania, Poland, Czechoslovakia, Romania, Hungary, Bulgaria, Albania, East Germany, Yugoslavia, or any state of the former Yugoslavia who entered the U.S. before December 31, 1990, and who filed an application for asylum on or before December 31, 1991.

b. Spouses and Children of Qualifying Individuals

The spouse and minor children of an individual who is granted cancellation or suspension under NACARA also qualified for permanent residence under NACARA. Unmarried adult sons and daughters (over 21 years old when their parents were granted suspension or cancellation) must have entered the U.S. before October 1, 1990 in order to qualify on the basis of a grant of suspension of deportation to their parents.

3. Application Procedures for NACARA Applications

The application period for NACARA benefits began on June 22, 1998 and ended on March 31, 2000.

a. Application Procedure

Applicants were required to use Form I-881, Application for Suspension of Deportation or Special Rule Cancellation of Removal (see Appendix II). The application fee to the INS was $215, except the maximum fee per family (husband, wife, unmarried children under 21 years old) was $430. Applications submitted to the Immigration Court were charged a single $100 for one applicant or for applications filed by two or more aliens in the same proceeding. The $100 fee was not required if the Form I-881 was denied by USCIS and referred to the Immigration Court. Every applicant over the age of 14 was required to complete a fingerprinting card for a $50 fee. The applicant needed to include:

- a birth certificate or other record of birth
- two photographs
- a completed Biographic Information Sheet (Form G-325A) if the applicant was between 14 and 79 years of age
- a report of medical examination
- a local police clearance from each jurisdiction where the alien has resided for six months or longer since arriving in the United States, if the applicant was at least 14 years of age
- a copy of the applicant's Arrival-Departure Record (Form I-94) or other evidence of inspection and admission or parole into the United States, if applicable
- one or more of the documents that prove continuous physical presence, as described earlier in this chapter
- a statement showing all departures from and arrivals in the United States since Dec. 1, 1995, and
- if the applicant is applying as the spouse, child, or unmarried son or daughter of another NACARA beneficiary, evidence of that relationship.

An applicant who has already used Form EOIR-40 (Application for Suspension of Deportation) in the Immigration Court before June 21, 1999, could apply to the former INS by submitting a copy of that application attached to a completed first page of Form I-881. The application needed to be filed at the regional service center indicated on the form.

b. Proving Your Case

People who meet the requirements of ABC class members mentioned above are automatically presumed to meet the requirement of "extreme hardship." All other applicants must show that they meet the extreme hardship standard. Even though ABC class members are presumed to meet the "extreme hardship" standard, it is best for all applicants to be prepared to present evidence to back up their claim. An applicant should prepare as much of the following evidence as possible about herself and her immediate family, remembering that deportation alone is not enough to establish "extreme hardship."

- The age of the people involved, both at the time of entry to the United States and at the time of application
- The age, number, and immigration status of the people who face the possibility of deportation. If there are children, then it would be helpful to show the extent to which their limited ability to speak the native language and to adjust to life in the country might make things more difficult for their adjustment to the new country

- The health condition of the persons who might be required to leave the U.S. including the children, spouse, or parents and the availability of any required medical treatment in the country to which the alien would be returned
- The possibility of obtaining employment in the country to which the people would be returned
- The length of residence in the United States
- The existence of other family members who are or will be legally residing in the United States
- The financial impact of the alien's departure
- The impact of a disruption of educational opportunities
- The psychological impact of the being forced to leave the United States
- The current political and economic conditions in the country to which the person would be returned
- Family and other ties to the country to which the people would be returned
- Contributions to and ties to a community in the United States, including the degree of integration into society
- Immigration history, including authorized residence in the United States, and
- The availability of other means of adjusting to permanent resident status.

c. Form I-881

Parts 1 and 2. These are self-explanatory.

Part 3: Presence in the United States. Here you needed to account for where you lived for at least six months at a time over the last ten years. It is important that you clearly documented your residences during the dates set out in the law, depending on whether you are applying as a Nicaraguan, Eastern European, or Central American.

Part 4, Question 1. Seeks similar information as was asked in Part 3, but concerning your employment.

Part 4, Question 3. Seeks to determine whether you have paid income taxes. If you have not, it is recommended that you take steps to complete income tax returns for the years you have not filed.

Part 5. Seeks to determine whether you may be entitled to permanent residency based upon marriage to a U.S. citizen or lawful permanent resident, or possibly whether you may be ineligible for cancellation of removal due to an earlier fraudulent marriage, or for other reasons like failure to support your prior spouse or child.

Another reason for asking these questions is to compare your answers with any prior answers you might have given to the INS (now the USCIS), to determine if you answered them differently. If you have, you should be prepared to explain why. Also, failure to include a child or spouse may make them ineligible to receive NACARA benefits later.

Part 7. While this question only asks for financial information regarding your parents, we recommend that you also include a supplement at the end of the questionnaire on page eight presenting other reasons for hardship to your children, spouse, or parents, or because of a medical condition, or simply because of the long residency in the U.S., which makes it difficult for either them or you to have to leave the U.S

Part 8. These questions are to determine whether there are any legal reasons why you should be denied cancellation of removal. The questions relate to specific legal grounds of inadmissibility. If you believe that any of the items in the boxes apply to you, you should check with an experienced lawyer. When considering if any of these items apply to you, consider whether you have:

- in any way encouraged or helped a family member to come to the U.S. illegally
- ever lied about anything related to an immigrant visa application
- been convicted of driving under the influence (DUI), or
- entered the U.S. under an exchange student visa (J visa).

Part 9. While these questions generally only allow you to answer yes or no, you could use additional pages to provide more information. These are some of the most important questions in the application. Remember in answering these questions that "hardship" includes everything from emotional to economic to physical. It relates to each individual in different ways and so almost anything which you believe is important will be relevant here.

Note: The NACARA rules have been subject to many changes since the original law was passed. We suggest that you contact a nonprofit immigration support organization in your area to find the latest news on NACARA.

4. Fast-Track NACARA Program for ABC and Other Asylum Applicants

Prior to NACARA, only an immigration judge could grant suspension or cancellation of removal. That meant that you could apply only if you were already in removal proceedings. Under the new program, however, USCIS asylum officers will decide cancellation of removal applications for certain NACARA applicants, including individuals who have

asylum applications pending with the USCIS Asylum Office, such as registered class members of the ABC settlement agreement.

It appears that USCIS processes pending asylum applications which are NACARA eligible as suspension of deportation applications first, and as asylum applications if the suspension case is not granted.

5. If a Deportation Order Has Been Entered

Until November 18, 1999, a person facing deportation had the legal right to ask that their case be reopened and considered under the NACARA rules. If you did not file under NACARA by the deadline, you should consult with an attorney right away. If you have been ordered deported and did not file a NACARA petition by the final date, the immigration service could take steps to remove you from the United States without any further hearings.

6. Appeals of Denials Under NACARA

The text of the NACARA law specifically bars judicial appeals (appeals made to the federal District Courts, Courts of Appeals and the Supreme Court). This means that the only appeal available is to an immigration judge or the Board of Immigration Appeals (BIA).

B. Haitian Immigrant Relief Act

The Haitian Refugee Immigration Fairness Act of 1998 (HRIFA) allowed certain citizens of Haiti to become lawful permanent residents, if they:

- were in the United States on December 31, 1995
- had been living in the United States for a continuous period beginning not later than December 31, 1995, and ending not earlier than the date the application for adjustment is filed (the applicant cannot have been outside the U.S. for more than 180 days at a time), and one of the following:
  - filed for political asylum before December 31, 1995, or
  - were paroled into the U.S. before December 31, 1995, or
  - are a child with Haitian citizenship, arrived in the United States without parents, and have remained without parents in the United States since arrival, or became orphaned after arrival or were abandoned by their parents or guardians prior to April 1, 1998, and have remained abandoned.

However, the deadline for applications passed on March 31, 2000. As of now, only dependents of principal applicants are still eligible to apply—unless you are eligible to file a motion to reopen under the 2000 "LIFE Act," which you would need to consult a lawyer to find out. Because the deadlines have passed, we do not cover the application procedures in this book.

All the grounds for inadmissibility still apply to Haitians under this law, except they will not be excluded if they are likely to become a public charge, don't meet Labor Certification requirements, are illegal entrants, unlawfully present, or lack the required entry documentation. If the person is ineligible based on other grounds of inadmissibility, they must be able to qualify for a waiver. (See Chapter 25.) If the application is denied it may be renewed before an immigration judge.

C. Amnesty

The Immigration Reform and Control Act of 1986 (IRCA) created a legalization program that granted amnesty to persons who had lived in the U.S. illegally since the beginning of 1982. The last day for filing amnesty applications was officially May 4, 1988. However, there are still people who haven't gotten a final answer on their application.

In October 2000, Congress passed legislation (the "USCISLIFE" Act) offering people who had joined certain class action lawsuits against the INS (as UCSIC was then called) an opportunity to apply for permanent residence. However, the application deadline has since passed (it was June 4, 2003). (The lawsuits alleged that the INS had improperly handled the 1986 amnesty program.) To qualify for a green card under this new legislation, you needed to prove that you really filed to be a member of one of the appropriate lawsuits (*CSS*, *LULAC*, or *Zambrano*), and that you otherwise qualified for amnesty, lived in the U.S. continuously from November 6, 1986 through May 4, 1988, and aren't otherwise inadmissible to the United States. You also needed to pass a basic citizenship skills test. The husbands, wives and unmarried children of such applicants were also eligible to live in the United States and receive work permits.

Another issue that was, until recently, winding through the court system was whether the INS (as USCIS was then called) was wrong to deny amnesty to applicants who, because of having been deported, had spent some time outside the U.S. during the crucial time period between 1982 and when their amnesty applications were submitted. The court in the case of *Proyecto San Pablo v. INS* (a class-action suit) said that the INS was indeed wrong, and ordered the immigration authorities to reopen the cases of anyone wrongfully denied for this reason and make a new decision on whether they deserved amnesty.

If you believe you might be eligible for amnesty under the *Proyecto San Pablo* case, see an attorney right away. The deadline to file your motion to reopen is one year after the USCIS sends you a notice telling you that you're eligible—and they sent out a number of notices in early 2003. If you never received the notice, your deadline is one year after USCIS finds out where to reach you (perhaps because you tell them). In any case, you should consult an attorney for assistance in evaluating your eligibility and preparing the paperwork. For more information, see Federal Register notice at www.uscis.gov/graphics/lawsregs/fr012903b.pdf.

D. Special Agricultural Workers (SAW)

IRCA also granted legal status to special agricultural workers (SAWs) who performed certain types of agricultural field labor for at least 90 days between May 1, 1985 and May 1, 1986. The deadline for filing applications under the SAW program officially expired on November 30, 1988. However, some SAW applicants who missed the deadline were allowed to file late applications if the former INS forced them not to apply or forced them to withdraw their applications.

One of the requirements to qualifying as a SAW is that the labor performed involved seasonal or perishable crops. There has been considerable court litigation over the Department of Agriculture's definition of seasonal or perishable crops. If you did not file for SAW status, but can prove you performed 90 days of field labor between May 1, 1985 and May 1, 1986, check with a lawyer or immigration assistance group to see if you can file late. Likewise, if you did apply but were turned down because the crops you worked with did not qualify, contact someone who knows the law to see if there may be a chance to file a new application.

E. Family Unity: Spouses and Children

Many families were faced with special problems caused by amnesty. While one family member qualified for amnesty benefits, that person's spouse or children did not qualify. This occurred when some family members arrived in the U.S. before January 1, 1982, while others arrived after that date. In SAW applications, there were problems when not everyone in the family worked in the fields. Those who did not could not qualify for immigration benefits under amnesty. Though visa petitions could be filed on their behalf, they faced long waits due to the preference category 2A and 2B quotas.

The Immigration Act of 1990 created a Family Unity program to help out in these cases. To qualify, you must be the spouse or unmarried child under age 21 of an amnesty recipient. You must have entered the U.S. no later than May 5, 1988 and have been living in the U.S. continuously since that date, and continuously eligible for a second preference family-based visa petition. Also, your qualifying relationship (such as marriage) to the amnesty recipient must have existed on May 5, 1988. Note that children will not lose their status when they turn 21, as long as they remain unmarried.

To apply for Family Unity, you must submit Form I-817, together with evidence of your eligibility and the appropriate fees (currently $140 but double-check the USCIS website at www.uscis.gov). Also include two photos and your old work permit card if you plan to apply for a work permit after you're approved. Evidence of your eligibility should include a copy of the notice of approval of the visa petition (I-130) that your family member filed on your behalf, a copy of any previous approvals of Family Unity, and copies of documents (such as school records, bills, doctor visits, driver's licenses) showing that you have lived in the U.S. continuously since the required date. Mail them to the USCIS Service Center that handles cases from your area; see Appendix I for a list, or check the USCIS website. After

your Family Unity status is approved, you can apply for a work permit on Form I-765.

Family Unity benefits may be terminated if the applicant committed fraud to obtain the status, or becomes inadmissible as an immigrant, or ineligible according to the Family Unity requirements, or the relationship to the legalization beneficiary ends. The 1996 Immigration Reform Law added an additional disqualification, for aliens who committed an act of juvenile delinquency, if it would be a felony offense if committed by an adult and if it included violence, threat of force or possible violence, but only if committed after September 1996.

An additional benefit of Family Unity status is that it stops the running of time for both the three- and ten-year overstay bars. (See Chapter 25 for a discussion of the overstay bars.) Finally, persons in Family Unity status are allowed to request advance permission to leave and reenter the U.S. ("Advance Parole") so that they may travel abroad.

Family Unity status does not turn into a green card. An amnesty relative who already has a green card must file a relative petition on behalf of the other family members. The Family Unity status can be extended over and over until a green card is obtained, however. ■

Nonimmigrant Visas: An Overview

There are many kinds of nonimmigrant (temporary) visas. Each is issued for a different purpose and each is known by a letter-number combination as well as a name. You may be familiar with the more popular types of nonimmigrant visas such as B-2 visitors, E-2 investors, or F-1 students. All of these fall into the general nonimmigrant group.

When you get a nonimmigrant visa, the U.S. government assumes you will perform a specific activity while you are in America. You are therefore given a specialized visa authorizing that activity, for a specific, limited time, and no other.

How is a nonimmigrant visa different from a green card? The most basic difference is that all green cards are permanent while all nonimmigrant visas are temporary. If you hold a green card, you are considered a permanent resident of the U.S. Your green card can only be taken away if you violate certain laws or regulations. The exact opposite is true of nonimmigrant visas—they're very easy for the government to take away from you. For example, if you travel to the U.S. on a nonimmigrant visa and the border authorities think you do not plan to go home, the visa will be taken away. After you've held a green card for a certain length of time, you can become an American citizen; a nonimmigrant visa, however, will never lead to U.S. citizenship.

A. Types of Nonimmigrant Visas

Nonimmigrant visas differ from each other in the kinds of privileges they offer, as well as how long they last. Here is a complete list of the nonimmigrant visas available.

A-1. Ambassadors, public ministers, or career diplomats, and their immediate family members.

A-2. Other accredited officials or employees of foreign governments, and their immediate family members.

A-3. Personal attendants, servants, or employees, and the immediate family members of A-1 and A-2 visa holders.

B-1. Business visitors.

B-2. Tourist visitors. (Also, tourists from certain countries are permitted to come to the U.S. without B-2 visas under what is known as the Visa Waiver Program. See Chapter 15 for a description of this program and the countries included.)

C-1. Foreign travelers in immediate and continuous transit through the U.S.

D-1. Crewmen who need to land temporarily in the U.S. and who will depart aboard the same ship or plane on which they arrived.

E-1. Treaty traders, their spouses and children.

E-2. Treaty investors, their spouses and children.

F-1. Academic or language students.

F-2. Immediate family members of F-1 visa holders.

F-3. Citizens or residents of Mexico or Canada commuting to the U.S. as academic or language students.

G-1. Designated principal resident representatives of foreign governments coming to the U.S. to work for an international organization, their staff members and immediate family members.

G-2. Other accredited representatives of foreign governments coming to the U.S. to work for an international organization, and their immediate family members.

G-3. Representatives of foreign governments, and their immediate family members who would ordinarily qualify for G-1 or G-2 visas except that their governments are not members of an international organization.

G-4. Officers or employees of international organizations and their immediate family members.

G-5. Attendants, servants, and personal employees of G-1 through G-4 visa holders, and their immediate family members.

H-1B. Persons working in specialty occupations requiring at least a bachelor's degree or its equivalent in on-the-job experience, and distinguished fashion models.

H-2A. Temporary agricultural workers coming to the U.S. to fill positions for which a temporary shortage of American workers has been recognized by the U.S. Department of Agriculture.

H-2B. Temporary workers of various kinds coming to the U.S. to perform temporary jobs for which there is a shortage of available qualified American workers.

H-3. Temporary trainees.

H-4. Immediate family members of H-1, H-2, or H-3 visa holders.

I. Bona fide representatives of the foreign press coming to the U.S. to work solely in that capacity, and their immediate family members.

J-1. Exchange visitors coming to the U.S. to study, work, or train as part of an exchange program officially recognized by the U.S. Information Agency.

J-2. Immediate family members of J-1 visa holders.

K-1. Fiancé(e)s of U.S. citizens coming to the U.S. for the purpose of getting married.

K-2. Minor, unmarried children of K-1 visa holders.

K-3. Spouses of U.S. citizens who have filed both a fiancé visa petition and a separate application to enter the U.S.

K-4. Minor, unmarried children of K-3 visa holders.

L-1. Intracompany transferees who work in positions as managers, executives, or persons with specialized knowledge.

L-2. Immediate family members of L-1 visa holders.

M-1. Vocational or other nonacademic students, other than language students.

M-2. Immediate families of M-1 visa holders.

M-3. Citizens or residents of Mexico or Canada commuting to the U.S. to attend a vocational program.

N. Children of certain special immigrants.

NATO-1, NATO-2, NATO-3, NATO-4 and NATO-5. Associates coming to the U.S. under applicable provisions of the NATO Treaty and their immediate family members.

NATO-6. Members of civilian components accompanying military forces on missions authorized under the NATO Treaty, and their immediate family members.

NATO-7. Attendants, servants, or personal employees of NATO-1 through NATO-6 visa holders, and their immediate family members.

O-1. Persons of extraordinary ability in the sciences, arts, education, business, or athletics.

O-2. Essential support staff of O-1 visa holders.

O-3. Immediate family members of O-1 and O-2 visa holders.

P-1. Internationally recognized athletes and entertainers, and their essential support staff.

P-2. Entertainers coming to perform in the U.S. through a government-recognized exchange program.

P-3. Artists and entertainers coming to the U.S. in a group for the purpose of presenting culturally unique performances.

P-4. Immediate family members of P-1, P-2, and P-3 visa holders.

Q-1. Exchange visitors coming to the U.S. to participate in international cultural-exchange programs.

Q-2. Immediate family members of Q-1 visa holders.

R-1. Ministers and other workers of recognized religions.

R-2. Immediate family members of R-1 visa holders.

S-1. People coming to the U.S. to supply critical information to federal or state authorities where it has been determined that their presence in the U.S. is essential to the success of a criminal investigation or prosecution.

S-5 or S-6. People coming to the U.S. to provide critical information to federal authorities or a court, who will be in danger as a result of providing such information, and are eligible to receive a reward for the information.

S-7. Immediate family members of S visa holders.

T. Women and children who are in the United States because they are victims of trafficking, who are cooperating with law enforcement, and who fear extreme hardship (such as retribution) if returned home.

TN. NAFTA professionals.

TO. Spouses or children of TN visa holders.

U. Victims of criminal abuse in the U.S., who are cooperating with law enforcement.

V. Spouses and minor unmarried children of lawful permanent residents who have been waiting three or more years to get a green card, whose initial visa petition was submitted to the INS before December 21, 2000.

By looking at these categories, you can probably see that some will apply to much larger groups of people than others. In this book, we have covered in detail those nonimmigrant visas utilized by the greatest majority of people. If you wish information on some of the lesser-used nonimmigrant visas, contact your USCIS local office or U.S. consulate for more information.

B.   Difference Between a Visa and a Status

A nonimmigrant visa is something you can see and touch. It is a stamp placed on a page in your passport. Your nonimmigrant visa gives you certain privileges, most importantly the right to request entry to the U.S. *Visas are entry documents.*

A visa stamp cannot be issued inside the U.S. It can be obtained only at a U.S. embassy or consulate outside the U.S.

There are, however, other privileges that come with visas, such as permission to work, study, or invest in the U.S. Different privileges are attached to different visas.

Status is the name given to the particular group of privileges you receive after being allowed to enter the U.S. with your visa. You can also apply for a status while you're in the U.S. Again, different groups of privileges go with different types of statuses and visas. However, the ability to enter the U.S. is not part of the status. Only an actual, physical visa can be used to enter the U.S., so if you apply for a particular status and then leave the U.S., you'll have to visit a U.S. consulate and apply for a visa before you return.

C.   Time Limits on Nonimmigrant Visas

Just as nonimmigrant visas vary in purpose, they also vary as to how long they last. Each nonimmigrant visa is given an expiration date, according to what the law allows for that particular category. Most nonimmigrant visas can be extended a certain number of times. The number and length of these extensions also vary according to the visa category and this, too, is fixed by law. In the individual nonimmigrant visa profiles contained this book, we will tell you the length of time each visa lasts and how many extensions are available. You may need to look at a combination of factors, such as:

- the expiration date of your petition or certificate of eligibility, if one is required
- the expiration date of your visa
- the number of entries permitted on your visa
- the date stamped on your I-94 card
- the expiration date of your passport (rules are different for Canadians—see Chapter 28), and
- the expiration date of your status.

1. Expiration Date of Your Visa Petition or Certificate of Eligibility

Most visas can be obtained by applying directly to your local U.S. consulate. However, to get H, L, O, P, and Q work visas, you must first have a petition approved by USCIS. F student visas, M student visas, and J exchange-visitors visas require that you first obtain certificates of eligibility from a U.S. school or employer. Such petitions and certificates of eligibility will indicate the desired starting and expiration dates of the visa.

When you enter the U.S. with one of these visas, you should also bring the certificate of eligibility or Notice of Approval for the petition. The CBP officer who admits you into the country will then know from the petition or certificate of eligibility, not the visa in your passport, how long you are permitted to stay. The officer will give you an I-94 card, which will show the date by which you must leave.

2. Expiration Date of Your Visa

A visa serves two purposes: it allows you to request entry to the U.S., and it gives you the right to engage in certain activities once you have arrived. Permissible activities vary with the type of visa. The expiration date on your visa does not show how long you can stay in the U.S. once you arrive (see the I-94 for that date), but it does indicate how long you have the right to enter or reenter the U.S. with visa privileges.

Nonimmigrant visas can be issued for any length of time up to a certain maximum allowed by law, depending on the type of visa. Visitor's visas, for example, can last indefinitely. (Remember, this means only that you have entry privileges indefinitely, not that you can stay forever.) Many other nonimmigrant visas can be issued for up to five years.

Citizens of some countries can't get visas issued for the maximum period usually allowed by law. The shorter time limitation is based on the nationality of the applicant, not the location of the consulate that issues the visa.

Remember that the visa controls only how long you have the right to enter the U.S., not how long you can stay. Even nationals of those countries who receive visas of shorter duration can have petitions or certificates of eligibility approved for the maximum length of stay. Then, when they do make an entry, they may stay for the full length of time indicated on the approved petition or certificate of eligibility—even if it's beyond the expiration date of their visa—and that date will be written on the I-94 card.

If your visa expires before your petition or certificate of eligibility, you can renew your visa at a U.S. consulate the next time you travel outside of the U.S. You can also choose to stay in the U.S. without traveling for the full term of your petition or certificate of eligibility. Then the fact that your visa may expire doesn't really matter.

LIMITED TRAVEL WHEN YOUR VISA HAS EXPIRED

If you have an expired visa in your passport but a current I-94 card, you can still do some traveling on a limited basis. Specifically, you are permitted to go to Canada, Mexico, or an island adjacent to the U.S. (such as the Bahamas or Bermuda) for up to 30 days, and return to the U.S. without getting a new visa. However, there are some limitations on this privilege. For one thing, you cannot apply for a new visa while you're away, because this will set a new security check into motion and the State Department doesn't want to risk people entering the U.S. while security checks are pending. For another thing, you are not allowed to use this procedure if you're from a country that the U.S. government has identified as supporting terrorism. As of this book's printing, those countries included North Korea, Cuba, Syria, Sudan, Iran, Iraq, and Libya.

The limited travel law is also very useful to Mexican nationals in the U.S. on work and study visas. This is because they are often hampered in simply visiting their homes by the fact that many types of visas to Mexican nationals are issued for only six months at a time.

3. Number of U.S. Entries Permitted on the Visa

Most visas are the multiple entry type. This means that until the visa expires, you may use it to go in and out of the U.S. an unlimited number of times. Some visas are the single entry type. If you hold such a visa, you may use it to enter the U.S. only once. When you leave, you can't return again with that same visa, even if time still remains before its expiration date.

SPECIAL REGISTRATION FOR CERTAIN PEOPLE VISITING THE U.S.

USCIS is imposing extra monitoring on certain people who come to the U.S. on nonimmigrant (temporary) visas. You won't necessarily know before you arrive whether you'll be subject to this additional monitoring; USCIS is trying to keep some of its criteria secret. Although there were press reports in 2003 saying that this program had been ended, in fact it was only modified, to reduce the re-registration requirements.

Phase I: Visitors to the U.S.

The USCIS officer who greets you at the border will look at what country you're from, whether you show up on a database of security risks, and whether your personal characteristics match USCIS's ideas of risk factors. If the officer decides that you are a risk, you will have to:

- be fingerprinted, photographed, and interviewed about your plans in the U.S.
- if you stay in the U.S. for more than 30 days, you may be asked to report in person to a USCIS office between day 30 and day 40 of your U.S. stay, to show that you are following your earlier-stated travel plan. (Until 2003, every person identified as subject to Special Registration had to do this; now, only selected ones will.)
- if you will stay in the U.S for more than one year, and if told when you entered that you would have to re-register, report in person to a USCIS office within ten days of having been here for a year
- send USCIS written notification if you change your address, your employer, or your school (unless you stay in the U.S. for fewer than 30 days)
- leave the U.S. only through a designated port of departure (there are currently about 55 such designated ports), and
- meet with a USCIS officer when you leave.

You will be given a packet of information more fully explaining these requirements when you enter the U.S.

Phase II: Certain Men Already in the U.S.

In November 2002, the former INS instituted "Phase II" of the registration program. You had to register at a local INS or USCIS office if you are a man who:

- was born on or before December 2, 1986
- is a citizen or national of one of the countries listed below
- entered the United States on or before certain dates in 2002, on a nonimmigrant (temporary) visa, and

- planned to stay in the United States until at least your required registration date (see below).

If you fit these criteria and failed to register, you could be deported. Here is the list of countries affected:

Afghanistan	Jordan	Saudi Arabia
Algeria	Kuwait	Somalia
Bahrain	Lebanon	Sudan
Bangladesh	Libya	Syria
Egypt	Morocco	Tunisia
Eritrea	North Korea	the United
Indonesia	Oman	Arab Emirates
Iran	Pakistan	Yemen
Iraq	Qatar	

The registration dates have all passed. Men from Iran, Iraq, Libya, Sudan, and Syria who entered the U.S. before September 10, 2002 were originally required to register by December 16, 2002, but this was extended to include the period between January 27 and February 7, 2003. Men from Afghanistan, Algeria, Bahrain, Eritrea, Lebanon, Morocco, North Korea, Oman, Qatar, Somalia, Tunisia, United Arab Emirates, and Yemen who entered the U.S. before October 1, 2002 were originally required to register between December 2, 2002 and January 10, 2003, but were also given the January 27 to February 7, 2003 extension. The registration period for men from Pakistan and Saudi Arabia who entered the U.S. before October 1, 2002 was between January 13, 2003 and February 21, 2003. The registration period for men from Bangladesh, Egypt, Jordan, Kuwait, and Indonesia who entered the U.S. before September 30, 2002 ran from February 24 to March 28, 2003.

There are exceptions to this registration requirement. You did not need to register if you are:

- a diplomat or other person on an A or G visa
- a lawful permanent resident (green card holder) or other immigrant alien, such as an approved asylee or refugee, or
- an asylum applicant who filed before November 22, 2002.

If you are in the U.S. illegally and have not yet registered, speak to an attorney—the former INS detained or arrested many men who went in to register. Also speak to an attorney if you've already missed the registration period.

4. Date Stamped on Your I-94 Card

When you enter the U.S. on a nonimmigrant visa, you will be given a small white card called an I-94 card. A CBP officer will stamp the card with a date as you enter the country. We have already mentioned that the date you get will come from either the immigration laws, or the date on your petition or certificate of eligibility, if you have one. It is this date and not the expiration date of the visa which controls how long you can stay.

U.S. government regulations state that when you enter the U.S., you should be admitted for the full amount of time remaining on your petition, if you have one. Normally, this is also the expiration date of your visa. In practice, the date on your I-94 card, the final date on your petition, and the expiration date of your visa will usually all be the same.

Occasionally, however, a CBP inspector will stamp the I-94 card giving you a shorter stay than the dates on your petition indicate. Although this is technically improper, it is best not to argue with the inspector. In such cases, if the date on your I-94 card is about to pass and you still wish to remain in the U.S., you can apply for an extension. Directions on how to apply for extensions are in the specific chapters on the various types of visas.

5. Expiration Date of Your Passport

You can't get into the U.S. without a valid passport. Mexicans with border crossing cards and Canadians are the only exceptions to this rule. Remember that visas are stamped inside your passport. When you are ready to receive the visa stamp, make sure you have a passport that is not about to expire. You will not normally be admitted to the U.S. with an expired passport, even if the visa inside is still current.

There is a simple solution to this problem. If your passport contains a visa that is still in effect but the passport itself has already expired, you should apply for a new passport but keep the old one with the current visa stamp. When entering the U.S, show both the new passport and the old one containing the valid visa. Then your visa will be honored for its full term.

6. Expiration of Your Status

If you are presently in the U.S. in valid nonimmigrant status, but want to switch to another nonimmigrant category, you can change your status without leaving the U.S. Make sure to apply before your stay expires. In that case, you will get a different nonimmigrant status but no new visa. For example, you could go from F-1 student status to H-1B specialty worker status in this way. Your new status will be written on a new I-94 card you receive when your request for change of status is approved. Your period

of authorized stay will be extended to the time allowed in the new status category.

D. At the Border

Even after obtaining a nonimmigrant visa, you aren't guaranteed entry into the United States. When you arrive at a U.S. airport, seaport, or land border post, you must present your visa, along with any supporting paperwork such as your proof of financial support or school acceptance. The person who reviews these materials will be part of a different arm of the U.S. government than you've dealt with before—called Customs and Border Protection, or CBP. The CBP inspector will examine your paperwork and ask questions to make sure you deserved the visa in the first place.

CBP inspectors have the power to deport someone requesting admission to the U.S. under two circumstances:

- The inspector believes you are making a misrepresentation about practically anything connected to your entering the U.S., such as your purpose in coming, intent to return, or prior immigration history.
- You do not have the proper documentation to support your entry to the U.S. in the category you are requesting.

If the inspector excludes you (called "Summary Exclusion"), you may not request entry for five years, unless you were entering under the Visa Waiver Program or the immigration authorities grant a special waiver. For this reason, it is extremely important to understand the terms of your requested status and to not make any misrepresentations.

If you are found inadmissible, you can ask to withdraw your application to enter the U.S. to prevent having the five-year ban on your record. The CBP may allow you to do so in some cases. You can also ask to see a judge if you fear you'd be persecuted after returning to your home country and deserve political asylum (see Chapter 12).

Assuming you don't have such problems, your passport will be stamped and you'll be given an I-94 card, as described in Section C, above. You may also be fingerprinted and photographed, as part of the government's new "US-VISIT" program. Starting in 2004, the government will be collecting this data and storing it electronically in order to better trace visitors.

E. Heightened Security Measures

Responding to the September 11, 2001 terrorist acts on the United States, Congress and the State Department have been scrutinizing every part of the visa application process and adding new requirements and security checks. They will no doubt continue strengthening or adjusting these measures in the future. Everyone applying for a visa to the U.S. can now expect delays due to background and security checks. Nearly every applicant is now required to appear for a personal visa interview, resulting in even longer waits at the consulates. Same-day visa processing is virtually a thing of the past. The waits are made even longer by the U.S. consulates' new practice regarding suspicious cases—these are being forwarded to the U.S. Federal Bureau of Investigation (FBI), thus adding weeks or even months to the decision-making process.

In addition, all 16- to 45-year-old male visa applicants must now submit Form DS-157 in addition to the usual application materials. This will affect mainly those applying for student and tourist visas. A few visa categories, mostly diplomatic ones, are exempted, including categories A-1, A-2, G-1, G-2, G-3, G-4, NATO-1, NATO-2, NATO-3, NATO-4, NATO-5, NATO-6, and TECRO E-1. This new form will be mandatory for young men from all countries in the world, not just for men from countries suspected of terrorist links. However, men from Middle Eastern countries are facing longer waits for visas than other applicants.

For new requirements affecting specific visa categories, such as tourists and students, see the chapters that follow.

F. Effect of Nonimmigrant Visas on Green Cards

A question people often ask is, "How does getting a nonimmigrant visa affect my ability to get a green card?" The answer is that usually, there is no effect at all. From a strictly legal standpoint, getting a nonimmigrant visa will not help you to get a green card, nor will it hurt you.

If you must have a nonimmigrant visa so you can go to the U.S. right away, but are definitely planning to apply for a green card later, you should probably not apply for a green card until you have less need to travel. When you can wait for the green card to come through without too much inconvenience, only then should you apply for one. That's because you may be blocked from entering for your temporary stay if you appear to have an "immigrant intent"—that is, plan to stay in the United States permanently.

There are certain nonimmigrant visa categories that allow you to apply for a green card without worrying about immigrant intent. By law, immigrant intent is not a factor for consideration in H-1A, H-1B, L, O, and P visa applications.

G. Nonimmigrant Visas and U.S. Taxes

Though nonimmigrants are, by definition, not permanent residents of the U.S., it is possible to become a *tax resident* simply by spending a certain amount of time in America each year. If you become a tax resident, your entire worldwide income must be reported to the U.S. government. It doesn't matter if a portion or all of that income was earned from investments or business activities carried on outside the U.S. The income still must be reported.

Becoming a tax resident does not necessarily mean that the U.S. government will actually tax all of your worldwide income. International treaties control whether or not you must pay U.S. taxes on income earned elsewhere. However, if you stay in the U.S. long enough to become a tax resident, you will have to at least report all income you have earned worldwide—a paperwork burden, if nothing else.

At what point do you become a tax resident? If you have been present in the U.S. for 183 days or more of the current year, you are a tax resident for the year. If you have been in the U.S. for a weighted total of 183 days during the previous three years, you are also a tax resident unless you spend fewer than 30 days in the U.S. in the current year. For determining the "weighted" total number of days, each day in the current year counts as one, each day in the previous year counts as only one-third of a day, and each day in the second previous year counts as only one-sixth of a day. This latter rule does not apply to certain foreign government employees, certain teachers, students, and professional athletes.

Provided you spend fewer than 183 days of the current year in the U.S., you will also avoid being classified as a tax resident if you maintain a tax home in another country and have a closer connection to that country than to the U.S. There are other exceptions to these rules. A tax treaty between the U.S. and your home country may also alter these rules. If you are unsure of your situation, consult with a tax accountant or lawyer.

If you do become a tax resident, you must file U.S. tax return Form 1040 each year by April 15th. Failure to follow U.S. tax laws may be considered a criminal offense. Failure to comply with U.S. tax laws can also make it more difficult for you to obtain permanent residency. To find out exactly how to comply with U.S. tax laws, consult a tax professional or the nearest office of the Internal Revenue Service (IRS) or visit its website at www.irs.gov. If you are found guilty of a tax crime, your nonimmigrant visa can be revoked and you may be deported.

H. Status Overstays and Automatic Cancellation of Visas

Some people may wish to obtain a nonimmigrant visa at a consulate other than one in their home country. This is called "third country national," or TCN, processing.

TCN processing is prohibited if you have been unlawfully present in the U.S. under a prior visa status. Even if you overstayed your status by just one day, your visa will be automatically canceled, you will not be eligible for TCN processing and you will have to return to your home country to apply for a new visa.

If you were admitted on an A, F, G, or J visa for duration of status (indicated as "D/S" on your Form I-94) and you remain in the U.S. beyond the time for which your status was conferred, you still may be eligible for TCN processing. You will be barred only if the USCIS (or the former INS) or an immigration judge has determined that you were unlawfully present. Six or more months of unlawful presence acquired after April 1, 1997, is also a ground of inadmissibility if you leave the U.S. (See Chapter 25 for more details.)

■

Business and Tourist Visitors: B-1 and B-2 Visas

Privileges

- You can come to the U.S. on a B-2 visa as a tourist visitor or on a B-1 visa as a business visitor. Often, B-1 and B-2 visas are issued together to allow flexibility on your U.S visits.

- B-1 and B-2 visas can be issued quickly in most countries.

- B-2 visitor's visas are sometimes issued for an indefinite period without an expiration date, meaning that one visitor's visa may last you a lifetime.

Limitations

- You may not be employed or operate your own business in the U.S. on a B-1 or B-2 visitor's visa.

- Although you may make any number of trips into the U.S. on a visitor's visa, the length of each visit is normally limited to between 30 days and six months. After that, you must either leave or apply for an extension of your stay.

- You may not legally use your visitor's visa to live permanently in the U.S.

This chapter explains who is eligible for a temporary visa for business or pleasure, and how to apply. Most consulates can approve and issue visitors' visas within days, although new security measures can delay their final decision by weeks or months.

A. Who Qualifies for a Visitor's Visa?

You qualify for a B-1 visa if you are coming to the U.S. as a visitor for a temporary business trip. You qualify for a B-2 visa if you are visiting the U.S. temporarily as a tourist or for medical treatment. Often, these two visas are issued together in combination so you have all the options under both. You must have the intent to return to your home country after your visit is over. Usually, you are required to have a home abroad to which you will return. You can apply for a visitor's visa at a U.S. consulate.

A B-1 visa allows you to be in the U.S. for business purposes such as making investments, buying goods, attending seminars, or performing other temporary work for an employer located outside the U.S. You may not, however, be employed or operate your own company. You may not be paid by a source inside the U.S. It is sometimes difficult to draw the line between permissible business activities and illegal employment on a B-1 visa.

Unlike the B-1 visitor, the B-2 tourist may not engage in business-related activities at all. A condition of being admitted on a B-2 visa is that you are visiting solely for purposes of pleasure or medical treatment.

⚠️ **There are severe penalties for persons who use fraudulent documents or make misrepresentations, or who attempt entry to the U.S. without proper documentation.** Individuals who commit one of these acts can be refused entry at the border or airport, deported from the U.S., and prevented from returning for five years. Accordingly, it is extremely important to understand the requirements of the visa classification you are requesting, and that you not make any misrepresentations of your intent or qualifications for a particular visa.

If you enter the U.S. with a B visa, your intention must be to come only as a temporary visitor. Tourists are usually given stays of up to six months and business visitors may stay as necessary up to a maximum of one year. The date when your permitted stay will expire will be shown on your Form I-94, a little white card that the CBP officer at the border or airport will put into your passport. Theoretically, you may leave the U.S. at the end of your stay, return the next day, and be readmitted for another stay. Alternatively, when your permitted stay has expired, you can apply for an extension of stay without leaving. (See Section C.)

If your travel history shows that you are spending most of your time in the U.S., the CBP will assume you have the intent to be more than just a temporary visitor. On this basis, you can be denied entry altogether, even though you do have a valid visa. Some people, thinking that they have found a loophole in the system, try to live in the U.S. permanently on a visitor's visa by merely taking brief trips outside the country every time their permitted stay expires. Do not expect this tactic to work for very long. However, those who want to have vacation homes in the U.S. and live in them for about six months each year may do so legally.

1. Exception to the Visitor's Visa Requirement: The Visa Waiver Program

Visa Waivers are available for people from countries that do not have a history of illegal immigration to the U.S. Currently there are 27 participating countries in the Visa Waiver Program, including: Andorra, Austria, Australia, Belgium, Brunei, Denmark, Finland, France, Germany, Iceland, Ireland, Italy, Japan, Liechtenstein, Luxembourg, Monaco, the Netherlands, New Zealand, Norway, Portugal, San Marino, Singapore, Slovenia, Spain, Sweden, Switzerland, and the United Kingdom. Nationals of these countries have the option of entering the U.S. for up to 90 days without a visa.

Each visitor who enters under the program must arrive with a transportation ticket to leave the U.S. They must also present what's called a "machine readable passport," that is, one with two lines of scannable characters at the bottom of the biographical information page. Those who come by land from Canada or Mexico may also enter without a visa, but must show evidence at the border of sufficient funds to live in the U.S. without working.

When you enter the U.S. under the Visa Waiver Program, you will not be allowed to change your status to another nonimmigrant classification or apply for a green card without first leaving the country. (The only exception is for persons who marry a U.S. citizen or are the unmarried children or parents of a U.S. citizen.)

Participation in the Visa Waiver Program is optional, not a requirement. Nationals from those countries qualifying for visa waivers can still get standard visitor's visas. You will have more flexibility and rights once you enter the U.S. if you come with a visa.

2. Applying for a Green Card From B-1 or B-2 Status

If you have a B-1 or B-2 visa, you can file for a green card if you're otherwise eligible for one, but being in the U.S. on a B visa gives you no advantage in doing so. Many people believe that if they physically go to the U.S. as a visitor, a way will somehow open up for them to stay. This is simply not a realistic expectation. In fact, even if you are fully qualified for a green card, unless your claim to it is through marriage to an American citizen (see Chapter 5), immigration law often requires you to leave the U.S. and make your application at a U.S. consulate or embassy in your home country. At that point, if you stayed past your visa's expiration date by six months or more, you will not be allowed to return to the U.S. for three or ten years.

Another problem for someone who applies for permanent residency after entering the U.S. on a B-1 or B-2 visa is that they may open themselves to a charge of having committed fraud or material misrepresentation in getting their nonimmigrant visa. This means that the USCIS or consulate believes that the person gave false information to gain entry to the U.S. or to get the visa. An allegation of fraud can ruin your chances of winning permanent residence.

3. Tips on Preparing the Paperwork

There are two types of paperwork you must submit to get a visitor's visa. The first consists of official government forms. The second is personal documents such as birth and marriage certificates.

It is vital that forms are properly filled out and all necessary documents are supplied. You may resent the intrusion into your privacy and the sizable effort it takes to prepare immigration applications, but realize the process is an impersonal matter to immigration officials. Your getting a visa is more important to you than it is to the U.S. government. Take the time and trouble to prepare your papers properly.

Documents submitted to U.S. consulates may be photocopied, but the original must carry a government seal. But add the following language to the photocopy, with your signature and the date:

> *Copies of documents submitted are exact photocopies of unaltered original documents and I understand that I may be required to submit original documents to an immigration or consular official at a later date.*
> *Signature* _____
> *Typed or Printed Name* _____
> *Date*_____

Documents will be accepted if they are in either English or the language of the country where the documents are being filed. An exception exists for papers filed at the U.S. consulates in Japan, where all documents must be translated into English. If the documents are not in an acceptable language as just explained, they must be accompanied by a full, word for word, written English translation. Any capable person may act as translator. It is not necessary to hire a professional. At the end of each translation, the following statement must appear:

> *I hereby certify that I translated this document from [language] to English. This translation is accurate and complete. I further certify that I am fully competent to translate from [language] to English.*
> *Signature* _____
> *Typed or Printed Name* _____
> *Date*_____

The translator should sign this statement but it does not have to be witnessed or notarized.

Later in this chapter we describe in detail the forms and documents needed to get your visitor's visa. A summary checklist of forms and documents appears at the end of the chapter.

B. The Application

Applying for a B visa is a one-step process. You file only one application, consisting of one or two government forms and some personal documents.

1. General Procedures

Technically, the law allows you to apply for a B visa at any U.S. consulate you choose. From a practical standpoint your case will be given greatest consideration at the consulate in your home country. Applying in some other country creates suspicion in the minds of the consular officers about your motives for choosing their consulate. (Often, when an applicant is having trouble at a home consulate, he will seek a more lenient office in some other country.)

Furthermore, if you have ever been present in the U.S. unlawfully, you cannot apply outside your own country. Even if you overstayed your status in the U.S. by just one day, you must return to your home country and apply for the visa from that consulate. There is an exception. If you were admitted to the U.S. for the duration of your status (indicated by a "D/S" on your I-94 form) and you remained in the U.S. beyond that time or purpose for which your status was conferred, you may still be able to apply in a third country. You will be barred from third-country national processing only if an immigration judge or USCIS (or INS) official has determined that you were unlawfully present. You may find that your success in applying as a third-country national depends on your country, the consulate, and the relative seriousness of your offense.

In some consulates, you can simply walk in with your passport and supporting documents, fill out the application form while you are there, and get your B visa within a few days or weeks. Other consulates insist on advance appointments. Since procedures among the consulates vary, you should always telephone or check their website in advance to find out about local policies. Allow plenty of time for a decision—security checks can add weeks or months to the processing time.

While there is a definite difference between B-1 and B-2 visas, the two are frequently issued together. In fact, the machine used to print the visas in your passport groups both B-1 and B-2 on the same stamp. If the consulate wishes you to have only one, the other will be crossed out by hand in your passport.

On entering the U.S. with your new B visa, you will be given an I-94 card. It will be stamped with the dates showing your authorized stay. You are normally permitted to remain in the U.S. for six months. Each time you exit and reenter the U.S., you will get a new I-94 card with a new period of authorized stay.

If your visa was issued as both B-1 and B-2 together, you should make it clear to the immigration inspector which visa you are using. Your I-94 card will show whether you were admitted as a B-1 business visitor or a B-2 tourist.

2. Forms

When you file at a U.S. consulate abroad, the consulate officials will provide you with certain forms, designated by a "DS" preceding a number. Instructions for completing DS forms and what to do with them once they are filled out will come with the forms. We do not include copies of these forms in this book, because some consulates create their own version. Copies of all non-"DS" forms are in Appendix II and on the USCIS website.

Form I-134

You must convince the consulate that once you arrive in the U.S. you are not likely to seek employment or go on public welfare. Form I-134, the Affidavit of Support, can be helpful to guarantee that someone is willing to take financial responsibility for you. (There is a newer affidavit of support, Form I-864, which contains much stricter legal requirements. It is not meant for nonimmigrant visas, so don't use it.)

If possible, the person you will be visiting in the U.S. should sign Form I-134 on your behalf. That person must be a U.S. citizen or green card holder. If you can prove that you are financially independent or are employed in your home country, an I-134 need not be filed on your behalf.

When you request someone in the U.S. to sign an Affidavit of Support, he or she will doubtless wish to know the legal extent of the financial obligation. In signing the Affidavit of Support, the person does not promise to support you. What he or she does promise to do is repay the

U.S. government for the total of any government support payments you might receive. The Affidavit of Support supposedly binds your relative to this obligation for three years, though most lawyers believe the form is flawed and no court would enforce it anyway.

3. Documents

To apply for a visitor's visa, you must show a passport valid for at least six months beyond your period of intended stay and two passport-type photographs. For details on the photo requirements, see http://travel.state.gov/photorequirements/html. You will also need documents showing your intent to leave the U.S. when your visa expires—evidence that your ties to your home country are so strong you will be highly motivated to return. Proof of such ties can include deeds verifying ownership of a home or other real property, written statements from you explaining that close relatives are staying behind, or a letter from your employer in your home country. The application fee is $100.

You must convince the consular officer that you will not need to work while in the U.S. Bring proof of your income and assets. Bank statements or personal financial statements are the appropriate documents for this purpose. Alternatively, if you will be visiting a relative or friend in the U.S. who is a U.S. citizen or green card holder and you will be dependent on that relative for support, ask that person to complete Form I-134, Affidavit of Support. Additionally, a letter from your relative or friend inviting you to visit and stating that you are welcome to stay with him or her is helpful.

If applying as a B-1 business visitor, bring a letter from your employer in your home country describing your job and telling what you will be doing for them in the U.S. The letter should explain that you will be paid only from sources outside the U.S., and state when you will be expected to return from your U.S. business trip.

4. Interviews

The consulate normally requires an interview before issuing a B visa. During the interview, a consular officer examines the application form for accuracy. Evidence of ties to your home country and the state of your financial resources are also checked. During the interview, you will surely be asked how long you intend to remain in the U.S. Any answer suggesting uncertainty about plans to return or an interest in applying for a green card is likely to result in a denial of your B visa. The officer will initiate various security checks to make sure you haven't been involved in criminal or terrorist activity. Because the U.S. is doing more comprehensive security checks than in the past, you are unlikely to receive a decision on your visa the same day as the interview.

5. Appeals

When a consulate turns down a B visa application, there is no way to make a formal appeal, although you are free to reapply as often as you like. (Check with your local consulate to be sure, however—some place limits on the number of repeat applications, or require you to wait a certain number of months before reapplying.) If your visa is denied, you will be told by the consular officer the reasons for the denial. Written statements of decisions are not normally provided in nonimmigrant cases. If a lack of evidence about a particular point is the problem, sometimes simply presenting more evidence on an unclear fact can bring a positive result. The most common reasons for denial are that the consular officer does not believe you intend to return to your home country when the time of your legal U.S. stay is up, or that the consular officer feels you will try to work illegally in the U.S.

Certain people who have been refused B visas reapply at a different consulate, trying to hide the fact that they were turned down elsewhere. If your application is denied, the last page in your passport will be stamped "Application Received" with the date and location of the rejecting consulate. A consular officer will recognize this notation as meaning some type of prior visa application has failed. It serves as a warning that your case merits close inspection. If what we have just told you makes you think it would be a good idea to overcome the problem by getting a new, unmarked passport, you should also know that permanent computer records are kept of all visa denials.

C. Extensions of Stay

After you are in the U.S. on your visa, any application for extension of stay must be filed before the date on your I-94 card passes. (Rules are different for Canadians. See Chapter 28.)

1. General Procedures

Your visit can be extended as long as you did not enter the U.S. on a visa waiver and your total stay will not exceed one year. You cannot usually get an extension of more than six additional months.

You may apply for an extension of stay by mailing forms and documents, including your I-94 card, to the USCIS regional service center having jurisdiction over the place you are visiting. Appendix I contains a list of all USCIS offices and their addresses. The filing fee for each application is currently $140. Checks and money orders are accepted. It is not advisable to send cash. We recommend submitting all papers by certified mail, return receipt requested, and keeping a copy of everything sent in.

If USCIS wants further information before acting on your case, all papers, forms and documents will be returned together with another form known as an *I-797*. The I-797 tells you what additional pieces of information or documents are expected. Supply the extra data and mail the whole package back to the USCIS regional service center.

Applications for extensions of stay for visitors are normally approved within two to four months. You must apply before the date on your I-94 card passes, but not more than 60 days before. If you file your application on time, you will be permitted to remain in the U.S. until receiving a decision, even if your authorized stay expires. When your application is approved, you will receive a Notice of Action Form I-797, indicating the approval with the new date on a tear-off card that's meant to serve as a new I-94 card.

If your application for an extension of stay is denied, you will be sent a written notice explaining the reasons for the negative decision. The most common reason for denial is that USCIS feels you are merely trying to prolong your U.S. stay indefinitely. When your application is denied, you will normally be given a period of 30 days to leave the U.S. voluntarily. Failure to leave within that time may result in your being deported.

There is no way of making a formal appeal to USCIS if your extension is turned down. You may challenge the decision in a U.S. district court, but the time and expense required for this approach usually makes it impractical.

Special Note for Visa Waiver Program. If you were admitted to the U.S. under the Visa Waiver Program, described in Section A1, you may not apply for an extension of stay unless there is a genuine emergency that prevents you from leaving the U.S. on time. If such an extension is needed, you should apply for it in person, not by mail, and you will not get more than 30 days' time to leave.

2. Extension Forms

Copies of all needed forms can be found in Appendix II or on the USCIS website.

Form I-539

Only one application form is needed for an entire family. If you have a spouse or children coming with you, you should also complete the I-539 supplement.

Part 1. These questions are self-explanatory. "A" numbers are usually given only to people who have previously applied for green cards or who have been in deportation proceedings.

Part 2, Question 1. Mark box "a."

Question 2. This question asks if you are also applying for a spouse or children. If so, you must complete the supplement, which asks for their names, dates of birth and passport information.

Part 3. In most cases, you will answer only the first item in this part, by putting in the date. You should put down a date not more than six months beyond the expiration of your current authorized stay.

Part 4, Questions 1–2. These questions are self-explanatory.

Question 3. The different parts to this question are self-explanatory; however, items "a" and "b" ask if an immigrant visa petition or adjustment of status application has ever been filed on your behalf. If you are applying for a green card through a relative, this would be Step One, as described in Chapter 5, or if you are applying for a green card through employment, this would be Step Two, as described in Chapter 8. If your relative or employer has filed the papers for either of these steps, the answer is "yes," and since you have therefore expressed a desire to live in the U.S. permanently, your extension application is very likely to be denied. If you have only begun the Labor Certification, the Step One of getting a green card through employment, this question should be answered "No."

Form I-134

You must convince USCIS that you can continue to stay in the U.S. without working. Form I-134, the Affidavit of Support, guarantees that someone is willing to take financial responsibility for you. See earlier discussion under Section B2.

3. Extension Documents

You must submit I-94 cards for yourself and any family members you have brought with you. (Canadian visitors do not usually get I-94 cards, but the rest of the procedures, forms and documents are the same. See Chapter 28.) You should also submit proof of the relationship between you and accompanying family members. You may verify a parent/child relationship by presenting the child's long-form birth certificate. Many countries, including Canada and England, issue both short- and long-form birth certificates. Where both are available, the long-form is needed because it contains the names of the parents while the short form does not. If you are accompanied by your spouse, you must establish that you are lawfully married by showing a civil marriage certificate. Church certificates are generally unacceptable. (There are a few exceptions, depending on the laws of your particular country. Canadians, for example, may use church certificates if the marriage took place in Quebec Province, but not elsewhere. If a civil certificate is available, however, you should always use it.)

You may have married in a country where marriages are not usually recorded. Tribal areas of Africa are an example. In such situations, call the nearest consulate or embassy of your home country for help with getting acceptable proof of marriage.

If you are a business visitor, you should include a letter from your foreign employer explaining why you need the extension of stay. If you are a tourist, you should, again, submit evidence that you do not need to work by showing proof of your own income and assets. Bank statements or personal financial statements are the best documents for this purpose. Alternatively, if you will be visiting a friend or relative in the U.S. who is a U.S. citizen or green card holder, you may have your relative complete Form I-134, Affidavit of Support, discussed above.

4. Extension Appeals

If your extension application is denied, you will receive a written decision by mail explaining the reasons for the denial. There is no way of making a formal appeal to USCIS for the denial of an extension of stay. If the problem is too little evidence, you can overcome this obstacle by adding more documents and resubmitting the entire application to the same USCIS office you have been dealing with, together with a written request that the case be reopened. The written request does not have to be in any special form. This is technically called a *Motion to Reopen*. There is a $110 fee to file this motion. You may not remain in the U.S. to wait for a decision on your Motion to Reopen.

Theoretically, when an extension of stay is denied you also have the option to file a legal action in a U.S. district court, but this does not give you the right to remain in the U.S. pending a decision either. Since extensions for visitor's visas are only granted for six months or less anyway, pursuing court action is not really practical.

If your application is denied, you should leave the U.S. within the period given to leave voluntarily. If you do this, you should be able to return without difficulty as a visitor at a later date. If you remain beyond your date of voluntary departure, you may have problems returning to the U.S. later. Recently, computers have been installed at each port of entry that tell the government of all your entries and departures.

For a more in-depth discussion of all aspects of getting and using a tourist visa (B-2), see *Student and Tourist Visas: How to Come to the U.S.*, by Ilona Bray & Richard A. Boswell (Nolo).

FORMS AND DOCUMENTS CHECKLIST

STEP ONE: APPLICATION (the only step)

Forms
- [ ] DS forms (available from U.S. consulates abroad).
- [ ] Form I-134 (if you will depend on someone else for financial support).

Documents
- [ ] Your passport, valid for at least six months.
- [ ] Two passport-type photos of you.
- [ ] Documents showing ownership of real estate in your home country.
- [ ] Documents showing that close family members or property are being left behind in your home country.
- [ ] Documents showing a job waiting on your return to your home country.
- [ ] Proof of financial support, such as:
  - [ ] Form I-134, Affidavit of Support from U.S. friend or relative, or
  - [ ] letter from a friend or relative inviting you to visit, stating you are welcome to stay with him or her.
- [ ] Bank statements.
- [ ] Personal financial statements.
- [ ] Evidence of your current sources of income.
- [ ] If you are coming to the U.S. on business, a letter from your foreign employer explaining the reason for your U.S. trip.

Form to Apply for an Extension of Stay
- [ ] Form I-539.
- [ ] Form I-134 (or proof of your independent sources of income).

Documents to Apply for an Extension
- [ ] I-94 cards.
- [ ] Financial documents to accompany Form I-134 or to show independent sources of income.

Temporary Specialty Workers: H-1B Visas

Privileges

- You can work legally in the U.S. for your H-1B sponsor.

- You may travel in and out of the U.S. or remain here continuously until your H-1B visa status expires.

- Visas are available for accompanying relatives.

Limitations

- You are initially restricted to working only for the employer who acted as your H-1B sponsor. Later, you can change jobs.

- Employers must have an attestation on file with the U.S. Labor Department before they can sponsor you for H-1B status.

- H-1B status can be held for no more than six years (with certain exceptions for applicants caught in agency backlogs). Then, you must return to your home country, unless you are eligible to change to another nonimmigrant category or apply for permanent residence.

- Accompanying relatives may stay in the U.S. with you, but they may not work, unless they qualify for a work visa in their own right.

UPDATE ON NURSING NONIMMIGRANT VISAS

As of September 1, 1995, the H-1A category for nonimmigrant nurses was eliminated, on the grounds that there was no longer a shortage of nurses. But by 1999, Congress realized that nurses were once again in short supply. Thus Congress passed the "Nursing Relief for Disadvantaged Areas Act of 1999," which went into effect on November 12, 1999 and will end June 13, 2005 (four years after regulations were promulgated). Unfortunately this didn't bring back the H-1A category.

Instead, it created a new visa category, H-1C, and only allotted 500 H-1C visas per year. Nurses can apply for temporary H-1C visas if they are registered, licensed to practice in the U.S. and in the state where the hospital is, and legally able to start work immediately. More significantly, the hospital that petitions them must meet a number of requirements, among them that they have at least 190 acute-care beds, that certain percentages of their patients are covered by Medicare and Medicaid, and that they are located in a Health Professional Shortage Area (HPSA). It is estimated that no more than 14 hospitals qualify. With individual nurses limited to a

three-year stay, this program doesn't look too promising as a source of visas for registered nurses.

The other option is to get a nonimmigrant H visa by satisfying the H-1B specialty occupation requirements, for which a bachelor's degree or the equivalent is the minimum entry requirement. Such applications will probably only be successful where the job actually requires a four-year nursing degree; owing, for example, to supervisory duties (head nurse), the need to conduct advanced procedures, or the industry's or employer's hiring standards and practices. Nurses may also qualify under the TN category (Canadians and Mexican nationals—see Chapter 28), or in limited circumstances, under the H-3 trainee category. (See Chapter 18.)

Nurses who were previously in the U.S. in H-1A status and who have been out of status for over six months should be sure to understand the grounds of inadmissibility and bars to getting a green card, as discussed in Chapter 25, in order to devise a strategy for regularizing their status.

This chapter will cover who is eligible for an H-1B temporary work visa, and how to apply.

A. Who Qualifies for an H-1B Visa?

To qualify for an H-1B visa, you must first have a job offer from a U.S. employer for duties to be performed in the U.S. The employer must have filed an LCA with the federal Department of Labor (DOL), which, among other things, certifies that the employer will be paying at least the average or "prevailing" wage for that type of job in the particular geographic area.

H-1B visas are available only to workers in occupations requiring highly specialized knowledge normally acquired through a college education, and to distinguished fashion models. To qualify for this visa, unless you are a fashion model, you need at least a bachelor's degree or substantial on-the-job experience that is the equivalent of a bachelor's degree. If you're qualifying through a bachelor's degree, it's preferable if it's not in a liberal arts or general business subject area, which USCIS tends to view as insufficiently specialized. If you don't have a bachelor's degree but will be attempting to qualify through work experience, USCIS usually wants to see three years of specialized training and/or work experience for every year of college that you would have attended.

You must be coming to the U.S. to perform services in a so-called "specialty occupation." If a license to practice your particular occupation is required by the U.S. state in which you will be working, then, in addition to your educational credentials, you must also have the appropriate license.

To get an H-1B visa, not only do your job qualifications have to meet the standards mentioned above, it is also necessary to have the correct type of background for the job you are offered. If your academic and professional credentials are strong, but they do not match the job, then you are not eligible for an H-1B visa.

H-1B visas are specifically *not* given to prominent business people without college degrees, even though they may have substantial on-the-job experience. O-1 visas are available to this group. (See Chapter 24.) H-1B visas are likewise not given to athletes and entertainers, who should consider instead O or P visas, discussed in Chapter 24. Professional nurses are eligible for H-1B visas only if the position they will occupy actually requires an RN degree—usually because the job duties are complex or there are supervisory duties involved.

To summarize, there are four requirements for getting an H-1B visa:

- you must be coming to the U.S. to perform services in a specialty occupation with a college degree or its equivalent in work experience, or be a distinguished fashion model
- you must have a job offer from a qualified U.S. employer for work to be performed in the U.S., and you must be offered at least the prevailing wage that is paid in the same geographic area for that type of job (or the actual wage paid to similar workers at that employer—whichever is the higher of the two wages)
- you must have the correct background to qualify for the job you have been offered, and
- your employer must have filed an attestation (LCA) with the DOL.

Your job must meet one of the following criteria:

- A bachelor's degree or higher degree (or the equivalent) is the minimum requirement for entry into the position.
- The degree requirement is common to the industry in parallel positions among similar organizations, or the duties of the position are so complex that it can be performed only by a person with a degree.
- The employer normally requires a degree or its equivalent for the position.
- The nature of the specific duties is so specialized and complex that knowledge required to perform the duties is usually associated with a bachelor's or higher degree.

Unlike many other nonimmigrant visas, you don't have to prove that you plan to return home at the end of your U.S. stay. In fact, you can (if you are separately eligible) have family members or employers submit applications for you to get a permanent green card at the same time that you're pursuing your H-1B visa—which would be the kiss of death for most other temporary visa applications. It's a different story, however, if you aren't eligible for a green card now but openly admit that you have no intention of leaving the U.S. after your visa expires—then your visa will be denied.

1. Job Criteria

Specialty occupations include but are not limited to accountants, architects, engineers, artists, dietitians, chiropractors, librarians, computer systems analysts, physical therapists, chemists, pharmacists, medical technologists, hotel managers (large hotels), and upper-level business managers.

Some occupations requiring licenses do not usually fall into the H-1B category because college degrees are not normally needed. Such occupations include many types of medical technicians, real estate agents, plumbers, and electricians. Unless a college degree is required, people in such occupations are limited to the more restrictive H-2B visa described in Chapter 17.

LIMITATIONS ON QUALIFYING PHYSICIANS

Although physicians can qualify for H-1B visas, they must either pass a certifying exam ("FLEX," "NBME," or "USMLE") and an English competency exam ("TOEFL"), be a graduate of an accredited medical school, or face limitations in the type of job they'll be allowed to perform here. Specifically, physicians who don't pass one of the exams can only work at a teaching or research job in a public or nonprofit private educational or research institution or agency. Jobs that primarily involve patient care will not qualify this group for H-1B visas (although some patient care is allowed if necessary within the teaching or research context). See 8 C.F.R. §214.2(h)(4)(viii).

ACADEMIC CREDENTIAL EVALUATIONS

Unless you are a distinguished fashion model, to qualify for an H-1B visa you must always hold at least a bachelor's degree or have its equivalent in work experience. However, not every country in the world operates on the same academic degree and grade level systems found in the U.S. If you were educated in some other country, USCIS, as part of judging your H-1B eligibility, will often ask for an academic credential evaluation from an approved consulting service to determine the American equivalent of your educational level.

Evaluations from accredited credential evaluation services are not binding on USCIS, but they are very persuasive. When the results are favorable, they strengthen your case. If, on the other hand, the evaluation shows that your credentials do not equal at least an American bachelor's degree, this can mean you will not qualify for an H-1B visa.

We recommend getting a credential evaluation in every case where non-U.S. education is a factor. We also advise getting the evaluation before USCIS asks for it. The service charge for an evaluation is around $100.

There are several qualified credential evaluation services recognized by USCIS. Two of them are:
International Education Research Foundation
P.O. Box 3665
Culver City, CA 90231-3665
Telephone: 310-258-9451
Fax: 310-342-7086
Website: www.ierf.org

Educational Credential Evaluators, Inc.
P.O. Box 514070
Milwaukee, WI 53203-3470
Telephone: 414-289-3400
Fax: 414-289-3411
Website: www.ece.org

The credential evaluation companies listed above evaluate only formal education. They do not rate job experience. Some U.S. universities also offer evaluations of foreign academic credentials but, unlike the credential evaluation services, many are willing to recognize work experience as having an academic equivalent. USCIS considers every three years of experience to be equivalent to one year of college. Therefore, if you lack a university education but can show many years of responsible experience, you are better off trying to get an evaluation from a U.S. college or university.

When sending your credentials to a U.S. university, include documents showing your complete academic background, as well as all relevant career achievements. Letters of recommendation from former employers are the preferred proof of work experience. Evidence of any special accomplishments, such as awards or published articles, should also be submitted.

2. Job Offer From a U.S. Employer for Work Performed Inside the U.S.

To get an H-1B visa, you need a specific job offer from a qualified employer for work to be performed inside the U.S. The employer will have to act as the petitioner in getting your H-1B visa.

Many people are surprised to learn that they require an employment offer before applying for a work visa. The idea behind it is that you are being granted an H-1B visa only because your services have been recognized as essential to a U.S. enterprise. Put another way, the U.S. government is issuing the visa not for your benefit, but to help the U.S. economy.

The petitioner may be a company or an individual. Whether or not you can form your own corporation and have that corporation act as your sponsoring employer is not completely clear under the law. When the company you own is a legitimate business corporation and is not dependent on your presence to operate, there should be no trouble in using the company as a petitioner. If, however, the corporation appears to be formed strictly for the purpose of getting you a visa, there are likely to be problems with the application.

The employer must also be offering you at least the prevailing wage that is paid for your type of job in that geographic area. Prevailing wage is defined as 5% below the "weighted average" salary. Labor attestation forms will require the employer to state the amount of the prevailing wage. The local job service or state labor department office does periodic surveys of salaries and can provide you with prevailing wage information. If you elect to rely on your own or a different survey, however, you will be required to identify the source of your information.

3. Specialty Occupation

The job offered can't be for just any type of work. The position must really require the skills of a highly educated person. For example, you may be a certified public accountant holding an advanced college degree. Public accounting clearly qualifies as a professional occupation. However, if you are offered a job as a bookkeeper, you will not get an H-1B visa because it doesn't take a highly educated accountant to carry out standard bookkeeping tasks.

4. Correct Background

You must have the correct background for the job you have been offered. For example, if you are a qualified nuclear scientist, but are offered a position managing a U.S. automobile factory, you will not be granted an H-1B visa because you have no background in automobile factory management. If, however, you are asked to manage a factory that produces the kinds of items where your nuclear

science background is required to perform the job duties, you would be eligible for the H-1B visa.

It is irrelevant that your native intelligence and general knowledge of business may make you quite capable of handling the automobile factory job. Likewise, reliability or willingness to work hard, characteristics difficult to find and much in demand by real-world employers, are not a USCIS consideration.

5. Approved Attestation

A business cannot sponsor you for an H-1B petition unless it first files an attestation, also known as a *Labor Condition Application* or LCA, with the DOL. The attestation is a document similar to a sworn declaration or written oath. It must include a number of statements ensuring that both U.S. and foreign workers are being treated fairly. These are discussed below in Section C.

6. Accompanying Relatives

When you qualify for an H-1B visa, your spouse and unmarried children under age 21 can apply for H-4 visas by providing proof of their family relationship to you. H-4 visas authorize your family members to stay with you in the U.S., but not to work there. Like you, however, your family members will have to prove that they are not inadmissible to the U.S. (see Chapter 25).

THE ROAD TO A GREEN CARD

Having an H-1B visa gives you no legal advantage in applying for a green card. Realistically, however, it is probably easier to get an employer to sponsor you for an H-1B visa than a green card, and coming to the U.S. first with an H-1B gives you the opportunity to decide if you really want to live in the U.S. permanently. Once you are in the U.S. with a work permit, it is also usually easier to find an employer willing to sponsor you for a green card.

B. Numerical Limitations

Currently, no more than 65,000 H-1B visa petitions can be approved each year. Also, not all of these 65,000 are available to everyone–a certain number are earmarked each year for countries who have signed free trade agreements with the U.S., for example Chile and Singapore. However, you're not subject to these limits if you'll be working for an institution of higher education, or a nonprofit or government research organization. If the quota gets used up in a given year, no more H-1B petitions can be approved until the start of the next fiscal year, October 1. The quota often gets used up.

Before the Step One visa petition can be submitted, the employer must file a Labor Condition Attestation (LCA) concerning its offered wage and working conditions.

The LCA takes between 14 days and four months for approval. Step One petitions are normally approved within three to six months. If visas are available within that fiscal year, they are usually issued within months after petition approval.

C. Employer Requirements

No employer can sponsor you for an H-1B petition unless it first files a Labor Condition Attestation (LCA) with the DOL. The LCA can be submitted up to six months before you plan to start work.

1. Employer's Attestation

An LCA is similar to a sworn declaration or a written oath. It must include the following information and statements:
- a list of occupations for which H-1B workers are needed
- a statement of the number of foreign workers to be hired in that occupation
- a statement of the wages to be paid the foreign workers, what the prevailing wage is for each worker, and where the employer obtained the prevailing wage information
- a written promise that foreign nationals will be paid the higher of the prevailing market wage for the position, or the actual wage paid to similarly situated workers working for the same employer, and will receive the same benefits as the U.S. coworkers
- a statement that there are no strikes or lockouts in progress involving the jobs to be filled by H-1B workers, and
- a statement that the employer has given notice of the filing of H-1B attestations to either the labor union representing the type of employee involved, or, if no union exists, that the employer has posted notice of the filing in a conspicuous place for other workers to see.

The law frowns on employers who rely too heavily on H-1B workers, however. Employers who are "H-1B dependent," or who have committed certain labor-related violations in the last five years, will have to make additional statements on the attestation form (except in cases where they're paying the worker more than $60,000 or the worker has a master's degree or higher). H-1B dependent means that their workforce includes:
- 25 or fewer full-time employees and eight or more H-1B employees
- 26 to 50 full-time employees and 13 or more H-1B employees, or
- 51 or more full-time employees and at least 15 percent H-1B employees.

The additional attestations that such employers must make include that:
- the H-1B worker will not displace U.S. workers
- if the employer places the employee with another employer or worksite, the original employer will first make certain that no U.S. workers will be displaced there, and
- the employer has made good faith efforts to recruit U.S. workers for the job, at the prevailing wage.

A separate LCA must be filed for each type of job the company wishes to fill with H-1B workers.

Filing the LCA is a very simple matter. Form ETA-9035 is completed, in duplicate, and mailed or faxed to a regional office of the DOL's Employment and Training Administration (ETA). A list of all regional DOL offices, together with addresses, telephone and fax numbers, is in Appendix I. The form can also be downloaded or submitted online at www.lca.doleta.gov. Filing online is recommended for the fastest response.

The form has all necessary statements already written out, with blanks to be filled in with the appropriate occupations, numbers of workers and salaries. The DOL will accept for filing all complete attestations; however, anyone, including other employees at the petitioning company, can file a complaint. The primary objective here is to require employers to pay H-1B workers at least the "prevailing wage" or average ("weighted average") salary for that type of job in the particular geographic area.

When the attestation is accepted, one of the original ETA-9035 forms will be returned to the employer with a DOL endorsement. A copy of the endorsed ETA-9035 must then be submitted to USCIS as a supporting Step One document.

2. Employer's Additional Obligation

Frequently, before agreeing to sponsor a worker for an H-1B visa, prospective employers ask what their liability is in filing a petition. Any employer who dismisses an H-1B worker before his or her authorized stay expires must pay for the trip back to the worker's home country. This is true even if the cause of the firing was the employee's own fault. This liability does not apply if the worker quits the job, but only if he or she is fired.

In addition, employers are prohibited from trying to keep hold of H-1B employees by forcing them to pay a penalty if they leave the job prior to a certain date. The employer can be fined up to $1,000 for this violation.

Employers also take on certain paperwork requirements, namely to make available at their offices for public inspection a copy of each H-1B worker's attestation and supporting documents. The file must also contain information about the company's wage system, benefits plan and more. Many employers seek the help of attorneys in complying with these requirements.

Employers should also know that they are required to pay new H-1B employees within 30 days of their entry into the U.S., or, if the employee is already in the U.S., within 60 days of the employee's approval as an H-1B worker. The employer is also prohibited from "benching" the H-1B worker, that is, putting the worker on involuntary, unpaid leave. This prohibition holds true even if the employer has insufficient work for the employee or the employee lacks a permit or license. Employees must be paid for any time spent in nonproductive status due to a decision by the employer.

D. Applying for an H-1B Visa

Once you have been offered a job and your U.S. employer has completed the preliminary attestation requirements, getting an H-1B visa is a two-step process. Some applicants expect their U.S. employers to handle the entire process for them and, indeed, many large companies have experienced staff specialists who will do this for highly desirable employees. Even smaller companies may be prepared to do whatever is necessary, including paying an immigration attorney's fees, to attract key employees. However, often it is the employee who is most interested in having the visa issued, and to U.S. employers, the red tape of hiring a foreign employee can be an unfamiliar nuisance.

As we give you step-by-step instructions for getting an H-1B visa, we will indicate that certain activities are to be performed by your employer and others are to be done by you. However, there is nothing to stop you from helping with the employer's work. For example, you can fill out forms intended to be completed by your employer and simply ask the employer to check them over and sign them. The less your U.S. employer is inconvenienced, the more it will be willing to act as sponsor for your visa.

1. Overview of Step One: The Petition

The petition is filed by your U.S. employer. All H-1B visa petitions are submitted to USCIS regional service centers in the U.S. The object of the petition is to prove four things:

- that you personally qualify for H-1B status
- that your future job is of a high enough level to warrant someone with your advanced skills
- that you have the correct background and skills to match the job requirements, and
- that your U.S. employer has the financial ability to pay your salary.

Be aware that an approved petition does not by itself give you any immigration privileges. It is only a prerequisite to Step Two, submitting your application for an H-1B visa. The petition must be approved before you are eligible for Step Two.

2. Overview of Step Two: The Application

The application is filed by you and your accompanying relatives, if any. The application is your formal request for an H-1B visa or status. (If you are Canadian, your Step Two procedures will be different from those of other applicants. See Chapter 28.) Step Two may be carried out in the U.S. at a USCIS service center (if you're already legally in the U.S.) or in your home country at a U.S. consulate there. If you file Step Two papers in the U.S., you will usually submit them together with those for Step One. When Step Two is dispatched at a U.S. consulate abroad, you must wait to file the application until the Step One petition is first approved.

If you are already in the U.S. legally on some other type of nonimmigrant visa, you qualify to apply for an H-1B status at a USCIS office inside the U.S. using a procedure known as *change of nonimmigrant status*. (If you were admitted as a visitor without a visa under the Visa Waiver Program, you may not carry out Step Two in the U.S. Currently there are 28 participating countries in the Visa Waiver Program, listed in Chapter 2.) Change of status is simply a technical term meaning you are switching from one nonimmigrant status to another. If approved, you will then be allowed to assume H status in the U.S. without requesting an H visa at a consulate abroad. You can keep the status as long as you remain in the U.S. or until your status expires, whichever comes first.

You will not, however, receive a visa stamp, which you need if your plans include traveling in and out of the U.S. Visa stamps are issued only at U.S. consulates abroad. Therefore, if you change your status and later travel outside the U.S., you will have to go to the U.S. consulate in your home country and repeat Step Two, obtaining the H-1B visa stamp in your passport before you can return.

3. Who's Who in Getting Your H-1B Visa

Getting an H-1B visa will be easier if you familiarize yourself with the technical names used for each participant in the process. During Step One, the petition, you are known as either the *beneficiary* or the *employee* and your U.S. employer is called the *petitioner* or the *employer*. The petitioner may be either a business or a person but usually it is a business. In Step Two, the application, you are called *applicant*, but your employer remains the petitioner or employer. If you are bringing your spouse and children with you as accompanying relatives, each of them is known as *applicant* as well.

4.   Tips on Handling the Paperwork

There are two types of paperwork you must submit to get an H-1B visa. The first consists of official government forms completed by you or your U.S. employer. The second is copies of personal documents, such as academic credentials and professional licenses.

It is vital that forms are properly filled out and all necessary documents are supplied. You or your U.S. employer may resent the intrusion into your privacy and the sizable effort it takes to prepare immigration applications, but you should realize the process is an impersonal matter to immigration officials. Your getting a visa is more important to you than it is to the U.S. government. There is no shortage of applicants.

The documents you or your U.S. employer supply to USCIS or the consulate do not have to be originals. Photocopies of all documents are acceptable as long as you have the originals in your possession and are willing to produce them upon request. But add the following language to the photocopy, with your signature and the date:

Copies of documents submitted are exact photocopies of unaltered original documents and I understand that I may be required to submit original documents to an immigration or consular official at a later date.
Signature _____
Typed or Printed Name _____
Date_____

Documents will be accepted if they are in either English, or, with papers filed at U.S. consulates abroad, the language of the country where the documents are being filed. An exception exists for papers filed at U.S. consulates in Japan, where all documents must be translated into English. If the documents are not in an acceptable language as just explained, they must be accompanied by a full, word for word, written English translation. Any capable person may act as translator. It is not necessary to hire a professional. At the end of each translation, the following statement must appear:

I hereby certify that I translated this document from [language] to English. This translation is accurate and complete. I further certify that I am fully competent to translate from [language] to English.
Signature _____
Typed or Printed Name _____
Date_____

The translator should sign this statement but it does not have to be witnessed or notarized.

Later in this chapter we describe in detail the forms and documents needed to get your H-1B visa. A summary checklist of forms and documents appears at the end of this chapter.

E.   Carrying Out Step One: The Petition

This section includes the information your employer needs to submit the petition.

1.   General Procedures

The U.S. employer submits the petition, consisting of forms and documents, by mail, in duplicate, to the USCIS regional service center having jurisdiction over your intended employer's place of business. USCIS regional service centers are not the same as USCIS local offices –for one thing, you cannot visit regional service centers in person. There are four USCIS regional service centers spread across the U.S. See the USCIS website at www.uscis.gov for the regional service centers' addresses and P.O. boxes.

The filing fee for each petition, if no change of status (Step Two, U.S. Filing) is being requested, is currently $130. Checks or money orders are accepted. It is not advisable to send cash. We recommend submitting all papers by certified mail, return receipt requested, and making a copy of everything sent in to keep in your records.

Within a few weeks after mailing in the petition, your employer should get back a written confirmation that the papers are being processed, together with a receipt for the fee. This notice will also give your immigration file number and tell approximately when you should expect to have a decision. If USCIS wants further information before acting on your case, all petition papers, forms, and documents will be returned to your employer with another form known as an *I-797*. The request for more information tells your employer what additional pieces of information or documents are expected. Your employer should supply the extra data and mail the whole package back to the service center.

H-1B petitions are normally approved within four months. When this happens, a Notice of Action Form I-797 will be sent to your employer, showing the petition was approved. If you plan to execute Step Two at a U.S. consulate abroad, USCIS will also notify the consulate of your choice, sending a complete copy of your file. Only the employer receives communications from USCIS about the petition, because technically it is the employer who is seeking the visa on your behalf.

 Faster processing—at a price. For $1,000 over and above the regular filing fees, USCIS promises "premium processing" of the visa petition, including a decision within 15 days. To use this service, the employer must fill out an additional application (Form I-907) and submit the application to a special USCIS service center address. For complete instructions, see the USCIS website at www.uscis.gov.

2. Petition Forms

Copies of all USCIS forms can be found in Appendix II and on the USCIS website.

Form I-129 and H Supplement

The basic form for Step One, the petition, is immigration Form I-129 and H Supplement. The I-129 form is used for many different nonimmigrant visas. In addition to the basic part of the form that applies to all types of visas, it comes with several supplements for each specific nonimmigrant category. Simply use the supplement that applies to you. Your employer must file the petition form in duplicate. Send in two signed originals. Copies are not acceptable.

The employer may choose to list more than one foreign employee may be listed on a single I-129 petition. This is done if the employer has more than one opening to be filled for the same type of job. If more than one employee is to be included, Supplement-1, which is also part of Form I-129, should be completed for each additional employee.

Most of the questions on the I-129 form are straightforward. If a question does not apply to you, answer it with "None" or "N/A." Those questions requiring explanations are as follows:

Part 1. These questions concern the employer only and are self-explanatory.

Part 2, Question 1. Question 1 should be answered "H-1B."

Questions 2–3. These questions are self-explanatory.

Question 4. This question asks you to indicate what action is requested from USCIS . Normally you will mark box "a" which tells USCIS to notify a U.S. consulate abroad of the petition approval so that you may apply for a visa there. If you will be filing your Step Two application in the U.S., mark box "b." If this petition is being filed as an extension, mark box "c."

Part 3. These questions are self-explanatory. If you previously held a U.S. work permit and therefore have a U.S. Social Security number, put down that number where asked. If you have a Social Security number that is not valid for employment, put down that number followed by "not valid for employment." If you have never had a Social Security number, put down "None."

Alien Registration Numbers, which all begin with the letter "A," are given only to people who have applied for green cards, received political asylum, or been in deportation proceedings. If you do have an "A" number, consult an immigration attorney before filing this application. If you do not have an "A" number, write down "None."

If you're in the U.S., your I-94 number is on the small white or green card that was stapled into your passport when you arrived. (Note: if your card is green, it means you used the Visa Waiver Program to enter, which means you won't be allowed to stay in the U.S. to apply for a change of status.)

If your present authorized stay has expired, you must disclose that where asked. If you have overstayed by six months or more, this may affect your ability to get an H-1B visa at a U.S. consulate; see a lawyer. But if you are out of status now, you cannot file Step Two inside the U.S.

Part 4. These questions are self-explanatory. Under recent changes in the law, the fact that you may have a separate green card petition or application in process does not prevent you from getting an H-1B visa.

Part 5. These questions are self-explanatory. The dates of intended employment should not exceed a total of three years, which is the maximum period of time for which an H-1B petition may be approved.

H Supplement, Top of Form. These questions are self-explanatory. Note, however, that there are a number of H-1B categories listed that we have not discussed, such as those for artists, entertainers and athletes. These occupations were eliminated from H-1B eligibility.

H Supplement, Section 1. Complete only the first four items, which are self-explanatory. The petitioner must sign this form in more than one place.

H Supplement, Sections 2–4. These do not apply to H-1B petitions and should be left blank.

Form I-129W

USCIS has recently begun requiring all petitioners to include Form I-129W with the petition, as an information-collecting device. Ignore Part B of the form, however—it comes from a dead law under which you had to pay an additional $1,000 with your H-1B petition, for a special training fund. The training fund and added fee were stopped in 2003 (but don't confuse this extinct $1,000 fee with the optional $1,000 fee for premium processing of your petition, which is still available). The form is self-explanatory.

3. Petition Documents

You must provide several documents with the petition.

a. Preliminary Attestation

Your employer must submit evidence that it has completed the attestation. This involves supplying a copy of the accepted Form ETA-9035.

b. Job Verification

Your employer must show that the job you have been offered really exists. To do this, the employer must produce either a written employment agreement with you or a written summary of an oral agreement. The terms of your employment, including job duties, hours, and salary, must be mentioned in the letter. It is acceptable that the employment be "at will" and not of any particular duration.

c. Proof of Professional-Level Job

Next should come evidence that the job being offered really requires a person who meets one of the four criteria discussed above, that is to say, someone with a bachelor's degree or the equivalent. Sometimes, as with positions for physicians, accountants, and similarly recognized professions, the high level of the work is common knowledge. In

such cases, the employment agreement will serve to prove both the existence and the level of the job.

Where it is not evident that the position is a "specialty occupation," additional documents are required. Then your employer should write out and submit a detailed description of all job functions, with an explanation of how advanced knowledge and education are essential to their performance. If it remains unclear that the job requires a high-level employee, still more job-level proof can be obtained by asking for written affidavits from experts, such as educators in the field or other employers in similar businesses, stating that jobs of this kind are normally held by highly qualified and degreed individuals.

d. Proof of Employer's Ability to Pay Your Salary

Your employer must be able to prove its existence and financial viability. If the employer is large and well known, it is usually enough to state the annual gross receipts or income, in the letter it submits describing the job opportunity and duties. If the employer is very small, USCIS may request documents to verify the existence and financial solvency of the employer's business. In that case, USCIS will specifically list the documents it wishes to see, including tax returns, profit and loss statements, etc.

Publicly held companies do not have to produce tax returns, accounting records, or bank statements. For them, annual reports of the past two years are accepted to prove ability to pay wages. Again, the larger the company, the less evidence the USCIS demands of its ability to pay additional salaries. When a company is nationally known, USCIS may require no proof of this at all.

e. Proof That You Are a Professional

To qualify for an H-1B visa, you must show evidence that you have a bachelor's degree or otherwise meet the criteria discussed above concerning "specialty occupations." This evidence should include copies of diplomas and transcripts from the colleges and universities you attended. USCIS insists on both a diploma and a transcript from a school where you graduated. If you attended a school but did not graduate, the transcript is required. If you attended any relevant training courses, include a copy of the certificate of completion. If you were educated outside the U.S., USCIS may request a credential evaluation from an approved evaluation service as explained in Section A, above.

f. Special Documents for Physicians

Graduates of medical schools outside the U.S. or Canada may not get H-1B visas as practicing physicians unless they have passed the USMLE licensing exam or an equivalent exam and satisfy the state licensing requirements if they will provide direct patient care services. If patient care will be provided, the physician must also have an unrestricted license to practice in a foreign state, or have graduated from a U.S. medical school. Passing the exam, however, is not required of foreign medical graduates who come to the U.S. to work solely in teaching or research positions at a public or nonprofit institution. In those cases, any patient-care activities must be incidental to the teaching or research functions.

Therefore, in addition to all other documents required from members of the professions, the petitioning employer must submit either a certificate showing you have passed the USMLE or an equivalent exam, or a statement certifying that you will be employed as either a teacher or researcher and that any patient care will be undertaken only as part of the teaching or research. This written statement does not have to be in any special form but simply in the petitioner's own words.

Foreign medical students attending medical school abroad may petition to be classified as an H-3 trainee if the hospital is approved by the American Medical Association or American Osteopathic Association. A hospital submits the petition, for either a residency or internship, if the alien will engage in employment as an extern during his or her medical school training.

4. Petition Interviews

USCIS rarely holds interviews on H-1B visa petitions. When it does, the interview is always with the employer. If you are in the U.S., you may be asked to appear as well. Interviews are requested only if USCIS doubts that the documents or information on Form I-129 and the H Supplement are genuine. Then the petition file is forwarded to the USCIS local office nearest your employer's place of business, and your employer is notified to appear there. The employer may also be asked to bring additional documents at that time. If, after the interview, everything is in order, the petition will be approved. The best way to avoid an interview is to have the employer document the petition well from the beginning.

5. Petition Appeals

If your job qualifications or the ability of the employer to pay your salary have been poorly documented, the petition will probably be denied. Your employer will then get a notice of USCIS's unfavorable decision, containing the reasons for the negative outcome, and an explanation of how to appeal.

The best way to handle an appeal is to try avoiding it altogether. Filing an appeal means arguing to USCIS that its reasoning was wrong. This is difficult to do successfully. If you think you can eliminate the reason your petition failed by improving your paperwork, disregard the appeals process and simply file a new petition, better prepared than the first.

If the petition was denied because your U.S. employer left out necessary documents that have since been located, the new documents should be sent, together with a written request that the case be reopened, to the same USCIS office that issued the denial. This is technically called a *Motion to Reopen*. There is a $110 fee to file this motion. Appeals often take a long time. A Motion to Reopen can be concluded faster than an appeal.

If your U.S. employer does choose to appeal, it must do so within 30 days of the date on the Notice of Denial. The appeal should be filed at the same USCIS office that issued the denial. There is a $110 filing fee. The USCIS will then forward the papers for consideration to the Administrative Appeals Unit in Washington, DC. In six to 18 months or more, your employer will get back a decision by mail. Fewer than 5% of all appeals are successful.

When an appeal has been denied, the next step is to make an appeal through the U.S. judicial system. Your employer may not file an action in court without first going through the appeals process available from USCIS. If the case has reached this stage and you are in the U.S. illegally, we strongly recommend seeking representation from a qualified immigration attorney.

F. Carrying Out Step Two: The Application (Consular Filing)

Anyone with an approved H-1B petition can apply for a visa at a U.S. consulate in his or her home country. You must be physically present to apply there. If you have been or are now working or living illegally in the U.S., you should see Chapter 25 regarding whether you can still get an H-1B visa from a U.S. consulate—or have become inadmissible or subject to the three- or ten-year bars on reentry.

If you are Canadian, your Step Two procedures will be different from those of other applicants. (See Chapter 28 for details.)

1. Benefits and Drawbacks of Consular Filing

A major benefit to consular filing is that only consulates issue visas. When you go through a U.S. filing, you get a status, not a visa. (See Chapter 14, Section B.) H-1B status confers the same right to work as an H-1B worker has, but it does not give you the ability to travel out of the U.S. and get back in again. If you want travel privileges, you will at some time have to go through the extra step of applying for a visa at a U.S. consulate, even though you have already applied for and received H-1B status in the U.S.

Anyone with an approved petition may apply for an H-1B visa at the appropriate consulate. That is not the case with U.S. applications for H-1B status. Only certain people are eligible to apply for H-1B status without leaving the U.S., as discussed in Section G, below. In fact, if you are in the U.S. illegally, consular filing is a must—but see Chapter 25 to make sure none of the grounds of inadmissibility will bar your return. You are not eligible to process a change of status application in the U.S. unless you are presently in status, meaning you have an unexpired visa (not including a visa waiver) or other right to be in the United States.

A further plus to consular filing is that consular offices ordinarily work much more quickly to issue nonimmigrant visas than USCIS offices do to process nonimmigrant statuses. Your waiting time for the paperwork to be finished will likely be much shorter at a U.S. consulate abroad than at most USCIS offices.

A drawback to consular filing is that if your petition is ultimately turned down, not only will you have to wait outside the U.S. until the problem is resolved, but other visas in your passport, such as a visitor's visa, may be canceled. It will then be impossible for you to enter the U.S. in any capacity. Consequently, if your H-1B visa case is not very strong, and freedom of travel is not essential to you, it might be wise to apply in the U.S., make up your mind to remain there for the duration of the H-1B status, and skip trying to get a visa from the consulate.

2. Application Procedures: Consular Filing

The law allows you to apply for an H-1B visa at any U.S. consulate you choose. However, your case will be given the greatest consideration at the consulate in your home country. Applying in some other country creates suspicion in the minds of the consul officers there about your motives for choosing their consulate. Often, when an applicant is having trouble at a home consulate, he will seek a more lenient office in some other country. This practice of consulate shopping is frowned on by officials in the system. Unless you have a very good reason for being elsewhere (such as a temporary job assignment in some other nation), it is smarter to file your visa application in your home country.

3. Overstays and Cancellation of Visas

If you have ever been present in the U.S. unlawfully, your visa will be automatically cancelled and you cannot apply as a third-country national (at a consulate outside your home country). Even if you overstayed your status in the U.S. by

just one day, you must return to your home country and apply for the visa from that consulate. There is an exception. If you were admitted to the U.S. for the duration of your status (indicated by a "D/S" on your I-94 form and most common with student visas) and you remained in the U.S. beyond that time for which your status was conferred, you will be barred from third-country national processing only if an immigration judge or USCIS (or former INS) officer has determined that you were unlawfully present. You may find that your success in applying as a third-country national will depend on your country, the consulate and the relative seriousness of your offense. Being unlawfully present is also a ground of inadmissibility if the period of unlawful presence is six months or more. (See Chapter 25.)

4. Awaiting Petition Approval

You may not file an application for an H-1B visa at a consulate before your petition has been approved. Once this occurs, the USCIS regional service center where the petition was originally submitted will forward a complete copy of your file to the U.S. consulate designated on Form I-129 in Step One. At the same time, a Notice of Action Form I-797 indicating approval will be sent directly to your U.S. employer. When your employer receives this, you should telephone the consulate to see if the petition file has arrived from USCIS. If the file is slow in coming, ask the consulate to consider granting approval of your H-1B visa based only on the Notice of Action. Many U.S. consulates are willing to do so.

Once the petition is approved, check with your local U.S. consulate regarding its application procedures. Many insist on advance appointments. Just getting an appointment can take several weeks, so plan ahead.

5. Application Forms: Consular Filing

When you file at a U.S. consulate abroad, the consulate officials will provide you with certain forms, designated by a "DS" preceding a number. Instructions for completing DS forms and what to do with them once they are filled out will come with the forms. We do not include copies of these forms in this book, because different consulates use different versions.

6. Application Documents: Consular Filing

You must show a valid passport and present one photograph taken according to the photo instructions at http://travel.state.gov/photorequirement.html. If the consulate has not yet received your USCIS file containing the paperwork from the approved petition, you will then need to show the original Notice of Action, Form I-797, which your employer received from USCIS by mail. Most consulates will issue H-1B visas based only on the Notice of Action, although some, particularly in South America and Asia, insist on seeing the complete USCIS file. If the consulate wants to see your file and it is late (more than a month) in arriving, request that the consulate investigate the file's whereabouts. You, too, can write the USCIS regional service center where your petition was processed, asking for the file.

For each accompanying relative, you must present a valid passport and one photograph taken according to the state department's photo instructions. You will also need documents verifying their family relationship to you. You may verify a parent/child relationship by presenting the child's long-form birth certificate. Many countries, including Canada and England, issue both short- and long-form birth certificates. Where both are available, the long form is needed, because it contains the names of the parents, while the short form does not.

If you are accompanied by your spouse, you must prove that you are lawfully married, by showing a civil marriage certificate. Church certificates are generally unacceptable. (There are a few exceptions, depending on the laws of your particular country. Canadians, for example, may use church marriage certificates if the marriage took place in Quebec Province, but not elsewhere. If a civil certificate is available, however, you should always use it.) You may have married in a country where marriages are not customarily recorded. Tribal areas of Africa are an example. In such situations, call the nearest consulate or embassy of your home country for help with getting acceptable proof of marriage.

You will be charged a $100 application fee for the visa. In addition, there may or may not be an issuance fee for the visa. H-1B visas are issued free to the citizens of some countries, but others may be charged fees that can be as high as $100. If the country of your nationality charges fees for visas to U.S. citizens who wish to work there, then the U.S. will charge people of your country a similar fee as well. Whether or not there is a fee is determined by your nationality, not by where you apply. Check with the nearest U.S. consulate to find out if there will be a fee in your case.

7. Application Interviews: Consular Filing

The consulate will normally require an interview before issuing an H-1B visa. During the interview, a consul officer will examine the data you gave in Step One for accuracy, especially regarding facts about your own qualifications.

8. Using Your H-1B Visa

On entering the U.S. with your new H-1B visa, you will be given an I-94 card. It will be stamped with a date showing how long you can stay. Normally, you are permitted to

remain up to the expiration date on your H-1B petition. Each time you exit and reenter the U.S., you will get a new I-94 card authorizing your stay up to the final date indicated on the petition.

SUMMARY EXCLUSION

The law empowers a CBP inspector at the airport or border to summarily (without allowing judicial review) bar entry to someone requesting admission to the U.S. if either of the following are true:
- The inspector thinks you are lying about practically anything connected with entering the U.S., including your purpose in coming, intent to return, and prior immigration history. This includes the use or suspected use of false documents.
- You do not have the proper documentation to support your entry to the U.S. in the category you are requesting.

If the inspector excludes you, you cannot be readmitted to the U.S. for five years, unless USCIS grants a special waiver. For this reason it is extremely important to understand the terms of your requested status, and to not make any misrepresentations. If you are found to be inadmissible, you may ask the CBP inspector to withdraw your application to enter the U.S. in order to prevent having the five-year deportation order on your record. The CBP may allow this in some exceptional cases.

9. Application Appeals: Consular Filing

When a consulate turns down an H-1B visa application, there is no way to make a formal appeal, although you are free to reapply as often as you like. Some consulates, however, will make you wait several months before allowing you to file another application, or limit the number of repeat applications you file. If your visa is denied, you will be told by the consul officer the reasons for the denial. Written statements of decisions are not normally provided in nonimmigrant cases. If a lack of evidence about a particular point is the problem, sometimes simply presenting more evidence on an unclear fact can change the result.

The most likely reasons for having an H-1B visa turned down are because you are found inadmissible or the consulate believes that you are not really qualified for an H-1B visa.

Certain people who have been refused visas reapply at a different consulate, attempting to hide the fact that they were turned down elsewhere. You should know that if your application is denied, the last page in your passport will be stamped "Application Received," with the date and location of the rejecting consulate. This notation shows that some type of prior visa application has failed. It serves as a warning to other consulates that your case merits close inspection. If what we have just told you makes you think it would be a good idea to overcome this problem by obtaining a new, unmarked passport, you should also know that permanent computer records are kept of all visa denials.

G. Carrying Out Step Two: The Application (U.S. Filing)

If you are physically present in the U.S., you may apply for H-1B status without leaving the country on the following conditions:

- you are simultaneously filing paperwork for or have already received an approved I-129 petition
- you entered the U.S. legally
- you have never worked in U.S. illegally, and
- the date on your I-94 card has not passed.

If you were admitted as a visitor without a visa under the Visa Waiver Program (see Chapter 2), you may not carry out Step Two in the U.S.

If you cannot meet the above terms, you may not file for H-1B status in the U.S. It is important to realize, however, that eligibility to apply in the U.S. has nothing to do with overall eligibility for an H-1B visa. Many applicants who are barred from filing in the U.S. but otherwise qualify for H-1B status may still apply successfully for an H-1B visa at U.S. consulates abroad. If you find you are not eligible for U.S. filing, read Section F, above.

1. Benefits and Drawbacks of U.S. Filing

Visas are never given inside the U.S. They are issued exclusively by U.S. consulates abroad. If you file in the U.S. and you are successful, you will get H-1B status but not the visa itself. H-1B status allows you to remain in the U.S. with H-1B privileges until the status expires, but should you leave the country for any reason before that time, you will have to apply for the visa itself at a U.S. consulate before returning to America. Moreover, the fact that your H-1B status has been approved in the U.S. does not guarantee that the consulate will also approve your visa. Some consulates may even regard your previously acquired H-1B status as a negative factor, an indication that you have deliberately tried to avoid the consulate's authority.

There is another problem that comes up only in U.S. filings. It is the issue of what is called *preconceived intent.* To approve a change of status, USCIS must believe that at the time you originally entered the U.S. as a visitor or with some other nonimmigrant visa, you did not intend to apply for a different status. If USCIS thinks you had a preconceived plan to change from the status you arrived with to a different status, it may deny your application. The preconceived intent issue is one less potential hazard you will face if you apply at a U.S. consulate abroad.

On the plus side of U.S. filing is that when problems do arise with your U.S. application, you can stay in the U.S. while they are being corrected, a circumstance most visa applicants prefer. If you run into snags at a U.S. consulate, you will have to remain outside the U.S. until matters are resolved.

2. Application Procedures: U.S. Filing

The general procedure for filing Step Two in the U.S. is to follow Step One as outlined in Section E, above, but to mark box "4b" in Part 2 of Form I-129, indicating that you will complete processing in the U.S. There is no separate application form for filing Step Two in the U.S. If you have an accompanying spouse or children, however, a separate Form I-539 must be filed for them.

When you apply for a change of status, the filing fee for a Step One petition is presently $130. The fee for your family is $140. Checks and money orders are accepted. It is not advisable to send cash. We recommend submitting all papers by certified mail, return receipt requested, and making a copy of everything sent in to keep for your records.

Within a few weeks of mailing in the application, you should get back a written notice of confirmation that the papers are being processed, together with a receipt for the fees. This notice will also tell you your immigration file number and approximately when to expect a decision. If USCIS wants further information before acting on your case, all application papers, forms and documents will be returned together with another form known as an *I-797*. The I-797 tells you what additional pieces of information or documents are expected. You should supply the extra data and mail the whole package back to the USCIS regional service center.

Applications for an H-1B status are normally approved within three to six months. When this happens, you will receive a Notice of Action Form I-797 indicating the dates for which your status is approved. A new I-94 card will be attached to the bottom of the form.

3. Application Forms: U.S. Filing

Copies of all USCIS forms can be found in Appendix II and on the USCIS website.

Form I-129

Follow the directions for Step One in Section E, above, except in Part 2, mark box "4b" instead of box "4a."

Form I-539 (for accompanying relatives only)

Only one application form is needed for an entire family, but if there is more than one accompanying relative, each additional one should be listed on the I-539 supplement.

Part 1. These questions are self-explanatory. "A" numbers are usually given only to people who have previously applied for green cards or who have been in deportation proceedings. If this describes you, you may need a lawyer's help.

Part 2, Question 1. Mark box "b," and write in "H-4."

Question 2. This question is self-explanatory.

Part 3. In most cases, you will mark Item 1 with the date requested in the Step One petition. You will also complete Items 3 and 4, which are self-explanatory.

Part 4, Questions 1–2. These questions are self-explanatory.

Question 3. The different parts to this question are self-explanatory; however, items "a" through "c" ask if an immigrant visa petition or adjustment of status application has ever been filed on your behalf. If you are applying for a green card through a relative, this would refer to Step One, as described in Chapter 5. If you are applying for a green card through employment, this would refer to Step Two as described in Chapter 8. If you have only begun the Labor Certification, the first step of getting a green card through employment, this question should be answered "no."

4. Application Documents: U.S. Filing

Each applicant must submit a copy of his or her I-94 card, the small white card you received on entering the U.S. Remember, if the date stamped on your I-94 card has already passed, you are ineligible for U.S. filing. If you entered the U.S. under the Visa Waiver Program and have a green I-94 card, you are also ineligible for U.S. filing. Canadians who are just visiting are not expected to have I-94 cards. Canadians with any other type of nonimmigrant status should have them.

For each accompanying relative, send in a copy of his or her I-94 card. You will also need documents verifying their family relationship to you. You may prove a parent/child relationship by presenting the child's long-form birth certificate. Many countries, including Canada and England, issue both short- and long-form birth certificates. Where both are available, the long form is needed because it contains the names of the parents while the short form does not.

If you are accompanied by your spouse, you must prove that you are lawfully married by showing a civil marriage certificate. Church certificates are usually unacceptable. (There are a few exceptions, depending on the laws of your particular country. Canadians, for example, may use church mar-

riage certificates if the marriage took place in Quebec Province, but not elsewhere. If a civil certificate is available, however, you should always use it.) You may have married in a country where marriages are not customarily recorded. Tribal areas of Africa are an example. In such situations, call the nearest consulate or embassy of your home country for help with getting acceptable proof of marriage.

5. Application Interviews: U.S. Filing

Interviews on H-1B change of status applications are rarely held. When an interview is required, the USCIS regional service center where you filed will send your paperwork to the local USCIS office nearest the location of your U.S. employer's institution. This office will in turn contact you for an appointment. (If USCIS has questions on the Step One petition rather than the application, your employer will be contacted.) USCIS may ask you to bring additional documents at that time.

If you are called for an interview, the most likely reason is that USCIS either suspects some type of fraud or believes you may be subject to a ground of inadmissibility. Interviews are usually a sign of trouble and can result in considerable delays. It's best to consult an experienced immigration attorney.

6. Application Appeals: U.S. Filing

If your application is denied, you will receive a written decision by mail explaining the reasons for the denial. There is no way of making a formal appeal to USCIS if your application to change status is turned down. If the problem is too little evidence, you may be able to overcome this obstacle by adding more documents and resubmitting the entire application to the same USCIS office you have been dealing with together with a written request that the case be reopened. The written request does not have to be in any special form. This is technically called a *Motion to Reopen.* There is a $110 fee to file this motion.

Remember that you may be denied the right to a U.S. filing without being denied an H-1B visa. When your application is turned down because you are found ineligible for U.S. filing, simply change your application to a consular filing.

Although there is no appeal to USCIS for the denial of an H-1B change of status application, you do have the right to file an appeal in a U.S. district court. It would be difficult to file such an appeal without employing an attorney at considerable expense. Such appeals are usually unsuccessful.

H. Extensions

H-1B visas can be extended for three years at a time, but you may not hold an H-1B visa for longer than a total of six years. Although an extension is usually easier to get than the

H-1B visa itself, it is not automatic. USCIS has the right to reconsider your qualifications based on any changes in the facts or law, and your employer must maintain a valid attestation for your position. As always, however, good cases that are well prepared will be successful.

To extend your H-1B visa, the petition and visa stamp will both have to be updated. As with the original application, you can file either in the U.S. or at a consulate. However, contrary to our advice on the initial visa procedures, extensions are best handled in the U.S. That is because visa stamps, which can only be issued originally at consulates, may be extended in the U.S.

Under legislation enacted in 2000, H-1B visa holders who are awaiting a decision on their green card application can get additional extensions of one year at a time. Either your application for a labor certification or your immigrant visa petition must have been pending 365 days or more.

1. Step One: Extension Petition

Extension procedures are identical with the procedures followed in getting the initial visa, except that less documentation is required. In addition to a copy of the previous employer's LCA (if it is valid for the extension period requested—or a new LCA if the old one is expired), you need only submit your I-94 card, a letter from the employer requesting your visa be extended and stating that you will continue to be employed in a specialty occupation as previously described, and a copy of your U.S. income tax returns for the previous two years, including the W-2 forms. (Be sure the tax returns reflect only H-1B employment before submitting them.)

a. Extension Petition Forms

Copies of all the required USCIS forms can be found in Appendix II and on the USCIS website.

WORKING WHILE YOUR EXTENSION PETITION IS PENDING

If you file your petition for an extension of H-1B status before your authorized stay expires, you are automatically permitted to continue working for up to 240 days while you are waiting for a decision. If, however, your authorized stay expires after you have filed for an extension but before you receive an approval, and more than 240 days go by without getting a decision on your extension petition, your work authorization ceases and you must stop working. You will not be able to continue working until your extension is finally approved.

Form I-129, H Supplement, and Form I-129W

Follow the directions for these forms in Section E, above. The only difference is that you will mark boxes "2b" and "4c" of Part 2.

Form I-539 (for accompanying relatives only)

Follow the directions for this form in Section G2, above, but mark box "1a" of Part 2.

b. Extension Petition Documents

You must submit a copy of your I-94 card. You should also submit the original Notice of Action I-797, a letter from your employer stating that your extension is required and a copy of your employer's LCA.

 Faster processing—at a price. For $1,000 over and above the regular filing fees, USCIS promises "premium processing" of the visa petition, including a decision within 15 days. To use this service, the employer must fill out an additional application (Form I-907) and submit the application to a special USCIS service center address. For complete instructions, see the USCIS website at www.uscis.gov.

2. Step Two: Visa Revalidation

Visas can be revalidated either in the U.S. or at a consulate.

a. Visa Revalidation: U.S. Filing

If you are physically in the U.S. and your H-1B status extension has been approved by USICS, you can have your visa revalidated by mail without leaving the country. The exception is if you're on the U.S. government's list of countries that sponsor terrorism, in which case you won't be allowed to revalidate your visa without leaving the U.S. first. When this book went to print, the listed countries included North Korea, Cuba, Syria, Sudan, Iran, Iraq, and Libya.

To request visa revalidation, you must fill out Form DS-156, and send it to the Department of State. Send it as soon as possible within the 60 days before your allowed stay expires (but don't send it any earlier, or the entire package will be returned to you). With the form you should submit as documents your passport (valid for at least six months), current I-94 card, a recent passport-sized photo stapled or glued to the form (full-face view, on a light background, 2" x 2"), a fee ($100 plus an additional "reciprocity fee" for nationals of certain countries), Notice of Action Form I-797, and a detailed letter from your employer describing your job duties. The fees may be paid by bank draft, corporate check, or money order, payable to the U.S. Department of State. You cannot pay by cash, credit card, or personal check.

Male visa applicants between the ages of 16 and 45, regardless of nationality and regardless of where they apply, must also complete and submit a form DS-157.

You should enclose a self-addressed, stamped envelope, or a completed Federal Express airbill or other courier service. Send the entire package by certified mail to:

If sending by postal service:
U.S. Department of State/Visa
P.O. Box 952099
St. Louis, MO 63195–2099

If sending by courier service:
U.S. Department of State/Visa (Box 2099)
1005 Convention Plaza
St. Louis, MO 63101–1200

The passport will be returned to you with a newly revalidated visa in around 12 weeks.

If your accompanying relatives are physically in the U.S., their H-4 visas may be revalidated by sending in their passports and I-94 cards together with yours. We strongly advise gathering your family together inside U.S. borders so you can take advantage of this simple revalidation procedure.

For more information and forms, see the State Department website at www.travel.state.gov/revals.html.

b. Visa Revalidation: Consular Filing

If you must leave the U.S. after your extension has been approved but before you had time to get your visa revalidated, you must get a new visa stamp issued at a consulate. Reread the procedures in Section F, above. The procedures for consular extensions are identical.

We would like to reemphasize that it is much more convenient to apply for a revalidated visa by mail through the State Department in Washington, DC, than it is to extend your H-1B visa through a consulate. If possible, try to schedule filing your extension application so that you can remain in the U.S. until it is complete.

I. Changing Employers

Once you've got H-1B status, the law offers you some protection if you lose your job. As long as you entered the U.S. lawfully, have never worked without permission, and haven't stayed past the date when your original H-1B status was to expire, you can accept a new job as soon as your new employer files an I-129 petition on your behalf. It's not a perfect system—you'll still have to leave the U.S. to get a new visa after the I-129 is approved, because people whose old visas have become invalid are not allowed to apply to change status within the U.S. But at least you won't be sitting around unemployed and out of status or out of the country while USCIS is making its decision on the new I-129 petition.

FORMS AND DOCUMENTS CHECKLIST

EMPLOYER ATTESTATION

Form
☐ Form ETA-9035.

STEP ONE: PETITION

Form
☐ Form I-129, I-129W, and H Supplement.

Documents
☐ Copy of employer's attestation Form ETA-9035.
☐ Written employment contract or written summary of an oral agreement.
☐ College and university diplomas.
☐ If you do not have a degree, evidence that your combined education and experience is equivalent to a degree.

STEP TWO: APPLICATION

Forms
☐ DS forms (available at U.S. consulates, for consular filing only).
☐ Form I-129 (U.S. filing only).
☐ Form I-129W (U.S. filing only).
☐ Form I-539 (U.S. filing, accompanying relatives only).

Documents
☐ Notice showing approval of the H-1B petition.
☐ Valid passport for you and each accompanying relative.
☐ A copy of I-94 card for you and each accompanying relative (U.S. filing only).
☐ One passport-type photo of you and each accompanying relative (consular filing only).

Temporary Nonagricultural Workers: H-2B Visas

Privileges

- You can work legally in the U.S. for your H-2B sponsor.
- You may travel in and out of the U.S. or remain here continuously until your H-2B visa expires.
- Visas are available for accompanying relatives.

Limitations

- You are restricted to working only for the U.S. employer who acted as your H-2B visa sponsor. If you wish to change jobs, you must get a new H-2B visa.
- H-2B visas can initially be approved for up to only one year. Additional one-year extensions are allowed. After a maximum of three years, you must return home and wait at least 12 months before applying for another H-2B visa, unless you qualify to change to another status.
- Accompanying relatives may stay in the U.S. with you, but they may not work.

The H-2B visa was created to allow people to come to the U.S. temporarily to fill nonagricultural jobs for which U.S. workers are in short supply. This chapter will explain who is eligible for an H-2B visa and how to apply.

A. Who Qualifies for an H-2B Visa?

You qualify for an H-2B visa if you are coming to the U.S. to accept a temporary or seasonal nonagricultural job from a U.S. employer and you have the correct background or skills or natural abilities needed by that employer. H-2B visas are aimed at skilled and unskilled workers, as compared to H-1B visas, which are intended for college-educated workers. To get an H-2B visa, it must be shown that there are no qualified Americans available to take the job you have been offered.

The term "temporary" refers to the employer's need for the duties performed by the position, regardless of whether the underlying position is permanent or temporary. Seasonal laborers, workers on short-term business projects, and those who come to the U.S. as trainers of other workers commonly get H-2B visas. H-2B visas are also frequently used for entertainers who cannot meet the criteria for O or P

visas. H-2B visas enable such entertainers to come to the U.S. for specific bookings. These bookings are considered temporary positions. Other jobs that have met the criteria include athletes, camp counselors, craftpersons, ski instructors, and home attendants for terminally ill patients. A job can be deemed temporary if it is a onetime occurrence, meets a seasonal or peak-load need, or fulfills an intermittent but not regular need of the employer. Although we've just given you some examples of jobs that meet the USCIS's definition of temporary, be aware that most jobs do not.

Finally, you are eligible for an H-2B visa only if you have the intention to return to your home county when the visa expires.

To summarize, there are four requirements for obtaining an H-2B visa:

- You must have a job offer from a U.S. employer to perform work that is either temporary or seasonal.
- You must have the correct background to qualify for the job you have been offered.
- There must be no qualified Americans willing or able to take the job. A Temporary Labor Certification is required.
- You must intend to return home when your visa expires.

TEMPORARY AGRICULTURAL WORKER: H-2A VISAS

Under the 1986 amendments to the U.S. immigration laws, temporary agricultural workers are now treated differently from all other types of temporary workers. Agricultural workers are now issued H-2A visas while all other temporary workers receive H-2B visas.

The rules for getting temporary agricultural worker visas are extremely complex and beyond the scope of this book. The basic requirements are that before a non-U.S. agricultural worker may be granted an H-2A visa, the prospective employer must attempt to find U.S. agricultural workers. The employer must search for U.S. workers not just in the employer's own immediate geographical area, but throughout the entire adjacent region of the country. The employer must do this by undertaking a multi-state recruitment effort.

Moreover, H-2A visas will not, as a practical matter, be issued to foreign workers who are already in the U.S. illegally. Due to the great amount of effort involved in obtaining H-2A visas, they will be attractive only to employers who urgently need to bring in a large crew of foreign laborers at one time to work on a particular harvest. Again, from a practical standpoint, the employer will either have to travel abroad or use the services of a foreign labor contractor to find these crews of temporary foreign workers. H-2A visas are not practical for bringing one temporary agricultural worker at a time to the U.S.

1.   Job Offer From a U.S. Employer

You need a specific job offer from a U.S. employer to get an H-2B visa. The employer will have to act as the petitioner in getting your H-2B visa. Many people are surprised to learn that they require an employment offer before applying for a work visa. The idea behind it is that you are being granted an H-2B visa because your services are essential to a U.S. company. Put another way, the U.S. government is issuing the visa not for your benefit, but to help your U.S. employer.

The petitioner may be a company or an individual. Generally, you cannot act as your own employer. An agent who books your talents for a variety of jobs can be the source of the job offer, if the salary is paid to you directly by the agent and not by the individual places where you perform. This is a common arrangement for entertainers.

The job you are offered can't be just any position. First, it must be one that meets the legal definition of temporary. To be considered temporary, the period of the employer's need for services should be one year or less, absent unusual circumstances.

Second, the employer's need must be either one-time, seasonal, based on a peakload need, or based on an intermittent need. An example of a one-time need would be a specific project, such as building a housing development. Seasonal needs are fairly self-explanatory—workers at a ski resort would be a good example. Peakload needs often occur around tourist or holiday seasons, when employers bring in extra workers that they let go afterwards. Intermittent needs are ones where the employer needs workers occasionally for short periods, but not for long enough to justify hiring someone permanently. Professional minor-league baseball players are a common example of employees who do seasonal work. (Major-league players will usually qualify for O visas. See Chapter 24.)

2.   Correct Background

You must have the correct background and abilities for the job you have been offered. For example, if you are a qualified insurance salesman but are offered a job supervising a catering project, you will not be granted an H-2B visa for that job because you have no background in catering. It is irrelevant that your native intelligence and general knowledge of business may make you quite capable of handling the catering job. Likewise, reliability or willingness to work hard, characteristics difficult to find and much sought after by real-world employers, are not a USCIS consideration. If you lack the required background in the job offered, the petition will fail.

H-2B visas can be issued to unskilled as well as skilled workers. If your job offer happens to be for employment as an unskilled worker, there are by definition no specific background qualifications for you to meet. Under these circumstances, your natural abilities may be a consideration, but you do not need to be concerned about having the correct background.

3.   No Qualified Americans

To obtain an H-2B visa, there must be no qualified Americans available to take the job you have been offered. A Temporary Labor Certification must be successfully completed to prove the unavailability of U.S. workers. This condition may or may not be hard to meet, depending on the type of job. Where the jobs are meant for skilled and unskilled workers rather than professionals, the competition

ENTERTAINMENT INDUSTRY WORKERS: SPECIAL CONSIDERATIONS

Entertainment industry workers, both the performers and the many diversified workers it takes to make a movie or stage a live performance, often need temporary U.S. work visas. H-1B visas are not available to entertainers or athletes. The better-known ones will qualify for O or P visas. (See Chapter 24.) The individual entertainment industry worker who is not well known, not part of a well-known group, or not part of an international production team is limited to an H-2B visa.

In these cases, there is a problem with both the temporariness of the job and the availability of similarly qualified American workers. The definition of temporariness is narrow for entertainment industry jobs, as it is for positions in other occupations. If, for example, a Las Vegas nightclub wants to book an act for only one week, USCIS will still say that the job is *not* temporary because nightclubs are always employing acts to perform there. The conclusion is that the job is not temporary even if the booking is. On the other hand, jobs for performers on tour are considered temporary, as are jobs for workers on motion pictures. That is because tours and motion picture productions always end.

Even if the job is clearly temporary, your U.S. employer must still get a clearance from the DOL acknowledging that no Americans are available to fill the job that is open. When such a clearance is requested, the DOL will in turn contact the appropriate U.S. entertainment industry union to see if the union can find an American worker to fill the position or has some other objection to a non-American taking the job. Since there are many competent U.S. entertainment industry workers looking for employment, getting union approval on an H-2B case may be difficult.

The availability of competing American workers is not a problem in several situations. H-2B visas are readily available to all performing and non-performing members of lesser known troupes coming to the U.S. on tour. We have already explained that in the view of USCIS, the touring factor makes a job temporary. Moreover, U.S. entertainment industry unions are usually reluctant to break up performing units. Therefore, an entire touring group, from performers to technicians and stage hands, can all get H-2B visas.

The offer of employment must be from a U.S. employer. The workers cannot be self-employed nor can they be working in the U.S. for a foreign company. Individual performers, therefore, normally have to get their H-2B visas through a central booking agent. This is acceptable, provided the booking agent acts as the employer in every respect, including being responsible for paying the salary.

Foreign entertainment industry working units, such as film companies, who wish to get H-2B visas will need to do one of two things to supply themselves with the required U.S. employer. They can be sponsored for visas by an established U.S. company which will act as the employer of each individual foreign employee. Alternatively, the foreign group may form its own U.S. corporation and have it act as the employer. U.S. corporations are set up by state governments in the U.S. state where the business will be headquartered. Forming a U.S. corporation is extremely simple and in most states can be accomplished in a matter of days. Information on how to form a U.S. corporation is available from the office of the Secretary of State located in each state capital.

 If you're forming a corporation, the following resources may help you:

- *Incorporator Pro*, the only do-it-yourself incorporation software that assures that you get the official corporation forms used in your state, by Anthony Mancuso (Nolo)
- *Incorporate Your Business: A 50-State Guide to Forming a Corporation*, by Anthony Mancuso (Nolo)
- *How to Form Your Own California Corporation*, by Anthony Mancuso (Nolo)

factor can be a problem. Many employers do go begging, however, for want of either qualified or willing U.S. applicants, especially in businesses requiring unusual skills or with odd working hours or other undesirable features.

4. Intent to Return to Your Home Country

H-2B visas are meant to be temporary. At the time of applying, you must intend to return home when the visa expires. If you have it in mind to take up permanent residence in the U.S., you are legally ineligible for an H-2B visa. The U.S. government knows it is difficult to read minds. Expect to be asked for evidence showing that when you go to America on an H-2B visa, you are leaving behind possessions, property, or family members as incentive for your eventual return.

5. Accompanying Relatives

When you qualify for an H-2B visa, your spouse and unmarried children under age 21 can get H-4 visas by providing proof of their family relationship to you. Like you, your family members will also have to show that they are not inadmissible (see Chapter 25). H-4 visas authorize your accompanying relatives to stay with you in the U.S., but not to work there.

B. Numerical Limits

No more than 66,000 H-2B visa petitions may be approved during the government year (fiscal year), which ends on September 30. This doesn't include accompanying spouses and children. The annual quota has not yet been exceeded and prospects are good that these visas will remain easily available in the future.

Temporary Labor Certification takes about four months. Petition approval usually takes an additional two to four months. After the petition is approved, visas are usually issued within several weeks.

C. Possibilities for a Green Card From H-2B Status

If you have an H-2B visa, you can file to get a green card if you are separately eligible for one, but being in the U.S. on an H-2B visa gives you no advantage in doing so. In fact, it will almost certainly prove to be a drawback. That is because H-2B visas, like most nonimmigrant visas, are intended only for those who plan to return home once their jobs or other activities in the U.S. are completed. However, if you apply for a green card, you are in effect making a statement that you never intend to leave the U.S. Therefore, USCIS will al-

low you to keep H-2B status while pursuing a green card, but only if you can convince USCIS that you did not intend to get a green card when you originally applied for the H-2B visa and that you will return home if you are unable to secure a green card before your H-2B visa expires. Doing this can be difficult. If you do not succeed, your H-2B status can be taken away.

It is also important to understand that even if you argue successfully and keep your H-2B status, the visa and the petition each carry an absolute maximum duration of one year and will probably expire before you get a green card. Once you have made a green card application, you will be absolutely barred from receiving an extension of your H-2B status. Should you, for any reason, lose your H-2B status, it may affect your green card application. (See Chapter 25.)

Another problem comes up if it is your current H-2B sponsoring employer who also wants to sponsor you for a green card. USCIS regulations provide that if you have an approved permanent Labor Certification sponsored by the same employer who petitioned for your H-2B visa, the H-2B visa will automatically be revoked. The only way you can apply for a green card through employment and retain an H-2B visa, even until its expiration date, is to have a different sponsoring employer for the green card than you had for the H-2B visa.

If what you really want is a green card, apply for it directly and disregard H-2B visas. Although the green card is harder to get and may take several years, in the long run you will be happier with the results. Also, relatively few jobs qualify as temporary for H-2B visa purposes and you may actually have a better chance of getting a green card through a given job than an H-2B visa.

D. Applying for an H-2B Visa

Once you have been offered a job, getting an H-2B visa is a three-step process. Often applicants expect their employers to handle the entire procedure for them and indeed, a number of large companies are equipped with experienced staff specialists who will do this for highly desirable employees. Even smaller companies may be prepared to do whatever is necessary, including paying an immigration attorney's fees, in order to attract a key employee. However, you should do as much as possible to help your employer through the paperwork.

1. Overview of Step One: Temporary Labor Certification

Temporary Labor Certification is filed by your U.S. employer. The process may not begin more than 120 days before you are needed. The object of the Temporary Labor Certification is to satisfy the U.S. government that there are no qualified American workers available to take the specific job that has been offered to you, and to determine whether the job is temporary in nature and therefore suitable for an H-2B visa. These things must be proven first to the DOL, and then to USCIS. Therefore, you will initially file Temporary Labor Certification papers with the DOL.

If all goes well, your Temporary Labor Certification will eventually be approved, but be aware that an approved Temporary Labor Certification does not by itself give you any immigration privileges. It is only a prerequisite to Steps Two and Three, submitting your petition and application for an H-2B visa. The judgment of the DOL on the Temporary Labor Certification is only advisory in nature. USCIS has the final word. However, USCIS gives great weight to the DOL's opinion, and if the Temporary Labor Certification is denied, it will be difficult to get an approval from USCIS in Step Two. In any event, without a response from the DOL on the Temporary Labor Certification, whether it be an approval or a denial, you are not eligible to go on with Steps Two and Three.

2. Overview of Step Two: The Petition

Step Two is called the petition. It is filed by your U.S. employer. All H-2B petitions are submitted to USCIS regional service centers in the U.S. The object of the petition is to prove four things:

- That the job is temporary or seasonal in nature. (Remember, the DOL's decision is only advisory.)
- That no qualified Americans are available for the job. (Once again, the DOL's decision is only advisory.)
- That you have the correct background, skills, and abilities to match the job requirements.
- That your U.S. employer has the financial ability to pay your salary.

Like the Temporary Labor Certification, an approved petition does not by itself give you any immigration privileges. It is only a prerequisite to Step Three, submitting your application. The petition must be approved before you are eligible for Step Three.

3. Overview of Step Three: The Application

Step Three is called the application. It is filed by you and your accompanying relatives, if any. The application is your formal request for an H-2B visa or status. (If you are Canadian, your Step Three procedures will be different from those of other applicants. See Chapter 28.) Step Three may be carried out in the U.S. at a USCIS office (if you're already in the U.S. legally) or in your home country at a

U.S. consulate there. If you file Step Three papers in the U.S., you will usually submit them at the same time as those for Step Two. When Step Three is dispatched at a U.S. consulate abroad, you must wait to file the application until the Step Two petition is first approved.

If you are already in the U.S. legally on some other type of nonimmigrant visa, you qualify to apply for an H-2B status at a USCIS office inside the U.S., using a procedure known as change of nonimmigrant status. (If you are admitted as a visitor without a visa under the Visa Waiver Program you may not carry out Step Three in the U.S. Currently there are 28 participating countries in the Visa Waiver Program; see Chapter 2 for a list.)

If a change of status is approved, you will then be treated as if you had entered the country with an H-2B visa and you can keep the status as long as you remain in the U.S. or until it expires, whichever comes first. You will not, however, receive a visa stamp, which you need if your plans include traveling in and out of the U.S. Visa stamps are issued only at U.S. consulates abroad. Therefore, if you change your status and later travel outside the U.S., you will have to go to the U.S. consulate in your home country and repeat Step Three over again, obtaining the H-2B visa stamp in your passport before you can return.

4. Who's Who in Getting Your H-2B Visa

Getting an H-2B visa will be easier if you familiarize yourself with the technical names used for each participant in the process. During Steps One and Two, the Temporary Labor Certification and the petition, you are known as the *beneficiary* or the *employee* and your U.S. employer is known as the *petitioner* or the *employer*. In Step Three, the application, you are referred to as *applicant*, but your employer remains the petitioner or employer. If you are bringing your spouse and children with you as accompanying relatives, each of them is known as *applicant* as well.

5. Tips on Handling the Paperwork

There are two types of paperwork you must submit to get an H-2B visa. The first consists of official government forms completed by you or your U.S. employer. The second is copies of personal documents such as academic credentials and evidence of previous job experience.

It is vital that forms are properly filled out and all necessary documents are supplied. You or your U.S. employer may resent the intrusion into your privacy and the sizable effort it takes to prepare immigration applications, but you should realize the process is an impersonal matter to immigration officials. Your getting a visa is more important to you than it is to the U.S. government. There is no shortage of applicants.

The documents you or your U.S. employer supply to USCIS or the consulate do not have to be originals. Photocopies of all documents are acceptable as long as you have the originals in your possession and are willing to produce them upon request. But add the following language to the photocopy, with your signature and the date:

> *Copies of documents submitted are exact photocopies of unaltered original documents and I understand that I may be required to submit original documents to an immigration or consular official at a later date.*
> *Signature _____*
> *Typed or Printed Name _____*
> *Date_____*

Documents will be accepted if they are in either English, or, with papers filed at U.S. consulates abroad, the language of the country where the documents are being filed (except in Japan, where all documents must be translated into English). If the documents are not in an acceptable language as just explained, they must be accompanied by a full, word for word, written English translation. Any capable person may act as translator. It is not necessary to hire a professional. At the end of each translation, the following statement must appear:

> *I hereby certify that I translated this document from [language] to English. This translation is accurate and complete. I further certify that I am fully competent to translate from [language] to English.*
> *Signature _____*
> *Typed or Printed Name _____*
> *Date_____*

The translator should sign this statement but it does not have to be witnessed or notarized.

Later in this chapter we describe the forms and documents needed to get your H-2B visa. A summary checklist of forms and documents appears at the end of this chapter.

E. Carrying Out Step One: Temporary Labor Certification

This section includes the information you need to get a Temporary Labor Certification.

1. General Procedures

Temporary Labor Certifications, consisting both of forms and documents, are filed in the U.S. at the local state employment agency office nearest the employer's place of business. We emphasize that this is an office of the state

government, not the federal DOL. State government employment agencies assist the DOL in the Temporary Labor Certification process by monitoring employers' efforts to locate American workers. However, a regional office of the DOL, where the file is sent after the state office finishes its work, makes the final decision on your Temporary Labor Certification. Unlike Labor Certifications for green cards, the DOL's decision is only advisory. In Step Two, the petition, USCIS does not have to accept the DOL's findings. However, USCIS weighs the DOL's opinion heavily and it will be difficult to get an H-2B visa without an approved Temporary Labor Certification.

States differ about the exact place and procedures for filing Temporary Labor Certifications. Some designate a single office to accept applications for the entire state while others use a system of several regional offices around the state. A call to the nearest office of the state employment agency in your employer's area of the country will tell you where and how to file Step One papers.

There is no filing fee for a Temporary Labor Certification. If possible, it is better for the employer to file in person so you can be sure that the arrival of the papers is recorded. When filing the papers in person, ask for a dated written receipt. The receipt should be kept in a safe place together with a complete copy of everything submitted. Then your employer can prove when your Temporary Labor Certification was filed and help to locate the papers should they get lost or delayed in processing. When filing by mail, send the papers by certified mail, return receipt requested, and again keep a complete copy for your records.

Because there is no uniformity in operating methods among the various state employment agencies, the length of time it takes to get a Temporary Labor Certification approved varies greatly from one state to another; however, all offices are supposed to give priority to Temporary Labor Certification applications. The application cannot be filed more than 120 days before the worker is needed, and it is likely to take about four months to get approval. In some states, it may take longer.

If you have good reason, most DOL offices will expedite the processing of a Temporary Labor Certification if you ask. Your employer must simply include a letter requesting expedited processing and explain why your presence on the job is needed immediately.

2. Advertising Procedures

The Temporary Labor Certification is similar to the Labor Certification process discussed in Chapter 8. In general, the procedure consists of the U.S. employer attempting to recruit U.S. workers for the position that has been offered to a foreign national. It is crucial to the success of the H-2B application for the employer to fail at this attempt. To demonstrate that American workers are in fact unavailable, the job must be publicly advertised. The employer must then wait to see if any qualified U.S. candidates come forward. The DOL has established a specific procedure for this advertising.

The procedure begins when the employer files Form ETA-750 with the state labor department. Once this form is submitted, the state labor department will send back a letter to the employer acknowledging receipt of the form and assigning an identification number known as a job order number to the case. The letter will also give instructions on how to advertise.

The employer must carry out the advertising procedures exactly as required. Three separate types of advertisements are necessary. First, the state labor department will enter a description of the position, identified by the job order number, in its statewide computer bank. For ten days, anyone throughout the state who contacts the labor department will have an opportunity to apply for the job.

Second, the petitioning employer must prepare a written advertisement for the classified section of a newspaper or professional journal. The ad must state the job title, salary, and working hours of the position as well as describe the duties and qualifications. It is important that the job descriptions in the ad match the one that appears in the ETA-750 form. The employer cannot reject an American job applicant for lacking any qualification not listed in both the ad and the form.

The advertisement should not give the name or address of the employer's company. Instead, it must contain the address of the state labor department and the job order number. Prospective U.S. job candidates will be asked to contact the state labor department office and make reference to this number. By having all job candidates contact them directly, the labor department is able to monitor the results of the ad placed by the employer.

Normally, the employer should place the advertisement in the classified section of a standard newspaper circulated in the city where the employer's place of business is located. If the city has only one daily newspaper, the ad should be placed there. If there are two or more daily newspapers in the area, as is common in larger cities, the employer may choose whichever one he prefers. The same ad must be run for three consecutive days.

Sometimes the letter from the state labor department will suggest that the employer advertise in a professional journal, trade journal, or national publication, instead of a local newspaper. The employer is not required to follow this suggestion, but unless there is a good business reason for not doing so, it is best to comply. When the ad is placed in a national newspaper or journal, it need appear only once instead of three times.

The third type of advertising required for Labor Certification is an official job notice posted at the employer's place of business. The notice must contain the identical language used in the newspaper or journal advertisement, but instead of giving the job order number, prospective candidates should be asked to contact a specific person in the company. The notice must be posted for at least ten business days on an employee bulletin board or other suitable location on the company premises.

If the job being offered is one represented by a labor union or collective bargaining group, that union or group must also be sent a notice that a Labor Certification application has been filed. This gives the union an opportunity to refer union members for the job.

3. Handling Job Applications

If anyone applies for the job by responding to the advertisement or state labor department listing, the labor department will collect resumes from the candidates and forward them to the employer. The employer must then review the resumes and be prepared to state in writing why each candidate does not meet the *minimum* qualifications for the job as described in the advertisement and on Form ETA-750. The same must be done with candidates who respond directly to the employer from the posting of the in-house notice. Even if a single requested qualification is missing from the resume, that is enough reason for the employer to reject an American job candidate in favor of you, if he wishes to do so. However, when some acceptable resumes do turn up, the employer must interview those people.

After the interview, if the employer is unsatisfied and still wishes to employ you, he should again put in writing why the U.S. job candidates were not suitable. Once an interview has been held, the employer is no longer limited to rejecting candidates only because they do not meet the job description as stated in the ad or the ETA-750 form. Poor work habits, lack of job stability, questionable character, and similar business considerations, if legitimate, are also satisfactory reasons. In addition, it sometimes comes out in an interview that the prospective worker's qualifications are not in fact what they appeared to be on the resume. This provides still another reason to turn down the U.S. candidate.

The DOL does not consider the fact that you may be more qualified than any other candidate to be a valid reason for rejecting a U.S. worker. Being the most qualified is not enough. You must be the *only* one who is qualified. The employer cannot be forced to hire an American who happens to apply for the job as a result of the required advertising, but if a qualified American does turn up and your prospective employer cannot find a solid business reason to reject him or her, the Temporary Labor Certification application filed on your behalf will fail.

If no suitable American job candidates present themselves, the Temporary Labor Certification will be approved. Then the stamped certification will be sent to your U.S. employer. Only the employer receives communications from the DOL because, technically, it is the company that is seeking Temporary Labor Certification in order to fill a staff need.

4. Temporary Labor Certification Form

A copy of this form can be found in Appendix II.

Form ETA-750, Part A Only

Form ETA-750, Part A, is the only form used in Step One, Temporary Labor Certification. It must be submitted in triplicate. Each of the three forms must be a signed original. Photocopies are not acceptable.

All questions on the ETA-750 should be answered truthfully, as on all government forms. Giving false information on a government form is a criminal offense and could lead to your deportation from the U.S.

The ETA-750 form is divided into Parts A and B. For a Temporary Labor Certification, use only Part A, which asks for a description of the job you are being offered. Be sure there are no qualifications listed in Part A that you, as the potential employee, cannot meet.

One of the questions asked in Part A is the number of years of work experience the job requires. You will eventually be asked to show that you have at least that much experience. When you count up how many years of relevant experience you have to offer, you may not include experience gained from working for your petitioning employer. You must be prepared to prove that you met the minimum experience and education requirements as stated in Part A of the ETA-750 before you started working for the petitioner, even if you have been employed there for some time.

You will remember that a purpose of Step One is to demonstrate to the DOL's satisfaction that there are no qualified Americans available for the job in question. The DOL does not normally evaluate your job fitness during Step One. This judgment is made by USCIS in Step Two. Nonetheless, the DOL will sometimes send your ETA-750 form back to your employer and ask for proof of your qualifications. This is not a proper request for the DOL to make. However, when the demands are not too difficult to meet, giving the DOL what it asks for is the easiest and quickest way to keep your case moving.

Although it is not mandatory to verify the employee's qualifications in Step One, don't lose sight of the fact that this will eventually have to be done in Step Two. In Step Two, it must be proven to USCIS that you can meet every qualification requested by the employer in Part A of Form ETA-750. A Temporary Labor Certification will be approved if no qualified U.S. job candidates come forward, but that doesn't guarantee you will eventually get an H-2B visa. If you can't meet the job qualifications either, the approved Temporary Labor Certification will turn out to be wasted effort. We also reemphasize that you must not only meet the job qualification, you must be able to prove you meet them. Section E5, below explains how to do this.

Now we will look at the ETA-750 form question by question. Most of the questions are straightforward.

Top of the Form. Write in red ink on the top "Temporary Labor Certification." This should assist in expediting your application.

Questions 1–11. These questions are self-explanatory.

Question 12. The DOL is concerned that a petitioning employer may offer a very low salary to discourage Americans from applying for the job. To ensure that such a tactic can't work, the DOL has salary guidelines that must be followed. The salary offer listed in Question 12 can be no more than 5% below the average salary paid to workers in the same type of job in the same geographical area where the employer's company is located. This average salary is called the prevailing wage. To find out the prevailing wage for your job, the local state employment agency office makes a wage survey for similar jobs in the area. Most state employment offices have on file wage surveys for various occupations and, upon request, will tell the employer the prevailing wage in response to a faxed request. Before beginning advertising or submitting the ETA-750 form, the employer may wish to call and ask for the amount of the prevailing wage so that he can judge if the salary being offered is high enough to meet Temporary Labor Certification requirements. If the salary listed in Question 12 is more than 5% below the prevailing wage, the Temporary Labor Certification will be turned down.

Question 13. Question 13 asks the employer to describe the job being offered. This question should be answered with as much detail as possible. Daily duties, typical projects, supervisory responsibilities, the kinds and use of any machinery or equipment, foreign language skills needed, and so forth should all be thoroughly explained. If there are special job conditions, such as the requirement to live in, or unusual physical demands, these too must be described. The employer should not fail to put down *any* skill or activity the job requires, no matter how obvious it may seem. The ability to reject U.S. workers will depend completely on how well the U.S. job candidates match up to the job description in Question 13. The more detailed the job description, the more possible reasons for rejecting American candidates.

While the employer should do his best to describe the position and its demands fully, he should not invent aspects of the job that don't exist or seem excessive for the industry. For example, suppose the job opening is for a trainer of bakery managers, but in the job description the employer states that all applicants must have a background in nuclear science. This sort of illogical requirement makes it clear to the state employment agency reviewer that the job description is not legitimate, but deliberately made up to discourage U.S. workers from applying.

When the job description lacks real-world credibility, the ETA-750 will be sent back and the employer will be asked to justify the more unusual requirements. If the state employment agency reviewer cannot be convinced that the job description reflects the employer's true needs, the Temporary Labor Certification will be denied.

The employer should also guard against asking for such a variety of requirements that the job seems more appropriate for two separate workers instead of one. For example, if the job is that of summer resort restaurant manager and the job description requires the applicant not only to manage the restaurant but to do the cooking as well, the reviewer might say the business really needs two people, a cook and a restaurant manager. Once again, this will result in the Temporary Labor Certification being denied.

Question 14. Question 14 asks for the minimum experience and education the job requires. The answer to this question should describe the demands of the job, not the personal qualifications of the potential H-2B visa recipient. For example, you may have a degree from a technical school representing two years of automotive mechanic's training, but if the position you have been offered is for a live-in housekeeper for the summer, being an automotive mechanic usually has nothing to do with being a housekeeper and therefore should not be mentioned in the answer to this question. Remember, it is the job offer that is being described, not you.

As with salary levels, the DOL also has specific guidelines on what the minimum number of years of experience and education should be for a certain kind of job. If your employer calls and asks, the local state employment agency office can tell him exactly the number of years of education and experience they consider a normal minimum for the particular job you have been offered. This number comes from looking up the job in a book called the *Dictionary of*

Occupational Titles (DOT), and it is available at government bookstores and most public libraries. However, the DOL is moving to using a Web-based database with the same information, called O*NET. See http://online.onetcenter.org.

The number of years listed for each job in the DOT controls what you may put down in answer to Question 14. You and your employer need not concern yourselves with the DOT other than to know it exists. Keep in mind that the number of years of experience and education it lists for each job is the total allowable years of both experience and education.

U.S. company personnel staff or others reading this book who may be working with Labor Certifications on a regular basis may find it useful to familiarize themselves with the DOT and its Specific Vocational Preparation classifications, which dictate the number of years of background presumed necessary for each job. The employer may divide up the years in any way he or she sees fit, as long as he or she doesn't go over the total. For example, if the DOT says the job you have been offered warrants a minimum of two years of background, your employer has a choice of requiring two years of education, two years of experience, or one of each. The employer may even divide it by months, requiring, say, six months of training or education and 18 months of experience.

Suppose the employer genuinely feels the company needs a person with more total years of education and experience than the DOT indicates. Then a letter from the employer should be submitted with the ETA-750 forms, giving the reason additional years of background are justified. The DOL will normally respect the employer's judgment if it seems reasonable. In Question 14, if the employer puts down a higher number of years than the DOT allows, it must be supported with an explanatory letter, or the Temporary Labor Certification will be denied. This letter does not have to be in any special form. A simple explanation in your employer's own words will do.

When a certain number of years appears in the box marked "experience," it is understood that this means experience in the same occupation as the job being offered. If the experience is in a different but relevant field, it should go in the box marked "related occupations."

Once again, if, in Question 14, the employer asks for a background of specific education or experience, make sure you yourself can meet these requirements. In Step Two, the petition, you will be asked to prove that you can fulfill the job criteria established in the ETA-750. If you cannot do so, you will not get an H-2B visa.

Question 15. Question 15 asks the employer to state essential requirements for the job (over and above years of formal education or work experience). Any special knowledge or skills detailed in Question 13, such as foreign language ability, familiarity with certain types of machinery, or special physical capabilities (the strength to do heavy lifting, for example) should be repeated here. When you reach Step Two, you will have to prove in some way that you can perform the skills listed in Question 15, but you will not have to show an exact number of years of education or on-the-job experience as you will for the qualifications listed in Question 14.

Questions 16 and 17. These questions are self-explanatory.

Questions 18 and 19. These questions ask for the exact dates you wish to be able to work in the U.S. Keep in mind that the H-2B status cannot be approved for more than 12 months at a time and therefore you should not request more than 12 months. The petition will be approved only through the dates requested on the Temporary Labor Certification. Remember, the dates you ask for are the dates you will get, so choose a starting date three or four months after you begin filing your papers to allow some lead time for visa processing.

Question 20. This question is self-explanatory.

Question 21. Question 21 asks your employer to describe past attempts to hire U.S. workers for the position being offered to you. At this stage, it is not essential that such efforts have already been made. If the U.S. employer has not yet tried to hire a worker for the job, he or she should write the following statement for Question 21:

"Advertisements and job posting to begin upon receipt of job order number."

If, however, your employer has already made some attempt to hire a U.S. worker, the nature of these efforts (newspaper ads, use of employment agencies, etc.) and the results should be described here. Of course, we assume any prior efforts to fill the job have failed, or the employer would not be trying to hire you.

5. Temporary Labor Certification Documents

Your U.S. employer must submit to the state employment agency proof and written results of the mandatory advertising procedure. A key document is the employer's written explanation of why each American who applied for the job was unsatisfactory. By far the most acceptable reason for turning down an applicant is failure to meet the requirements as stated on the Form ETA-750 and in the newspaper or journal advertisement, but other reasons are also considered adequate, as long as they reflect valid business concerns.

The pages from the publications where the advertisement appeared must be torn out and submitted. If the ad ran in a newspaper for three days, three pages must be presented, one for each day, even though the exact same ad was published on all three days. Photocopies of the ad are not acceptable. Your employer must obtain a copy of every publication in which the ad appeared and actually tear out the entire page so the date shows.

The submission of all these documents normally completes the Temporary Labor Certification procedure. Once your employer has sent them in, the forms and documents are eventually forwarded from the state employment agency to the regional certifying office of the DOL for a decision. If the paperwork has been carefully prepared, the Temporary Labor Certification should be approved on the first try. Sometimes, papers are returned to the employer with a request for additional information or instructions to remedy a defect in the advertising. After mistakes and deficiencies have been corrected, the papers should be returned to the DOL.

When your employer has finally gotten the paperwork the way the DOL wants it, the employer will get back a decision either granting or denying the Temporary Labor Certification.

FOREIGN LANGUAGE REQUIREMENTS

According to the DOL, foreign language capability is not a valid requirement for most jobs, except perhaps the occupations of foreign language teacher or translator. By foreign language capability we mean the ability to speak English plus at least one other language. Many Temporary Labor Certification job descriptions contain a foreign language requirement because petitioning employers know it is a good way to decrease the chances that qualified Americans will apply for the job.

If your employer wants a foreign language capability in the job description, the employer must prove this need is real by preparing and submitting a signed statement explaining the business reasons why. The statement does not have to be in any particular form but it should answer obvious questions like: What is it about the employer's business that makes knowledge of a foreign language necessary? Why does this position require knowledge of a foreign language if someone else in the company already speaks that language? Why couldn't the company simply hire a translator as a separate employee or use a translator on a part-time basis when the need arises? The employer must show that the need for the employee to speak a foreign language is very great and that no alternative arrangement will be an adequate substitute.

A good example of how to approach this problem is an employer who owns a restaurant in a resort and is trying to justify a foreign language requirement for a seasonal waiter. Here, the employer can explain that a large percentage of the restaurant's customers speak the particular foreign language in question and expect to be addressed in that language when they come in to eat. If the restaurant's clientele demand it, it is reasonable that all employees of this restaurant who have contact with the public be able to speak the language of the customers.

The DOL doesn't like foreign language requirements, because it is well aware that most people who apply for Temporary Labor Certifications have the ability to speak a language other than English. The DOL regards this as a poor excuse to keep a U.S. worker from taking a job. Therefore, it is usually best not to include a language requirement, especially if the Temporary Labor Certification is likely to be approved anyway. If, however, the occupation being certified is relatively unskilled, as in the case of the seasonal waiter, a language requirement supported by strong documents showing a real business need may mean the difference between success and failure of the Temporary Labor Certification.

6. Temporary Labor Certification Appeals

If the DOL thinks the Temporary Labor Certification is unsatisfactory, it will be denied and the employer will receive a written decision explaining the reasons. The most common reason for denial is that the job is not temporary in nature. No appeal is available. The Temporary Labor Certification, however, is considered to be only advisory and therefore an H-2B visa petition may be filed with USCIS even though the Temporary Labor Certification is denied. You will have to convince USCIS, however, that the DOL was wrong.

F. Carrying Out Step Two: The Petition

This section includes the information you need to complete the petition.

1. General Procedures

The U.S. employer submits the petition, consisting of Form I-129 and documents, by mail, in duplicate, to the USCIS regional service center having jurisdiction over your intended employer's place of business. USCIS regional service centers are not the same as USCIS local offices—for one thing, you cannot visit service centers in person. There are four USCIS regional service centers spread across the U.S. Appendix I contains a list of all USCIS regional service centers with their addresses, but you should check the USCIS website at www.uscis.gov for the correct P.O. box number.

The filing fee for each petition, if no change of status is being requested, is currently $130. Checks or money orders are accepted. It is not advisable to send cash. We recommend submitting all papers by certified mail, return receipt requested, and making a copy of everything sent in to keep in your records.

Within a few weeks after mailing in the petition, your employer should get back a written confirmation that the papers are being processed, together with a receipt for the fees. This notice will also give your immigration file number and tell approximately when you should expect to have a decision. If USCIS wants further information before acting on your case, all petition papers, forms, and documents will be returned to your employer with another form known as an I-797. The I-797 tells your employer what additional pieces of information or documents are expected. Your employer should supply the extra data and mail the whole package back to the regional service center, with the I-797 on top.

H-2B petitions are normally approved within two to four months. When this happens, a Notice of Action Form I-797 will be sent to your employer showing the petition was approved. If you plan to execute Step Two at a U.S. consulate abroad, USCIS will also notify the consulate of your choice, sending a complete copy of your file. Only the employer receives communications from USCIS about the petition because technically it is the employer who is seeking the visa on your behalf.

 Faster processing—at a price. For $1,000 over and above the regular filing fees, USCIS promises "Premium Processing" of the visa petition, including a decision within 15 days. To use this service, the employer must fill out an additional application (Form I-907) and submit the application to a special USCIS Service Center address. For complete instructions, see the USCIS website at www.uscis.gov.

2. Petition Forms

Copies of all the required USCIS forms can be found in Appendix II and on the USCIS website.

Form I-129 and H Supplement

The basic form for Step Two, the petition, is Form I-129 and H Supplement. The I-129 form is used for many different nonimmigrant visas. In addition to the basic part of the form that applies to all types of visas, it comes with several supplements for each specific nonimmigrant category. Simply use the supplement that applies to you. Your employer must file the petition form in duplicate. Send in two signed originals. Copies are not acceptable.

Your employer may choose to list more than one foreign employee on a single I-129 petition. This is done if the employer has more than one opening to be filled for the same type of job. If more than one employee is to be included, Supplement-1, which is also part of Form I-129, should be completed for each additional employee.

Most of the questions on the I-129 form are straightforward. If a question does not apply to you, answer it with "None" or "N/A."

Part 1. These questions concern the employer only and are self-explanatory.

Part 2, Question 1. Enter "H-2B."

Questions 2–3. These questions are self-explanatory.

Question 4. This question asks you to indicate what action is requested from USCIS. Normally you will mark box "a," which tells USCIS to notify a U.S. consulate abroad of the petition approval so that you may apply for a visa there. If you will be filing your Step Three application in the U.S., mark box "b." If this petition is being filed as an extension, mark box "c."

Question 5. This question is self-explanatory.

Part 3. These questions are self-explanatory. If you previously held a U.S. work permit and therefore have a U.S. Social Security number, put down that number where asked. If you have a Social Security number that is not valid for employment, put down that number followed by "not valid for employment." If you have never had a Social Security number, put down "None." If you've ever used a false Social Security card, see an attorney—this may make you inadmissible.

Alien Registration Numbers, which all begin with the letter "A," are given only to people who have applied for green cards, received political asylum or have been in deportation proceedings. If you have an "A" number, consult an attorney. If you do not have an "A" number, write down "None."

If your present authorized stay has expired, you must disclose that where asked. This makes you ineligible to file Step Three inside the U.S. You may still apply for a visa at a U.S. consulate, but the fact that you remained in the U.S. illegally may affect your ability to get an H-2B visa at a U.S. consulate. You are required to have the intention to return to your home country when your status expires. If you have already lived in the U.S. illegally for a substantial period of time, it will be difficult to convince a consulate that you won't do it again. (See Chapter 25 for more detail on problems which arise from having been out of status in the U.S.)

Part 4. These questions are self-explanatory. If you have a green card petition or application in process it is less likely that your H-2B visa will be approved. If your H-2B employer is sponsoring you for a green card, you will not qualify for the H-2B visa.

Part 5. These questions are self-explanatory. The dates of intended employment should coincide with the dates shown on the Temporary Labor Certification. An H-2B petition cannot be approved beyond its expiration date.

H Supplement, Top of Form. These questions are self-explanatory.

H Supplement, Section 1. Do not complete this section.

H Supplement, Section 2. This question asks if the employment is seasonal or temporary, and asks for your employer to explain why the need is temporary. Temporary employment is defined in Section A2a, above.

H Supplement, Sections 3-4. These do not apply to H-2B petitions and should be left blank.

3. Petition Documents

You must provide several documents with the petition.

a. Temporary Labor Certification

You must submit your approved Temporary Labor Certification. This is actually the ETA-750 form, Part A, which has been returned to your employer with a red and blue approval stamp. You must submit the original approved form. A copy is not acceptable. If the Temporary Labor Certification was denied, the ETA-750 will be sent back without an approval stamp together with a letter from the DOL stating that Temporary Labor Certification cannot be issued.

Whether the Temporary Labor Certification was approved or denied, all of the documentation submitted to the labor department with the ETA-750 will be returned to your employer. The approved Temporary Labor Certification or letter of denial together with all documentation submitted in Step One must be submitted again in Step Two.

b. Employer's Statement of Need

Your employer must provide a detailed explanation of why the job is temporary, and if the need is seasonal or intermittent, whether the need is expected to occur again. If the job is temporary because it is tied into a specific project of the employer and will terminate upon completion of the project, a copy of the employer's contract for that project should be attached to his affidavit.

c. Proof of Your Job Qualifications

Documents to prove your own qualifications for the job also go with the petition. There must be evidence that you have the minimum education and experience called for in the advertisements and job description on Form ETA-750. If special requirements were written in Question 15 of Part A of the form, you must prove you have those skills or abilities as well.

Evidence of job experience should include letters or notarized affidavits from previous employers. These do not have to be in any special form but simply in your former employer's own words. The letters should clearly indicate what your position was with the company, your specific job duties, and the length of time you were employed. If letters from previous employers are unavailable, you may be able to prove your work experience with your personal tax returns or by affidavits from former coworkers. Proof of special knowledge or skills can be supplied through notarized affidavits, either from you or someone else who can swear you have the special ability (such as skill to use a particular machine or speak a foreign language) required. These, too, need not be in any special form.

If your employer asked for a specific type or amount of education, diplomas and transcripts from schools attended must be shown to verify your education. USCIS insists on both a diploma and a transcript from each school where you graduated. (Keep in mind that if you have a college-level diploma in a major field of study related to the type of job you have been offered, you probably qualify for an H-1B visa. H-1B visas are more desirable in many ways than H-2B visas, so if you think you may qualify, read Chapter 16.) If you attended a school but did not graduate, the transcript is required. If you were educated outside the U.S., USCIS may request a credential evaluation.

d. Special Documents for Entertainment Industry Workers

Frequently, entertainers will tour the U.S. instead of remaining in one location. If that is the case with your job, your employer must provide a copy of the touring route schedule, including cities and dates of performance.

4. Petition Interviews

USCIS rarely holds interviews on H-2B visa petitions but when they do, the interview is always with the employer. If you are in the U.S., you may be asked to appear as well. Interviews are requested only if USCIS doubts that the documents or information on Form I-129 or H Supplement are genuine. Then the petition file is forwarded to the USCIS local office nearest your employer's place of business and your employer is notified to appear there. The employer may also be asked to bring additional documents at that time. If, after the interview, everything seems in order, the petition will be approved. The best way to avoid an interview is to have the employer document the petition well, from the beginning.

5. Petition Appeals

When your job qualifications, the temporariness of the position or the ability of the employer to pay your salary have been poorly documented, the petition will probably be denied. Your employer will get a notice of USCIS's unfavorable decision, with the reasons for the negative outcome and an explanation of how to appeal.

The best way to handle an appeal is to try avoiding it altogether. Filing an appeal means arguing to USCIS that its reasoning was wrong. This is difficult to do successfully. If you think you can eliminate the reason why your petition failed by improving your paperwork, it makes sense to disregard the appeals process and simply file a new petition, being careful to see that it is better prepared than the first.

If the petition was denied because your U.S. employer left out necessary documents that have since been located, the new documents should be sent, together with a written request that the case be reopened, to the same USCIS office that issued the denial. This is technically called a *Motion to Reopen*. There is a $110 fee to file this motion. Appeals often take a long time. A Motion to Reopen can be concluded faster than an appeal.

If your U.S. employer does choose to appeal, it must be done within 30 days of the date on the Notice of Denial. The appeal should be filed at the same USCIS office that issued the denial. There is a $110 filing fee. USCIS will then forward the papers for consideration to the Administrative Appeals Unit in Washington, DC. In six months or more, your employer will get back a decision by mail. Few appeals are successful.

When an appeal to USCIS has been denied, the next step is to make an appeal through the U.S. judicial system. Your employer may not file an action in court without first going through the appeals process available from USCIS. If the case has reached this stage and you are illegally present in the U.S., seek representation from a qualified immigration attorney.

G. Carrying out Step Three: The Application (Consular Filing)

Anyone with an approved H-2B petition can apply for a visa at a U.S. consulate in his or her home country. You must be physically present to apply there. If you have been or are now working or living illegally in the U.S., you may have problems or be ineligible to get an H-2B visa from a U.S. consulate, even if you otherwise qualify. (See Chapter 25.)

1. Benefits and Drawbacks of Consular Filing

The biggest benefit to consular filing is that only consulates issue visas. When you go through a U.S. filing you get a status, not a visa. (See Chapter 14, Section B.) An H-2B status approval by USCIS confers the same right to work as you receive after entering the U.S. on an H-2B visa, but it does not give you the ability to travel out of the U.S. and get back in again. Therefore, if you want travel privileges, you will at some time have to go through the extra step of applying for a visa at a U.S. consulate, even though you have already applied for and received H-2B status in the U.S.

Moreover, anyone with an approved petition may apply for an H-2B visa at the appropriate consulate. That is not the case with U.S. applications for H-2B status. You are not eligible to process a change of status application in the U.S. unless your presence and activities in the U.S. have always been legal. If you are in the U.S. illegally, consular filing may be your only option. However, if you have been out of status over six or 12 months and depart the U.S. there will be a three- or ten-year wait, respectively, before you can be readmitted to the U.S. (See Chapter 25.)

A drawback to consular filing comes from the fact that you must be physically present in the country where the consulate is located to file there. If your petition is ultimately turned down because of an unexpected problem, not only will you have to wait outside the U.S. until the problem is resolved, but other visas in your passport, such as a visitor's visa, may be canceled. It will then be impossible for you to enter the U.S. in any capacity. Consequently, if your H-2B visa case is not very strong and freedom of travel is not essential to you, it might be wise to apply in the U.S., make up your mind to remain there for the duration of the H-2B status, and skip trying to get a visa from the consulate.

2. Application Procedures: Consular Filing

Technically, the law allows you to apply for an H-2B visa at any U.S. consulate you choose. However, if you have ever overstayed your visa status by even one day, you have to apply in your home country. From a practical standpoint, your case will be given the greatest consideration at the consulate in your home country. Applying in some other country creates suspicion in the minds of the consular officers there about your motives for choosing their consulate. Often, when an applicant is having trouble at a home consulate, he will seek a more lenient office in some other country. This practice of consulate shopping is frowned on. Unless you have a very good reason for being elsewhere (such as a temporary job assignment in some other nation),

ACADEMIC CREDENTIAL EVALUATIONS

Not every country in the world operates on the same academic degree and grade level systems found in the U.S. If you were educated in some other country, USCIS may ask for an academic credential evaluation from an approved consulting service to determine the American equivalent of your educational level.

Evaluations from accredited credential evaluation services are not binding on USCIS. When the results are favorable, that is, when they show you have the equivalent of the educational level required by your U.S. employer, credential evaluations strengthen your case.

We recommend obtaining a credential evaluation in every case where non-U.S. education is a factor. We also advise getting the evaluation before USCIS asks for it. If the evaluation is favorable, include it with your petition. If the evaluation is unfavorable, and your credentials prove to be less than the equivalent of what your employer has asked for, do not submit the results unless USCIS insists you do so. Consider discussing this with your employer, who may decide to ask for less education when he fills out Form ETA-750, Part A. Also note that if the credential evaluation shows that you have the educational equivalent of a U.S. university bachelor's degree or more, you are eligible for an H-1B visa and should apply for that instead. H-1B visas are explained in Chapter 16.

Before sending a credential evaluation service your academic documents, you may want to call in advance to discuss your prospects over the telephone. You may get some idea of the likelihood for receiving good results. If your prospects are truly bleak, you may decide not to order the evaluation and to save the service charge, which is typically around $100.

There are several qualified credential evaluation services recognized by USCIS. Two of them are:

International Education Research Foundation
P.O. Box 3665
Culver City, CA 90231-3665
Telephone: 310-258-9451
Fax: 310-342-7086
Website: www.ierf.org

Educational Credential Evaluators, Inc.
P.O. Box 514070
Milwaukee, WI 53203-3470
Telephone: 414-289-3400
Fax: 414-289-3411
Website: www.ece.org

The credential evaluation companies listed above will evaluate only formal education. They will not evaluate job experience. Some U.S. universities offer evaluations of foreign academic credentials and will recognize work experience as having an academic equivalent. Therefore, if you lack formal education but can show many years of responsible experience, you are better off trying to get an evaluation from a U.S. college or university.

When sending your credentials to a U.S. university, include documents showing your complete academic background, as well as all relevant career achievements. Letters of recommendation from former employers are the preferred proof of work experience. Evidence of any special accomplishments, such as awards or published articles, should also be submitted. USCIS can be influenced, but not bound by, academic evaluations from U.S. colleges and universities.

---

it is smarter to file your visa application in your home country.

You may not file an application for an H-2B visa at a consulate before your petition has been approved. Once this occurs, the USCIS regional service center where the petition was originally submitted will forward a complete copy of your file to the U.S. consulate designated on Form I-129 in Step Two. At the same time, a Notice of Action Form I-797 indicating approval will be sent directly to your U.S. employer. Once your employer receives this, telephone the consulate to see if the petition file has arrived from USCIS. If the file is slow in coming, ask the consulate to consider granting approval of your H-2B visa based only on the Notice of Action. Many U.S. consulates are willing to do so.

Once the petition is approved, check with your local U.S. consulate about the application procedures and getting your H-2B visa. Many insist on advance appointments. Just getting an appointment can take several weeks, so plan ahead.

3. Application Forms: Consular Filing

When you file at a U.S. consulate abroad, the consulate officials will provide you with certain forms, designated by a "DS" preceding a number. Instructions for completing DS forms and what to do with them once they are filled out will come with the forms. We do not include copies of these forms in this book because different consulates sometimes create different versions.

4. Application Documents: Consular Filing

You are required to show a valid passport and present one photograph taken in accordance with the photo instructions at http://travel.state.gov/photorequirements/html. If the consulate has not yet received your USCIS file containing the paperwork from the approved Temporary Labor Certification and petition, you will then need to show the original Notice of Action, Form I-797, which your employer received from USCIS by mail. Most consulates will issue H-2B visas based only on the Notice of Action, although some, particularly in Latin America and Asia, insist on seeing the complete USCIS file. If the consulate wants to see your file and it is late (more than a month) in arriving, request that the consulate investigate the file's whereabouts. You, too, can write the USCIS regional service center where your petition was processed, asking for the file.

For each accompanying relative, you must present a valid passport and one photograph taken in accordance with the State Department's photo instructions. You will also need documents verifying their family relationship to you.

Verify a parent/child relationship by presenting the child's long-form birth certificate. Many countries, including Canada and England, issue both short- and long-form birth certificates. Where both are available, the long form is needed because it contains the names of the parents while the short form does not.

If you are accompanied by your spouse, prove that you are lawfully married by showing a valid civil marriage certificate. Church marriage certificates are generally unacceptable. (There are a few exceptions, depending on the laws of your particular country. Canadians, for example, may use church marriage certificates if the marriage took place in Quebec Province, but not elsewhere. If a civil certificate is available, however, you should always use it.) You may have married in a country where marriages are not customarily recorded. Tribal areas of Africa are an example. In such situations, call the nearest consulate or embassy representing your home country for advice in locating acceptable proof of marriage.

You will need documents establishing your intent to leave the U.S. when your status expires. The consulate will want to see evidence that ties to your home country are so strong you will be highly motivated to return. Proof of such ties can include deeds verifying ownership of a house or other real property, written statements from you explaining that close relatives are staying behind, or letters from a company showing that you have a job waiting when you return from the U.S.

5. Application Interviews: Consular Filing

The consulate will frequently require an interview before issuing an H-2B visa. During the interview, a consul officer will examine the data you gave in Step One for accuracy, especially regarding facts about your own qualifications. Evidence of ties to your home country will also be checked. During the interview, you will surely be asked how long you intend to remain in the U.S. Any answer indicating that you are unsure about plans to return or have an interest in applying for a green card is likely to result in a denial of your H-2B visa.

6. Using Your H-2B Visa

On entering the U.S. with your new H-2B visa, you will be given an I-94 card. It will be stamped with a date showing how long you can stay. Normally, you are permitted to remain up to the expiration date on your H-2B petition. Each time you exit and reenter the U.S., you will get a new I-94 card authorizing your stay up to the final date indicated on the petition.

SUMMARY EXCLUSION

The law empowers a CBP inspector at the airport or border to summarily (without allowing judicial review) bar entry to someone requesting admission to the U.S. if either of the following are true:

- The inspector thinks you are lying about practically anything connected with entering the U.S., including your purpose in coming, intent to return and prior immigration history. This includes the use or suspected use of false documents.
- You do not have the proper documentation to support your entry to the U.S. in the category you are requesting.

If the inspector excludes you, you cannot be re-admitted to the U.S. for five years, unless USCIS grants a special waiver. For this reason it is extremely important to understand the terms of your requested status, and to not make any misrepresentations. If you are found to be inadmissible, you may ask the CBP inspector to withdraw your application to enter the U.S. in order to prevent having the five-year deportation order on your record. The CBP may allow this in some exceptional cases.

7. Application Appeals: Consular Filing

When a consulate turns down an H-2B visa application, there is no way to make a formal appeal, although you are free to reapply as often as you like. (Check with your local consulate to be sure, however—some place limits on the number of repeat applications, or require you to wait a certain number of months before reapplying.) If your visa is denied, you will be told by the consul officer the reasons for the denial. Written statements of decisions are not normally provided. If a lack of evidence about a particular point is the problem, sometimes simply presenting more evidence on an unclear fact can change the result.

The most common reason for denial of an H-2B visa is that the consul officer did not believe you intend to return to your home country when the visa expires. This is particularly common if you have previously lived in the U.S. illegally. The other most likely reasons are that you are found inadmissible or the consulate believes that you are not really qualified for the job.

Certain people who have been refused H-2B visas reapply at a different consulate, attempting to hide the fact that they were turned down elsewhere. You should know that if your application is denied, the last page in your pass-port will be stamped "Application Received" with the date and location of the rejecting consulate. This notation shows that some type of prior visa application has failed. It serves as a warning to other consulates that your case merits close inspection. If what we have just told you makes you think it would be a good idea to overcome this problem by obtaining a new, unmarked passport, you should also know that permanent computer records are kept of all visa denials.

H. Carrying Out Step Three: The Application (U.S. Filing)

If you are physically present in the U.S., you may apply for H-2B status without leaving the country on the following conditions:

- you have already obtained a Temporary Labor Certification
- you are simultaneously filing paperwork for or have already received an approved petition
- you entered the U.S. legally and not under the Visa Waiver Program
- you have never worked illegally in the U.S.
- the date on your I-94 card has not passed, and
- you are admissible to (and not deportable from) the U.S.

If you are admitted as a visitor without a visa under the Visa Waiver Program, you may not carry out Step Three in the U.S. Currently there are 28 participating countries in the Visa Waiver Program, listed in Chapter 2.

If you cannot meet these terms, you may not file for H-2B status in the U.S. It is important to realize, however, that eligibility to apply for change of status in the U.S. will not necessarily result in ineligibility for an H-2B visa. Many applicants who are barred from filing in the U.S. but otherwise qualify for H-2B status may apply successfully for an H-2B visa at U.S. consulates abroad. To determine if you are eligible for consular filing, read Section G, above, and Chapter 25 on inadmissibility.

1. Benefits and Drawbacks of U.S. Filing

Visas are never given inside the U.S. They are issued exclusively by U.S. consulates abroad. If you file in the U.S. and you are successful, you will get H-2B status, but not a visa. H-2B status allows you to remain in the U.S. with H-2B privileges until the status expires, but should you leave the country for any reason before that time, you will have to apply for the visa itself at a U.S. consulate before returning to America. Moreover, the fact that your H-2B status has been approved in the U.S. does not guarantee that the consulate will also approve your visa. Some consulates may even regard your previously acquired H-2B status as a negative factor, an indication that you have deliberately tried to avoid the consulate's authority.

There is another problem which comes up only in U.S. filings. It is the issue of what is called *preconceived intent.* In order to approve a change of status, USCIS must believe that at the time you originally entered the U.S. as a visitor or with some other nonimmigrant visa, you did not intend to apply for a different status. If USCIS thinks you had a preconceived plan to change from the status you arrived with to a different status, USCIS will deny your application. The preconceived intent issue is one less potential hazard you will face if you apply at a U.S. consulate abroad.

On the plus side of U.S. filing, if you come from a place where it is difficult to obtain U.S. visas, such as Latin America or India, your chances for success may be better in the U.S. Another benefit is that when problems do arise with your U.S. application, you can stay in the U.S. while they are being corrected, a circumstance most visa applicants prefer. If you run into snags at a U.S. consulate, you will have to remain outside the U.S. until matters are resolved.

2. Application Procedures: U.S. Filing

For filing Step Three in the U.S., follow Step Two as outlined above, but mark box "b" in Question 4 of Part 2 of Form I-129, indicating that you will complete processing in the U.S. There is no separate application form for filing Step Two in the U.S. If you have an accompanying spouse or children, however, a separate Form I-539 must be filed for them. The filing fee for a Step Two petition is presently $130. Your family must pay $140 with Form I-539. Checks and money orders are accepted. It is not advisable to send cash. We recommend submitting all papers by certified mail, return receipt requested, and making a copy of everything sent in to keep for your records.

Within a week or two after mailing in the application, you should get back a written notice of confirmation that the papers are being processed, together with a receipt for the fees. This notice will also tell you your immigration file number and approximately when to expect a decision. If USCIS wants further information before acting on your case, all application papers, forms, and documents will be returned, together with another form known as an I-797. The I-797 tells you what additional pieces of information or documents are expected. You should supply the extra data and mail the whole package back to the USCIS regional service center.

Applications for an H-2B status are normally approved within two to four months. When this happens, you will receive a Notice of Action Form I-797 indicating the dates for which your status is approved. A new I-94 card will be attached to the bottom of the form.

3. Application Forms: U.S. Filing

Copies of all the required USCIS forms can be found in Appendix II and on the USCIS website.

Form I-129

Follow the directions for Step Two in Section F2, above, except in Part 2, Question 4, mark box "b" instead of box "a."

Form I-539 (for accompanying relatives only)

Only one application form is needed for an entire family, but if there is more than one accompanying relative, each additional one should be listed on the I-539 supplement.

Part 1. These questions are self-explanatory. "A" numbers are usually given only to people who have previously applied for green cards or who have been in deportation proceedings. See an attorney if you have an A number.

Part 2, Question 1. Mark box "b," and write in "H-4."

Question 2. This question is self-explanatory.

Part 3. In most cases, you will mark Item 1 with the date requested in the Step Two petition. You will also complete Items 3 and 4, which are self-explanatory.

Part 4, Questions 1–2. These questions are self-explanatory.

Question 3. The different parts to this question are self-explanatory; however, items "a" through "c" ask if an immigrant visa petition or adjustment of status application has ever been filed on your behalf. If you are separately applying for a green card through a relative, this would be Step One, as described in Chapter 5. If you are separately applying for a green card through employment, this would be Step Two as described in Chapter 8. If you have only begun the Labor Certification, the first step of getting a green card through employment, this question should be answered "no." Answering any of these questions "yes" may make you ineligible for an H-2B status.

4. Application Documents: U.S. Filing

Each applicant must submit a copy of his or her I-94 card, the small white card you received on entering the U.S. Remember, if the date stamped on your I-94 card has already passed, you are ineligible for U.S. filing. If you entered the U.S. under the Visa Waiver Program and have a green I-94 card, you are also ineligible for U.S. filing. Canadians who are just visiting are not expected to have I-94 cards. Canadians with any other type of nonimmigrant status should have them.

You are required to document your qualifications for H-2B status. When you file the application together with the H-2B petition, the documents you submitted as part of Step Two will do double duty as the documents for Step Three.

For each accompanying relative, send in a copy of his or her I-94 card. You will also need documents verifying their family relationship to you. You may verify a parent/child relationship by presenting the child's long-form birth certificate. Many countries, including Canada and England, issue both short- and long-form birth certificates. Where both are available, the long form is needed because it contains the names of the parents while the short form does not.

If you are accompanied by your spouse, you must establish that you are lawfully married by showing a valid civil marriage certificate. Church certificates are generally unacceptable. (There are a few exceptions, depending on the laws of your particular country. Canadians, for example, may use church marriage certificates if the marriage took place in Quebec Province, but not elsewhere. If a civil certificate is available, however, you should always use it.) You may have married in a country where marriages are not customarily recorded. Tribal areas of Africa are an example. In such situations, call the nearest consulate or embassy of your home country for help with getting acceptable proof of marriage.

We have emphasized that in order to qualify for an H-2B visa, you must have the intention of returning to your home country when your visa expires. Consulates will demand evidence that ties to your home country are strong enough to motivate your eventual return. In a U.S. filing, USCIS does not always ask for proof of this. However, we strongly advise you to submit such evidence anyway. Proof of ties to your home country can include deeds verifying ownership of a house or other real property, written statements from you explaining that close relatives are staying behind, or a letter from a company in your home country showing that you have a job waiting when you return from the U.S.

5. Application Interviews: U.S. Filing

Interviews on H-2B change of status applications are rarely held. When an interview is required, the USCIS regional service center where you filed will send your paperwork to the local USCIS office nearest your U.S. employer's place of business. This office will in turn contact you for an appointment. (If USCIS has questions on the petition rather than the application, your employer will be contacted.) USCIS may ask you to bring additional documents at that time.

If you are called for an interview, the most likely reason is that USCIS either suspects some type of fraud or has doubts about your intent to return home after the H-2B visa expires. Interviews are a sign of trouble and can delay your application.

6. Application Appeals: U.S. Filing

If your application is denied, you will receive a written decision by mail explaining the reasons for the denial. There is no way of making a formal appeal to USCIS if your application is turned down. If the problem is too little evidence, you may be able to overcome this obstacle by adding more documents and resubmitting the entire application to the same USCIS office you have been dealing with, together with a written request that the case be reopened. The written request does not have to be in any special form. This is technically called a *Motion to Reopen*. There is a $110 fee to file this motion.

Remember that you may be denied the right to a U.S. filing without being denied an H-2B visa. When your application is turned down because you are found ineligible for U.S. filing, simply change your application to a consular filing—unless you will face inadmissibility problems as described in Chapter 25.

Although there is no appeal to USCIS for the denial of an H-2B change of status application, you do have the right to file an appeal in a U.S. district court. It would be difficult to file such an appeal without employing an immigration attorney at considerable expense. Such appeals are usually unsuccessful.

I. Extensions

H-2B visas may be extended for one year at a time, but you may not hold H-2B status for longer than a total of three years. Therefore, if your visa was first issued for the one-year maximum, you may be allowed two one-year extensions. Extensions are not automatic, nor are they easier to get than the original visa. In fact, extensions are sometimes more difficult to obtain because the longer you remain on a particular job, the less likely the DOL and USCIS are to believe that the job is truly temporary. Moreover, USCIS has the right to reconsider your qualifications based on any changes in the facts or law. When the original application for an H-2B visa was weak, it is not unusual for an extension request to be turned down. As always, however, good cases that are well prepared will be successful.

To extend your H-2B visa, the Temporary Labor Certification, petition and visa stamp will all have to be updated. As with the original application, you can file either in the U.S. or at a consulate. However, contrary to our advice on the initial visa procedures, in the case of extensions we highly recommend U.S. filing. That is because visa stamps, which can only be issued originally at consulates, may be extended in the U.S.

1. Step One: Temporary Labor Certification

The process for getting an extension of the Temporary Labor Certification is identical in every respect with the one used to obtain the original Temporary Labor Certification. See Section E, above.

2. Step Two: Extension Petition

Extension procedures are identical to the procedures followed in getting the initial visa. Fully document your application so that your case is not delayed if USCIS cannot locate your previous file.

WORKING WHILE YOUR EXTENSION PETITION IS PENDING

If you file your petition for an extension of H-2B status before your authorized stay expires, you are automatically permitted to continue working for up to 240 days while you are waiting for a decision. If, however, your authorized stay expires after you have filed for an extension but before you receive an approval, and more than 240 days go by without getting a decision on your extension petition, your work authorization ceases and you must stop working.

---

a. Extension Petition Forms

Copies of all the required USCIS forms can be found in Appendix II and on the USCIS website.

Form I-129 and H Supplement

Follow the directions for this form under Step Two in Section F2, above. The only difference is that you will mark boxes "2b" and "4c" of Part 2.

Form I-539 (for accompanying relatives only)

Follow the directions for this form under Step Three in Section H3, above, but mark box "1a" of Part 2.

b. Extension Petition Documents

Submit the new Temporary Labor Certification and Notice of Action indicating the approval that your employer received on the original petition. All your personal U.S. income tax returns and W-2 forms for the time period you have already been working in the U.S. on an H-2B visa are required as well. Once USCIS has these documents, it will notify the employer if any further data are needed.

3. Step Three: Visa Revalidation

This section includes information you need to complete the visa revalidation.

a. Visa Revalidation: U.S. Filing

If you are physically in the U.S. and your H-2B status extension has been approved by USCIS, you can have your visa revalidated by mail without leaving the country. The exception is if you carry the passport of a country that is on the U.S. government's list of countries that sponsor terrorism, in which case you won't be allowed to revalidate your visa without leaving the U.S. first. When this book went to print, the listed countries included North Korea, Cuba, Syria, Sudan, Iran, Iraq, and Libya.

To revalidate your visa, you must fill out Form DS-156, and send it to the Department of State. With Form DS-156, you should also submit as documents your passport (valid for at least six months), a recent passport-sized photo (full frontal view, on a light background, 2" x 2", stapled or glued to the form), the fee (currently $100 plus a "reciprocity fee" for nationals of certain countries), your current I-94 card, Notice of Action Form I-797, and a detailed letter from your employer describing your job duties. The fees may be paid by bank draft, corporate check, or money order, payable to the U.S. Department of State. You cannot pay by cash, credit card, or personal check. Male visa applicants between the ages of 16 and 45, regardless of nationality and regardless of where they apply, must also complete and submit a form DS-157. Enclose a self-addressed, stamped envelope, or a completed Federal Express or other courier service airbill. You should send in your visa revalidation application as soon as possible within the 60 days before your allowed stay expires (but don't send it any earlier or the entire package will be returned to you). Send the entire package by certified mail to:

If sending by postal service:
U.S. Department of State/Visa
P.O. Box 952099
St. Louis, MO 63195-2099

If sending by courier service:
U.S. Department of State/Visa (Box 2099)
1005 Convention Plaza
St. Louis, MO 63101-1200

The passport will be returned to you with a newly revalidated visa in around 12 weeks.

If your accompanying relatives are physically in the U.S., their H-4 visas may be revalidated by sending in their passports and I-94 cards together with yours. We strongly advise gathering your family together inside U.S. borders so you can take advantage of this simple revalidation procedure.

For more information on this process and the forms, see the State Department website at www.travelstate.gov/revals.html.

b.   Visa Revalidation: Consular Filing

If you must leave the U.S. after your extension has been approved but before you had time to get your visa revalidated, you must get a new visa stamp issued at a consulate. Read the section above. The procedures for consular extensions are identical.

We would like to reemphasize that it is much more convenient to apply for a revalidated visa by mail through the State Department in Washington, DC, than it is to extend your H-2B visa through a consulate. If possible, you should try to schedule filing your extension application so that you can remain in the U.S. until it is complete.

FORMS AND DOCUMENTS CHECKLIST

STEP ONE: TEMPORARY LABOR CERTIFICATION

Form

☐ Form ETA-750, Part A only.

Documents

☐ Tear sheets from newspapers or journals where advertisements were printed.

☐ Evidence employer posted notice of job opening within place of business.

☐ Employer's written statement of recruitment results.

☐ Employer's written statement explaining why the job is temporary or seasonal.

☐ If you are a touring entertainment industry worker, a written schedule of dates and cities where you will be working.

STEP TWO: PETITION

Forms

☐ Form I-129 and H Supplement.

Documents

☐ Approved Temporary Labor Certification.

☐ All documents submitted to DOL in Step One.

☐ Written employment contract.

☐ Detailed written statement from the employer explaining why the position is temporary or seasonal.

☐ If the position is temporary because it is tied to a specific project, a copy of the U.S. employer's contract for that particular project.

☐ Employer's annual report, if it is a public company.

☐ Letters from banks or bank statements indicating the average account balance of the employer's business, if it is a private company.

☐ Accountant's financial statements, including profit and loss statements and balance sheets of the employer's company for the past two years, if available.

☐ Tax returns of the employer's company for the past two years (if it is a private company), if available.

☐ Diplomas from schools attended.

☐ Transcripts from schools attended.

☐ Letters from former employers describing previous experience in detail.

STEP THREE: APPLICATION

Forms

☐ DS forms (available at U.S. consulates abroad for consular filing only).

☐ Form I-129, and H Supplement (U.S. filing only).

☐ Form I-539 (U.S. filing only).

Documents

☐ Notice of approval of the H-2B visa petition.

☐ Valid passport for you and each accompanying relative.

☐ Copy of I-94 card for you and each accompanying relative (U.S. filing only).

☐ One passport-type photo of you and each accompanying relative (consular filing only).

☐ Long-form birth certificate for you and each accompanying relative.

☐ Marriage certificate if you are married and bringing your spouse.

☐ If either you or your spouse have ever been married, copies of divorce and death certificates showing termination of all previous marriages.

☐ Documents showing ownership of real estate in your home country.

☐ Documents showing that close family members or property are being left behind in your home country.

☐ Documents showing a job is waiting on your return to your home country.

Temporary Trainees: H-3 Visas

Privileges

- You can participate in a training program offered by a U.S. company and you can work legally in the U.S. for the company that is training you.
- Visas can be issued quickly.
- You may travel in and out of the U.S. or remain here continuously until your H-3 status expires.
- Visas are available for accompanying relatives.

Limitations

- Your primary activity in the U.S. must be receiving training. Any work you perform for the U.S. company must be incidental to the training program. You are restricted to working only for the employer who admitted you to the training program and acted as sponsor for your H-3 visa. If you wish to change training programs, you must get a different H-3 visa.
- Visas can initially be approved for the time needed to complete the training program, although there is usually a maximum of two years permitted. Extensions of a year at a time may be allowed, but only if the original training program has not yet been completed, and only within the overall two-year maximum.
- Accompanying relatives may stay in the U.S. with you, but they may not work, unless they obtain permission to do so in their own right.

A. How to Qualify

You qualify for an H-3 visa if you are coming to the U.S. for on-the-job training to be provided by a U.S. company. Productive employment in the U.S. can be only a minor part of the total program. The purpose of the training should be to further your career in your home country. Similar training opportunities must be unavailable there.

There are no numerical limits. Step One petitions are normally approved within two to four months. Visas are usually issued within several weeks after petition approval.

Training programs supporting H-3 visas exist most often in two situations. A company with branches in foreign countries will often train foreign employees in their U.S. branches before sending them to work overseas. Another common training situation occurs when a U.S. company wishes to establish a beneficial business relationship with a foreign company. A good way to do this is by bringing in some of the foreign company's personnel and teaching them about the U.S. business. These people then develop personal ties with the U.S. company.

To qualify for an H-3 visa, you must possess the necessary background and experience to complete the U.S. training program successfully. In addition, you are eligible for an H-3 visa only if you intend to return to your home country when the visa expires. Be aware that very few training programs meet the USCIS's strict qualifications for such programs.

1. Training Program

You need a specific offer to participate in a job training program from a U.S. company or U.S. government agency. The job training slot you are invited to fill can't be in just any occupation. It must be one that will further your career abroad. Many types of occupations qualify, however. For example, you could be coming for training in agriculture, commerce, communications, finance, government, or virtually any other field. (However, physicians are ineligible to use this category.) The training program must be formal in structure with a curriculum, books, and study materials.

2. Training Is Unavailable in Your Home Country

One of the more difficult requirements for getting an H-3 visa is that the training you will receive in the U.S. must be unavailable to you in your home country. This does not mean that the training cannot exist there, but only that you, personally, do not have access to it.

3. Productive Employment Is Only a Minor Part

Although you can work on an H-3 visa, employment must be merely incidental and necessary to the training activities. If the employment aspect takes up so much time that the company could justify hiring a full-time U.S. worker to perform these duties, your H-3 visa will be denied. As a rule, if more than half of your time will be spent on productive employment, you will not qualify for an H-3 visa.

4. Correct Background

You must have the correct background for the training position you are offered. For example, if the training position is as an intern with a U.S. law firm, intended to further your career as an international lawyer, you will have to show that you have a law degree.

5. Intent to Return to Your Home Country

H-3 visas are meant to be temporary. At the time of applying, you must intend to return home when the visa expires. If you have it in mind to take up permanent residence in the U.S., you are ineligible for an H-3 visa. The U.S. government knows it is difficult to read minds. Expect to be asked for evidence showing that when you complete your training, you will go back home and use it there.

If you are training for work that doesn't exist in your home country, you'll have trouble. For example, if you will be in a training program for offshore oil drilling and you come from a country that is landlocked and has no oil, no one will believe you plan to take the skills learned in the U.S. back home.

You will also be asked for evidence that you are leaving behind possessions, property, or family members as incentives for your eventual return.

6. Accompanying Relatives

When you qualify for an H-3 visa, your spouse and unmarried children under age 21 can get H-4 visas, by providing proof of their family relationship to you. H-4 visas authorize your family members to stay with you in the U.S., but not to work there. They may, however, study at U.S. schools.

APPLYING FOR A GREEN CARD FROM AN H-3 STATUS

If you have an H-3 visa, you can file to get a green card if you are separately eligible for one. However, being in the U.S. on an H-3 visa gives you no advantage in doing so, and in fact may prove to be a drawback. That is because H-3 visas, like most nonimmigrant visas, are intended only for those who plan to return home once their training or other activities in the U.S. are completed.

If you apply for a green card, you are in effect making a statement that you never intend to leave the U.S. Therefore, USCIS will allow you to keep H-3 status while pursuing a green card only if you are able to convince USCIS that you did not intend to get a green card when you originally applied for the H-3 visa and that you will return home if you are unable to secure a green card before your H-3 visa expires. Proving these things can be difficult. If you do not succeed, your H-3 status may be taken away. Should this happen, it will in no way affect your green card application. You will simply risk being without your nonimmigrant visa until you get your green card. However, if you are out of status for over six or 12 months, or work without authorization, you may not be able to get your green card. Read Chapter 25 regarding inadmissibility and bars to adjustment of status before you overstay six months or depart the U.S.

If your method of applying for a green card is through employment, as discussed in Chapter 8, there is an even more difficult problem. The ultimate purpose of the H-3 visa is furtherance of your career abroad. By applying for a green card through employment you are making it clear that you are really utilizing the H-3 visa to establish a career in the U.S. and so are no longer qualified for H-3 status. Therefore, although you are permitted to apply for the green card, your H-3 status may be revoked.

If what you really want is a green card, apply for it directly and disregard H-3 visas. Although it may be more difficult to get a green card, which frequently takes several years, in the long run you will be happier with the results—not to mention the fact that you will be obeying the law by not trying to hide your true intentions.

B. H-3 Visa Overview

Once you have been offered a training position by a U.S. company, getting an H-3 visa is a two-step process. We have already explained how having foreign trainees can be beneficial to U.S companies. When this is the case, H-3 applicants often expect their U.S. employers to handle the entire process for them and indeed, many large companies are equipped with staff specialists who will do this for highly desirable trainees. Even smaller companies may be prepared to do whatever is necessary, including paying an immigration attorney's fees, in order to attract a trainee who may later prove valuable to them. However, in many cases it is the trainee who is most interested in having the visa issued, and to U.S. employers, the red tape of taking on a foreign trainee can be an unfamiliar nuisance.

As we give you step-by-step instructions for getting an H-3 visa, we will tell you what activities are to be performed by your employer and which others are to be done by you. There is nothing to stop you from helping with the work. For example, you can fill out forms intended to be completed by your employer and simply ask the employer to check them over and sign them. Unless your employer volunteers to help, or you are sure the company simply can't live without you, we recommend doing the paperwork yourself. The less your U.S. employer is inconvenienced, the more the company will be willing to act as sponsor for your visa.

1. Overview of Step One: The Petition

The petition is filed by your U.S. employer. All H-3 petitions are submitted to the USCIS regional service centers in the U.S. The object of the petition is to prove four things:
- that a qualifying formal training position has been offered to you by a U.S. company
- that you have the correct background for the training
- that the training is unavailable to you in your home country, and
- that the training will further your career in your home country.

Be aware that an approved petition does not by itself give you any immigration privileges. It is only a prerequisite to Step Two, submitting your application for an H-3 visa. The petition must be approved before you are eligible for Step Two.

2. Overview of Step Two: The Application

The application is filed by you and your accompanying relatives, if any. The application is your formal request for an H-3 visa or status. (If you are Canadian, your Step Two procedure will be different from those of other applicants. See Chapter 28, Canadians: Special Rules.) Step Two may be carried out in the U.S. at a USCIS office or in your home country at a U.S. consulate there. If you file Step Two papers in the U.S., you will usually submit them together with those for Step One. When Step Two is done at a U.S. consulate abroad, you must wait to file the application until the Step One petition is first approved.

If you are already in the U.S. legally on some other type of nonimmigrant visa, you may qualify to apply for an H-3 status at a USCIS office inside the U.S., using a procedure known as *change of nonimmigrant status*. (If you are admitted as a visitor without a visa under the Visa Waiver Program, you may not carry out Step Two in the U.S. Currently there are 28 participating countries in the Visa Waiver Program, listed in Chapter 2.)

If a change of status is approved, you will then be treated as if you had entered the country with an H-3 visa and you can keep the status as long as you remain in the U.S. or until it expires, whichever comes first.

You will not, however, receive a visa stamp, which you need if your plans include traveling in and out of the U.S. Visa stamps are issued only at U.S. consulates abroad. Therefore, if you change your status and later travel outside the U.S., you will have to go to the U.S. consulate in your home country and repeat Step Two, getting the H-3 visa stamp in your passport, before you can return.

3. Who's Who in Getting Your H-3 Visa

Getting an H-3 visa will be easier if you familiarize yourself with the technical names used for each participant in the process. During Step One, the petition, you are known as the *beneficiary* or the *trainee* and your U.S. employer is known as the *petitioner* or the *employer*. In Step Two, the application, you are referred to as *applicant*, but your employer remains the petitioner or employer. If you are bringing your spouse and children with you as accompanying relatives, each of them is known as *applicant* as well.

4. Tips on Handling the Paperwork

There are two types of paperwork you must submit to get an H-3 visa. The first consists of official government forms completed by you or your U.S. employer. The second is personal documents, such as academic credentials and professional licenses.

It is vital that forms are properly filled out and all necessary documents are supplied. You or your U.S. employer may resent the intrusion into your privacy and the sizable effort it takes to prepare an immigration applications but you should realize the process is an impersonal matter to immigration officials. Your getting a visa is more important to you than it is to the U.S. government. There is no shortage of applicants.

The documents you or your U.S. employer supply to USCIS or the consulate do not have to be originals. Photocopies of all documents are acceptable as long as you have the originals in your possession and are willing to produce them upon request. But add the following language to the photocopy, with your signature and the date:

> *Copies of documents submitted are exact photocopies of unaltered original documents and I understand that I may be required to submit original documents to an immigration or consular official at a later date.*
> *Signature _____*
> *Typed or Printed Name _____*
> *Date_____*

Documents will be accepted if they are in either English, or, with papers filed at U.S. consulates abroad, the language of the country where the documents are being filed (except in Japan, where all documents must be translated into English). If the documents are not in an acceptable language as just explained, they must be accompanied by a full, word for word, written English translation. Any capable person may act as translator. It is not necessary to hire a professional. At the end of each translation, the following statement must appear:

> *I hereby certify that I translated this document from [language] to English. This translation is accurate and complete. I further certify that I am fully competent to translate from [language] to English.*
> *Signature _____*
> *Typed or Printed Name _____*
> *Date_____*

The translator should sign this statement but it does not have to be witnessed or notarized.

Later in this chapter we describe in detail the forms and documents needed to get your H-3 visa. A summary checklist of forms and documents appears at the end of this chapter.

C. Carrying Out Step One: The Petition

This section includes the information you need to submit the petition.

1. General Procedures

The U.S. employer submits the petition, consisting of forms and documents, by mail, in duplicate, to the USCIS regional service center having jurisdiction over your intended employer's place of business. USCIS regional service centers are not the same as USCIS local offices—for one thing, you cannot visit regional service centers in person. There are four regional service centers spread across the U.S. Appendix I contains a list of all regional service centers with their addresses, but check the USCIS website for the correct P.O. box.

The filing fee for each petition, if no change of status (Step Two, U.S. Filing) is being requested, is currently $130. Checks or money orders are accepted. It is not advisable to send cash. We recommend submitting all papers by certified mail, return receipt requested, and making a copy of everything sent in to keep in your records.

Within a few weeks of mailing in the petition, your employer should get back a written confirmation that the papers are being processed, together with a receipt for the fees. This notice will also give your immigration file number and tell approximately when you should expect to have a decision. If USCIS wants further information before acting on your case, all petition papers, forms, and documents will be returned to your employer with another form known as an I-797. The I-797 tells your employer what additional pieces of information or documents are expected. Your employer should supply the extra data and mail the whole package back to the USCIS regional service center, with the I-797 on top.

H-3 petitions are normally approved within two to four months. When this happens, a Notice of Action Form I-797 will be sent to your employer showing the petition was approved. If you plan to execute Step Two at a U.S. consulate abroad, USCIS will also notify the consulate of your choice, sending the consulate a complete copy of your file. Only the employer receives communications from USCIS about the petition because technically it is the employer who is seeking the visa on your behalf.

 Faster processing—at a price. For $1,000 over and above the regular filing fees, USCIS promises "premium processing" of the visa petition, including a decision within 15 days. To use this service, the employer must fill out an additional application (Form I-907) and submit the application to a special USCIS Service Center address. For complete instructions, see the USCIS website at www.uscis.gov.

2. Petition Forms

Copies of all USCIS forms can be found in Appendix II andon the USCIS website.

Form I-129 and H Supplement

The basic form for Step One, the petition, is immigration Form I-129 and H Supplement. The I-129 form is used for many different nonimmigrant visas. In addition to the basic part of the form that applies to all types of visas, it comes with several supplements for each specific nonimmigrant category. Simply use the supplement that applies to you. Your employer must file the petition form in duplicate. Send in two signed originals. Copies are not acceptable.

Your employer may choose to list more than one foreign employee may be listed on a single I-129 petition. This is done if the employer has more than one opening to be filled for the same type of training position. If more than one employee is to be included, Supplement-1, which is also part of Form I-129, should be completed for each additional employee.

Most of the questions on the I-129 form are straightforward. If a question does not apply to you, answer it with "None" or "N/A."

Part 1. These questions concern the employer only and are self-explanatory.

Part 2, Question 1. Question 1 should be answered "H-3."

Questions 2–3. These questions are self-explanatory.

Question 4. This question asks you to indicate what action is requested from USCIS. Normally you will mark box "a" which tells USCIS to notify a U.S. consulate abroad of the petition approval so that you may apply for a visa there. If you will be filing your Step Two application in the U.S., mark box "b." If this petition is being filed as an extension, mark box "c."

Question 5. This question is self-explanatory.

Part 3. These questions are self-explanatory. If you previously held a U.S. work permit and therefore have a U.S. Social Security number, put down that number where asked. If you have a Social Security number that is not valid for employment, put down that number followed by "not valid for employment." If you have never had a Social Security number, put down "None."

Alien Registration Numbers, which all begin with the letter "A," are given only to people who have applied for green cards, received political asylum, or have been in deportation proceedings. If you have an "A" number, consult an attorney. If you do not have an "A" number, write down "None."

If your present authorized stay has expired, you must disclose that where asked. This may affect your ability to get an H-3 visa at a U.S. consulate, especially if you have been out of status for a long time, but if you are out of status now, you cannot file Step Two inside the U.S.

Part 4. These questions are self-explanatory. If a green card petition has been filed on your behalf, you will probably not be able to get an H-3 visa, since you are required to have the intention to return to your home country after the training program is completed.

Part 5. These questions are self-explanatory. The dates of intended training should not exceed a total of two years, which is the maximum period of time for which an H-3 petition may be approved. The maximum reduces to 18 months if you are applying for a training program in special education of disabled children.

H Supplement, Top of Form. These questions are self-explanatory.

H Supplement, Sections 1–3. These do not apply to H-3 petitions and should be left blank.

H Supplement, Section 4. Each question in this section is self-explanatory. Remember that the training should be unavailable to you in your home country and you must have the intention to return to your home country after it is completed. USCIS is very suspicious of most H-3 petitions. Therefore, Section 4 requires a written explanation of why the employer is willing to incur the cost of training you. There should be some logical way in which your training will financially benefit the U.S. employer, such as to help it with business abroad after you return to your home country.

3. Petition Documents

You must provide several documents with the petition.

a. Describing the Training Program

Your employer must submit a detailed statement describing the type of training and giving the number of hours that will be devoted to classroom instruction, on-the-job training, productive employment, and unsupervised work or study. Also, include a description of the curriculum, giving the names of any textbooks to be used and the specific subjects to be covered.

b. Showing Training Is Unavailable in Your Home Country

Your employer must prove that you cannot receive the same training in your home country. This is best shown by letters or affidavits from authorities in your home country who are leaders of industry, officials in government, or administrators in universities. The letters should give the name and position of the writer. In these letters it should be stated that the writer is acquainted with the training program you intend to pursue in the U.S. and that similar training is not available in your home country. It may take a lot of effort to get these statements, but without them, your H-3 visa stands little chance of approval.

c. Showing How Training Will Further Your Career

Ideally, the H-3 training program will be related to your current occupation at home. In that case, your U.S. employer can show the nature of your present job with a letter from your foreign employer explaining how the training will further your career in your home country. If you are not now employed in the occupation for which you hope to get U.S. training, it would be very helpful to your case to have a letter from a company in your homeland offering you a job based on the completion of your training

in the U.S. If you can't get a letter containing a specific job offer for the future, you will have to present evidence that jobs in the field for which you are training are available. Your U.S. employer must then submit a general statement from a leader in the industry for which you will be trained or an official of the government department of labor in your home country, confirming that there is a demand for persons with the type of training you will receive.

d. Proving You Are Qualified for the Training Program

If the nature of the training you will receive requires special background for entering the program, the employer must submit evidence with the petition showing that you have that background. For example, if the training is at a professional level, such as internships for lawyers or engineers, your employer must submit evidence that you are already qualified to practice law or engineering at home. The employer should also submit copies of your diplomas, and if you have previous professional work experience, letters from your foreign employers describing the nature and length of your previous employment.

4. Petition Interviews

USCIS rarely holds interviews on H-3 visa petitions but when it does, the interview is always with the employer. If you are in the U.S., you may be asked to appear as well. Interviews are requested only if USCIS doubts that the documents or information on Form I-129 or H Supplement are genuine. Then the petition file is forwarded to the USCIS local office nearest your employer's place of business and your employer is notified to appear there. The employer may also be asked to bring additional documents at that time. If, after the interview, everything seems in order, the petition will be approved. The best way to avoid an interview is to have the employer document the petition well from the beginning.

5. Petition Appeals

If the existence of a legitimate training position or the unavailability of such training in your home country has been poorly documented, the petition will probably be denied. Your employer will then get a notice of USCIS's unfavorable decision, stating the reasons for the negative outcome and how to appeal.

The best way to handle an appeal is to try avoiding it altogether. Filing an appeal means arguing to USCIS that its reasoning was wrong. This is not something USCIS likes to hear. If you think you can eliminate the reason why your petition failed by improving your paperwork, it makes sense to disregard the appeals process and simply file a new petition, being careful to see that it is better prepared than the first.

If the petition was denied because your U.S. employer left out necessary documents that have since been located, the new documents should be sent, together with a written request that the case be reopened, to the same USCIS office that issued the denial. This is technically called a *Motion to Reopen*. There is a $110 fee to file this motion. Appeals often take a long time. A Motion to Reopen can be concluded faster than an appeal.

If your U.S. employer does choose to appeal, it must be done within 30 days of the date on the Notice of Denial. The appeal should be filed at the same USCIS office that issued the denial. There is a $110 filing fee. USCIS will then forward the papers for consideration to the Administrative Appeals Unit in Washington, DC. In six months or more, your employer will get back a decision by mail. Only a small number of appeals are successful.

When an appeal to USCIS has been denied, the next step is to make an appeal through the U.S. judicial system. Your employer may not file an action in court without first going through the appeals process available from USCIS. If the case has reached this stage and you are illegally present in the U.S., seek representation from a qualified immigration attorney, as you are now in danger of being deported.

D. Carrying Out Step Two: The Application (Consular Filing)

➡ If you are Canadian, your Step Two procedures will be different from those of other applicants. (See Chapter 28 for details.)

Anyone with an approved H-3 petition can apply for a visa at a U.S. consulate in his or her home country. You must be physically present to apply there. If you have been or are now working or living illegally in the U.S., you may not be able to get an H-3 visa from a U.S. consulate even if you otherwise qualify. Read Chapters 14 and 25 to determine whether you are admissible to the U.S. as a nonimmigrant and otherwise qualified to apply for a visa.

1. Benefits and Drawbacks of Consular Filing

The biggest benefit to consular filing is that only consulates issue visas. When you go through a U.S. filing, you get a status, not a visa. (See Chapter 14, Section B.) An H-3 status does not give you the ability to travel out of the U.S. and get back in again. Therefore, if you want travel privileges, you will at some time have to go through the extra step of applying for a visa at a U.S. consulate, even though you have already applied for and received H-3 status in the U.S.

Moreover, anyone with an approved petition may apply for an H-3 visa at the appropriate consulate. That is not the case with U.S. applications for H-3 status. You are not eligible to process a status application in the U.S. unless your presence and activities in the U.S. have been consistent with your immigration status. If you are in the U.S. illegally, consular filing may be the only option, but see Chapter 25 to make sure that you won't be blocked from returning.

A drawback to consular filing is that you must be physically present in the country where the consulate is located to file there. If your petition is ultimately turned down, not only will you have to wait outside the U.S. until the problem is resolved, but other visas in your passport, such as a visitor's visa, may be canceled. It will then be impossible for you to enter the U.S. at all. Consequently, if your H-3 visa case is not very strong and freedom of travel is not essential to you, it might be wise to apply in the U.S., make up your mind to remain there for the duration of the H-3 status and skip trying to get a visa from the consulate.

2. Application General Procedures: Consular Filing

Technically, the law allows you to apply for an H-3 visa at any U.S. consulate you choose. However, from a practical standpoint, your case will be given the greatest consideration at the consulate in your home country. Applying in some other country creates suspicion. Often, when an applicant is having trouble at a home consulate, he will seek a more lenient office in some other country. This practice of consulate shopping is frowned on. Unless you have a very good reason for being elsewhere (such as a temporary job assignment in some other nation), it is smarter to file your visa application in your home country.

You may not file an application for an H-3 visa at a consulate before your petition has been approved. Once this occurs, the USCIS regional service center where the petition was originally submitted will forward a complete copy of your file to the U.S. consulate designated on Form I-129 in Step One. At the same time, a Notice of Action Form I-797 indicating approval will be sent directly to your U.S. employer. Once your employer receives this, telephone the consulate to see if the petition file has arrived from USCIS. If the file is slow in coming, ask the consulate to consider granting approval of your H-3 visa based only on the Notice of Action. Many U.S. consulates are willing to do so.

Once the petition is approved, check with the U.S. consulate to find out its application procedures for getting your H-3 visa. Many insist on advance appointments. Just getting an appointment can take several weeks, so plan ahead.

3. Application Forms: Consular Filing

When you file at a U.S. consulate abroad, the consulate officials will provide you with certain forms, designated by a "DS" preceding a number. Instructions for completing DS forms and what to do with them once they are filled out will come with the forms. We do not include copies of these forms in this book, because different consulates may use different versions of the forms.

4. Application Documents: Consular Filing

You must show a valid passport and present one photograph taken in accordance with the photo instructions at http://travel.state.gov/photorequirements/html. If the consulate has not yet received your USCIS file containing the paperwork from the approved petition, you will then need to show the original Notice of Action, Form I-797, which your employer received from USCIS by mail. Most consulates will issue H-3 visas based only on the Notice of Action, although some, particularly in South America and Asia, insist on seeing the complete USCIS file. If the consulate wants to see your file and it is late (more than a month) in arriving, you should request that the consulate investigate the file's whereabouts. You, too, can write the USCIS regional service center where your petition was processed, asking them to look for the file.

For each accompanying relative, you must present a valid passport and one photograph taken in accordance with the State Department's photo instructions. You will also need documents verifying their family relationship to you. You may verify a parent/child relationship by presenting the child's long-form birth certificate. Many countries, including Canada and England, issue both short- and long-form birth certificates. Where both are available, the long form is needed because it contains the names of the parents while the short form does not.

If you are accompanied by your spouse, prove that you are lawfully married by showing a valid civil marriage certificate. Church certificates are generally unacceptable. (There are a few exceptions, depending on the laws of your particular country. Canadians, for example, may use church marriage certificates if the marriage took place in Quebec Province, but not elsewhere. If a civil certificate is available, however, use it.) You may have married in a country where marriages are not customarily recorded. Tribal areas of Africa are an example. In such situations, call the nearest U.S. consulate or embassy for advice on locating acceptable proof of marriage.

You will need documents establishing your eventual intent to leave the U.S. (when your visa expires). The consulate will want to see evidence that ties to your home country are so strong you will be highly motivated to return. Proof of such ties can include deeds verifying ownership of a house or other real property, written statements from you explaining that close relatives are staying behind or letters from a company showing that you have a job waiting when you return from the U.S.

5. Application Interviews: Consular Filing

The consulate will normally require an interview before issuing an H-3 visa. During the interview, a consul officer will examine the data you gave in Step One for accuracy, especially regarding facts about your own qualifications. Evidence of ties to your home country will also be checked. During the interview, you will surely be asked how long you intend to remain in the U.S. Any answer indicating that you are unsure about plans to return or have an interest in applying for a green card is likely to result in a denial of your H-3 visa. Once you are approved, you will probably be asked to return later for your visa. Many cases are approved only provisionally, however, awaiting the completion of security checks.

6. Using Your H-3 Visa

On entering the U.S. with your new H-3 visa, you will be given an I-94 card. It will be stamped with a date showing how long you can stay. Normally, you are permitted to remain up to the expiration date on your H-3 petition. Each time you exit and reenter the U.S., you will get a new I-94 card authorizing your stay up to the final date indicated on the petition.

SUMMARY EXCLUSION

The law empowers CBP inspector at the airport or border to summarily (without allowing judicial review) bar entry to someone requesting admission to the U.S. if either of the following are true:

- The inspector thinks you are lying about practically anything connected with entering the U.S., including your purpose in coming, intent to return and prior immigration history. This includes the use or suspected use of false documents.
- You do not have the proper documentation to support your entry to the U.S. in the category you are requesting.

If the inspector excludes you, you cannot be readmitted to the U.S. for five years, unless USCIS grants a special waiver. For this reason it is extremely important to understand the terms of your requested status, and to not make any misrepresentations. If you are found to be inadmissible, you may ask the CBP inspector to withdraw your application to enter the U.S. in order to prevent having the five-year deportation order on your record. The CBP may allow this in some exceptional cases.

7. Application Appeals: Consular Filing

When a consulate turns down an H-3 visa application, there is no way to make a formal appeal, although you are free to reapply as often as you like. (Check with your local consulate to be sure, however—some place limits on the number of repeat applications, or require you to wait a certain number of months before reapplying.) If your visa is denied, you will be told by the consul officer the reasons for the denial. Written statements of decisions are not normally provided in nonimmigrant cases. If a lack of evidence about a particular point is the problem, sometimes simply presenting more evidence on an unclear fact can change the result.

The most common reason for denial of an H-3 visa is that the consul officer does not believe you intend to return to your home country when the visa expires. Another likely reason is that you are found inadmissible or the consulate believes that you are not really qualified for the training position.

Certain people who have been refused H-3 visas reapply at a different consulate, attempting to hide the fact that they were turned down elsewhere. You should know that if your application is denied, the last page in your passport will be stamped "Application Received," with the date and location of the rejecting consulate. This notation shows that some type of prior visa application has failed. It serves as a warning to other consulates that your case merits close inspection. If what we have just told you makes you think it would be a good idea to overcome this problem by obtaining a new, unmarked passport, you should also know that permanent computer records are kept of all visa denials.

E. Carrying Out Step Two: The Application (U.S. Filing)

If you are physically present in the U.S., you may apply for H-3 status without leaving the country on the following conditions:

- you are simultaneously filing paperwork for or have already received an approved petition
- you entered the U.S. legally
- you have never worked illegally in the U.S., and
- the date on your I-94 card has not passed.

If you were admitted as a visitor without a visa under the Visa Waiver Program, you may not carry out Step Two in the U.S. Currently there are 28 participating countries in the Visa Waiver Program, listed in Chapter 2.

If you cannot meet these terms, you may not file for H-3 status in the U.S. It is important to realize, however, that eligibility to apply in the U.S. has nothing to do with overall eligibility for an H-3 visa. Many applicants who are barred from filing in the U.S. but otherwise qualify for H-3 status can apply successfully for an H-3 visa at U.S. consulates abroad. If you find you are not eligible for U.S. filing, read Section E, above, and be sure to understand Chapter 25's discussion of overstays and inadmissibility before departing the U.S.

1. Benefits and Drawbacks of U.S. Filing

Visas are never given inside the U.S. They are issued exclusively by U.S. consulates abroad. If you file in the U.S. and you are successful, you will get H-3 status but not a visa. H-3 status allows you to remain in the U.S. with H-3 privileges until the status expires, but should you leave the country for any reason before that time, you will have to apply for the visa itself at a U.S. consulate before returning to the U.S. Moreover, the fact that your H-3 status has been approved in the U.S. does not guarantee that the consulate will also approve your visa. Some consulates may even regard your previously acquired H-3 status as a negative factor, an indication that you have deliberately tried to avoid the consulate's authority.

There is another problem which comes up only in U.S. filings. It is the issue of what is called *preconceived intent*. To approve a change of status, USCIS must believe that at the time you originally entered the U.S. as a visitor or with some other nonimmigrant visa, you did not intend to apply for a different status. If USCIS thinks you had a preconceived plan to change from the status you arrived with to a different status, it may deny your application. The preconceived-intent issue is one less potential hazard you will face if you apply at a U.S. consulate abroad.

On the plus side of U.S. filing, when problems do arise with your U.S. application, you can stay in the U.S. while they are being corrected, a circumstance most visa applicants prefer. If you run into snags at a U.S. consulate, you will have to remain outside the U.S. until matters are resolved.

2. Application Procedures: U.S. Filing

The general procedure for filing Step Two in the U.S. is to follow Step One as outlined above, but to mark box "b" in Part 2, Question 4, of Form I-129, indicating that you will complete processing in the U.S. There is no separate application form for filing Step Two in the U.S. If you have an accompanying spouse or children, however, a separate Form I-539 must be filed for them (with accompanying $140 fee).

When you apply for a change of status, the filing fee for a Step One petition is presently $130. Checks and money orders are accepted. It is not advisable to send cash. We recommend submitting all papers by certified mail, return

receipt requested, and making a copy of everything sent in to keep for your records.

Within a few weeks after mailing in the application, you should get back a written notice of confirmation that the papers are being processed, together with a receipt for the fees. This notice will also tell you your immigration file number and approximately when to expect a decision. If USCIS wants further information before acting on your case, all application papers, forms and documents will be returned together with another form known as an I-797. The I-797 tells you what additional pieces of information or documents are expected. You should supply the extra data and mail the whole package back to the USCIS regional service center.

Applications for an H-3 status are normally approved within four months. When this happens, you will receive a Notice of Action Form I-797 indicating the dates for which your status is approved. A new I-94 card is attached to the bottom of the form.

3. Application Forms: U.S. Filing

Copies of all the required USCIS forms can be found in Appendix II and on the USCIS website.

Form I-129

Follow the directions in Section C2, above, except in Part 2, Question 4, mark box "b" instead of box "a."

Form I-539 (for accompanying relatives only)

Only one application form is needed for an entire family, but if there is more than one accompanying relative, each additional one should be listed on the I-539 supplement.

Part 1. These questions are self-explanatory. "A" numbers are usually given only to people who have previously applied for green cards or political asylum or who have been in deportation proceedings. If you have an A number, consult an attorney.

Part 2, Question 1. Mark box "b," and write in "H-4."

Question 2. This question is self-explanatory.

Part 3. In most cases, you will mark Item 1 with the date requested in the Step One petition. You will also complete Items 3 and 4, which are self-explanatory.

Part 4, Questions 1–2. These questions are self-explanatory.

Question 3. The different parts to this question are self-explanatory; however, items "a" through "c" ask if an immigrant visa petition or adjustment of status application has ever been filed on your behalf. (If you are separately applying for a green card through a relative, this would be Step One, in Chapter 5. If you are separately applying for a green card through employment, this would be Step Two in

Chapter 8.) If you have only begun the Labor Certification, the first step of getting a green card through employment, this question should be answered "no." Answering any of these questions "yes" may make you ineligible for H-3 status.

4. Application Documents: U.S. Filing

Each applicant must submit a copy of his or her I-94 card, the small white card you received on entering the U.S. If the date stamped on your I-94 card has already passed, you are ineligible for U.S. filing. If you entered the U.S. under the Visa Waiver Program and have a green I-94 card, you are also ineligible for U.S. filing. Canadians who are just visiting are not expected to have I-94 cards. Canadians with any other type of nonimmigrant status should have them.

You must document your qualifications for H-3 status. When you file the application together with the H-3 petition, the documents you submitted as part of Step One will do double duty as the documents for Step Two. If the petition was submitted first and then approved, you can simply submit a copy of Form I-797, Notice of Action instead.

For each accompanying relative, send in a copy of his or her I-94 card. You will also need documents verifying their family relationship to you. You may verify a parent/child relationship by presenting the child's long-form birth certificate. Many countries, including Canada and England, issue both short- and long-form birth certificates. Where both are available, the long form is needed because it contains the names of the parents, while the short form does not.

If you are accompanied by your spouse, you must prove that you are lawfully married, by showing a civil marriage certificate. Church marriage certificates are generally unacceptable. (There are a few exceptions, depending on the laws of your particular country. Canadians, for example, may use church marriage certificates if the marriage took place in Quebec Province, but not elsewhere. If a civil certificate is available, however, you should always use it.) You may have married in a country where marriages are not customarily recorded. Tribal areas of Africa are an example. In such situations, call the nearest consulate or embassy of your home country for advice on locating acceptable proof of marriage.

We have emphasized that to qualify for an H-3 visa, you must have the intention of returning to your home country when your visa expires. Consulates will demand evidence that ties to your home country are strong enough to motivate your eventual return. In a U.S. filing, USCIS does not always ask for proof of this. However, we strongly advise you to submit such evidence anyway. Proof of ties to your home country can include deeds verifying ownership of a house or other real property, written statements from you explaining that close relatives are staying behind or letters from a company in your home country showing that you have a job waiting when you return from the U.S.

5. Application Interviews: U.S. Filing

Interviews on H-3 change of status applications are rarely held. When an interview is required, the USCIS regional service center where you filed will send your paperwork to the USCIS local office nearest your U.S. employer's place of business. This office will in turn contact you for an appointment. (If USCIS has questions on the petition rather than the application, your employer will be contacted.) USCIS may ask you to bring additional documents at that time.

If you are called for an interview, the most likely reason is that USCIS either suspects some type of fraud or has doubts about your intent to return home after the H-3 visa expires. Because they are not common and usually a sign of trouble, these interviews can result in considerable delays.

6. Application Appeals: U.S. Filing

If your application is denied, you will receive a written decision by mail explaining the reasons for the denial. There is no way of making a formal appeal to USCIS if your application is turned down. If the problem is too little evidence, you may be able to overcome this obstacle by adding more documents and resubmitting the entire application to the same USCIS office you have been dealing with, together with a written request that the case be reopened. The written request does not have to be in any special form. This is technically called a *Motion to Reopen*. There is a $110 fee to file this motion.

Remember that you may be denied the right to a U.S. filing without being denied the right to eventually take up that status after getting an H-3 visa. When your application is turned down because you are found ineligible for U.S. filing, simply change your application to a consular filing. (See Chapter 25, however, before departing the U.S., to make sure you are not subject to the three- or ten-year bars on returning.)

Although there is no appeal to USCIS for the denial of an H-3 change of status application, you can file an appeal in a U.S. district court. However, it would be difficult to file such an appeal without employing an immigration attorney at considerable expense. Such appeals are usually unsuccessful.

F. Extensions

H-3 visas can be extended for up to a total of two years' time in H-3 status. Although an extension is usually easier to get than the status itself, it is not automatic. USCIS has the right to reconsider your qualifications based on any changes in the facts or law. When the original application for an H-3 visa was weak, it is not unusual for an extension request to be turned down. As always, however, good cases that are well prepared will be successful.

To extend your H-3 visa, the petition, I-94 card, and visa stamp will all have to be updated. As with the original application, you can file either in the U.S. or at a consulate. However, contrary to our advice on the initial visa procedures, for extensions we highly recommend U.S. filing. That is because visa stamps, which can only be issued originally at consulates, may be extended in the U.S.

1. Step One: Extension Petition

Extension procedures are identical to the procedures followed in getting the initial visa. The petition should be fully documented in the same manner as it was for the initial petition, including a letter from the employer requesting your status be extended, with an explanation of why the training has not yet been completed and a copy of your U.S. income tax returns for the previous year, including W-2 forms.

WORKING WHILE YOUR EXTENSION PETITION IS PENDING

If you file your petition for an extension of H-3 status before your authorized stay expires, you are automatically permitted to continue working for up to 240 days while you are waiting for a decision. If, however, your authorized stay expires after you have filed for an extension but before you receive an approval, and more than 240 days go by without getting a decision on your extension petition, your work authorization ceases.

---

a. Extension Petition: Forms

Copies of all the required USCIS forms can be found in Appendix II and on the USCIS website.

Form I-129 and H Supplement

Follow the directions in Section C2, above. The only difference is that you will mark boxes "2b" and "4c" of Part 2.

Form I-539 (for accompanying relatives only)

Follow the directions in Section E3, above, but mark box "a" of Part 2, Question 1.

b. Extension Petition: Documents

You must submit a copy of your I-94 card. You should also submit the original Notice of Action I-797, a letter from your employer stating that your extension is required and the reason why your training is not yet completed, and a copy of your personal U.S. income tax returns for the past year, including form W-2. (Be sure no employment other than that for your H-3 employer is reflected in your tax documents.)

2. Step Two: Visa Revalidation

This section includes information you need to complete the extension petition.

a. Visa Revalidation: U.S. Filing

If you are physically in the U.S. and your H-3 status extension has been approved by USCIS, you can have your visa revalidated by mail without leaving the country. The exception is if you carry the passport of a country that is on the U.S. government's list of countries that sponsor terrorism, in which case you won't be allowed to revalidate your visa without leaving the U.S. first. When this book went to print, the listed countries included North Korea, Cuba, Syria, Sudan, Iran, Iraq, and Libya.

To revalidate your visa, fill out Form DS-156, and send it to the Department of State. With the form you should also submit as documents your passport (valid for at least six months), a recent passport-sized photo (2" x 2", full face view, on a light background, stapled or glued to the form), the fee ($100 plus a "reciprocity fee" for nationals of certain countries), your current I-94 card, Notice of Action Form I-797, and a detailed letter from your employer describing your training and job duties.

The fees may be paid by bank draft, corporate check, or money order, payable to the U.S. Department of State. You cannot pay by cash, credit card, or personal check.

Male visa applicants between the ages of 16 and 45, regardless of nationality and regardless of where they apply, must also complete and submit a form DS-157.

Enclose a self-addressed, stamped envelope, or a completed Federal Express or other courier service airbill. You should send in your visa revalidation application as soon as possible within the 60 days before your allowed stay expires (but don't send it any earlier, or the entire package will be returned to you). Send the entire package by certified mail to:

If sending by postal service:
U.S. Department of State/Visa
P.O. Box 952099
St. Louis, MO 63195–2099

If sending by courier service:

U.S. Department of State/Visa (Box 2099)

1005 Convention Plaza

St. Louis, MO 63101–1200

The passport will be returned to you with a newly revalidated visa in around 12 weeks.

If your accompanying relatives are physically in the U.S., their H-4 visas may be revalidated by sending in their passports and I-94 cards together with yours. We strongly advise gathering your family together inside U.S. borders so you can take advantage of this simple revalidation procedure.

For more information on this process and the forms, see the State Department website at www.travel.state.gov/revals.html.

b. Visa Revalidation: Consular Filing

If you must leave the U.S. after your extension has been approved but before you had time to get your visa revalidated, you must get a new visa stamp issued at a consulate. Reread Section F, above. The procedures for consular extensions are identical.

We would like to reemphasize that it is much more convenient to apply for a revalidated visa by mail through the State Department in Washington, D.C., than it is to extend your H-3 visa through a consulate. If possible, you should try to schedule filing your extension petition so that you can remain in the U.S. until it is complete.

FORMS AND DOCUMENTS CHECKLIST

STEP ONE: PETITION

Forms

☐ Form I-129 and H Supplement.

Documents

☐ Detailed statement from the U.S. employer describing the training program.

☐ Documents proving previous, relevant experience.

☐ Diplomas showing the completion of any necessary education.

☐ Letters or affidavits from companies in your home country or from your own government stating that similar training is unavailable in your home country.

☐ Proof of opportunities to use your training at home:

　☐ letter from a foreign employer explaining how the training will further your career in your home country, or

　☐ letter from your home country's labor department describing job opportunities for persons with the type of training you will receive in the U.S.

STEP TWO: APPLICATION

Forms

☐ DS forms (available from U.S. consulates abroad for consular filing only).

☐ Form I-129 (U.S. filing only).

☐ Form I-539 (U.S. filing only for accompanying relatives).

Documents

☐ Notice of approval of the H-3 visa petition.

☐ Valid passport for you and each accompanying relative.

☐ Copy of I-94 card for you and each accompanying relative (U.S. filing only).

☐ One passport-type photo of you and each accompanying relative (consular filing only).

☐ Long-form birth certificate for you and each accompanying relative.

☐ Marriage certificate if you are married and bringing your spouse.

☐ Documents showing ownership of real estate in your home country.

☐ Documents showing that close family members or property are being left behind in your home country.

☐ Documents showing a job is waiting on your return to your home country.

Intracompany Transfers: L-1 Visas

Privileges

- You can be transferred to the U.S. and work legally for a U.S. company that is a branch, subsidiary, affiliate, or joint venture partner of a company that already employs you outside of the U.S.

- Visas can be issued quickly.

- You may travel in and out of the U.S. or remain there continuously until your L-1 status expires.

- Visas are available for accompanying relatives, and your spouse will be permitted to accept employment in the U.S.

- If you have an L-1 visa for an executive or managerial level position in the U.S. company and want to apply for a green card through employment (see Chapter 8), you can do so and skip a major step of that process.

Limitations

- You are restricted to working only for the U.S. employer who acted as your L-1 visa sponsor, and the U.S. company must be a branch, subsidiary, affiliate, or joint venture partner of the company that currently employs you outside the U.S.

- Visas can initially be approved for only up to three years. Extensions of two years at a time may be allowed until you have been in the U.S. for a total of seven years if you are a manager or executive. Persons with specialized knowledge can get extensions until their total stay is only five years.

- Accompanying relatives may stay in the U.S. with you, but your children may not work, unless they get work authorization through a separate basis for eligibility.

A. How to Qualify

There are no quota restrictions. Petitions are normally approved within three to four months. Visas are usually issued within several weeks after petition approval.

You qualify for an L-1 visa if you have been employed outside the U.S. as a manager, executive, or person with specialized knowledge for at least one out of the past three years, and you are transferred to the U.S. to be employed in a position that utilizes your special knowledge and skills. The one-year period of required employment is reduced to six months if your employer has filed a blanket petition and been granted Blanket L approval (described in Subsection 3, below).

The U.S. company to which you are transferring must be a branch, subsidiary, affiliate, or joint venture partner of your non-U.S. employer. The non-U.S. company must remain in operation while you have the L-1 visa. "Non-U.S. company" means that it is physically located outside the U.S. Such a company may be a foreign division of a U.S.-based business or it may have originated in a country outside the U.S. Either one fits the definition of a non-U.S. company. The company must continue operations for the

duration of your visa, and you should show that you can expect to be transferred back upon your return.

To get an L-1 visa, it is not necessary that either your non-U.S. or prospective U.S. employer be operating in a particular business structure. Many legal forms of doing business are acceptable, including, but not restricted to, corporations, limited corporations, partnerships, joint ventures, and sole proprietorships. The employer may also be a nonprofit or religious organization.

Although you are generally expected to work full-time in the U.S., you can work somewhat less if you dedicate a significant portion of your time to the job, on a regular and systematic basis.

1. Manager, Executive, or Person With Specialized Knowledge

To be eligible for an L-1 visa, the job you hold with the non-U.S. company must be that of manager, executive, or person with specialized knowledge. You must have worked in that position a total of at least one year out of the past three years. That year must have been spent outside the U.S. For immigration purposes, the definitions of manager, executive, and specialized knowledge are more restricted than their everyday meanings.

a. Managers

A manager is defined as a person who has all of the following characteristics:

- He or she manages the organization or a department, subdivision, function, or component of the organization.
- He or she supervises and controls the work of other supervisory, professional, or managerial employees or manages an essential function, department, or subdivision of the organization.
- He or she has the authority to hire and fire or recommend these and other personnel decisions regarding those persons supervised. If no employees are supervised, the manager must work at a senior level within the organization or function.
- He or she has the authority to make decisions concerning the day-to-day operations of the portion of the organization that he or she manages.

First-line supervisors are lower management personnel who directly oversee nonmanagement workers. A first-line supervisor is not normally considered a manager unless the employees supervised are professionals. The word "professional" here means a worker holding a university degree.

A manager coming to work for a U.S. office that has been in operation for at least one year also qualifies for a green card as a priority worker. See Chapter 8 for details.

b. Executives

An executive is defined as a person whose primary role includes that:

- He or she directs the management of the organization or a major function or component of it.
- He or she sets the goals or policies of the organization or a part or function of it.
- He or she has extensive discretionary decision-making authority.
- He or she receives only general supervision or direction from higher level executives, a board of directors, or the stockholders of the organization.

An executive coming to work for a U.S. office that has been in operation for at least one year also qualifies for a green card as a priority worker. Again, see Chapter 8 for details.

c. Persons With Specialized Knowledge

The knowledge that is referred to in the term "specialized knowledge" must specifically concern the employer company, its products, services, research, equipment, techniques, management or other interests and its application in international markets, or advanced knowledge of the company's processes and procedures. The consular officers will be looking for knowledge that is not held commonly throughout the industry, but is truly specialized. They will also be looking to see that such knowledge is not readily available in the United States.

2. Branch, Subsidiary, Affiliate, or Joint Venture Partner

L-1 visas are available only to employees of companies outside the U.S. that have related U.S. branches, subsidiaries, affiliates, or joint venture partners. There is also a special category of international accounting firms. For visa purposes, these terms have specific definitions.

a. Branches

Branches are simply different operating locations of the same company. The clearest example of this is a single international corporation that has branch offices in many countries.

b. Subsidiaries

In a subsidiary relationship, one company must own a controlling percentage of the other company, that is, 50% or more. For L-1 purposes, when two companies are in the same corporate or limited form, and at least 50% of the stock of a company in the U.S. is owned by a non-U.S. company, or vice versa, this is a classic subsidiary relationship.

c. Affiliates

Affiliate business relationships are more difficult to demonstrate than those of branches or subsidiaries because there is no direct ownership between the two companies. Instead, they share the fact that both are controlled by a common third entity, either a company, group of companies, individual, or group of people.

There are two methods of ownership that will support an L-1 visa based on an affiliate relationship. The first is for one common person or business entity to own at least 50% of the non-U.S. company and 50% of the U.S. company. If no single entity owns at least 50% of both companies, the second possibility is for each owner of the non-U.S. company to also own the U.S. company, and in the same percentages. For example, if five different people each own 20% of the stock of the non-U.S. company, then the same five people must each own 20% of the U.S. company for an affiliate relationship to exist.

d. Joint Venture Partners

A joint venture exists when there is no common ownership between the two companies, but they have jointly undertaken a common business operation or project. To qualify for L-1 purposes, each company must have veto power over decisions, take an equal share of the profits, and bear the losses on an equal basis.

In a situation where both the U.S. and non-U.S. companies are in the corporate or limited form and the majority of the stock of both is publicly held, unless they are simply branches of the same company that wish to transfer employees between them, the joint venture relationship is the only one that is practical for L-1 qualifying purposes. The ownership of a publicly held company is too vast and diverse to prove any of the other types of qualifying business relationships.

e. International Accounting Firms

The Immigration Act of 1990 made it clear that L-1 visas are available to employees and partners of international accounting firms. In the case of big accounting firms, the partnership's interests between one country and another are not usually close enough for them to qualify as affiliates under normal L-1 visa rules. For this reason, the managers of such companies that could not, in the past, be transferred to U.S. international accounting firms, are now considered qualified to support L-1 visa petitions for their employees. This is provided the firm is part of an international accounting organization with an internationally recognized name. These rules are intended to apply only to a limited number of very large and prominent firms.

3. Blanket L-1 Visas: Privileges for Large Companies

Large U.S. companies (other than nonprofits) that are branches, subsidiaries, or affiliates of non-U.S. companies may obtain what is known as a blanket L-1 status. Blanket L-1 status enables qualified U.S. companies that require frequent transferring of non-U.S. employees to their related U.S. companies to do so easily. Instead of submitting individual petitions for each transferee, the company itself gets a general approval for transferring employees, which eliminates much of the time and paperwork in each individual case. If a non-U.S. company has more than one U.S. branch, subsidiary, or affiliate, it need obtain only one blanket L-1 petition for all of its related U.S. companies.

It is the company itself and not the individual employee that qualifies for this program. Although this procedure is not used often, there are enormous benefits when a company obtains blanket L-1 status. The company need apply only once to receive a blanket L-1 status, and when the company does so, it may easily bring key employees into the U.S. as needed, bypassing the USCIS individual petition process and the inevitable delays that come with it. We wish to make clear that although a U.S. company must be a branch, subsidiary, or affiliate of a non-U.S. company to qualify, it is the U.S. company that petitions for and receives the blanket L-1 status.

Initially, a blanket L-1 petition can be approved for only three years. However, if the company continues to qualify, at the end of three years it can obtain an indefinite renewal. L-1 visas are available under the blanket program to executives and managers of the blanket L-1 status company as well as those employees considered to be specialized knowledge professionals. The definitions for manager and executives wanting blanket L-1 visas are the same as for those who apply for individual L-1 visas. However, this specialized knowledge category differs from the one for individual L-1 applicants. Individual L-1 visas may be given to those who simply have specialized knowledge. For the blanket visa, they must be considered professionals as well.

If a company has the need and meets the following requirements, it should obtain a blanket L-1 petition:

- The petitioning U.S. company to which employees may be transferred must be a branch, subsidiary, or affiliate of a company outside the U.S. (Note that a joint venture partnership is not a qualifying business relationship for blanket L-1 status purposes.)
- Both the U.S. company and its related non-U.S. company must be engaged in actual commercial trade or rendering of services.
- The U.S. company must have been engaged in business for at least one year.
- The U.S. company must have a total of at least three branches, subsidiaries, or affiliates, although all three need not be located in the U.S.
- The company and any related U.S. companies must either have:
  - successfully obtained L-1 visas for at least ten of its employees during the past 12 months
  - combined annual sales of at least $25 million, irrespective of the related company outside the U.S., or
  - a total of at least 1,000 employees actually working in the U.S.

4. Specialized Knowledge Professionals

This category is only for employees of companies with blanket L-1 status. It is a more stringent substitute for the specialized knowledge category available to individual L-1 applicants. USCIS's regulations require that an individual have specialized knowledge, as defined above, and that he or she further be a member of the professions as that term is defined in immigration law. The law specifically lists architects, engineers, lawyers, physicians, surgeons, teachers in elementary and secondary schools, colleges, academies, or seminaries. However, the term profession has been more liberally interpreted in other contexts, to include any occupation that requires theoretical and practical knowledge to perform the occupation in such fields as architecture, physical and social sciences, business specialties, and the arts, requiring completion of a university education reflected by at least a bachelor's degree in a specific occupational specialty, as long as that degree is the minimum requirement for entry to that occupation.

Under this definition, the following occupations have been found to be professional: registered nurse, accountant, computer systems analyst, physical therapist, chemist, pharmacist, medical technologist, hotel manager, fashion designer, commercial airline pilot of 747s or other large aircraft, and upper-level business managers.

Other occupations may also be considered professional, as long as they meet the criteria discussed above

5. Accompanying Relatives

When you qualify for an L-1 visa, your spouse and unmarried children under age 21 can get L-2 visas by providing proof of their family relationship to you. L-2 visas authorize your accompanying relatives to stay with you in the U.S., but only your spouse will be permitted to work there.

To take advantage of the right to work, your spouse will, after arriving in the United States, need to apply for a work permit. This is done on Form I-765. In filling out the form, your spouse should write "spouse of L nonimmigrant" in Question 15, and "A-18" in Question 16.

Your spouse will need to mail this form, together with proof of your visa status, a copy of his or her I-94 card, the filing fee and two photos, to the appropriate USCIS Service Center for your geographic region. For the address and other information, call USCIS Information at 800-375-5283 or see the USCIS website (www.uscis.gov).

B. Possibilities for a Green Card From L-1 Status

If you are eligible for or now have an L-1 visa as either a manager or an executive, you may also be eligible for a green card through employment as explained in Chapter 8. In addition to your eligibility, you also have the benefit of being able to get the green card without going through the rigorous procedures of Labor Certification, which is usually the first step required for those seeking green cards through

employment. The purpose of the Labor Certification procedure is to show that there are no U.S. workers available to take the U.S. job that has been offered to you. However, if you qualify for L-1 status as a manager or executive, you also fall under a green card preference category called *priority workers*. This category is exempt from Labor Certification requirements.

We wish to stress that in order to use L-1 eligibility to qualify for a green card, you need not have actually gotten an L-1 visa. Showing that you are eligible to get one is sufficient. Chapter 8 will give you full instructions on how to get a green card using an L-1 visa or L-1 visa eligibility.

C. Applying for an L-1 Visa

Once you have been offered a job transfer to the U.S., getting an L-1 visa is a two-step process. Often applicants expect their U.S. employers to handle the entire process for them and indeed, a number of large companies are equipped with staff specialists who will do this for highly desirable employees. Even smaller companies may be prepared to do whatever is necessary, including paying an immigration attorney's fees, in order to transfer a key employee. However, in many cases it is the employee who is most interested in the U.S. transfer, and to a U.S.-based company, the red tape of transferring a foreign employee can be an unfamiliar nuisance.

As we give you step-by-step instructions for getting an L-1 visa, we will indicate that certain activities are to be performed by the U.S. company and others are to be done by you. However, there is nothing to stop you from helping with the work. For example, you can fill out forms and ask the appropriate official in the company to check them over and sign them. It is completely legal as well as in your best interest to assist whenever possible.

1. Summary of Step One: The Petition

The petition is filed by your U.S. employer company. All L-1 petitions, both individual and blanket, are submitted to USCIS regional service centers in the U.S. The object of the individual L-1 petition is to prove three things:

- that you have been employed outside the U.S. for at least one of the past three years as an executive, manager, or person with specialized knowledge
- that the company you worked for outside the US. has a branch, subsidiary, affiliate, or joint venture partner company in the U.S., and
- that the U.S. entity requires your services to fill a position of the same or similar level as the one you presently hold outside of the U.S.

The object of the blanket L-1 petition is to prove five things:

- that the petitioning U.S. company is in a branch, subsidiary, or affiliate relationship with a company outside of the U.S.
- that the U.S. company has been engaged in actual trade or the rendering of services
- that the U.S. company has been in business for at least one year
- that the U.S. company has a total of at least three U.S. branches, subsidiaries, or affiliates, and
- that the U.S. company and its other U.S. related business entities have:
  - successfully obtained L-1 visas for at least ten employees in the past year
  - combined total annual sales of at least $25 million, or
  - a combined total of at least 1,000 employees working in the U.S.

An approved petition, either individual or blanket, does not by itself give the transferee any immigration privileges. It is only a prerequisite to Step Two, submitting the application for an L-1 visa. The petition must be approved before you are eligible for Step Two.

 Faster processing—at a price. For $1,000 over and above the regular filing fees, the USCIS promises "premium processing" of the visa petition, including a decision within 15 days. To use this service, the employer must fill out an additional application (Form I-907) and submit the application to a special USCIS Service Center address. For complete instructions, see the USCIS website at www.uscis.gov.

2.   Summary of Step Two: The Application

The application is filed by you and your accompanying relatives, if any. The application is your formal request for an L-1 visa or status. (If you are Canadian, your Step Two procedures will be different from those of other applicants. See Chapter 28.) Step Two may be carried out in the U.S. at a USCIS office (if you're already in the U.S. legally) or in your home country at a U.S. consulate there. If you file Step Two papers in the U.S., you will usually submit them at the same time as those for Step One. When Step Two is dispatched at a U.S. consulate abroad, you must wait to file the application until the Step One petition is first approved.

If you are already in the U.S. legally on some other type of nonimmigrant visa, you qualify to apply for an L-1 status at a USCIS office inside the U.S. using a procedure known as *change of nonimmigrant status*. (If you were

admitted as a visitor without a visa under the Visa Waiver Program, you may not carry out Step Two in the U.S. Currently there are 28 participating countries in the Visa Waiver Program, as listed in Chapter 2.)

If a change of status is approved, you will then be treated as if you had entered the country with an L-1 visa and you can keep the status as long as you remain in the U.S. or until it expires, whichever comes first.

You will not, however, receive a visa stamp, which you need if your plans include traveling in and out of the U.S. Visa stamps are issued only at U.S. consulates abroad. Therefore, if you change your status and later travel outside the U.S., you will have to go to the U.S. consulate in your home country and repeat Step Two, obtaining the L-1 visa stamp in your passport, before you can return.

3.   Who's Who in Getting Your L-1 Visa

Getting an L-1 visa will be easier if you familiarize yourself with the technical names used for each participant in the process. During Step One, the petition, you are known as either the *beneficiary* or the *employee* and the U.S. company to which you are being transferred is called the *petitioner* or the *employer*. In Step Two, the application, you are referred to as *applicant*, but your U.S. employer remains the *petitioner* or *employer*. If you are bringing your spouse and children with you as accompanying relatives, they are known as *applicants* as well.

4.   Tips on Handling the Paperwork

There are two types of paperwork you must submit to get an L-1 visa. The first consists of official government forms completed by you or your employer. The second is personal and business documents such as birth certificates, marriage certificates, school transcripts, diplomas, company financial statements, and company tax returns.

It is vital that forms are properly filled out and all necessary documents are supplied. You or your U.S. employer may resent the intrusion into your privacy and the sizable effort it takes to prepare immigration applications, but you should realize the process is an impersonal matter to immigration officials. Your getting a visa is more important to you than it is to the U.S. government. There is no shortage of applicants.

The documents you or your U.S. employer supply to USCIS or the consulate do not have to be originals. Photocopies of all documents are acceptable as long as you have the originals in your possession and are willing to produce them upon request. But add the following language to the photocopy, with your signature and the date:

ACADEMIC CREDENTIAL EVALUATIONS

Because it is almost always necessary that you hold at least a bachelor's degree, evidence that you are personally eligible as a specialized knowledge professional should include copies of diplomas and transcripts from the colleges and universities you attended. However, not every country operates on the same academic degree and grade level systems found in the U.S. If you were educated in some other country, USCIS or the U.S. consulate will often ask for an academic credential evaluation from an approved consulting service to determine the U.S. equivalent of your educational level.

When the results of a credential evaluation are favorable, they strengthen your case. If, however, the evaluation shows that your credentials do not equal at least a U.S. bachelor's degree, this can mean you will not qualify as a specialized knowledge professional.

We recommend obtaining a credential evaluation in every case where non-U.S. education is a factor. In addition, we advise getting the evaluation before USCIS or the consulate has the opportunity to ask for it. When the evaluation is favorable, include it with your application—it saves time if USCIS or the consulate decides to request it later. You should also reconsider applying for an L-1 visa under the blanket program as you probably will not qualify.

Before sending a credential evaluation service your academic documents, you may want to call in advance to discuss your prospects over the telephone. Usually, you can get some idea of the likelihood for receiving good results. If your prospects are truly bleak, you may decide not to order the evaluation and to save the service charge, which is typically around $100.

There are several qualified credential evaluation services recognized by USCIS. Two of them are:

International Education Research Foundation
P.O. Box 3665
Culver City, CA 90231-3665
Telephone: 310-258-9451
Fax: 310-342-7086
Website: www.ierf.org

Educational Credential Evaluators, Inc.
P.O. Box 514070
Milwaukee, WI 53203-3470
Telephone: 414-289-3400
Fax: 414-289-3411
Website: www.ece.org

The credential evaluation companies listed above will evaluate only formal education. They will not evaluate job experience. Some U.S. universities also offer evaluations of foreign academic credentials but will recognize work experience as having an academic equivalent. Therefore, if you lack a university education but can show many years of responsible experience, you are better off trying to get an evaluation from a U.S. college or university.

When sending your credentials to a U.S. university, include documents showing your complete academic background, as well as all relevant career achievements. Letters of recommendation from former employers are the preferred proof of work experience. Evidence of any special accomplishments, such as awards or published articles, should also be submitted.

USCIS and the U.S. consulates can be influenced but not bound by academic evaluations from U.S. colleges and universities.

Copies of documents submitted are exact photocopies of unaltered original documents and I understand that I may be required to submit original documents to an immigration or consular official at a later date.
Signature _____
Typed or Printed Name _____
Date _____

Documents will be accepted if they are in either English, or, with papers filed at U.S. consulates abroad, the language of the country where the documents are being filed (except in Japan, where all documents must be translated into English). If the documents are not in an acceptable language as just explained, they must be accompanied by a full, word for word, written English translation. Any capable person may act as translator. It is not necessary to hire a professional. At the end of each translation, the following statement must appear:

I hereby certify that I translated this document from [language] to English. This translation is accurate and complete. I further certify that I am fully competent to translate from [language] to English.

Signature _____

Typed or Printed Name _____

*Date*_____

The translator should sign this statement but it does not have to be witnessed or notarized.

Later in this chapter we describe in detail the forms and documents needed to get your L-1 visa. A summary checklist of forms and documents appears at the end of the chapter.

D. Carrying Out Step One: The Petition

There are two different types of L-1 visa petitions, individual and blanket. Individual L-1 petitions are used when a company wishes to transfer one or just a few employees on an infrequent basis. Blanket L-1 petitions are reserved for large corporations that transfer many employees to the U.S. each year. We have already discussed the advantages to a blanket L-1 status. Remember that blanket L-1 petitions are filed to get blanket L-1 status for the U.S. company, while individual petitions are filed for each potential transferee.

If your non-U.S. employer wants to transfer you to the U.S. and regularly transfers others, ask whether the company already has an approved blanket petition. If so, ask your potential U.S. employer to issue you three copies of a document known as a Certificate of Eligibility, Form I-129S, and one copy of the Notice of Action Form I-797, indicating approval of the blanket L-1 petition. These items will prove that the company does indeed have an approved blanket L-1 petition. Once you have these papers, you may skip Step One, go directly to Step Two, the application, and follow the directions for applicants in blanket L-1 cases.

If the U.S. company does transfer many employees to the U.S. but has not obtained a blanket L-1 visa, you might suggest that it look into getting one.

1. General Procedures

The U.S. employer submits the petition (individual or blanket), consisting of forms and documents, by mail, in duplicate, to the USCIS regional service center having jurisdiction over your intended employer's place of business. USCIS regional service centers are not the same as USCIS local offices—for one thing, you cannot visit them in person. There are four USCIS regional service centers spread across the U.S. Appendix I contains a list of all USCIS regional service centers with their addresses, but check the USCIS website for the appropriate P.O. box (www.uscis.gov).

The filing fee for each petition is currently $130. (Individual and blanket petitions are both done on the same USCIS form, Form I-129.) Checks or money orders are accepted. It is not advisable to send cash. Submit all papers by certified mail, return receipt requested, and make a copy of everything sent in to keep in your records.

Within a few weeks after mailing in the petition, your employer should get back a written confirmation that the papers are being processed, together with a receipt for the fee. This notice will also give your immigration file number (if it's an individual petition) and tell approximately when you should expect to have a decision. If USCIS wants further information before acting on the case, all petition papers, forms, and documents will be returned to your employer with a request for additional pieces of information or documents. Your employer should supply the extra data and mail the whole package back to the regional service center.

L-1 petitions are normally approved within three to four months. A Notice of Action Form I-797 will be sent to your employer showing the petition was approved. If you plan to execute Step Two at a U.S. consulate abroad, USCIS will also notify the consulate of your choice, sending a complete copy of your file. Only the employer receives communications from USCIS about the petition, because technically it is the employer who is seeking the visa on your behalf.

2. Petition Forms

Copies of the required USCIS forms can be found in Appendix II and on the USCIS website.

Form I-129 and L Supplement

The basic form for Step One, the petition, is immigration Form I-129 and L Supplement. The I-129 form is used for many different nonimmigrant visas. In addition to the basic part of the form that applies to all types of visas, it comes with several supplements for each specific nonimmigrant category. Simply use the supplement that applies to you. Your employer must file the petition form in duplicate. Send in two signed originals. Copies are not acceptable.

Most of the questions on the I-129 form are straightforward. If a question does not apply to you, answer it with "None" or "N/A."

Part 1. These questions concern the employer only and are self-explanatory.

Part 2, Question 1. Question 1 should be answered "L-1" if you're a manager or executive, "L-1B" if you're a person with specialized knowledge, and "LZ" for a blanket petition.

Questions 2–3. These questions are self-explanatory.

Question 4. This question asks you to indicate what action is requested from USCIS. Normally you will mark box "a" which tells USCIS to notify a U.S. consulate abroad of the petition approval so that you may apply for a visa there. If you will be filing your Step Two application in the U.S., mark box "b." If this petition is being filed as an extension, mark box "c."

Part 3. If this is a blanket petition, Part 3 does not apply. On the top line, write "N/A, Blanket petition, see L Supplement for individual employee details." If this is an individual petition, these questions are self-explanatory. If you previously held a U.S. work permit and therefore have a U.S. Social Security number, put down that number where asked. If you have a Social Security number that is not valid for employment, put down that number followed by "not valid for employment." If you have never had a Social Security number, put down "None." If you've used a false Social Security card, see an attorney—you could be found inadmissible.

Alien Registration Numbers, which all begin with the letter "A," are given only to people who have applied for green cards, received political asylum, or have been in deportation proceedings. If you do have an "A" number, put that number down and explain how you got it, such as "number issued from previous green card petition filed by my brother." However, you should consult an attorney if you were in deportation proceedings. If you do not have an "A" number, write down "None."

If your present authorized stay has expired, you must disclose that where asked. This should not affect your ability to get an L-1 visa at a U.S. consulate, but if you are out of status now, you cannot file Step Two inside the U.S. (See Chapter 25.)

Part 4. These questions are self-explanatory. The fact that you may have a green card petition or application in process does not prevent you from getting an L-1 visa.

If you are filing a blanket petition, Part 4 does not apply. Write in "N/A, Blanket petition."

Part 5. These questions are self-explanatory. The dates of intended employment should not exceed a total of three years. This is the maximum period of time for which an L-1 petition may be approved.

L Supplement

This supplement is self-explanatory. Section 1 is completed for all individual petitions. Section 2 is completed for blanket petitions.

3.   Petition Documents

You must provide several documents with the petition.

For individual petitions, provide the documents described in Subsections a through d, below. For blanket petitions, provide the documents described in Subsections c through e.

a.   Proof of Employment Abroad

Your U.S. employer must supply documents proving that you were employed outside the U.S. by the non-U.S. company for at least one of the past three years. The best way to prove this is by providing copies of any wage statements you may have received. In Canada this is the T-4, in England, the P.A.Y.E. You should also submit your personal income tax return filed in your home country for the most recent year. If this is unavailable, a notarized statement from the bookkeeping department or accountant of your non-U.S. employer may be used; however, you should also submit a statement explaining why the tax returns are unavailable. For example, you might state that tax returns are not required in your home country or that the returns haven't been prepared yet.

b.   Proof That You Are a Manager, Executive, or Person With Specialized Knowledge

Your U.S. employer must submit evidence that your employment abroad fits the USCIS definition of manager, executive, or person with specialized knowledge, and that your employment in the U.S. will be of a similar type. To prove this, submit detailed statements from both the U.S. and non-U.S. employers explaining your dates of employment, qualifications, salary, and specific duties as well as the number and kind of employees you supervise. If the petition is based on specialized knowledge, the statements should also describe the nature of the specialized knowledge and how it will be used in your U.S. job. The statements should also include a description of the job you'll be doing in the U.S., including the duties, and evidence that the position is executive, managerial, or requires specialized knowledge. These statements may be in your employer's own words and do not have to be in any special form.

c. Proof That the U.S. and Non-U.S. Companies Are Engaged in Trade or the Rendering of Services

The petitioning U.S. employer should submit as many documents as possible to show that both the U.S. and non-U.S. companies are financially healthy and presently engaged in trade or the rendering of services. Such documents would include:

- copies of the articles of incorporation or other legal charters
- any business registration certificates
- company tax returns for the past two years
- company annual reports or financial statements for the past two years, including balance sheets and profit/loss statements
- payroll records for the past two years
- letters of reference from chambers of commerce
- promotional literature describing the nature of the company
- letters from banks indicating average account balances, and
- copies of leases or deeds for business premises.

d. Proof of a Qualifying Business Relationship Between the U.S. and Non-U.S. Companies

The U.S. employer must submit documents showing that the U.S. and non-U.S. companies are in a branch, subsidiary, affiliate, or joint venture relationship. There are many different types or business organizations that may qualify to support L-1 visa petitions, ranging from privately owned companies to large corporations whose stock is publicly traded. The types of documents that are submitted will differ from case to case depending on the legal structure of the companies involved as well as the nature of the relationship. Business documents will also vary greatly from one country to another, as some types of business structures are unique to a particular country and cannot be found elsewhere. Therefore, it is impossible to list all the documents that can be used to show the existence of one of the four qualifying business relationships, as they differ with each case. The petitioning employer must simply keep the elements of the four types of relationship in mind and produce all documents possible to demonstrate that one of them applies to his company.

If a company is in the corporate or limited company form, whether privately or publicly held, articles of incorporation, stock certificates showing ownership of the companies, and statements from the secretaries of the corporations explaining the percentages of stock ownership are required to prove any of the four qualifying business relationships. Remember that in subsidiary and affiliate relationships, at least 50% of the stock must be involved for the relationship to qualify. If the corporations are privately held, notarized affidavits from the secretary or other record keeper of each company verifying the names of the officers and directors, as well as copies of minutes of shareholder meetings appointing the officers and directors, should be submitted.

If one or both companies are not in the corporate form, other proof of who owns the company, such as business registration certificates, business licenses, and affidavits from company officials attesting to the identity of the owners should be submitted. The purpose of identifying the owners is to show commonality of ownership between the U.S. and non-U.S. companies.

In the case of joint venture partnerships, the U.S. employer must submit a copy of the joint venture agreement, together with as much of the above-mentioned documentation concerning each company as possible.

e. Additional Documents for Blanket L-1 Petitions

In addition to the above company documents, the following items must be provided:

- documents showing that the employer has an office in the U.S. that has been doing business for one year or more
- documents showing that the employer has three or more domestic or foreign branches, subsidiaries, or affiliates, and either:
  - documents showing the U.S. company and any related companies have successfully obtained L-1 visas for at least ten of its employees during the past 12 months (copies of individual Notice of Action Forms I-797 will be sufficient)
  - documents showing the U.S. company and any related U.S. companies have combined annual sales of at least $25 million (such as company tax returns, audited accountant's financial statements, or the annual report to shareholders), or
  - documents showing the U.S. company and any related U.S. companies have a total of at least 1,000 employees actually working in the U.S. (such as the most recent quarterly state unemployment tax return and federal employment tax return Form 940).

4. Petition Interviews

USCIS rarely holds interviews on L-1 visa petitions. When it does, the interview is always with the employer. If you are in the U.S., you may be asked to appear as well. Interviews are requested only if USCIS doubts that the documents or information on Form I-129 and the L supplement are genuine. Then the petition file is forwarded to the USCIS local office nearest your employer's place of business and your employer is notified to appear there. The employer may also be asked to bring additional documents at that time. If, after the interview, everything is in order, the petition will be approved. The best way to avoid an interview is to have the employer document the petition well from the beginning.

5. Petition Appeals

When your job qualifications or the ability of the employer to pay your salary have been poorly documented, the petition will probably be denied. Your employer will then get a notice of USCIS's unfavorable decision, stating the reasons for the negative outcome and how to appeal. In the alternative, USCIS may request additional information by sending you a Form I-797 and a list of information and/or documents it needs to determine your eligibility. You must respond to such a request within the specified time period (usually about three months) or your petition will be decided on the basis of the already submitted documentation.

The best way to handle an appeal is to try avoiding it altogether. Filing an appeal means arguing to USCIS that its reasoning or facts were wrong. This is difficult to do successfully. If you think you can eliminate the reason your petition failed by improving your paperwork, it makes sense to disregard the appeals process and simply file a new petition, better prepared than the first.

If the petition was denied because your U.S. employer left out necessary documents that have since been located, the new documents should be sent, together with a written request that the case be reopened, to the same USCIS office that issued the denial. This is technically called a *Motion to Reopen*. There is a $110 fee to file this motion. Appeals often take a long time. A Motion to Reopen can be concluded faster than an appeal.

If your U.S. employer does choose to appeal, it must be done within 30 days of the date on the Notice of Denial. The appeal should be filed at the same USCIS office that issued the denial. There is a $110 filing fee. USCIS will then forward the papers for consideration to the Administrative Appeals Unit in Washington, D.C. In six months or more, your employer will get back a decision by mail. Less than 5% of all appeals are successful.

When an appeal to USCIS has been denied, the next step is an appeal through the U.S. judicial system. (Your employer may not file an action in court without first going through the USCIS appeals process.) If the case has reached this stage and you are in the U.S. illegally, seek representation from a qualified immigration attorney, as you are now in danger of being deported.

E. Carrying Out Step Two: The Application (Consular Filing)

If you are Canadian, your Step Two procedures will be different from those of other applicants. See Chapter 28 for details.

Anyone with an approved L-1 petition or any qualified employee of a company holding an approved blanket L-1 petition can apply for a visa at a U.S. consulate in his or her home country. You must be physically present in order to apply there. However, if you have been or are now working or living illegally in the U.S., see Chapter 25 to see if you will be found inadmissible and barred from returning for three or ten years.

1. Benefits and Drawbacks of Consular Filing

The most important benefit to consular filing is that only consulates issue visas. When you go through a U.S. filing, you get a status, not a visa. (See Chapter 14.) An L-1 status confers the same right to work as an L-1 visa, but it does not give you the ability to travel out of the U.S. and get back in again. Therefore, if you want travel privileges, you will at some time have to go through the extra step of applying for a visa at a U.S. consulate, even though you have already applied for and received L-1 status in the U.S.

You are not eligible to process a status application in the U.S. unless you are presently in status. If you are in the U.S. illegally, consular filing is a must. (On the other hand, if you have been out of status for more than six months, you may be barred from reentering the U.S. for up to ten years. See Chapter 25.)

A further plus to consular filing is that consular offices normally work much more quickly to issue nonimmigrant visas than USCIS offices do to process nonimmigrant statuses. Your waiting time for the paperwork to be finished may be much shorter at a U.S. consulate abroad than at most USCIS offices.

A drawback to consular filing is that you must be physically present in the country where the consulate is located to file there. If your petition is ultimately turned down because of an unexpected problem, not only will you have to wait outside the U.S. until the problem is resolved, but other visas in your passport, such as a visitor's visa, may be canceled. It will then be impossible for you to enter the U.S. at all. Consequently, if your L-1 visa case is not very strong and freedom of travel is not essential to you, it might be wise to apply in the U.S., make up your mind to remain there for the duration of the L-1 status and skip trying to get a visa from the consulate.

2. Application Procedures: Consular Filing

Technically the law allows you to apply for an L-1 visa at any U.S. consulate you choose. However, from a practical standpoint, your case will be given the greatest consideration at the consulate in your home country. Applying in some other country creates suspicion there about your motives for choosing their consulate. Often, when an applicant is having trouble at a home consulate, he will seek a more lenient office in some other country. This practice of consulate shopping is frowned on. Unless you have a very good reason for being elsewhere (such as a temporary job assignment in some other nation), it is smarter to file your visa application in your home country.

Furthermore, if you have been present in the U.S. unlawfully, in general you cannot apply as a third-country national. Even if you overstayed your status in the U.S. by just one day, you must return to your home country and apply for the visa from that consulate. Overstaying will also result in the automatic cancellation of your visa. There is an exception. If you were admitted to the U.S. for the duration of your status (indicated by a "D/S" on your I-94 form) and you remained in the U.S. beyond that time, you may still be able to apply as a third-country national. You will be barred from third-country national processing only if an immigration judge has determined that you were unlawfully present.

You may not file an application for an L-1 visa at a consulate before your petition has been approved. Once this occurs, the USCIS regional service center where the petition was originally submitted will forward a complete copy of your file to the U.S. consulate designated on Form I-129 in Step One. At the same time, a Notice of Action Form I-797 indicating approval will be sent directly to your U.S. employer. Once your employer receives this, telephone the consulate to see if the petition file has arrived from USCIS. If the file is slow in coming, ask the consulate to consider granting approval of your L-1 visa based only on the Notice of Action. Many U.S. consulates are willing to do so. If your U.S. employer has approved L-1 blanket status, the U.S. company will issue a Certificate of Eligibility directly to you. This is used as a substitute for the Notice of Action in individual L-1 cases.

Once the petition is approved, check with the U.S. consulate regarding its application procedures. Many insist on advance appointments. Just getting an appointment can take several weeks. Be aware that heightened U.S. security procedures are adding weeks to visa processing times around the world.

3. Application Forms: Consular Filing

When you file at a U.S. consulate abroad, the consulate officials will provide you with certain forms, designated by a "DS" preceding a number. Instructions for completing DS forms and what to do with them once they are filled out will come with the forms. We do not include copies of these forms in this book, because different consulates sometimes create different versions of the forms.

4. Application Documents: Consular Filing

You are required to show a valid passport and present one photograph taken in accordance with the photo instructions at http://travel.state.gov/photorequirements/html. If the consulate has not yet received your USCIS file containing the paperwork from the approved petition, you will then need to show the original Notice of Action, Form I-797, which your employer received from USCIS by mail, or your Certificate of Eligibility Form I-129S. Most consulates will issue L-1 visas based only on the Notice of Action or Certificate of Eligibility, although some, particularly in South America, insist on seeing the complete USCIS file. If the consulate wants to see your file and it is late (more than a month) in arriving, request that the consulate investigate the file's whereabouts. You, too, can write the USCIS regional service center where the petition was processed, requesting that they look for the file.

For each accompanying relative, you must present a valid passport and one photograph taken in accordance with the State Department's photo instructions. You will also need documents verifying their family relationship to you. You may verify a parent/child relationship by presenting the child's long-form birth certificate. Many countries, including Canada and England, issue both short- and long-form birth certificates. Where both are available, the long form is needed because it contains the names of the parents while the short form does not.

If you are accompanied by your spouse, you must prove that you are lawfully married by showing a civil marriage certificate. Church marriage certificates are generally unacceptable. (There are a few exceptions, depending on the laws of your particular country. Canadians, for example, may use church marriage certificates if the marriage took place in Quebec Province, but not elsewhere. If a civil certificate is available, however, you should always use it.) You may have married in a country where marriages are not customarily recorded. Tribal areas of Africa are an example. In such situations, ask the U.S. consulate or embassy what it will accept as proof of marriage.

5. Additional Application Documents for Blanket L-1 Visas: Consular Filing

In addition to all those documents listed above for applicants in individual L-1 cases, applicants having U.S. employers with approved blanket L-1 visa petitions must submit some extra documents. The first of these is a copy of the Notice of Action showing approval of the blanket petition, Form I-797. Your U.S. employer will give this form directly to you and you will, in turn, submit it with your application. This document is a substitute for the Notice of Action sent to the consulate by USCIS in individual L-1 cases.

Since your own eligibility for an L-1 classification is not proven in the Step One portion of a blanket L-1 petition case as it is with individual L-1 cases, you must now document your own eligibility.

a. Proof of Employment Abroad

You must present documents proving that you were employed outside of the U.S. by the non-U.S. company for at least one of the past three years. The best way to prove this is by providing copies of any wage statements you may have received. In Canada this is the T-4, in England, the P.A.Y.E. You should also submit your personal income tax return filed in your home country for the most recent year. If this is unavailable, a notarized statement from the bookkeeper or accountant of the non-U.S. employer may be used; however, you should also submit a statement explaining why the tax returns are unavailable. For example, you might state that tax returns are not required in your home country or that the returns haven't been prepared yet.

b. Proof That You Are a Manager, Executive, or Specialized Knowledge Professional

You must submit evidence that your employment abroad fits the USCIS definition of manager, executive, or specialized knowledge professional, and that your employment in the U.S. will be of a similar type. To prove this, detailed statements from both the U.S. and non-U.S. employers explaining your specific duties as well as the number and kind of employees you supervise must be presented.

If the application is based on specialized knowledge, the statements should also describe the nature of the specialized knowledge you possess, the reason why only you have that knowledge, and how it will be used in your U.S. job. Specialized knowledge must pertain to the individual company. It cannot be knowledge that is available from others in the open job market. The statements your employer submits should be in his own words and do not have to be in any special form.

You must also submit documents showing you meet USCIS's definition of professional. This usually requires you to show that you have a degree from a college or university. Evidence should include copies of diplomas and transcripts from the colleges and universities you attended. The consulate insists on both a diploma and a transcript from a school where you graduated. If you attended a school but did not graduate, the transcript is required. If you were educated outside of the U.S., the consulate may request a credential evaluation from an approved evaluation service as explained in "Academic Credential Evaluations,", above.

6. Application Interviews: Consular Filing

The consulate will frequently require an interview before issuing an L-1 visa. During the interview, a consul officer will examine the data you gave in Step One for accuracy, especially regarding facts about your own qualifications. Once you are approved, you will proably be asked to return later for your visa. Many cases are approved only provisionally, however, awaiting the completion of security checks.

7. Using Your L-1 Visa

On entering the U.S. with your new L-1 visa, you will be given an I-94 card. It will be stamped with a date indicating how long you can stay. Normally, you are permitted to remain up to the expiration date on your L-1 petition or, in a blanket L-1 case, the Certificate of Eligibility. If you are coming to the U.S. on a blanket L-1 visa, your U.S. employer will provide you with Certificate of Eligibility Forms I-129S in triplicate and a copy of the Notice of Action indicating approval of the blanket L-1 petition. In addition to the I-94 card, upon your entry the I-129S will be stamped by an immigration (CBP) inspector and you will be required to keep one copy, together with your I-94 card. Each time you exit and reenter the U.S., you will get a new I-94 card authorizing your stay up to the final date indicated on the petition or Certificate of Eligibility.

SUMMARY EXCLUSION

The law empowers a CBP inspector at the airport to summarily (without allowing judicial review) bar entry to someone requesting admission to the U.S. if either of the following are true:

- The inspector thinks you are lying about practically anything connected with entering the U.S., including your purpose in coming, intent to return, and prior immigration history. This includes the use or suspected use of false documents.
- You do not have the proper documentation to support your entry to the U.S. in the category you are requesting.

If the inspector excludes you, you cannot be re-admitted to the U.S. for five years, unless USCIS grants a special waiver. For this reason it is extremely important to understand the terms of your requested status, and to not make any misrepresentations. If you are found to be inadmissible, you may request to withdraw your application to enter the U.S. in order to prevent having the five-year deportation order on your record. The CBP may allow this in some exceptional cases.

8. Application Appeals: Consular Filing

When a consulate turns down an L-1 visa application, there is no way to make a formal appeal, although you are free to reapply as often as you like. (Check with your local consulate to be sure, however—some place limits on the number of repeat applications, or require you to wait a certain number of months before reapplying.) If your visa is denied, the reasons for the denial will be explained by the consul officer. Written statements of decisions are not normally provided in nonimmigrant cases. If a lack of evidence about a particular point is the problem, sometimes simply presenting more evidence can change the result. The most common reason for denial of an L-1 visa is that you are found inadmissible.

Certain people who have been refused L-1 visas reapply at a different consulate, attempting to hide the fact that they were turned down previously. You should know that if your application is denied, the last page in your passport will be stamped "Application Received" with the date and location of the rejecting consulate. This notation shows that some type of prior visa application has failed. It serves as a warning to other consulates that your case merits close inspection. If what we have just told you makes you think it would be a good idea to overcome this problem by obtaining a new, unmarked passport, you should also know that permanent computer records are kept of all visa denials.

F. Carrying Out Step Two: The Application (U.S. Filing)

If you are physically present in the U.S., you may apply for L-1 status without leaving the country, on the following conditions:

- you are simultaneously filing paperwork for or have already received an approved petition for an individual L-1, or you have a Certificate of Eligibility for a blanket L-1
- you entered the U.S. legally
- you have never worked illegally in the U.S., and
- the date on your I-94 card has not passed.

If you were admitted as a visitor without a visa under the Visa Waiver Program, you may not carry out Step Two in the U.S. Currently there are 28 participating countries in the Visa Waiver Program, as listed in Chapter 2.

If you cannot meet these terms, you may not file for L-1 status in the U.S. It is important to realize, however, that eligibility to apply in the U.S. has nothing to do with overall eligibility for an L-1 visa. Many applicants who are barred from filing in the U.S. but otherwise qualify for L-1 status may (as long as they're not inadmissible) apply successfully for an L-1 visa at U.S. consulates abroad. If you find you are not eligible for U.S. filing, read Section E, above.

1. Benefits and Drawbacks of U.S. filing

Visas are never given inside the U.S. They are issued exclusively by U.S. consulates abroad. If you file in the U.S. and you are successful, you will get L-1 status but not the visa itself. L-1 status allows you to remain in the U.S. with L-1 privileges until the status expires, but should you leave the country for any reason before that time, you will have to apply for the visa itself at a U.S. consulate before returning to America. Moreover, the fact that your L-1 status has been approved in the U.S. does not guarantee that the consulate will also approve your visa.

There is another problem which comes up only in U.S. filings. It is the issue of what is called *preconceived intent*. To approve a change of status, USCIS must believe that at the time you originally entered the U.S. as a visitor or with some other nonimmigrant visa, you did not intend to apply for a different status. If USCIS thinks you had a preconceived plan to change from the status you arrived with to a different status, it may deny your application. The preconceived intent issue is one less potential hazard you will face if you apply at a U.S. consulate abroad.

On the plus side of U.S. filing, when problems do arise with your U.S. application, you can stay in the U.S. while they are being corrected. If you run into snags at a U.S. consulate, you will have to remain outside the U.S. until matters are resolved.

2.   Application General Procedures: U.S. Filing

The general procedure for filing Step Two in the U.S. is to follow Step One as outlined in Section E, above, but to mark box "b" in Part 2 of Form I-129, indicating that you will complete processing in the U.S. There is no separate application form for filing Step Two in the U.S. If you have an accompanying spouse or children, however, a separate Form I-539 must be filed for them.

When you apply for a change of status, the filing fee for a Step One petition (Form I-129) is presently $130. Your family must pay $140 with their Form I-539 (no matter how many family members are included). Checks and money orders are accepted. It is not advisable to send cash. We recommend submitting all papers by certified mail, return receipt requested, and making a copy of everything sent in to keep for your records.

Within a few weeks of mailing in the application, you should get back a written notice of confirmation that the papers are being processed, together with a receipt for the fees. This notice will also tell you your immigration file number and approximately when to expect a decision. If USCIS wants further information before acting on your case, all application papers, forms and documents will be returned together with another form known as an *I-797*. The I-797 tells you what additional pieces of information or documents are expected. Supply the extra data and mail the whole package back to the USCIS regional service center by the deadline given, usually 12 weeks.

Applications for an L-1 status are normally approved within two to four months. When this happens, you will receive a Notice of Action Form I-797 indicating the dates for which your status is approved, and a new I-94 card, which is attached to the bottom of the form.

3.   Application Forms: U.S. Filing

Copies of all the required USCIS forms can be found in Appendix II and on the USCIS website.

Form I-129

Follow the directions in Section D2, except in Part 2, Question 4, mark box "b" instead of box "a."

Form I-539 (for accompanying relatives only)

Only one application form is needed for an entire family, but if there is more than one accompanying relative, each additional one should be listed on the I-539 supplement.

Part 1. These questions are self-explanatory. "A" numbers are usually given only to people who have previously applied for green cards or who have been in deportation proceedings. Consult an attorney if you have an A number. "Current nonimmigrant status" means the type of visa that the person has, such as B-2 visitor or F-2 family member of student.

Part 2, Question 1. Mark box "b," and write in "L-2."

Question 2. This question is self-explanatory.

Part 3. In most cases, you will mark Item 1 with the date requested in the Step One petition. You will also complete Items 3 and 4, which are self-explanatory.

Part 4, Questions 1–2. These questions are self-explanatory.

Question 3. The different parts to this question are self-explanatory; however, items "a" through "c" ask if an immigrant visa petition or adjustment of status application has ever been filed on your behalf. If you are separately applying for a green card through a relative, this would be Step One, as described in Chapter 5. If you are separately applying for a green card through employment, this would be Step Two as described in Chapter 8. If you have only begun the Labor Certification, the first step of getting a green card through employment, this question should be answered "no."

4.   Application Documents: U.S. Filing

Each applicant must submit a copy of his or her I-94 card, the small white card you received on entering the U.S. Remember, if the date stamped on your I-94 card has already passed, you are ineligible for U.S. filing. Canadians who are just visiting are not expected to have I-94 cards. Canadians with any other type of nonimmigrant status should have them.

For each accompanying relative, send in a copy of his or her I-94 card. You will also need documents verifying their family relationship to you. You may verify a parent/child relationship by presenting the child's long-form birth certificate. Many countries, including Canada and England, issue both short- and long-form birth certificates. Where both are available, the long form is needed because it contains the names of the parents while the short form does not.

If you are accompanied by your spouse, you must prove that you are lawfully married by showing a valid civil marriage certificate. Church marriage certificates are generally unacceptable. (There are a few exceptions, depending on the laws of your particular country. Canadians, for example, may use church marriage certificates if the marriage took place in Quebec Province, but not elsewhere. If a civil certificate is available, however, you should always use it.) You may have married in a country where marriages are not customarily recorded. Tribal areas of Africa are an example. In such situations call the nearest consulate or embassy representing your home country for help with getting acceptable proof of marriage.

5. Additional Application Documents for Blanket L-1 Visa: U.S. Filing

In addition to all those documents listed above for applicants in individual L-1 cases, applicants having U.S. employers with approved blanket L-1 visa petitions must submit some extra documents. The first of these is the Notice of Action indicating approval of the blanket petition, Form I-797. Your U.S. employer will give this form directly to you and you will in turn submit it with your application. This document is a substitute for the Notice of Action sent by USCIS in individual L-1 cases.

Since your own eligibility for an L-1 classification is not proven in the Step One portion of a blanket L-1 petition case as it is in individual L-1 cases, you must document your own eligibility as part of Step Two.

a. Proof of Employment Abroad

You must supply documents proving that you were employed outside the U.S. by the non-U.S. company for at least one of the past three years. The best way to prove this is by providing copies of any wage statements you may have received. In Canada this is the T-4, in England, the P.A.Y.E. You should also submit your personal income tax return filed in your home country for the most recent year. If this is unavailable, a notarized statement from the bookkeeper or accountant of the non-U.S. employer may be used. However, you should also submit a statement explaining why

the tax returns are unavailable. For example, you might state that tax returns are not required in your home country or that the returns haven't been prepared yet.

b. Proof You Are a Manager, Executive, or Specialized Knowledge Professional

You must submit evidence that your employment abroad fits the USCIS definition of manager, executive, or specialized knowledge professional, and that your employment in the U.S. will be of a similar type. To prove this, submit detailed statements from both the U.S. and non-U.S. employers explaining your specific duties as well as the number and kind of employees you supervise. If the application is based on specialized knowledge you possess, the statements should also describe the nature of the specialized knowledge, the reason why only you have that knowledge, and how it will be used in your U.S. job. The specialized knowledge must have the characteristic of being special to the individual company. It cannot be knowledge that is available from others in the open job market. The statements your U.S. employer submits may be in the employer's own words and do not have to be in any special form.

You must also submit documents showing you meet the definition of professional. This usually requires you to show that you have a degree from a college or university. Evidence should include copies of diplomas and transcripts from the colleges and universities you attended. USCIS insists on both a diploma and a transcript from a school where you graduated. If you attended a school but did not graduate, the transcript is required. If you were educated outside of the U.S., USCIS may request a credential evaluation from an approved evaluation service as explained in "Academic Credential Evaluations," above.

6. Application Interviews: U.S. Filing

Interviews on L-1 change of status applications are rarely held. When an interview is required, the USCIS regional service center where you filed will send your paperwork to the local USCIS office nearest your U.S. employer's place of business. This office will in turn contact you for an appointment. (If USCIS has questions on the petition rather than the application, your employer will be contacted.) USCIS may ask you to bring additional documents at that time.

If you are called for an interview, the most likely reason is that USCIS either suspects some type of fraud, doubts the existence of the company, or believes you may be subject to a ground of inadmissibility. Interviews are usually a sign of trouble and can result in considerable delays.

7. Application Appeals: U.S. Filing

If your application is denied, you will receive a written decision by mail explaining the reasons for the denial. There is no way of making a formal appeal to USCIS if your application to change status is turned down. If the problem is too little evidence, you may be able to overcome this obstacle by adding more documents and resubmitting the entire application to the same USCIS office you have been dealing with, together with a written request that the case be reopened. The written request does not have to be in any special form. This is technically called a *Motion to Reopen*. There is a $110 fee to file this motion.

Remember that you may be denied the right to a U.S. filing without being denied an L-1 visa. When your application is turned down because you are found ineligible for U.S. filing, simply change your application to a consular filing. But before you depart the U.S., be sure that none of the bars to returning (such as being out of status in the U.S. for a long time before departing) or other grounds of inadmissibility, apply. If you depart and one of these problems exists, you may be stuck outside the U.S. for a long time before you can reenter.

Although there is no appeal to USCIS for the denial of an L-1 change of status application, you do have the right to file an appeal in a U.S. district court. It would be difficult to file such an appeal without employing an attorney at considerable expense. Such appeals are usually unsuccessful.

G. Extensions

L-1 visas can be extended for three years at a time, but you may not hold an L-1 visa for longer than a total of seven years if you are a manager or executive, or five years if you're a person with specialized knowledge. Although an extension is usually easier to get than the L-1 visa itself, it is not automatic. USCIS has the right to reconsider your qualifications based on any changes in the facts or law. As always, however, good cases that are well prepared will usually be successful.

To extend your L-1 visa, the petition and visa stamp will both have to be updated. Like the original application procedures, you can file either in the U.S. or at a consulate. However, contrary to our advice on the initial visa procedures, extensions are best handled in the U.S. That is because visa stamps, which can only be issued originally at consulates, may be extended in the U.S.

1. Step One: Extension Petition

Extension procedures are identical to the procedures followed in getting the initial visa, except that less documen-tation is generally required. However, the best practice is to fully document an extension application as well as the initial request, since USCIS will probably not have the original file and papers onsite, and it could cause a long delay if they have to request the old file to decide the extension request.

a. Extension Petition Forms

Copies of all the required USCIS forms can be found in Appendix II and on the USCIS website.

Form I-129 and L Supplement

Follow the directions in Section D2. The only difference is that you will mark boxes "2b" and "4c" of Part 2.

Form I-539 (for accompanying relatives only)

Follow the directions for Section F3, but mark box "1a" of Part 2.

b. Extension Petition Documents

In addition to the same documents you filed the first time, you must submit your I-94 card. You should also submit the original Notice of Action I-797 (approval notice), a letter from your employer stating that your extension is required, a copy of your personal U.S. income tax returns for the past two years, including W-2 forms, and a copy of your employer's most recent U.S. income tax return.

WORKING WHILE YOUR EXTENSION PETITION IS PENDING

If you file your petition for an extension of L-1 status before your authorized stay expires, you are automatically permitted to continue working under the same terms of your L-visa, for up to eight months (240 days) while you are waiting for a decision. If, however, your authorized stay expires after you have filed for an extension but before you receive an approval, and more than eight months (240 days) go by without getting a decision on your extension petition, you must stop working.

---

2. Step Two: Visa Revalidation

Visas can be revalidated either in the U.S. or at a consulate.

a. Visa Revalidation: U.S. Filing

If you are physically in the U.S. and your L-1 status extension has been approved by USCIS, you can have your visa revalidated by mail without leaving the country. The exception is if you carry the passport of a country that is on the U.S. government's list of countries that sponsor terrorism, in which case you won't be allowed to revalidate your visa without leaving the U.S. first. When this book went to print, the listed countries included North Korea, Cuba, Syria, Sudan, Iran, Iraq, and Libya.

To revalidate your visa, you must fill out Form DS-156 and send it to the Department of State. You should send in your visa revalidation application as soon as possible within the 60 days before your allowed stay expires (but don't send it any earlier, or the entire package will be returned to you). With the form you should also submit as documents your passport (valid for at least six months), a recent passport-sized photo (2" x 2", full face view, on a light background, stapled or glued to the form), a fee ($100), your current I-94 card, your Employment Petition on Notice of Action Form I-797, and a detailed letter from your employer describing your job duties and justifying your need for the visa. Nationals of certain countries must also pay a "reciprocity fee." The fees may be paid by bank draft, corporate check, or money order, payable to the U.S. Department of State. You cannot pay by cash, credit card, or personal check.

Male visa applicants between the ages of 16 and 45, regardless of nationality and regardless of where they apply, must also complete and submit a form DS-157.

You should enclose a self-addressed, stamped envelope, or a completed Federal Express or other courier service airbill. Send the entire package by certified mail to

If sending by postal service:
U.S. Department of State/Visa
P.O. Box 952099
St. Louis, MO 63195–2099

If sending by courier service:
U.S. Department of State/Visa (Box 2099)
1005 Convention Plaza
St. Louis, MO 63101–1200

The passport will be returned to you with a newly revalidated visa in around seven weeks. For more information on this process, see the State Department website at www.travel.state.gov/revals.html.

If your accompanying relatives are physically in the U.S., their L-2 visas may be revalidated by sending in their passports and I-94 cards together with yours. We strongly advise gathering your family together inside U.S. borders so you can take advantage of this simple revalidation procedure.

b. Visa Revalidation: Consular Filing

If you must leave the U.S. after your extension has been approved but before you had time to get your visa revalidated, you must get a new visa stamp issued at a consulate. Read Section G, above. The procedures for consular extensions are identical.

We would like to reemphasize that it is much more convenient to apply for a revalidated visa by mail through the State Department than it is to extend your L-1 visa through a consulate. Try to schedule filing your extension petition so that you can remain in the U.S. until it is complete.

3. Blanket L-1 Extensions

This refers to the extension of the blanket status itself that is given to the company. This is not an explanation of how you may extend your own visa if you arrived in the U.S. under your company's blanket L-1 visa. Extensions for individual L-1 visa holders and those who obtained visas under the blanket program are handled in the same manner as explained above, except that a Certificate of Eligibility Form I-129S must also be submitted.

A company holding an approved blanket L-1 petition will have to extend that petition only one time. After the initial three-year approval period, the blanket L-1 visa petition can be extended with indefinite validity.

a. Blanket L-1 Extension Forms

A new Form I-129 and L Supplement has to be filed. For instructions on filling out this Form, see Section D, above.

b. Blanket L-1 Extension Documents

The only documents required to extend the blanket L visa petition are as follows:
- a copy of the previous Notice of Action, Form I-797, and
- a written list of the names of all transferees admitted under the blanket L-1 petition for the previous three years; for each person, include the position held, name of the specific company where the person worked, the date of initial admission, and the date of final departure.

FORMS AND DOCUMENTS CHECKLIST

STEP ONE: PETITION

Forms

- [ ] Form I-129 and L Supplement.

Documents

- [ ] Documents proving one year of employment outside the U.S. during the last three years.
- [ ] Documents proving employment outside of U.S. as an executive, manager, or person with specialized knowledge.
- [ ] A statement describing your proposed job's duties, salary, and dates of employment.
- [ ] Articles of incorporation or other legal charter or business license of the non-U.S. company.
- [ ] Articles of incorporation or other legal charter or business license of the U.S. company.
- [ ] Legal business registration certificate of the non-U.S. company.
- [ ] Legal business registration certificate of the U.S. company.
- [ ] Tax returns of the non-U.S. company for the past two years.
- [ ] Tax returns of the U.S. company for the past two years, if available.
- [ ] Copies of all outstanding stock certificates, if the business is a corporation.
- [ ] Notarized affidavit from the secretary of the corporation, or, if the business is not a corporation, from the official record keeper of the business, stating the names of each owner and percentages of the company owned.
- [ ] If the business relationship is a joint venture, a copy of the written joint venture agreement.
- [ ] Annual shareholder reports of the U.S. and non-U.S. companies, if publicly held.
- [ ] Accountant's financial statements, including profit and loss statements and balance sheets of the non-U.S. company for the past two years.
- [ ] Accountant's financial statements, including profit and loss statements and balance sheets of the U.S. company for the past two years, if available.
- [ ] Payroll records of the non-U.S. company for the past two years.
- [ ] Payroll records of the U.S. company for the past two years, if available.

- [ ] Letters of reference from Chambers of Commerce for the non-U.S. company.
- [ ] Promotional literature describing the nature of U.S. employer's business.
- [ ] Letters from banks or bank statements indicating the average account balance of the U.S. business.
- [ ] Copy of a business lease or deed for business premises of the U.S. business.
- [ ] If more than half the stock of either the U.S. or non-U.S. company is publicly held, statements from the secretary of the corporation describing how the companies are related.

Additional Documents for Blanket Petitions

- [ ] Copies of the Notice of Action Forms I-797 showing at least ten L-1 approvals during the past year
- [ ] Company income tax returns, audited accountant's financial statements, or the annual shareholders' report, showing combined annual sales for all of the related U.S. employer companies totaling at least $25 million, or
- [ ] The most recent quarterly state unemployment tax return and federal employment tax return Form 940 showing at least 1,000 employees for all of the related U.S. employer business locations.

STEP TWO: APPLICATION

Forms

- [ ] DS forms (available at U.S. consulates abroad for consular filing only).
- [ ] Form I-129 (U.S. filing only) with L Supplement.
- [ ] Form I-539 (U.S. filing only, for accompanying relatives).

Documents

- [ ] Form I-797 indicating approval of the L-1 petition.
- [ ] Valid passport for you and each accompanying relative.
- [ ] Copy of I-94 card for you and each accompanying relative (U.S. filing only).
- [ ] One passport-type photo of you and each accompanying relative (consular filing only).

Treaty Traders: E-1 Visas

Privileges

- You can work legally in the U.S. for a U.S. company for whom more than 50% of its business is trade between the U.S. and your home country.

- Visas can be issued quickly.

- You may travel in and out of the U.S. or remain here continuously until your E-1 visa expires.

- There is no legal limitation on the number of extensions that may be granted. Because of the initial duration of an E-1 visa (two years) as well as the limitless extensions, E-1 visas can allow you to live in the U.S. on a prolonged basis, provided you continue to maintain E-1 qualifications.

- Visas are available for accompanying relatives and your spouse can get a permit to accept employment in the U.S.

Limitations

- Visas are available only to nationals of countries having trade treaties with the U.S.

- You are restricted to working only for the specific employer or self-owned business that acted as your E-1 visa sponsor.

- Visas can initially be approved for up to two years. Extensions of up to two more years at a time may be allowed.

- Accompanying relatives may stay in the U.S. with you, but your children may not work, unless they qualify to do so in their own right.

A. How to Qualify

There are no quota restrictions for E-1 visas. U.S. filed applications are usually approved within two to four months. Applications made at U.S. consulates are usually approved and visas issued within four to eight weeks. There are several requirements for qualifying for an E-1 visa.

1. Citizen of a Treaty Country

E-1 visas are available to citizens of only selected countries which have trade treaties with the U.S. and wish to come to the U.S. to carry on trade between the U.S. and their home country. Those countries with treaties currently in effect are:

Argentina, Australia, Austria, Belgium, Bolivia, Bosnia & Herzegovina, Brunei, Canada, Colombia, Costa Rica, Croatia, Denmark, Estonia, Ethiopia, Finland, France, Germany, Greece, Honduras, Iran, Ireland, Israel, Italy, Japan, Jordan, Korea (South), Latvia, Liberia, Luxembourg, Mexico, Netherlands, Norway, Oman, Pakistan, Paraguay, Philippines, Slovenia, Spain, Suriname, Sweden, Switzerland, Taiwan, Thailand, Togo, Turkey, United Kingdom, Yugoslavia.

Because treaty provisions are subject to change, be sure your country has one in force before proceeding with your application. The complete list is kept at Volume 9 of the Foreign Affairs Manual, § 41.51 Exh. 1.

2. Company Owned by Citizens of a Qualifying Country

To qualify for an E-1 visa, you must be coming to the U.S. to trade on behalf of or develop and direct the operations of a business, at least 50% of which is owned by citizens of your treaty country. The company may be owned by you or others. If the company is owned in part or in whole by others, and some or all of them already live in the U.S., those people may need to have E-1 visas themselves before the company can act as an E-1 sponsor for you. Specifically:

- at least 50% of the company must be owned by citizens of a single trade treaty country, and
- the owners from the single trade treaty country must either live outside the U.S. and be classifiable for E-1 status or live inside the U.S. with E-1 visas.

This second condition can be a little confusing. Some examples may help to make it clearer.

EXAMPLE 1: The company is owned 100% by one person. The owner is a citizen of a trade treaty country and lives outside the U.S. in his home country. He would qualify for E-1 status if he sought to enter the U.S.

In this case the owner does not need to already have an E-1 visa for the company to support your E-1 visa application. He has already fulfilled the alternative condition by living outside the U.S. and being eligible for such status.

EXAMPLE 2: The company is owned in equal shares by two individuals. Each owner is a citizen of the same trade treaty country. One owner lives in the U.S. on a green card. The other still lives in his home country and is classifiable as an E-1.

In this case, neither owner needs an E-1 visa for the company to support your E-1 application, because 50% of the owners have fulfilled the qualifying conditions. If, however, we changed this example so that both owners lived in the U.S., at least one of them would need an E-1 visa to fulfill the required conditions. (Green card holders do not qualify as E-1 principals.)

EXAMPLE 3: The company is owned in equal shares by 100 people. Thirty owners are citizens of a particular trade treaty country but live in the U.S. Thirty other owners are citizens of the same trade treaty country and they are living in their home country, but are eligible as E-1 visa holders. The remaining 40 owners are U.S. citizens.

In this situation, if the company is to act as an E-1 sponsor for others, 20 of the 30 owners who are citizens of the trade treaty country but live in the U.S. must hold E-1 visas. Remember that only 50 of the owners need to be citizens of the treaty country. Of those 50, each must either live outside the U.S. and be classifiable as E-1s or live in the U.S. on an E-1 visa. In our example, 30 live outside the U.S. Therefore, only 20 of the trade treaty country citizens living inside the U.S. need have E-1 visas to make up the necessary 50% total of qualifying owners.

Additionally, USCIS's regulations allow a different test in the case of large multinational corporations in which it is difficult to determine ownership by stock ownership. Therefore, in the situation where a corporation's stock is sold exclusively in the country of incorporation, it may be presumed to have the nationality of the country where the stocks are exchanged.

3. You Must Be a 50% Owner or Key Employee

E-1 visas may be issued only to the principal owners or key employees of the qualifying business, provided all have the same treaty nationality. To qualify as a principal owner, you must control at least 50% of the company, possess operational control through a managerial position or similar corporate device, or be in a position to control the enterprise by other means. To qualify as a key employee you must be considered an executive, supervisor, supervisory role executive, or person whose skills are essential to the enterprise.

a. Executives and Supervisors

For E-2 classification purposes, the main thrust of the position must be executive or supervisory, and give the employee ultimate control and responsibility for the operation of at least a major part of the enterprise. USCIS will examine the following to determine whether a given position fits the bill:

- an "executive" position is normally one that gives the employee great authority in determining policy and direction of the enterprise;
- "supervisory" positions normally entail responsibility for supervising a major portion of an enterprise's operations and do not usually involve direct supervision of low-level employees, and
- whether the individual applicant's skills, experience, salary, and title are on a par with executive or supervisory positions, and whether the position carries overall authority and responsibility in the overall context of the enterprise, such as discretionary decision making, policy-setting, direction and management of business operations, and supervision of other professional and supervisory personnel.

b. Essential Employees

USCIS's regulations are vague on what constitutes the essentiality of an employee. The employee's skills do not have to be unique or "one of a kind" but they should be indispensable to the success of the investment. They will be evaluated on a case-by-case basis. However, if the skills possessed by the employee are commonplace or readily available in the U.S. labor market, it will be difficult to show that the employee is essential.

Specifically, USCIS will consider the following to determine whether an individual who is a non-executive, non-supervisor and who is not at least a 50% owner, should be classified as an E-2 employee because of the essentiality of his or her skills:

- the degree of expertise in the area of operations involved; the degree of experience and training with the enterprise
- whether U.S. workers possess the individual's skills or aptitude
- the length of the applicant's specific skill or aptitude
- the length of time required to train an individual to perform the job duties of the position
- the relationship of the individual's skills and talents to the overall operations of the entity, and
- the salary the special qualifications can command.

Knowledge of a foreign language and/or culture will not by itself constitute the degree of essentiality required.

4. Fifty-One Percent of the Company's Trade Must Be Between the U.S. and Your Home Country

More than 50% of the company's trade must be between the U.S. and the treaty nation citizen's home country. For example, if you are from the U.K. and are in the business of importing English antiques to the U.S., more than 50% of your inventory, as measured by its cash value, must have been imported directly from the U.K. If some other company does the importing and your business simply buys the British goods once they reach the U.S., you will not qualify for the visa, because your company is not directly engaged in trade with the U.K.

The law is liberal in its definition of what constitutes trade. The most straightforward example is the import or export of a tangible product, but exchange of monies or services can also qualify. For example, the transfer of technology through scientifically knowledgeable employees or the rendering of services have been recognized as trade. Activities other than the sale of goods that have been officially recognized by the U.S. Department of State as trade for E-1 purposes include international banking, the practice of law, the sale of insurance, the provision of international transportation, the sale of communications services, some news gathering activities, and the sale of tickets by tourist agencies.

5. Substantial Trade

A company must be carrying on a substantial amount of trade between the U.S. and the home country in order for the company to successfully support your E-1 application. The term "substantial" is not defined in the law by a strict numerical measure. In fact it is not specifically defined at all, though USCIS regulations state that there must be a "continuous flow" of trade items between the two countries.

What is considered substantial depends on the type of business. For example, a business that imports heavy machinery may not have to show a huge number of sales, but will have to show a greater dollar volume of business than a business importing candy bars to meet the requirement of substantial trade.

There are three general tests—dollars, volume, and frequency—that can normally be relied on to measure substantiality. The company must be able to meet the minimum standards of all three.

a. Dollar Amount of Trade

The dollar amount (not the retail value) of the inventory, services, or other commodities purchased from or sold to the treaty country should exceed $200,000 per year. However, some consulates require the sales or purchases to equal or exceed as much as $500,000, while others may accept as little as $50,000. A specific sum is not written into the law. The individual consul officer has the authority to require varying amounts in different cases. Still, experience shows that anything under the $200,000 mark is a weak case.

b. Volume

If the company sells products, to satisfy the volume test, its import or export trade must be enough to create full-time business in the U.S. The company's initial shipment must fill at least an entire warehouse or retail store. If the company sells services, the volume should be large enough to support the E-1 visa holder and at least one other worker. Some businesses do not meet the volume test when they are first starting up, but grow to the required size as time goes on. Purchasing a growing business may be one way to fulfill the volume requirement immediately.

c. Frequency

The company must import to or export from the U.S. with sufficient frequency to maintain a full inventory at all times. One shipment is not enough. Importation or exportation must be ongoing.

 These measures have been primarily derived from our own experience and not the immigration laws. It is possible for an E-1 visa to be approved with a smaller amount of trade than we have described in our three tests. With E-1 visas, a great deal is left to the judgment of the USCIS or consul officer evaluating the application.

6. Intent to Leave the U.S.

E-1 visas are meant to be temporary. At the time of application, you must intend to depart the U.S. when your business there is completed. As previously mentioned, you are not required to maintain a foreign residence abroad.

The U.S. government knows it is difficult to read minds. Expect to be asked for evidence showing that when you go to the U.S. on an E-1 visa, you eventually plan to leave. In many nonimmigrant categories, you are asked to show proof that you keep a house or apartment outside the U.S. as an indication that you eventually intend to go back to your home country. You do not need to keep a home outside the U.S. to qualify for an E-1 visa—but it would help, nonetheless. You will certainly be asked to show that you have some family members, possessions, or property elsewhere in the world as an incentive for your eventual departure from the U.S.

7. Accompanying Relatives

When you qualify for an E-1 visa, your spouse and unmarried children under age 21 can also get E-1 visas by providing proof of their family relationship to you. Your spouse will also be permitted to work in the U.S.

To take advantage of the right to work, your spouse will, after arriving in the U.S., need to apply for a work permit. This is done on Form I-765. In filling out the form, your spouse should write "spouse of E nonimmigrant" in Question 15, and "A-17" in Question 16.

Your spouse will need to mail this form, together with proof of your visa status, a copy of his or her I-94 card, the filing fee and two photos, to the appropriate USCIS Service Center for your geographic region. For the address and other information, call USCIS Information at 800-375-5283 or see the USCIS website (www.uscis.gov).

POSSIBILITIES FOR A GREEN CARD FROM E-1 STATUS

If you have an E-1 visa, you can file to get a green card, but being in the U.S. on an E-1 visa gives you no advantage in doing so, and in fact may prove to be a drawback. That is because E-1 visas, like all nonimmigrant visas, are intended only for those who plan on leaving the U.S. once their jobs or other activities there are completed.

If you apply for a green card, you are in effect making a statement that you never intend to leave the U.S. Therefore, the U.S. government may allow you to keep E-1 status while pursuing a green card, but only if you can convince it that you did not intend to get a green card when you originally applied for the E-1 visa, and that you will leave the U.S. if you are unable to secure a green card before your E-1 visa expires. Proving these things can be difficult. If you do not succeed, your E-1 visa may be taken away. Should this happen, it may affect your green card application, since being out of status or working without authorization may be a bar to getting a green card in the U.S., or may create a waiting period of three or ten years if you depart the U.S. and apply for a visa. (See Chapter 25.)

B. Applying for an E-1 Visa

Getting an E-1 visa is a one-step process.

1. The Application

Once you have opened a qualifying company engaged in trade between your home country and the U.S., or been offered a job as a key employee of a qualifying company owned by others from your country, getting an E-1 visa is a one-step process.

Some applicants seeking E-1 visas as key employees expect their sponsoring employers to handle the entire process for them and indeed, a number of large companies are equipped with experienced workers who will do this for highly desirable employees. Other companies are prepared to pay an immigration attorney's fees as an expense of trying to attract a key staff member. However, in many cases it is the employee who is most interested in having the visa issued, and, to employers, the red tape of having a foreign employee can be an unfamiliar nuisance.

As we give you step-by-step instructions for getting an E-1 visa, we will indicate that certain activities are to be performed by your employer and others are to be performed by you, recognizing that in the case of an E-1 visa you yourself may be the principal owner of the qualifying business. However, there is nothing to stop you from helping with the work. For example, you can fill out forms intended to be completed by your employer and simply ask him to check them over and sign them. The less your sponsoring employer is inconvenienced, the more the company will be willing to act as sponsor for your E-1 visa. Of course if you are the principal owner of a qualifying business, all the paperwork responsibilities will fall on you.

The one step required to get an E-1 visa is called the application. The object of the application is to show that the conditions to getting an E-1 visa discussed earlier in this chapter have been met. It is filed by you and your accompanying relatives, if any. The application may be carried out in the U.S. at a USCIS office (if you're already legally in the U.S.) or in your home country at a U.S. consulate there. The vast majority of nonimmigrant visa applications are filed at consulates. That is because most cases don't qualify for U.S. filing.

If you are already in the U.S. legally on some other type of nonimmigrant visa, you qualify to apply for an E-1 status at a USCIS office inside the U.S., using a procedure known as *change of nonimmigrant status*. (If you were admitted as a visitor without a visa under the Visa Waiver Program, you may not carry out the application step in the U.S. Currently there are 28 participating countries in the Visa Waiver Program, listed in Chapter 2.)

Change of Status is simply a technical term meaning you are switching from one nonimmigrant status to another. If a change of status is approved, you will then be treated as if you had entered the country with an E-1 visa and you can keep the status as long as you remain in the U.S. or until it expires, whichever comes first.

You will not, however, receive a visa stamp, which is what you need if your plans include traveling in and out of the U.S. Visa stamps are issued only at U.S. consulates abroad. Therefore, if you change your status and later travel outside the U.S., you will have to go to the U.S. consulate in your home country and repeat the application over again, obtaining the E-1 visa stamp in your passport before you can return.

Although it is not a requirement, one item you or your sponsoring employer may wish to add to the paperwork package is a cover letter. Cover letters act as a summary and index to the forms and documents, and are often used by immigration attorneys or U.S. companies that process many visas for their employees. Cover letters begin with a statement summarizing the facts of the case and explaining why the particular applicant is eligible for the visa. This statement is followed by a list of the forms and documents submitted. If it is carefully written, a cover letter can make the case clearer and easier to process for the consular or USCIS officer evaluating it. This is particularly important in an E-1 visa case where the documentation by itself may require explanation. Cover letters must be individually tailored to each case, so if you don't think you can write a good one, just leave it out and submit only your forms and documents; or consult with an attorney.

2. Tips on Handling the Paperwork

There are two types of paperwork you must submit to get an E-1 visa. The first consists of official government forms completed by you or your employer. The second is personal and business documents, such as birth and marriage certificates, school transcripts and diplomas, and company financial statements and tax returns.

It is vital that forms are properly filled out and all necessary documents are supplied. You or your U.S. employer may resent the intrusion into your privacy and the sizable effort it takes to prepare immigration applications but you should realize the process is an impersonal matter to immigration officials. Your getting a visa is more important to you than it is to the U.S. government. There is no shortage of applicants.

The documents you or your U.S. employer supply to USCIS or the consulate do not have to be originals. Photocopies of all documents are acceptable as long as you have the originals in your possession and are willing to produce them upon request. But add the following language to the photocopy, with your signature and the date:

> Copies of documents submitted are exact photocopies of unaltered original documents and I understand that I may be required to submit original documents to an immigration or consular official at a later date.
> Signature_____
> Typed or Printed Name_____
> Date_____

Documents will be accepted if they are in either English, or, with papers filed at U.S. consulates abroad, the language of the country where the documents are being filed (except in Japan, where all documents must be translated into English). If the documents are not in an acceptable language as just explained, they must be accompanied by a full, word for word, written English translation. Any capable person may act as translator. It is not necessary to hire a professional. At the end of each translation, the following statement must appear:

> I hereby certify that I translated this document from [language] to English. This translation is accurate and complete. I further certify that I am fully competent to translate from [language] to English.
> Signature_____
> Typed or Printed Name_____
> Date_____

The translator should sign this statement but it does not have to be witnessed or notarized.

Later in this chapter, we describe in detail the forms and documents needed to get your E-1 visa. A summary checklist of forms and documents appears at the end of the chapter.

3. Who's Who in Getting Your E-1 Visa

Getting an E-1 visa will be easier if you familiarize yourself with the technical names used for each participant in the process. You are known as the *applicant*. The applicant can be either the owner or a key employee, depending on whether or not it is you who owns the company. The business is known as the *qualifying business* or *qualifying company*, the *employer*, or the *sponsoring business*. If you are bringing your spouse and children with you as accompanying relatives, they are known as *applicants* as well.

C. The Application: Consular Filing

Anyone who owns a qualifying business or who has been offered a job in the U.S. as a key employee by a qualifying business can apply for an E-1 visa at a U.S. consulate in his or her home country. You must be physically present in order to apply there. If you have been or are now working or living illegally in the U.S., you may be ineligible to get an E-1 visa from a U.S. consulate even if you otherwise qualify. Read Chapter 25 to understand the issues and risks involved.

1. Benefits and Drawbacks of Consular Filing

The most important benefit to consular filing is that only consulates issue visas. When you go through a U.S. filing you get a status, not a visa. (See Chapter 14.) An E-1 status confers the same right to work as an E-1 visa, but it does not give you the ability to travel in and out of the U.S. Therefore, if you want travel privileges, you will at some time have to go through the extra step of applying for a visa at a U.S. consulate, even though you have already applied for and received E-1 status in the U.S.

Moreover, you are not eligible to process a status application in the U.S. unless you are presently in status. If you are in the U.S. illegally, consular filing is a must, although you may not be eligible to return without a long wait (see Chapter 25).

A further plus to consular filing is that consular offices may work more quickly to issue nonimmigrant visas than USCIS service centers may to process nonimmigrant statuses. Your waiting time for the paperwork to be finished will probably be much shorter at a U.S. consulate abroad than at most USCIS offices.

A drawback to consular filing comes from the fact that you must be physically present in the country where the consulate is located to file there. If your petition is ultimately turned down because of an unexpected problem, not only will you have to wait outside the U.S. until the problem is resolved, but other visas in your passport, such as a visitor's visa, may be canceled. It will then be impossible for you to enter the U.S. at all. Consequently, if your E-1 visa case is not very strong and freedom of travel is not essential to you, it might be wise to apply in the U.S., make up your mind to remain there for the duration of the E-1 status and skip trying to get a visa from the consulate.

2. Application General Procedures: Consular Filing

Technically, the law allows you to apply for an E-1 visa at any U.S. consulate you choose, although if you have even overstayed your status in the U.S. by as little as one day, you are required to apply at your home consulate. However, from a practical standpoint your case will be given greatest consideration at the consulate in your home country. Applying in some other country creates suspicion. Often, when an applicant is having trouble at a home consulate he will seek a more lenient office in some other country. This practice of consulate shopping is frowned upon. Unless you have a very good reason for being elsewhere (such as a temporary job assignment in some other nation), it is smarter to file your visa application in your home country.

In some consulates you can simply walk in with your application paperwork and get your E-1 visa application rolling. Most insist that you submit your forms and documents in advance, and then give you an appointment for a personal interview several weeks later. Since procedures among consulates vary, telephone in advance to ask about local policies.

On entering the U.S. with your new E-1 visa, you will be given an I-94 card. It will be stamped with a date indicating how long you can stay. Normally you are permitted to remain for two years at a time, without regard to when your visa actually expires. Each time you exit and reenter the U.S., you will get a new I-94 card authorizing your stay for an additional one- or two-year period. If you do not wish to leave the U.S. after that time, you can apply for extensions of stay, which are issued in two-year increments for as long as you maintain your E-1 status qualifications.

3. Application Form: Consular Filing

When you file at a U.S. consulate abroad, the consulate officials will provide you with certain forms, designated by a "DS" preceding a number. Most consulates use Form DS-156 together with a supplemental form especially for E visa applicants called a DS-156E. Instructions for completing these forms and what to do with them once they are filled out will come with the forms. We do not include copies of these forms in this book, because different consulates sometimes create different versions.

4. Application Documents: Consular Filing

All E-1 applicants must show a valid passport and present one photograph taken in accordance with the photo instructions at http://travel.state.gov/photorequirements.html. For each accompanying relative, you must also present a valid passport and one photograph. You will also need documents verifying their family relationship to you. You may verify a parent/child relationship by presenting the child's long-form birth certificate. Many countries, including Canada and England, issue both short- and long-form birth certificates. Where both are available, the long form is needed because it contains the names of the parents while the short form does not.

If you are accompanied by your spouse, you must establish that you are lawfully married by showing a civil marriage certificate. Church marriage certificates are generally unacceptable. (There are a few exceptions, depending on the laws of your particular country. Canadians, for example, may use church marriage certificates if the marriage took place in Quebec Province, but not elsewhere. If a civil certificate is available, however, you should always use it.) You may have married in a country where marriages are not customarily recorded. Tribal areas of Africa are an example. In such situations, ask the nearest U.S. consulate or embassy what it will accept as proof of marriage.

You will need documents establishing your intent to leave the U.S. when your business in the U.S. is completed. The consulate will want to see evidence of ties to some other country so strong that you will be highly motivated to return there. Proof of such ties can include deeds verifying ownership of a house or other real property, written statements from you explaining that close relatives live elsewhere, or letters from a company outside the U.S. showing that you have a job waiting when you return from America. We have already explained that technically you should not be required to prove that you are maintaining a residence outside the U.S. in order to get an E-1 visa. As a practical matter, however, a consular officer may ask for evidence that you do have assets of some kind located outside the U.S. If you want your visa to be approved you will have to produce this evidence.

Some additional documents are necessary, as outlined below.

a. Proof of Your Nationality

You must prove that you are a citizen of one of the trade treaty countries. Your passport showing your nationality must therefore be presented.

b. Proof of the Nationality of the Qualifying Business Owners

You must show that the qualifying business is owned by citizens of one of the trade treaty countries. If you are not the owner yourself, you will need to show that both you and those who do own the company are citizens of the same treaty country, usually by showing copies of their passports.

Although you will be doing work for the qualifying company in the U.S., the company and its owners may or may not be located there. Therefore, documents must be presented showing where each of the owners is living currently. Affidavits from each of these owners stating their places of residence will serve this purpose. If any are living in the U.S., copies of their passports and I-94 cards are also needed to demonstrate that they hold valid E-1 visas.

Remember, if the owners of the company live in the U.S., at least 50% must also hold E-1 visas for the business to support your own E-1 application.

You will need to prove that you or other nationals of your country own not just a small part, but a majority of the qualifying business. If the qualifying business is a corporation, you should submit copies of all stock certificates, together with a notarized affidavit from the secretary of the corporation listing the name of each shareholder and the number of shares each owns. The affidavit must account for all the shares issued to date. Remember, at least 50% must be owned by nationals of your treaty country.

If the qualifying business is not incorporated, instead of copies of stock certificates you will need to present legal papers proving the existence and ownership of the company. These may be partnership agreements, business registration certificates, or business licenses, together with a notarized affidavit from an official of the company certifying who owns the business and in what percentages.

c.   Proof That You Are a Key Employee

If you are not the majority owner of the company, you must submit evidence that your job in the U.S. will fit the USCIS definition of executive or supervisor or supervisory role essential employee. To prove this, detailed statements from the sponsoring business explaining your specific duties as well as the number and kind of employees you will supervise must be presented. If the application is based on your special position as an employee, the statements should also describe the nature of the essential knowledge or experience and how it will be used and why it is essential in your U.S. job. These required statements may be in your employer's own words and do not have to be in any special form.

d.   Proof of the Existence of an Active Business

You should submit as many documents as possible to show that your E-1 visa application is based on a real, ongoing business. Such evidence should include:

- articles of incorporation or other business charter of the qualifying company
- bank statements for the qualifying company
- credit agreements with suppliers
- letters of credit issued
- leases or deeds for business premises and warehouse space
- tax returns filed in the past two years, if any, including payroll tax returns, and
- promotional literature or advertising.

If the business is newly formed, there will be no tax returns yet. You should then submit a detailed business plan including financial projections for the next five years.

e.   Proof That a Majority of the Company's Trade Is Between the U.S. and Your Home Country

More than 50% of the company's total trade must consist of commerce between your treaty home country and the U.S. This is best shown by presenting copies of all import or export documents from the previous 12 months, including purchase or sale orders, bills of lading and customs entry documents, contracts with suppliers outside of the U.S, and a balance sheet from the qualifying company showing the total amount of inventory for the same period. Comparison of the balance sheet with the import or export documents will show the percentage of the company's trade devoted to commerce between the U.S. and the trade treaty country. The dollar amount of the imports or exports between the U.S. and your home country must total more than 50% of the entire inventory.

f.   Proof That the Trade Is Substantial

The qualifying company's trade between the U.S. and your home treaty country must be substantial, meeting the three tests previously described: dollar, volume and frequency. The same documents presented to prove that the majority of the company's trade is between the U.S. and your home treaty country will also serve to show that the trade is substantial.

5.   Application Interviews: Consular Filing

Consulates will normally require an interview before issuing an E-1 visa. During the interview, a consular officer will examine the forms and documents for accuracy, especially regarding facts about the substantiality of the business and the nationality of the owners. Evidence of ties to your home country will also be checked. During the interview, you will surely be asked how long you intend to remain in the U.S. Any answer indicating uncertainty about plans to return or an interest in applying for a green card may result in a denial of your E-1 visa. (See Section A6.)

Once your E-1 visa is approved, you will probably be asked to return later to pick it up. However, your visa may be approved only provisionally, awaiting security checks, which can add weeks or months to the process.

6.   Using Your E-1 Visa

On entering the U.S. with your new E-1 visa, you will be given a small white card known as an I-94. It will be stamped with a date indicating how long you can stay. Keep track of the whereabouts of this card, and make spare copies to keep in a safe place. You'll need it to prove your entry and to apply for extensions.

Each time you exit and reenter the U.S., you will get a new I-94 card.

SUMMARY EXCLUSION

The law empowers a CBP inspector at the airport to summarily (without allowing judicial review) bar entry to someone requesting admission to the U.S. if either of the following are true:

- The inspector thinks you are lying about practically anything connected with entering the U.S., including your purpose in coming, intent to return, and prior immigration history. This includes the use or suspected use of false documents.
- You do not have the proper documentation to support your entry to the U.S. in the category you are requesting.

If the inspector excludes you, you cannot be re-admitted to the U.S. for five years, unless USCIS grants a special waiver. For this reason it is extremely important to understand the terms of your requested status, and to not make any misrepresentations. If you are found to be inadmissible, you may request to withdraw your application to enter the U.S. in order to prevent having the five-year deportation order on your record. the CBP may allow this in some exceptional cases.

7. Application Appeals: Consular Filing

When a consulate turns down an E-1 visa application, there is no way to make a formal appeal, although you are free to reapply as often as you like. Some consulates, however, will make you wait several months before allowing you to file another application, or limit the total number of repeat applications you can file. If your visa is denied, you will be told by the consul officer the reasons for the denial. Written statements of decisions are not normally provided in non-immigrant cases. If a lack of evidence about a particular point is the problem, sometimes simply presenting more evidence on an unclear fact can change the result.

The most likely reasons for having an E-1 visa turned down are because the consular officer does not believe that your trade is substantial enough, or you are found inadmissible.

Certain people who have been refused visas reapply at a different consulate, attempting to hide the fact that they were turned down elsewhere. If your application is denied, the last page in your passport will be stamped "Application Received," with the date and location of the rejecting consulate. This notation shows that some type of prior visa

application has failed. It serves as a warning to other consulates that your case merits close inspection. If what we have just told you makes you think it would be a good idea to overcome this problem by obtaining a new, unmarked passport, you should also know that permanent computer records are kept of all visa denials.

D. The Application: U.S. Filing

If you are physically present in the U.S., you may apply for E-1 status without leaving the country on the following conditions:

- you entered the U.S. legally and not on a visa waiver
- you have never worked illegally
- the date on your I-94 card has not passed, and
- you are admissible and none of the bars to changing status apply to you (see Chapter 25).

If you were admitted as a visitor without a visa under the Visa Waiver Program, you may not carry out the application step in the U.S. Currently there are 28 participating countries in the Visa Waiver Program, listed in Chapter 2.

If you cannot meet these terms, you may not file for E-1 status in the U.S. However, eligibility to apply in the U.S. has nothing to do with overall eligibility for an E-1 visa. Applicants who are barred from filing in the U.S. but otherwise qualify for E-1 status can sometimes apply successfully for an E-1 visa at U.S. consulates abroad. If you find you are not eligible for U.S. filing, see Section C, above, and read Chapter 25 (to make sure you won't be barred from returning) before devising a strategy.

1. Benefits and Drawbacks of U.S. Filing

Visas are never given inside the U.S. They are issued exclusively by U.S. consulates abroad. If you file in the U.S. and you are successful, you will get E-1 status but not the visa itself. E-1 status allows you to remain in the U.S. with E-1 privileges until the status expires, but should you leave the country for any reason before that time, you will have to apply for the visa itself at a U.S. consulate before returning to the U.S. Moreover, the fact that your E-1 status has been approved in the U.S. does not guarantee that the consulate will approve your visa. Some consulates may even regard your previously acquired E-1 status as a negative factor, an indication that you have deliberately tried to avoid the consulate's authority.

There is another problem which comes up only in U.S. filings. It is the issue of what is called "preconceived intent." To approve a change of status, USCIS must believe that at the time you originally entered the U.S. as a visitor or with some other nonimmigrant visa, you did not intend to apply for a different status. If USCIS thinks you had a preconceived plan to change from the status you arrived with to a different status, it may deny your application. The preconceived intent issue is one less potential hazard you will face if you apply at a U.S. consulate abroad.

On the plus side of U.S. filing, when problems do arise with your U.S. application, you can stay in the U.S. while they are being corrected, a circumstance most visa applicants prefer. If you run into snags at a U.S. consulate, you will have to remain outside the U.S. until matters are resolved.

2. Application Procedures: U.S. Filing

In the U.S., the application, consisting of both forms and documents, is sent by mail to the USCIS regional service center having jurisdiction over the intended place of business. The USCIS regional service centers are not the same as USCIS local offices—for one thing, you cannot visit them in person. There are four USCIS regional service centers spread across the U.S. Appendix I contains a list of all USCIS regional service centers and their addresses, but check the USCIS website (www.uscis.gov) for the correct P.O. box.

The fee for applying to change to E status (on Form I-129) is $130. Your family must pay an additional $140 with their Form I-539. Checks or money orders are accepted. It is not advisable to send cash. We recommend submitting all papers by certified mail, return receipt requested, and making a copy of everything sent in to keep in your records.

Within a few weeks after mailing in the application, you should get back a written notice of confirmation that the papers are being processed, together with a receipt for the fees. This notice will also tell you your immigration file number and approximately when to expect a decision. If USCIS wants further information before acting on your case, all application papers, forms and documents, will be returned together with another form known as an *I-797*. The I-797 tells you what additional pieces of information or documents are expected. You should supply the extra data and mail the whole package back to the USCIS regional service center—again, keeping a copy for your records.

Applications for an E-1 status are normally approved within six months. You will receive a Notice of Action Form I-797 indicating the dates for which your status is approved. A new I-94 card will be attached to the bottom of the form.

Faster USCIS approval—at a price. For $1,000 over and above the regular filing fees, USCIS promises "premium processing" of the visa petition, including a decision within 15 days. To use this service, you must fill out an additional application (Form I-907) and submit the application to a special USCIS Service Center address. For complete instructions, see the USCIS website at www.uscis.gov.

3. Application Forms: U.S. Filing

Copies of all USCIS forms can be found in Appendix II and on the USCIS website.

Form I-129 and E Supplement

The basic form for the application is Form I-129 and the E Supplement. The I-129 form is used for many different nonimmigrant visas and comes with several supplements for each nonimmigrant category. Simply tear out and use the supplement that applies to you. You must file the form in duplicate. Send in two signed originals.

Most of the questions on the I-129 form are straightforward. If a question does not apply to you, answer it with "None" or "N/A." Those questions requiring explanations are as follows:

Part 1. These questions are self-explanatory.

Part 2, Question 1. Question 1 should be answered "E-1."

Questions 2-3. These questions are self-explanatory.

Question 4. This question asks you to indicate what action is requested from USCIS. Normally you will mark box "b."

Part 3. These questions are self-explanatory. If you previously held a U.S. work permit and therefore have a U.S. Social Security number, put down that number where asked. If you have a Social Security number that is not valid for employment, put down that number followed by "not valid for employment." If you have never had a Social Security number, put down "None." (Read Chapter 25 before listing a false number.)

Alien Registration Numbers, which all begin with the letter "A," are given only to people who have applied for green cards, received political asylum, or been in deportation proceedings. If you do have an "A" number, consult with an attorney before proceeding. If you do not have an "A" number, write down "None."

Your "current nonimmigrant status" is the type of visa you're carrying, such as "B-2 visitor" or "F-1 student." If your present authorized stay has expired, you cannot file your application inside the U.S. You must use consular processing. (But watch out for the three- or ten-year bars that might prevent your return. See Chapter 25.)

Part 4. These questions are self-explanatory. Having a green card petition or application in process may affect your ability to get an E-1 status. To qualify for an E-1 status, you must intend to return to your home country after your business needs are completed in the U.S.

Part 5. These questions are self-explanatory. The dates of intended employment should not exceed one year, which is the maximum period of time for which an initial E-1 status may be approved. Extensions may be approved for two years at a time.

E Supplement

This form is self-explanatory. Fill in all parts except Section 4.

Form I-539 (for accompanying relatives only)

Only one application form is needed for an entire family, but if there is more than one accompanying relative, each additional one should be listed on the I-539 supplement.

Part 1. These questions are self-explanatory. "A" numbers are usually given only to people who have previously applied for green cards, political asylum, or been in deportation proceedings.

Part 2, Question 1. Mark box "b," and write in "E-1."

Question 2. This question is self-explanatory.

Part 3. In most cases you will mark Item 1. You will also complete Items 3 and 4, which are self-explanatory.

Part 4, Questions 1–2. These questions are self-explanatory.

Question 3. The different parts to this question are self-explanatory; however, Items "a" through "c" ask if an immigrant visa petition or adjustment of status application has ever been filed on your behalf. If you are separately applying for a green card through a relative, this would be Step One, as described in Chapter 5. If you are separately applying for a green card through employment, this would be Step Two as described in Chapter 8. If you have only begun the Labor Certification, the first step of getting a green card through employment, this question should be answered "no."

4. Application Documents: U.S. Filing

Each applicant must submit a copy of his or her I-94 card, the small white card you received on entering the U.S. Remember, if the date stamped on your I-94 card has already passed, you are ineligible for U.S. filing. Canadians who are just visiting are not expected to have I-94 cards. Canadians with any other type of nonimmigrant status should have them.

For each accompanying relative, send in a copy of his or her I-94 card. You will also need documents verifying their family relationship to you. You may verify a parent/child relationship by presenting the child's long-form birth certificate. Many countries, including Canada and England, issue both short- and long-form birth certificates. Where both are available, the long form is needed because it contains the names of the parents while the short form does not.

If you are accompanied by your spouse, you must establish that you are lawfully married by showing a civil marriage certificate. Church marriage certificates are generally unacceptable. (There are a few exceptions, depending on the laws of your particular country. Canadians, for example, may use church marriage certificates if the marriage took place in Quebec Province, but not elsewhere. If a civil certificate is available, however, you should always use it.) You may have married in a country where marriages are not customarily recorded. Tribal areas of Africa are an example. In such situations call the nearest consulate or embassy of your home country for help with getting acceptable proof of marriage.

We have emphasized that in order to qualify for an E-1 you must have the intent to eventually leave the U.S. when your business is completed. We have also explained how consulates will demand proof that ties to your home country or some other place outside the U.S. are strong enough to motivate your eventual departure. In a U.S. filing, USCIS does not always ask for proof of this. However, we strongly advise you to submit such evidence anyway. Proof of ties to some other country can include deeds verifying ownership of a house or other real property, written statements from you explaining that close relatives are living elsewhere, or letters from a company outside the U.S. showing that you have a job waiting when you leave America.

Some additional documents are necessary, as described below.

a. Proof of Your Nationality

You must prove that you are a citizen of one of the trade treaty countries. Your passport showing your nationality must therefore be presented.

b. Proof of the Nationality of the Qualifying Business Owners

You must show that the qualifying business is owned by citizens of one of the trade treaty countries. If you are not the owner yourself, you will need to show that both you and those who do own the company are citizens of same treaty country, usually by submitting copies of their passports.

Although you will be doing work for the qualifying company in the U.S., the company and its owners may or may not be located there. Therefore, documents must be presented showing where each of the owners is living currently. Affidavits from each of these owners stating their places of residence will serve this purpose. If any are living in the U.S., copies of their passports and I-94 cards are also needed to demonstrate that they hold valid E-1 visas. Remember, if the owners of the company live in the U.S. at least 50% must also hold E-1 visas for the business to support your own E-1 application.

You will need to prove that you or other nationals of your country own not just a small part, but a majority of the qualifying business. If the qualifying business is a corporation, you should submit copies of all stock certificates, together with a notarized affidavit from the secretary of the corporation listing the name of each shareholder and the number of shares each owns. The affidavit must account for all the shares issued to date. Remember, at least 50% must be owned by nationals of your treaty country.

If the qualifying business is not incorporated, instead of copies of stock certificates you will need to present legal papers proving the existence and ownership of the company. These may be partnership agreements, business registration certificates, or business licenses, together with a notarized affidavit from an official of the company certifying who owns the business and in what percentages.

c.   Proof That You Are a Key Employee

If you are not the majority owner of the company, you must submit evidence that your job in the U.S. will fit the USCIS definition of executive, supervisor, supervisory role, or essential employee. To prove this, detailed statements from the sponsoring business explaining your specific duties, as well as the number and kind of employees you will supervise, must be presented. If the application is based on your being an essential employee, the statements should also describe the nature of the essential knowledge or experience, the reason why only you have that knowledge, and how it will be used in your U.S. job. Remember that the essential expertise/knowledge must be generally unavailable from anyone else either inside or outside the company. These required statements may be in your employer's own words and do not have to be in any special form.

d.   Proof of the Existence of an Active Business

Submit as many documents as possible to show that your E-1 visa application is based on a real, ongoing, and active business. Such evidence should include:

- articles of incorporation or other business charter of the qualifying company
- bank statements for the qualifying company
- credit agreements with suppliers
- letters of credit issued
- leases or deeds for business premises and warehouse space
- tax returns filed in the past two years, if any, including payroll tax returns, and
- promotional literature or advertising.

If the business is newly formed, there will be no tax returns yet. You should then submit a detailed business plan including financial projections for the next five years.

e.   Proof That a Majority of the Company's Trade Is Between the U.S. and Your Home Country

More than 50% of the company's total trade must consist of commerce between your treaty home country and the U.S. This is best shown by presenting copies of all import or export documents from the previous 12 months, including purchase or sale orders, bills of lading and customs entry documents, contracts with suppliers outside of the U.S., and a balance sheet from the qualifying company showing the total amount of inventory for the same period. Comparison of the balance sheet with the import or export documents will show the percentage of the company's trade devoted to commerce between the U.S. and the trade treaty country. The dollar amount of the imports or exports between the U.S. and your home country must total more than 50% of the entire inventory.

f.   Proof That the Trade Is Substantial

The qualifying company's trade between the U.S. and your home treaty country must be substantial, meeting the three tests previously described: dollar, volume, and frequency. The same documents presented to prove that the majority of the company's trade is between the U.S. and your home treaty country will also serve to show that the trade is substantial.

5.   Application Interviews: U.S. Filing

Interviews on E-1 change of status applications are rarely held. When an interview is required, the USCIS regional service center where you filed will send your paperwork to the USCIS local office nearest your U.S. place of business. This office will in turn contact you for an appointment. USCIS may ask you to bring additional documents at that time.

If you are called for an interview, the most likely reason is that USCIS either suspects some type of fraud or has doubts about your intent to leave the U.S. after the E-1 status expires. Because they are not common and usually a sign of trouble, these interviews can result in considerable delays.

6. Application Appeals: U.S. Filing

If your application is denied, you will receive a written decision by mail explaining the reasons for the denial. There is no way of making a formal appeal to USCIS if your application to change status is turned down. If the problem is too little evidence, you may be able to overcome this obstacle by adding more documents and resubmitting the entire application to the same USCIS office you have been dealing with, together with a written request that the case be reopened. The written request does not have to be in any special form. This is technically called a *Motion to Reopen.* There is a $110 fee to file this motion.

You may be denied the right to a U.S. filing without being denied an E-1 visa. When your application is turned down because you are found ineligible for U.S. filing, simply change your application to a consular filing. (Read Chapter 25 to make sure you won't be barred from reentering the U.S. if you've lived there illegally.)

Although there is no appeal to USCIS for the denial of an E-1 change of status application, you do have the right to file an appeal in a U.S. district court. It would be difficult to file such an appeal without employing an immigration attorney at considerable expense. Such appeals are usually unsuccessful.

E. Extensions

E-1 visas can be extended for up to five years at a time and E-1 status stays can be extended for two years at a time. When you enter the U.S. with an E-1 visa, your authorized stay as indicated on your I-94 card, which is limited to two years at a time, may elapse before the expiration date of your visa. Therefore, depending on your situation, you may need to extend just your I-94 card, your visa or both. Although an extension is usually easier to get than the E-1 visa itself, it is not automatic. USCIS or the consulate has the right to reconsider your qualifications based on any changes in the facts or law. When the original application for an E-1 visa or status was weak, it is not unusual for an extension request to be turned down. As always, however, good cases that are well prepared will be successful.

You can file for an extension of your visa either in the U.S. or at a consulate. However, contrary to our advice on the initial application, if your visa needs to be extended we highly recommend U.S. filing. That is because visa stamps,

which can only be issued originally at consulates, may be extended in the U.S. If you have received an E-1 status but never applied for a visa, U.S. extensions of your status as indicated on your I-94 card are also advisable. However, if you have an E-1 visa that is still valid but your I-94 card is about to expire, it is generally better to leave the U.S. and return again instead of trying to extend your I-94 card in the U.S. When you return to the U.S. on your valid E-1 visa, you will automatically receive a new I-94 card and a new one- or two-year period of authorized stay. By leaving and reentering, no extension application will be needed and there will be no reevaluation of your qualifications.

1. Extension Applications: U.S. Filing

The general procedures for an E-1 extension are the same as those described in Section E, above. The forms and documents are identical. As with the original application, the paperwork, together with a $130 filing fee and an additional $140 for your family, should be mailed to the USCIS regional service center nearest your place of business.

WORKING WHILE YOUR EXTENSION APPLICATION IS PENDING

If you file your application for an extension of E-1 status before your authorized stay expires, you are automatically permitted to continue working for up to 240 days while you are waiting for a decision. If, however, your authorized stay expires after you have filed for an extension but before you receive an approval, and more than 240 days go by without getting a decision on your extension application, your work authorization ends and you must stop working.

2. Extension Application Forms

Copies of all USCIS forms can be found in Appendix II and on the USCIS website.

Form I-129 and E Supplement

Follow the directions in Section D3, above. The only difference is that you will mark boxes "2b" and "4c" of Part 2.

Form I-539 (for accompanying relatives only)

Follow the directions in Section D3, above, but mark box "1a" of Part 2.

3. Extension Application Documents

You must submit a copy of your I-94 card. You should also submit a copy of the original Notice of Action I-797, if your status was previously approved or extended in the U.S., or a copy of your complete passport including the E-1 visa stamp if you have an actual visa, a letter from your employer stating that your extension is required, and a copy of your personal and business U.S. income tax returns for the past two years, including payroll tax returns.

F. Visa Revalidation: U.S. Filing

If you are physically in the U.S. and have been granted an extension on your I-94 card, you can have your visa revalidated by mail without leaving the country. The exception is if you carry the passport of a country that is on the U.S. government's list of countries that sponsor terrorism, in which case you won't be allowed to revalidate your visa without leaving the U.S. first. When this book went to print, the listed countries included North Korea, Cuba, Syria, Sudan, Iran, Iraq, and Libya.

To do this, you must fill out Form DS-156 and send it to the Department of State. With the form, you should submit your passport (valid for at least six more months), current I-94 card, a recent passport-sized photo (2" x 2", full face view, on a light background, stapled or glued to the form), a fee ($100 plus an additional "reciprocity fee" for nationals of certain countries), updated evidence of continuing trade between the U.S. and your home treaty country, a detailed letter from your employer describing your job duties and explaining why you are needed in the U.S., and a written statement from you declaring that you intend to leave the U.S. when your E-1 status ends.

The fees may be paid by bank draft, corporate check, or money order, payable to the U.S. Department of State. You cannot pay by cash, credit card, or personal check.

Male visa applicants between the ages of 16 and 45, regardless of nationality and regardless of where they apply, must also complete and submit a form DS-157.

You should send in your visa revalidation application as soon as possible within the 60 days before your allowed stay expires (but don't send it any earlier, or the entire package will be returned to you). You should enclose a self-addressed, stamped envelope, or a completed Federal Express or other courier service airbill. Send the entire package by certified mail to:

If sending by postal service:
U.S. Department of State/Visa
P.O. Box 952099
St. Louis, MO 63195–2099

If sending by courier service:
U.S. Department of State/Visa (Box 2099)
1005 Convention Plaza
St. Louis, MO 63101–1200

The passport will be returned to you with a newly revalidated visa in about 12 weeks.

If your accompanying relatives are physically in the U.S., their E-1 visas may be revalidated by sending in their passports and I-94 cards, together with yours. Again, there may be a charge for each visa revalidated. If your E-1 visa has expired, we strongly advise gathering your family together inside U.S. borders so you can take advantage of this simple revalidation procedure.

For more information, see the State Department website at www.travel.state.gov/revals.html.

G. Visa Revalidation: Consular Filing

If you are outside of the U.S. when your visa stamp expires, you must have a new visa stamp issued at a consulate. Reread procedures for the application, consular filing, in Section D. The procedures for consular visa extensions are identical. If you are outside the U.S. with a valid visa, you need only reenter and a new I-94 card authorizing your stay for one year will be given to you.

FORMS AND DOCUMENTS CHECKLIST

STEP ONE: APPLICATION (THE ONLY STEP)

Forms

- ☐ DS forms (available at U.S. consulates abroad for consular filing only).
- ☐ Form I-129 and E Supplement (U.S. filing only).
- ☐ Form I-539 (U.S. filing only for accompanying relatives).

Documents

- ☐ Valid passport for you and each accompanying relative.
- ☐ One photo of you and each accompanying relative (consular filing only).
- ☐ Copy of I-94 card for you and each accompanying relative (U.S. filing only).
- ☐ Long-form birth certificate for you and each accompanying relative.
- ☐ Marriage certificate if you are married and bringing your spouse.
- ☐ If either you or your spouse have ever been married before, copies of divorce and death certificates showing termination of all previous marriages.
- ☐ Documents showing ownership of real estate in your home country, if possible.
- ☐ Documents showing that close family members or property are being left behind in your home country.
- ☐ Documents showing that a job is waiting on your return to your home country.
- ☐ If trade involves the import or export of goods, copies of shipping documents and customs invoices for all shipments during the past two years.
- ☐ If trade involves the sale of services, a detailed statement and itemized breakdown showing that the trade is between the U.S. and your home country.
- ☐ Copies of all outstanding stock certificates, if the qualifying business is a corporation.
- ☐ Notarized affidavit from the secretary of the qualifying corporation, or, if the business is not a corporation, from the official record keeper of the business, stating the names of each owner and percentages of company owned.
- ☐ Passport or proof of citizenship for each owner of the qualifying business.
- ☐ Articles of incorporation or other legal charter or business license of the qualifying company.
- ☐ Tax returns of the qualifying company for the past two years, if available.
- ☐ Accountant's financial statements, including profit and loss statements and balance sheets, of the qualifying company for the past two years, if available.
- ☐ Payroll records of the qualifying company for the past two years, if available.
- ☐ Promotional literature describing the nature of the qualifying business.
- ☐ Letters from banks, or bank statements, indicating the average account balance of the qualifying business.
- ☐ Copy of a business lease or deed for U.S. business premises of the qualifying business.
- ☐ If the qualifying company is a new business, a comprehensive business plan with financial projections for the next five years.
- ☐ If you are not a majority owner of the qualifying business, evidence that your position in the U.S. will be as an executive, supervisor, or essential employee.

Treaty Investors: E-2 Visas

Privileges

- You can work legally in the U.S. for a U.S. business in which a substantial cash investment has been made by you or other citizens of your home country.

- Visas can be issued quickly.

- You may travel in and out of the U.S. or remain here continuously until your E-2 visa and status expire.

- There is no legal limitation on the number of extensions that may be granted. Because of the two-year initial duration of an E-2 visa, as well as the limitless extensions, E-2 visas can allow you to live in the U.S. on a prolonged basis, provided you continue to maintain E-2 qualifications.

- Visas are available for accompanying relatives and your spouse will be permitted to accept employment in the U.S.

Limitations

- Visas are available only to nationals of countries having trade treaties with the U.S.

- You are restricted to working only for the specific employer or self-owned business that acted as your E-2 visa sponsor.

- Visas can initially be approved for up to two years. Extensions of up to two more years at a time may be allowed.

- Accompanying relatives may stay in the U.S. with you, but your children may not work (unless they obtain their own status and visa to do so).

A. How to Qualify

There are no numerical limits on E-2 visas. U.S.-filed applications are usually approved within two to four months. Applications made at U.S. consulates are usually approved and visas issued within two to four weeks.

You qualify for an E-2 visa if you are a citizen of a country that has an investor treaty with the U.S. and you are coming to the U.S. to work for a U.S. business supported by a substantial cash investment from nationals of your home country. You can own the business yourself or you may be a key employee of a business that is at least 50% owned by other nationals of your home country. The investment must be made in a U.S. business that is actively engaged in trade or the rendering of services. Investment in stocks, land speculation, or holding companies does not qualify.

Do not confuse E-2 treaty investor nonimmigrant visas with green cards through investment discussed in Chapter 10. The E-2 visa is a completely different type of visa with completely different requirements. Remember, all nonimmigrant visas are temporary, while green cards are permanent. Moreover, a green card through investment requires a dollar investment of $1 million or more, while an E-2 visa has no dollar minimum. Again, see Chapter 10 to compare.

Citizenship in a country having an investor treaty with the U.S. is an E-2 visa requirement. Legal residence is not enough. In fact, with the exception of E-2 applicants from the U.K., you need not be presently residing in your country of citizenship in order to qualify for an E-2 visa. When you are a citizen of more than one nation, you may qualify for an E-2 visa if at least one of them has an investor treaty with the U.S.

Finally, in order to get an E-2 visa, you must plan to leave the U.S. when your business is completed, although you are not required to maintain a foreign residence abroad. Furthermore, USCIS regulations state that as long as you intend to depart the U.S. at the end of your stay, the fact that you have an approved permanent labor certification or have filed or received approval of an immigrant visa petition should not by itself be a reason to deny your application. However, the State Department's regulations merely state that the intent to depart the U.S. at the end of E-2 status is required without specifically referring to the allowance for permanent residence petitions. This may mean that E-2 applications requested at a foreign consulate will demand a higher standard of proof that you will depart, and may still deny your visa if you're separately applying for permanent residence.

To summarize, there are six requirements for getting an E-2 visa:

1. You must be a citizen of a country that has an investor treaty with the U.S.
2. You must be coming to work in the U.S. for a company you own or one that is at least 50% owned by other nationals of your home country.
3. You must be either the owner or a key employee of the U.S. business.
4. You or the company must have made a substantial cash investment in the U.S. business.
5. The U.S. business must be actively engaged in trade or the rendering of services.
6. You must intend to leave the U.S. when your business there is completed.

1. Citizen of a Treaty Country

E-2 visas are available to citizens of only selected countries that have investor treaties with the U.S. Those countries with treaties currently in effect are:

Albania	Finland	Pakistan
Argentina	France	Panama
Armenia	Georgia	Paraguay
Australia	Germany	Philippines
Austria	Grenada	Poland
Azerbaijan	Honduras	Romania
Bahrain	Iran	Senegal
Bangladesh	Ireland	Slovenia
Belgium	Italy	Slovak Republic
Bolivia	Jamaica	Spain
Bosnia & Herzegovina	Japan	Sri Lanka
Bulgaria	Jordan	Suriname
Cameroon	Kazakhstan	Sweden
Canada	Korea (South)	Switzerland
Colombia	Kyrgyzstan	Taiwan
Congo (Brazzaville)	Latvia	Thailand
Congo (Democratic	Liberia	Togo
Republic of Kinshasa)	Luxembourg	Trinidad and
Costa Rica	Mexico	Tobago
Croatia	Moldova	Tunisia
Czech Republic	Mongolia	Turkey
Ecuador	Morocco	Ukraine
Egypt	Netherlands	United Kingdom
Estonia	Norway	Yugoslavia
Ethiopia	Oman	

Additional treaties are pending and will go into effect within the next several years. Check with the appropriate consulate to make sure a treaty is in force before you apply. The list is kept at Volume 9 of the Foreign Affairs Manual, §41.51 Exh. 1.

2. Company Owned by Citizens of a Qualifying Country

To get an E-2 visa, you must be coming to the U.S. to work for a business that is at least 50% owned by citizens of your treaty country. The company may be owned by you or others. If the company is owned in part or in whole by others, and some or all of them already live in the U.S., those people may need to have E-2 visas themselves before the company can act as an E-2 sponsor for you. Specifically:

- at least 50% of the company must be owned by citizens of a single investor treaty country, and
- the owners from the single investor treaty country must either live outside the U.S. and be able to be classified as treaty investors or live inside the U.S. with E-2 visas.

This second condition can be a little confusing. Some examples may help to make it clearer.

EXAMPLE 1: The company is owned 100% by one person. The owner is a citizen of an investor treaty country and lives outside the U.S. in his home country.

In this case the owner does not need an E-2 visa for the company to support your E-2 visa application, but must be able to satisfy the criteria for an E-2 visa if he or she were to apply.

EXAMPLE 2: The company is owned in equal shares by two individuals. Each owner is a citizen of the same investor treaty country. One owner lives in the U.S. on a green card. The other still lives in his home country.

In this case, the owner living abroad must be classifiable for E-2 status. If, however, we changed this example so that both owners lived in the U.S., the owner who is a green card holder would be prohibited by regulations from being a qualifying employer, so the other owner would have to be in E status.

EXAMPLE 3: The company is owned in equal shares by 100 people. Thirty owners are citizens of a particular investor treaty country but live in the U.S. Thirty other owners are citizens of the same investor treaty country and they are living in their home country. The remaining 40 owners are U.S. citizens.

In this situation, if the company is to act as an E-2 visa sponsor for others, 20 of the 30 owners who are citizens of the investor treaty country but live in the U.S. must hold E-2 visas. Remember that only 50 of the owners need to be citizens of the treaty country. Of those 50, each must either live outside the U.S. and be classifiable for E-2 status or live in the U.S. on an E-2 visa. In our example, 30 live outside the U.S. Therefore, only 20 of the investor treaty country citizens living inside the U.S. need to have E-2 visas to make up the necessary 50% total of qualifying owners.

Additionally, USCIS regulations allow a different test in the case of large multinational corporations in which it is difficult to determine ownership by stock ownership. Therefore, in the situation where a corporation's stock is sold exclusively in the country of incorporation, it may be presumed to have the nationality of the country where the stocks are exchanged.

3. You Must Be a 50% Owner, or Supervisor, Executive, or "Key Employee"

E-2 visas may be issued only to the principal owners or key employees of the qualifying business, provided all have the same treaty nationality. To qualify as a principal owner, you must own at least 50% of the company, possess operational control through a managerial position or similar corporate device, or be in a position to control the enterprise by other means. To qualify as a key employee you must be considered an executive, supervisor, someone in a supervisory role, or person whose skills are essential to the enterprise.

a. Executives and Supervisors

For E-2 classification purposes, the main thrust of the position must be executive or supervisory, and give the employee ultimate control and responsibility for the operation of at least a major part of the enterprise. USCIS will consider the following to determine whether a given position fits the bill:

- an "executive" position is normally one that gives the employee great authority in determining policy and direction of the enterprise;
- "supervisory" positions normally entail responsibility for supervising a major portion of an enterprise's operations and do not usually involve direct supervision of low-level employees, and
- whether the individual applicant's skills, experience, salary, and title are on a par with executive or supervisory positions, and whether the position carries overall authority and responsibility in the context of the enterprise, such as discretionary decision-making, policy-setting, direction and management of business

operations, and supervision of other professional and supervisory personnel.

b. Essential Employees

USCIS regulations are somewhat vague on what constitutes the essentiality of an employee. The employee's skills do not have to be unique or "one of a kind" but they should be indispensable to the success of the investment. They will be evaluated on a case-by-case basis. However, if the skills possessed by the employee are commonplace or readily available in the U.S. labor market, it will be difficult to show that the employee is essential.

Specifically, USCIS will consider the following to determine whether an individual who is a non-executive, non-supervisor and who is not at least a 50% owner, should be classified as an E-2 employee because of the essentiality of his or her skills:

- the degree of expertise in the area of operations involved
- the degree of experience and training with the enterprise
- whether U.S. workers possess the individual's skills or aptitude
- the length of the applicant's specific skill or aptitude
- the length of time required to train an individual to perform the job duties of the position
- the relationship of the individual's skills and talents to the overall operations of the entity, and
- the salary the special qualifications can command.

Knowledge of a foreign language and/or culture will not by themselves constitute the degree of essentiality required.

4. Substantial Investment

A substantial cash investment must be made in the U.S. business in order for the business to successfully support an E-2 visa application. The term substantial is not defined in the law by a strict numerical measure. In fact it is not specifically defined at all. At a minimum, the investment must produce a return that is much higher than a mere income to support you and your family. What is considered substantial depends on the type of business. For example, an automobile manufacturer will have to show a greater dollar amount of investment than a retail toy store in order to meet the requirement of substantial investment.

There are three general tests—dollars, capitalization, and jobs—that, in our experience, can normally be relied on to measure substantiality. The investment must be able to meet the minimum standards of all three.

a.   Dollar Amount of Investment

The dollar amount of the cash business investment should normally exceed $200,000. However, some consulates require as much as $500,000 or more, while others may accept an investment of less than $100,000. A specific sum is not written into the law. The individual consular officer has the authority to require varying amounts in different cases depending on the type of business. Still, experience shows that anything under the $200,000 mark is a weak case.

In order for investment dollars to be counted into the total amount, they must be spent on the U.S. business. Money invested in a house to be used as the investor's residence will not be considered when a decision is made on whether or not the investment meets the dollar requirement. Mortgage values and other borrowed money can be included in the dollar totals. If borrowed funds make up the investment, the investor must be personally liable for the debt or it must be secured by personal assets. Capital investment must be irrevocably committed to the venture, although the investor may utilize escrow as a way of protecting him or herself against loss of capital in case the visa is not issued.

b.   Capitalization

To satisfy the capitalization test, the investment must be large enough to start and operate a business of the type in which the investment is made. This means that different dollar amounts of capitalization will be considered sufficient in different cases. A restaurant, for example, needs a large enough investment to furnish the restaurant, buy, build, or lease the actual restaurant building, pay wages until the business generates enough income to support its staff, purchase food, and pay for initial advertising. The $200,000 minimum dollar amount mentioned above may or may not be enough, depending on the size and type of restaurant. On the other hand, if the business will be the construction and management of a shopping center or office complex, several million

dollars may be necessary to adequately capitalize such a project. An investment is not considered substantial unless it is large enough to capitalize the venture properly, so that it has a realistic chance of success.

The investment amount must also be substantial in proportion to the overall cost of the enterprise. USCIS uses an "inverted sliding scale" for this determination: the lower the total cost of the enterprise, the higher the investment must be in order to qualify, and vice versa.

c.   The Investment Must Not Constitute a "Marginal Enterprise" and Job Creation

A business investment will not be considered substantial for E-2 visa purposes if the business is likely to generate only enough income to support the owners and their families. The business should operate at a sufficient volume to make hiring Americans necessary, and the cash flow should be large enough to pay their salaries. Regardless of the dollars invested, a small family-operated business, such as a retail store, will rarely qualify to support E-2 visa applications if jobs are created only for the owners.

USCIS's regulations place a burden on the investor to show a business plan that indicates that the business will provide more than a subsistence living for the investor starting five years after the onset of normal business activities.

⚠ **These measurement tests have been derived from our own experience and are not all set forth in immigration law.** It is possible for an E-2 visa to be approved with a less substantial business investment than we have described in our tests. With E-2 visas, a great deal is left to the judgment of the USCIS or consular officer evaluating the application.

5.   Active Business

The investment must be in a for-profit business that is actively engaged in trade or the rendering of services, which meets the applicable legal requirements for doing business in the state or region. Investment in holding companies, stocks, bonds, and land speculation will not support an E-2 visa application, since they are not considered "active."

The test is whether or not the business requires active supervisory or executive oversight on a day-to-day basis. Clearly, retail, wholesale, and manufacturing operations require such supervision, while stock purchases and land speculation do not. There are some types of investments, especially in real estate, where the line between a qualifying and non-qualifying business investment is difficult to draw.

For example, if you purchase and rent out a single home or duplex, this is not the type of investment that will support an E-2 visa application, even if the dollar amount is adequate. If you purchase and rent out an eight- or ten-unit apartment building, that is probably a marginal case. As the number of rental units becomes greater, the need for daily management increases, and the case for an E-2 visa becomes stronger.

6. Intent to Leave the U.S.

E-2 visas are meant to be temporary. At the time of application, you must intend to depart the U.S. when your business there is completed. As previously mentioned, you are not required to maintain a foreign residence abroad. Furthermore, USCIS regulations state that as long as you intend to depart the U.S. at the end of your stay, the fact that you have an approved permanent labor certification or have filed or received approval of an immigrant visa petition should not by itself be used as a reason to deny your application. However, the State Department's regulations merely state that the intent to depart the U.S. at the end of E-2 status is required, without specifically referring to the allowance for permanent residence petitions. This may mean that E-2 applications requested at a foreign consulate will demand a higher standard of proof that you will depart, and may still deny visas where permanent residence is contemplated. Furthermore, if you are applying as a representative of foreign media, the State Department's rules specify that the consul should first consider your application under the "I" visa rules, under which you must show a definitive intent to depart and not pursue permanent residence. Remember, all nonimmigrant visas are intended to be temporary.

The U.S. government knows it is difficult to read minds. Expect to be asked for evidence showing that when you go to the U.S. on an E-2 visa, you eventually plan to leave. In many nonimmigrant categories, you are asked to show proof that you keep a house or apartment outside the U.S. as an indication of your intent to eventually go back to your home country. You do not need to keep a home outside the U.S. to qualify for an E-2 visa—but it would help. You will certainly be asked to show that you do have some family members, possessions, or property elsewhere in the world as an incentive for your eventual departure from the U.S.

7. Accompanying Relatives

When you qualify for an E-2 visa, your spouse and unmarried children under age 21 can also get E-2 visas by providing proof of their family relationship to you. Your spouse, but not your children, will be permitted to accept employment in the U.S.

To take advantage of the right to work, your spouse will, after arriving in the United States, need to apply for a work permit. This is done on Form I-765. In filling out the form, your spouse should write "spouse of E nonimmigrant" in Question 15, and "A-17" in Question 16.

Your spouse will need to mail this form, together with proof of your visa status, a copy of his or her I-94 card, the filing fee and two photos, to the appropriate USCIS Service Center for your geographic region. For the address and other information, call USCIS Information at 800-375-5283 or see the USCIS website (www.uscis.gov).

POSSIBILITIES FOR A GREEN CARD FROM E-2 STATUS

If you have an E-2 visa, you can file to get a green card, but being in the U.S. on an E-2 visa gives you no advantage in doing so, and in fact may prove to be a drawback. That is because E-2 visas, like all nonimmigrant visas, are intended only for those who plan on leaving the U.S. once their jobs or other activities there are completed. If you apply for a green card, you are in effect making a statement that you never intend to leave the U.S. Therefore, the U.S. government will allow you to keep E-2 status while pursuing a green card, but only if you can convince the government that you did not intend to get a green card when you originally applied for the E-2 visa, and that you will leave the U.S. if you are unable to secure a green card before your E-2 visa expires.

Proving those things can be difficult. If you do not succeed, your E-2 visa may be taken away. Should this happen, it may affect your green card application, since being out of status or working without authorization may be a bar to getting a green card in the U.S., or may create a waiting period if you depart the U.S. and apply for a visa. (See Chapter 25.)

B. E-2 Visa Overview

Getting an E-2 visa is a one-step process.

1. The Application

Once you have made a qualifying investment in the U.S. or have been offered a job as a key employee of a qualifying company owned by people from your country, getting an E-2 visa is a one-step process. Some applicants seeking E-2 visas as key employees expect their sponsoring employers to handle the entire process for them. Indeed, a number of large companies are equipped with experienced workers who will do this for highly desirable employees. Other companies are prepared to pay an immigration attorney's fees as an expense of trying to attract a key staff member. However, in many cases it is the employee who is most interested in having the visa issued, and to employers, the red tape of having a foreign employee can be an unfamiliar nuisance.

As we give you step-by-step instructions for getting an E-2 visa, we will indicate that certain activities are to be performed by your employer and others are to be performed by you, recognizing that in the case of an E-2 visa you, yourself, may be the principal owner of the qualifying business. However, there is nothing to stop you from helping with the work. For example, you can fill out forms intended to be completed by your employer and simply ask him or her to check them over and sign them. The less your sponsoring employer is inconvenienced, the more the company will be willing to act as sponsor for your E-2 visa. Of course if you are the principal owner of a qualifying business, all the paperwork responsibilities will fall on you.

The one step required to get an E-2 visa is called the application. The object of the application is to show that the conditions to getting an E-2 visa discussed earlier in this chapter have been met. It is filed by you and your accompanying relatives, if any. The application may be carried out in the U.S. at a USCIS office (if you're already in the U.S. legally) or in your home country at a U.S. consulate there. The vast majority of nonimmigrant visa applications are filed at consulates. That is because most cases don't qualify for U.S. filing.

If you are already in the U.S. legally on some other type of nonimmigrant visa, you may qualify to apply for an E-2 status at a USCIS office inside the U.S., using a procedure known as change of nonimmigrant status. If you have been admitted as a visitor without a visa under the Visa Waiver Program, currently available only to nationals of the countries listed in Chapter 2, you may not carry out the application step in the U.S.

"Change of status" is simply a technical term meaning you are switching from one nonimmigrant status to another. If a change of status is approved, you will then be treated as if you had entered the country with an E-2 visa and you can keep the status as long as you remain in the U.S. or until it expires, whichever comes first.

You will not, however, receive a visa stamp, which is what you need if your plans include traveling in and out of the U.S. Visa stamps are issued only at U.S. consulates abroad. Therefore, if you change your status and later travel outside the U.S., you will have to go to the U.S. consulate in your home country and repeat the application over again, obtaining the E-2 visa stamp in your passport before you can return.

Although it is not a requirement, one item you or your sponsoring employer may wish to add to the paperwork package is a cover letter. Cover letters act as a summary and index to the forms and documents, and are often used by immigration attorneys or U.S. companies that process many visas for their employees. Cover letters begin with a statement summarizing the facts of the case and explaining why the particular applicant is eligible for the visa. This statement is followed by a list of the forms and documents submitted. If it is carefully written, a cover letter can make the case clearer and easier to process for the consular or USCIS officer evaluating it. This is particularly important in an E-2 visa case where the documentation by itself may require explanation. Cover letters must be individually tailored to each case, so if you don't think you can write a good one, consult an attorney or leave it out and submit only your forms and documents.

2. Who's Who in Getting Your E-2 Visa

Getting an E-2 visa will be easier if you familiarize yourself with the technical names used for each participant in the process. You are known as the *applicant*. The applicant can be either the owner or a key employee, depending on whether or not it is you who owns the company. The business is known as the *qualifying business* or *qualifying company*, the *employer*, or the *sponsoring business*. If you are bringing your spouse and children with you as accompanying relatives they are known as *applicants* as well.

3. Tips on Handling the Paperwork

There are two types of paperwork you must submit to get an E-2 visa. The first consists of official government forms completed by you or your employer. The second is personal and business documents, such as birth and marriage certificates, school transcripts and diplomas, and company financial statements and tax returns.

It is vital that forms are properly filled out and all necessary documents are supplied. You or your U.S. employer may resent the intrusion into your privacy and the sizable effort it takes to prepare immigration applications but you should realize the process is an impersonal matter to immigration officials. Your getting a visa is more important to you than it is to the U.S. government. There is no shortage of applicants.

The documents you or your U.S. employer supply USCIS or the consulate do not have to be originals. Photocopies of all documents are acceptable as long as you have the originals in your possession and are willing to produce them upon request. But add the following language to the photocopy, with your signature and the date:

Copies of documents submitted are exact photocopies of unaltered original documents and I understand that I may be required to submit original documents to an immigration or consular official at a later date.

Signature_____

Typed or Printed Name_____

Date_____

Documents will be accepted if they are in either English, or, with papers filed at U.S. consulates abroad, the language of the country where the documents are being filed. An exception exists for papers filed at U.S. consulates in Japan, where all documents must be translated into English. If the documents are not in an acceptable language as just explained, they must be accompanied by a full, word for word, written English translation. Any capable person may act as translator. It is not necessary to hire a professional. At the end of each translation, the following statement must appear:

I hereby certify that I translated this document from [language] to English. This translation is accurate and complete. I further certify that I am fully competent to translate from [language] to English.

Signature_____

Typed or Printed Name_____

Date_____

The translator should sign this statement but it does not have to be witnessed or notarized.

Later in this chapter we describe in detail the forms and documents needed to get your E-2 visa. A summary checklist of forms and documents appears at the end of this chapter.

C. The Application: Consular Filing

Anyone who has made a qualifying investment or who has been offered a job in the U.S. as a key employee by a qualifying business can apply for an E-2 visa at a U.S. consulate in his or her home country. You must be physically present in order to apply there. If you have been or are now working or living illegally in the U.S., you may be ineligible to get an E-2 visa from a U.S. consulate even if you otherwise qualify. Read Chapter 25 to understand the issues and risks involved.

1. Benefits and Drawbacks of Consular Filing

The most important benefit to consular filing is that only consulates issue visas. When you go through a U.S. filing you get a status, not a visa. (See Chapter 14, Section B.) An E-2 status confers the same right to work as an E-2 visa, but it does not give you the ability to travel in and out of the U.S. Therefore, if you want travel privileges, you will at some time have to go through the extra step of applying for a visa at a U.S. consulate, even though you have already applied for and received E-2 status in the U.S.

You are not eligible to process a status application in the U.S. unless your presence and activities in the U.S. have always been legal. If you are in the U.S. illegally, consular filing is a must, although you may not be eligible to return within three or ten years, depending on the length of your illegal stay (see Chapter 25).

A further plus to consular filing is that some consular offices may work more quickly to issue nonimmigrant visas than USCIS service centers may to process nonimmigrant statuses. Your waiting time for the paperwork to be finished may be shorter at a U.S. consulate abroad.

A drawback to consular filing comes from the fact that you must be physically present in the country where the consulate is located to file there. If your application is ultimately turned down because of an unexpected problem, not only will you have to wait outside the U.S. until the problem is resolved, but other visas in your passport, such as a visitor's visa, may be canceled. It will then be impossible for you to enter the U.S. at all. Consequently, if your E-2 visa case is not very strong and freedom of travel is not essential to you, it might be wise to apply in the U.S., make up your mind to remain there for the duration of the E-2 status, and skip trying to get a visa from the consulate.

2. Application General Procedures: Consular Filing

Technically, the law allows you to apply for an E-2 visa at any U.S. consulate you choose, although if you have even overstayed your status in the U.S. by as little as one day, you are required to apply at your home consulate. Because unlawful presence in the U.S. may also constitute a ground of inadmissibility, be sure to read Chapters 14 and 25 before proceeding. However, from a practical standpoint your case will be given greatest consideration at the consulate in your home country. Applying in some other country creates suspicion. Often, when an applicant is having trouble at a home consulate he will seek a more lenient office in some other country. This practice of consulate shopping is frowned upon. Unless you have a very good reason for being elsewhere (such as a temporary job assignment in some other nation), it is smarter to file your visa application in your home country.

Check with your local U.S. consulate regarding its application procedures for getting your E-2 visa. Most insist that you submit your forms and documents in advance, and then give you an appointment for a personal interview several weeks later.

3. Application Forms: Consular Filing

When you file at a U.S. consulate abroad, the consulate officials will provide you with certain forms, designated by a "DS" preceding a number. Most consulates use Form DS-156 together with a supplemental form especially for E visa applicants called a DS-156E. Instructions for completing these forms and what to do with them once they are filled out will come with the forms. We do not include copies of these forms in this book since different consulates often issue different versions.

4. Application Documents: Consular Filing

All E-2 applicants must show a valid passport and present one photograph taken in accordance with the photo instructions at http://travel.state.gov/photorequirements/html. For each accompanying relative you must present a valid passport and one photograph. You will also need documents verifying their family relationship to you. You may verify a parent/child relationship by presenting the child's long-form birth certificate. Many countries, including Canada and England, issue both short- and long-form birth certificates. Where both are available, the long form is needed because it contains the names of the parents while the short form does not.

If you are accompanied by your spouse, you must establish that you are lawfully married by showing a civil marriage certificate. Church marriage certificates are generally unacceptable. (There are a few exceptions, depending on the laws of your particular country. Canadians, for example, may use church marriage certificates if the marriage took place in Quebec Province, but not elsewhere. If a civil certificate is available, however, you should always use it.) You may have married in a country where marriages are not customarily recorded. Tribal areas of Africa are an example. In such situations, ask the U.S. consulate or embassy what documents it will accept as proof of marriage.

You will need documents establishing your intent to leave the U.S. when your business in the U.S. is completed. The consulate will want to see evidence of ties to some other country so strong that you will be highly motivated to return there. Proof of such ties can include deeds verifying ownership of a house or other real property, written statements from you explaining that close relatives live elsewhere, or letters from a company outside the U.S. showing that you have a job waiting when you return from America. We have already explained that technically you should not be required to prove that you are maintaining a residence outside the U.S. in order to get an E-2 visa. As a practical matter, however, a consular officer may ask for evidence that you do have assets of some kind located outside the U.S.

a. Proof of Your Nationality

You must prove that you are a citizen of one of the investment treaty countries. Your passport showing your nationality must therefore be presented.

b. Proof of the Nationality of the Qualifying Business Owners

You must show that the qualifying business is owned by citizens of one of the investment treaty countries. If you are not the owner yourself, you will need to show that both you and those who do own the company are citizens of the same treaty country, usually by showing copies of their passports.

Although you will be doing work for the qualifying company in the U.S., the company and its owners may or may not be located there. Therefore, documents must be presented showing where each of the owners is living currently. Affidavits from each of these owners stating their places of residence will serve this purpose. If any are living in the U.S., copies of their passports and I-94 cards are also needed to demonstrate that they hold valid E-2 visas. Remember, if the owners of the company live in the U.S., at least 50% must also hold E-2 visas for the business to support your own E-2 application.

You will need to prove that you or other nationals of your country own not just a small part, but a majority of the qualifying business. If the qualifying business is a corporation, you should submit copies of all stock certificates, together with a notarized affidavit from the secretary of the corporation listing the name of each shareholder and the number of shares each owns. The affidavit must account for all the shares issued to date. Remember, at least 50% must be owned by nationals of your treaty country.

If the qualifying business is not incorporated, instead of copies of stock certificates you will need to present legal papers proving the existence and ownership of the company. These may be partnership agreements, business registration certificates, or business licenses, together with a notarized affidavit from an official of the company certifying who owns the business and in what percentages.

c. Proof That You Are a Key Employee

If you are not the majority owner of the company, you must submit evidence that your job in the U.S. will fit the USCIS definition of supervisor, executive, essential employee, or person with predominantly supervisory job duties. To prove this, detailed statements from the sponsoring business explaining your specific duties, as well as the number and kind of employees you will supervise must be presented. If the application is based on your essentiality as an employee, the statements should also describe the nature of the essential knowledge or experience, how it will be used, and why it is essential in your U.S. job. These required statements may be in your employer's own words and do not have to be in any special form.

d. Proof of the Existence of an Active Business

You should submit as many documents as possible to show that your E-2 visa application is based on a real, ongoing business. Such evidence should include:

- articles of incorporation or other business charter of the qualifying company
- bank statements for the qualifying company
- credit agreements with suppliers
- letters of credit issued
- leases or deeds for business premises and warehouse space
- tax returns filed in the past two years, if any, including payroll tax returns, and
- promotional literature or advertising.

If the business is newly formed, there will be no tax returns yet. You should then submit a detailed business plan including financial projections for the next five years.

e. Documents Showing That U.S. Business Investment Is Substantial

The business investment made in the U.S. qualifying company must be substantial, meeting the three tests previously described: dollars, capitalization, and jobs. Documents to prove this will include:

- bank wire transfer memos showing money sent to the U.S. from abroad
- contracts and bills of sale for purchase of capital goods and inventory
- leases, deeds, or contracts for purchase of business premises
- construction contracts and blueprints for building a business premise, comprehensive business plans with cash flow projections for the next five years, showing how the enterprise will support more than you (and your family) by then
- U.S. employment tax returns showing the number of employees on the qualifying company's payroll (if any), and
- accountant's financial statements for the business, including balance sheets.

If the business in the U.S. is new, you may not have tax returns or employment records, but you must present evidence that the investment that has been made will provide sufficient capitalization for that type of business. Documents such as market surveys, written summaries of trade association statistics, or written reports from qualified business consultants will serve this purpose.

5. Application Interviews: Consular Filing

The consulate will usually require an interview before issuing an E-2 visa. During the interview, a consular officer will examine the forms and documents for accuracy, especially regarding facts about the substantiality of the business and the nationality of the owners. Evidence of ties to your home country will also be checked. During the interview, you will surely be asked how long you intend to remain in the U.S. Any answer indicating uncertainty about plans to return or an interest in applying for a green card may result in a denial of your E-2 visa.

6. Using Your E-2 Visa

On entering the U.S. with your new E-2 visa, you will be given an I-94 card. It will be stamped with a date indicating how long you can stay. Normally you are permitted to remain for two years at a time, without regard to when your visa actually expires. Each time you exit and reenter the U.S., you will get a new I-94 card authorizing your stay for an additional one- or two-year period, or if you do not wish to leave the U.S. after that time, you can apply for extensions of stay which are issued in two-year increments for as long as you maintain your E-2 status qualifications.

7. Application Appeals: Consular Filing

When a consulate turns down an E-2 visa application, there is no way to make a formal appeal, although you are free to reapply as often as you like. Some consulates, however, will make you wait several months before allowing you to file another application, or limit the total number of repeat applications you can file. If your visa is denied, you will be told by the consular officer the reasons for the denial. Written statements of decisions are not normally provided in nonimmigrant cases. If a lack of evidence about a particular point is the problem, sometimes simply presenting more evidence on an unclear fact can change the result.

The most likely reasons for having an E-2 visa turned down are because the consular officer does not believe that your investment is substantial enough, or you are found inadmissible.

Certain people who have been refused visas reapply at a different consulate, attempting to hide the fact that they were turned down elsewhere. If your application is denied, the last page in your passport will be stamped "Application Received," with the date and location of the rejecting consulate. This notation shows that some type of prior visa application has failed. It serves as a warning to other consulates that your case merits close inspection.

If what we have just told you makes you think it would be a good idea to overcome this problem by obtaining a new, unmarked passport, you should also know that permanent computer records are kept of all visa denials.

SUMMARY EXCLUSION

The law empowers a CBP inspector at the airport to summarily (without allowing judicial review) bar entry to someone requesting admission to the U.S. if either of the following are true:

- The inspector thinks you are lying about practically anything connected with entering the U.S., including your purpose in coming, intent to return, and prior immigration history. This includes the use or suspected use of false documents.
- You do not have the proper documentation to support your entry to the U.S. in the category you are requesting.

If the inspector excludes you, you cannot be re-admitted to the U.S. for five years, unless USCIS grants a special waiver. For this reason it is extremely important to understand the terms of your requested status, and to not make any misrepresentations. If you are found to be inadmissible, you may request to withdraw your application to enter the U.S. in order to prevent having the five-year deportation order on your record. The CBP may allow this in some exceptional cases.

D. The Application: U.S. Filing

If you are physically present in the U.S., you may apply for E-2 status without leaving the country on the following conditions:

- you entered the U.S. legally and not under the Visa Waiver Program
- you have never worked illegally
- the date on your I-94 card has not passed, and
- you are admissible and none of the bars to changing status apply to you (see Chapter 25).

If you were admitted as a visitor without a visa under the Visa Waiver Program, you may not carry out the application step in the U.S. Currently there are 28 participating countries in the Visa Waiver Program, listed in Chapter 2.

 If you cannot meet these terms, you may not file for E-2 status in the U.S. It is important to realize, however, that eligibility to apply in the U.S. has nothing to do with overall eligibility for an E-2 visa. Many applicants who are barred from filing in the U.S. but otherwise qualify for E-2 status can apply successfully for an E-2 visa at U.S. consulates abroad. If you find you are not eligible for U.S. filing, see Section C, above, and read Chapter 25 before devising a strategy.

1. Benefits and Drawbacks of U.S. Filing

Visas are never given inside the U.S. They are issued exclusively by U.S. consulates abroad. If you file in the U.S., and you are successful, you will get E-2 status but not the visa itself. E-2 status allows you to remain in the U.S. with E-2 privileges until the status expires. However, should you leave the country for any reason before that time, you will have to apply for the visa itself at a U.S. consulate before returning to America. Moreover, the fact that your E-2 status has been approved in the U.S. does not guarantee that the consulate will approve your visa. Some consulates may even regard your previously acquired E-2 status as a negative factor, an indication that you have deliberately tried to avoid the consulate's authority.

There is another problem which comes up only in U.S. filings. It is the issue of what is called "preconceived intent." To approve a change of status, USCIS must believe that at the time you originally entered the U.S. as a visitor or with some other nonimmigrant visa, you did not intend to apply for a different status. If USCIS thinks you had a preconceived plan to change from the status you arrived with to a different status, they may deny your application. The preconceived intent issue is one less potential hazard you will face if you apply at a U.S. consulate abroad.

On the plus side of U.S. filing, if problems do arise with your U.S. application, you can stay in the U.S. while they are being corrected, a circumstance most visa applicants prefer. If you run into snags at a U.S. consulate, you will have to remain outside the U.S. until matters are resolved.

2. Application General Procedures: U.S. Filing

The application, consisting of both forms and documents, is sent by mail to the USCIS regional service center having jurisdiction over the intended place of business. USCIS regional service centers are not the same as USCIS local offices—for one thing, you cannot visit them in person. There are four USCIS regional service centers spread across the U.S. Appendix I contains a list of all USCIS regional service centers and their addresses, but check the USCIS website (www.uscis.gov) for the appropriate P.O. box.

The filing fee for each Form I-129 is $130. Your family must pay an additional $140 with their Form I-539 (the fee remains the same no matter how many family members are included in the application). Checks or money orders are accepted. It is not advisable to send cash. We recommend submitting all papers by certified mail, return receipt requested, and making a copy of everything sent in to keep in your records.

Within a few weeks after mailing in the application, you should get back a written notice of confirmation that the papers are being processed, together with a receipt for the fees. This notice will also tell you your immigration file number and approximately when to expect a decision. If USCIS wants further information before acting on your case, all application papers, forms and documents, will be returned together with another form known as an I-797. The I-797 tells you what additional pieces of information or documents are expected. You should supply the extra data and mail the whole package back to the regional service center, with the I-797 form on top—again, keeping a copy for your records.

Applications for an E-2 status are normally approved within two to eight weeks. When this happens, you will receive a Notice of Action Form I-797, indicating the dates for which your status is approved. A new I-94 card will be attached to the bottom of the form.

Faster decisions—at a price. For $1,000 over and above the regular filing fees, USCIS promises "premium processing" of the visa petition, including a decision within 15 days. To use this service, the employer must fill out an additional application (Form I-907) and submit the application to a special USCIS Service Center address. For complete instructions, see the USCIS website at www.uscis.gov.

3. Application Forms: U.S. Filing

Copies of all USCIS forms are in Appendix II and on the USCIS website.

Form I-129 and E Supplement

When filing in the U.S., the basic form for the application is Form I-129 and E Supplement. The I-129 form is used for many different nonimmigrant visas, and comes with several supplements for each specific nonimmigrant category. Simply tear out and use the supplement that applies to you. Your employer must file the form in duplicate. Send in two signed originals. Copies are not acceptable.

Most of the questions on the I-129 form are straightforward. If a question does not apply to you, answer it with "None" or "N/A." Those questions requiring explanations are as follows:

Part 1. These questions are self-explanatory.

Part 2, Question 1. Question 1 should be answered "E-2."

Questions 2–3. These questions are self-explanatory.

Question 4. This question asks you to indicate what action is requested from USCIS. Normally you will mark box "b."

Part 3. These questions are self-explanatory. If you previously held a U.S. work permit and therefore have a U.S. Social Security number, put down that number where asked. If you have a Social Security number that is not valid for employment, put down that number followed by "not valid for employment." If you have never had a Social Security number, put down "None." (Read Chapter 25 before listing a false number.)

Alien Registration Numbers, which all begin with the letter "A," are given only to people who have applied for green cards, received political asylum, or been in deportation proceedings. If you do have an "A" number, consult an attorney before proceeding. If you do not have an "A" number, write down "None."

Your "current nonimmigrant status" is the type of visa you're carrying, such as "B-2 visitor" or "F-1 student." If your present authorized stay has expired, you cannot file your application inside the U.S. You must use consular processing, but see Chapter 25 if you overstayed your visa by six months or more.

Part 4. These questions are self-explanatory. Having a green card petition or application in process may affect your ability to get an E-2 status. To qualify for an E-2 status, you must intend to return to your home country after your business needs are completed in the U.S.

Part 5. These questions are self-explanatory. The dates of intended employment should not exceed one year, which is the maximum period of time for which an initial E-2 status may be approved. Extensions may be approved for two years at a time.

E Supplement

This form is self-explanatory. Fill in all parts except Section 3.

Form I-539 (for accompanying relatives only)

Only one application form is needed for an entire family, but if there is more than one accompanying relative, each additional one should be listed on the I-539 supplement.

Part 1. These questions are self-explanatory. "A" numbers are usually given only to people who have previously applied for green cards or who have been in deportation proceedings. See an attorney if you have one.

Part 2. Question 1. Mark box "b," and write in "E-2."

Question 2. This question is self-explanatory.

Part 3. In most cases you will mark Item 1. You will also complete Items 3 and 4, which are self-explanatory.

Part 4. Questions 1–2. These questions are self-explanatory.

Question 3. The different parts to this question are self-explanatory; however, Items "a" through "c" ask if an immigrant visa petition or adjustment of status application has ever been filed on your behalf. If you are separately applying for a green card through a relative, this would be Step One, as described in Chapter 5. If you are separately applying for a green card through employment, this would be Step Two as described in Chapter 8. If you have only begun the Labor Certification, the first step of getting a green card through employment, this question should be answered "no."

4. Application Documents: U.S. Filing

Each applicant must submit a copy of his or her I-94 card, the small white card you received on entering the U.S. Remember, if the date stamped on your I-94 card has already passed, you are ineligible for U.S. filing.

For each accompanying relative, send in a copy of his or her I-94 card. You will also need documents verifying their family relationship to you. You may verify a parent/child relationship by presenting the child's long-form birth certificate. Many countries, including Canada and England, issue both short- and long-form birth certificates. Where both are available, the long form is needed because it contains the names of the parents while the short form does not.

If you are accompanied by your spouse, you must establish that you are lawfully married by showing a civil marriage certificate. Church marriage certificates are generally unacceptable. (There are a few exceptions, depending on the laws of your particular country. Canadians, for example, may use church marriage certificates if the marriage

took place in Quebec Province, but not elsewhere. If a civil certificate is available, however, you should always use it.) You may have married in a country where marriages are not customarily recorded. Tribal areas of Africa are an example. In such situations call the nearest consulate or embassy of your home country for help with getting acceptable proof of marriage.

We have emphasized that in order to qualify for an E-2 you must have the intent to eventually leave the U.S. when your business is completed. Consulates will demand proof that ties to your home country or some other place outside the U.S. are strong enough to motivate your eventual departure. In a U.S. filing, USCIS does not always ask for proof of this. However, we strongly advise you to submit such evidence anyway. Proof of ties to some other country can include deeds verifying ownership of a house or other real property, written statements from you explaining that close relatives are living elsewhere, or letters from a company outside the U.S. showing that you have a job waiting when you return to your country.

Some additional documents are necessary, as described below.

a. Proof of Your Nationality

You must prove that you are a citizen of one of the investment treaty countries. Your passport showing your nationality must therefore be presented.

b. Proof of the Nationality of the Qualifying Business Owners

You must show that the qualifying business is owned by citizens of one of the investment treaty countries. If you are not the owner yourself, you will need to show that both you and those who do own the company are citizens of the same treaty country, usually by submitting copies of their passports. Although you will be doing work for the qualifying company in the U.S., the company and its owners may or may not be located there. Therefore, documents must be presented showing where each of the owners is living currently. Affidavits from each of these owners stating their places of residence will serve this purpose. If any are living in the U.S., copies of their passports and I-94 cards are also needed to demonstrate that they hold valid E-2 visas. Remember, if the owners of the company live in the U.S. at least 50% must also hold E-2 visas for the business to support your own E-2 application.

You will need to prove that you or other nationals of your country own not just a small part, but a majority of the qualifying business. If the qualifying business is a corporation, you should submit copies of all stock certificates, together with a notarized affidavit from the secretary of the corporation, listing the name of each shareholder and the number of shares each owns. The affidavit must account for all the shares issued to date. Remember, at least 50% must be owned by nationals of your treaty country.

If the qualifying business is not incorporated, instead of copies of stock certificates you will need to present legal papers proving the existence and ownership of the company. These may be partnership agreements, business registration certificates, or business licenses, together with a notarized affidavit from an official of the company certifying who owns the business and in what percentages.

c. Proof That You Are a Key Employee

If you are not the majority owner of the company, you must submit evidence that your job in the U.S. will fit the USCIS definition of executive, supervisor, person in a supervisory role, or essential employee. To prove this, detailed statements from the sponsoring business explaining your specific duties, as well as the number and kind of employees you will supervise, must be presented. If the application is based on your being an essential employee, the statements should also describe the nature of the essential knowledge or experience, the reason why only you have that knowledge, and how it will be used in your U.S. job. Remember that the essential expertise/knowledge must be generally unavailable from anyone else either inside or outside the company. These required statements may be in your employer's own words and do not have to be in any special form.

d. Proof of the Existence of an Active Business

Submit as many documents as possible to show that your E-2 visa application is based on a real, ongoing and active business. Such evidence should include:

- articles of incorporation or other business charter of the qualifying company
- bank statements for the qualifying company
- credit agreements with suppliers
- letters of credit issued
- leases or deeds for business premises and warehouse space
- tax returns filed in the past two years, if any, including payroll tax returns, and
- promotional literature or advertising.

If the business is newly formed, there will be no tax returns yet. You should then submit a detailed business plan, including financial projections for the next three years.

e. Proof That U.S. Business Investment Is Substantial

The business investment made in the U.S. qualifying company must be substantial, meeting the three tests previously described: dollars, capitalization, and jobs. Documents to prove this will include:

- bank wire-transfer memos showing money sent to the U.S. from abroad
- contracts and bills of sale for purchase of capital goods and inventory
- leases, deeds, or contracts for purchase of business premises
- construction contracts and blueprints for building a business premises
- comprehensive business plans with cash flow projections for the next three years
- U.S. employment tax returns showing the number of employees on the qualifying company's payroll, and
- accountant's financial statements for the business, including balance sheets.

If the business in the U.S. is new, you may not have tax returns or employment records, but you must present evidence that the investment which has been made will provide sufficient capitalization for that type of business. Documents such as market surveys, written summaries of trade-association statistics, or written reports from qualified business consultants will serve this purpose.

5. Application Interviews: U.S. Filing

Interviews on E-2 change of status applications are rarely held. When an interview is required, the USCIS regional service center where you filed will send your paperwork to the USCIS local office nearest your U.S. place of business. This office will in turn contact you for an appointment. USCIS may ask you to bring additional documents at that time.

If you are called for an interview, the most likely reason is that the USCIS either suspects some type of fraud or has doubts about your intent to leave the U.S. after the E-2 status expires. Because they are not common and usually a sign of trouble, these interviews can result in considerable delays.

6. Application Appeals: U.S. Filing

If your application is denied, you will receive a written decision by mail explaining the reasons for the denial. There is no way of making a formal appeal to USCIS if your application to change status is turned down. If the problem is too little evidence, you may be able to overcome this obstacle by adding more documents and resubmitting the entire application to the same USCIS office you have been dealing with, together with a written request that the case be reopened. The written request does not have to be in any special form. This is technically called a *Motion to Reopen*. There is a $110 fee to file this motion.

You may be denied the right to a U.S. filing without being denied an E-2 visa. When your application is turned down because you are found ineligible for U.S. filing, simply change your application to a consular filing. (Read Chapter 25 to make sure you won't be barred from returning.)

Although there is no appeal to USCIS for the denial of an E-2 change of status application, you do have the right to file an appeal in a U.S. district court. It would be difficult to file such an appeal without employing an immigration attorney at considerable expense. Such appeals are usually unsuccessful.

E. Extensions

E-2 visas can be extended for up to five years at a time and E-2 status stays can be extended for two years at a time. When you enter the U.S. with an E-2 visa, your authorized stay as indicated on your I-94 card, which is limited to two years, may elapse before the expiration date of your visa. Therefore, depending on your situation, you may need to extend just your I-94 card, your visa, or both. Although an extension is usually easier to get than the E-2 visa itself, it is not automatic. USCIS or the consulate has the right to reconsider your qualifications based on any changes in the facts or law. When the original application for an E-2 visa or status was weak, it is not unusual for an extension request to be turned down. As always, however, good cases that are well prepared will be successful.

You can file for an extension of your visa either in the U.S. or at a consulate. However, contrary to our advice on the initial application, if your visa needs to be extended we highly recommend U.S. filing. That is because visa stamps, which can only be issued originally at consulates, may be extended in the U.S. If you have received an E-2 status but never applied for a visa, U.S. extensions of your status as indicated on your I-94 card are also advisable. However, if you have an E-2 visa that is still valid but your I-94 card is about to expire, it is generally better to leave the U.S. and return again instead of trying to extend your I-94 card in the U.S. When you return to the U.S. on your valid E-2 visa, you will automatically receive a new I-94 card and a new one- or two-year period of authorized stay. By leaving and reentering, no extension application will be needed and there will be no reevaluation of your qualifications.

1. Extension Application: U.S. Filing

The general procedures for an E-2 extension are the same as those described in Section E, above. The forms and documents are identical. As with the original application, the paperwork, together with a $130 filing fee and an additional $140 for your family, should be mailed to the USCIS regional service center nearest your place of business.

WORKING WHILE YOUR EXTENSION APPLICATION IS PENDING

If you file your application for an extension of E-2 status before your authorized stay expires, you are automatically permitted to continue working for up to 240 days while you are waiting for a decision. If, however, your authorized stay expires after you have filed for an extension, but before you receive an approval, and more than 240 days go by without getting a decision on your extension application, your work authorization ceases and you must stop working.

---

2. Extension Application Forms

Copies of all the required USCIS forms are in Appendix II and on the USCIS website.

Form I-129 and E Supplement

Follow the directions in Section D3, above. The only difference is that you will mark boxes "2b" and "4c" of Part 2.

Form I-539 (for accompanying relatives only)

Follow the directions in Section D3, above, but mark box "1a" of Part 2.

3. Extension Application Documents

You must submit a copy of your I-94 card. You should also submit a copy of the original Notice of Action I-797, if your status was previously approved or extended in the U.S., or a copy of your complete passport, including an E-2 visa stamp if you have an actual visa, a letter from your employer stating that your extension is required, and a copy of your personal and business U.S. income tax returns for the past two years, including payroll tax returns.

F. Visa Revalidation: U.S. Filing

If you are physically in the U.S. and have been granted an extension on your I-94 card, you can have your visa revalidated by mail without leaving the country. The exception is if you carry the passport of a country that is on the U.S. government's list of countries that sponsor terrorism, in which case you won't be allowed to revalidate your visa without leaving the U.S. first. When this book went to print, the listed countries included North Korea, Cuba, Syria, Sudan, Iran, Iraq, and Libya.

To do this, you must fill out Form DS-156 and send it to the Department of State. With the form, you should submit as documents your passport (valid for at least six months), a recent passport-sized photo (2" x 2", full face view, on a light background, stapled or glued to the form), a fee ($100 plus a "reciprocity fee" for nationals of certain countries), your current I-94 card, updated evidence of continuing investment, a detailed letter from your employer describing your job duties and explaining why you are needed in the U.S., and a written statement from you declaring that you intend to leave the U.S. when your E-2 status ends. The fees may be paid by bank draft, corporate check, or money order, payable to the U.S. Department of State. You cannot pay by cash, credit card, or personal check.

Male visa applicants between the ages of 16 and 45, regardless of nationality and regardless of where they apply, must also complete and submit a form DS-157.

You should send in your visa revalidation application as soon as possible within the 60 days before your allowed stay expires (but don't send it any earlier, or the entire package will be returned to you). Enclose a self-addressed, stamped envelope, or a completed Federal Express or other courier service airbill. Send the entire package by certified mail to:

If sending by postal service:
U.S. Department of State/Visa
P.O. Box 952099
St. Louis, MO 63195-2099

If sending by courier service:
U.S. Department of State/Visa (Box 2099)
1005 Convention Plaza
St. Louis, MO 63101-1200

The passport will be returned to you with a newly revalidated visa in about 12 weeks.

If your accompanying relatives are physically in the U.S., their E-2 visas may be revalidated by sending in their passports and I-94 cards together with yours. Again, there may be a charge for each visa revalidated. If your E-2 visa has expired, we strongly advise gathering your family together inside U.S. borders so you can take advantage of this simple revalidation procedure.

For more information on this process, see the State Department website at www.travel.state.gov/revals.html.

G. Visa Revalidation: Consular Filing

If you are outside of the U.S. when your visa stamp expires, you must have a new visa stamp issued at a consulate. Reread procedures for the application, consular filing, in Section D. The procedures for consular visa extensions are identical. If you are outside the U.S. with a valid visa, you need only reenter and a new I-94 card authorizing your stay for one year will be given to you.

FORMS AND DOCUMENTS CHECKLIST

STEP ONE: APPLICATION (THE ONLY STEP)

Forms

- [ ] DS forms (available from U.S. consulates abroad for consular filing only).
- [ ] Form I-129 and Supplement E (U.S. filing only).
- [ ] Form I-539 (U.S. filing only for accompanying relatives).

Documents

- [ ] Valid passport for you and each accompanying relative.
- [ ] One photo of you and each accompanying relative (consular filing only).
- [ ] Copy of I-94 card for you and each accompanying relative (U.S. filing only).
- [ ] Long-form birth certificate for you and each accompanying relative.
- [ ] Marriage certificate if you are married and bringing your spouse.
- [ ] If either you or your spouse have ever been married, copies of divorce and death certificates showing termination of all previous marriages.
- [ ] Documents showing ownership of real estate in your home country, if possible.
- [ ] Documents showing that close family members or property are being left behind in your home country.
- [ ] Documents showing that a job is waiting on your return to your home country.
- [ ] Copies of all outstanding stock certificates, if the qualifying business is a corporation.
- [ ] Notarized affidavit from the secretary of the qualifying corporation, or, if the business is not a corporation, from the official record keeper of the business, stating the names of each owner and percentages of the company owned.

- [ ] Passport or proof of citizenship for each owner of the qualifying business.
- [ ] Articles of incorporation or other legal charter or business license of the qualifying company.
- [ ] Tax returns of the qualifying company for the past two years, if available.
- [ ] Accountant's financial statements, including profit and loss statements and balance sheets, of the qualifying company for the past two years, if available.
- [ ] Payroll records of the qualifying company for the past two years, if available.
- [ ] Promotional literature describing the nature of the qualifying business.
- [ ] Letters from banks, or bank statements, indicating the average account balance of the qualifying business.
- [ ] Copy of a business lease or deed for the U.S. business premises of the qualifying business.
- [ ] If the qualifying company is a new business, a comprehensive business plan with financial projections for the next three years.
- [ ] If you are not majority owner of the qualifying business, evidence that your position in the U.S. will be as an executive, supervisor, or essential employee.
- [ ] Bank wire-transfer memos showing money sent to the U.S. from abroad.
- [ ] Contracts for purchase and bills of sale for purchase of capital goods and inventory.
- [ ] Lease agreements for the business premises, or contracts to purchase or deeds for business real estate, or construction contracts and blueprints for building the business premises.
- [ ] If the qualifying company is a new business, documents showing that the investment is large enough to capitalize the business, such as market surveys, written trade-association statistics, or written reports from qualified business consultants.

Students: F-1 and M-1 Visas

There are two primary types of student visas: F-1 and M-1. F-1 visas are issued to full-time academic or language students. M-1 visas are issued to vocational or other nonacademic students. Both visas are obtained in exactly the same manner. However, the privileges and limitations of the two visas differ.

F-1 Privileges

- You may come to the U.S. as a full-time academic or language student enrolled in a program leading to a degree or certificate. (Students not requiring student visas include tourists who are taking a class or two for recreational purposes, those who have a spouse or parent in the U.S. with an A, E, G, H, J, L, or NATO visa or status, or a worker in H status, as long as it does not interfere with his or her nonimmigrant status.)

- You can transfer from one school to another or switch academic programs by going through a simple procedure to notify USCIS of the change.

- You may work legally in a part-time job on campus. Also, you may get special permission to work off campus if it is economically urgent or if the job provides practical training for your field of study.

- You may travel in and out of the U.S. or remain there until the completion of your studies.

- Visas are available for accompanying relatives.

F-1 Limitations

- You must first be accepted as a student by an approved school in the U.S. before you can apply for an F-1 visa. (Once accepted by the school, you may be able to apply for your student status without leaving the U.S.)

- You may not work legally off campus without special permission.

- You are restricted to attending only the specific school for which your visa currently has been approved.

- Accompanying relatives may stay in the U.S. with you, but they may not work.

- You may not obtain an F visa to study at a public elementary school or a publicly funded adult education program.

- You may not obtain an F visa to study at a public secondary school unless you prepay the full cost of such program for a maximum of one year.

- You may not obtain F status to study at a private elementary or secondary school, or private adult education program, and then transfer to or attend publicly funded elementary, secondary, or adult education programs.

- An individual who violates the above regulations regarding study at a public elementary, secondary, or publicly funded adult education program or who changes such enrollment from such a private school or program to such a public program (without receiving prior approval and paying the full cost for a period not to exceed one year) will be inadmissible to the U.S. for five years.

M-1 Privileges

- You may come to the U.S. as a full-time vocational or nonacademic student enrolled in a program leading to a degree or certificate.

- You can transfer from one school to another, though it becomes more difficult after your first six months of study.

- You may get permission to work for up to six months after your studies are done. The job must be considered practical training for your field of study.

- You may travel in and out of the U.S. or remain there until the completion of your studies, up to a maximum of one year. If you have not completed your program in a year or by the time indicated on your I-20M form, whichever is less, you must apply for an extension.

- Visas are available for accompanying relatives.

M-1 Limitations

- You must first be accepted by an approved school.

- You are restricted to attending only the specific school for which your visa has been currently approved. You can transfer from one school to another only if you apply for and receive permission from USCIS to do so. Once you are six months into the program of studies, you are prohibited from transferring except under truly exceptional circumstances.

- You are never permitted to change your course of study.

- You may not work during your studies.

- Accompanying relatives may stay in the U.S. with you, but they may not work.

This chapter will discuss who is eligible for an academic (F-1) or vocational (M-1) visa, and how to apply for one.

For a more in-depth discussion of all aspects of getting and using a student visa, see *Student and Tourist Visas: How to Come to the U.S.*, by Ilona Bray & Richard A. Boswell (Nolo).

A. Who Qualifies for a Student Visa?

If you are coming to the U.S. to study full-time in a program leading to a degree, diploma, or certificate, you must be entering a U.S. government-approved school to qualify for a student visa. Academic and language students get F-1 visas, while vocational and technical school students get M-1 visas. The primary differences are that F-1 visas may be held for a much longer time than M-1 visas, and F-1 students have greater opportunities to get work permits.

To qualify for a student visa, you must already be accepted by the school of your choice and have enough money to study full-time without working. You must be able to speak, read, and write English well enough to understand the course work or, alternatively, the school can offer special tutoring or instruction in your native tongue to help overcome any language barriers. In addition to your academic and financial qualifications, you must prove that you intend to return to your home country when your program of studies is over.

At every government-approved school there is a person on the staff known as the designated school official (DSO). The DSO is recognized by USCIS and the consulates as having primary responsibility for dealing with foreign students.

To summarize, there are six requirements for obtaining a student visa. You must:

- be coming to the U.S. as a full-time student
- be enrolled in a program which leads to the attainment of a specific vocational or educational objective
- have been accepted by a school approved by the U.S. government
- have sufficient knowledge of English to be able to understand the course work; alternatively, the school can offer you either instruction in your native language or special English tutoring
- have enough money or financial support to study full-time without working, and
- intend to return home when your studies are completed.

Now we will explain each of these requirements in detail.

COMING TO THE U.S. TO LOOK FOR A SCHOOL

As a prospective student, you can come to the U.S. as a tourist for the purpose of locating a school you want to attend. If you do this, however, be sure to tell the consul at your interview that this is your intent so that s/he can make the appropriate annotation in your passport (such as "Prospective Student—school not yet selected"). Otherwise USCIS will presume that you committed fraud by applying for a visitor visa when you intended to come to the U.S. to study. USCIS will then refuse your application to convert to student status.

An interest in certain subjects may bar you from entry. If you're planning to study a subject with international security implications such as biochemistry, nuclear physics, or missile telemetry, and you're from a country on the U.S. government's list of supporters of terrorism, you may not be allowed a student visa. At the time this book went to print, the Bush administration was working to identify subject areas that it felt should only be offered to international students who've been individually screened by a special panel of experts.

1. Full-Time Student

How much time is "full-time" study? This depends on what kind of program you are pursuing. The different types of programs are classified for immigration purposes as:

- undergraduate college or university programs
- postgraduate college or university programs
- programs of specialized college-level schools
- high school and primary school programs, and
- technical, vocational, or other nonacademic programs.

The time requirements of full-time enrollment vary for each one.

Undergraduate college or university programs. If you are an undergraduate at a U.S. college or university, you must be enrolled in at least 12 semester or quarter hours of instruction per term. An exception to this is if you are in your last term and need fewer than 12 semester hours to graduate.

Postgraduate college or university programs. If you are a graduate student, full-time studies are whatever the designated school official says they are. For example, a graduate student may be working on a dissertation and taking no classes at all, but still be considered a full-time student, if the designated school official approves.

Programs of specialized college-level schools. When your course of studies is at a specialized school offering recognized college-level degrees or certificates in language, liberal arts, fine arts, or other nonvocational programs, you must be attending at least 12 hours of class per week. This means 12 hours by the clock, not 12 semester hours.

High school and primary school programs. Primary school or high school students must attend the minimum number of class hours per week that the school requires for normal progress toward graduation. However, the school may recommend a lesser load for a foreign student with a limited understanding of English.

Technical, vocational, or other nonacademic programs. To be classified as a full-time student in a technical, vocational, or other type of nonacademic program, you must attend at least 18 clock hours per week, if the courses consist mostly of classroom study. If the courses are made up primarily of laboratory work, 22 clock hours per week is the minimum.

PERMISSION TO TAKE A REDUCED LOAD

When you are unable to carry a full-time course load due to health problems or academic issues, you may be permitted to keep your student status even though you are not going to school full time. However, your course load cannot be reduced to less than six semester or quarter hours, or half the clock hours required for a full course of study. A reduced course load to less than half time is only acceptable for defined medical reasons or for your final school term if the school determines that fewer courses are needed to complete your course of study.

No special USCIS application is necessary to take a reduced load. However, USCIS has the right to challenge your status at a later date. Therefore, get a written statement from your DSO explaining that he or she believes it is medically or academically necessary for you to reduce your course load, and giving the reasons why.

2. Program Leading to the Attainment of a Specific Educational or Vocational Objective

In order to qualify for a student visa, you must be enrolled in a program that leads to the attainment of a specific educational or vocational objective. You must also maintain a full-time course load, as described above.

3. Government-Approved School

Student visas are issued only to students who attend U.S. schools that have received prior approval from USCIS for enrollment of foreign students. Virtually all public and accredited private colleges, universities, and vocational schools have been approved. To become approved, the school must take the initiative and file a formal application with USCIS. If you do not plan to attend a public school or a fully accredited college or university, before you apply for either an F-1 or M-1 visa you should check to be sure that the school you have selected has been approved by USCIS to accept foreign students.

4. Knowledge of English

To qualify for a student visa, you must know the English language well enough to pursue your studies effectively. Most U.S. colleges and universities will not admit students whose native language is not English until they first pass an English proficiency test such as the "TOEFL." Tests can be arranged in your home country. Your chosen school in the U.S. will tell you if such a test is required and how to go about taking it.

Usually, consul officials let each school decide for itself who is and is not qualified to study there. Still, occasionally even when a school is willing to admit you without a strong knowledge of English, the U.S. consulate may refuse to issue a student visa because it thinks your English is not good enough. You may still be able to satisfy the consulate if the school you plan to attend is willing to supply English language tutoring or, alternatively, offer a course of studies in your native tongue.

5. Adequate Financial Resources

You must show that you have enough money to complete your entire course of studies without working. At the time you apply for a student visa, you must have enough cash on hand to cover all first-year expenses. In addition, you must be able to show a reliable source of money available to pay for subsequent years. This is normally accomplished by having your parents or other close relatives promise in writing to finance your education, and submit proof of their ability to do so.

6. Intent to Return to Your Home Country

Student visas are meant to be temporary. At the time of applying, you must intend to return home when your studies are completed. If you have it in mind to take up permanent residence in the U.S., you are legally ineligible for a student visa. The U.S. government knows it is difficult to read minds. Therefore, you can expect to be asked for evidence showing that when you go to the U.S. on a student visa, you are leaving behind possessions, property, or family members as an incentive for your eventual return. It is also helpful if you can show that you have a job waiting at home after graduation.

If you are studying to prepare yourself for an occupation in which no jobs are available in your home country, neither USCIS nor the U.S. consulate will believe that you are planning to return home. To avoid trouble with getting a student visa, be sure to choose a field of study that will give you career opportunities in your home country when you graduate.

7. Accompanying Relatives

When you qualify for an F-1 or M-1 visa, your spouse and unmarried children under age 21 can get F-2 or M-2 visas by providing proof of their family relationship to you and by showing that you have sufficient financial resources to support them in the U.S. so that they will have no need to work. F-2 and M-2 visas authorize your accompanying relatives to stay with you in the U.S., but not to work there.

Family members may also enroll in elementary or secondary school (kindergarten through 12th grade), or in any avocational or recreational studies. They may not, however, enroll full time in a degree-granting course of post-secondary study.

B. How Long It Takes to Get the Visa

There are no quota restrictions. Applications filed at consulates were formerly approved within one or two days, but now added security procedures mean that you should expect a wait of two or three months. Some consulates will, at least, give students priority when scheduling appointments. Applications filed in the U.S. are approved within a few months.

C. How Long the Visa Will Last

The expiration date on your student visa indicates how long you have the right to request entry to the U.S. in order to assume student privileges. It doesn't tell how long you may stay once you arrive. This is controlled by the duration of your student status.

Duration of status is the period of time it is expected to take for you to complete your studies. When you enter the U.S. using a valid student visa, you will be given a small white card called an I-94 card. With all other types of non-immigrant visas, a USCIS officer normally stamps the I-94

card with a date as you enter the country and it is this date, not the expiration date of the visa, which controls how long you can stay. However, many student I-94 cards, particularly for F-1 students, are not stamped with a specific date. Instead, the I-94 card is marked "D/S" for duration of status. This means that you may remain in the U.S. in a student status for as long as it takes to complete your educational objectives, provided you finish within what USCIS and your school consider a reasonable period of time. The following specific rules control the time you may spend in the U.S. as a student:

- F-1 and M-1 students, and their accompanying family members, can arrive in the United States up to 30 days before the start of classes.
- Both F-1 and M-1 visas are issued for the estimated length of time it will take to complete your proposed program of studies. Consulates will use their judgment in deciding the expiration date of the visa. Normally it is expected that academic programs for F-1 students will last longer than vocational or nonacademic programs for M-1 students. Therefore, M-1 visas will generally not be approved for a program lasting longer than a total of 12 months.
- Once you arrive in the U.S., you may remain in student status without requesting an extension, for up to the date indicated on the paperwork from your school, plus a 60-day (F-1) or 30-day (M-1) grace period provided that you remain enrolled in an approved program of studies, and you maintain your full-time student status and do not become inadmissible or deportable. If you receive the school's permission to withdraw from your studies, your grace period will be 15 days.
- If your student status expires because your maximum stay (time indicated on I-20A-B for F students; time indicated on I-20M-N for M students) is up, you can apply to your designated school official for an extension of stay. To receive an extension, you will have to show that you are still enrolled in an approved program, you are still eligible for nonimmigrant student status, and that there is a good reason why it is taking you extra time to complete your studies. You must do so within 30 days of the I-20 expiration date. If that date passes, you are out of status and will have to return home and get a new visa.

POSSIBILITIES FOR A GREEN CARD FROM STUDENT STATUS

If you have an F-1 or M-1 visa, you are not barred from filing for a green card, but being in the U.S. on a student visa gives you no direct advantage in doing so. Earning a degree may, however, help you indirectly, especially if you happen to be studying in a field where there is a shortage of qualified U.S. workers. (A key element in getting a green card through employment is proving that there are not enough American workers available to fill a position for which you are qualified.) College graduates also have a number of other advantages in applying for a green card through employment. (See Chapter 8 for details.)

Keep in mind, however, that student visas, like all nonimmigrant visas, are meant to be temporary. They are intended only for those who plan on returning home once their studies in the U.S. are completed. Therefore, if you decide to apply for a green card before your studies are finished, the U.S. government will allow you to maintain student status while pursuing a green card, but only if you are able to convince them of two things: first, that you did not intend to get a green card when you originally applied for the F-1 or M-1 visa, and second, that you will return home if you are unable to secure a green card before your student status expires. Proving these things can be difficult. If you do not succeed, your student visa may be taken away. If this happens, it will not directly affect your green card application. You will simply risk being without a nonimmigrant visa until you get your green card—meaning you'll have to return home in the interim.

If you instead choose to stay out of status for even six or 12 months and then depart the U.S., it may result in a three- or ten-year bar to your returning to the U.S. However, current USCIS interpretations state that a student who goes out of status does not begin to accumulate time toward these six- or 12-month periods until a USCIS official or an immigration judge makes a ruling that the person is out of status. This means that if you stop attending school for some reason, you will not begin to accrue time toward the overstay bars unless you come to the government's attention. This could happen, for example, if you request reinstatement of student status and the USCIS denies it. Then you would begin to accrue time toward the six- or 12-month "overstay bars" as of the date of USCIS's decision. (See Chapter 25 for a discussion of how being out of status can affect your ability to get a green card.)

D. Applying for a Student Visa

Once a school has accepted you, getting either an F-1 or M-1 visa is a one-step process.

1. Overview of the Application Procedures

Certain portions of the application are technically the responsibility of the school you will be attending. Some applicants expect their schools to handle the entire procedure for them, but this rarely happens. The only part of the student visa application you should expect your school to complete is a form known as the Certificate of Eligibility (SEVIS I-20). You will use this certificate in preparing your application for a student visa.

The application is your formal request for a student visa or status. (If you are Canadian, your application procedures will be different from those of other applicants. See Chapter 28.) It is filed by you and your accompanying relatives, if any. The application process may, under certain circumstances, be carried out in the U.S. at a USICS office, or in your home country at a U.S. consulate.

The vast majority of nonimmigrant visa applications are filed at consulates. That is because most cases don't qualify for U.S. filing. You are not eligible for U.S. filing if you planned to file for a student status before you entered the U.S. on some other type of visa, unless your visitor visa was so annotated. If a USICS officer believes you had a preconceived intent to become a student when you entered the U.S., your application will be turned down. In recent years, USICS has become especially strict about preconceived intent in student cases. That is why an overwhelming percentage of student cases filed in the U.S. are not approved.

If you are already in the U.S. legally on some other type of nonimmigrant visa, you may qualify to apply for a student status at a USICS office inside the U.S. using a procedure known as "change of nonimmigrant status." (If you were admitted as a visitor without a visa under the Visa Waiver Program, you may not carry out the application step in the U.S. Currently there are 28 participating countries in the Visa Waiver Program; see Chapter 2 for a list.)

Change of status is simply a technical term meaning you are switching from one nonimmigrant status to another. If a change of status is approved, you will then be treated as if you had entered the country with a student visa, and you can keep the status as long as you remain in the U.S. or until it expires, whichever comes first.

You will not, however, receive a visa stamp, which is what you will eventually need if your plans include traveling in and out of the U.S. Visa stamps are issued only at U.S. consulates abroad. Therefore, if you change your status and later travel outside the U.S., you will have to go to the U.S.

consulate in your home country and repeat the application process over again, obtaining the student visa stamp in your passport before you can return. (However, Canadians don't need to obtain visas in advance; see Chapter 28.)

2. Who's Who in Getting Your Student Visa

Getting an F-1 or M-1 visa will be easier if you familiarize yourself with the technical names used for each participant in the process. You are known as the *student* or the *applicant*. Your U.S. government-approved school is referred to as the *school*. Each government-approved school is required to appoint at least one individual who has responsibility for visa processing and other school-related immigration matters of foreign students. That individual is known as the *designated school official* (or DSO). If you are bringing your spouse and children with you as accompanying relatives, they are known as *applicants* as well.

3. Tips on Handling the Paperwork

There are two types of paperwork you must submit to get a student visa. The first consists of official government forms completed by you or your U.S. school. The second is personal and financial documents, such as school transcripts and diplomas, bank statements, and guarantees of support.

It is vital that forms are properly filled out and all necessary documents are supplied. You may resent the intrusion into your privacy and the sizable effort it takes to prepare immigration applications, but you should realize the process is an impersonal matter to immigration officials. Your getting a visa is more important to you than it is to the U.S. government. There is no shortage of applicants.

The documents you supply to USCIS or consulate do not have to be originals. Photocopies of all documents are acceptable as long as you have the originals in your possession and are willing to produce them upon request. But add the following language to the photocopy, with your signature and the date:

> *Copies of documents submitted are exact photo-copies of unaltered original documents and I understand that I may be required to submit original documents to an immigration or consular official at a later date.*
> *Signature _____*
> *Typed or Printed Name _____*
> *Date_____*

Documents will be accepted if they are in either English, or, with papers filed at U.S. consulates abroad, the language of the country where the documents are being filed. An exception exists for papers filed at U.S. consulates in Japan, where all documents must be translated into English. If the documents are not in an acceptable language as just explained, they must be accompanied by a full, word for word, written English translation. Any capable person may act as translator. It is not necessary to hire a professional. At the end of each translation, the following statement must appear:

> *I hereby certify that I translated this document from [language] to English. This translation is accurate and complete. I further certify that I am fully competent to translate from [language] to English.*
> *Signature _____*
> *Typed or Printed Name _____*
> *Date_____*

The translator should sign this statement, but it does not have to be witnessed or notarized.

Later in this chapter we describe in detail the forms and documents needed to get your student visa. A summary checklist of forms and documents appears at the end of this chapter.

E. The Application: Consular Filing

Anyone with a Certificate of Eligibility (SEVIS I-20) from a U.S. school indicating acceptance by the school into a full-time program can apply for an F-1 or M-1 visa at a U.S. consulate in his or her home country. You must be physically present in order to apply there.

⚠ **If you have been or are now working or living illegally in the U.S., you may not be eligible to reenter the U.S. for many years.** Be sure to read and understand Chapter 25 before your out-of-status period exceeds six or 12 months, and before you depart the U.S. or file any applications with USCIS or the consulate.

1. Benefits and Drawbacks of Consular Filing

The most important benefit to consular filing is that only consulates issue visas. When you go through a U.S. filing you get a status, not a visa. (See Chapter 14.) An F-1 or M-1 status confers the same right to attend school as an F-1 or M-1 visa, but it does not give you the ability to travel in and out of the U.S. Therefore, if you want travel privileges, you will at some time have to go through the extra step of applying for a visa at a U.S. consulate, even though you have already applied for and received student status in the U.S.

However, if you had an immigrant visa petition filed on your behalf after entering in F or M status, you may be denied a nonimmigrant visa if you depart the U.S., as the consul may not believe you will leave the U.S. In that case you may be better off staying in the U.S. until you get your green card.

If you are in the U.S. illegally, consular filing is a must. You are not eligible to process a status application in the U.S. unless you have maintained your nonimmigrant status since your last entry. Again, however, if you've been in the U.S. illegally for six months or more, and leave for a consulate, you may be barred from returning for at least three years.

A further advantage to consular filing is that some consular offices work more quickly than some USCIS offices do. Know the reputation and track record of a foreign U.S. consulate before applying for a visa there.

A drawback to consular filing comes from the fact that you must be physically present in the country where the consulate is located in order to apply there. If your petition is ultimately turned down, the consular officer may, depending on the reasons for the denial, stop you from entering the U.S. on any nonimmigrant visa. In fact, he or she may cancel some other nonimmigrant visa you already have, including a visitor's visa. It will then be impossible for you to enter the U.S. at all. Consequently, if your F-1 or M-1 visa case is not very strong and freedom of travel is not essential to you, it might be wise to apply in the U.S., make up your mind to remain there for the duration of the student status, and skip trying to get a visa from the consulate.

THIRD COUNTRY PROCESSING

The immigration law amendments of 1996 limited who can obtain a nonimmigrant visa at a consulate other than one in your home country, called "third country national," or TCN, processing.

TCN processing is prohibited when you have been unlawfully present in the U.S. under a prior visa status. Even if you overstayed your status by just one day, the visa will be automatically canceled, you will be ineligible for TCN processing, and you will have to return to your home country to apply for a new visa at the consulate there.

If you were admitted to the U.S. for duration of status (indicated as "D/S" on your Form I-94), however, you still may be able to do TCN processing even though you remained in the U.S. too long. This applies to people in A, F, G, and J status. In this situation, you will be barred from TCN processing only if USCIS or an immigration judge determined that you were unlawfully present. (In general though, unlawful presence need not be determined by a judge or USCIS officer if you overstayed your I-20 date.)

Unlawful presence of six months or more after April 1, 1997 is also a ground of inadmissibility, if you left the U.S. and are requesting reentry. (See Chapter 25.)

2. Application General Procedures: Consular Filing

Technically, the law allows you to apply for an F-1 or M-1 visa at any U.S. consulate you choose (but see above, "Third Country Processing").

Once you have obtained the SEVIS I-20 Certificate of Eligibility, check with the nearest U.S. consulate to find out its application procedures for getting your F-1 or M-1 visa. Many insist on advance appointments. Appointments can take weeks to get, so plan ahead. You will need to pay a $100 visa-processing fee. In addition, you may need to pay a separate visa issuance fee, depending on whether your home country charges similar fees to visitors from the U.S.—ask the U.S. consulate about this "reciprocity fee."

3. Application Forms: Consular Filing

The consulate officials will provide you with certain forms, designated by a "DS" preceding a number. Instructions for completing DS forms and what to do with them once they are filled out will come with the forms. For security reasons, all males between the ages of 16 and 45 will have to submit an extra biographical form, called the DS-157. We do not include copies of these forms in Appendix II since different consulates often use different versions.

In addition to the DS forms, the consulate will need a copy of Form SEVIS I-20, which is completed by your school. You must have been accepted, met any special requirements for foreign students (such as proficiency in English), and proven you have the ability to pay for your education without working before the school will be authorized to complete its part of this form on your behalf. Ask your school to provide you with the completed form.

4.   Application Documents: Consular Filing

In addition to the forms, you'll have to gather or prepare various documents in support of your application to the consulate, as described below.

Passports and photos. You are required to show a valid passport and present one photograph taken in accordance with the photo instructions at http://travel.state.gov/photorequirements/html. For each accompanying relative, you must present a valid passport and one photograph. You will also need documents verifying their family relationship to you. You may verify a parent/child relationship by presenting the child's long-form birth certificate. Many countries, including Canada and England, issue both short- and long-form birth certificates. Where both are available, the long form is needed because it contains the names of the parents while the short form does not.

If you are accompanied by your spouse, you must establish that you are lawfully married by showing a civil marriage certificate. Church certificates are generally unacceptable. (There are a few exceptions, depending on the laws of your particular country. Canadians, for example, may use church marriage certificates if the marriage took place in Quebec Province, but not elsewhere. If a civil certificate is available, however, you should always use it.) You may have married in a country where marriages are not customarily recorded. Tribal areas of Africa are an example. In such situations, ask the consulate or embassy for advice on what it will accept as proof of marriage.

Evidence of intent to return. You will need documents establishing your intent to leave the U.S. when your studies in the U.S. are completed. The consulate will want to see evidence of ties to some other country so strong that you will be highly motivated to return there. Proof of such ties can include deeds verifying ownership of a house or other real property, written statements from you explaining that close relatives live there, or letters from a company showing that you have a job waiting when you return from the U.S.

Evidence of academic qualifications. If you will be attending a U.S. college or university, some consular officers will require you to prove that you are academically qualified to pursue the program, even though the school itself has already accepted you. Therefore, you should present evidence of all of your previous education, in the form of official transcripts and diplomas from schools you attended. If these documents are not available, submit detailed letters by officials of the schools you previously attended describing the extent and nature of your education.

Evidence of sufficient funds. Most important, you must submit documents showing you presently have sufficient funds available to cover all tuition and living costs for your first year of study. The Certificate of Eligibility, Form SEVIS I-20, gives the school's estimate of what your total annual expenses will be. Specifically, you must show you have that much money presently available. You must also document that you have a source of funds to cover expenses in future years without your having to work.

The best evidence of your ability to pay educational expenses is a letter from a bank, or a bank statement, either in the U.S. or abroad, showing an account in your name with a balance of at least the amount of money it will take to pay for your first year of education.

Alternatively, you can submit a written guarantee of support signed by an immediate relative, preferably a parent, together with your relative's bank statements. Unless your relative can show enough assets to prove he or she can support you without additional income, you should also show that your relative is presently employed. You can document this by submitting a letter from the employer verifying your relative's work situation.

Although the guarantee of support may be in the form of a simple written statement in your relative's own words, we suggest you use Form I-134, called an *Affidavit of Support.* A copy of this form is in Appendix II and on the USCIS website. The questions on Form I-134 are self-explanatory. Be aware that the form was designed to be filled out by someone living in the U.S. Since it is quite likely that the person who will support you is living outside the U.S., any questions that apply to U.S. residents should be answered "N/A."

Additional documents for flight trainees. If you're applying for an F or M visa for U.S. flight training, you will be required to submit written information and documents specifying the following:

- your reason for the training (be specific)
- current employer and your position
- who is paying for the training (name and relationship)
- your most recent flight certifications and ratings
- information on what kind of aircraft the training is for (document must be signed by a school official in the U.S.)
- certified take-off weight of the aircraft type (document must be signed by a school official in the U.S.), and
- current rank or title if you are presently working as an active pilot.

5. Application Interviews: Consular Filing

Most consulates will require an interview before issuing a student visa. During the interview, a consular officer will examine the forms and documents for accuracy. Documents proving your ability to finance your education will be carefully checked, as will evidence of ties to your home country. During the interview you will surely be asked how long you intend to remain in the U.S. Any answer indicating uncertainty about plans to return home or an interest in applying for a green card is likely to result in a denial of your student visa.

Because of new security requirements, you are unlikely to be approved for your visa on the same day as your interview. The consular officer will need to compare your name against various databases of people with a history of criminal activity, violations of U.S. immigration laws, or terrorist affiliations. This can add weeks or months to the processing of your visa, particularly if you come from a country that the U.S. suspects of supporting terrorism.

6. Using Your Student Visa

On entering the U.S. with your new F-1 or M-1 visa, you will be given an I-94 card. This will be stamped showing you have been admitted for duration of status (D/S). Also shown is the name of the school you have been authorized to attend.

Each time you exit and reenter the U.S., you will get a new I-94 card authorizing your stay for duration of status. When you have stayed in the U.S. on an M-1 visa for a year (or whatever time you were given) and you wish to remain longer, you will have to apply for only one extension of your I-20 to your designated school official. F-1 students can apply for extensions of stay as long as they continue to

maintain their eligibility for the status, and their DSO grants an extension of their I-20 time to complete studies.

SUMMARY EXCLUSION

The law empowers a CBP inspector at the airport to summarily (without allowing judicial review) bar entry to someone requesting admission to the U.S. if either of the following are true:

- The inspector thinks you are lying about practically anything connected with entering the U.S., including your purpose in coming, intent to return, and prior immigration history. This includes the use or suspected use of false documents.
- You do not have the proper documentation to support your entry to the U.S. in the category you are requesting.

If the inspector excludes you, you cannot be readmitted to the U.S. for five years, unless USCIS grants a special waiver. For this reason it is extremely important to understand the terms of your requested status, and to not make any misrepresentations. If you are found to be inadmissible, you may request to withdraw your application to enter the U.S. in order to prevent having the five-year deportation order on your record. The CBP may allow this in some exceptional cases.

---

7. Application Appeals: Consular Filings

When a consulate turns down an F-1 or M-1 visa application, there is no way to make a formal appeal, although you are free to reapply as often as you like (unless the individual consulate sets limits on repeat applications or makes you wait a certain number of months before reapplying). If your visa is denied, you will be told by the consular officer the reasons for the denial. Written statements of decisions are not normally provided in nonimmigrant cases. If a lack of evidence about a particular point is the problem, sometimes simply presenting more evidence on an unclear fact can change the result. The most common reasons for denial of a student visa are that the consular officer does not believe you intend to return home when your studies are completed, you are viewed as a security risk, or you have failed to prove an ability to pay for your education without working.

Certain people who have been refused student visas reapply at a different consulate, attempting to hide the fact that they were turned down elsewhere. You should know that if your application is denied, the last page in your passport will be stamped "Application Received," with the date and location of the rejecting consulate. This notation shows that some type of prior visa application has failed. It serves as a warning to other consulates that your case merits close inspection. If what we have just told you makes you think it would be a good idea to overcome this problem by obtaining a new, unmarked passport, you should also know that permanent computer records are kept of all visa denials.

F. Applying for a Student Visa When You Have Not Yet Been Accepted by a U.S. School

The requirement that you must first be accepted by a school in the U.S. before applying for a student visa sometimes creates a dilemma. You may want to travel to the U.S. before being accepted in order to make a final selection of schools or complete the school application. Under these circumstances you may enter the U.S. on a visitor's visa (see Chapter 15); however, you must advise the U.S. consulate issuing the visitor's visa that you are a prospective student. The consulate will then ask for proof of your ability to pay for your education as well as evidence that you are otherwise qualified for a student visa. If you are found qualified, the visitor's visa will be marked with the notation "prospective student." This notation will enable you to enter the U.S. as a visitor and, after being accepted into school, apply for student status without leaving the country. The procedure for a U.S. filing is discussed next.

G. The Application: U.S. Filing

If you are physically present in the U.S., you may apply for F-1 or M-1 status without leaving the country on the following conditions:
- you have been accepted as a student by a U.S. government-approved school and the school has given you a Certificate of Eligibility, Form I-20
- you entered the U.S. legally and not under the Visa Waiver Program
- you have never worked in the U.S. illegally
- the date on your I-94 card has not passed, and
- you are not inadmissible.

If you are admitted as a visitor without a visa under the Visa Waiver Program, you may not carry out the application step in the U.S. Currently there are 28 participating countries in the Visa Waiver Program; see Chapter 2 for a list.

⚠ **If you cannot meet these terms, you may not file for F-1 or M-1 status in the U.S.** However, eligibility to apply while you're in the U.S. has nothing to do with overall eligibility for an F-l or M-1 visa. Applicants who are barred from filing in the U.S. but otherwise qualify for student status can sometimes apply successfully for an F-1 or M-1 visa at U.S. consulates abroad. If you find you are not eligible for U.S. filing, read Section E, above, and Chapter 25 (regarding the bars to change and adjustment of status), before filing an application or departing the U.S.

1. Benefits and Drawbacks of U.S. Filing

Visas are never given inside the U.S. They are issued exclusively by U.S. consulates abroad. If you file in the U.S. and are successful, you will get student status but not the visa itself. Student status allows you to remain in the U.S. with student privileges until the status expires, but should you leave the country for any reason before that time, you will have to apply for the visa itself at a U.S. consulate before returning to the U.S. Moreover, the fact that your F-1 or M-1 status has been approved in the U.S. does not guarantee that the consulate will also approve your visa.

There is another problem which comes up only in U.S. filings. It is the issue of what is called *preconceived intent.* To approve a change of status, USCIS must believe that at the time you originally entered the U.S. as a visitor or with some other nonimmigrant visa, you did not intend to apply for a different status. If USCIS thinks you had a preconceived plan to change from the status you arrived with to a different status, it may deny your application. The preconceived intent issue is one less potential hazard you will face if you apply at a U.S. consulate abroad.

On the plus side of U.S. filing, when problems do arise with your U.S. application, you can stay in the U.S. while they are being corrected, a circumstance most visa applicants prefer. If you run into snags at a U.S. consulate, you will have to remain outside the U.S. until matters are resolved.

Overall, USCIS offices do not favor change of status applications. Your student application will stand a better chance of approval at most consulates than it will if filed in the U.S. But understand the pitfalls involved in departing the U.S. (discussed in Chapter 25, especially if you have lived here unlawfully) before making your decision.

2. Application General Procedures: U.S. Filing

The change of status application, Form I-539 and documents, is sent by mail to the USCIS regional service center having jurisdiction over the intended school. USCIS regional service centers are not the same as USCIS local offices—for one thing, you cannot visit the regional service centers in person. There are four USCIS regional service centers spread across the U.S. Appendix I contains a list of all USCIS regional service centers and their addresses.

The filing fee for each application is currently $140. Checks and money orders are accepted. It is not advisable to send cash. We recommend submitting all papers by certified mail, return receipt requested, and making a copy of everything sent in to keep for your records.

Within a few weeks of mailing in the application, you should get back a written notice of confirmation that the papers are being processed, together with a receipt for the fees. This notice will also tell you your immigration file number and approximately when to expect a decision. If USCIS wants further information before acting on your case, all application papers, forms, and documents will be returned, together with another form known as an *I-797*. The I-797 tells you what additional pieces of information or documents are expected. You should supply the extra data and mail the whole package back to the regional service center—again, keeping a copy for your records.

Waiting times for F-1 or M-1 status approval range from two weeks to five months. You will receive a Notice of Action Form I-797 indicating the dates for which your status is approved. A new I-94 card will be attached to the bottom of the form. You will also be issued an I-20 Student ID.

3. Application Forms: U.S. Filing

Copies of all the USCIS forms you must complete are in Appendix II and on the USCIS website.

Form I-20

You must submit a completed Form SEVIS I-20, called Certificate of Eligibility. It is completed by your school. You must have been accepted, met any special requirements for foreign students (such as proficiency in English), and proven you have the ability to pay for your education without working, before the school will be authorized to complete its part of this form on your behalf. Ask your school to provide you with a completed copy.

Form I-539

Only one application form is needed for an entire family. If you have a spouse or children coming with you, you should also complete the I-539 Supplement.

Part 1. These questions are self-explanatory. "A" numbers are usually given only to people who have previously applied for green cards or who have been in deportation proceedings. If you have an A number, consult an attorney. If you don't, write "None." Your "current nonimmigrant status" refers to the visa you're currently carrying, such as "B-2 visitor."

Part 2. Question 1. Mark box "b" followed by "F-1" or "M-1."

Question 2. This question asks if you are also applying for a spouse or children. If so, you must complete the Supplement, which asks for their names, dates of birth, and passport information.

Part 3. In most cases you will answer only the first item in this part, by putting in the date. You should put down the date shown on your I-20 as the anticipated completion time of your studies.

Part 4, Questions 1–2. These questions are self-explanatory.

Question 3. The different parts to this question are self-explanatory; however, items "a" through "c" ask if an immigrant visa petition or adjustment of status application has ever been filed on your behalf. If you are separately applying for a green card through a relative, this would be Step One, as described in Chapter 5. If you are separately applying for a green card through employment, this would be Step Two, as described in Chapter 8. If your relative or employer has filed the papers for either of these steps, the answer is "yes," and since you have therefore expressed a desire to live in the U.S. permanently, your application is very likely to be denied. If you have only begun the Labor Certification, the Step One of getting a green card through employment, this question should be answered "no."

4. Application Documents: U.S. Filing

In addition to the forms, you'll have to gather or prepare various documents in support of your application, as described below.

I-94 card. Each applicant must submit an I-94 card, the small white card you received on entering the U.S. Remember, if the date stamped on your I-94 card has already passed, you are ineligible for U.S. filing. Canadians who are just visiting are not expected to have I-94 cards. Canadians with any other type of nonimmigrant status should have them.

For accompanying relatives. For each accompanying relative, send in an I-94 card. You will also need documents verifying their family relationship to you. You may verify a parent/child relationship by presenting the child's long-form birth certificate. Many countries, including Canada and England, issue both short- and long-form birth certificates. Where both are available, the long form is needed because it contains the names of the parents, while the short form does not.

If you are accompanied by your spouse, you must prove that you are lawfully married by showing a civil marriage certificate. Church certificates are generally unacceptable. (There are a few exceptions, depending on the laws of your particular country. Canadians, for example, may use church marriage certificates if the marriage took place in Quebec Province, but not elsewhere. If a civil certificate is available, however, you should always use it.) You may have married in a country where marriages are not customarily recorded. Tribal areas of Africa are an example. In such situations, call the nearest consulate or embassy of your home country for help with getting acceptable proof of marriage.

Evidence of intent to return. We have emphasized that in order to qualify for either an F-1 or M-1 visa, you must have the intention of returning to your home country when your studies are completed. Although consulates will demand evidence that ties to your home country are strong enough to motivate your eventual return, in a U.S. filing, USCIS does not always ask for this. However, submit such evidence anyway. Proof of ties to your home country can include deeds verifying ownership of a house or other real property, written statements from you or your parents explaining that close relatives are staying behind, or letters from a company in your home country showing that you have a job waiting when you return from the U.S.

Evidence of academic qualifications. If you will be attending a U.S. college or university, some USCIS officers will require you to prove that you are academically qualified to pursue the program, even though the school itself has already accepted you. Therefore, present evidence of all of your previous education, in the form of official transcripts and diplomas from schools you attended. If these documents are not available, submit detailed letters written by officials of the schools you previously attended, describing the extent and nature of your education.

Evidence of sufficient funds. Most important, you must submit documents showing you presently have sufficient funds available to cover all tuition and living costs for your first year of study. The Certificate of Eligibility, Form SEVIS I-20, gives the school's estimate of what your total annual expenses will be. Specifically, you must show you have that much money presently available. You must also document that you have a source of funds to cover expenses in future years without your having to work.

The best evidence of your ability to pay educational expenses is a bank statement or letter from a bank, either in the U.S. or abroad, showing an account in your name with a balance of at least the amount of money it will take to pay for your first year of education.

Alternatively, you can submit a written guarantee of support signed by an immediate relative, preferably a parent, together with your relative's bank statements. Unless your relative can show enough assets to prove he or she can support you without additional income, you should also show that your relative is presently employed. Document

this by submitting a letter from the employer verifying your relative's work situation.

Although the guarantee of support may be in the form of a simple written statement in your relative's own words, we suggest you use Form I-134, called an Affidavit of Support. (Do not use the new Form I-864.) A copy of this form is in Appendix II and on the USCIS websites. The questions on Form I-134 are self-explanatory. However, be aware that the form was designed to be filled out by someone living in the U.S. Since it is quite likely that the person who will support you is living outside the U.S., any questions that apply to U.S. residents should be answered "N/A."

Additional documents for flight trainees. If you're applying for an F or M visa for U.S. flight training, you will be required to submit written information and documents specifying the following:

- your reason for the training (be specific)
- current employer and your position
- who is paying for the training (name and relationship)
- your most recent flight certifications and ratings
- information on what kind of aircraft the training is for (document must be signed by a school official in the U.S.)
- certified take-off weight of the aircraft type (document must be signed by a school official in the U.S.), and
- current rank or title if you are presently working as an active pilot.

5. Application Interviews: U.S. Filing

Interviews on student change of status applications are rarely held. When an interview is required, the USCIS regional service center where you filed will send your paperwork to the USCIS local office nearest your intended school. This office will in turn contact you for an appointment. USCIS may ask you to bring additional documents at that time.

If you are called for an interview, the most likely reason is that USCIS either suspects some type of fraud or has doubts about your intent to leave the U.S. after the student status expires. Because they are not common and usually a sign of trouble, these interviews can result in considerable delays.

6. Application Appeals: U.S. Filing

If your application is denied, you will receive a written decision by mail explaining the reasons for the denial. There is no way of making a formal appeal to USCIS if your application is turned down. If the problem is too little evidence, you may be able to overcome this obstacle by adding more documents and resubmitting the entire application to the same USCIS office you have been dealing with, together with a written request that the case be reopened. The written request does not have to be in any special form. This is technically called a *Motion to Reopen*. There is a $110 fee to file this motion.

Remember that you may be denied the right to a U.S. filing without being denied a student visa. When your application is turned down only because you are found ineligible for U.S. filing (change of status), you may be able to change your application to a consular filing. However, be sure you are eligible for a consular filing and not subject to the overstay bars—see Chapter 25.

Although there is no appeal to USCIS for the denial of a student change of status application, you do have the right to file an appeal in a U.S. district court. It would be difficult to file such an appeal without employing an immigration attorney at considerable expense. Such appeals are usually unsuccessful.

SCHOOLS' RESPONSIBILITIES TO TRACK INTERNATIONAL STUDENTS

As of 2002, schools must make various reports to USCIS concerning international students. When a school issues an I-20 to a student, it will be required to notify the U.S. consulate in the student's home country. When that consulate approves the student's visa, it will be required to notify USCIS.

During the student's time at school, the school will have to keep USCIS up to date on the student's status and whereabouts through a database called SEVIS. To finance this database, international students will now have to pay a fee in addition to the usual visa fees. That fee may well be around $100—however, at the time this book went to print, the government was still arguing about how high it could set the fee. The information and documents that schools are required to routinely make available to USCIS for each international student include:

- name, date and place of birth, country of citizenship
- current address
- visa classification, date of visa issuance or classification granted
- in-school status (full-time or part-time)
- date when studies began
- degree program and field of study
- whether the student has been certified for practical training and the dates of such certification

- date that studies were terminated, and the reason, if known
- written application for admission, transcripts or other course records, proof of financial responsibility, and other documents that the school evaluated in admitting the student
- number of credits completed per semester
- photocopy of Form I-20 ID, and
- record of any academic disciplinary actions due to criminal convictions.

On top of maintaining this database, the school must actually report news of each international student to USCIS each semester, no later than 30 days after the deadline for class registration. The information the schools must report includes: whether each student has enrolled, identification of any F-1 student who has dropped below a full course of study without authorization, and the student's current address.

In addition, the school has 21 days in which to report various changes in your situation (meaning that you must report all of these to the school as soon as possible—you have only ten days in the case of address changes). These changes include: your failure to maintain F-1 status or complete your educational program, a change in your address or name, your early graduation or graduation prior to the program end date on your form SEVIS I-20, or any disciplinary action the school has taken against you.

H. Extensions

Student visas and student statuses can be extended to allow necessary continuation of your studies. F-1 statuses as written on the Form I-20 must be extended if your studies exceed the time limits stated on that form. F-1 student I-20s can be extended by the designated school official. The new period will extend to the end of the revised estimated completion date of your academic program. M-1 statuses can be extended after one year for a maximum of one more year.

Your authorized stay as indicated on your Form I-20 may last longer than the expiration date of your visa or it may expire before your visa expires. Therefore, depending on your situation, you may need to extend your I-20 date, your visa, or both. Statuses as written on the Forms I-20 can be extended only by your DSO in the U.S. Student visas can be extended only at consulates (but you can wait until your next trip outside the U.S.). Extensions are not automatic. Your DSO or the consular officers have the right to reconsider your qualifications based on any changes in the facts or law. When it appears you are not making progress toward your academic or vocational objectives, it is not unusual for an extension request to be turned down. As always, however, good cases will be successful.

For those who must extend the duration of status as shown on the I-20 ID student copy, contact your DSO, who is responsible for making the extension and forwarding the information and paperwork to USCIS. Be sure, however, to request your extension before the end date on your I-20. If you are unable to complete your educational program before that date, and you don't request an extension by then, you are out of status and must apply for reinstatment, or leave the U.S.

THIS IS A VERY STRONG APPEAL MR. HODGEKISS BUT I'M AFRAID....

It is possible for your visa to expire before your duration of status period (as indicated on your I-20) is up. If you should leave the U.S. for any reason after your visa has expired, you must have a new visa issued at a consulate in order to return. If you do not leave the U.S., you do not need to have a valid visa; your I-20 and I-94 control your status period while in the U.S. (See Section C, above.)

I.   Work Permission for Students

When you have F-1 student status, you can work only under limited circumstances. M-1 students have almost no rights to work. In many cases these work privileges do not come automatically with the visa. You are often expected to file a separate application. There are a number of different types of work situations recognized as permissible for those with F-1 student status, and different rules apply to each one. Each situation is described in this section.

1.   On-Campus Employment

F-1 students are permitted to work in an on-campus job for up to 20 hours per week when school is in session. During vacation periods, you can work on campus full-time. No special permission or application is required, as long as the job does not displace U.S. residents. Students working on campus can be employed by the school itself or any independent companies serving the school's needs, such as cafeteria suppliers providing food on campus premises.

2.   Employment As Part of a Scholarship

F-1 students may also be employed as part of the terms of a scholarship, fellowship, or assistantship. The job duties must be related to your field of study. No special work permission or application is required. This is true even when the actual location of the job is off campus.

3.   Practical Training

Both F-1 and M-1 students are eligible to apply for work permission on the basis of practical training. Practical training for F-1 students can be either curricular or post-completion ("optional" or "OPT"). Curricular practical training occurs before graduation as part of your study program, while post-completion takes place afterward.

Curricular practical training is available only to F-1 students who have been enrolled in school for at least nine months. The nine-month enrollment requirement can be waived for graduate students requiring immediate participation in curricular practical training. All requests for curricular practical training are approved by the designated school official, who notifies USCIS.

Only the following types of work situations qualify as curricular practical training:

- alternate work/study programs
- internships, whether required or not required by the curriculum
- cooperative education programs, and
- required practicums offered though cooperative agreements with the school.

Both F-1 and M-1 students can get permission to work in post-completion practical training (OPT) after graduating. F-1 students, however, are not eligible for post-completion practical training if they have already worked for more than one year in curricular practical training.

Post-completion practical training can be approved for up to one year for F-1 students and six months for M students. Part-time practical training taken is deducted from the total period available at one-half the full-time rate. F-1 students are eligible for a new one-year period of post-completion optional practical training after every level of higher education they complete. For example, a student could do one year of OPT upon completing a Bachelor's degree, an additional year after a Master's, and then, if the student newly enrolls in a doctoral program, a third year once the Ph.D. is completed. Both the designated school official and USCIS must approve all applications for post-completion practical training. (Instructions are given in Section 6, below.)

4. Economic Necessity

Only F-1 students are eligible for work permission based on economic necessity. You will remember that in order to obtain a student visa, you were required to show that you had enough money on hand to cover all of your first-year costs. Therefore, work permission on the basis of economic necessity will never be granted during your first year of studies.

As an F-1 student, you can request work permission after the first year if there has been an unforeseen change in your financial situation and if you meet the following conditions:

- you have maintained F-1 student status for at least one academic year
- you are in good standing at your school
- you are a full-time student
- you will continue to be a full-time student while working
- you will not work for more than 20 hours per week while school is in session, and
- you have tried but failed to find on-campus employment.

USCIS recognizes as unforeseen circumstances such things as losing a scholarship, unusually large devaluation of your home country's currency, unexpected new restrictions enacted by your government that prevent your family from sending money out of the country, large increases in your tuition or living expenses, unexpected changes in the ability of your family to support you, or other unanticipated expenses such as medical bills that are beyond your control. Work permission can be granted for one year at a time, and must be renewed each year. Instructions on how to apply for work permission are given later in this chapter.

You should consider your situation carefully before deciding to file a request for employment authorization based on economic necessity. If the application is denied, USCIS may decide that you are not eligible to continue in your student status, since you are basically telling USCIS that you don't have sufficient funds to support yourself.

5. How to Apply for Work Permission Based on Economic Need

Check with your DSO or the local USCIS whether the application is filed in your district USCIS office or the service center. Before bringing your application to USCIS, your DSO will first review the paperwork to decide whether or not you meet all the requirements for work permission. If you appear to qualify, you will be given a written recommendation for employment, endorsed by the designated school official on Form I-20 ID. You should submit the endorsed form to USCIS with your other work application papers. The filing fee is currently $120. It is very important to keep the fee receipt USCIS will give you so you can prove that the I-765 was filed.

USCIS is required to make a decision on your employment authorization application within 90 days. If the decision is in your favor, you will receive a work authorization identification card. Most USCIS offices will attempt to decide your application within a few weeks.

If, for some reason, you are not given a decision within 90 days, you will, at your request, be granted an interim employment authorization that will last for 240 days. To receive an interim card, you must return in person to the USCIS local office and show your fee receipt. Then your interim work authorization card will be issued.

If 240 days pass and you still have not received a final decision on the I-765, you must stop working. Interim work authorization cards cannot be renewed. However, if you reach this point, you have the option to file a new I-765 application and, if you do not get a decision on the new application within 90 days, you will then be entitled to another interim work authorization. You may not begin to work before receiving some sort of USCIS approval.

If your request for work permission is denied, you will receive a written decision by mail explaining the reason for the denial. There is no way of making a formal appeal to USCIS if your request is turned down. If you have new evidence of why you should be allowed to work, you may submit it to the same USCIS office that made the original decision and request that your case be reconsidered. This is technically called a *Motion to Reopen* and you must pay a $110 filing fee. You may also challenge the decision in U.S. district court but the time and expense required for this approach usually makes it impractical.

a.   Work Application Forms

Copies of all the needed USCIS forms are in Appendix II and on the USCIS website.

Form I-765

Block above Question 1. Mark the first box, "Permission to accept employment."

Questions 1–9. These questions are self-explanatory.

Question 10. You will not usually have an Alien Registration Number unless you previously applied for a green card, were in deportation proceedings or have had certain types of immigration applications denied. All Alien Registration Numbers begin with the letter "A." If you have no "A" number but you entered the U.S. with a valid visa, you should have an I-94 card. In this case, insert the admission number from the I-94 card here.

Questions 11–15. These questions are self-explanatory.

Question 16. Answer this question "(c))(3)(iii)."

b.   Work Application Documents

You will need to submit your I-20 ID (student copy). You will also need documents to support your claim that an unexpected change in circumstances is creating your economic need. Such proof might include letters from government officials of your home country stating that there has been an unusual devaluation of the national currency or that your country's laws have changed and prevent your family from sending money out of the country to help support you as they once did. Depending on the situation, other items you might present are documents from your school showing a substantial tuition increase or bills from hospitals and doctors evidencing a costly family illness or birth of a child. If someone who has been supporting you is no longer able to do so, you can present a statement from a doctor or a death certificate showing that the person has become ill or died. You can also show documents demonstrating that the person who has been supporting you is having financial problems and so is unable to continue with your support.

6.   Application for Work Permission Based on Practical Training

Both F-1 and M-1 foreign students may apply for work permission to accept practical training employment. Practical training employment is any position where the work is directly related to the student's course of studies.

a.   General Procedures for F-1 Students

As an F-1 student, you must apply for permission to take practical training before completion of your study program. You may not apply until you have been enrolled as a student for at least nine months. If you apply before your full course of study is completed, you may be granted permission to take practical training only if it is necessary to fulfill a specific requirement of your particular academic program or if the work will be scheduled exclusively during regular school vacations. If the practical training will begin after you graduate, you may work simply because you wish to do so.

When practical training is to start after your studies are completed, an application for work permission must be filed not more than 60 days before your graduation. You can be granted permission to work in a practical training position for a total of no more than 12 months. You must have an offer of employment.

The application, consisting of both forms and documents, should be submitted to the USCIS service center designated for where you are attending school. Before mailing your application to USCIS, your designated school official will review the paperwork to decide whether or not you meet all the requirements for work permission. If you appear to qualify, he or she will give you a written recommendation for employment, endorsed on Form I-20 ID. Submit the endorsed form to USCIS with your other work application papers. The filing fee is currently $120. Keep the fee receipt USCIS will give you so you can prove that the I-765 was filed in case USCIS loses it.

If USCIS wants further information before acting on your case, USCIS may send you a form known as an I-797. The I-797 tells you what additional pieces of information or documents are expected. Supply the extra data and mail the whole package back.

Most USCIS offices will make a decision on your application within several weeks. The law requires USCIS to make a decision on your employment authorization application within 90 days. If the decision is in your favor, you will receive a work authorization card.

If, for some reason, you are not given a decision within 90 days, you will, at your request, be granted an interim employment authorization which will last for 240 days. To receive an interim card, you must go in person to USCIS local office nearest your school and show your fee receipt. Then your interim work authorization card will be issued.

If 240 days pass and you still have not received a final decision on the I-765, you must stop working. Interim work authorization cards cannot be renewed. However, if you reach this point, you have the option to file a new I-765 application and, if you do not get a decision on the new application within 90 days, request another interim work authorization card.

If your request for work permission is denied, you will receive a written decision by mail explaining the reason for the denial. There is no way of making a formal appeal to USCIS if your request is turned down. If you have new evidence, you may submit it to the same USCIS office that made the original decision and request that your case be reconsidered. This is technically called a *Motion to Reopen* and you must pay a $110 filing fee. You may also challenge the decision in U.S. district court, but the time and expense required for this approach usually make it impractical.

SPECIAL RULES FOR F-1 STUDENTS WHO TAKE PRACTICAL TRAINING AS A REQUIRED PART OF THEIR STUDIES

If, prior to graduation, you accept practical training employment that is a required part of your studies, as is frequently done by students on fellowships, only 50% of your employment time will be deducted from the allotted 12-month total. Practical training in this special situation is called curricular practical training and has the effect of allowing you to work for a total of 24 months prior to graduation instead of only 12. If you work for six months in curricular practical training, you are required to deduct only three months from your allotment, meaning you may still accept nine months of additional practical training employment prior to graduation and the full 12 months after graduation. If, however, you work more than 20 hours per week, you lose the benefit of this special rule. Under these circumstances, once again you must deduct the whole amount of time you worked, meaning you are limited to a maximum of 12 months of practical training prior to graduation.

b. General Procedures for M-1 Students

As an M-1 student, you can apply for permission to take practical training only after you have completed your entire program of studies. Applications for work permission must be filed not more than 60 days before your graduation. M-1 students can be granted permission to work in a practical training position only for a period of one month for each four months of study, with a total overall maximum of six months. While the time periods for getting practical training work permission for F-1 students differ from those for M-1 students, the procedures, forms, and documents are exactly the same.

The application, consisting of both forms and documents, should be submitted by mail to the USCIS service center responsible for your school's location. Before mailing your application, your designated school official will review the paperwork to decide whether or not you meet all the requirements for work permission. If you appear to qualify, he or she will endorse your Form I-20 ID. Submit the endorsed form to USCIS with your other work application papers. The filing fee is currently $120. It is very important to keep the fee receipt USCIS will send you so you can prove that the I-765 was filed.

Most USCIS offices will make a decision on your application within several weeks. The law requires USCIS to make a decision on your employment authorization application within 90 days. If the decision is in your favor, you will receive a work authorization card.

If, for some reason, you are not given a decision within 90 days, you will, at your request, be granted an interim employment authorization which will last for 240 days. To receive an interim card, you must go in person to USCIS local office nearest your school and show your fee receipt. Then your interim work authorization card will be issued.

If 240 days pass and you still have not received a final decision on the I-765, you must stop working. Interim work authorization cards cannot be renewed. However, if you reach this point, you have the option to file a new I-765 application and, if you do not get a decision on the new application within 90 days, you will then be entitled to another interim work authorization card.

If your request for work permission is denied, you will receive a written decision by mail explaining the reason for the denial. There is no way of making a formal appeal to USCIS if your request is turned down. If you have new evidence, you may submit it to the same USCIS office that made the original decision and request that your case be reconsidered. This is technically called a *Motion to Reopen* and you must pay a $110 filing fee. You may also challenge the decision in U.S. district court, but the time and expense required for this approach usually make it impractical.

c. Work Application Forms

Copies of all the required USCIS forms are in Appendix II and on the USCIS website.

Form I-765

Block above Question 1. Mark the first box, "Permission to accept employment."

Questions 1–9. These questions are self-explanatory.

Question 10. You will not usually have an Alien Registration Number unless you previously applied for a green card, were in deportation proceedings or have had certain types of immigration applications denied. All Alien Registration Numbers begin with the letter "A." If you have no "A" number but you entered the U.S. with a valid visa, you should have an I-94 card. In this case, put down the admission number from the I-94 card.

Questions 11–15. These questions are self-explanatory.

Question 16. If you are an F-1 student, answer this question "(c)(3)(i)." If you are an M-1 student, answer this question "(c)(6)."

d. Work Application Documents

You must submit as documents your I-94 card and I-20 ID student copy. If your practical training is post-completion, you must have a job offer. Submit a letter from your U.S. employer explaining the details of the work you will perform. The job description should show clearly that the work is in the same field as your course of studies.

J. School Transfers

Requirements for transfers are different for F-1 students and M-1 students.

1. Applications for Transfers of F-1 Students

As an F-1 student, you may transfer from one school to another following a specific procedure. You must be a full-time student at the time—otherwise you will have to request reinstatement to student status. You must notify USCIS of the change, as well as the designated school officials at both your old and new schools. Applications to transfer are made by submitting Form SEVIS I-20, together with your I-20 ID copy, to the designated school official at your new school who will, in turn, forward the paperwork to USCIS. You must submit the paperwork to the designated school official no more than 15 days after enrolling in the new school. A letter must be sent to the designated school official at the school you are leaving, telling him or her that you have transferred. This letter should be sent by certified mail. A copy of the letter should also be included when you submit Form I-20. Your I-20 ID student copy, which you have submitted as a document, will eventually be returned to you by USCIS (not the designated school official). On it will be written a notation showing that you have been authorized to transfer schools.

Transfers are denied only if it is discovered that you have in some way violated your student status. You cannot appeal a refusal of permission to transfer through USCIS. In fact, because your request will be refused only if a violation of your status has been discovered, in addition to denying you permission to transfer, USCIS may also order you to leave the U.S. or face deportation. If this occurs, it is at this point (under current USCIS interpretations) that you will begin to accrue time out of status toward the three- or ten-year bars. (See Chapter 25.) If you have new evidence to prove that you have not in fact been out of status, you may submit it to the same USCIS office that made the original decision and request that your case be reconsidered. This is technically called a *Motion to Reopen* and with it you must pay a $110 filing fee. You may also challenge the decision in U.S. district court, but the time and expense required for this approach usually make it impractical.

2. Applications for Transfers of M-1 Students

As an M-1 student, you can transfer from one school to another, but only during your first six months of study, unless the transfer is required by circumstances beyond your control. You must request permission for the transfer from USCIS.

Applications to transfer are made by submitting Form SEVIS I-20, issued by the school to which you will transfer, together with your I-20 ID student copy, to the USCIS local office having jurisdiction over the location of your new school. Appendix I contains a list of USCIS local offices with their addresses and phone numbers. You must apply at least 60 days before you wish to transfer. Provided you file your application on time, you may enroll in the new school 60 days after filing, even if you have not yet received USCIS's decision. If you transfer schools without following these procedures, you are considered out of status.

Transfer applications are normally approved in one or two months. Upon approval, the I-20 ID, which you have submitted as a document, will be returned directly to you. On it will be written a notation showing that you have been authorized to transfer to the new school. If your request to transfer is denied, you will receive a written decision by mail explaining the reason. USCIS has discretion to deny your application to transfer for any legitimate reason. There is no way of making a formal appeal to USCIS if your request is turned down.

If you have new evidence, you may submit it to the same USCIS office that made the original decision and request that your case be reconsidered. This is technically called a *Motion to Reopen* and you must pay a $110 filing fee. You may also challenge the decision in U.S. district court, but the time and expense required for this approach usually make it impractical.

K. Changes in Course of Studies

F-1 students can change their courses of studies within the same school as long as they remain in qualifying programs. No formal permission from USCIS is required to change major areas of studies.

M-1 students are never permitted to change courses of studies. If an M-1 student wishes to make such a change, he or she will have to return to a consulate and apply for a completely new student visa.

FORMS AND DOCUMENTS CHECKLIST

STEP ONE: APPLICATION (THE ONLY STEP)

Forms

- ☐ Form SEVIS I-20 (from your school).
- ☐ DS forms (available at U.S. consulates abroad for consular filing only).
- ☐ Form I-539 (U.S. filing only).

Documents

- ☐ Valid passport for you and each accompanying relative.
- ☐ I-94 card for you and each accompanying relative (U.S. filing only).
- ☐ One photo of you and each accompanying relative (consular filing only).
- ☐ Long-form birth certificate for you and each accompanying relative.
- ☐ Marriage certificate if you are married and bringing your spouse.
- ☐ If either you or your spouse have ever been married, copies of divorce and death certificates showing termination of all previous marriages.
- ☐ Transcripts and diplomas showing your previous education.
- ☐ Proof of financial support:
  - ☐ Form I-134, Affidavit of Support, for you and each accompanying relative, or
  - ☐ financial documents showing sufficient funds to attend school for at least one year without working.
- ☐ Proof that you will return home after your studies, such as:
  - ☐ documents showing that close family members or property are being left behind in your home country.
  - ☐ documents showing ownership of real estate in your home country.
  - ☐ documents showing a job is waiting on your return to your home country.

APPLICATION FOR PERMISSION TO WORK

ECONOMIC NECESSITY

Form

- ☐ Form I-765.

Documents

- ☐ I-20 ID student copy.
- ☐ I-94 card.
- ☐ Evidence of change in financial circumstances.

PRACTICAL TRAINING

Form

- ☐ Form I-765.

Documents

- ☐ I-20 ID student copy.
- ☐ I-94 card.
- ☐ Letter from prospective employer (for post-completion training only).

APPLICATION FOR TRANSFER

Forms

None.

Documents

- ☐ I-20 from new school and I-20 ID student copy.
- ☐ If F-1, notice of transfer sent to old school.
- ☐ If M-1, new evidence of financial resources.

Exchange Visitors: J-1 Visas

Privileges

- You may come to the U.S. to participate in a specific exchange visitor program approved by the U.S. Department of State (DOS) (formerly the U.S. Information Agency (USIA)). DOS has approved a large array of such special programs, sponsored by schools, businesses, and a variety of organizations and institutions, meant to foster international cooperation through exchange of information. The programs are intended for students, scholars, trainees in business and industry, teachers, research assistants, and international visitors on cultural missions.

- You may work legally in the U.S. if work is part of your approved program or if you receive permission to work from the official program sponsor.

- You may travel in and out of the U.S. or remain there until the completion of your exchange visitor program.

- Visas are available for accompanying relatives.

- Your accompanying relatives may work in the U.S. if they receive special permission from USCIS and the money is not needed to support you.

Limitations

- Your activities are restricted to studying, working, or otherwise participating in the specific exchange visitor programs for which your visa has been approved.

- You must first be accepted as a participant in an exchange visitor program approved by the DOS before you can apply for a J-1 visa.

- Exchange visitors participating in certain types of programs may be required to return to their home countries for at least two years before they are permitted to get a green card or change to another nonimmigrant status or to have an L or H visa petition approved on their behalf.

This chapter will explain who is eligible for a J-1 exchange visitor visa and how to apply for one.

A. Who Qualifies for a J-1 Visa?

You qualify for a J-1 exchange visitor visa if you are coming to the U.S. as a student, scholar, trainee, teacher, professor, research assistant, medical graduate, or international visitor who is participating in a program of studies, training, research, or cultural enrichment specifically designed for such individuals by the U.S. Department of State (DOS), through its Bureau of Educational and Cultural Affairs (ECA). You must already be accepted into the program before you can apply for the visa.

Some common programs for which J-1 visas are issued include the Fulbright Scholarship program, specialized training programs for foreign medical graduates, and programs for foreign university professors teaching or doing research in the U.S.

You must have enough money to cover your expenses while you are in the U.S. as an exchange visitor. Those funds may come from personal resources, or when the J-1 visa is based on work activities, the salary may be your means of support. If you are a J-1 student, the money may also come from a scholarship.

You must be able to speak, read, and write English well enough to participate effectively in the exchange program of your choice. In addition to all other qualifications, you are eligible for a J-1 visa only if you intend to return to your home country when the program is over.

To summarize, there are five requirements for getting a J-1 visa:

- you must be coming to the U.S. to work, study, teach, train, consult, or observe U.S. culture in a specific exchange visitor program approved by the DOS
- you must already have been accepted into the program
- you must have enough money to cover your expenses while in the U.S.
- you must have sufficient knowledge of English to be able to participate effectively in the exchange visitor program you have chosen, and
- you must intend to return home when your status expires.

1. An Exchange Visitor Program Approved by the DOS

J-1 visas allow you to study, teach, do research, or participate in cultural activities in the U.S. as part of any program specifically approved by the DOS. Sponsors of acceptable programs may be foreign or U.S. government agencies, private foreign and U.S. organizations, or U.S. educational institutions. Such groups wanting program approval must apply to the DOS. Those making successful applications will be authorized to issue what are known as Certificates of Eligibility to J-1 visa applicants. They indicate that the applicant has been accepted into an approved program. Each approved program appoints an administrator known as the *responsible officer*. The responsible officer plays a formal part in dealing with the immigration process for program applicants.

There are over 1,500 DOS-approved programs in existence. Current information about exchange visitor programs is available from DOS at http://exchanges.state.gov.

2. Acceptance Into the Program

Before applying for a J-1 visa, you must first apply for acceptance into the DOS-approved program of your choice. Application is made directly to the program sponsor. Until you have been accepted, you do not qualify for a J-1 visa.

3. Financial Support

You must establish that you have enough money to cover all expenses while you are in the U.S. The money may come from you, your family, or scholarships and salaries that are part of the program itself. Since most exchange visitor programs involve either employment or scholarships, this particular requirement is usually easy to meet.

4. Knowledge of English

To qualify for an exchange visitor visa, you must know English well enough to participate effectively in the exchange visitor program. If your program is for students, you should know that most U.S. colleges and universities will not admit people whose native language is not English unless they first pass an English proficiency test such as the "TOEFL." Tests can sometimes be arranged in your home country. The school will tell you if such a test is required and how to go about taking it.

Consular officials usually let each school decide for itself who is and is not qualified to study there. Still, the consulate may refuse to issue an exchange visitor visa based on its own judgment that you do not know enough English to function as a U.S. student.

5. Intent to Return to Your Home Country

Exchange visitor visas are meant to be temporary. At the time of applying, you must intend to return home when your program in the U.S. is completed. If you have it in mind to take up permanent residence in the U.S., you are legally ineligible for an exchange visitor visa.

The U.S. government knows it is difficult to read minds. Expect to be asked for evidence showing that when you go to the U.S. on a J-1 visa, you are leaving behind possessions, property or family members as incentives for your eventual return. It is also helpful to show that you have a job waiting at home when your program is completed. If you are studying or training to prepare yourself for an occupation in which no jobs are available in your home country, neither USCIS nor the U.S. consulate will believe that you are planning to return there. To avoid trouble, choose a field of study that will give you career opportunities at home when you are finished.

6. Foreign Medical Graduates: Additional Qualifications

If you are coming to the U.S. as a foreign medical graduate for the purpose of continuing your medical training or education, there are some added requirements. First, you must have passed Parts I and II of the U.S. National Board of Medical Examiners examination or its equivalent. Information on taking the exam is available from:

Educational Commission for Foreign Medical
  Graduates
3624 Market Street, Fourth Floor
Philadelphia, PA 19104-2685
Telephone: 215-386-5900
Fax: 215-387-9963
www.ecfmg.org

Like all J-1 visa applicants, foreign medical graduates must prove they will return home when their status expires. However, your evidence must include a written guarantee from the government in your home country verifying that employment will be available to you when your U.S. medical training is completed.

Foreign medical graduates applying for J-1 visas should understand that they are legally required to return home for at least two years before becoming eligible to apply for green cards (with a possible waiver for those who receive job offers to work in underserved areas). Pay especially close attention to Section D1, below.

7. Accompanying Relatives

When you qualify for a J-1 visa, your spouse and unmarried children under age 21 can get J-2 visas by providing proof of their family relationship to you. J-2 visas authorize your accompanying relatives to stay with you in the U.S., but not to work there unless they first obtain special permission from USCIS.

B. How Long It Takes to Get the Visa

There are no quota restrictions for J-1 visas. Applications filed at consulates are usually approved in a matter of weeks. Applications filed in the U.S. are approved in about three months.

C. How Long the J-1 Visa Will Last

How long you'll be allowed to stay in the U.S. on your J-1 visa depends on the type of program you'll be participating in (Subsections 1 through 14, below) and the dates of your participation.

In seeking a J-1 visa, you will be asked to present a Certificate of Eligibility, formerly known as Form IAP-66, now reworked and renumbered as SEVIS DS-2019. This form is provided to you by the sponsor of the exchange visitor program in which you will take part. The form will list the specific dates you are expected to be participating in the program. Upon entering the U.S. with a J-1 visa, you will be authorized to remain only up to the final date indicated on the Certificate of Eligibility.

The Certificate of Eligibility is usually issued for the period of time needed to complete the particular exchange visitor program for which your J-1 visa is approved. USCIS regulations, however, place some maximum time limits on J-1 visas according to the type of program.

1. Students

Most students may remain in the U.S. for the duration of their programs plus an additional 18 months of practical

training employment (the student must apply for practical training). Practical training is any employment directly related to the subject matter of the student's major field of study. Remaining in the U.S. for the additional 18 months of practical training is at the student's discretion. Post-doctoral training is limited to 36 months minus any previously used practical training time.

However, students between the ages of 15 and 18½ who are participating in a high school exchange program (living with a U.S. host family or residing at an accredited U.S. boarding school) are limited to one year's stay. They cannot work, except at odd jobs such as babysitting or yard work.

2. Teachers, Professors, Research Scholars, and People With Specialized Skills

Exchange visitors in any of these categories may be issued J-1 visas for no more than three years, plus 30 days in which to prepare to depart the U.S.

3. International Visitors

International visitors whose purpose it is to promote cultural exchange, such as those working in the cultural/ethnic pavilions of Disney's Epcot Center, may be issued J-1 visas for no more than one year plus 30 days in which to prepare to depart the U.S. Persons qualifying under this category may also be eligible for Q visas.

4. Foreign Medical Graduate Students

Foreign medical graduates may be issued J-1 visas for the length of time necessary to complete their training programs, up to a usual maximum of seven years (with limited exceptions) plus 30 days in which to prepare to depart the U.S.

5. Other Medically Related Programs

Participants in any medically related programs other than those for foreign medical graduates may be issued J-1 visas for the duration of their educational programs plus 18 months of practical training. However, the total time of both program participation and practical training may not be more than three years.

6. Business and Industrial Trainees

Business and industrial trainees may be issued J-1 visas for a maximum of 18 months, except interns, who are limited to 12 months. Trainees in flight programs may be issued J-1 visas for a maximum of 24 months; however, flight students must provide extra documentation about their plans, for security reasons.

7. Employees of the International Communications Agency

Participants in this particular exchange visitor program may be issued J-1 visas for up to ten years or even longer if the director of the International Communications Agency makes a special request to USCIS.

8. Research Assistants Sponsored by the National Institutes of Health

Participants in the NIH research assistants exchange visitor program may be issued J-1 visas for a period of up to five years.

9. Au Pairs

Au pairs who are between age 18 and 26 may come to the U.S. on J-1 visas to live in and perform child care (but no other housework) for U.S. families. Au pairs may work no more than ten hours per day, 45 hours per week, be paid at least the minimum wage, and must attend an institution of higher education to earn at least six hours of academic credit. As of this writing, only a few agencies have been approved to issue Form IAP-66 for bringing au pairs to the U.S. Stays are limited to only one year and cannot be extended. If this program interests you, check the State Department website at http://exchanges.state.gov.

10. Government Visitors

Visitors may be invited by the U.S. government to participate in exchanges which strengthen professional and personal ties between key foreign nationals and Americans and American institutions. They may be issued J-1 visas for the length of time necessary to complete the program, but no more than 18 months.

11. Camp Counselors

Youth workers over the age of 18 coming to serve as counselors in U.S. summer camps may be issued J-1 visas for no more than four months.

12. Summer Work Travel

Post-secondary students may use a J-1 visa to work and travel in the United States for a four-month period during their summer vacations, through programs conducted by Department of State-designated sponsors.

13. Short-Term Scholars

Professors and other academics participating in short-term activities such as seminars, workshops, conferences, study tours, or professional meetings may be granted up to six months on a J-1 visa.

14. Exceptions to the General Rules

Any exchange visitor may be allowed to remain in the U.S. beyond the limitations stated above if exceptional circumstances arise that are beyond the exchange visitor's control, such as illness.

D. Students: Comparing J-1 Visas to F-1 and M-1 Visas

Students coming to the U.S. often have a choice between J-1 exchange visitor visas and M-1 or F-1 student visas. Student visas are discussed in Chapter 22. J-1 programs for students are very limited as to the level of education and types of subjects that can be studied, while F-1 and M-1 visas can be issued for almost any type of education program imaginable, including vocational, secondary, and high school programs as well as all courses of study at colleges and universities.

Assuming there is an exchange visitor program that will fit your needs as a student, there are certain advantages to holding a J-1 visa. It is much easier to get work permission as an exchange visitor than it is on a student visa. With a J-1 visa you may remain in the U.S. for up to 18 months after you graduate for the purpose of working in a practical training position. F-1 student visa holders are limited to 12 months of practical training employment and M-1 students are limited to only six months.

F-1 and M-1 student visas, however, are more flexible than exchange visitor visas in several ways. With a student visa, you may transfer from one school to another or change courses of study quite freely. After graduation, you may enroll in a new educational program without having to obtain a new visa. On a J-1 visa, you must remain in the exact program for which your visa was issued. Most important, certain J-1 visa programs *automatically make you subject to a two-year home residency requirement,* which will cause problems should you later want to apply for a green card or change to another nonimmigrant status, or have a nonimmigrant worker "L" or "H" visa petition approved.

1. Possibilities for a Green Card From J-1 Status

Keep in mind that J-1 visas, like all nonimmigrant visas, are meant to be temporary. They are intended only for those who plan on returning home once the exchange program in the U.S. is completed. Should you decide to apply for a green card before your program is finished, the U.S. government will allow you to keep J-1 status while pursuing a green card, but only if you are able to convince them that you did not intend to get a green card when you originally applied for the J-1 visa and that you will return home if you are unable to secure a green card before your exchange visitor status expires. Proving these things can be difficult. If you do not succeed, your J-1 visa may be taken away. Some program sponsors have been known to withdraw J-1 privileges after an exchange visitor has applied for a green card.

The most serious drawback to applying for a green card from J-1 status is that many J-1 visas are granted subject to a two-year home residency requirement. If you choose an exchange visitor program that carries this requirement, it means that you must return to your home country and remain there for at least two years before you are eligible to either apply for a green card, be approved for a change of status, or have an L or H visa petition approved for yourself, even if you marry a U.S. citizen or have some other compelling reason to want a green card.

It is possible to apply for a waiver of the home residency requirement. Although the procedures for filing waiver applications are simple, getting approval can be extremely difficult, especially for foreign medical graduates. Most exchange visitors can get waivers if the governments of their home countries consent to it. If not, and in the case of all foreign medical graduates as well as most Fulbright scholars, even if the home government does consent, waiver applications are approved only under compelling circumstances. Most are simply denied.

The reason for this is that many J-1 visa programs are set up and financed by foreign governments for the specific purpose of getting U.S. training for their citizens. The foreign governments hope that those who are trained will eventually return and use their new skills to benefit their homeland. Were the U.S. government to interfere with these goals by allowing J-1 visa holders to remain in the U.S., there would be political discord between the U.S. and the other nations involved. Therefore, the U.S. makes every effort to see that J-1 exchange visitors keep their bargains and fulfill the home residency requirements.

Not all J-1 visa holders are subject to a home residency requirement. It applies only to participants in the following types of exchange visitor programs:

- programs for foreign medical graduates coming to the U.S. to receive additional medical training
- programs where the expenses of the participants are paid by the U.S., a foreign government, or international organization, and
- programs for teaching individuals certain skills that are in short supply in their home countries. The DOS maintains a list of such skills and the countries where they are especially needed. The skills list can be accessed at http://exchanges.state.gov/education/jexchanges.

The Certificate of Eligibility, Form DS-2019, which you will receive when you are accepted into an approved J-1 program, has a space on it showing whether or not your J-1 visa is subject to a home residency requirement. If it is, the U.S. consulate issuing the visa will have you sign a declaration stating that you understand your obligation to return to your home country for at least two years before being allowed to apply for a green card or other U.S. visa. The consulate will also make a notation of the home residency requirement in your passport.

Be aware that the consulate does not have the power to decide who will or won't be subject to a home residency requirement. The facts of your situation, not the consulate's notation on your visa or DS2019, determine whether you must meet this requirement. Some consulates routinely mark all J-1 visas subject to the home residency requirement, no matter what the facts. The consulate's notation is a strong indication that you are probably subject to the home residency requirement, but it is not the final word. If you have doubts about the correctness of the consulate's notation, it is worth checking into the matter.

E. J-1 Overview

Getting a J-1 visa is a one-step process.

1. The Application

Certain portions of the application are technically the responsibility of the sponsor of the particular exchange visitor program in which you will participate. Some applicants expect the responsible officer of their program to handle the entire procedure for them, but this rarely happens. The only part of the J-1 visa application you should expect your program sponsor to complete is the Certificate of Eligibility. You will use this certificate in preparing your application for a J-1 visa or status.

The application is your formal request for a J-1 visa or status. (If you are Canadian, your application procedures will be different from those of other applicants. See Chapter 28.) It is filed by you and your accompanying relatives, if any. The application process may be carried out in the U.S. at a USCIS office or in your home country at a U.S. consulate there.

The vast majority of nonimmigrant visa applications are filed at consulates. That is because most cases don't qualify for U.S. filing. You are not eligible for U.S. filing if you planned to file for a J-1 status before you entered the U.S. on some other type of temporary visa. Such a preplanned change is technically called *preconceived intent*. If a USCIS officer believes you had a preconceived intent to become an exchange visitor when you entered the U.S., your application will be turned down. An overwhelming percentage of student exchange visitor applications filed in the U.S. are not approved for this reason. (See Section G1, below.)

2. Who's Who in Getting Your J-1 Visa

Getting a J-1 visa will be easier if you familiarize yourself with the technical names used for each participant in the process. You are known as the *exchange visitor* or the *applicant.* Your U.S. employer or school is referred to as the *exchange visitor program sponsor,* and the individual at the employer or school responsible for J-1 visa processing is known as the *responsible official.* If you will be bringing your spouse and children with you as accompanying relatives, they are known as *applicants* as well.

3. Tips on Handling the Paperwork

There are two types of paperwork you must submit to get a J-1 visa. The first consists of official government forms completed by you or your program sponsor. The second is personal documents, such as birth and marriage certificates, school transcripts, and diplomas.

It is vital that forms are properly filled out and all necessary documents are supplied. You may resent the intrusion into your privacy and the sizable effort it takes to prepare immigration applications, but you should realize the process is an impersonal matter to immigration officials. Your getting a visa is more important to you than it is to the U.S. government. There is no shortage of applicants.

The documents you supply to USCIS or the consulate do not have to be originals. Photocopies of all documents are acceptable as long as you have the originals in your possession and are willing to produce them upon request. But add the following language to the photocopy, with your signature and the date:

> *Copies of documents submitted are exact photocopies of unaltered original documents and I understand that I may be required to submit original documents to an immigration or consular official at a later date.*
> *Signature _____*
> *Typed or Printed Name _____*
> *Date_____*

Documents will be accepted if they are in either English, or, with papers filed at U.S. consulates abroad, the language of the country where the documents are being filed (except in Japan, where all documents must be translated into English). If the documents are not in an acceptable language as just explained, they must be accompanied by a full, word for word, written English translation. Any capable person may act as translator. It is not necessary to hire a professional. At the end of each translation, the following statement must appear:

> *I hereby certify that I translated this document from [language] to English. This translation is accurate and complete. I further certify that I am fully competent to translate from [language] to English.*
> *Signature _____*
> *Typed or Printed Name _____*
> *Date_____*

The translator should sign this statement but it does not have to be witnessed or notarized.

Later in this chapter we describe in detail the forms and documents needed to get your J-1 visa. A summary checklist of forms and documents appears at the end of this chapter.

F. The Application: Consular Filing

Anyone with a Certificate of Eligibility (SEVIS Form DS-2019) from an exchange visitor program sponsor can apply for a J-1 visa at a U.S. consulate in his or her home country. You must be physically present in order to apply there.

If you have been or are now working or living illegally in the U.S., read Chapter 25 to see if you can still get a J-1 visa from a U.S. consulate without facing time bars or a finding of inadmissibility.

1.   Benefits and Drawbacks of Consular Filing

The most important benefit of consular filing is that only consulates issue visas. When you go through a U.S. filing you get a status, not a visa. (See Chapter 14.) A J-1 status confers the same right to work or attend school as a J-1 visa, but it does not give you the ability to travel in and out of the U.S. Therefore, if you want travel privileges, you will at some time have to go through the extra step of applying for a visa at a U.S. consulate, even though you have already applied for and received exchange visitor status in the U.S.

You are usually not eligible to process a status application in the U.S. unless you are currently maintaining legal status. If you are in the U.S. illegally, consular filing may be your only option (but again, watch out for the time bars described in Chapter 25).

A further plus to consular filing is that consular offices may work more quickly than USCIS offices do. Your waiting time for the paperwork to be finished may be shorter at a U.S. consulate abroad.

A drawback to consular filing comes from the fact that you must be physically present in the country where the consulate is located in order to file there. If your application is ultimately turned down because it is suspected you are not going to return home when your participation in the exchange visitor program is completed, the consular officer will stop you from entering the U.S. on any nonimmigrant visa. He or she may even cancel some other nonimmigrant visa you already have, including a visitor's visa. It will then be impossible for you to enter the U.S. Consequently, if your J-1 visa case is not very strong and freedom of travel is not essential to you, it might be wise to apply in the U.S. (if you're eligible to), make up your mind to remain there for the duration of the exchange visitor status, and skip trying to get a visa from the consulate.

2.   Application General Procedures: Consular Filing

Technically, the law allows you to apply for a J-1 at any U.S. consulate you choose. However, from a practical standpoint, your case will be given greatest consideration at the consulate in your home country. Applying in some other country creates suspicion about your motives for choosing their consulate. Often, when an applicant is having trouble at a home consulate he will seek a more lenient office in some other country. This practice of consulate shopping is frowned on. Unless you have a very good reason for being

elsewhere (such as a temporary job assignment in some other nation), it is smarter to file your visa application in your home country.

Furthermore, if you have been present in the U.S. unlawfully, in general you cannot apply as a third-country national. Even if you overstayed your status in the U.S. by just one day, your visa will be automatically cancelled and you must return to your home country and apply for the visa from that consulate. There is an exception. If you were admitted to the U.S. for the duration of your status (indicated by a "D/S" on your I-94 form) and you remained in the U.S. beyond the authorized period of stay, you may still be able to apply as a third-country national. Under current regulations, you will be barred from third-country national processing only if an immigration judge or USCIS officer has determined that you were unlawfully present. Because of the ambiguity, you may find that your success in applying as a third-country national will depend on your country, the consulate and the relative seriousness of your offense.

You may not file an application for a J-1 visa at a consulate until a DOS-approved exchange visitor program sponsor has given you a Certificate of Eligibility, SEVIS Form DS-2019.

Once you have obtained the Certificate of Eligibility, check with your local U.S. consulate regarding its application procedures for getting your J-1 visa. Many insist on advance appointments.

3.   Application Forms: Consular Filing

When you file at a U.S. consulate abroad, the consulate officials will provide you with certain forms, designated by a "DS" preceding a number. Instructions for completing DS forms and what to do with them once they are filled out will come with the forms. We do not include copies of these forms in this book since different consulates often use different versions.

In addition to the DS forms, the consulate will need a copy of SEVIS Form DS-2019, which is prepared by the exchange visitor program sponsor. You do not fill out or sign any part of it. After your program sponsor completes the form, it will give the form to you for you to submit, together with your other forms and documents, to the consulate for processing.

4.   Application Documents: Consular Filing

In addition to the forms, you'll have to gather or prepare various documents in support of your aplication to the consulate, as described below.

Passport and photos. You are required to show a valid passport and present one photograph taken in accordance with the photo instructionsat http://travel.state.gov/photorequirements/html.

For accompanying family. For each accompanying relative, you must present a valid passport and one photograph. You will also need documents verifying their family relationship to you. You may verify a parent/child relationship by presenting the child's long-form birth certificate. Many countries, including Canada and England, issue both short- and long-form birth certificates. Where both are available, the long form is needed, because it contains the names of the parents while the short form does not.

If you are accompanied by your spouse, establish that you are lawfully married by showing a civil marriage certificate. Church certificates are generally unacceptable. (There are a few exceptions depending on the laws of your particular country. Canadians, for example, may use church marriage certificates if the marriage took place in Quebec Province, but not elsewhere. If a civil certificate is available, however, you should always use it.) You may have married in a country where marriages are not customarily recorded. Tribal areas of Africa are an example. In such situations, ask the U.S. consulate for advice on what it will accept as proof of marriage.

Evidence of intent to return. You will need documents establishing your intent to leave the U.S. when your visa expires. The consulate will want to see evidence that ties to your home country are so strong you will be highly motivated to return. Proof of such ties can include deeds verifying ownership of a house or other real property, written statements from you explaining that close relatives are staying behind, or letters from a company outside the U.S. showing that you have a job waiting when you return from America.

Evidence of sufficient funds. If you will be attending school in the U.S., and neither employment nor a scholarship is part of your exchange visitor program, you must present evidence that you have sufficient funds available to cover all of your costs for the first year of study and that you also have a source of funds to cover your expenses in future years, so that you will be able to study full time without working. If your particular exchange visitor program provides you with a scholarship or employment, evidence of such support in the form of a letter from the program sponsor will satisfy this requirement.

If the exchange visitor program sponsor will not be furnishing you with financial support, you will have to show either that you can meet your own expenses without working, or that a close relative is willing to guarantee your support. The best evidence of your ability to pay educational expenses is a bank statement or letter from a bank, either in the U.S. or abroad, showing an account in your name with a balance of at least one year's worth of expenses in it. Alternatively, you can submit a written guarantee of support signed by an immediate relative, preferably a parent, together with your relative's bank statements. Unless your relative can show enough assets to prove he or she is able to support you without additional income, you should also show that your relative is presently employed. You can document this by submitting a letter from the employer verifying your relative's work situation.

Although the guarantee of support may be in the form of a simple written statement in your relative's own words, we suggest you use Form I-134, called an Affidavit of Support. A copy of this form is in Appendix II. The ques-tions on Form I-134 are self-explanatory. However, the form was designed to be filled out by someone living in the U.S. Since it is quite likely that the person who will support you is living outside the U.S., any questions that apply to U.S. residents should be answered "N/A."

Additional documents for flight trainees. If you're applying for a J visa for U.S. flight training, you will be required to submit written information and documents specifying the following:

- your reason for the training (be specific)
- current employer and your position
- who is paying for the training (name and relationship)
- your most recent flight certifications and ratings
- information on what kind of aircraft the training is for (document must be signed by a school official in the U.S.)
- certified take-off weight of the aircraft type (document must be signed by a school official in the U.S.), and
- current rank or title if you are presently working as an active pilot.

5. Application Interviews: Consular Filing

The consulates will frequently require an interview before issuing an exchange visitor visa. During the interview, a consul officer will examine the forms and documents for accuracy. Documents proving your ability to support yourself while you are in the U.S. will be carefully checked as will evidence of ties to your home country. During the interview, you will surely be asked how long you intend to remain in the U.S. Any answer indicating uncertainty about plans to return home or an interest in applying for a green card is likely to result in a denial of your J-1 visa. If you are subject to the two-year home residency requirement, the consul officer will probably discuss this with you to make certain you understand what it means. Keep in mind that if you want a green card, a home residency requirement can significantly delay your reaching this goal.

Because of new security requirements, you are unlikely to be approved for your visa on the same day as your interview. The consular officer will need to compare your name against various databases of people with a history of criminal activity, violations of U.S. immigration laws or terrorist affiliations. This can add weeks or months to the processing of your visa, particularly if you come from a country that the U.S. suspects of supporting terrorism.

6. Using Your J-1 Visa

Once you've received your J-1 visa, it's time to think about traveling to the U.S. You'll be allowed to enter up to 30 days before the start of your classes or program, but no earlier. On entering the U.S. with your new J-1 visa, you will be given an I-94 card. It will be stamped "D/S" indicating that you can stay until the completion of your program. As a practical matter, however, you are permitted to remain up to the expiration date on your SEVIS Form DS-2019 Certificate of Eligibility. Each time you exit and reenter the U.S., you will get a new I-94 card.

SUMMARY EXCLUSION

The law empowers a CBP inspector at the airport to summarily (without allowing judicial review) bar entry to someone requesting admission to the U.S. if either of the following are true:

- The inspector thinks you are lying about practically anything connected with entering the U.S., including your purpose in coming, intent to return, and prior immigration history. This includes the use or suspected use of false documents.
- You do not have the proper documentation to support your entry to the U.S. in the category you are requesting.

If the inspector excludes you, you cannot be re-admitted to the U.S. for five years, unless USCIS grants a special waiver. For this reason it is extremely important to understand the terms of your requested status, and to not make any misrepresentations. If you are found to be inadmissible, you may request to withdraw your application to enter the U.S. in order to prevent having the five-year deportation order on your record. The CBP may allow this in some exceptional cases.

---

7. Application Appeals: Consular Filings

When a consulate turns down a J-1 visa application, there is no way to make a formal appeal, although you are free to reapply as often as you like. (Check with your local consulate to be sure, however—some place limits on the number of repeat applications, or require you to wait a certain number of months before reapplying.) If your visa is denied, you will be told by the consular officer the reasons for the denial. Written statements of decisions are not normally provided in nonimmigrant cases. If a lack of evidence about a particular point is the problem, sometimes simply presenting more evidence can change the result. The most common reasons for denial of an exchange visitor visa are that the consular officer does not believe you intend to return home upon the completion of your program or, if you will be a student, that you have failed to prove you can pay for your education without working.

Certain people who have been refused J-1 visas reapply at a different consulate, attempting to hide the fact that they were turned down elsewhere. You should know that if your application is denied, the last page in your passport will be stamped "Application Received," with the date and location of the rejecting consulate. This notation shows that some type of prior visa application has failed. It serves as a warning to other consulates that your case merits close inspection. If what we have just told you makes you think it would be a good idea to overcome this problem by obtaining a new, unmarked passport, you should also know that permanent computer records are kept of all visa denials.

G. The Application: U.S. Filing

If you are physically present in the U.S., you may apply for J-1 status without leaving the country on the following conditions:

- you have been accepted as an exchange visitor by a DOS-approved exchange visitor program sponsor and in recognition of your acceptance, the program sponsor has given you a Certificate of Eligibility, Form DS-2019
- you entered the U.S. legally and not under the Visa Waiver Program
- you have never worked illegally in the U.S.
- the date on your I-94 card has not passed, and
- you are not subject to any grounds of inadmissibility or bars to changing status (see Chapter 25).

If you are admitted as a visitor without a visa under the Visa Waiver Program, you may not carry out the application step in the U.S. Currently there are 28 participating countries in the Visa Waiver Program, listed in Chapter 2.

⚠ **If you cannot meet these terms, you may not file for J-1 status in the U.S.** It is important to realize, however, that eligibility to apply while you're in the U.S. has nothing to do with overall eligibility for a J-1 visa. Many applicants who are barred from filing in the U.S. but otherwise qualify for exchange visitor status can apply successfully for a J-1 visa at a U.S. consulate abroad. If you find you are not eligible for U.S. filing, read Section F. However, be sure to read and understand the issues and problems involving inadmissibility and penalties for overstaying visas, discussed in Chapter 25, before proceeding.

1. Benefits and Drawbacks of U.S. Filing

Visas are never given inside the U.S. They are issued exclusively by U.S. consulates abroad. If you file in the U.S. and you are successful, you will get J-1 status but not the visa itself. J-1 status allows you to remain in the U.S. with J-1 privileges until the status expires, but should you leave the country for any reason before that time, you will have to apply for the visa itself at a U.S. consulate before returning to America. Moreover, the fact that your exchange visitor status has been approved in the U.S. does not guarantee that the consulate will approve your visa. Some consulates may even regard your previously acquired status as a negative factor, an indication that you have deliberately tried to avoid the consulate's authority.

There is another problem which comes up only in U.S. filings. It is the issue of what is called *preconceived intent* (defined earlier in this chapter). USCIS is especially strict in this area on student program applications. In order to approve a change of status, USCIS must believe that at the time you originally entered the U.S. as a visitor or with some other nonimmigrant visa, you did not intend to apply for a different status. If USCIS thinks you had a preconceived plan to change from the status you arrived with to a different status, USCIS will deny your application. The preconceived intent issue is one less potential hazard you will face if you apply at a U.S. consulate abroad.

On the plus side of U.S. filing, if you come from a place where it is difficult to obtain U.S. visas, such as Latin America or Asia, your chances for success may be better in the U.S. Another benefit is that when problems do arise with your U.S. application, you can stay in the U.S. while they are being corrected, a circumstance most visa applicants prefer. If you run into snags at a U.S. consulate you will have to remain outside the U.S. until matters are resolved.

Overall, USCIS offices disfavor change of status applications if they are submitted or if other action is taken too soon after you received your nonimmigrant visa and entered the U.S. consulate. Many USCIS offices use a 30/60 day rule to charge applicants with fraud or "preconceived intent" if they behave in a way which is inconsistent with their visitor visa within 30 or 60 days. For example, if you are admitted in visitor status on June 1, 2004, and you commence unauthorized employment or seek to change to F or J status on June 15, 2004, USCIS will presume that you already had that intent to change status or commence employment at the time you entered. That presumption is conclusive for 30 days; from 31-60 days it is rebuttable, which means a consulate or USCIS office may or may not deny your application, depending on what your circumstances are. At day 61 after entry, the presumption no longer operates.

2. Application Procedures: U.S. Filing

The application, consisting of both forms and documents, is sent by mail to USCIS regional service center having jurisdiction over the location of the DOS-approved program that has accepted you. USCIS regional service centers are not the same as USCIS local offices. There are four USCIS regional service centers spread across the U.S. Appendix I contains a list of all USCIS regional service centers and their addresses, but check the USCIS website, www.uscis.gov, for the appropriate P.O. box.

The filing fee for each change of status application is currently $140. Checks and money orders are accepted. It is not advisable to send cash. We recommend submitting all papers by certified mail, return receipt requested, and making a copy of everything sent in to keep for your records.

Within a few weeks of mailing in the application, you should get back a written notice of confirmation that the papers are being processed, together with a receipt for the fees. The notice will also tell you your immigration file number and approximately when to expect a decision.

If USCIS wants further information before acting on your case, it will send a form known as an *I-797* (Request for Evidence or RFE). The I-797 tells you what additional pieces of information or documents are expected. You should supply the extra data and mail the package back to the USCIS regional service center, with the I-797 form on top.

Applications for a J-1 status are normally approved within two to four months. You'll receive an I-94 card with your new status and a date indicating how long you can remain in the U.S. Normally, this will be 30 days later than the last date shown on the DS-2019, Certificate of Eligibility.

3. Application Forms: U.S. Filing

Copies of all USCIS forms you must complete are in Appendix II and on the USCIS website.

Form DS-2019

This form is prepared by the exchange visitor program sponsor. You do not fill out or sign any part of it. Your program sponsor completes the form, and gives the form to you for you to submit, together with your other forms and documents, to USCIS for processing.

Form I-539

Only one application form is needed for an entire family. If you have a spouse or children coming with you, you should also complete the I-539 supplement page.

Part 1. These questions are self-explanatory. "A" numbers are usually given only to people who have previously applied for green cards or who have been in deportation proceedings. If you have an A number, consult an attorney. If you don't, write "None." Your "current nonimmigrant status" refers to the visa you're now carrying, such as "B-2 visitor."

Part 2, Question 1. Mark box "b" followed by "J-1."

Question 2. This question asks if you are also applying for a spouse or children. If so, you must complete the supplement, which asks for their names, dates of birth, and passport information.

Part 3. In most cases you will answer only the first item in this part, by putting in the date. You should put down the date shown on your DS-2019 as the anticipated completion time of your exchange visitor program.

Part 4, Questions 1–2. These questions are self-explanatory.

Question 3. The different parts to this question are self-explanatory; however, items "a" through "c" ask if an immigrant visa petition or adjustment of status application

has ever been filed on your behalf. (If you are separately applying for a green card through a relative, this would be Step One, as described in Chapter 5. If you are separately applying for a green card through employment, this would be Step Two as described in Chapter 8.) If your relative or employer has filed the papers for either of these steps, the answer is "yes," and since you have therefore expressed a desire to live in the U.S. permanently, your application is very likely to be denied. If you have only begun the Labor Certification, the Step One of getting a green card through employment, this question should be answered "no."

4. Application Documents: U.S. Filing

In addition to the forms, you must gather or prepare various documents in support of your application, as described below.

Form I-94. Each applicant must submit a copy of his or her I-94 card, the small white card you received on entering the U.S. Remember, if the date stamped on your I-94 card has already passed, you are ineligible for U.S. filing. Canadians who are just visiting are not expected to have I-94 cards. Canadians with any other type of nonimmigrant status should have them.

For accompanying relatives. For each accompanying relative, send in a copy of his or her I-94 card. You will also need documents verifying their family relationship to you. You may verify a parent/child relationship by presenting the child's long-form birth certificate. Many countries, including Canada and England, issue both short- and long-form birth certificates. Where both are available, the long form is needed because it contains the names of the parents while the short form does not.

If you are accompanied by your spouse, you must establish that you are lawfully married by showing a civil marriage certificate. Church certificates are generally unacceptable. (There are a few exceptions, depending on the laws of your particular country. Canadians, for example, may use church marriage certificates if the marriage took place in Quebec Province, but not elsewhere. If a civil certificate is available, however, you should always use it.) You may have married in a country where marriages are not customarily recorded. Tribal areas of Africa are an example. In such situations, call the nearest consulate or embassy of your home country for help with getting acceptable proof of marriage.

Evidence of Intent to Return. We have emphasized that in order to qualify for a J-1 visa, you must have the intention of returning to your home country upon the completion of your exchange visitor program. Consulates will demand evidence that ties to your home country are strong enough to motivate your eventual return. In a U.S. filing, USCIS does not always ask for proof of this. However, we strongly advise you to submit such evidence anyway. Proof of ties to your home country can include deeds verifying ownership of a house or other real property, written statements from you explaining that close relatives are staying behind, or letters from a company in your home country showing that you have a job waiting when you return from the U.S.

Evidence of Sufficient Funds. If you will be attending school in the U.S. and neither employment nor a scholarship is part of your exchange visitor program, you must present evidence that you have sufficient funds available to cover all of your costs for the first year of study and that you also have a source of funds to cover your expenses in future years so that you will be able to study full time without working. If your particular exchange visitor program provides you with a scholarship or employment, evidence of such support in the form of a letter from the program sponsor will satisfy this requirement.

If the exchange visitor program sponsor will not be furnishing you with financial support, you will have to show either that you can meet your own expenses without working or that a close relative is willing to guarantee your support. The best evidence of your ability to pay educational expenses is a bank statement or letter from a bank, either in the U.S. or abroad, showing an account in your name with a balance of at least one year's worth of expenses in it. Alternatively, you can submit a written guarantee of support signed by an immediate relative, preferably a parent, together with your relative's bank statements. Unless your relative can show enough assets to prove he or she is able to support you without additional income, you should also show that your relative is presently employed. You can document this by submitting a letter from the employer verifying your relative's work situation.

Although the guarantee of support may be in the form of a simple written statement in your relative's own words, we suggest you use Form I-134, called an Affidavit of Support. A copy of this form is in Appendix II and on the USCIS website. The questions on Form I-134 are self-explanatory; however, you should be aware that the form was designed to be filled out by someone living in the U.S. If the person who will support you is living outside the U.S., any questions that apply to U.S. residents should be answered "N/A."

Additional documents for flight trainees. If you're applying for a J visa for U.S. flight training, you will be required to submit written information and documents specifying the following:

- your reason for the training (be specific)
- current employer and your position
- who is paying for the training (name and relationship)
- your most recent flight certifications and ratings
- information on what kind of aircraft the training is for (document must be signed by a school official in the U.S.)
- certified take-off weight of the aircraft type (document must be signed by a school official in the U.S.), and
- current rank or title if you are presently working as an active pilot.

5. Application Interviews: U.S. Filing

Interviews on exchange visitor change of status applications are rarely held. When an interview is required, USCIS regional service center where you originally filed your application will send your paperwork to the USCIS local office nearest the location of your exchange visitor program. This office will in turn contact you for an appointment. USCIS may ask you to bring additional documents at that time.

If you are called for an interview, the most likely reason is that USCIS either suspects some type of fraud or has doubts about your intent to return home after you complete your exchange visitor program. Because they are not common and are usually a sign of trouble, these interviews can result in considerable delays.

6. Application Appeals: U.S. Filing

If your application is denied, you will receive a written decision by mail explaining the reasons for the denial. There is no way of making a formal appeal to USCIS when your application is turned down. If the problem is too little evidence, you may be able to overcome this obstacle by adding more documents and resubmitting the entire application to the same USCIS office you have been dealing with, together with a written request that the case be reopened. The written request does not have to be in any special form. This is technically called a *Motion to Reopen*. There is a $110 fee to file this motion.

Remember that you may be denied the right to a U.S. filing without being denied a J-1 visa. When your application is turned down because you are found ineligible for U.S. filing, simply change your application to a consular filing (unless you would face time bars or inadmissibility as described in Chapter 25).

Although there is no appeal to USCIS for the denial of a J-1 change of status application, you do have the right to file an appeal in a U.S. district court. It would be difficult to file such an appeal without employing an immigration attorney at considerable expense. Such appeals are usually unsuccessful.

As of 2002, schools must make various reports to USCIS concerning international students, including scholars on J visas. When a program issues an IAP-66 to a scholar, it will be required to notify the U.S. consulate in the scholar's home country. When that consulate approves the J visa, it will be required to notify USCIS. During the scholar's time in the U.S., the program sponsor will have to keep USCIS up to date on the scholar's status and whereabouts through a database called SEVIS. To finance this database, international scholars will now have to pay a fee in addition to the usual visa fees. That fee may well be around $100—however, at the time this book went to print, the government was still arguing about how high it could set the fee.

The information and documents that program sponsors are required to make available to the USCIS for each international scholar include:

- name, date and place of birth, country of citizenship
- current address
- visa classification, date of visa issuance, or classification granted
- academic or program status (full-time or part-time)
- whether the scholar has been certified for work authorization and the dates of such certification, and
- date that program was terminated, and the reason, if known.

On top of maintaining this database, the school must actually report news of various changes in the scholar's status or activities to USCIS. Most importantly, the school has 21 days in which to advise USCIS that your address has changed—and you must report address changes to your school within only ten days of your move.

H. Extensions

J-1 visas and statuses can be extended in the U.S. to enable you to complete your particular exchange visitor program. However, since J-1 statuses are usually granted for the period of time considered reasonable for the type of exchange visitor program in which you are participating, extensions

are not easy to get. USCIS has the right to reconsider your qualifications based on any changes in the facts or law, and will want to hear a compelling reason why you have been unable to complete your exchange visitor program within normal time limits. As always, however, good cases that are well prepared will be successful.

When you enter the U.S. on a J-1 visa, your authorized stay as indicated on your I-94 card is the duration of your status, limited by the time period on your Certificate of Eligibility. However, if you come from a country where J-1 visa time privileges are especially limited, your visa may expire before your I-94 card does. In such a situation, if you wish to leave the U.S. and then reenter to complete your exchange visitor program, you will have to extend your visa. To extend the visa that is stamped in your passport, you must apply at a U.S. consulate abroad.

1. I-94 Extension Procedures

Whether and how you can extend your J-1 stay depends on whether you were admitted for the duration of your status (with a "D/S" mark on your I-94) or until a specific date. It's easier with a D/S mark—in that case you can simply explain the situation to your RO (most of them like you to give them at least 30 days notice) and ask the RO to prepare a new Form DS-2019 showing the new expected completion date. The RO then notifies the State Department, and your extension becomes official.

If, however, you were admitted until a specific date, you must not only get a new Form DS-2019, but also seek actual approval from USCIS (if you don't want to leave the U.S.) or the State Department (if you're willing to leave and either reenter or reapply through a U.S. consulate).

To apply within the U.S., you would use Form I-539 (the form used for changing status, which you may have used once already—it's in Appendix II and on the USCIS website). You'd also need to enclose the appropriate fee (currently $140), your new Form DS-2019, copies of your old DS-2019 and your I-94 (and those of your family members, if any), and a letter from your program sponsor stating how long the extension is needed for, and explaining in as much detail as possible why you are unable to complete your program within the expected amount of time. Mail your package to the USCIS regional service center indicated on its website at www.uscis.gov. It may take several months to get an answer from USCIS, so plan ahead so that your permitted stay doesn't expire while the application is pending.

To apply from overseas, your procedure depends on whether not only your I-94, but also your J-1 visa has run out. If only the I-94 has run out, you can simply arrive at the airport with your existing J-1 visa, your new DS-2019, your old DS-2019, and, to be safe, all the supporting materials you used to get your J-1 visa in the first place. You will be given a new I-94 showing your new departure date.

If not only your I-94 but also your J-1 visa has run out, you'll need to reapply for everything through a U.S. consulate. In addition to your new DS-2019, you'll need to gather all the materials you used to apply for your original visa, as described in Section F, above.

WORKING WHILE YOUR EXTENSION APPLICATION IS PENDING

If you file your application for extension of J-1 status before your authorized stay expires, you are automatically authorized to continue working for up to 240 days while waiting for a decision. If, however, your authorized stay expires after you have filed for an extension but before you receive an approval, and more than 240 days go by without getting a decision on your extension application, you must stop working.

I. Waivers of Foreign Home Residency Requirements

You may be participating in the type of exchange visitor program that makes it mandatory for you to spend two years residing in your home country after completing your program before you are eligible to apply for a green card or other U.S. visa. If you wish to escape this obligation and apply for a green card immediately, you will first have to apply for a waiver of the home residency requirement. You cannot get around the requirement by spending two years in a third country or by switching to a different visa status within the U.S.

There are special procedures that must be followed in applying for a waiver of the home residency requirement. (Although the presence of this requirement is considered a ground of inadmissibility in green card cases, you should not follow the standard procedures for waivers of inadmissibility as discussed in Chapter 25.)

Under procedures begun in 2002, you start the waiver application process by submitting a request to the U.S. Department of State (DOS) on Form DS-3035, together with two self-addressed, stamped, legal-size envelopes and $230. The address to which you'll send your application, if using regular mail, is U.S. Dept. of State/Waiver Review Division, P.O. Box 952137, St. Louis, MO 63195-2137. If sending your application by a courier service, the address is U.S. Dept. of State/Waiver Review Division (Box 952137), 1005 Convention Plaza, St. Louis, MO 63101-1200.

On your application form, you'll have to indicate which of the five grounds for a waiver you wish yours to be considered under. The five grounds include:

- **No objection from your home government.** Unless you are a foreign medical graduate, the easiest way to obtain a waiver is by having your home government consent to it through a "No Objection Letter." In this letter, your government would assert that it doesn't mind your staying in the U.S. to apply for a green card—despite the fact that it may have helped finance your exchange program participation. Contact your home country's embassy in Washington, DC to request such a letter.

- **Request by an interested U.S Government Agency.** If you're working on a project of interest to an agency of the U.S. government, and that agency decides that your continued stay is vital to one of its programs, it may support your request for a waiver.

- **Fear of persecution in your home country.** If you can show that you would be persecuted upon return to your home country based on your race, religion, or political opinion, you can apply for a waiver. Note that, unlike applicants for political asylum, you cannot qualify if you fear persecution based only on your nationality or membership in a particular social group. Also, the standard is higher than in ordinary asylum cases, in which applicants need only prove a "reasonable fear" of persecution—you, by contrast, must show that you "would be" persecuted upon return. If you meet this standard, you'd probably be better off skipping the waiver process and submitting a separate application for political asylum.

- **Exceptional hardship to your U.S. citizen or permanent resident spouse or child.** If your spouse or any of your children is a U.S. citizen or permanent resident, and you can show that your departure from the U.S.

would cause them exceptional hardship, you may be granted a waiver. However, USCIS will demand a greater showing of hardship than the "mere" emotional pain of separation, or economic or language difficulties. The classic exceptional hardship case is one in which your family member has a medical problem that would be worsened by your departure or by traveling with you to your home country; or if the family member would be persecuted if he or she departed with you.

- **Request by a state department of health.** If you're a foreign medical graduate with an offer of full-time employment at a healthcare facility in an area that's been designated as having a shortage of doctors, and you agree to begin working there within 90 days of receiving the waiver and to continue working there full-time for at least three years, you may be granted a waiver.

After the DOS receives your application, it will send you a case number and instructions on what to do next. You'll be asked to put together a packet of personal documents and other materials and return them to the DOS. While you're waiting, you can check on the status of your case by calling 202-663-1600. When the Waiver Review Division has completed its evaluation of your application, it will send a recommendation on your case to USCIS, with a copy to you.

If and only if the DOS agreed that your waiver should be granted, you can continue with your application to USCIS. This is done by submitting Form I-612, together with a copy of your I-94 card, proof of any included family members' relationship to you (marriage or birth certificates), documents supporting your claim, including the DOS recommendation, and a fee (currently $195) to the USCIS service center for your geographical region.

As you can see, the waiver application process is complex and often depends on persuading reluctant government officials that you fit into a category whose boundaries are not clearly defined. For this reason, before you attempt to apply for a waiver of the home residency requirement, we strongly advise you to get help from an experienced immigration lawyer.

1. Waiver Application Forms

Copies of these forms are in Appendix II.

Form DS-3035

This DOS form is the one used to start your waiver application. It can be obtained in the Appendix to this book or on the DOS website at www.state.gov.

The form itself is fairly simple to fill out. Question 9, which asks whether the application "include[s] J-2," is asking whether you have any spouse or children in J-2 visa status

who are asking for a waiver along with you. On Question 10, your "Alien Registration Number" is an eight-digit number following the letter A that you would have been assigned if you applied for a work permit or certain other immigration benefits. If you don't have one, simply answer "none."

Form I-612

This form is used for your waiver application to USCIS after the DOS recommends your case.

Questions 1–3. These questions are self-explanatory.

Question 4. This question asks why you believe that you are subject to the home residency requirement. If your exchange visitor program was financed by the U.S. government or the government of your home country, check box "A." If as part of your program you received a grant or scholarship paid for by the U.S. government or a foreign government, check box "B" and put down the name of the foreign country or U.S. government agency that sponsored the financial aid. If the skills you have acquired in the U.S. are on the list of occupations that have few qualified workers in your home country, called the skills list (available via http://exchanges.state.gov), check box "C." If you came to the U.S. as a foreign medical graduate for the purpose of receiving medical training, check box "D."

Question 5. If returning to your home country for two years will result in an exceptional hardship to your spouse or child who is a U.S. citizen or U.S. permanent resident, mark box "A." If you are afraid to return to your home country because you fear possible racial, religious, or political persecution, check box "B." If you are eligible for a waiver for any other reason, such as having received a No Objection Letter from the government of your home country, handwrite this onto the form.

Questions 6–14. These questions are self-explanatory.

Questions 15 and 16. These questions are self-explanatory and apply only to those requesting waivers based on a claim of exceptional hardship to a U.S. citizen or U.S. permanent resident spouse or child. If you are seeking a waiver on some other grounds, answer these questions "N/A."

2. Waiver Application Documents

No matter which category you apply under, various documents will be necessary to obtain a home country residency waiver.

a. No Objection Letters

If at all possible, you should seek a No Objection Letter from the government of your home country. If your exchange visitor program was paid for by the U.S. government, you can request a similar letter from your sponsoring agency. When such a letter is issued, it goes as a direct diplomatic communication from your home country or the U.S. agency to the DOS and you will receive a copy. A No Objection Letter will usually mean an approval on your waiver application (except in those cases involving foreign medical graduates).

b. Documents From Interested U.S. or State Government Agencies

Each government agency uses its own criteria in determining whether or not to act on your behalf and each has its own procedures. Clearly, if you are rendering vital services directly to a government agency, that agency will probably agree to assist you. If you are unable to find such an agency, the DOS will frequently act as the interested party. Because there are no standard procedures, you should contact the particular agency directly. If the agency does decide to assist you, it will create any necessary documents and submit them directly to the DOS. In all likelihood, the agency will want to issue a statement in writing clearly explaining to the DOS why you are important to them. Remember that state government agencies can only recommend waivers for foreign medical graduates. U.S. government agencies can recommend waivers for anyone.

c. Documents Showing Exceptional Hardship to a U.S. Citizen or Green Card Holder

Under these circumstances, it is you who must submit the documents. For a waiver application based on a claim of hardship to succeed, the hardship must be unanticipated and unavoidable. For example, if you came to the U.S. with a J-1 visa and while here married a U.S. citizen who is now sponsoring you for a green card, the hardships that your U.S. spouse may suffer if you return to your home country for two years will not normally support a waiver application. That is because the U.S. government feels you should have anticipated these problems at the time of your marriage and so the hardship is self-imposed.

If your family is in fact subject to an exceptional hardship, prepare a notarized affidavit in your own words describing the hardship and explaining why that hardship is beyond your control. The cases most likely to succeed involve one or more of the following situations:

- Your U.S. spouse or child has serious medical problems and his or her health may be jeopardized by returning with you to your home country.
- The education of your U.S. spouse or child will be harmfully disrupted by returning with you to your home country.
- Your U.S. spouse or child will have to endure serious financial difficulties or unhealthy living conditions by returning with you to your home country.

- You are unable to locate employment in your home country to support your family.
- Your spouse has elderly or ill parents living in the U.S. who would be deprived of necessary care if he or she returned with you to your home country.

Also include letters and statements from people in positions of authority who know of your situation and can vouch for the hardship you'd face. Your family doctor, your children's schoolteacher, and therapists whom you've seen for counseling would all be good sources of support.

d. Documents Showing Danger of Racial, Religious, or Political Persecution

Under these circumstances, it is you who must submit the documents. You must be able to show that, should you return to your home country, you will be singled out for or have good reason to fear persecution. The persecution that you anticipate must be based on race, religion, or political beliefs. If you have been persecuted in the past and can produce evidence of that, such as newspaper reports showing you were jailed or affidavits from people in your home country who personally witnessed your persecution, your case stands a reasonable chance of success. If you cannot prove that you have been persecuted previously, you will have to present evidence that you are a member of a certain group of people that is routinely persecuted in your home country. Such evidence should be in the form of newspaper articles, human rights reports about your home country from organizations such as Human Rights Watch and Amnesty International, or affidavits from experts knowledgeable in the affairs of your home country, describing the nature of the persecution. Before applying for a waiver based on persecution, you should see an experienced immigration attorney.

e. Documents for Foreign Medical Graduate Waivers

If you're seeking a waiver as a foreign medical graduate with a job offer to serve in an area with a shortage of physicians, contact the department of health in your prospective employer's state for more information. Your employer should be able to help you identify the proper office to supply the documentation, which will include such items as your employment contract with the health care facility, proof that it is in an underserved area, and proof that your employer has made reasonable efforts to recruit a U.S. physician for the job. You will also need to supply your curriculum vitae. If your U.S. stay was funded by your home government, you will also need a letter from it stating that it has no objection to your applying for a U.S. green card.

J. Working As an Exchange Visitor

Special rules apply for you to be able to work.

1. Without Special Permission

Exchange visitors are permitted to work in the U.S. if the job is part of the particular exchange program in which they are participating. Many J-1 programs, such as those for college and university professors or graduate medical students, are specifically created to engage the exchange visitor in employment. Others, like those for graduate students, often involve part-time employment in the form of teaching or research assistantships. The job may be located on or off the school premises. As long as the employment is part of the program, no special work permission is required.

2. With Special Permission

Working outside the bounds of your program often requires special permission.

a. Practical Training

If your J-1 visa was issued for a study program, you may accept work that is not specifically part of the program but is related to the subject matter of your studies. This can include work that begins after your program is completed (but no more than 30 days after) with an 18-month aggregate limit. Such employment is called practical training. You must have written permission from the responsible officer of your exchange visitor program to accept a practical training position. USCIS plays no role in granting permission for practical training.

b. Economic Necessity

Remember that in order to get a J-1 visa you must show that you have sufficient financial resources to support yourself while participating in an exchange visitor program. As we discussed earlier, such resources may be in the form of scholarships or salary earned for work that is part of or related to the program. However, if unforeseen financial problems arise after you arrive in the U.S., you may get work permission for employment that is unrelated to your exchange visitor program if the employment will not adversely affect your ability to be a full-time participant in the exchange visitor program. There is no special application, but you must have written approval from the responsible officer of your exchange visitor program.

3. Employment for Accompanying Relatives

Your accompanying spouse or minor children may apply to USCIS for permission to work. However, they cannot get work permission if the money earned helps to support you, or is needed to support you.

If your accompanying spouse or children want to work, they must file separate applications for employment authorization. This can be done by completing Form I-765 and filing it with the USCIS service center nearest to where your program in the U.S. is being carried out. Together with their Forms I-765 they must submit copies of their I-94 cards, two photos, and a filing fee of $120 each. They must also include a written statement explaining why the employment is for purposes other than supporting the J-1 visa holder and including any supporting evidence. USCIS also likes to see a monthly budget, detailing your sources of in-

come and your expenses. It is very important to keep the fee receipt USCIS will send them so they can prove that the I-765 was filed.

USCIS is required to make a decision on employment authorization applications within 90 days. If the decision is in your accompanying relative's favor, he or she will receive a work authorization card.

If the decision is not made within 90 days, your relative will, at his or her request, be granted an interim employment authorization which will last for 240 days. To receive an interim card, your relative must visit a local USCIS district office and show the fee receipt. Then an interim work authorization card will be issued.

If 240 days pass and your relative still hasn't received a final decision on the I-765, he or she must stop working. Interim work authorization cards cannot be renewed. However, if this point is reached, your relative has the option to file a new I-765 application and, if a decision on the new application is not made within 90 days, another interim work authorization card may be issued.

Form I-765

(This form is needed for your accompanying relatives to get work authorization.)

Block above Question 1. Mark the first box, "Permission to accept employment."

Questions 1–8. These questions are self-explanatory.

Question 9. This asks for your relative's Social Security number, including all numbers he or she has ever used. If he or she has never used a Social Security number, answer "None." If your relative has a nonworking Social Security number, write down the number followed by the words "Nonworking, for tax purposes only." If he or she has ever used a false number, give that number followed by the words "Not my valid number," but see Chapter 25 before proceeding.

Question 10. Your relative will not usually have an Alien Registration Number unless he or she previously applied for a green card, was in deportation proceedings or had certain types of immigration applications denied. All Alien Registration Numbers begin with the letter "A." If your relative has no "A" number but entered the U.S. with a valid visa, he or she should have an I-94 card. In this case, answer Question 10 by putting down the admission number from the I-94 card.

Questions 11–15. These questions are self-explanatory.

Question 16. Answer this question "(c)(5)."

K. Annual Reports for Foreign Medical Graduates

All foreign medical graduates training in the U.S. on J-1 visas are required to file annual reports with the USCIS local office having jurisdiction over their places of training. The reports are filed on Form I-644, which is self-explanatory. A copy of this form can be obtained from your program sponsor. A complete list of USCIS local offices with their addresses and phone numbers is in Appendix I. Failure to file this report each year will result in your visa being canceled.

FORMS AND DOCUMENTS CHECKLIST

STEP ONE: APPLICATION (THE ONLY STEP)

Forms

☐ Form DS-2019 (available from exchange visitor program sponsor).

☐ DS forms (available from U.S. consulates abroad for consular filing only).

☐ Form I-539 (U.S. filing only).

Documents

☐ Valid passport for you and each accompanying relative.

☐ One passport-type photo of you and each accompanying relative (Consular filing only).

☐ I-94 card for you and each accompanying relative (U.S. filing only).

☐ Long-form birth certificate for you and each accompanying relative.

☐ Marriage certificate if you are married and bringing your spouse.

☐ If either you or your spouse have ever been married, copies of divorce and death certificates showing termination of all previous marriages.

☐ If attending school, transcripts and diplomas showing your previous education.

☐ If employment is not part of the program, proof of financial support:

   ☐ Form I-134, Affidavit of Support, for you and each accompanying relative, or

   ☐ financial documents showing sufficient funds to participate in the exchange program for at least one year without working.

☐ Documents showing that close family members or property are being left behind in your home country.

☐ Documents showing a job is waiting on your return to your home country.

☐ Documents showing ownership of real estate in your home country.

APPLICATION FOR EXTENSIONS OF STAY

Forms

☐ Form DS-2019 (available from exchange visitor program sponsor).

Documents

Written explanation for request.

APPLICATION FOR WAIVER OF TWO-YEAR HOME RESIDENCY BASED ON EXCEPTIONAL HARDSHIP OR POLITICAL PERSECUTION

Forms

☐ Form I-612.

☐ Form DS-3035.

Documents

Some combination of the following, depending on the basis for your waiver request:

☐ No Objection Letter from your home government.

☐ Notarized affidavit explaining the nature of the hardship your family will suffer.

☐ Documents showing you have a spouse or child who is a U.S. citizen or green card holder.

☐ Documents to support the existence of the hardship.

☐ If application for waiver is based on likely persecution if you return to your home country:

   ☐ documents showing you were previously persecuted

   ☐ documents explaining the nature of the persecution in your home country, or

   ☐ documents verifying that you belong to a group of people that will be singled out for persecution.

☐ Documents from state department of health services in support of foreign medical graduate waiver.

☐ Your curriculum vitae.

Temporary Workers in Selected Occupations: O, P, and R Visas

Privileges

- You can work legally in the U.S. for your O, P, or R sponsor.

- O, P, and R visas can be issued quickly.

- You may travel in and out of the U.S. for as long as your visa stamp and status are valid. You may remain in the U.S. only as long as your status remains valid.

- Visas are available for accompanying relatives.

Limitations

- You are restricted to working only for the employer who acted as your visa sponsor. If you wish to change jobs, you must get a new visa.

- Accompanying relatives may stay in the U.S. with you but they may not work.

A. Who Qualifies for an O, P, or R Visa?

The Immigration Act of 1990 created a number of highly specialized temporary work visa categories. O and P visas are for certain outstanding workers in the sciences, arts, education, business, entertainment, and athletics. R visas are for religious workers. A job offer from a U.S. employer is a basic requirement for all these visas. The O, P, and R visa categories are quite narrow in scope.

There are no quota restrictions for O, P, and R visas. Step One petitions are normally approved within two to seven months. Visas are usually issued within several weeks after petition approval.

1. O-1 Visas: Persons of Extraordinary Ability in the Arts, Athletics, Science, Business, and Education

O-1 visas are available to persons of proven extraordinary ability in the sciences, arts, education, business, or athletics. To be considered a person of extraordinary ability, you must have sustained national or international acclaim, or, if you work in motion pictures or television productions, you must have a demonstrated record of extraordinary achievement. O-1 visas can be given only on the basis of individual qualifications. Membership in a group or team is not by itself enough to get you the visa. In addition, the alien must be coming to work or perform at an event or a series of events in the area of extraordinary ability.

a. Extraordinary Ability in Science, Education, Business, or Athletics

To meet O-1 standards, you must be able to show that you have extraordinary ability and that you have received sustained national or international acclaim. This can be demonstrated if you have gotten a major, internationally recognized award, such as a Nobel Prize, or if you have accomplished at least three of the following:

- receipt of a nationally recognized prize or award for excellence

- membership in associations that require outstanding achievements of their members in your field of expertise, as judged by recognized national or international experts

- publication of material in professional or major trade publications or major media about you and your work

- participation on a panel or individually as a judge of the work of others in your field

- making an original scientific, scholarly, or business-related contribution that is of major significance in the field

- authorship of scholarly articles in professional journals or major media

- previous employment in a critical or essential capacity for an organization with a distinguished reputation, or

- commanding or having commanded a high salary or other outstanding remuneration for your services.

Or, if the above criteria do not readily apply to the occupation, the petitioner may submit comparable evidence in order to show that the applicant is "extraordinary" even though the above evidence is not available. Be sure to explain why the above criteria do not apply.

b. Alien of Extraordinary Ability in the Arts

If the applicant is applying as an O-1 alien of extraordinary ability in the arts (defined as any field of creative activity, including but not limited to fine, visual, culinary, and performing arts), he or she must be coming to the U.S. to perform in the area of extraordinary ability and must be recognized as being prominent in his or her field of endeavor. The person can demonstrate his or her recognition with documents showing that he or she has been nominated for or has received significant national or international awards or prizes in the particular field, such as an Oscar, Emmy, Grammy, or Director's Guild Award, or at least three of the following forms of documentation:

- Evidence that the person has performed, and will perform, services as a lead or starring participant in productions or events that have a distinguished reputation as evidenced by critical reviews, advertisements, publicity releases, publication contracts, or endorsements.
- Evidence that the person has achieved national or international recognition for achievements evidenced by critical reviews or other published materials by or about him or her in major newspapers, trade journals, magazines, or other publications.
- Evidence that the person has performed, and will perform, in a lead, starring, or critical role for organizations and establishments that have a distinguished reputation evidenced by articles in newspapers, trade journals, publications, or testimonials.
- Evidence that the person has a record of major commercial or critically acclaimed successes, as evidenced by such indicators as title, rating, standing in the field, box office receipts, motion pictures, or television ratings and other occupational achievements reported in trade journals, major newspapers, or other publications.
- Evidence that the person has received significant recognition for achievements from organizations, critics, government agencies or other recognized experts in the field. Such testimonials must be in a form that clearly indicates the author's authority, expertise, and knowledge of her achievements.
- Evidence that the person has either commanded a high salary or will command a high salary or other substantial remuneration for services in relation to others in the field, as evidenced by contracts or other reliable evidence.

If the above criteria do not lend themselves to the applicant's situation, the employer may submit alternative but comparable evidence in order to establish the applicant's eligibility.

Although O-1 principals and O-3 aliens are permitted to pursue permanent residence while in nonimmigrant O status, this is not true of O-2s, who must have the intent to depart, and maintain a residence abroad, during their stay.

SPECIAL RULES FOR WORKERS ON TELEVISION AND MOVIE PRODUCTIONS

If you're an artist, entertainer, director, technical, or creative staffperson seeking a visa to work on a television or motion picture production, certain special rules apply to you. First, you must prove not merely a "high level of achievement," but a "very high level of accomplishment" in the motion picture and television industry. You'll need to show evidence that your skill and recognition is significantly higher than that ordinarily encountered. You'll need to show the same sorts of evidence as other artists, but you won't have the option of showing comparable evidence if you can't come up with anything on the USCIS's list.

---

2. O-2 Visas: Support Staff for Those With O-1 Visas

O-2 visas are available to those who work as essential support personnel of O-1 athletes and entertainers. O-2 visas are not available in the fields of science, business, or education. O-2 workers must be accompanying O-1 artists or athletes and be an integral part of the actual performance. The O-2 worker must also have critical skills and experience with the particular O-1 worker that is not general in nature and cannot be performed by a U.S. worker.

In the case of motion picture or television productions, there must be a preexisting, long standing working relationship between the O-2 applicant and the O-1 worker. If significant portions of the production will take place both in and out of the U.S., O-2 support personnel must be deemed necessary for the achievement of continuity and a smooth, successful production. O-2 visa holders are not allowed to pursue permanent residence in the U.S. while on their nonimmigrant visa.

3. O-3 Visas: Accompanying Relatives of Those With O-1 and O-2 Visas

O-3 visas are available to accompanying spouses and unmarried children under age 21 of O-1 or O-2 visa holders. O-3 visas allow relatives to remain in the U.S., but they may not work. They may seek permanent residence while in O-3 status.

4. P-1 Visas: Outstanding Athletes, Athletic Teams, and Entertainment Companies

P-1 visas are available to athletes or athletic teams that have been internationally recognized as outstanding for a long and continuous period of time. Entertainment companies that have been nationally recognized as outstanding for a long time also qualify. A written statement from an appropriate labor union or peer group confirming the group's stature in the industry is a required document in these cases. Unlike O visas, which always rest on the capabilities of individuals, P-1 visas can be issued based on the expertise of a group. However, don't be surprised to find a lot of overlap between uses and qualifications for O and P visas.

In the case of entertainment companies, each performer who wishes to qualify for a P-1 visa must have been an integral part of the group for at least one year, although up to 25% of them can be excused from the one-year requirement, if necessary. This requirement may also be waived in exceptional situations, where due to illness or other unanticipated circumstances, a critical performer is unable to travel. The one-year requirement is for performers only. It does not apply to support personnel. It also does not apply to anyone at all who works for a circus, including performers.

Like O-1 visas, P-1 visas are issued only for the time needed to complete a particular event, tour, or season. You may also be allowed some extra time for vacation, as well as promotional appearances and stopovers incidental and/or related to the event. Individual athletes, however, may remain in the U.S. for up to ten years.

a. Athletes

To qualify as a P-1 athlete, you or your team must have an internationally recognized reputation in the sport. Evidence of this must include a contract with a major U.S. sports league, team, or international sporting event, and at least two of the following:

- proof of your, or your team's, previous significant participation with a major U.S. sports league
- proof of your participation in an international competition with a national team
- proof of your previous significant participation with a U.S. college in intercollegiate competition
- written statement from an official of a major U.S. sports league or the governing body of the sport, detailing how you or your team is internationally recognized
- written statement from the sports media or a recognized expert regarding your international recognition
- evidence that you or your team is internationally ranked, or
- proof that you or your team has received a significant honor or award in the sport.

b. Entertainers

P-1 visas are not available to individual entertainers, but only to members of groups with international reputations. Evidence of that reputation must be shown with the following:

- proof that your group has been performing regularly for at least one year
- a statement listing each member of your group and the exact dates each has been regularly employed by that group, and
- proof of your group's sustained international recognition, as shown by either its nomination for, or receipt of, significant international awards or prizes, or at least three of the following:
  - proof that your group has or will star or take a leading role in productions or events with distinguished reputations
  - reviews or other published material showing that your group has achieved international recognition and acclaim for outstanding achievement in the field
  - proof that your group has and will star or take a leading role in productions or events for organizations with distinguished reputations
  - proof of large box office receipts or ratings showing your group has a record of major commercial or critically acclaimed successes
  - proof that your group has received significant recognition for achievements from organizations, critics, government agencies, or other recognized experts, or
  - proof that your group commands a high salary or other substantial remuneration.

c. Circuses

Circus performers and essential personnel do not need to have been part of the organization for one year to get a P-1 visa, provided the particular circus itself has a nationally recognized reputation as outstanding.

d. Waiver for Nationally Known Entertainment Groups

USCIS may waive the international recognition requirement for groups that have only outstanding national reputations, if special circumstances would make it difficult for your group to prove its international reputation. Such circumstances could include your group having only limited access to news media, or problems based on your group's geographical location.

e. Waiver of One-Year Group Membership

USCIS may waive the one-year group membership requirement for you if you are replacing an ill or otherwise unexpectedly absent but essential member of a P-1 entertainment group. This requirement may also be waived if you will be performing in any critical role of the group's operation.

5. P-2 Visas: Participants in Reciprocal Exchange Programs

P-2 visas are available to artists or entertainers, either individually or as part of a group, who come to the U.S. to perform under a reciprocal exchange program between the U.S. and one or more other countries. All essential support personnel are included. The legitimacy of the program must be evidenced by a formal, written exchange agreement. In addition, a labor union in the U.S. must have either been involved in the negotiation of the exchange or have agreed

to it. The U.S. individual or group being exchanged must have skills and terms of employment comparable to the person or group coming to the U.S.

6. P-3 Visas: Culturally Unique Groups

P-3 visas are available to artists or entertainers who come to the U.S., either individually or as part of a group, to develop, interpret, represent, teach, or coach in a program that is considered culturally unique. The program may be of either a commercial or non-commercial nature.

A P-3 alien must be coming to the U.S. to participate in a cultural event or events that will further the understanding or development of his art form. In addition, the individual will have to submit:

- Statements from recognized experts showing the authenticity of his or her, or the group's skills in performing, presenting, coaching, or teaching the unique or traditional art form and giving credentials showing the basis of his or her knowledge of his or her or the group's skill, or
- Evidence that his or her, or the group's performance is culturally unique, as shown by reviews in newspapers, journals, or other published materials, and that their performance will be culturally unique.

Essential support personnel of P-3 aliens should also request classification under the P-3 category. The documentation for P-3 support personnel should include:

- A consultation from a labor organization with expertise in the area of the alien's skill
- A statement describing why the support person has been essential in the past, critical skills, and experience with the principal alien, and
- A copy of the written contract or a summary of the terms of the oral agreement between the alien and the employer.

7. P-4 Visas: Accompanying Relatives of Those With P-1, P-2, and P-3 Visas

P-4 visas are issued to the accompanying relatives of any P visa workers. The accompanying relatives are permitted to remain in the U.S., but they cannot work unless granted work authorization in their own right.

8. R-1 Visas: Religious Workers

An R-1 visa is available to a person who has been a member of a legitimate religious denomination for at least two years and has a job offer in the U.S. to work for an affiliate of that same religious organization. R-1 visas may be issued to both members of the clergy and lay religious workers. The maximum stay is five years.

The criteria for qualifying are the same as those for religious workers applying for special immigrant green cards discussed in Chapter 11, with one big difference. Unlike the green card category, it is not necessary that R-1 visa workers were employed by the religious organization before getting the visa. They need only have been members for two years.

Usually, people qualifying for R-1 visas also qualify for green cards as special immigrants and may prefer to apply directly for a green card.

9. R-2 Visas: Accompanying Relatives of Those With R-1 Visas

Accompanying relatives of R-1 visa holders can get R-2 visas. This allows them to stay in the U.S., but not to work.

POSSIBILITIES FOR A GREEN CARD FROM O, P, OR R STATUS

Having an O, P, or R visa gives you no legal advantage in applying for a green card. Realistically, however, it is probably easier to get an employer to sponsor you for an O, P, or R visa than for a green card, and coming to the U.S. first with a temporary work visa gives you the opportunity to decide if you really want to live in the U.S. permanently. Once you are in the U.S. with a work permit, it is also usually easier to find an employer willing to sponsor you for a green card.

O and P visa holders are not required to have the intention of returning to their home countries. Accordingly, applying for a green card while in the U.S. on an O or P visa will not jeopardize your status. R visa holders are required to have the intention of returning home once the visa or status expires. Therefore, if you apply for a green card, it may be difficult to obtain or renew an R visa. Many religious workers qualify for green cards as special immigrants. If you are a religious worker and want to remain in the U.S. permanently, you should read Chapter 11 before applying for an R visa.

B. O, P, and R Visa Overview

Once you have been offered a job, getting an O, P, or R visa is a two-step process. Some applicants expect their U.S. employers to handle the entire process for them and, indeed, many large companies and institutions have experienced staff specialists who will do this for highly desirable employees. This is particularly likely in the case of a large sports or entertainment organization. Even smaller companies may be prepared to do whatever is necessary, including paying an immigration attorney's fees, to attract key employees. However, often it is the employee who is most interested in having the visa issued, and to U.S. employers, the red tape of hiring a foreign employee can be an unfamiliar nuisance.

As we give you step-by-step instructions for getting a visa, we will indicate that certain activities are to be performed by your employer and others are to be done by you. However, there is nothing to stop you from helping with the work. For example, you can fill out forms intended to be completed by your employer and simply ask the employer to check them over and sign them. The less your U.S. employer is inconvenienced, the more the company will be willing to act as sponsor for your visa.

1. Step One: The Petition

Step One is called the *petition*. It is filed by your U.S. employer on Form I-129. All O, P, and R visa petitions are submitted to USCIS regional service centers in the U.S. The object of the petition is to prove four things:

- that you qualify for O, P, or R status
- that your future job is of a high enough level or appropriate nature to warrant someone with your advanced or specialized skills
- that you have the correct background and skills to match the job requirements, and
- in the case of O and P visas, that appropriate labor unions or similar organizations have been consulted concerning your eligibility.

Be aware that an approved petition does not by itself give you any immigration privileges. It is only a prerequisite to Step Two, submitting your application for an O, P, or R visa. The petition must be approved before you are eligible for Step Two.

2. Step Two: The Application

Step Two is called the *application*. It is filed by you and your accompanying relatives, if any. The application is your formal request for an O, P, or R visa or status. (If you are Canadian, your Step Two procedures will be different from those of other applicants. See Chapter 28.)

Step Two may be carried out in the U.S. at a USCIS office (if you're already in the U.S. legally) or in your home country at a U.S. consulate there. If you file Step Two papers in the U.S., you will usually submit them together with those for Step One. When Step Two is done at a U.S. consulate abroad, you must wait to file the application until the Step One petition is first approved.

If you are already in the U.S. legally on some other type of nonimmigrant visa, you qualify to apply for an O, P, or R status at a USCIS office inside the U.S. using a procedure known as *change of nonimmigrant status*. (If you are admitted as a visitor without a visa under the Visa Waiver Program, you may not carry out Step Two in the U.S. Currently there are 28 participating countries in the Visa Waiver Program; listed in Chapter 2.)

"Change of Status" is simply a technical term meaning you are switching from one nonimmigrant status to another. If a change of status is approved, you will then be treated as if you had entered the country with an O, P, or R visa. You can keep the status as long as you remain in the U.S. or until it expires, whichever comes first.

You will not, however, receive a visa stamp, which you need if your plans include traveling in and out of the U.S. Again, visa stamps are issued only at U.S. consulates abroad. Therefore, if you change your status and later travel outside the U.S., you will have to go to the U.S. consulate in your home country and repeat Step Two, obtaining the O, P, or R visa stamp in your passport before you can return.

3. Who's Who in Getting Your O, P, or R Visa

Getting an O, P, or R visa will be easier if you familiarize yourself with the technical names used for each participant in the process. During Step One, the petition, you are known as either the *beneficiary* or the *employee* and your U.S. employer is called the *petitioner* or the *employer*. The petitioner may be a business, an institution or a person but usually it is a business or institution. In Step Two, the application, you are called the *applicant*, but your employer remains the *petitioner* or *employer*. If you are bringing your spouse and children with you as accompanying relatives, each of them is known as an *applicant* as well.

4. Tips on Handling the Paperwork

There are two types of paperwork you must submit to get an O, P, or R visa. The first consists of official government forms completed by you or your U.S. employer. The second is personal documents such as professional credentials and critical reviews.

It is vital that forms are properly filled out and all necessary documents are supplied. You or your U.S. employer may resent the intrusion into your privacy and the sizable effort it takes to prepare immigration applications, but realize the process is an impersonal matter to immigration officials. Your getting a visa is more important to you than it is to the U.S. government. There is no shortage of applicants.

The documents you or your U.S. employer supply to USCIS or the consulate do not have to be originals. Photo-copies of all documents are acceptable as long as you have the originals in your possession and are willing to produce them upon request. But add the following language to the photocopy, with your signature and the date:

> *Copies of documents submitted are exact photocopies of unaltered original documents and I understand that I may be required to submit original documents to an immigration or consular official at a later date.*
> *Signature* _____
> *Typed or Printed Name* _____
> *Date* _____

Documents will be accepted if they are in either English, or, with papers filed at U.S. consulates abroad, the language of the country where the documents are being filed. An exception exists for papers filed at U.S. consulates in Japan, where all documents must be translated into English. If the documents are not in an acceptable language as just explained, they must be accompanied by a full, word for word, written English translation. Any capable person may act as translator. It is not necessary to hire a professional. At the end of each translation, the following statement must appear:

> *I hereby certify that I translated this document from [language] to English. This translation is accurate and complete. I further certify that I am fully competent to translate from [language] to English.*
> *Signature* _____
> *Typed or Printed Name* _____
> *Date* _____

The translator should sign this statement but it does not have to be witnessed or notarized.

Later in this chapter we describe in detail the forms and documents needed to get your O, P, or R visa. A summary checklist of forms and documents appears at the end of this chapter.

C. Step One: The Petition

The U.S. employer submits the petition, consisting of forms and documents, by mail, in duplicate, to the USCIS regional service center having jurisdiction over your intended employer's place of business. USCIS regional service centers are not the same as USCIS local offices. There are four USCIS regional service centers spread across the U.S. Appendix I contains a list of all USCIS regional service centers with their addresses, but check the USCIS website, www.uscis.gov, for the appropriate P.O. box.

The filing fee for each petition, if no change of status is being requested, is currently $130. Checks or money orders are accepted. It is not advisable to send cash. We recommend submitting all papers by certified mail, return receipt requested, and making a copy of everything sent in, for your records.

Although the service center is likely to take a long time to make a decision on the petition, you are not allowed to submit the petition more than six months before the event that requires your services.

Within a few weeks of mailing in the petition, your employer should get back a written confirmation that the papers are being processed, together with a receipt for the fees. This notice will also give your immigration file number and tell approximately when you should expect to have a decision. If USCIS wants further information before acting on your case, it may send you a request for information or documents on Form I-797. Your employer should supply the extra data and mail the whole package back to the USCIS regional service center.

O, P, and R petitions are normally approved two to four months. A Notice of Action Form I-797 will be sent to your employer showing the petition was approved. If you plan to execute Step Two at a U.S. consulate abroad, USCIS will also notify the consulate of your choice, sending them a complete copy of your file. Only the employer receives communications from USCIS about the petition because technically it is the employer who is seeking the visa on your behalf.

Faster decisions—at a price. For $1,000 over and above the regular filing fees, USCIS promises "premium processing" of the visa petition, including a decision within 15 days. To use this service, the employer must fill out an additional application (Form I-907) and submit the application to a special USCIS Service Center address. For complete instructions, see the USCIS website at www.uscis.gov.

1. Petition Forms

Copies of all USCIS forms are in Appendix II and on the USCIS website.

Form I-129 and O/P/Q/R Supplement

The basic form for Step One, the petition, is immigration Form I-129 and O/P/Q/R Supplement. The I-129 form is used for many different nonimmigrant visas. In addition to the basic part of the form that applies to all types of visas, it comes with several supplements for each specific nonimmi-grant category. Simply use the supplement that applies to you. Your employer must file the petition form in duplicate. Send in two signed originals. Copies are not acceptable.

The employer can choose to list more than one foreign employee on a single I-129 petition. This is done if the employer has more than one opening to be filled for the same type of job or if it is a group petition. Supplement-1, which is also part of Form I-129, should be completed for each additional employee.

Most of the questions on the I-129 form are straightforward. If a question does not apply to you, answer it with "None" or "N/A." Those questions requiring explanations are as follows:

Part 1. These questions concern the employer only and are self-explanatory.

Part 2. Question 1. Question 1 should be answered "O-1," "O-2," "P-1," "P-2," "P-3," or "R-1" as appropriate.

Questions 2–3. These questions are self-explanatory.

Question 4. This question asks you to indicate what action is requested from USCIS. Normally you will mark box "a" which tells USCIS to notify a U.S. consulate abroad of the petition approval so that you may apply for a visa there. If you will be filing your Step Two application in the U.S., mark box "b." If this petition is being filed as an extension, mark box "c."

Part 3. These questions are self-explanatory. If you previously held a U.S. work permit and therefore have a U.S. Social Security number, put down that number where asked. If you have a Social Security number that is not valid for employment, put down that number followed by "not valid for employment." If you have never had a Social Security number, put down "None." If you've used a false Social Security card, see Chapter 25—you could be found inadmissible.

Alien Registration Numbers, which all begin with the letter "A," are given only to people who have applied for green cards, received political asylum, or been in deportation proceedings. If you have an "A" number, you may want to consult with an attorney before proceeding. If you do not have an "A" number, write down "None."

If your present authorized stay has expired, you must disclose that where asked. This may affect your ability to get an O, P, or R visa at a U.S. consulate (see Chapter 25), but if you are out of status now, you cannot file Step Two inside the U.S.

Part 4. These questions are self-explanatory. The fact that you may have a green card petition or application in process does not prevent you from getting a visa if you are an O-1 or O-3 or P-1, but it will bar related categories such as O-2.

Part 5. These questions are self-explanatory. The dates of intended employment for O and P visas should not exceed the period of your employment contract. If you are applying for an R visa, put no more than five years, which is the maximum period of time for which an R petition may be approved.

O & P Supplement (for O and P petitions only)

Most of this form is self-explanatory. It asks if the required written consultations with labor unions have been provided. See Section 2b, just below.

Q & R Supplement (for R petitions only)

Section 1 of this form applies only to Q visas, a very limited category that is not covered here. Section 2 is for R visas and should be completed in full and is self-explanatory.

2.   Petition Documents

You must submit several documents with the petition.

a.   Job Verification

Your employer must show that the job you have been offered really exists. To do this, he or she must produce either a written employment contract with you or a written summary of an oral contract. The terms of your employment, including job duties, hours, salary, and other benefits, must be mentioned in the document. If you will be going on tour, a tour schedule should be included. For O and P visas, the employer should also submit a detailed written statement explaining the nature of the employer, the specific events or activities in which you will be participating, and why your participation is needed. P-2 petitions must also include a copy of the formal reciprocal exchange agreement, as well as a statement from the sponsoring organization that explains how the particualr exchange relates to the underlying agreement.

b.   Special Requirements for O & P Visas

Documents for O and P visas should include:
- certificates showing prizes or awards won
- certificates of membership in associations
- copies of articles published about you and your work
- publications written by you
- letters from leaders in your field explaining your significant accomplishments, and
- letters from previous employers, showing your salary and explaining your importance to them.

If you are part of a group, documents explaining the prestige and accomplishments of your group and details about each of its members, including dates of employment, should also be provided.

All O and P visa petitions must be accompanied by a consultation report or written advisory opinion from an appropriate peer group, labor union, and/or management organization, concerning the nature of the work to be done and your qualifications. Alternatively, you may request USCIS to obtain an advisory opinion for you, but this will significantly delay your case.

For O-1 petitions, the opinion can simply be a letter stating that the organization has no objection to your getting an O-1 visa. In P-1 petitions, the opinion must explain the reputation of either you or your team and the nature of the event in the U.S. The opinion in all O-2 cases and for P-1 visa support personnel must contain an explanation of why you are essential to the performance and the nature of your working relationship with the principal performer. It must also state whether or not U.S. workers are available or assert that significant production activities will take place both in and out of the U.S. and, therefore, your presence is required for continuity.

P-2 advisory opinions must verify the existence of a viable exchange program. P-3 opinions must evaluate the cultural uniqueness of the performances, state that the events are mostly cultural in nature, and give the reason why the event or activity is appropriate for P-3 classification.

USCIS maintains a list of organizations willing to supply advisory opinions. The list can be found on the USCIS website at www.uscis.gov (click "Immigration Laws, Regulations, and Guides," then "Operation Instructions," then "OI 214," then scroll down to OI 214.2 and click just below, on "EX 214.2h"). However, you are free to get an opinion from a group that is not on the USCIS list. Some of them charge for this service, around $250.

c.   Special Requirements for R Visas

Documents required for an R visa petition are identical to those required to get a green card as a special immigrant in the religious worker category (see Chapter 11), except you need not show that you previously worked for the religious organization. It is only necessary that you have been a member of the organization. You should submit all diplomas and certificates showing your academic and professional qualifications. In addition, submit a detailed letter from the religious organization in the U.S. explaining its structure and number of followers in both your home country and the U.S., as well as the details of your job offer in the U.S. including job title, duties, salary, and qualification demands. Finally, you should include written verification that you have been a member of that organization for at least two years.

3. Petition Interviews

USCIS rarely holds interviews on O, P, or R visa petitions. When it does, the interview is always with the employer. If you are in the U.S., you may be asked to appear as well. Interviews are requested only if USCIS doubts that the documents or information on Form I-129 and the O, P, Q, R supplement are genuine. Then, the petition file is forwarded to the USCIS local office nearest your employer's place of business, and your employer is notified to appear there. The employer may also be asked to bring additional documents at that time. If, after the interview, everything is in order, the petition will be approved. The best way to avoid an interview is to have the employer document the petition correctly from the beginning.

4. Petition Appeals

If you have poorly documented your qualifications, the petition will probably be denied. Your employer will then get a notice of USCIS's unfavorable decision, a written statement of the reasons for the negative outcome, and an explanation of how to appeal, or a request for evidence (I-797) specifically requesting information or documentation.

The best way to handle an appeal is to try avoiding it altogether. Filing an appeal means arguing to USCIS that its reasoning was wrong. This is difficult to do successfully. If you think you can eliminate the reason your petition failed by improving your paperwork, it makes sense to disregard the appeals process and simply file a new petition, better prepared than the first.

If the petition was denied because your U.S. employer left out necessary documents that have since been located, the new documents should be sent together with a written request that the case be reopened to the same USCIS office that issued the denial. This is technically called a *Motion to Reopen*. There is a $110 fee to file this motion. Appeals often take a long time. A Motion to Reopen can be concluded faster than an appeal.

If your U.S. employer does choose to appeal, it must be done within 30 days of the date on the Notice of Denial. The appeal should be filed at the same USCIS office that issued the denial. There is a $110 filing fee. USCIS will then forward the papers for consideration to the Administrative Appeals Unit in Washington, DC. In six months or more your employer will get back a decision by mail. Fewer than 5% of all appeals are successful.

When an appeal to USCIS has been denied, the next step is to make an appeal through the U.S. judicial system. Your employer may not file an action in court without first going through the appeals process available from USCIS. If the

case has reached this stage and you are in the U.S. illegally, we strongly recommend seeking representation from a qualified immigration attorney, as you are now in danger of being deported.

D. Step Two: The Application (Consular Filing)

If you are Canadian, your Step Two procedures will be different from those of other applicants. See Chapter 28 for details.

Anyone with an approved O, P, or R petition can apply for a visa at a U.S. consulate in his or her home country. You must be physically present to apply there. If you have been or are now working or living illegally in the U.S., be sure to read and understand the grounds of inadmissibility and bars to re-entering the U.S. discussed in Chapter 25.

THIRD COUNTRY PROCESSING

The immigration law amendments of 1996 changed the rules about obtaining a nonimmigrant visa at a consulate other than one in your home country—called "third country national," or TCN, processing.

TCN processing is prohibited when you have been unlawfully present in the U.S. under a prior visa status. Even if you overstayed your status by just one day, the visa will be automatically canceled, you will be ineligible for TCN processing, and you will have to return to your home country to apply for a new visa at the consulate there.

If you were admitted for duration of status (indicated as "D/S" on your Form I-94), however, you still may be able to do TCN processing even though you remained in the U.S. beyond the time for which your status was conferred. This applies to individuals in A, F, G, and J status. In this situation, you will be barred from TCN processing only if USCIS or an immigration judge has determined that you were unlawfully present.

Unlawful presence of six months or more after April 1, 1997 is also a ground of inadmissibility, provided you leave the U.S. and request reentry. (See Chapter 25.)

AT THE AIRPORT OR BORDER

The law empowers a CBP inspector at the airport to summarily (without allowing judicial review) bar entry to someone requesting admission to the U.S. if either of the following are true:

- The inspector thinks you are making a misrepresentation about practically anything connected with entering the U.S., including your purpose in coming, intent to return, and prior immigration history. This includes the use or suspected use of false documents.
- You do not have the proper documentation to support your entry to the U.S. in the category you are requesting.

If the inspector excludes you, you cannot request entry for five years, unless USCIS grants a special waiver. For this reason it is extremely important to understand the terms of your requested status, and to not make any misrepresentations. If you are found to be inadmissible, you may request to withdraw your application to enter the U.S. in order to prevent having the five-year entry bar on your record. The CBP may allow this in some exceptional cases.

1. Benefits and Drawbacks of Consular Filing

The most important benefit to consular filing is that only consulates issue visas. When you go through a U.S. filing you get a status, not a visa. (See Chapter 14.) An O, P, or R status confers the same right to work as an O, P, or R visa, but it does not give you the ability to travel in and out of the U.S. Therefore, if you want travel privileges, you will at some time have to go through the extra step of applying for a visa at a U.S. consulate, even though you have already applied for and received status in the U.S.

Moreover, you are not eligible to process a change of status application in the U.S. unless your presence and activities in the U.S. have always been legal. If you are in the U.S. illegally, consular filing is a must (though see Chapter 25 about whether you'll be barred from returning).

A further plus to consular filing is that consular offices may work more quickly to issue nonimmigrant visas than some USCIS offices do to process nonimmigrant statuses. Your waiting time for the paperwork to be finished may be much shorter at a U.S. consulate abroad.

A drawback to consular filing comes from the fact that you must be physically present in the country where the consulate is located to file there. If your application is ultimately turned down because of an unexpected problem, not only will you have to wait outside the U.S. until the problem is resolved, but other visas in your passport, such as a visitor's visa, may be canceled. It will then be impossible for you to enter the U.S. at all. Consequently, if your case is not very strong and freedom of travel is not essential to you, it might be wise to apply in the U.S., make up your mind to remain there for the duration of the O, P, or R status, and skip trying to get a visa from the consulate.

2. Application General Procedures: Consular Filing

Technically, the law allows you to apply for an O, P, or R visa at any U.S. consulate you choose.

You may not file an application for an O, P, or R visa at a consulate before your petition has been approved. Once it is approved, the USCIS regional service center where the petition was originally submitted will forward a complete copy of your file to the U.S. consulate designated on Form I-129 in Step One. At the same time, a Notice of Action Form I-797 indicating approval will be sent directly to your U.S. employer. Once your employer receives this, telephone the consulate to see if the petition file has arrived from USCIS. If the file is slow in coming, ask the consulate to consider granting approval of your visa based only on the Notice of Action. Many U.S. consulates are willing to do so.

Once the petition is approved, you can simply walk into many consulates with your application paperwork and get your O, P, or R visa immediately. Others insist on appointments. Telephone in advance to ask about local policies.

On entering the U.S. with your new visa, you will be given an I-94 card. It will be stamped with a date showing how long you can stay. Normally, you are permitted to remain up to the expiration date on your Step One petition. Each time you exit and reenter the U.S., you will get a new I-94 card authorizing your stay up to the final date indicated on the petition.

3. Application Forms: Consular Filing

When you file at a U.S. consulate abroad, the consulate officials will provide you with certain forms, designated by a "DS" preceding a number. Instructions for completing DS forms and what to do with them once they are filled out will come with the forms. We do not include copies of these forms in this book, because different consulates sometimes issue different versions of the forms.

4. Application Documents: Consular Filing

You must show a valid passport and present one photograph taken according to the photo instructions at http://travel.state.gov/photorequirements/html. If the consulate has not yet received your USCIS file containing the paperwork from the approved petition, you will then need to show the original Notice of Action, Form I-797, which your employer received from USCIS by mail. Most consulates will issue O, P, and R visas based only on the Notice of Action, although some, particularly in South America and Asia, insist on seeing the complete USCIS file. If the consulate wants to see your file and it is late (more than a month) in arriving, you should request that the consulate investigate the file's whereabouts. You, too, can write the USCIS regional service center where your petition was processed, asking them to look for the file.

For each accompanying relative, you must present a valid passport and one photograph taken according to the State Department's photo instructions. You will also need documents verifying their family relationship to you. You may verify a parent/child relationship by presenting the child's long-form birth certificate. Many countries, including Canada and England, issue both short- and long-form birth certificates. Where both are available, the long form is needed because it contains the names of the parents while the short form does not.

If you are accompanied by your spouse, you must prove that you are lawfully married by showing a civil marriage certificate. Church certificates are generally unacceptable. (There are a few exceptions, depending on the laws of your particular country. Canadians, for example, may use church marriage certificates if the marriage took place in Quebec Province, but not elsewhere. If a civil certificate is available, however, you should always use it.) You may have married in a country where marriages are not customarily recorded. Tribal areas of Africa are an example. In such situations ask the U.S. consulate regarding what it accepts as proof of marriage.

There will be a minimum $100 fee for the visa. Also, if the country of your nationality charges fees for visas to U.S. citizens who wish to work there, then the U.S. will charge people of your country a similar fee as well. Whether or not this fee is added is determined by your nationality, not by where you apply. This is called a reciprocity fee. Check with the nearest U.S. consulate to find out if there will be a fee in your case.

5. Application Interviews: Consular Filing

The consulate will frequently require an interview before issuing an O, P, or R visa. During the interview, a consul officer will examine the data you gave in Step One for accuracy, especially regarding facts about your own qualifications. In the case of R-1 visas, evidence of ties to your home country will also be checked.

During the interview, you will surely be asked how long you intend to remain in the U.S. Any answer indicating uncertainty about plans to return or an interest in applying for a green card is likely to result in a denial of your R-1 visa.

Note that O-1/O-3 and P-1 visas do not require you to have the intention to return home.

6. Application Appeals: Consular Filing

When a consulate turns down an O, P, or R visa application, there is no way to make a formal appeal, although you are free to reapply as often as you like. Some consulates, however, will make you wait several months before allowing you to file another application, or place limits on the total number of repeat applications you can file. If your visa is denied, you will be told by the consular officer the reasons for the denial. Written statements of decisions are not normally provided in nonimmigrant cases. If a lack of evidence about a particular point is the problem, sometimes simply presenting more evidence on an unclear fact can change the result.

The most likely reasons for having an O or P visa turned down are because you are found inadmissible. The most likely reason for having an R visa turned down is that the consulate does not believe you intend to return to your home country.

Certain people who have been refused visas reapply at a different consulate, attempting to hide the fact that they were turned down elsewhere. You should know that if your application is denied, the last page in your passport will be stamped "Application Received" with the date and location of the rejecting consulate. This notation shows that some type of prior visa application has failed. It serves as a warning to other consulates that your case merits close inspection. If what we have just told you makes you think it would be a good idea to overcome this problem by obtaining a new, unmarked passport, you should also know that permanent computer records are kept of all visa denials.

E. Step Two: The Application (U.S. Filing)

If you are physically present in the U.S., you may apply for O, P, or R status without leaving the country, on the following conditions:

- you are simultaneously filing paperwork for or have already received an approved visa petition
- you entered the U.S. legally and not under the Visa Waiver Program
- you have never worked illegally in the U.S.
- the date on your I-94 card has not passed, and
- you are not inadmissible and none of the bars to change of status apply (see Chapter 25).

If you were admitted as a visitor without a visa under the new Visa Waiver Program, you may not carry out Step Two in the U.S. Currently there are 28 participating countries in the Visa Waiver Program, listed in Chapter 2.

⚠ **If you cannot meet these terms, you may not file for O, P, or R status in the U.S.** It is important to realize, however, that eligibility to apply while you're in the U.S. has nothing to do with overall eligibility for an O, P, or R visa. Many applicants who are barred from filing in the U.S. but otherwise qualify for O, P, or R status apply successfully for a visa at U.S. consulates abroad. If you find you are not eligible for U.S. filing, read Section D. Read Chapter 25 to make sure you are not subject to any waiting periods or ground of inadmissibility before leaving the U.S.

1. Benefits and Drawbacks of U.S. Filing

Visas are never given inside the U.S. They are issued exclusively by U.S. consulates abroad. If you file for a "change of status" in the U.S. and you are successful, you will get O, P, or R status but not the visa itself. O, P, or R status allows you to remain in the U.S. with O, P, or R privileges until the status expires, but should you leave the country for any reason before that time, you will have to apply for the visa itself at a U.S. consulate before returning to America. Moreover, the fact that your status has been approved in the U.S. does not guarantee that the consulate will also approve your visa. Some consulates may even regard your previously acquired status as a negative factor, an indication that you have deliberately tried to avoid the consulate's authority.

There is another problem that comes up only in U.S. filings. It is the issue of what is called *preconceived intent.* To approve a change of status, USCIS must believe that at the time you originally entered the U.S. as a visitor or with some other nonimmigrant visa, you did not intend to apply for a different status. If USCIS thinks you had a preconceived plan to change from the status you arrived with to a different status, it may deny your application. The preconceived intent issue is one less potential hazard you will face if you apply at a U.S. consulate abroad.

On the plus side of U.S. filing, if problems do arise with your U.S. application, you can stay in the U.S. while they are being corrected, a circumstance most visa applicants prefer. If you run into snags at a U.S. consulate, you will have to remain outside the U.S. until matters are resolved.

2. Application General Procedures: U.S. Filing

The general procedure for filing Step Two in the U.S. is to follow Step One as outlined above, but to mark box "4b" in Part 2 of Form I-129, indicating that you will complete processing in the U.S. There is no additional application form for filing Step Two in the U.S. If you have an accompanying spouse or children, however, a separate Form I-539 must be filed for them.

When you apply for a change of status, the filing fee for a Step One petition is presently $130 (with Form I-129), and an additional $140 for your family (with their Form I-539). Checks and money orders are accepted. It is not advisable to send cash. We recommend submitting all papers by certified mail, return receipt requested, and making a copy of everything sent in to keep for your records.

Within a week or two after mailing in the application, you should get back a written notice of confirmation that the papers are being processed, together with a receipt for the fees. This notice will also tell you your immigration file number and approximately when to expect a decision. If USCIS wants further information before acting on your case, it will send a request for evidence on a form known as an I-797. The I-797 tells you what additional pieces of information or documents are expected. You should supply the extra data and mail the whole package back to the USCIS regional service center, with the I-797 on top.

Applications for O, P, and R status are normally approved within two to four months. You will receive a Notice of Action Form I-797 indicating the dates for which your status is approved. A new I-94 card is attached to the bottom of the form.

3. Application Forms: U.S. Filing

Copies of all needed USCIS forms are in Appendix II and on the USCIS website.

Form I-129

Follow the directions in Section C1, above, except in Part 2, mark box "4b" instead of box "4a."

Form I-539 (for accompanying relatives only)

Only one application form is needed for an entire family, but if there is more than one accompanying relative, each additional one should be listed on the I-539 supplement.

Part 1. These questions are self-explanatory. "A" numbers are usually given only to people who have previously applied for green cards or who have been in deportation proceedings. Consult an attorney to make sure these past issues won't affect the current application.

Part 2. Question 1. Mark box "b," and write in "O-3," "P-4" or ""R-2," as appropriate.

Question 2. This question is self-explanatory.

Part 3. In most cases you will mark Item 1 with the date requested in the Step One petition. You will also complete Items 3 and 4, which are self-explanatory.

Part 4. Questions 1–2. These questions are self-explanatory.

Question 3. The different parts to this question are self-explanatory; however, items "a" through "c" ask if an immigrant visa petition or adjustment of status application has ever been filed on your behalf. If you are separately applying for a green card through a relative, this would be Step One, as described in Chapter 5. If you are separately applying for a green card through employment, this would be Step Two as described in Chapter 8. If you have only begun the Labor Certification, the first step of getting a green card through employment, this question should be answered "no." An answer of "yes" to any of these questions will not affect your ability to get an O or P visa, but may make you ineligible for an R visa, which requires you to have the intention of returning to your home country after the visa expires.

4. Application Documents: U.S. Filing

Each applicant must submit a copy of his or her I-94 card, the small white card you received on entering the U.S. Remember, if the date stamped on your I-94 card has already passed, you are ineligible for U.S. filing. If you entered the U.S. under the Visa Waiver Program and have a green I-94 card, you are also ineligible for U.S. filing. Canadians who are just visiting are not expected to have I-94 cards. Canadians with any other type of nonimmigrant status should have them.

For each accompanying relative, send in a copy of his or her I-94 card. You will also need documents verifying their family relationship to you. You may prove a parent/child relationship by presenting the child's long-form birth certificate. Many countries, including Canada and England, issue both short- and long-form birth certificates. Where both are available, the long form is needed because it contains the names of the parents while the short form does not.

If you are accompanied by your spouse, you must prove that you are lawfully married by showing a civil marriage certificate. Church certificates are usually unacceptable. (There are a few exceptions, depending on the laws of your particular country. Canadians, for example, may use church marriage certificates if the marriage took place in Quebec Province, but not elsewhere. If a civil certificate is available, however, you should always use it.) You may have married in a country where marriages are not customarily recorded. Tribal areas of Africa are an example. In such situations call the nearest consulate or embassy of your home country for help with getting acceptable proof of marriage.

5. Application Interviews: U.S. Filing

Interviews on change of status applications are rarely held. When an interview is required, the USCIS regional service center where you filed will send your paperwork to the local USCIS office nearest the location of your U.S. employer's place of business or institution. This office will in turn contact you for an appointment. (If USCIS has questions on the Step One petition rather than the application, your employer will be contacted.) USCIS may ask you to bring additional documents at that time.

If you are called for an interview, the most likely reason is that USCIS either suspects some type of fraud or believes you may be subject to a ground of inadmissibility. Interviews are usually a sign of trouble and can result in considerable delays.

6. Application Appeals: U.S. Filing

If your application is denied, you will receive a written decision by mail explaining the reasons for the denial. There is no way of making a formal appeal to USCIS if your application is turned down. If the problem is too little evidence, you may be able to overcome this obstacle by adding more documents and resubmitting the entire application to the same USCIS office you have been dealing with, together with a written request that the case be reopened. The written request does not have to be in any special form. This is technically called a *Motion to Reopen*. There is a $110 fee to file this motion.

Remember that you may be denied the right to a U.S. filing without being denied an O, P, or R visa. When your application is turned down because you are found ineligible for U.S. filing, simply change your application to a consular filing; but see Chapter 25 to make sure you won't be found inadmissible and barred from returning to the U.S.

Although there is no appeal to USCIS for the denial of a change of status application, you do have the right to file an appeal in a U.S. district court. It would be difficult to file such an appeal without employing an immigration attorney at considerable expense. Such appeals are usually unsuccessful.

F. Extensions

O and P visas can be extended for the time needed, without limitation. R visas are limited to a total of five years, however. Although an extension is usually easier to get than the O, P, or R visa itself, it is not automatic. USCIS has the right to reconsider your qualifications based on any changes in the facts or law. As always, however, good cases that are well prepared will be successful.

To extend your O, P, or R visa, the petition and visa stamp will both have to be updated. As with the original application, you can file either in the U.S. or at a consulate. However, contrary to our advice on the initial visa procedures, O and P extensions are best handled in the U.S. That is because visa stamps, which can only be issued originally at consulates, may be extended in the U.S. R extensions must be issued at consulates.

1. Extension Petition

Extension procedures are identical to the procedures followed in getting the initial visa, except that less documentation is generally required. However the best practice is to fully document the extension request with all of the documents submitted with the initial petition, as USCIS will probably not have the file on site. In addition to the employer's attestation, you should also submit the documents described in Subsection b, below.

WORKING WHILE YOUR EXTENSION PETITION IS PENDING

If you file your petition for an extension of O, P, or R status before your authorized stay expires, you are automatically permitted to continue working for up to 240 days while you are waiting for a decision. If, however, your authorized stay expires after you have filed for an extension but before you receive an approval, and more than 240 days go by without getting a decision on your extension petition, continued employment is not authorized and you must stop working.

a. Extension Petition Forms

Copies of all needed USCIS forms are in Appendix II and on the USCIS website.

Form I-129 and Supplement

Follow the directions in Section C1, above. The only difference is that you will mark boxes "2b" and "4c" of Part 2.

Form I-539 (for accompanying relatives only)

Follow the directions in Section E3, above, but mark box "1a" of Part 2.

b. Extension Petition Documents

You must submit a copy of your I-94 card. You should also submit a copy of the original Notice of Action I-797, a letter from your employer stating that your extension is required, and a copy of your personal U.S. income tax returns for the past two years, including Form W-2. Be sure that only authorized employment is reflected on your tax documents before submitting them.

2. Visa Revalidation

Visas can be revalidated either in the U.S. or at a consulate.

a. Visa Revalidation: U.S. Filing

If you are physically in the U.S. and your O or P status extension has been approved by USCIS, you can have your visa revalidated by mail without leaving the country. The exception is if you carry the passport of a country that is on the U.S. government's list of countries that sponsor terrorism, in which case you won't be allowed to revalidate your visa without leaving the U.S. first. When this book went to print, the listed countries included North Korea, Cuba, Syria, Sudan, Iran, Iraq, and Libya.

To do this, you must fill out Form DS-156, and send it to the Department of State. With the form you should also submit as documents your passport (valid for at least six months), a recent passport-sized photo (2" x 2", full face view, on a light background, stapled or glued to the form), a fee ($100 plus a "reciprocity fee" for nationals of certain countries), your current I-94 card, Notice of Action Form I-797 and a detailed letter from your employer describing your job duties. The fees may be paid by bank draft, corporate check, or money order, payable to the U.S. Department of State. You cannot pay by cash, credit card, or personal check.

Male visa applicants between the ages of 16 and 45, regardless of nationality and regardless of where they apply, must also complete and submit a form DS-157.

You should send in your visa revalidatoin application as soon as possible within the 60 days before your allowed stay expires (but don't send it any earlier, or the entire package will be returned to you). Enclose a self-addressed, stamped envelope or a completed Federal Express or other courier service airbill. Send the entire package by certified mail.

If sending by postal service, send to:

U.S Department of State/Visa
P.O. Box 952099
St. Louis, M.O. 63195-2099

If sending by courier service:

U.S. Department of State/Visa (Box 2099)
1005 Convention Plaza
St. Louis, M.O. 63101-1200

The passport will be returned to you with a newly revalidated visa in about 12 weeks. For more information on this process, see the State Department website at www.travel.state.gov/revals.html.

If your accompanying relatives are physically in the U.S., their O-3 and P-4 visas may be revalidated by sending in their passports and I-94 cards together with yours. We strongly advise gathering your family together inside U.S. borders so you can take advantage of this simple revalidation procedure.

R visa holders cannot revalidate their visas in the U.S.

b.   Visa Revalidation: Consular Filing

If you must leave the U.S. after your extension has been approved but before you had time to get your visa revalidated, you must get a new visa stamp issued at a consulate. Read Section D, above. The procedures for consular extensions are identical.

We would like to reemphasize that it is much more convenient to apply for a revalidated visa by mail through the U.S. State Department than it is to extend your O or P visa through a consulate. If possible, schedule filing your extension application when you can remain in the U.S. until it is complete. Again, R visas do not qualify for this special procedure.

FORMS AND DOCUMENTS CHECKLIST

STEP ONE: PETITION

Forms

☐ Form I-129 and O/P/Q/R Supplement.

Documents

☐ Written employment contract or written summary of an oral contract.

☐ College and university diplomas.

☐ Employer's written statement explaining the nature of the employer, the specific events or activities you will be participating in and why your participation is needed.

Additional Documents for O & P Visas

☐ Consultation report.

☐ Certificates showing prizes or awards won.

☐ Certificates of membership in associations.

☐ Copies of articles published about you and your work.

☐ Publications written by you.

☐ Letters from leaders in your field explaining your significant accomplishments.

☐ Letters from previous employers showing your salary and explaining your importance to them.

☐ For P-2 visas, a copy of the formal reciprocal exchange agreement and a statement from the sponsoring organization explaining how the particular exchange relates to the underlying agreement.

☐ If part of a group:

　☐ documentation explaining the prestige and accomplishments of your group, and

　☐ details about each of its members.

Additional Documents for R Visas

☐ Diplomas and certificates showing your academic and professional qualifications.

☐ Detailed letter from the U.S. religious organization, fully describing the operation of the organization both in and out of the U.S.

☐ Letter from the U.S. organization giving details of your U.S. job offer, including how you will be paid.

☐ Written verification that you have been a member of that same organization outside the U.S. for at least two years.

☐ Evidence that the religious organization in the U.S. qualifies as a tax-exempt organization under §501(c) of the Internal Revenue Code.

STEP TWO: APPLICATION

Forms

☐ DS forms (available at U.S. consulates abroad for consular filing only).

☐ Form I-129 (U.S. filing only).

☐ Form I-539 (U.S. filing only for accompanying relatives).

Documents

☐ Notice showing approval of the visa petition.

☐ Valid passport for you and each accompanying relative.

☐ A copy of I-94 card for you and each accompanying relative (U.S. filing only).

☐ One photo of you and each accompanying relative (Consular filing only).

Inadmissibility

A. Grounds of Inadmissibility

The U.S. government keeps a list of conditions or characteristics which it has decided are undesirable or pose a threat to the health and safety of others. People who have these conditions are not allowed to enter the country. These people are called *inadmissible*. Inadmissibility creates problems in green card applications. Technically, those who want nonimmigrant visas can also be inadmissible. In reality, inadmissibility is often not as closely checked in nonimmigrant applications.

There are many reasons why someone may be unwanted in the U.S. Each of these reasons represents a different category of inadmissibility. The list of such grounds includes affliction with various physical and mental disorders, commission of crimes, and participation in terrorist or subversive activity.

Just because you fall into one of the categories of inadmissibility does not mean you are absolutely barred from getting a green card or otherwise entering the U.S. Some grounds of inadmissibility may be legally excused or waived. Others may not. But determining how to appeal for a waiver is complicated and you should consult with an attorney if you are in this situation. Recent rulings by the Board of Immigration Appeals make it difficult to clear a crime off your record for immigration purposes, even if, under state law, the record of criminal conviction has been "expunged" or removed.

Below is a chart summarizing the grounds of inadmissibility, whether or not a waiver is available, and the special conditions you must meet in order to get a waiver. For more detail, see I.N.A § 212, 8 U.S.C. §1182.

B. Reversing an Inadmissibility Finding

You may be judged inadmissible at any time after you have filed an application for a green card, nonimmigrant visa, or other immigration status. If you are found inadmissible, your application will be denied. Even if you manage to hide your inadmissibility long enough to receive a green card or visa and be admitted into the U.S., if the problem is ever discovered later, you can be deported.

There are four ways to overcome a finding of inadmissibility:

- In the case of physical or mental illness only, you may be able to correct the condition. Some criminal grounds of inadmissibility can be removed through a court proceeding that sets aside the criminal conviction.
- You can prove that you really don't fall into the category of inadmissibility that USCIS believes you do.
- You can prove that the accusations of inadmissibility against you are false.
- You can apply for a waiver of inadmissibility.

1. Correcting Grounds of Inadmissibility

If you have had a physical or mental illness that is a ground of inadmissibility and you have been cured of the condition by the time you submit your green card application, you will no longer be considered inadmissible for that reason. If the condition is not cured by the time you apply, you may still be eligible for a waiver of inadmissibility.

2. Proving Inadmissibility Does Not Apply

Proving that you're not really inadmissible is mainly useful for overcoming criminal and ideological grounds of inadmissibility. When dealing with criminal grounds of inadmissibility, it is very important to consider both the type of crime committed and the nature of the punishment to see whether your criminal activity really constitutes a ground of inadmissibility. For example, with some criminal activity, only actual convictions are grounds of inadmissibility. If you have been charged with a crime and the charges were then dropped, you may not be inadmissible.

Another example involves crimes of moral turpitude. Crimes of moral turpitude are those showing dishonesty or basically immoral conduct. Commission of acts that constitute a crime of moral turpitude can be a ground of inadmissibility, even with no conviction. Crimes with no element of moral turpitude, however, are often not considered grounds of inadmissibility. Laws differ from state to state

GROUNDS OF INADMISSIBILITY

Ground of Inadmissibility	Waiver Available	Conditions of Waiver
Health Problems		
Persons with communicable diseases of public health significance, in particular tuberculosis and HIV (AIDS).	Yes	Waiver available to the spouse or the unmarried son or daughter or the unmarried minor lawfully adopted child of a U.S. citizen or permanent resident, or of an alien who has been issued an immigrant visa; or to an individual who has a son or daughter who is a U.S. citizen, or a permanent resident, or an alien issued an immigrant visa, upon compliance with USCIS's terms and regulations.
Persons with physical or mental disorders which threaten their own safety or the property, welfare or safety of others.	Yes	Special conditions required by USCIS, at its discretion.
Drug abusers or addicts.	No	(But doesn't include single-use experimentation.)
Persons who fail to show that they have been vaccinated against certain vaccine-preventable diseases.	Yes	The applicant must show either that he or she subsequently received the vaccine; that the vaccine is medically inappropriate as certified by a civil surgeon; or that having the vaccine administered is contrary to the applicant's religious beliefs or moral convictions.
Criminal and Related Violations		
Persons who have committed crimes involving moral turpitude.	Yes	Waivers are not available for commission of crimes such as attempted murder or conspiracy to commit murder, or murder, torture, or drug crimes, except for persons previously admitted as permanent residents, if they have been convicted of aggravated felony since such admission or if they have less than seven years of lawful continuous residence before deportation proceedings are initiated against them. Waivers for all other offenses are available only if the applicant is a spouse, parent, or child of a U.S. citizen or green card holder; or the only criminal activity was prostitution or the actions occurred more than 15 years before the application for a visa or green card is filed and the alien shows that he or she is rehabilitated and is not a threat to U.S. security.
Persons with two or more criminal convictions.	Yes	"
Prostitutes or procurers of prostitutes.	Yes	"
Diplomats or others involved in serious criminal activity who have received immunity from prosecution.	Yes	"
Drug offenders.	No	Except for simple possession of less than 30 grams of marijuana. There may also be an exception for simple possession or use by juvenile offenders.
Drug traffickers.	No	
Immediate family members of drug traffickers who knowingly benefited from the illicit money within the last five years.	No	But note that the problem "washes out" after five years.
National Security and Related Violations		
Spies, governmental saboteurs, or violators of export or technology transfer laws.	No	

GROUNDS OF INADMISSIBILITY

Ground of Inadmissibility	Waiver Available	Conditions of Waiver
Persons intending to overthrow the U.S. government.	No	
Persons intending to engage in unlawful activity.	No	
People subject to special registration who fail to have their departure confirmed and recorded are presumed to fall into this category	No	
Terrorists and members or representatives of foreign terrorist organizations.	No	
Persons whose entry would have adverse consequences for U.S. foreign policy, unless the applicant is an official of a foreign government, or the applicant's activities or beliefs would normally be lawful under the U.S. constitution.	No	
Voluntary members of totalitarian parties.	Yes	An exception is made if the membership was involuntary, or is or was when the applicant was under 16 years old, by operation of law, or for purposes of obtaining employment, food rations, or other "essentials" of living. An exception is also possible for past membership if the membership ended at least two years prior to the application (five years if the party in control of a foreign state is considered a totalitarian dictatorship). If neither applies, a waiver is available for an immigrant who is the parent, spouse, son, daughter, brother, or sister of a U.S. citizen, or a spouse, son, or daughter of a permanent resident.
Nazis	No	
Economic Grounds	No	
Any person who, in the opinion of a USCIS or consular official, is likely to become a "public charge," that is, receive public assistance or welfare in the United States. The official can consider factors such as the person's age, health, family and work history, and previous use of public benefits.	No	However, the applicant may cure the ground of inadmissibility by overcoming the reasons for it or obtaining an Affidavit of Support from a family member or friend.
Family-sponsored immigrants and employment-sponsored immigrants where a family member is the employment sponsor (or such a family member owns 5% of the petitioning business) whose sponsor has not executed an Affidavit of Support (Form I-864).	No	But an applicant may cure the ground of inadmissibility by subsequently satisfying affidavit of support requirements.
Nonimmigrant public benefit recipients (where the individual came as nonimmigrant and applied for benefits when he or she was not eligible or through fraud). Five-year bar to admissibility.	No	But ground of inadmissibility expires after five years.
Labor Certifications and Employment Qualifications		
Persons without approved labor certifications, if one is required in the category under which the green card application is made.	No	But see Chapter 8, for a discussion of the national interest waiver.
Graduates of unaccredited medical schools, whether inside or outside of the U.S., immigrating to the U.S. in a Second or Third Preference category based on their profession, who have not both passed the foreign medical graduates exam and shown proficiency in English. (Physicians qualifying as special immigrants, who have been practicing medicine in the U.S., with a license, since January 9, 1978 are not subject to this exclusion.)	No	

GROUNDS OF INADMISSIBILITY

Ground of Inadmissibility	Waiver Available	Conditions of Waiver
Uncertified foreign healthcare workers seeking entry based on clinical employment in their field (not including physicians).	Yes	But applicant may show qualifications by submitting a certificate from the Commission on Graduates of Foreign Nursing Schools or the equivalent.
Immigration Violators		
Persons who entered the U.S. without inspection by the INS or CBP.	Yes	Available for certain battered women and children who came to the U.S. escaping such battery or who qualify as self-petitioners. Also available for individuals who had visa petitions or labor certifications on file before January 14, 1998 or before April 30, 2001, with proof of physical presence in the U.S. on December 21, 2000. ($1,000 penalty required for latter waiver.) Does not apply to applicants outside of the U.S.
Persons who were deported after a hearing and seek readmission within ten years.	Yes	Discretionary with USCIS.
Persons who have failed to attend removal (deportation) proceedings (unless they had reasonable cause for doing so). Five-year bar to reentry.	Yes	Advance permission to apply for readmission. Discretionary with USCIS.
People who have been summarily excluded from the U.S. and again attempt to enter within five years	Yes	Discretionary with USCIS.
Persons who made misrepresentations during the immigration process.	Yes	The applicant must be the spouse or child of a U.S. citizen or green card holder. A waiver will be granted if the refusal of admission would cause extreme hardship to that relative. Discretionary with USCIS.
Persons who made a false claim to U.S. citizenship.	No	
Individuals subject to a final removal (deportation) order under the Immigration and Naturalization Act §274C (Civil Document Fraud Proceedings).	Yes	Available to permanent residents who voluntarily left the U.S., and for those applying for permanent residence as immediate relatives or based on other family petitions, if the fraud was committed solely to assist the person's spouse or child and provided that no fine was imposed as part of the previous civil proceeding.
Student visa abusers (persons who improperly obtain F-1 status to attend a public elementary school or adult education program, or transfer from a private to a public program except as permitted). Five-year bar to admissibility.	No	
Certain individuals twice removed (deported or removed after aggravated felony). Twenty-year bar to admissibility for those twice deported.	Yes	Discretionary with USCIS (advance permission to apply for readmission).
Individuals unlawfully present (time counted only after April 1, 1997 and after the age of 18). Presence for 180-364 days results in three-year bar to admissibility. Presence for 365 or more days creates ten-year bar to admissibility. Bars kick in only when the individual departs the U.S. and seeks reentry after a period of unlawful presence.	Yes	A waiver is provided for an immigrant who has a U.S. citizen or permanent resident spouse or parent to whom refusal of the application would cause extreme hardship. There is also a complex body of law concerning when a person's presence can be considered "lawful," for example if one has certain applications awaiting decision by USCIS or is protected by battered spouse/child provisions of the immigration laws.

GROUNDS OF INADMISSIBILITY

Ground of Inadmissibility	Waiver Available	Conditions of Waiver
Individuals unlawfully present after previous immigration violations. (Applies to persons who were in the U.S. unlawfully for an aggregate period over one year, who subsequently reenter without being properly admitted. Also applies to anyone ordered removed who subsequently attempts entry without admission.)	No	
Stowaways.	No	This is a permanent ground of inadmissibility. However, after being gone for ten years an applicant can apply for advance permission to reapply for admission.
Smugglers of illegal aliens.	Yes	Waivable if the applicant was smuggling in persons who were immediate family members at the time, and either is a permanent resident or is immigrating under a family-based visa petition as an immediate relative; the unmarried son or daughter of a U.S. citizen or permanent resident; or the spouse of a U.S. permanent resident.

Document Violations

Persons without required current passports or visas.	No	Except certain limited circumstance waivers. Under new "summary removal" procedures, CBP may quickly exclude for five years persons who arrive without proper documents or make misrepresentations during the inspection process.

Draft Evasion and Ineligibility for Citizenship

Persons who are permanently ineligible for citizenship.	No	
Persons who are draft evaders, unless they were U.S. citizens at the time of evasion or desertion.	No	

Miscellaneous Grounds

Practicing polygamists.	No	
Guardians accompanying excludable aliens.	No	
International child abductors. (The exclusion does not apply if the applicant is a national of a country that signed the Hague Convention on International Child Abduction.)	No	
Unlawful voters (voting in violation of any federal, state or local law or regulation).	No	
Former U.S. citizens who renounced citizenship to avoid taxation.	No	

on which crimes are considered to involve moral turpitude and which are not.

Still other factors that may help you are the brevity of any prison terms, how long ago the crime was committed, the number of convictions in your background, conditions of plea bargaining, and available pardons. Sometimes a conviction can be "vacated" if you can show it was unlawfully obtained or you were not advised of its immigration consequences, though under recent case law, USCIS may refuse to recognize this.

As you can see, proving that a criminal ground of inadmissibility does not apply in your case is a complicated business. You need to have a firm grasp not only of immigration law, but the technicalities of criminal law as well. If you have a criminal problem in your past, you may be able to get a green card, but not without the help of an experienced immigration lawyer.

3. Proving a Finding of Inadmissibility Is Factually Incorrect

When your green card or nonimmigrant visa application is denied because you are found inadmissible, you can try to prove that the finding of inadmissibility is factually incorrect. For example, if a USCIS medical examination shows that you have certain medical problems, you can present reports from other doctors stating that the first diagnosis was wrong and that you are free of the problem condition. If you are accused of lying on a visa application, you can present evidence proving you told the truth, or that any false statements were made unintentionally.

C. Particularly Troublesome Grounds of Inadmissibility

Below is a discussion of some of the grounds which have the most significant impact on those planning to immigrate and/or obtain nonimmigrant visas.

1. Affidavit of Support Required for Family-Based Petitions

Most family-based immigrants (and employment-based immigrants where the applicant's relatives submitted the visa petition or own at least 5% of the petitioning company) must submit an affidavit of support on Form I-864, signed by the petitioner, in order to apply for permanent residence. This form also satisfies or helps the immigrant show that he or she is not likely to become a public charge. Note that this form is not required for other employment-based petitions or nonimmigrant visas.

There are two exceptions to the Form I-864 requirement. First, if the immigrant beneficiary has already worked in the U.S. for a total of 40 "quarters" (as defined by the Social Security Administration) or about ten years, no I-864 needs to be submitted on his or her behalf. Second, if the immigrant beneficiary is a child who will become a U.S. citizen immediately upon approval or entry to the U.S. for a green card (as discussed in Chapter 27) no I-864 needs to be submitted on his or her behalf.

The requirements for this affidavit of support are very different from those of its predecessor, Form I-134. The newer form is legally enforceable by the government for any means-tested public benefits utilized by the sponsored immigrant. It is also enforceable by the immigrant family member against the sponsor for support. And it requires that the sponsor show that he or she has at least 125% of income for a similar family size, according to the federal Poverty Guidelines.

The person who is sponsoring the immigrant petition must file Form I-864 even if his or her income doesn't meet the Poverty Guidelines level. However, another person (a "joint sponsor") may add her income to the sponsor's if she meets the 125% income requirement for her own household and she is:

- willing to be jointly liable
- a U.S. legal permanent resident or citizen
- over 18 years old, and
- residing in the U.S.

The joint sponsor files a separate Form I-864.

In addition, other household members may join their income to that of the main sponsor to help reach the 125% level, but only if they have been living with the sponsor for six months and they agree to be jointly liable by filing form I-864A ("Contract Between Sponsor and Household Member").

Personal assets of the sponsor or the immigrant (such as property, bank account deposits, and personal property such as automobiles) may also be used to supplement the sponsor's income, if the primary sponsor's actual income does not add up to 125% of the federal Poverty Guidelines. The assets (minus any debts or liens) will only be counted at one-fifth their value.

Sponsors must also notify USCIS within 30 days of the sponsor's change of address, using Form I-865. Failure to do so is punishable by fines of $250-$5,000.

If you are a sponsor and have questions about meeting the eligibility or the scope of your legal responsibility (which may last ten or more years or until the immigrant permanently leaves the country, dies, or naturalizes) consult an immigration attorney.

2. Summary Exclusion Law

The summary exclusion law empowers a Customs and Border Protection (CBP) inspector at the airport or other entry point to summarily (without allowing judicial review) exclude and deport someone requesting admission to the U.S. if either of the following are true:

- The inspector thinks you are making a misrepresentation about practically anything connected to your right to enter the U.S., such as your purpose in coming, intent to return, or prior immigration history. This includes the use or suspected use of false documents.
- You do not have the proper documentation to support your entry to the U.S. in the category you are requesting.

If the inspector excludes you, you may not request entry for five years, unless a special waiver is granted. (This will not be applied to persons entering under the Visa Waiver Program, according to a 1999 decision by the Board of Immigration Appeals.) For this reason it is extremely important to understand the terms of your requested status and to not make any misrepresentations. If the inspector intends to find you inadmissible, you may request to withdraw your application to enter the U.S. in order to prevent having the five-year order on your record. The CBP may allow you to do so in some cases.

3. Bars to Getting Your Green Card in the U.S. ("Adjusting Status")

The rules concerning who is allowed to adjust status (get your green card in the U.S. without having to go through an overseas consulate) are complicated. If you entered the U.S. properly—by being inspected by a USCIS official—and maintained your nonimmigrant status (in particular, didn't let your visa expire or do anything unauthorized), you can probably get your green card without leaving the U.S. Most persons who marry U.S. citizens or are the parent or unmarried child, under age 21, of a U.S. citizen can adjust their status even if they have fallen out of status or worked without authorization, as long as they did not enter without being properly inspected, or as a crewman or stowaway. All others need to use the penalty and grandfather clause.

a. The Penalty and Grandfather Clauses

If you are out of status, have worked without authorization or entered the U.S. without inspection, you can apply for adjustment only if you are grandfathered, or included within the old rule (§245(i)), which allowed adjustment of otherwise ineligible applicants who paid the $1,000 penalty fee. The old penalty law expired in the fall of 1997.

Presently, the only people who may still adjust status by paying a penalty are those who had a visa petition or Labor Certification on file by January 14, 1998, as well as those whose visa petition or Labor Certification was on file by April 30, 2001, and who can also prove that they were in the U.S. on December 21, 2000. (Unmarried children younger than 17 years old and the spouses or unmarried children younger than 21 years old of legalized aliens who are qualified for and have applied for benefits under the Family Unity program do not have to pay the penalty fee.)

b. Special Exception for Certain Employment-Based Green Card Applicants

If you are getting your green card through the First, Second, or Third Preference employment category (as a priority worker, advanced degree professional, person of exceptional ability, or skilled worker, professional, or other worker) or as a special immigrant, you can have worked without authorization or fallen out of status for up to 180 days and still apply to adjust status.

This exception applies only if at the time of filing the green card application, your last entry to the U.S. was legal, you have maintained continuous legal status, and you have not violated the terms of your status or other terms of admission, other than during a 180-day aggregate period.

4. Unlawful Presence and the Overstay Bars

People become inadmissible if they are "unlawfully present" in the U.S. for six months after April 1, 1997, subsequently leave the U.S., and then seek admission by applying for an immigrant or nonimmigrant visa from overseas. Such persons are subject to a three-year waiting period before they can return to the U.S.; the period is ten years if they were unlawfully present for one year or more after April 1, 1997.

This bar does not apply to someone who stays in the U.S. to adjust status—so anyone eligible to adjust status should take advantage of this and not leave the U.S. until they get their green card.

a. What Is Unlawful Presence?

If you have no choice but to apply for your green card overseas, through consular processing, it will become very important to calculate exactly how many of the days you spent in the U.S. were "unlawful." It is actually easier to say what unlawful presence isn't than what it is. You will not be found to be unlawfully present for purposes of the three- and ten-year bars:

- for time spent under the age of 18
- for time spent as a bona fide asylum applicant (including time while administrative or judicial review

is pending), unless you were employed without authorization

- for time spent under Family Unity protection
- for time spent as a battered spouse or child who shows a substantial connection between the status violation or unlawful entry and the abuse, or
- for time spent after you were lawfully admitted but were waiting for a USCIS decision on a valid and timely filed application for change or extension of status (as long as you did not work without authorization), but only up to a maximum of 120 days.

Furthermore, the following persons present in the U.S. will not have time counted as unlawful presence:

- persons with properly filed applications for adjustment of status who have their applications pending with USCIS
- aliens admitted to the U.S. as refugees
- aliens granted asylum
- certain aliens granted withholding of deportation/removal
- aliens present under a current grant of Deferred Enforced Departure (DED)
- certain aliens under a current grant of Temporary Protected Status (TPS), and
- certain Cuban-Haitian entrants.

b. Special Rules About Unlawful Presence

As you work on counting up your unlawful presence, you'll also need to factor in the following rules:

- No period of time prior to April 1, 1997, counts toward unlawful presence for overstay bar purposes.
- Periods of unlawful presence are not counted in the aggregate for purposes of the three- and ten-year bars—in order words, you have to be present for a block of time which constitutes six or 12 months; USCIS will not add up three months during one stay and three months during another stay to find that you were unlawfully present for six months.
- An alien admitted for "duration of status" ("D/S") (such as a student or exchange visitor) will begin to accrue unlawful presence only if either an immigration judge finds the alien has violated status and is deportable, or, USCIS, in the course of adjudicating an application, determines that a status violation has occurred.
- An alien admitted until a specified date will begin to accrue unlawful presence either when the date on the I-94 (or any extension) has passed, or if USCIS or an immigration judge makes a finding of a status violation, whichever comes first.

- Where the unlawful presence determination is based on a USCIS or immigration judge finding of a status violation, the unlawful presence clock starts to run from the date determined to be when the status violation began.
- A grant of voluntary departure (V/D or V/R for "voluntary return") constitutes a period of authorized stay. This includes the period between the date of the V/D order and the date by which the alien must depart. If the alien fails to depart by the date specified in the V/D order, the unlawful presence clock starts running.

c. Aliens Not Considered to Be in a Period of Stay

The following persons are unlawfully present for overstay bar purposes:

- aliens under an order of supervision
- aliens granted deferred action status
- aliens with pending applications for cancellation of removal
- aliens with pending applications for withholding of removal
- aliens issued voluntary departure prior to, during or following proceedings
- aliens granted satisfactory departure, and
- aliens in federal court litigation.

d. Waiver of Three- or Ten-Year Waiting Periods

There is a waiver available for persons who are the spouse, son, or daughter of a U.S. citizen or permanent resident, if the applicant can show that being kept out of the U.S. for three or ten years would cause the U.S. citizen extreme hardship. Note that hardship to the immigrant applicant doesn't count.

Extreme hardship usually means more hardship than is normally experienced by family separation; economic hardship is not usually sufficient to meet this requirement. These waivers are hard to get; see a lawyer for help.

5. Changes in Availability of the Fraud Waiver

Prior to the enactment of the Immigration Reform Act of 1996, children could serve as qualifying relatives for parents who needed a waiver for having made misrepresentations or using false documents. The fraud waiver is now only available to applicants whose U.S. citizen or permanent resident spouse or parent would, if the waiver were denied, suffer extreme hardship.

6. False Citizenship Claims and Illegal Voting

Congress also added new inadmissibility categories for which there is no waiver at all. This includes making a false claim that one is a U.S. citizen for the purpose of obtaining immigration benefits or to get benefits under any state or federal law, or voting illegally in a federal, state, or local election.

7. Special Rules in Asylum-Based Green Card Applications

The rules and grounds of inadmissibility are different for asylum than for other green card applications. Some grounds of inadmissibility, including public charge, affidavit of support, Labor Certification, and documentary requirements, do not even apply to a refugee or asylee applicant for permanent residence.

Most other grounds of inadmissibility are waivable if the person can show USCIS that it would be in the public interest, humanitarian interests, or would assure family unity to grant the waiver. This means that the asylee or refugee applicant does not need to have one of the special qualifying relatives (spouse or parent) to get a green card, assuming that there is a ground of inadmissibility which requires a waiver.

8. The Permanent Bar for Illegal Entry and Unlawful Presence

In addition to the three- and ten-year bars described above, a separate and more serious provision punishes certain people who've entered the U.S. illegally. If illegal entrants spend a total of one year's unlawful time in the U.S. or are ordered deported by an immigration judge (even after spending less than one year in the U.S.), and they then leave and return or attempt to return to the United States illegally, they become permanently inadmissible. This so-called permanent bar is found at I.N.A. §212(a)(9)(C), 8 U.S.C. §1182(a)(9)(C).

Unlike the three- and ten-year time bars, you can accumulate a year's unlawful time through various short stays— your unlawful time doesn't have to be continuous to count against you. Like the three- and ten-year bars, however, no unlawful time before April 1, 1997 (the date the law took effect) counts.

> EXAMPLE: Maria lived in the U.S. illegally from 1995 to 2001, when she returned to Mexico. In 2002, she illegally crossed the border to the U.S., met a U.S. citizen with whom she fell in love, and got married in 2003. When she tried to apply for a green card based on her marriage,

however, she was told that she was permanently barred from applying. The reason: She had spent more than a year in the U.S. illegally after April 1, 1997, then left and returned by entering illegally.

There is a waiver you can request if you're otherwise eligible for a green card, but only after a full ten years have passed since leaving the U.S.

D. Applying for a Waiver

By obtaining a waiver, you don't eliminate or disprove the ground of inadmissibility. Instead you ask USCIS to overlook the problem and give you a green card or visa anyway.

All green card and visa application forms ask questions designed to find out if any grounds of inadmissibility apply in your case. When the answers to the questions on these forms clearly show that you are inadmissible, you may be authorized to begin applying for a waiver immediately upon filing your application. In most cases, however, the consulate or USCIS office insists on having your final visa interview before ruling that you are inadmissible. If the USCIS office or consulate handling your case decides to wait until your final interview before finding you inadmissible, it will delay your ability to file for a waiver. This may in turn greatly delay your getting a green card or visa. Waivers can take many months to process.

Once it is determined that a waiver is necessary, you will be given Form I-601 to complete and file with a $170 filing fee. The form and fee are just the beginning of the waiver application process, however. For USCIS to evaluate your case, it will also need to see convincing evidence that you deserve the waiver. For example, in cases where your eligibility depends on having a "qualifying relative," you'd need to include a birth or marriage certificate showing that you are truly related to that person, as well as proof that your relative is a U.S. citizen or permanent resident. In a medical waiver, you'd normally need to prove that your health costs will be covered and that the nature of your condition and your personal behavior make it unlikely that you'll pass the disease to others.

Note that if you file your waiver application with a U.S. consulate abroad, you will have to wait for the consulate to send your application to a USCIS office. The consulate cannot approve the waiver.

Once again, there are many technical factors that control whether or not a waiver of inadmissibility is granted. If you want to get one approved, you stand the best chance of success by hiring a good immigration lawyer. ∎

Naturalization: Becoming a U.S. Citizen

Privileges

- You can carry a U.S. passport.
- As a U.S. citizen, you cannot be deported or lose your citizenship even if you commit a crime or choose to live elsewhere in the world, unless you misrepresented yourself to get citizenship or were ineligible at the time.
- As a U.S. citizen, you can petition for the green cards of close relatives.
- You can pass on U.S. citizenship to your children, both those who are already born and those born after your naturalization.
- You become eligible to vote.

Limitations

- If, after you have become a naturalized citizen, it is discovered that you were not eligible for naturalization or that you were not really eligible for a green card when you acquired it, then your citizenship will be revoked and you may be subject to deportation.
- You may have to renounce the citizenship of your home country when taking the citizenship oath, depending on the laws of your home country regarding dual citizenship.

A. Who Qualifies to Naturalize?

Except in rare cases, no one can become a naturalized U.S. citizen without first getting a green card. To qualify for citizenship, you must have held the green card and been physically present in the U.S. for a certain period of time. You should also be a person of good moral character (see Section 5, below), have a knowledge of the English language, and be familiar with U.S. government and history. You must be attached to the principles of the U.S. Constitution, and be willing to take an oath of allegiance to the United States. In addition, you must be at least 18 years of age.

Children under age 18 who hold green cards may be naturalized if they have a U.S. citizen parent. No specific period of residency is required. (See Chapter 27.)

Most people, in order to qualify for naturalization, are required to have held green cards for a minimum of five years. At least one-half of that time must be spent physically inside U.S. boundaries. You must also show that your five-year period of permanent residence has not been interrupted by substantial time spent abroad. If you leave the country and remain absent for a year or more, this wipes out any time counted toward the five-year total and you must start adding up your time all over again. Even worse, USCIS could find that you abandoned your U.S. residence altogether, and take your green card away. Absences of less than six months do not affect the five-year waiting period.

Absences of less than one year but more than six months may also wipe out your accumulated time, unless you can prove that your absence did not interrupt your continuous residence. You can show that you did not interrupt your continuous residence by submitting documents that show, for example: that you maintained your employment in the U.S. during the absence; that your immediate family remained in the U.S.; that you maintained full access to your U.S. home; or that you did not obtain employment while abroad. If USCIS believes such documents show that you in fact maintained continuous residence, you will be able to count that time toward the five-year period.

If you are married to a U.S. citizen, you need only to have held a green card for a minimum of three years to qualify for naturalization. If you had a "conditional" green card for the first two years, this counts toward the three years. You must have been married to the citizen for all three years.

Asylees need wait only four years from the date of their approval for permanent residence (green card). Refugees need wait only five years from the date they entered the U.S., regardless of when they obtained their permanent residence. At least half that time must have been spent physically inside U.S. boundaries. The rules about long absences that apply to those with five-year waiting periods apply to those with three- and four-year waiting periods as well.

If your U.S.-citizen spouse is employed abroad by the U.S. government, and you will be leaving to join him or her abroad, there is no waiting period and no required residency period to get U.S. citizenship. You may apply for naturalization as soon as you receive your green card.

⚠️ **The decision to file for naturalization is not a simple one.** An applicant should consider first whether there could be a problem of inadmissibility or a defect in their original permanent resident status. Filing an application for naturalization could cause the discovery of legal problems in permanent residency status, causing USCIS to start deportation or removal proceedings.

1. Local Residence Requirement

To qualify for naturalization, in addition to having lived in the U.S. for the necessary time period, you must have resided for at least three months within the state or USCIS district where you file your application. If you should move out of the state or district while your naturalization application is pending, the application may be transferred to your new district, but you will have to live there for three months before you are eligible to naturalize.

2. When Can You File?

Because of long delays in naturalization processing at many USCIS offices, you are permitted to file a naturalization application up to three months before your required period of U.S. residency has been completed. If you file even earlier, USCIS will send back your application for you to refile later.

3. Special Benefits for Former Members of the U.S. Armed Forces

Special laws often apply to non-Americans who once actively served in the U.S. armed forces. In some cases, these laws eliminate the residence and waiting period requirements applicable to most green card holders. In certain situations, ex-military personnel may even be able to become naturalized U.S. citizens without first getting green cards.

The types of naturalization benefits available to you as a former member of the U.S. armed forces are controlled by the particular war in which you fought and the time period during which you served in that war. The list of wars and military units that qualify you for special citizenship benefits is long. If you ever served in a U.S. military unit, check with a consulate to see what benefits are available to you based

on your former U.S. military activities; or see *Becoming a U.S. Citizen: A Guide to the Law, Exam & Interview,* by Ilona Bray (Nolo).

POSTHUMOUS CITIZENSHIP FOR SOLDIERS KILLED IN ACTION

The law allows family members of noncitizens who died from injury or disease caused during active duty with the U.S. Armed Forces during specified periods of military hostilities—most recently, the war in Iraq—to apply for citizenship for their dead relative. To apply, fill out and send Form N-644, together with a $60 fee, to the USCIS Service Center that handles your geographical area. Form N-644, and more detailed instructions, are available on the USCIS website at www.uscis.gov.

Posthumous citizenship is an honorary status commemorating the person's bravery and sacrifice; it does not convey any immigration benefits. In particular, it does not allow family members of the deceased soldier to apply for green cards or other immigration status as the relative of a U.S. citizen.

---

4. Showing Good Moral Character

You don't need to do a lot to prove your good moral character to USCIS—although if you've been active in community or religious organizations, mentioning these in the appropriate part of the application will help show your good character. The most important thing, however, is to show that you haven't demonstrated bad moral character.

People believed to have demonstrated bad moral character within the last five years are ineligible to become naturalized U.S. citizens. The definition of "moral character" is a complicated one, but individuals are barred from showing good moral character during the five-year period preceding the application if they:

- committed one or more crimes of moral turpitude (such as theft or crimes involving dishonesty, fraud, or malice)
- were convicted of an aggravated felony after November 20, 1990
- were convicted of murder at any time
- were convicted of two or more offenses, and the combined sentences add up to at least five years
- violated any law relating to a controlled substance, except for a single offense for posession of marijuana of 30 grams or less

- were confined to a jail or prison a total of 180 days or more, or
- have given false testimony to obtain any benefits under immigration laws, if made under oath and with the purpose of obtaining those benefits.

Various other acts also serve to bar the applicant from naturalization if they were committed during the five-year period, including involvement in prostitution or commercialized vice, practicing polygamy, illegal gambling, habitual alcoholism, and in most cases, willful failure to support dependents or having an extramarital affair that destroyed an existing marriage.

USCIS may use other acts or information not included in this list to find that an applicant lacks "good moral character." USCIS will not approve an application while the applicant is on probation or parole, but that does not in itself serve as a bar to eligibility. Finally, if an applicant falls into one of the above moral turpitude categories but it is outside the five-year period before the application, USCIS may still consider it in deciding the moral character issue. If the applicant can show he or she has reformed since the act or conviction, and there are no new bad acts during the five-year period, the application can be approved.

Receiving welfare or public benefits in the years before you apply for citizenship does not affect the determination of your good moral character unless you used fraud to obtain those benefits. Unlike your application for lawful permanent residence, you can't be denied citizenship simply because you are likely to become a "public charge."

Applicants who have one or more of these good moral character issues should see an immigration attorney before filing a naturalization application, since by applying for naturalization you bring yourself to the attention of USCIS. If you are ineligible, you risk being deported, in addition to having your application denied.

B. The Application

Naturalization is a one-step application process, followed by an interview. The papers for this application are filed at the USCIS service center having jurisdiction over your place of residence in the U.S. If you are one of those people entitled to naturalization without fulfilling a U.S. residency requirement and you live outside the U.S., you may apply at any USCIS office you choose.

After your application is processed, you will be called for an interview at the USCIS office nearest you. Depending on where in the U.S. you filed your application, you will probably have to wait more than a year before your interview is scheduled.

At the interview, you will be tested on your knowledge of U.S. history and government. You must also be able to show that you can read, write, and speak English. The requirements of reading and writing English are waived for anyone who is over the age of 50 and has been a permanent resident of the U.S. for at least 20 years. The English requirements are also waived for anyone who has been a permanent resident of the U.S. for at least 15 years and is over the age of 55.

If you are over 65 and have lived in the U.S. as a permanent resident for at least 20 years, you can also take an easier version of the history and government test, featuring only 25 potential questions instead of the usual 100.

USCIS is also required to accommodate people with disabilities. If the disability prevents you from learning English or U.S. history and government, you can, with the help of your doctor, apply for a waiver of these requirements.

1. General Procedures

Your completed application, consisting of forms and documents, is filed at the USCIS service center having jurisdiction over your place of residence. Although all naturalization applications were previously filed at local USCIS offices or suboffices, USCIS changed this procedure. The forms must be filed with the service center by mail.

You will be called to the local USCIS office for fingerprinting first, and later for an interview. After you are fingerprinted, USCIS will send the prints to the FBI and will schedule your interview only after the FBI check is completed.

The current filing fee for the application is $260 plus $50 for fingerprint processing. If you're over age 79, you need not submit the $50, because you won't be fingerprinted. If you file in person, ask for a receipt so that you can later prove on what date your application was submitted. The receipt number will also help to locate your file should it get lost or delayed in processing. When filing by mail, send the papers by certified mail, return receipt requested. In either case, keep a complete copy of everything sent or filed, for your records.

2. Where to File

Mail your citizenship application to the service center with jurisdiction over your place of residence, as follows:

If you live in Arizona, California, Hawaii, or Nevada mail your application to:

USCIS California Service Center
Attention N-400 Unit
P.O. Box 10400
Laguna Niguel, CA 92607-0400

If you live in Alaska, Colorado, Idaho, Illinois, Indiana, Iowa, Kansas, Michigan, Minnesota, Missouri, Montana, Nebraska, North Dakota, Ohio, Oregon, South Dakota, Utah, Washington, Wisconsin, or Wyoming mail your application to:

USCIS Nebraska Service Center
Attention N-400 Unit
P.O. Box 87400
Lincoln, NE 68501-7400

If you live in Connecticut, Delaware, Maine, Maryland, Massachusetts, New Hampshire, New Jersey, New York, Pennsylvania, Puerto Rico, Rhode Island, Vermont, Virginia, Washington, DC, West Virginia, or the Virgin Islands, mail your application to:

USCIS Vermont Service Center
Attention N-400 Unit
75 Lower Weldon Street
St. Albans, VT 05479-0001

If you live in Alabama, Arkansas, Florida, Georgia, Kentucky, Louisiana, Mississippi, New Mexico, North Carolina, Oklahoma, South Carolina, Tennessee, or Texas mail your application to:

USCIS Texas Service Center
Attention N-400 Unit
P.O. Box 851204
Mesquite, TX 75185-1204

3. Forms

Copies of all the required USCIS forms can be found in Appendix II and on the USCIS website.

Form N-400

The application for naturalization is started by filing Form N-400. All questions on this form are self-explanatory. You will remember that in order to become a naturalized citizen, you must be at least 18 years of age. Therefore, your minor children cannot be naturalized with you. However, after you are naturalized, they can apply for what are known as certificates of citizenship.

This form also asks for a complete history of all your absences from the U.S. since getting your green card. If you have made a great number of brief trips, such as might be the case if you live near the Canadian or Mexican borders, you may put down "numerous brief trips."

Do your best, however, to approximate the dates, or at least the years. Alternately, you could mention a time of

year, like "Regular trips around my mother's birthday in May." You can expect detailed questions about the length of your trips at your naturalization interview.

If you have been away from the U.S. for more than six months at a time, there is a presumption that you gave up your U.S. residence for naturalization purposes. This does not necessarily mean that you lost your green card, but it does mean that the three- or five-year residency requirement starts over again. Before filing again, you would then have to wait another four years and a day from your return to the U.S. if you need five years to qualify for naturalization; and two years and a day from your return to the U.S. if you need three years to qualify.

If you were away at any time for one year or more, you normally lose your U.S. residency for naturalization purposes. In addition, you risk being found to have abandoned your residence altogether, in which case your green card could be taken away from you and you could be placed in removal proceedings.

4. Documents

You will be required to submit a copy of your green card (both sides) and three color immigration-type photographs. Instructions for photographs may be found in Appendix II (Form M-378). No other specific documentation is required unless you wish to qualify for particular exceptions or waivers. When you go to the USCIS office for the personal interview, you will be asked to bring your green card and sometimes the marriage certificate and divorce decrees of you and your spouse and previous spouses, if any. USCIS offices differ in their policies concerning what documents you are expected to bring with you. You will be told exactly what is expected on your notice to appear for the interview.

5. The Naturalization Test and Interview

Several months to a year or more after you file your naturalization application, USCIS will send you a written notice to appear for an interview. If you have not already passed an approved U.S. citizenship examination as a participant in the amnesty program, you will be tested on your knowledge of U.S. government and history at your interview. You may want to consider enrolling in an accredited citizenship class, frequently given by local high schools or community colleges. If you are over age 65 and have held a green card for at least 20 years, the test will include fewer possible questions; see www.uscis.gov/graphics/services/natz/6520q.pdf for the list. You may also choose to take the test in your own language.

USCIS uses a standardized test for naturalization, but you may be asked only some of the questions. The USCIS officer can exercise discretion on what to ask. Here are some typical questions:

- When did the U.S. declare its independence from England?
- What do the stripes on the U.S. flag represent?
- What is the name of the form of government used in the U.S.?
- What are the three branches of the U.S. government and the function of each?
- What special name is given to the first ten amendments to the U.S. Constitution, and what are some of the special rights granted by these amendments?
- How many members are there in the U.S. House of Representatives and in the U.S. Senate? How long are each of their terms of office?
- Who are the U.S. senators from your state?
- Who is the secretary of state?
- Where is the capital of your state?
- Who is the governor of your state?
- Who is the U.S. representative from your congressional district?
- Who elects the president of the United States?
- How long is the term of office of the president?
- If both the president and vice president should die in office, who becomes president?
- How many justices sit on the Supreme Court?
- What is the name of the national anthem and who wrote it?
- What were some of the reasons for the American Civil War?

A complete set of the 100 possible questions can be found on the USCIS website at www.uscis.gov/graphics/services/natz/100q.pdf.

As the USCIS officer reviews your application and asks you the history and government questions, he or she will be listening to, and therefore testing, your English language ability. In addition, you will be asked to write a short sentence in English, such as "He has a very big dog." See www.uscis.gov/graphics/services/natz/natzsamp.htm for a list of sample sentences. Many people are denied citizenship because they spent so much time memorizing the 100 questions that they forgot to work on their written English skills.

At your naturalization interview, USCIS may also look into any other factors that might indicate that you are ineligible for naturalization. Technically, USCIS is required to investigate your eligibility prior to your interview date so any problem issues can be discussed at that time. However, some USCIS offices put off this investigation until after you

have taken the naturalization test. If the procedure at the USCIS office where you filed your application is to delay the investigation until after the test, and some ground of ineligibility is then discovered, you may be asked to submit more documents by mail or be called back for a second interview on the question of your eligibility. Current procedures require USCIS to make a decision on your application within four months after your interview.

Once you have passed your test and it has been established that you are eligible for naturalization, your application will be approved. If you do not pass the exam, you will be given an opportunity to take it again a few months later.

6. Swearing-In Ceremony

To finally become a citizen you must be sworn in. This involves taking an oath to maintain allegiance to the United States and uphold the U.S. Constitution. Most ceremonies are administrative, meaning you will not go before a judge. In certain circumstances, however, judicial naturalizations take place.

The swearing-in ceremony is normally a happy occasion. When it is completed, you will be a U.S. citizen. Any of your children under the age of 18 who hold green cards, although they are not old enough to be sworn in themselves, will automatically become U.S. citizens too, as long as they live with you.

7. Appeals

If your application is denied, you will be given a written decision stating the reasons. You may file an appeal directly with USCIS. Previously, appeals were handled by the courts rather than administratively through USCIS. If your application is denied, USCIS will provide you with instructions and necessary forms for filing an appeal.

Another option is to address the underlying problem and then reapply for naturalization. Reapplying is often easier than convincing USCIS it was wrong the first time.

If your administrative appeal is unsuccessful, you may file another appeal with a federal court. Do not attempt a naturalization appeal without a lawyer. Unless your naturalization is being denied only because you failed the exam or did not have the required residence in the U.S., denial could jeopardize your green card status as well.

For more detailed information on naturalization, including eligibility, the application process and special exceptions and waivers, see *Becoming a U.S. Citizen: A Guide to the Law, Exam & Interview*, by Ilona Bray (Nolo). ■

Discovering Claims to U.S. Citizenship

A. Who Qualifies for U.S. Citizenship?

U.S. citizenship can be obtained in one of four ways:
- birth in the U.S.
- birth to U.S. citizen parents ("acquisition")
- naturalization, or
- citizenship or naturalization of parents after obtaining a green card ("derivation").

If you were born on U.S. soil, became a naturalized U.S. citizen or were born to U.S. citizen parents, and you have been living in the U.S., the fact that you have U.S. citizenship is probably clear-cut. However, many people born or living outside the U.S. are already U.S. citizens but don't know it.

Some of these people were born in the U.S. but have lived most of their lives in other countries. They may now believe that their long absence from the U.S. and voting or military activities elsewhere have stripped them of U.S. citizenship.

Another group is made up of people who have U.S. citizens in their direct line of ancestry. These people don't realize that even though they were born elsewhere and their U.S. ancestors have not lived in the U.S. for a long time, U.S. citizenship may have still been passed down the line.

The members of still another group do live in the U.S. They are children of U.S. citizens who don't realize that minor children with green cards can acquire citizenship automatically without naturalization.

1. Birth in the U.S.

Under U.S. law, a child born on U.S. soil automatically acquires U.S. citizenship unless the child is born to a foreign government official who is in the U.S. as a recognized diplomat. Anyone born with U.S. citizenship will retain it for life unless he or she performs some act to intentionally lose it, such as filing an oath of renunciation.

2. Acquisition of Citizenship Through Birth to U.S. Citizen Parents

In many circumstances, even though a child is born outside the U.S., if at least one parent was a U.S. citizen at the time of the child's birth, he or she automatically "acquires" U.S.

citizenship. When this child marries and has children, those children may also acquire U.S. citizenship at birth.

The laws governing whether or not a child born outside U.S. boundaries acquires U.S. citizenship from his or her parents have changed several times. The law that was in effect on the date of the child's birth determines whether he or she acquired U.S. citizenship from a parent or grandparent. If there is anyone in your direct line of ancestry whom you believe may be a U.S. citizen, it is worth your time to read what the U.S. laws were on the date of your birth and theirs.

Most laws controlling the passage of U.S. citizenship from parent to child require that the parent, the child or both have a period of residence in the U.S. Sometimes the residence is required to be for a specified length of time and sometimes it is not. When the law doesn't say exactly how long the residence period must be, you can assume that even a brief time, such as a month, might be enough. The key element is often not the amount of time but whether or not USCIS or the consulate believes it was a residence and not a visit. If the period of stay has the character of a residence, the length of time doesn't matter.

a. Prior to May 24, 1934

Before 1934, the law provided that only U.S. citizen fathers could pass citizenship on to their children. The rules were very simple. In order to pass on U.S. citizenship, the father must have resided in the U.S. at some time before the child's birth. The length of the residence and the time it took place were not specified. Technically, a day or a week would be enough if it could be regarded as a residence and not just a visit. Once a child obtained U.S. citizenship at birth through a U.S. citizen father, under the law at this time there were no conditions to retaining it. These rules also applied to illegitimate children, provided the U.S. citizen father had at some time, legally legitimated the child. U.S. citizenship was then acquired at the time of legitimation, without regard to the child's age.

This law has been challenged several times as discriminatory, with some courts holding that citizenship could also be passed by the mother to the children. Congress finally addressed this issue in 1994 and amended the law, retroactively, to provide that either parent could pass his or her U.S. citizenship to children.

Consider that if you were born before May 24, 1934 and either of your parents was a U.S. citizen, that citizenship might have been passed on to you. Consider also, that if either of your parents was born before May 24, 1934, they may have acquired U.S. citizenship from either of their parents which they then passed on to you under laws in existence at a later date. A check of the family tree may well be worth your while.

b.   May 25, 1934 to January 12, 1941

If you were born between May 25, 1934 and January 12, 1941, you acquired U.S. citizenship at birth on the conditions that both your parents were U.S. citizens and at least one had resided in the U.S. prior to your birth. The law at this time placed no additional conditions on retaining U.S. citizenship acquired in this way.

You could also get U.S. citizenship if only one of your parents was a U.S. citizen, as long as that parent had a prior U.S. residence. If your U.S. citizenship came from only one parent, you too would have been required to reside in the U.S. for at least two years between the ages of 14 and 28 in order to retain the citizenship you got at birth. Alternately, you could retain citizenship if your non-citizen parent naturalized before you turned 18 and you began living in the U.S. permanently before age 18. Otherwise, your citizenship would be lost. If the one U.S. citizen parent was your father and your birth was illegitimate, the same rules applied provided your father legally legitimated you. Citizenship was passed at the time of legitimation without regard to your age, provided you had met the retention requirements.

c.   January 13, 1941 to December 23, 1952

If you were born between January 13, 1941 and December 23, 1952, both your parents were U.S. citizens and at least one had a prior residence in the U.S., you automatically acquired U.S. citizenship at birth, with no conditions to retaining it.

If only one parent was a U.S. citizen, that parent must have resided in the U.S. for at least ten years prior to your birth, and at least five of those years must have been after your parent reached the age of 16. With a parent thus qualified, you then acquired U.S. citizenship at birth, but with conditions for retaining it. To keep your citizenship, you must have resided in the U.S. for at least two years between the ages of 14 and 28. Alternately, you could retain citizen-

ship if your non-citizen parent naturalized before you turned 18 and you began living in the U.S. permanently before age 18. As a result of a U.S. Supreme Court decision, if you were born after October 9, 1952, your parent still had to fulfill the residence requirement in order to confer citizenship on you, but your own residence requirements for retaining U.S. citizenship were abolished. If your one U.S. citizen parent was your father and your birth was illegitimate, the same rules applied provided you were legally legitimated prior to your 21st birthday and you were unmarried at the time of legitimation.

d.   December 24, 1952 to November 13, 1986

If at the time of your birth both your parents were U.S. citizens and at least one had a prior residence in the U.S., you automatically acquired U.S. citizenship, with no other conditions for retaining it.

If only one parent was a U.S. citizen at the time of your birth, that parent must have resided in the U.S. for at least ten years, and at least five of those years must have been after your parent reached the age of 16. To retain your citizenship, you must have resided in the U.S. for two years between ages 14 and 28. If your one U.S. citizen parent is your father and your birth was illegitimate, the same rules apply provided you were legally legitimated prior to your 21st birthday and you were unmarried at the time of legitimation.

e.   November 14, 1986 to Present

If at the time of your birth, both your parents were U.S. citizens and at least one had a prior residence in the U.S., you automatically acquired U.S. citizenship, with no conditions for retaining it.

If only one parent was a U.S. citizen at the time of your birth, that parent must have resided in the U.S. for at least five years and at least two of those years must have been after your parent reached the age of 14. Even with only one U.S. citizen parent, there are still no conditions to retaining your citizenship. If your one U.S. citizen parent is your father and your birth was illegitimate, the same rules apply provided you were legally legitimated prior to your 18th birthday. Additionally, your father must have established paternity prior to your 18th birthday, either by acknowledgment, or by court order, and must have stated, in writing, that he would support you financially until your 18th birthday.

3.   Exception to Requirements for Retaining Citizenship

It is not unusual for a child born and raised outside the U.S. to have acquired U.S. citizenship at birth from parents or grandparents without knowing it. The child, ignorant of the laws and circumstances affecting his birthright, then proceeds to lose U.S. citizenship by failing to fulfill U.S. residency requirements.

Congress sought to address this by adding a law for people who once held U.S. citizenship but lost it by failing to fulfill the residency requirements that were in effect before 1978. Such persons can regain their citizenship by simply taking the oath of allegiance to the United States. It is not necessary that the person apply for naturalization. Contact a U.S. consulate or USCIS office for more information. The relevant statute is 8 U.S.C. §1435(d)(1), I.N.A. §324(d)(1).

4. Automatic Derivation of U.S. Citizenship Through Naturalized Parents

When one or both parents are or become naturalized U.S. citizens, the children become U.S. citizens automatically, provided they have green cards and are under age 18 at the time. The law calls this "derivation" of citizenship. Becoming a U.S. citizen in this way has a special benefit because the child does not have to participate in a naturalization ceremony and can thereby avoid taking an oath renouncing allegiance to any country but the U.S.

There are a number of people whose parents have been naturalized who do not realize they are U.S. citizens because they never went through a naturalization ceremony themselves. The laws on automatic naturalization of children have varied over the years. Once again, whether or not you achieved U.S. citizenship in this manner is determined by the laws as they were when your parents' naturalization took place.

a. Parents Naturalized Before May 24, 1934

If either parent became naturalized prior to your 21st birthday and you held a green card at the time, you automatically derived U.S. citizenship. This applied to you if you were an illegitimate child of your father and had been legally legitimated or an illegitimate child of your mother, whether legitimated or not. Adopted children and stepchildren did not qualify.

b. Parents Naturalized From May 24, 1934 to January 12, 1941

If both parents became naturalized prior to your 21st birthday and you held a green card at the time, you automatically derived U.S. citizenship. This applied to you if you were an illegitimate child of your father and had been legally legitimated or an illegitimate child of your mother, whether legitimated or not. Adopted children did not qualify.

If only one parent became naturalized prior to your 21st birthday, you acquired U.S. citizenship automatically if you had held a green card for at least five years. The five years could have taken place before or after your parent was naturalized (as long as they started before you turned 21), so if you hadn't held a green card that long when the naturalization occurred, you automatically became a U.S. citizen whenever you finally accumulated the five-year total.

c. Parents Naturalized From January 13, 1941 to December 23, 1952

You derived U.S. citizenship if you held a green card and both parents were naturalized prior to your 18th birthday (or the non-naturalized parent was dead, or if your parents were legally separated, the parent having legal custody was naturalized). At this time, the law did not permit either illegitimate or adopted children to derive citizenship in this manner.

d. Parents Naturalized From December 24, 1952 to October 4, 1978

You derived U.S. citizenship if you were unmarried, held a green card at the time and both parents were naturalized, prior to your 16th birthday. You must also have received your green card before your 18th birthday. If only one parent naturalized, you can only derive citizenship if the other parent was dead, or they were legally separated and the naturalized parent had custody. This applied to you if you were an illegitimate child of your father and had been legally legitimated or an illegitimate child of your mother, whether legitimated or not. Adopted children and stepchildren did not qualify.

e. Parents Naturalized October 5, 1978 to February 26, 2001

You derived U.S. citizenship if one of your parents was a U.S. citizen when you were born and never ceased to be a citizen, and your other parent was naturalized prior to your 18th birthday, and you were unmarried at the time, or the naturalization of both parents occurred while you were unmarried. You must be lawfully admitted as a permanent resident (have a green card) under both of these scenarios. This applies to all children, including those who are illegitimate and adopted. However, adopted children born prior to December 29, 1981 or after November 14, 1986, derived U.S. citizenship only if the adoption occurred prior to their 16th birthday.

f. Parent Born in U.S. or Naturalized February 27, 2001 to Present

You derived U.S. citizenship if one of your parents was born in the U.S. or naturalized prior to your 18th birthday while you were living in the U.S., in the legal and physical custody of that parent. You must also have had a green card (permanent residence). This law applies to both natural and adopted children.

Notice that, for the first time in the history of this law, children may derive citizenship through a parent who was born in the U.S. rather than only through a parent who later naturalizes. This has the practical effect of turning many children into citizens the instant that they obtain their green card through one U.S. citizen parent. In recognition of this instant citizenship, USCIS does not require Affidavits of Support (Form I-864) to be submitted with such children's green card applications.

NATURALIZATION FOR CERTAIN OVERSEAS CHILDREN

Children who live overseas can also gain citizenship through a citizen parent. The child must be under 18 and the parent must have lived in the U.S. for at least five years, at least two of which were after the age of 14. In addition, children in this situation must enter the U.S. on a nonimmigrant visa (a tourist visa, for example) and submit an application to USCIS for a certificate of citizenship (the child's citizenship is not automatic in this situation).

If you plan to apply for this, get started as soon as possible—the entire process, including interview and approval of the certificate, must be completed before the child's 18th birthday. This can be difficult, with many USCIS offices backed up for years with these applications.

B. Obtaining Proof of U.S. Citizenship

If you have a legitimate claim to U.S. citizenship, in order to establish that claim you must apply for some kind of citizenship document. When you were born on U.S. soil and there is a record of your birth, a standard U.S. birth certificate issued by a state government is your primary proof of U.S. citizenship. Birth certificates issued by hospitals are not official records and do not serve as proof of citizenship. If you were naturalized, you have a naturalization certificate. However, if your birth took place outside the territorial U.S, and you acquired U.S. citizenship at birth from your parents or derived it through your parents' naturalization, you will have neither of these documents and so you must try to acquire a substitute. Three other types of documents may be obtained which will be recognized as proof of U.S. citizenship. They are:

- U.S. passports
- certificates of citizenship, or
- certificates of consular registration of birth.

1. U.S. Passports

If you were born abroad to U.S. citizen parents, you can apply for a U.S. passport in the same way as someone born in the U.S. However, you will have the added requirement of establishing your citizenship claim. Passports are available from either passport offices in the U.S. (run by the U.S. Department of State) or at U.S. consulates abroad, but our experience shows that you have a better chance for success in making your case at a U.S. consulate abroad. Wherever you apply, you will be required to present proof of your parents' U.S. citizenship and evidence that they, and you, complied with any applicable U.S. residency requirements. Review the sections on birth to a U.S. citizen for what you must prove under these circumstances. You will need to present documents such as birth or citizenship records of your parent or grandparent and work or tax records establishing U.S. residency for your parent or grandparent.

2. Certificates of Citizenship

Certificates of citizenship are issued only inside the U.S. by USCIS offices. Anyone with a claim to U.S. citizenship can apply for a certificate of citizenship. In most cases it is more difficult and takes much longer to get a certificate of citizenship than a U.S. passport. However, in situations where your U.S. citizenship was obtained automatically through the naturalization of a parent, certificates of citizenship applications are the best choice. In fact, at the time a parent is naturalized, the children can, upon the parent's request, be issued certificates of citizenship simultaneously with their naturalization certificates.

Certificates of citizenship not requested simultaneously with a parent's naturalization must be applied for later, on Form N-600. (Except that a slightly different form, numbered N-600K, must be used by children living overseas who apply for citizenship through their parents, as described in "Naturalization for Certain Overseas Children," above.) The current fee is $145 for minor adopted children, and $185 for others. A copy of this form is in Appendix II and on the USCIS website. Most of the questions on the N-600 are self-explanatory. We offer the following suggestion in answering Question 14.

Question 14. Question 14 asks you to list all documents being submitted. We recommend you answer this question "See Cover Letter." Then prepare a letter explaining the basis of your claim to U.S. citizenship and describing the documents you are offering as proof. These should include your parents' birth certificates, marriage certificate, and citizenship or naturalization certificates. You should also present your own birth certificate, marriage certificates, and any divorce decrees to show legal changes in your name since birth. If you are not applying as the child of a naturalized citizen, your letter should also list whatever evidence you will be presenting to show that you have met any residency requirements as described in the section in this chapter on birth to a U.S. citizen.

Form N-600 and the documents, together with the cover letter, should be submitted to the USCIS local office having jurisdiction over your place of residence in the U.S. Appendix I contains a list of USCIS local offices with their current addresses and phone numbers. Interviews on your application are usually required. In many of the busier USCIS offices, it takes well over a year to get a decision on an application for certificate of citizenship.

3. Certificates of Consular Registration of Birth

Certificates of consular registration of birth are issued by a U.S. consulate abroad. If your parents were U.S. citizens but were not physically in the U.S. when you were born, they may have registered your birth with a U.S. consulate to establish your right to U.S. citizenship and create an official birth record. For you to have acquired a certificate of consular registration of birth, your parents must have registered your birth at a consulate within five years after you were born.

Multiple copies can be issued at the time of registration but duplicates cannot be obtained later. Therefore, parents should request at least several copies. In issuing the certificate, the consulate asks to see evidence that any residence requirements the law placed on your parents were fulfilled. The consular registration is conclusive proof of U.S. citizenship, but if your parents did not take the steps to get one when you were a child, there is no way of obtaining one now.

If your parents did not register your birth in time, you may either apply for a passport through a passport office in the U.S. or at a U.S. consulate abroad, or you may apply for a certificate of citizenship through the USCIS in the U.S. You can typically get the passport much faster than the certificate of citizenship.

C. Dual Citizenship

If a child is born on U.S. soil and either or both parents are citizens of another country, it is quite possible that the child may have dual citizenship. Whether or not a dual citizenship is created depends on the laws of the parents' country. A child born in the U.S. is always a U.S. citizen in the eyes of the U.S. government, no matter what the laws of the parents' homeland. (The only exception to this rule is children born of foreign diplomats.) However, if the foreign country recognizes the child as a citizen, the U.S. will recognize the non-U.S. citizenship as well.

Whenever a child is born to U.S. citizen parents but the birth takes place outside U.S. territory, again, the child may acquire dual citizenship. In this situation, the child will, depending on the laws of the country where the birth took place, usually have the nationality of the country in which he or she was actually born, in addition to U.S. citizenship through the nationality of the parents. U.S. law recognizes dual citizenship under these circumstances, and if you have acquired dual citizenship in this manner, under U.S. law you will be entitled to maintain dual status for your lifetime.

In addition, a person who becomes a U.S. citizen through naturalization can retain his or her previous citizenship if his or her original country allows dual citizenship. ■

Canadians and Mexicans: Special Rules

Many Canadians believe they are disfavored by the U.S. immigration system. Actually, the exact opposite is true, as the following description of rules for Canadians show. Some of the special rules also apply to Mexican citizens.

A. Visitors and Other Nonimmigrants

Canadian citizens do not require visas to enter the U.S. For the casual tourist or business visitor, this is a big benefit. With the exception of E-1 and E-2 treaty traders and investors, and K-1 and K-2 visas (fiancé(e)s and their children), Canadians have no need to go to a U.S. consulate and get nonimmigrant visas.

If a Canadian is coming to the U.S. directly from Canada, no passport is required either, although some proof of Canadian citizenship must be shown at the border. However, Canadians arriving from countries outside the Western Hemisphere will be asked to show a passport. Also, E-1 and E-2 treaty traders and investors, as well as K fiancé(e)s and children, require both visas and passports. Canadian landed immigrants who have a common nationality with Canadian nationals (such as those from the United Kingdom) also require visas and passports, a policy that began in 2003.

Despite the benefits, you must still prove that you don't fall into one of the inadmissibility categories barring U.S. entry. Anyone coming into the U.S. can be examined regarding his or her health, criminal, and other history, to see whether the person falls into one of the grounds of inadmissibility described in Chapter 25.

B. Tourists and Business Visitors

Even though a nonimmigrant visa is not usually required, Canadians still must show that they are eligible to enter the U.S. For visitors, this may mean something as simple as answering a few questions from a CBP inspector at a U.S. port of entry. On other occasions, a Canadian visitor might be asked to prove that he or she has enough money to last during the U.S. trip. Visitors may also have to show that they still keep Canadian residences to which they can return.

Canadian visitors are not normally issued I-94 cards as are people from all other countries. This is another advantage. Canadians are not expected to have this document on hand for purposes of proving status in the U.S. If you want an I-94, however, you can request one.

C. Special Work Privileges for Canadian and Mexican Visitors

Canadians and Mexicans are granted some special work privileges.

1. Working Without a Visa

The North American Free Trade Agreement (NAFTA) includes a program permitting Canadian and Mexican visitors who are coming to the U.S. to do certain kinds of work in the U.S. without having work visas. There are no other countries whose citizens are afforded these privileges.

To take advantage of this opportunity, you must show written proof that you are engaging in one of the occupations included in the program. A letter from your employer verifying the work to be done will serve this purpose. If relevant, you should also offer evidence that you are qualified for the job, such as copies of diplomas or licenses. These documents are presented to a U.S. immigration officer on your entry to the U.S. No fee or special application is needed for Canadians. However, Mexican nationals must obtain a valid entry document (Form I-186 or Form I-586) prior to arriving at the port of entry. The types of work that Canadians and Mexicans may do in the U.S. without work visas are:

- Performing research and design functions for a company located in Canada or Mexico.
- Supervising a crew harvesting agricultural crops; only the owner of the company qualifies.
- Purchasing for a company located in Canada or Mexico.

- Conducting other commercial transactions for a company located in Canada or Mexico.
- Doing market research for a company located in Canada or Mexico.
- Attending trade fairs.
- Taking sales orders and negotiating contracts for a company located in Canada or Mexico.
- Transporting goods or passengers into the U.S.
- Picking up goods and passengers in the U.S., only for direct transport back to Canada or Mexico.
- Performing normal duties as a customs broker. The goods must be exports from the U.S. to Canada or Mexico.
- Servicing equipment or machinery after sales.
- Performing any professional services, provided no salary is paid from within the U.S.
- Performing financial services for a company located in Canada.
- Consulting in the fields of public relations and advertising.
- Conducting tours that originate or have significant portions taking place in Canada.
- Performing language translation and acting as an interpreter for a company located in Canada.

2. Simplified Procedures and Substitutes for H and L Visas

Canadians entering the U.S. to take jobs with U.S. companies as H-1 and H-2 temporary workers or L-1 intracompany transferees should obtain approved visa petitions. To get such a petition, you must follow the Step One procedures for these visas described in earlier chapters of this book. Once the petition is approved, however, as a Canadian you need not perform Step Two. Instead, you can simply go to a port of entry, present the petition approval, and be admitted. (Be sure to have your passport stamped to show your entry.) You will also need proof of your Canadian citizenship, such as a passport or birth certificate.

Your accompanying spouse and children will be admitted on showing proof of their family relationship to you. This requires presenting a marriage certificate for your spouse and long-form birth certificates for your children.

When you enter the U.S., you will be given an I-94 card. This will indicate your immigration status and give the dates of the time period for which you may remain in the country. If you leave and return again before this period expires, you need only present the I-94 card, together with your petition approval or Certificate of Eligibility, and you will be allowed to reenter.

a. L-1 Visa Alternative

Instead of going through the USCIS petition process, you can choose to take all your L-1 paperwork, both forms and documents, along with the required fee, directly to a port of entry. There, an immigration officer will decide on the spot whether you qualify for L-1 status (you cannot send them your paperwork in advance). When your status is approved, you will be given an I-94 card and admitted to the U.S. immediately. The petition is then forwarded to the appropriate service center in the U.S. and the final decision on the petition is made in about 60 days, and mailed to you.

⚠ **If you're flying to the U.S., you may have to submit your paperwork to a preflight inspector before you board the plane.** In that case, plan to arrive several hours before your flight to make sure you're approved before the plane departs.

Although this method is much faster than going through normal USCIS petition procedures, if you are denied entry, your rights of appeal are limited. In addition, border inspectors are usually less experienced in deciding cases than USCIS office personnel, and therefore, may be reluctant to approve a more difficult case. When your situation is complicated, you are probably better off having your petition approved in advance at the service center and not using this alternative procedure.

b. H-1 Visa Alternative: TN Status

For people who practice certain professional occupations, an alternative to filing a USCIS petition is available for H-1 cases as well. This is called TN status. TN status lasts one year, and can be renewed in one-year increments, with no limit on renewals. You don't always have to be coming for a job—TN status can also be used by people coming for temporary training related to their professsion, or to conduct seminars.

At present, only the occupations listed below qualify for TN status. A bachelor's or licensure degree from a college or university is required, unless an alternative is shown in parentheses. You must have a U.S. employer; TN status is not available for self-employment in the U.S. For some professions, there are requirements in addition to a degree. These too are shown in parentheses. Whenever a license is required, either a Federal Canadian or Mexican, or a U.S. licensing agency from any province or state is acceptable. The occupations are:

- Accountant
- Architect (degree or license)
- Computer systems analyst

- Disaster relief claims adjuster (degree or three years' experience)
- Economist
- Engineer (degree or license)
- Forester (degree or license)
- Graphic designer (degree and three years' experience)
- Hotel manager (licensure degree or diploma or certificate plus three years' experience)
- Industrial designer (degree or certificate or diploma plus three years' experience)
- Interior designer (degree or certificate or diploma plus three years' experience)
- Land surveyor (degree or license)
- Landscape architect
- Lawyer (member of Canadian, Mexican, or U.S. bar)
- Librarian (master's degree)
- Management consultant (degree or five years' experience)
- Mathematician (including statistician)
- Medical professions:
    - Clinical lab technologist
    - Dentist (professional degree or license)
    - Dietitian (degree or license)
    - Medical lab technologist (degree or certificate or diploma plus three years experience)
    - Nutritionist
    - Occupational therapist (degree or license)
    - Pharmacist (degree or license)
    - Physician (teaching or research position only)
    - Physio/physical therapist (degree or license)
    - Psychologist
    - Recreational therapist
    - Registered nurse (license)
    - Veterinarian (professional degree or license)
- Range manager
- Research assistant (for colleges or universities only)
- Scientific technician (degree not required if you are working with professionals in: agricultural sciences, astronomy, biology, chemistry, engineering, forestry, geology, geophysics, meteorology, physics)
- Scientist working as:
    - Agronomist
    - Agriculturist
    - Animal breeder
    - Animal scientist
    - Apiculturist
    - Astronomer
    - Biochemist
    - Biologist
    - Chemist
    - Dairy scientist
    - Entomologist
    - Epidemiologist
    - Geneticist
    - Geochemist
    - Geologist
    - Geophysicist
    - Horticulturist
    - Meteorologist
    - Pharmacologist
    - Physicist
    - Plant breeder
    - Poultry scientist
    - Soil scientist
    - Zoologist
- Social worker
- Silviculturist
- Teacher (at a college, university, or seminary only)
- Technical publications writer (degree, or diploma, or certificate plus three years' experience)
- Urban planner
- Vocational counselor.

The person seeking TN status must be coming temporarily, to engage in business activities at a professional level. A person who intends to separately apply for a green card while in the U.S. can be denied TN status, because he or she violates the requirement that he or she intend to stay only temporarily. He or she must also meet the minimum requirements for the profession or occupation in question, as set forth in Appendix 1603.D.1 to Annex 1603 of NAFTA (also found at 8 C.F.R. 2145.6(c)). Furthermore, the person must not be self-employed in the U.S. Although the basic requirements are the same for Canadians and Mexicans, the procedures are distinct.

Procedures for Canadians

There is no annual limit for Canadian TNs. A Canadian professional worker may be admitted to the U.S. without advance petition approval or labor certification. In order to apply, the applicant merely proceeds directly to any U.S. port of entry (border, airport, or preflight inspection station). There, an immigration or NAFTA officer will adjudicate the application, and you'll need to proceed directly to the United States. Although no formal application form is required, you must pay a fee (currently $50, or $56 if you're crossing the border by car). Your spouse and unmarried minor children may accompany you, but may not work in the U.S. Family members must bring proof of the family relationship, such as a marriage or birth certificate. They will be given "TD" status. A Canadian applicant will need to present the following documents to be given TN status:

- evidence of Canadian citizenship, such as a birth certificate, citizenship identification card, certificate of citizenship, or passport
- description of proposed employment activity at a professional level, including a detailed description of your daily job duties, the job requirements (such as educational level or license), your salary and benefits, and how long your services will be needed for, up to one year (all described in a job offer letter)
- evidence of your qualifications to perform at a professional level, as demonstrated by degrees, licenses, memberships, or other relevant credentials that establish professional status, and a resume (optional), and
- evidence of the particular profession as one listed in Appendix 1603.D.1 to Annex 1603 of NAFTA.

The application should include a letter from the prospective employer, confirming that the applicant will perform the professional activity for the employer, stating also that the duration will be temporary and how long it will last. The letter should also describe in detail the need for professional services, the job duties, salary, and other essential terms, and how the applicant's educational and work experience confirm his or her professional status. The letter should also state and describe how the applicant complies with any state licensing or other requirements.

When admitted, the TN professional will be given an I-94 card indicating authorized status for up to one year. This period can be extended in one year increments without leaving the U.S. An extension may be requested on form I-129, filed at the Northern Service Center in Nebraska (regardless of where you live), or it may be requested by departing the U.S. prior to the first status expiration and reentering at the port of entry by presenting the above-listed documents.

Procedures for Mexicans

There is currently an annual cap of 5,500 TNs from Mexico. However, the application procedures have recently gotten easier. As of January 2004, Mexican TN applicants no longer need to obtain an approved Labor Condition Application (LCA), nor to have their employer file a petition with USCIS.

Applicants who are overseas can simply present themselves at a U.S. consular post to apply for TN status and an entry visa. The applicant will need to bring the same types of documents as described under "Procedures for Canadians," above. (Contact the consulate, however, to doublecheck its procedures—since this part of the program is new, special requirements may be announced after this book has gone to print.)

If the applicant is already in the U.S., he or she can apply for a change of status. This application is made on Form I-539, and must be sent to the USCIS.

Applicants can also bring their spouses and children to the U.S., (in "TD" status) by providing proof of the family relationship, such as a birth or marriage certificate. Family members with TD status cannot legally work in the U.S.

Upon entering the U.S., the Mexican TN professional will be given an I-94 card indicating an authorized stay of up to one year. This period can be extended in one-year increments without leaving the United States. To file for an extension, send Form I-129, together with the same types of documents you used for your initial application, with the USCIS Nebraska Service Center. If you don't mind leaving the U.S., you can also request an extension by departing before your status has expired and revisiting a U.S. consulate.

Advantages and disadvantages of TN status. The advantages of the treaty professional procedure are that you avoid potentially long delays from filing a petition in the U.S. TN status is also useful for Canadians and Mexicans who have used up their six years of H-1B status, but wish to continue working in the United States. Similarly, it's helpful for H-1B applicants who find that the annual supply of H-1B visas has run out. And, because the list of professions qualifying for TN status is fairly broad, it's useful for some people whose profession could never qualify them for an H-1B visa in the first place.

The main disadvantage is that professional workers using the TN instead of a standard H-1 visa must intend to return to Canada or Mexico when their work in the U.S. is finished, and receive only one-year periods of status at a time. Therefore, if you plan to apply for a green card, you should, if possible, get a standard H-1 visa, which does not have these restrictions. (Unfortunately, not all categories of TN status qualify for an H-1B visa.)

In addition, if you have a difficult case and you are denied entry as a treaty professional, there is no avenue of appeal. When a standard H-1 visa petition is denied, or if you apply for TN status extension or change of status by filing an application with the service center, you have the ability to appeal the decision through both USCIS and, eventually, the U.S. courts.

3. Treaty Traders and Treaty Investors

NAFTA allows Canadians to obtain E-1 and E-2 visas. Canadians wishing to get E-1 or E-2 status are treated exactly like persons of all other nationalities. This means that you must obtain an actual visa stamp in your passport before you can enter the U.S. with an E-1 or E-2 status. Therefore, you should follow all of the procedures discussed in Chapters 20 and 21. This is the only nonimmigrant category where a visa is required of Canadians.

Although getting an E visa could formerly be done in one day at a U.S. consulate in Canada, consulates are now requiring that you attend an interview on one day, then return on a later day to pick up your passport and visa.

4. Fiancés

See Chapter 7 for instructions on obtaining a fiancé visa. Your other option, of course, is to enter the U.S. with no visa, get married, and then file for a green card within the U.S. You would risk, however, a finding that you had used fraud when you entered the U.S. as a supposed nonimmigrant, with the actual intent of staying permanently. (See Chapter 25.)

D. Simplified Procedures for Students and Exchange Visitors

Canadians entering the U.S. as F-1 students, M-1 students, or J-1 exchange visitors also have a simplified way of getting status. First you must get an approved Certificate of Eligibility form. The Certificate of Eligibility for F-1 and M-1 students is Form I-20. For J-1 exchange visitors it is form DS-2019. These are described in Chapters 22 and 23.

Once you have a Certificate of Eligibility, you may go directly to a port of entry and present it to a U.S. immigration inspector together with proof of your Canadian citizenship. You should also have available evidence of how you will be supported financially while in the U.S. On showing these documents, you will be admitted as a student or exchange visitor. Your accompanying spouse and children will be admitted on showing proof of their family relationship to you. This requires presenting a marriage certificate for your spouse and long-form birth certificates for your children.

When you enter the U.S., you will receive an I-94 card indicating your immigration status and giving the dates of the period for which you may remain in the country. Your stay will usually be for duration of status, marked "D/S" on the I-94 card. This means you can stay until your studies are completed. If you leave the U.S. before your status expires and want to return, you need only present the I-94 card and Certificate of Eligibility at the port of entry and you will be admitted again.

E. Preflight Inspections

Another benefit Canadians enjoy is access to the procedure known as "preflight inspection." There are U.S. immigration offices located at most of the Canadian international airports. When Canadians fly to the U.S., they clear U.S. immigration and customs before boarding the plane. This service is considered to be a timesaving advantage.

There is a negative side to preflight inspection. In situations where a Canadian's eligibility to enter the U.S. is questionable, if the U.S. immigration inspector does not believe the Canadian traveler should be admitted, the inspector can prevent the Canadian from boarding the plane. Without preflight inspection, travelers to the U.S. can at least land on U.S. soil and are usually granted enough time in the country to stay and argue their case. However, a new law punishes those individuals who arrive without the proper documentation and those who make a misrepresentation to a CBP inspector, by making them inadmissible for a visa and unable to request entry for five years. Because of this you should be extremely cautious about presenting yourself for inspection. (See Chapters 14 and 25 for more details.) ∎

Directory of DHS and DOL Offices

DHS Central Office

U.S. Department of Homeland Security
Washington, DC 20528

USCIS Headquarters

425 I ("Eye") Street NW

Washington, DC 20536

Information: 800-375-5283

Form Requests: 800-876-3676

Website: www.uscis.gov

CBP Headquarters

1300 Pennsylvania Avenue, NW

Washington, DC 20229

202-354-1000

Website: www.customs.ustreas.gov

ICE Headquarters

425 I ("Eye") Street NW

Washington, DC 20536

202-514-2895

Website: www.ice.gov

USCIS Regional Service Centers

NOTE: Most Service Centers require that you mail each type of application to a different post office box number. Before mailing anything, check the USCIS website at www.uscis.gov/graphics/fieldoffices/statemap.htm.

CALIFORNIA SERVICE CENTER

USCIS CSC
P.O. Box 30111
Laguna Niguel, CA 92677-0111
Status inquiries: 800-375-5283

NEBRASKA SERVICE CENTER

USCIS NSC
850 S Street
Lincoln, NE 68508
Status inquiries: 800-375-5283

TEXAS SERVICE CENTER

USCIS TSC
P.O. Box 851488
Dallas, TX 75185-1488
Status inquiries: 800-375-5283
Premium Processing inquiries
    via fax: 214-962-5525
    via email: TSC-Premium.Processing@dhs.gov

VERMONT SERVICE CENTER

USCIS VSC
75 Lower Welden St.
St. Albans, VT 05479
Status inquiries: 800-375-5283

USCIS District Offices and Suboffices

NOTE: The below list contains street addresses, which are not always the same as the mailing address. For more information, see your District Office website, via www.uscis.gov/graphics/fieldoffices/alphaa.htm.

ALABAMA

USCIS Atlanta District Office
Martin Luther King, Jr., Federal Building
77 Forsyth Street SW
Atlanta, GA 30303

ALASKA

USCIS Anchorage District Office
620 East 10th Avenue, Suite 102
Anchorage, AK 99501

ARIZONA

USCIS Tucson Suboffice
6431 South Country Club Road
Tucson, AZ 85706-5907

USCIS Phoenix District Office
2035 North Central Avenue
Phoenix, AZ 85004

ARKANSAS

USCIS New Orleans District Office
701 Loyola Avenue
New Orleans, LA 70113

USCIS Fort Smith Suboffice
4991 Old Greenwood Road
Fort Smith, AR 72903

CALIFORNIA

USCIS Fresno Suboffice
865 Fulton Mall
Fresno, CA 93721

USCIS Los Angeles District Office
300 North Los Angeles Street, Room 1001
Los Angeles, CA 90012

USCIS Sacramento Suboffice
650 Capitol Mall
Sacramento, CA 95814

USCIS San Diego District Office
880 Front Street, Suite 1234
San Diego, CA 92101

USCIS San Francisco District Office
444 Washington Street
San Francisco, CA 94111

USCIS San Jose Suboffice
1887 Monterey Road
San Jose, CA 95112

USCIS Santa Ana Suboffice
34 Civic Center Plaza
Federal Building
Santa Ana, CA 92701

COLORADO

USCIS Denver District Office
4730 Paris Street
Denver, CO 80239

CONNECTICUT

USCIS Boston District Office
John F. Kennedy Federal Building
Government Center
Boston, MA 02203

USCIS Hartford Suboffice
450 Main Street, 4th Floor
Hartford, CT 06103-3060

DELAWARE

USCIS Philadelphia District Office
1600 Callowhill Street
Philadelphia, PA 19130

USCIS Dover Satellite Office
1305 McD Drive
Dover, DE 19901

DISTRICT OF COLUMBIA

USCIS Washington District Office
4420 N. Fairfax Drive
Arlington, VA 22203

FLORIDA

USCIS Miami District Office
7880 Biscayne Boulevard
Miami, FL 33138

USCIS Jacksonville Suboffice
4121 Southpoint Boulevard
Jacksonville, FL 32216

USCIS Orlando Suboffice
9403 Tradeport Drive
Orlando, FL 32827

USCIS Tampa Suboffice
5524 West Cypress Street
Tampa, FL 33607-1708

USCIS West Palm Beach Satellite Office
326 Fern Street
West Palm Beach, FL 33401

GEORGIA

USCIS Atlanta District Office
Martin Luther King, Jr., Federal
Building
77 Forsyth Street SW
Atlanta, GA 30303

GUAM

USCIS Honolulu District Office
595 Ala Moana Boulevard
Honolulu, HI 96813

HAWAII

USCIS Honolulu District Office
595 Ala Moana Boulevard
Honolulu, HI 96813

IDAHO

USCIS Helena District Office
2800 Skyway Drive
Helena, MT 59602

USCIS Boise Suboffice
1185 South Vinnell Way
Boise, ID 83709

ILLINOIS

USCIS Chicago District Office
10 West Jackson Boulevard
Chicago, IL 60604

Chicago USCIS Adjudications Office
230 S. Dearborn, 23rd floor
Chicago, IL 60604

Chicago USCIS Citizenship Office
539 S. LaSalle
Chicago, IL 60605

INDIANA

USCIS Chicago District Office
10 West Jackson Boulevard
Chicago, IL 60604

USCIS Indianapolis Suboffice
950 N. Meridian St., Room 400
Indianapolis, IN 46204

IOWA

USCIS Omaha District Office
3736 South 132nd Street
Omaha, NE 68144

KANSAS

USCIS Kansas City District Office
9747 Northwest Conant Avenue
Kansas City, MO 64153

USCIS Wichita Satellite Office
271 West 3rd Street North, Suite
1050
Wichita, KS 67202-1212

KENTUCKY

USCIS New Orleans District
701 Loyola Avenue
New Orleans, LA 70113

USCIS Louisville Suboffice
Gene Snyder U.S. Courthouse and
Customhouse
Room 390
601 West Broadway
Louisville, KY 40202

LOUISIANA

USCIS New Orleans District
701 Loyola Avenue
New Orleans, LA 70113

MAINE

USCIS Portland District Office
176 Gannett Drive
South Portland, ME 04106

MARYLAND

USCIS Baltimore District Office
Fallon Federal Building
31 Hopkins Plaza
Baltimore, MD 21201

MASSACHUSETTS

USCIS Boston District Office
John F. Kennedy Federal Building
Government Center
Boston, MA 02203

MICHIGAN

USCIS Detroit District Office
333 Mt. Elliot
Detroit, MI 48207

MINNESOTA

USCIS St. Paul District
2901 Metro Drive, Suite 100
Bloomington, MN 55425

MISSISSIPPI

USCIS New Orleans District
701 Loyola Avenue
New Orleans, LA 70113

USCIS Jackson Suboffice
100 West Capitol Street
Jackson, MS 36269

MISSOURI

USCIS Kansas City District
9747 Northwest Conant Avenue
Kansas City, MO 64153

MONTANA

USCIS Helena District Office
2800 Skyway Drive
Helena, MT 59602

NEBRASKA

USCIS Omaha District Office
3736 South 132nd Street
Omaha, NE 68144

NEVADA

USCIS Phoenix District Office
2035 North Central Avenue
Phoenix, AZ 85004

USCIS Las Vegas Suboffice
3373 Pepper Lane
Las Vegas, NV 89120-2739

USCIS Reno Suboffice
1351 Corporate Boulevard
Reno, NV 89502

NEW HAMPSHIRE

USCIS Boston District Office
John F. Kennedy Federal Building
Government Center
Boston, MA 02203

USCIS Manchester Satellite Office
803 Canal Street
Manchester, NH 03101

NEW JERSEY

USCIS Newark District Office
Peter Rodino, Jr., Federal Building
970 Broad Street
Newark, NJ 07102

USCIS Cherry Hill Suboffice
1886 Greentree Road
Cherry Hill, NJ 08003

NEW MEXICO

USCIS El Paso District Office
1545 Hawkins Boulevard, Suite 167
El Paso, TX 79925

USCIS Albuquerque Suboffice
1720 Randolph Road SE
Albuquerque, NM 87106

NEW YORK

USCIS Buffalo District Office
Federal Center
130 Delaware Avenue
Buffalo, NY 14202

USCIS New York City District Office
26 Federal Plaza
New York City, NY 10278

USCIS Albany Suboffice
1086 Troy-Schenectady Road
Latham, NY 12110

NORTH CAROLINA

USCIS Atlanta District Office
Martin Luther King, Jr., Federal
Building
77 Forsyth Street SW
Atlanta, GA 30303

USCIS Charlotte Suboffice
6130 Tyvola Centre Drive
Charlotte, NC 28217

NORTH DAKOTA

USCIS St. Paul District Office
2901 Metro Drive, Suite 100
Bloomington, MN 55425

OHIO

USCIS Cleveland District Office
A.J.C. Federal Building
1240 East Ninth Street, Room 501
Cleveland, OH 44199

USCIS Cincinnati Suboffice
J.W. Peck Federal Building
550 Main Street, Room 4001
Cincinnati, OH 45202

OKLAHOMA

USCIS Dallas District Office
8101 North Stemmons Freeway
Dallas, TX 75247

USCIS Oklahoma City Suboffice
4400 SW 44th Street
Oklahoma City, OK 73119

OREGON

USCIS Portland, Oregon District
Office
511 NW Broadway
Portland, OR 97209

PENNSYLVANIA

USCIS Philadelphia District Office
1600 Callowhill Street
Philadelphia, PA 19130

USCIS Pittsburgh Suboffice
1000 Liberty Avenue
Federal Building, Room 314
Pittsburgh, PA 15222-4181

PUERTO RICO

USCIS San Juan District Office
San Patricio Office Center
7 Tabonuco Street, Suite 100
Guaynabo, Puerto Rico 00968

USCIS Charlotte Amalie Suboffice
Nisky Center, Suite 1A
First Floor South
Charlotte Amalie, St. Thomas
U.S. Virgin Islands 00802

USCIS San Croix Suboffice
Sunny Isle Shopping Center
Christiansted, St. Croix
U.S. Virgin Islands 00820

RHODE ISLAND

USCIS Boston District Office
John F. Kennedy Federal Building
Government Center
Boston, MA 02203

USCIS Providence Suboffice
200 Dyer Street
Providence, RI 02903

SOUTH CAROLINA

USCIS Atlanta District Office
Martin Luther King, Jr., Federal
Building
77 Forsyth Street SW
Atlanta, GA 30303

USCIS Charleston Satellite Office
170 Meeting Street, Fifth Floor
Charleston, SC 29401

SOUTH DAKOTA

USCIS St. Paul District Office
2901 Metro Drive, Suite 100
Bloomington, MN 55425

TENNESSEE

USCIS New Orleans District Office
701 Loyola Avenue
New Orleans, LA 70113

USCIS Memphis Suboffice
Suite 100
1341 Sycamore View Road
Memphis, TN 38134

TEXAS

USCIS Dallas District Office
8101 North Stemmons Freeway
Dallas, TX 75247

USCIS El Paso District Office
1545 Hawkins Boulevard, Suite 167
El Paso, TX 79925

USCIS Harlingen District Office
1717 Zoy Street
Harlingen, TX 78552

USCIS Houston District Office
126 Northpoint
Houston, TX 77060

USCIS San Antonio District Office
8940 Fourwinds Drive
San Antonio, TX 78239

UTAH

USCIS Denver District Office
4730 Paris Street
Denver, CO 80239

USCIS Salt Lake City Suboffice
5272 South College Drive, #100
Murray, UT 84123

VERMONT

USCIS Portland District Office
176 Gannett Drive
South Portland, ME 04106

USCIS St. Albans Suboffice
64 Gricebrook Road
St. Albans, VT 05478

VIRGIN ISLANDS

USCIS San Juan District Office
San Patricio Office Center
7 Tabonuco Street, Suite 100
Guaynabo, Puerto Rico 00968

USCIS Charlotte Amalie Suboffice
Nisky Center, Suite 1A
First Floor South
Charlotte Amalie, St. Thomas
U.S. Virgin Islands 00802

San Croix Suboffice
Sunny Isle Shopping Center
Christiansted, St. Croix
U.S. Virgin Islands 00820

VIRGINIA

USCIS Washington District Office
4420 N. Fairfax Drive
Arlington, VA 22203

USCIS Norfolk Suboffice
5280 Henneman Drive
Norfolk, VA 23513

WASHINGTON

USCIS Seattle District Office
815 Airport Way South
Seattle, WA 98134

USCIS Spokane Suboffice
U.S. Courthouse
920 W. Riverside, Room 691
Spokane, WA 99201

USCIS Yakima Suboffice
415 North 3rd Street
Yakima, WA 98901

WEST VIRGINIA

USCIS Philadelphia District Office
1600 Callowhill Street
Philadelphia, PA 19130

USCIS West Virginia Satellite Office
210 Kanawha Boulevard West
Charleston, WV 25302

USCIS Pittsburgh Suboffice
1000 Liberty Avenue
Federal Building, Room 314
Pittsburgh, PA 15222-4181

WISCONSIN

USCIS Chicago District Office
10 West Jackson Boulevard
Chicago, IL 60604

USCIS Milwaukee Suboffice
310 E. Knapp Street
Milwaukee, WI 53202

WYOMING

USCIS Denver District Office
4730 Paris Street
Denver, CO 80239

Regional Department of Labor Offices

Region	States
ATLANTA Atlanta Federal Center Room 6M12 61 Forsyth Street, SW Atlanta, GA 30303 Tel: 404-562-2092	Alabama, Florida, Georgia, Kentucky, Mississippi, North Carolina, South Carolina, Tennessee
BOSTON JFK Federal Building Room E-350 Boston, MA 02203 Tel: 617-565-3630	Connecticut, Maine, Massachusetts, New Hampshire, Rhode Island, Vermont
CHICAGO 230 South Dearborn St. Room 628 Chicago, IL 60604 Tel: 312-353-0313	Ilinois, Indiana, Michigan, Minnesota, Ohio, Wisconsin
DALLAS 525 Griffin Street Room 317 Dallas, TX 75202 Tel: 214-767-8263	Arkansas, Louisiana, New Mexico, Oklahoma, Texas
DENVER 1999 Broadway Street Suite 1780 P.O. Box 46550 Denver, CO 80202-5716 Tel: 303-844-1650	Colorado, Montana, North Dakota, South Dakota, Utah, Wyoming

Region	States
KANSAS CITY 1100 Main St., Suite 1050 City Center Square Kansas City, MO 64105 Tel: 816-426-3796	Iowa, Kansas, Missouri, Nebraska
NEW YORK 201 Varick Street Room 755 New York, NY 10014 Tel: 212-337-2139	New York, New Jersey, Puerto Rico, Virgin Islands
PHILADELPHIA The Curtis Center 3535 Market Street Room 13300 Philadelphia, PA 19104 Tel: 215-596-6336	Delaware, District of Columbia, Maryland, Pennsylvania, Virginia, West Virginia
SAN FRANCISCO 71 Stevenson St. Suite 830 San Francisco, CA 94119 Tel: 415-975-4610	Arizona, California, Guam, Hawaii, Nevada
SEATTLE 1111 Third Avenue Ssuite 900 Seattle, WA 98101-3212 Tel: 206-553-7700	Alaska, Idaho, Oregon, Washington

APPENDIX II

Tear-Out Immigration Forms

Note: Some of these forms originally came with instructions from the INS or other agency. We have not included the instructions here. Most of them can be viewed on or downloaded from the USCIS website at www.uscis.gov.

AR-11	Alien's Change of Address Card
DS-3035	J-1 Visa Waiver Review Application
ETA-750	Part A: Offer of Employment
ETA-750	Part B: Statement of Qualifications of Alien
ETA-9035	Labor Condition Application for H-1B Nonimmigrants
G-325A	Biographic Information
I-129	Petition for a Nonimmigrant Worker
I-129F	Petition for Alien Fiancé(e)
I-129W	H-1B Data Collection and Filing Fee Exemption
I-130	Petition for Alien Relative
I-131	Application for Travel Document
I-134	Affidavit of Support
I-140	Immigrant Petition for Alien Worker
I-191	Application for Advance Permission to Return to Unrelinquished Domicile
I-360	Petition for Amerasian, Widow(er), or Special Immigrant
I-485	Application to Register Permanent Resident or Adjust Status
	Supplement A to Form I-485 Adjustment of Status Under Section 245(i)
I-526	Immigrant Petition by Alien Entrepreneur
I-539	Application to Extend/Change Nonimmigrant Status
	Supplement 1 to Form I-539
I-539	Supplement A Filing Instructions for V Nonimmigrant Status
I-589	Application for Asylum and for Withholding of Removal
I-590	Registration for Classification as Refugee
I-600	Petition to Classify Orphan as an Immediate Relative

I-600A	Application for Advance Processing of Orphan Petition
I-601	Application for Waiver of Ground of Excludability
I-612	Application for Waiver of the Foreign Residence Requirement
I-730	Refugee/Asylee Relative Petition
I-751	Petition to Remove the Conditions on Residence
I-765	Application for Employment Authorization
I-817	Application for Family Unity Benefits
I-821	Application for Temporary Protected Status
I-829	Petition by Entrepreneur to Remove Conditions
I-864	Affidavit of Support Under Section 213A of the Act
I-864A	Contract Between Sponsor and Household Member
I-864P	2003 Poverty Guidelines (Minimum Income Requirement For Use in Completing Form I-864)
I-865	Sponsor's Notice of Change of Address
I-881	Application for Suspension of Deportation or Special Rule Cancellation of Removal
M-378	Color Photograph Specifications
N-400	Application for Naturalization
N-565	Application for Replacement Naturalization/Citizenship Document
N-600	Application for Certificate of Citizenship
N-600/N-643	Supplement A, Application for Transmission of Citizenship Through a Grandparent
N-600K	Application for Citizenship and Issuance of Certificate under Section 322
N-648	Medical Certification for Disability Exceptions

Department of Homeland Security
Bureau of Citizenship and Immigration

Alien's Change of Address Card

NAME (Last in CAPS)	(First)	(Middle)	I AM IN THE UNITED STATES AS: ☐ Visitor ☐ Permanent Resident ☐ Student ☐ Other . . . . (Specify)

COUNTRY OF CITIZENSHIP	DATE OF BIRTH	**A**	COPY NUMBER FROM ALIEN CARD

PRESENT ADDRESS	(Street or Rural Route)	(City or Post Office)	(State)	(ZIP Code)

(IF ABOVE ADDRESS IS TEMPORARY) I expect to remain there _____ years _____ months

LAST ADDRESS	(Street or Rural Route)	(City or Post Office)	(State)	(ZIP Code)

I WORK FOR OR ATTEND SCHOOL AT: (Employer's Name or Name of School)

(Street Address or Rural Route)	(City or Post Office)	(State)	(ZIP Code)

PORT OF ENTRY INTO U.S.	DATE OF ENTRY INTO U.S	IF NOT A PERMANENT RESIDENT, MY STAY IN THE U.S. EXPIRES ON: (Date)
SIGNATURE	DATE	

AR-11 (Rev. 06/17/03)Y

ALIEN'S CHANGE OF ADDRESS CARD

This card is to be used by all aliens to report change of address within 10 days of such change.

The collection of this information is required by Section 265 of the I&N Act (8 U.S.C. 1305). The data used by the Bureau of Citizenship and Immigration Service for statistical and record purposes and may be furnished to federal, state, local and foreign law enforcement officials. Failure to report is punishable by fine or imprisonment and/or deportation.

This card is not evidence of identity, age, or status claimed.

Public Reporting Burden. Under the Paperwork Reduction Act, an agency may not conduct or sponsor an information collection and a person is not required to respond to an information collection unless it displays a currently valid OMB control number. We try to create forms and instructions that are accurate, can be easily understood, and which impose the least possible burden on you to provide us with information. Often this is difficult because some immigration laws are very complex. This collection of information is estimated to average 5 minutes per response, including the time for reviewing instructions, searching existing data sources, gathering and maintaining the data needed, and completing and reviewing the collection of information. Send comments regarding this burden estimate or any other aspect of this collection of information, including for reducing this burden to: Bureau of Citizenship and Immigration Services, HQRFS, 425 I Street, N.W., Room 4034, Washington, DC 20536; OMB No. 1615-0007. *Do not mail your completed form to this address.* **MAIL YOUR FORM TO THE ADDRESSES SHOWN BELOW:**

U.S. DEPARTMENT OF HOMELAND SECURITY
Bureau of Citizenship and Immigration Services
Change of Address
P.O. Box 7134
London, KY 40742-7134

For commercial overnight or fast freight

U.S. DEPARTMENT OF HOMELAND SECURITY
Bureau of Citizenship and Immigration Services
Change of Address
1084-I South Laurel Road
London, KY 40744

U. S. Department of State

OMB No. 1405-0135
EXPIRATION DATE: 03/31/2005
ESTIMATED BURDEN: 2 Hours

J-1 VISA WAIVER REVIEW APPLICATION INSTRUCTIONS

PLEASE DO NOT STAPLE ANY DOCUMENTS

PLEASE AVOID TWO-SIDED DOCUMENTS AND USE ONLY 8 1/2" X 11" PAPER

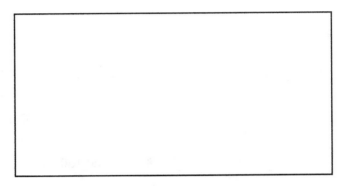

Please **PRINT** your full name and address in **UPPERCASE** letters in the box above. This is the address we will use to mail you a copy of our recommendation regarding your waiver application. You must include a self-addressed stamped envelope with your application.

FEE INFORMATION

PLEASE SEND YOUR APPLICATION, SUPPORTING DOCUMENTS, AND FEE PAYMENT TO

U. S. Department of State
P. O. Box 952137
St. Louis, MO 63195-2137

The application fee is $230 **PER J-1 APPLICANT**. Please send a cashier's check or money order in U.S. currency drawn on a U.S. bank, Made payable to **THE U.S. DEPARTMENT OF STATE**. Include your name, date and place of birth on whatever form of payment you submit.

DO NOT SUBMIT MORE THAN ONE APPLICATION FEE PER PERSON

We will contact you regarding the next step in processing your application. You should receive a reply and information package within 6 weeks of submitting your data sheet and fee.

DO NOT CALL TO VERIFY THAT THE APPLICATION HAS ARRIVED

PAPERWORK REDUCTION ACT

*The response time is an estimated average including the time needed to look for, get, and provide the information required. You do not have to provide the information requested if the OMB approval has expired. We would appreciate any comments on the estimated response and cost burdens, and recommendations for reducing them. Please send your comments to: U.S. Department of State (A/RPS/DIR) Washington, DC 20520.

U.S. Department of State
J-1 VISA WAIVER REVIEW APPLICATION

TYPE OR PRINT YOUR ANSWERS IN THE SPACE PROVIDED

1. _____
   Last Name

2. _____
   First Name   Middle Name

3. _____
   Date of Birth   Place of Birth *(City and Country)*

4. Nationality or last legal permanent residence as shown on IAP-66 or

   _____

5. I am requesting a recommendation for a waiver based on *(Check one)*

   ☐ Exceptional Hardship ☐ Persecution ☐ Interested Gov. Agency
   ☐ No Objection Statement ☐ State Health Agency Request

6. Date & Place of first entrance to U.S. on original Exchange Visitor (J-1)visa:

   _____
   Date of Entry   Port of Entry

7. Present Address

   _____
   _____
   _____

   Home Phone _____

   Business _____

   Fax Number _____

   E-Mail _____

8. Last U.S. Address *(If not currently living in U.S.)*

   _____
   _____
   _____

9. Does this application include J-2   ☐ Yes ☐ No

   If your spouse is in J-1 status, he or she must apply separately for a waiver.

10. INS alien registration number: _____

    I am represented by the following attorney or organization and want all correspondence sent to the following

    Name of Attorney or Organization _____

    Address _____

    _____   If an Attorney, please sign here

    _____   _____

11. List all exchange visitor programs in which you participated beginning with the first program

    _____ _____ _____
    _____ _____ _____

12. Give an explanation for any period of time in the U.S. not covered by your IAP-66 or DS-2019.

13. Did your exchange visitor program include U.S. Government funds, funds from your own government, or funds from an international organization? ☐ Yes ☐ No

_____
Signature

_____
Date *(mm-dd-yyyy)*

U.S. DEPARTMENT OF LABOR
Employment and Training Administration

APPLICATION
FOR
ALIEN EMPLOYMENT CERTIFICATION

IMPORTANT: READ CAREFULLY BEFORE COMPLETING THIS FORM

PRINT legibly in ink or use a typewriter. If you need more space to answer questions on this form, use a separate sheet. Identify each answer with the number of the corresponding question. SIGN AND DATE each sheet in original signature.

To knowingly furnish any false information in the preparation of this form and any supplement thereto or to aid, abet, or counsel another to do so is a felony punishable by $10,000 fine or 5 years in the penitentiary, or both (18 U.S.C. 1001).

PART A. OFFER OF EMPLOYMENT

1. Name of Alien *(Family name in capital letters, First, Middle, Maiden)*

2. Present Address of Alien *(Number, Street, City and Town, State, ZIP Code or Province, Country)*

3. Type of Visa *(If in U.S.)*

The following information is submitted as evidence of an offer of employment.

4. Name of Employer *(Full name of organization)*

5. Telephone *(Area Code and Number)*

6. Address *(Number, Street, City or Town, County, State, ZIP Code)*

7. Address Where Alien Will Work *(if different from item 6)*

8. Nature of Employer's Business Activity	9. Name of Job Title	10. Total Hours Per Week		11. Work Schedule *(Hourly)*	12. Rate of Pay	
		a. Basic	b. Overtime		a. Basic	b. Overtime
				a.m.	$	$
				p.m.	per	per hour

13. Describe Fully the Job to be Performed *(Duties)*

14. State in detail the MINIMUM education, training, and experience for a worker to perform satisfactorily the job duties described in Item 13 above.

15. Other Special Requirements

EDU-CATION *(Enter number of years)*	Grade School	High School	College	College Degree Required *(specify)*
				Major Field of Study

TRAIN-ING	No. Yrs.	No. Mos.	Type of Training

EXPERI-ENCE	Job Offered		Related Occupation	Related Occupation *(specify)*
	Number			
	Yrs.	Mos.	Yrs.	Mos.

16. Occupational Title of Person Who Will Be Alien's Immediate Supervisor ▶ ▶

17. Number of Employees Alien will Supervise ▶

◀ ENDORSEMENTS *(Make no entry in section - for government use only)*

Date Forms Received	
L.O.	S.O.
R.O.	N.O.
Ind. Code	Occ. Code
Occ. Title	

Replaces MA 7-50A, B and C (Apr. 1970 edition) which is obsolete.

ETA 750 (Oct. 1979)

18. COMPLETE ITEMS ONLY IF JOB IS TEMPORARY			19. IF JOB IS UNIONIZED *(Complete)*	
a. No. of Openings To Be Filled By Aliens Under Job Offer	b. Exact Dates You Expect To Employ Alien		a. Number of Local	b. Name of Local
	From	To		
				c. City and State

20. STATEMENT FOR LIVE-AT-WORK JOB OFFERS *(Complete for Private Household Job ONLY)*							
a. Description of Residence		b. No. Persons Residing at Place of Employment				c. Will free board and private room not shared with anyone be provided?	*("X" one)*
("X" one)	Number of Rooms	Adults		Children	Ages		
☐ House			BOYS				☐ YES ☐ NO
☐ Apartment			GIRLS				

21. DESCRIBE EFFORTS TO RECRUIT U.S. WORKERS AND THE RESULTS. *(Specify Sources of Recruitment by Name)*

22. Applications require various types of documentation. Please read PART II of the instructions to assure that appropriate supporting documentation is included with your application.

23. EMPLOYER CERTIFICATIONS

By virtue of my signature below, I HEREBY CERTIFY the following conditions of employment.

a. I have enough funds available to pay the wage or salary offered the alien.

b. The wage offered equals or exceeds the prevailing wage and I guarantee that, if a labor certification is granted, the wage paid to the alien when the alien begins work will equal or exceed the prevailing wage which is applicable at the time the alien begins work.

c. The wage offered is not based on commissions, bonuses, or other incentives, unless I guarantee a wage paid on a weekly, bi-weekly or monthly basis.

d. I will be able to place the alien on the payroll on or before the date of the alien's proposed entrance into the United States.

e. The job opportunity does not involve unlawful discrimination by race, creed, color, national origin, age, sex, religion, handicap, or citizenship.

f. The job opportunity is not:

(1) Vacant because the former occupant is on strike or is being locked out in the course of a labor dispute involving a work stoppage.

(2) At issue in a labor dispute involving a work stoppage.

g. The job opportunity's terms, conditions and occupational environment are not contrary to Federal, State or local law.

h. The job opportunity has been and is clearly open to any qualified U.S. worker.

24. DECLARATIONS

DECLARATION OF EMPLOYER ➤ *Pursuant to 28 U.S.C. 1746, I declare under penalty of perjury the foregoing is true and correct.*

SIGNATURE	DATE

NAME *(Type or Print)*	TITLE

AUTHORIZATION OF AGENT OF EMPLOYER ➤ *I HEREBY DESIGNATE the agent below to represent me for the purposes of labor certification and I TAKE FULL RESPONSIBILITY for accuracy of any representations made by my agent.*

SIGNATURE OF EMPLOYER	DATE

NAME OF AGENT *(Type or Print)*	ADDRESS OF AGENT *(Number, Street, City, State, ZIP Code)*

PART B. STATEMENT OF QUALIFICATIONS OF ALIEN

FOR ADVICE CONCERNING REQUIREMENTS FOR ALIEN EMPLOYMENT CERTIFICATION: *If alien is in the U.S., contact nearest office of Immigration and Naturalization Service. If alien is outside U.S., contact nearest U.S. Consulate.*

IMPORTANT: READ ATTACHED INSTRUCTIONS BEFORE COMPLETING THIS FORM.

Print legibly in ink or use a typewriter. If you need more space to fully answer any questions on this form, use a separate sheet. Identify each answer with the number of the corresponding question. Sign and date each sheet.

1. Name of Alien *(Family name in capital letters)*	First name	Middle name	Maiden name

2. Present Address *(No., Street, City or Town, State or Province and ZIP Code*	Country	3. Type of Visa *(If in U.S.)*

4. Alien's Birthdate *(Month, Day, Year)*	5. Birthplace *(City or Town, State or Province)*	Country	6. Present Nationality or Citizenship *(Country)*

7. Address in United States Where Alien Will Reside

8. Name and Address of Prospective Employer if Alien has job offer in U.S.	9. Occupation in which Alien is Seeking Work

10. "X" the appropriate box below and furnish the information required for the box marked

a. ☐ Alien will apply for a visa abroad at the American Consulate in ———➤   City in Foreign Country / Foreign Country

b. ☐ Alien is in the United States and will apply for adjustment of status to that of a lawful permanent resident in the office of the Immigration and Naturalization Service at ———➤   City / State

11. Names and Addresses of Schools, Colleges and Universities Attended *(Include trade or vocational training facilities)*	Field of Study	FROM		TO		Degrees or Certificates Received
		Month	Year	Month	Year	

SPECIAL QUALIFICATIONS AND SKILLS

12. Additional Qualifications and Skills Alien Possesses and Proficiency in the use of Tools, Machines or Equipment Which Would Help Establish if Alien Meets Requirements for Occupation in Item 9.

13. List Licenses *(Professional, journeyman, etc.)*

14. List Documents Attached Which are Submitted as Evidence that Alien Possesses the Education, Training, Experience, and Abilities Represented

Endorsements	DATE REC. DOL
	O.T. & C.
(Make no entry in this section — FOR Government Agency USE ONLY)	

(Items continued on next page)

15. WORK EXPERIENCE. *List all jobs held during past three (3) years. Also, list any other jobs related to the occupation for which the alien is seeking certification as indicated in item 9.*

a. NAME AND ADDRESS OF EMPLOYER

NAME OF JOB	DATE STARTED Month Year	DATE LEFT Month Year	KIND OF BUSINESS

DESCRIBE IN DETAILS THE DUTIES PERFORMED, INCLUDING THE USE OF TOOLS, MACHINES, OR EQUIPMENT	NO. OF HOURS PER WEEK

b. NAME AND ADDRESS OF EMPLOYER

NAME OF JOB	DATE STARTED Month Year	DATE LEFT Month Year	KIND OF BUSINESS

DESCRIBE IN DETAIL THE DUTIES PERFORMED, INCLUDING THE USE OF TOOLS, MACHINES, OR EQUIPMENT	NO. OF HOURS PER WEEK

c. NAME AND ADDRESS OF EMPLOYER

NAME OF JOB	DATE STARTED Month Year	DATE LEFT Month Year	KIND OF BUSINESS

DESCRIBE IN DETAIL THE DUTIES PERFORMED, INCLUDING THE USE OF TOOLS, MACHINES, OR EQUIPMENT	NO. OF HOURS PER WEEK

16. DECLARATIONS

DECLARATION OF ALIEN ➤ ➤ *Pursuant to 28 U.S.C. 1746, I declare under penalty of perjury the foregoing is true and correct.*

SIGNATURE OF ALIEN	DATE

AUTHORIZATION OF AGENT OF ALIEN ➤ ➤ *I hereby designate the agent below to represent me for the purposes of labor certification and I take full responsibility for accuracy of any representations made by my agent.*

SIGNATURE OF ALIEN	DATE

NAME OF AGENT *(Type or print)*	ADDRESS OF AGENT *(No., Street, City, State, ZIP Code)*

Labor Condition Application for H-1B Nonimmigrants

U.S. Department of Labor
Employment and Training Administration

Form ETA 9035
OMB Approval: 1205-0310
Expiration Date: 19 JAN 2004

A. Employer's Information

❗ If you want the application returned by mail, leave the Return Fax Number blank.

1. Return Fax Number
(☐☐☐) ☐☐☐ - ☐☐☐☐

2. Employer's Full Legal Name

3. Employer's Address (Number and Street)

4. Employer's City
State   Zip/Postal Code

5. Employer's EIN Number
☐☐ - ☐☐☐☐☐☐☐

6. Employer's Phone Number
(☐☐☐) ☐☐☐ - ☐☐☐☐
Extension

B. Rate of Pay

1. Wage Rate (or Rate From) (Required):
$ ☐☐☐☐☐☐☐ . 0 0

2. Rate Up To (Optional):
$ ☐☐☐☐☐☐☐ . 0 0

3. Rate is Per:
○ Year   ○ Week
○ Month ○ Hour
○ 2 Weeks

4. Is this position part-time?
○ Yes
○ No

❗ **Please Note: Part-time hours worked by nonimmigrant(s) will be in the range of hours stated on the INS Form(s) I-129.**

C. Period Of Employment and Occupation Information

❗ **Please Note: The Date Information MUST be in MM/DD/YYYY format**

1. Begin Date
☐☐ / ☐☐ / ☐☐☐☐

2. End Date
☐☐ / ☐☐ / ☐☐☐☐

3. Occupational Code
☐ ①②③④⑤⑥⑦⑧⑨⓪
☐ ①②③④⑤⑥⑦⑧⑨⓪
☐ ①②③④⑤⑥⑦⑧⑨⓪

4. Number of H-1B Nonimmigrants
☐ ①②③④⑤⑥⑦⑧⑨⓪
☐ ①②③④⑤⑥⑦⑧⑨⓪
☐ ①②③④⑤⑥⑦⑧⑨⓪

5. Job Title

D. Information relating to Work Location for the H-1B Nonimmigrants

❗ This section is **REQUIRED**

❗ **Do NOT write "Same As Above". This section MUST be filled out.**

1. City
State

2. Prevailing Wage
$ ☐☐☐☐☐☐ . 0 0

5. Year Source Published

3. Wage is Per:
○ Year   ○ Week
○ Month ○ Hour
○ 2 Weeks

4. Wage Source
○ SESA
○ Collective Bargaining Agreement
○ Other

If OTHER is chosen as the Wage Source, Numbers 5 and 6 in this section MUST be filled out.

6. Other Wage Source

Page Link
☐ 3 1 3 7 7 5

❗ If filing the form electronically, the Page Link field will be automatically created for you upon printing. If filing the form manually, please ensure that the Page Link field contains a 6 digit number that is repeated on all 3 pages.

26277

Form ETA 9035 - Page 1 of 3

| Labor Condition Application for H-1B Nonimmigrants | U.S. Department of Labor Employment and Training Administration | Form ETA 9035 OMB Approval: 1205-0310 Expiration Date: 19 JAN 2004 |

D. Subsection A Information For Additional or Subsequent Work Location

! This Section should be completed only if filing for more than 1 work location.

1. City

State

2. Prevailing Wage $ [ ] . 0 0

3. Wage is Per:
- ○ Year
- ○ Month
- ○ 2 Weeks
- ○ Week
- ○ Hour

4. Wage Source
- ○ SESA
- ○ Collective Bargaining Agreement
- ○ Other

If OTHER is chosen as the Wage Source, Numbers 5 and 6 in this section MUST be filled out.

5. Year Source Published

6. Other Wage Source

E. Employer Labor Condition Statements

! **Please Note: In order for your application to be processed, you MUST read section E of the Labor Condition Application cover pages under the heading "Employer Labor Condition Statements" and agree to all 4 labor condition statements summarized below:**

(1) Wages: Pay nonimmigrants at least the local prevailing wage or the employer's actual wage, whichever is higher, and pay for non-productive time. Offer nonimmigrants benefits on the same basis as U.S. workers.

(2) Working Conditions: Provide working conditions for nonimmigrants which will not adversely affect the working conditions of workers similarly employed.

(3) Strike, Lockout, or Work Stoppage: No strike or lockout in the occupational classification at the place of employment.

(4) Notice: Notice to union or to workers at the place of employment. A copy of this form to H-1B workers.

I have read and agree to Employer Labor Condition Statements 1, 2, 3, and 4 as set forth in Section E of the Labor Condition Application Cover Pages.   ○ Yes   ○ No

F. Additional Employer Labor Condition Statments

! **Please Note: In order for your application to be processed, you MUST read Section F - Subsections 1 and 2 of the Labor Condition Application cover pages under the heading "Additional Employer Labor Condition Statements" and choose one of the 3 alternatives (A, B, or C) listed below in Subsection 1. If you mark Alternative B, you MUST read Section F - Subsection 2 of the cover pages under the heading "Additional Employer Labor Condition Statements" and indicate your agreement to all 3 additional statements summarized below in Subsection 2.**

1. Subsection 1
Choose ONE of the following 3 alternatives:

A ○ **Employer is not H-1B dependent and is not a willful violator.**

B ○ **Employer is H-1B dependent and/or a willful violator.**

C ○ **Employer is H-1B dependent and/or a willful violator BUT will use this application ONLY to support H-1B petitions for exempt nonimmigrants.**

2. Subsection 2
If Alternative B in Subsection 1 is marked, the following Additional Labor Condition Statements are applicable:

A. **Displacement: Non-displacement of the U.S. workers in employer's work force;**

B. **Secondary Displacement: Non-displacement of U.S. workers in another employer's work force; and**

C. **Recruitment and Hiring: Recruitment of U.S. workers and hiring of U.S. worker applicant(s) who are equally or better qualified than the H-1B nonimmigrant(s).**

I have read and agree to Additional Labor Conditional Statements 2 A, B, and C.   ○ Yes   ○ No

Page Link

| 3 | 1 | 3 | 7 | 7 | 5 |

! If filing the form electronically, the Page Link field will be automatically created for you upon printing. If filing the form manually, please ensure that the Page Link field contains a 6 digit number that is repeated on all 3 pages.

26277

Form ETA 9035 - Page 2 of 3

| Labor Condition Application for H-1B Nonimmigrants | **U.S. Department of Labor**
Employment and Training Administration | **Form ETA 9035**
OMB Approval: 1205-0310
Expiration Date: 19 JAN 2004 |

G. Public Disclosure Information

Public disclosure information will be kept at:

! You must choose one of the two options listed in this Section.

○ Employer's principal place of business

○ Place of employment

H. Declaration of Employer

! By signing this form, I, on behalf of the employer, attest that the information and labor condition statements provided are true and accurate; that I have read the sections E and F of the cover pages (Form ETA 9035CP), and that I agree to comply with the Labor Condition Statements as set forth in the cover pages and with the Department of Labor regulations (20 CFR part 655, Subparts H and I). I agree to make this applicaton, supporting documentation, and other records, available to officials of the Department of Labor upon request during any investigation under the Immigration and Nationality Act.

1. First Name of Hiring or Other Designated Official   MI

2. Last Name of Hiring or Other Designated Official

3. Hiring or Other Designated Official Title

5. Date ☐☐ / ☐☐ / ☐☐☐☐

4. Signature - Do NOT let signature extend beyond the box

I. Contact Information

1. Contact First Name   MI

2. Contact Last Name

3. Contact Phone Number   Extension
(☐☐☐) ☐☐☐ - ☐☐☐☐   ☐☐☐☐

J. U.S. Government Agency Use Only

By virtue of my signature below, I hereby acknowledge this application certified for

Date Starting _____ and Date Ending _____

_____
Signature and Title of Authorized DOL Official   ETA Case Number   Date

The Department of Labor is not the guarantor of the accuracy, truthfulness, or adequacy of a certified labor condition application.

K. Complaints

Complaints alleging misrepresentation of material facts in the labor condition application and/or failure to comply with the terms of the labor condition application may be filed with any office of the Wage and Hour Division of the United States Department of Labor. Complaints alleging failure to offer employment to an equally or better qualified U.S. worker, or an employer's misrepresentation regarding such offer(s) of employment, may be filed with: U.S Department of Justice * 10th Street and Constitution Avenue, NW * Washington, DC * 20530.

Page Link: 3 1 3 7 7 5

! If filing the form electronically, the Page Link field will be automatically created for you upon printing. If filing the form manually, please ensure that the Page Link field contains a 6 digit number that is repeated on all 3 pages.

26277

Reset   Form ETA 9035 - Page 3 of 3

U.S. Department of Justice
Immigration and Naturalization Service

OMB No. 1115-0066
BIOGRAPHIC INFORMATION

(Family name)	(First name)	(Middle name)	☐ MALE ☐ FEMALE	BIRTHDATE (Mo.-Day-Yr.)	NATIONALITY	FILE NUMBER A-

ALL OTHER NAMES USED (Including names by previous marriages)	CITY AND COUNTRY OF BIRTH	SOCIAL SECURITY NO. (If any)

	FAMILY NAME	FIRST NAME	DATE, CITY AND COUNTRY OF BIRTH (If known)	CITY AND COUNTRY OF RESIDENCE.
FATHER				
MOTHER (Maiden name)				

HUSBAND (If none, so state) OR WIFE	FAMILY NAME (For wife, give maiden name)	FIRST NAME	BIRTHDATE	CITY & COUNTRY OF BIRTH	DATE OF MARRIAGE	PLACE OF MARRIAGE

FORMER HUSBANDS OR WIVES (if none, so state) FAMILY NAME (For wife, give maiden name)	FIRST NAME	BIRTHDATE	DATE & PLACE OF MARRIAGE	DATE AND PLACE OF TERMINATION OF MARRIAGE

APPLICANT'S RESIDENCE LAST FIVE YEARS. LIST PRESENT ADDRESS FIRST

STREET AND NUMBER	CITY	PROVINCE OR STATE	COUNTRY	FROM MONTH	YEAR	TO MONTH	YEAR
						PRESENT TIME	

APPLICANT'S LAST ADDRESS OUTSIDE THE UNITED STATES OF MORE THAN ONE YEAR

STREET AND NUMBER	CITY	PROVINCE OR STATE	COUNTRY	FROM MONTH	YEAR	TO MONTH	YEAR

APPLICANT'S EMPLOYMENT LAST FIVE YEARS. (IF NONE, SO STATE) LIST PRESENT EMPLOYMENT FIRST

FULL NAME AND ADDRESS OF EMPLOYER	OCCUPATION (SPECIFY)	FROM MONTH	YEAR	TO MONTH	YEAR
				PRESENT TIME	

Show below last occupation abroad if not shown above. (Include all information requested above.)				

THIS FORM IS SUBMITTED IN CONNECTION WITH APPLICATION FOR: ☐ NATURALIZATION ☐ STATUS AS PERMANENT RESIDENT ☐ OTHER (SPECIFY):	SIGNATURE OF APPLICANT	DATE
Submit all four pages of this form.	If your native alphabet is other than roman letters, write your name in your native alphabet here:	

PENALTIES: SEVERE PENALTIES ARE PROVIDED BY LAW FOR KNOWINGLY AND WILLFULLY FALSIFYING OR CONCEALING A MATERIAL FACT.

APPLICANT: BE SURE TO PUT YOUR NAME AND ALIEN REGISTRATION NUMBER IN THE BOX OUTLINED BY HEAVY BORDER BELOW.

COMPLETE THIS BOX (Family name)	(Given name)	(Middle name)	(Alien registration number)

Form G-325A (Rev. 09/11/00) Y

(1) Ident.

U.S. Department of Justice
Immigration and Naturalization Service

OMB No.1115-0168
Petition for a Nonimmigrant Worker

START HERE - Please Type or Print.	**FOR INS USE ONLY**

Part 1. Information about the employer filing this petition. If the employer is an individual, use the top name line. Organizations should use the second line.

Family Name	Given Name	Middle Initial

Company or Organization Name

Address - Attn:

Street Number and Name		Apt. #
City	State or Province	
Country	Zip/Postal Code	

IRS Tax #

Part 2. Information about this petition.
(See instructions to determine the fee.)

1. **Requested Nonimmigrant Classification**
   (Write classification symbol at right)

2. **Basis for Classification** *(Check one)*
   a. ☐ New employment
   b. ☐ Continuation of previously approved employment without change
   c. ☐ Change in previously approved employment
   d. ☐ New concurrent employment

3. **Prior Petition.** If you checked other than "New Employment" in item 2. (above) give the most recent prior petition number for the worker(s):

4. **Requested Action:** *(Check one)*
   a. ☐ Notify the office in Part 4 so the person(s) can obtain a visa or be admitted (NOTE: a petition is not required for an E-1, E-2 or R visa).
   b. ☐ Change the person(s) status and extend their stay since they are all now in the U.S. in another status (see instructions for limitations). This is available only where you check "New Employment" in item 2, above.
   c. ☐ Extend or amend the stay of ther person(s) since they now hold this status.

   Total number of workers in petition:
   (See instructions for where more than one worker can be included.)

Part 3. Information about the person(s) you are filing for.
Complete the blocks below. Use the continuation sheet to name each person included in this petition.

If an entertainment group, give their group name

Family Name	Given Name	Middle Initial
Date of Birth *(Month/Day/Year)*	Country of Birth	
Social Security #	A #	

If in the United States, complete the following:

Date of Arrival *(Month/Day/Year)*	I-94 #
Current Nonimmigrant Status	Expires *(Month/Day/Year)*

FOR INS USE ONLY (right column)

Returned _____

Resubmitted _____

Reloc Sent _____

Reloc Rec'd _____

Receipt

Interviewed
☐ Petitioner
☐ Beneficiary

Class: _____
# of Workers: _____
Priority Number: _____
Validity Dates: From _____
To _____

☐ **Classification**
☐ Consulate/POE/PFI Notified
At: _____
☐ Extension Granted
☐ COS/Extension Granted

Partial Approval *(explain)*

Action Block

To Be Completed by Attorney or Representative, if any
☐ Fill in box if G-28 is attached to represent the applicant

VOLAG#

ATTY State License #

Continued on back.

Form I-129 (Rev. 12/10/01) Y

Part 4. Processing Information.

a. If the person named in Part 3 is outside the U.S. or a requested extension of stay or change of status cannot be granted, give the U.S. consulate or inspection facility you want notified if this petition is approved.

Type of Office *(Check one)*: ☐ Consulate   ☐ Pre-flight inspection   ☐ Port of Entry

Office Address *(City)*   U.S. State or Foreign Country

Person's Foreign Address

b. Does each person in this petition have a valid passport?
   ☐ Not required to have passport   ☐ No - explain on separate paper   ☐ Yes

c. Are you filing any other petitions with this one?   ☐ No   ☐ Yes - How many? _____

d. Are applications for replacement/initial I-94's being filed with this petition?   ☐ No   ☐ Yes - How many? _____

e. Are applications by dependents being filed with this petition?   ☐ No   ☐ Yes - How many? _____

f. Is any person in this petition in exclusion or deportation proceedings?   ☐ No   ☐ Yes - explain on separate paper

g. Have you ever filed an immigrant petition for any person in this petition? ☐ No   ☐ Yes - explain on separate paper

h. If you indicated you were filing a new petition in Part 2, within the past 7 years has any person in this petition:

   1) ever been given the classification you are now requesting?   ☐ No   ☐ Yes - explain on separate paper

   2) ever been denied the classification you are now requesting?   ☐ No   ☐ Yes - explain on separate paper

i. If you are filing for an entertainment group, has any person in this petition not been with the group for at least 1 year?   ☐ No   ☐ Yes - explain on separate paper

Part 5. Basic information about the proposed employment and employer. *Attach the supplement relating to the classification you are requesting.*

Job Title   Nontechnical Description of Job

Address where the person(s) will work if different from the address in Part 1.

Is this a full-time position?
   ☐ No - Hours per week   ☐ Yes   Wages per week or per year

Other Compensation *(Explain)*   Value per week or per year   Dates of intended employment From: To

Type of Petitioner - *Check*   ☐ U.S. citizen or permanent resident   ☐ Organization   ☐ Other - explain on separate paper

Type of Business: Year established:

Current Number of Employees   Gross Annual Income   Net Annual Income

Part 6. Signature. *Read the information on penalties in the instructions before completing this section.*

I certify, under penalty of perjury under the laws of the United States of America, that this petition, and the evidence submitted with it, is all true and correct. If filing this on behalf of an organization, I certify that I am empowered to do so by that organization. If this petition is to extend a prior petition, I certify that the proposed employment is under the same terms and conditions as in the prior approved petition. I authorize the release of any information from my records, or from the petitioning organization's records, which the Immigration and Naturalization Service needs to determine eligibility for the benefit being sought.

Signature and Title   Print Name   Date

Please Note: If you do not completely fill out this form and the required supplement, or fail to submit required documents listed in the instructions, then the person(s) filed for may not be found eligible for the requested benefit, and this petition may be denied.

Part 7. Signature of person preparing form, if other than above.

I declare that I prepared this petition at the request of the above person and it is based on all information of which I have any knowledge.

Signature   Print Name   Date

Firm Name and Address

E Classification
Supplement to Form I-129

U.S. Department of Justice
Immigration and Naturalization Service

Name of person or organization filing petition:	Name of person you are filing for:

Classification Sought *(Check one):*
☐ E-1 Treaty trader   ☐ E-2 Treaty investor

Name of country signatory to treaty with U.S.

Section 1.   **Information about the Employer Outside the U.S. (If any)**

Name	Address
Alien's Position - Title, duties and number of years employed	Principal Product, Merchandise or Service
Total Number of Employees	

Section 2.   **Additional information about the U.S. Employer**

The U.S. company is, to the company outside the U.S. *(Check one)*:
☐ Parent   ☐ Branch   ☐ Subsidiary   ☐ Affiliate   ☐ Joint Venture

Date and Place of Incorporation or establishment in the U.S.

Nationality of Ownership *(Individual or Corporate)*

Name	Nationality	Immigration Status	% Ownership

Assets	Net Worth	Total Annual Income
Staff in the U.S.	Executive Manager	Specialized Qualifications or Knowledge
Nationals of Treaty Country in E or L Status		
Total number of employees in the U.S.		

Total number of employees the alien would supervise; or describe the nature of the specialized skills essential to the U.S. company.

Section 3.   **Complete if filing for an E-1 Treaty Trader**

Total Annual Gross Trade/Business of the U.S. company   For Year Ending

$

Percent of total gross trade which is between the U.S. and the country of which the treaty trader organization is a national.

Section 4.   **Complete if filing for an E-2 Treaty Investor**

Total Investment:	Cash	Equipment	Other
	$	$	$
	Inventory	Premises	Total
	$	$	$

Name of person or organization filing petition:

Name of person or total number of workers or trainees you are filing for:

List the alien's and any dependent family members' prior periods of stay in H classification in the U.S. for the last six years. Be sure to list only those periods in which the alien and/or family members were actually in the U.S. in an H classification. If more space is needed, attach an additional sheet.

Classification sought *(Check one)*:

☐ H-1A Registered professional nurse
☐ H-1B1 Specialty occupation
☐ H-1B2 Exceptional services relating to a cooperative research and development project administered by the U.S. Department of Defense
☐ H-1B3 Artist, entertainer or fashion model of national or international acclaim
☐ H-1B4 Artist or entertainer in unique or traditional art form

☐ H-1B5 Athlete
☐ H-1BS Essential Support Personnel for H-1B entertainer or athlete
☐ H-2A Agricultural worker
☐ H-2B Nonagricultural worker
☐ H-3 Trainee
☐ H-3 Special education exchange visitor program

Section 1. Complete this section if filing for H-1A or H-1B classification.

Describe the proposed duties

Alien's present occupation and summary of prior work experience

Statement for H-1B specialty occupations only:

By filing this petition, I agree to the terms of the labor condition application for the duration of the alien's authorized period of stay for H-1B employment.

Petitioner's Signature   Date

Statement for H-1B specialty occupations and DOD projects:

As an authorized official of the employer, I certify that the employer will be liable for the reasonable costs of return transportation of the alien abroad if the alien is dismissed from employment by the employer before the end of the period of authorized stay.

Signature of authoried official of employer   Date

Statement for H-1B DOD projects only:

I certify that the alien will be working on a cooperative research and development project or a coproduction project under a reciprocal Government-to-governement agreement administered by the Department of Defense.

DOD project manager's signature   Date

Section 2. Complete this section if filing for H-2A or H-2B classification.

Employment is: ☐ Seasonal   Temporary need is: ☐ Unpredictable
(Check one)   ☐ Peakload   *(Check one)*   ☐ Periodic
                  ☐ Intermittent   ☐ Recurrent annually
                  ☐ One-time occurrence

Explain your temporary need for the alien's services (attach a separate paper if additional space is needed).

Continued on back.

Section 3. Complete this section if filing for H-2A classification.

The petitioner and each employer consent to allow government access to the site where the labor is being performed for the purpose of determining compliance with H-2A requirements. The petitioner further agrees to notify the Service in the manner and within the time frame specified if an H-2A worker absconds or if the authorized employment ends more than five days before the relating certification document expires, and pay liquidated damages of ten dollars for each instance where it cannot demonstrate compliance with this notification requirement. The petitioner also agrees to pay liquidated damages of two hundred dollars for each instance where it cannot be demonstrated that the H-2A worker either departed the United States or obtained authorized status during the period of admission or within five days of early termination, whichever comes first.

The petitioner must execute Part A. If the petitioner is the employer's agent, the employer must execute Part B. If there are joint employers, they must each execute Part C.

Part A. Petitioner:

By filing this petition, I agree to the conditions of H-2A employment, and agree to the notice requirements and limited liabilities defined in 8 CFR 214.2(h)(3)(vi).

Petitioner's signature   Date

Part B. Employer who is not petitioner:

I certify that I have authorized the party filing this petition to act as my agent in this regard. I assume full responsibility for all representations made by this agent on my behalf, and agree to the conditions of H-2A eligibility.

Employer's signature   Date

Part C. Joint Employers:

I agree to the conditions of H-2A eligibility.

Joint employer's signature(s)   Date

Joint employer's signature(s)   Date

Joint employer's signature(s)   Date

Joint employer's signature(s)   Date

Joint employer's signature(s)   Date

Section 4. Complete this section if filing for H-3 classification.

If you answer "yes" to any of the following questions, attach a full explanation.

a. Is the training you intend to provide, or similar training, available in the alien's country? ☐ No ☐ Yes
b. Will the training benefit the alien in pursuing a career abroad? ☐ No ☐ Yes
c. Does the training involve productive employment incidental to training? ☐ No ☐ Yes
d. Does the alien already have skills related to the training? ☐ No ☐ Yes
e. Is this training an effort to overcome a labor shortage? ☐ No ☐ Yes
f. Do you intend to employ the alien abroad at the end of this training? ☐ No ☐ Yes

If you do not intend to employ this person abroad at the end of this training, explain why you wish to incur the cost of providing this training, and your expected return from this training.

U.S. Department of Justice
Immigration and Naturalization Service

L Classification
Supplement to Form I-129

Name of person or organization filing petition: | Name of person you are filing for:

This petition is *(Check one)*: ☐ An individual petition   ☐ A blanket petition

Section 1. Complete this section if filing an individual.

Classification sought *(Check one)*: ☐ L-1A manager or executive   ☐ L-1B specialized knowledge

List the alien's, and any dependent family member's prior periods of stay in an L classification in the U.S. for the last seven years. Be sure to list only those periods in which the alien and/or family members were actually in the U.S. in an L classification.

Name and address of employer abroad

Dates of alien's employment with this employer. Explain any interruptions in employment.

Description of the alien's duties for the past 3 years.

Description of alien's proposed duties in the U.S.

Summarize the alien's education and work experience.

The U.S. company is, to the company abroad: *(Check one)*
☐ Parent   ☐ Branch   ☐ Subsidiary   ☐ Affiliate   ☐ Joint Venture

Describe the stock ownership and managerial control of each company.

Do the companies currently have the same qualifying relationship as they did during the one-year period of the alien's employment with the company abroad?   ☐ Yes   ☐ No *(Attach explanation)*

Is the alien coming to the U.S. to open a new office?
☐ Yes *(Explain in detail on separate paper)*   ☐ No

Section 2. Complete this section if filing a Blanket Petition.

List all U.S. and foreign parent, branches, subsidiaries and affiliates included in this petition. *(Attach a separate paper if additional space is needed.)*

Name and Address   Relationship

Explain in detail on separate paper.

O and P Classification
Supplement to Form I-129

U.S. Department of Justice
Immigration and Naturalization Service

Name of person or organization filing petition: Name of person or group or total number of workers you are filing for:

Classification sought *(Check one)*:

☐ O-1 Alien of extraordinary ability in sciences, art, education, or business.
☐ P-2 Artist or entertainer for reciprocal exchange program
☐ P-2S Essential Support Personnel for P-2.

Explain the nature of the event

Describe the duties to be performed

If filing for O-2 or P support alien, dates of the alien's prior experience with the O-1 or P alien.

Have you obtained the required written consulation(s)?   ☐ Yes - attached   ☐ No - Copy of request attached
If not, give the following information about the organization(s) to which you have sent a duplicate of this petition.

O-1 Extraordinary ability

Name of recognized peer group   Phone #

Address   Date sent

O-1 Extraordinary achievement in motion pictures or television

Name of labor organization   Phone #

Address   Date sent

Name of management organization   Phone #

Address   Date sent

O-2 or P alien

Name of labor organization   Phone #

Address   Date Sent

U.S. Department of Justice
Immigration and Naturalization Service

O & R Classifications
Supplement to Form I-129

Name of person or organization filing petition: Name of person you are filing for:

Section 1.   **Complete this section if you are filing for a Q international cultural exchange alien.**

I hereby certify that the participant(s) in the international cultural exchange program:
- is at least 18 years of age,
- has the ability to communicate effectively about the cultural attributes of his or her country of nationality to the American public, and
  has not previously been in the United States as a Q nonimmigrant unless he/she has resided and been physically present outside the U.S.
- for the immediate prior year.

I also certify that the same wages and working conditions are accorded the participants as are provided similarly employed U.S. workers.

Petitioner's signature   Date

Section 2.   **Complete this section if you are filing for an R religious worker.**

List the alien's, and any dependent family members, prior periods of stay in R classification in the U.S. for the last six years. Be sure to list only those periods in which the alien and/or family members were actually in the U.S. in an R classification.

Describe the alien's proprosed duties in the U.S.

Describe the alien's qualifications for the vocation or occupation.

Description of the relationship between the U.S. religious organization and the organization abroad of which the alien was a member.

Supplement-1

Attach to Form I-129 when more than one person is included in the petition. *(List each person separtely. Do not include the person you named on the form).*

Family Name		Given Name	Middle Initial	Date of Birth *(Month/Day/Year)*
Country of Birth		Social Security No.		A#

IF IN THE U.S.	Date of Arrival *(Month/Day/Year)*		I-94#	
	Current Nonimmigrant Status:		Expires on *(Month/Day/Year)*	

Country where passport issued	Expiration Date *(Month/Day/Year)*	Date Started with group

Family Name		Given Name	Middle Initial	Date of Birth *(Month/Day/Year)*
Country of Birth		Social Security No.		A#

IF IN THE U.S.	Date of Arrival *(Month/Day/Year)*		I-94#	
	Current Nonimmigrant Status:		Expires on *(Month/Day/Year)*	

Country where passport issued	Expiration Date *(Month/DayYyear)*	Date Started with group

Family Name		Given Name	Middle Initial	Date of Birth *(Month/Day/Year)*
Country of Birth		Social Security No.		A#

IF IN THE U.S.	Date of Arrival *(Month/Day/Year)*		I-94#	
	Current Nonimmigrant Status:		Expires on *(Month/Day/Year)*	

Country where passport issued	Expiration Date *(Month/Day/Year)*	Date Started with group

Family Name		Given Name	Middle Initial	Date of Birth *(Month/Day/Year)*
Country of Birth		Social Security No.		A#

IF IN THE U.S.	Date of Arrival *(Month/Day/Year)*		I-94#	
	Current Nonimmigrant Status:		Expires on *(Month/Day/Year)*	

Country where passport issued	Expiration Date *(Month/Day/Year)*	Date Started with group

Family Name		Given Name	Middle Initial	Date of Birth *(Month/Day/Year)*
Country of Birth		Social Security No.		A#

IF IN THE U.S.	Date of Arrival *(Month/Day/Year)*		I-94#	
	Current Nonimmigrant Status:		Expires on *(Month/Day/Year)*	

Country where passport issued	Expiration Date *(Month/Day/Year)*	Date Started with group

Continued on back.

Supplement-1

Attach to Form I-129 when more than one person is included in the petition. *(List each person separtely. Do not include the person you named on the form).*

Family Name		Given Name	Middle Initial	Date of Birth *(Month/Day/Year)*
Country of Birth		Social Security No.		A#
IF IN THE U.S.	Date of Arrival *(Month/Day/Year)*		I-94#	
	Current Nonimmigrant Status:		Expires on *(Month/Day/Year)*	
Country where passport issued		Expiration Date *(Month/Day/Year)*	Date Started with group	

Family Name		Given Name	Middle Initial	Date of Birth *(Month/Day/Year)*
Country of Birth		Social Security No.		A#
IF IN THE U.S.	Date of Arrival *(Month/Day/Year)*		I-94#	
	Current Nonimmigrant Status:		Expires on *(Month/Day/Year)*	
Country where passport issued		Expiration Date *(Month/Day/Year)*	Date Started with group	

Family Name		Given Name	Middle Initial	Date of Birth *(Month/Day/Year)*
Country of Birth		Social Security No.		A#
IF IN THE U.S.	Date of Arrival *(month/day/year)*		I-94#	
	Current Nonimmigrant Status:		Expires on *(Month/Day/Year)*	
Country where passport issued		Expiration Date *(Month/Day/Year)*	Date Started with group	

Family Name		Given Name	Middle Initial	Date of Birth *(Month/Day/Year)*
Country of Birth		Social Security No.		A#
IF IN THE U.S.	Date of Arrival *(Month/Day/Year)*		I-94#	
	Current Nonimmigrant Status:		Expires on *(Month/Day/Year)*	
Country where passport issued		Expiration Date *(Month/Day/Year)*	Date Started with group	

Family Name		Given Name	Middle Initial	Date of Birth *(Month/Day/Year)*
Country of Birth		Social Security No.		A#
IF IN THE U.S.	Date of Arrival *(Month/Day/Year)*		I-94#	
	Current Nonimmigrant Status:		Expires on *(Month/Day/Year)*	
Country where passport issued		Expiration Date *(Month/Day/Year)*	Date Started with group	

OMB No. 1115-0071

Petition for Alien Fiancé(e)

DO NOT WRITE IN THIS BLOCK

Case ID#	Action Stamp	Fee Stamp
A#		
G-28 or Volag #		

The petition is approved for status under Section 101(a)(15)(k). It is valid for four months from date of action.	AMCON: _____ ☐ Personal Interview ☐ Previously Forwarded ☐ Document Check ☐ Field Investigations

Remarks:

A. Information about you.

1. Name (Family name in CAPS)   (First)   (Middle)

2. Address (Number and Street)   (Apartment Number)

(Town or City)   (State/Country)   (Zip/Postal Code)

3. Place of Birth (Town or City)   (State/Country)

4. Date of Birth (Mo/Day/Yr)   **5. Sex** ☑ Male ☑ Female   **6. Marital Status** ☐ Married ☐ Single ☐ Widowed ☐ Divorced

7. Other Names Used (including maiden name)

8. Social Security Number (if any)   **9. Alien Registration Number** (if any)

10. Names of Prior Husband/Wives   **11. Date(s) Marriages(s)**

12. If you are a U.S. citizen, complete the following:
My citizenship was acquired through (check one)

☐ Birth in the U.S.   ☐ Naturalization

Give number of certificate, date and place it was issued

☐ Parents
Have you obtained a certificate of citizenship in your own name?
☐ Yes   ☐ No
If "Yes," give number of certificate, date and place it was issued.

13. Have you ever filed for this or any other alien fiancé(e) before?   ☐ Yes   ☐ No
If you checked "yes," give name of alien, place and date of filing, and result.

B. Information about your alien fiancé(e).

1. Name (Family name in CAPS)   (First)   (Middle)

2. Address (Number and Street)   (Apartment Number)

(Town or City)   (State/Country)   (Zip/Postal Code)

3. Place of Birth (Town or City)   (State/Country)

4. Date of Birth (Mo/Day/Yr)   **5. Sex** ☐ Male ☐ Female   **6. Marital Status** ☐ Married ☐ Single ☐ Widowed ☐ Divorced

7. Other Names Used (including maiden name)

8. Social Security Number (if any)   **9. Alien Registration Number** (if any)

10. Names of Prior Husbands/Wives   **11. Date(s) Marriages(s)**

12. Has your fiancé(e) ever been in the U.S.?
☐ Yes   ☐ No

13. If your fiancé(e) is currently in the U.S., complete the following:
He or she last arrived as a (visitor, student, exchange alien, crewman, stowaway, temporary worker, without inspection, etc.)

Arrival/Departure Record (I-94)   **Date arrived** (Month/Day/Year)

Date authorized stay expired, or will expire, as shown on Form I-94

INITIAL	RESUBMITTED	RELOCATED		COMPLETED		
		Rec'd	Sent	Approved	Denied	Returned

B. Information about your alien fiancé(e)   (Continued)

14. List all children of your alien fiancé(e) (if any)

(Name)	(Date of Birth)	(Country of Birth)	(Present Address)

15. Address in the United States where your fiancé(e) intends to live

(Number and Street)	(Town or City)	(State)

16. Your fiancé(e)'s address abroad

(Number and Street)	(Town or City)	(Province)	(Country)	(Phone Number)

17. If your fiancé(e)'s native alphabet uses other than Roman letters, write his or her name and address abroad in the native alphabet:

(Name)	(Number and Street)	(Town or City)	(Province)	(Country)

18. Is your fiancé(e) related to you?   ☐ Yes   ☐ No
If you are related, state the nature and degree of relationship, e.g., third cousin or maternal uncle, etc.

19. Has your fiancé(e) met and seen you?   ☐ Yes   ☐ No

Describe the circumstances under which you met. If you have not personally met each ether, explain how the relationship was established, and explain in detail any reasons you may have for requesting that the requirement that you and your fiancé(e) must have met should not apply to you.

20. Your fiancé(e) will apply for a visa abroad at the American Consulate in _____   _____
(City)   (Country)

(Designation of a consulate outside the country of your fiancé(e)'s last residence does not guarantee acceptance for processing by that consulate. Acceptance is at the discretion of the designated consulate.)

C. Other information

If you are serving overseas in the Armed Forces of the United States, please answer the following:

I presently reside or am stationed overseas and my current mailing address is _____

I plan to return to the United States on or about _____

Penalties: **You may, by law, be imprisoned for not more than five years, or fined $250,000, or both, for entering into a marriage contract for the purpose of evading any provision of the immigration laws and you may be fined up to $10,000 or imprisoned up to five years, or both, for knowingly and willfully falsifying or concealing a material fact or using any false document in submitting this petition.**

Your Certification:
I am legally able to and intend to marry my alien fiancé(e) within 90 days of his or her arrival in the United States. I certify, under penalty of perjury under the laws of the United States of America, that the foregoing is true and correct. Furthermore, I authorize the release of any information from my records which the Immigration and Naturalizaton Service needs to determine eligibility for the benefit that I am seeking.

Signature _____ (Date) _____ (Phone Number) _____

Signature of Person Preparing Form, If Other Than Above:

I declare that I prepared this document at the request of the person above and that it is based on all information of which I have any knowledge.

Print Name _____ (Address) _____ (Signature) _____ (Date) _____

G-28 ID _____   **Volag** _____

H-1B Data Collection and Filing Fee Exemption

Petitioner's Name: [   ]

PART A.   General

Employer Information - *(check all items that apply)*   Yes   No

1. Is the petitioner a dependent employer?   ☐   ☐
2. Has the petitioner ever been found to be a willful violator?   ☐   ☐
3. Is the beneficiary an exempt H -1B nonimmigrant?   ☐   ☐
   a. If yes, is it because the beneficiary's annual rate of pay is equal to at least $60,000?   ☐   ☐
   b. Or is it because the beneficiary has a master's or higher degree in a speciality related to the employment?   ☐   ☐

Beneficiary' s Last Name	First Name	Middle Name
[ ]	[ ]	[ ]

Attention To or In Care Of	Current Residential Address - Street	Apt. #
[ ]	[ ]	[ ]

City	State	Zip Code
[ ]	[ ]	[ ]

Beneficiary's Highest Level of Education. Please check only one box.

☐ NO DIPLOMA

☐ HIGH SCHOOL GRADUATE - high school DIPLOMA or the equivalent (for example ,GED)

☐ Some college credit, but less than one year

☐ One or more years of college, no degree

☐ Associate's degree *(for example: AA, AS)*

☐ Bachelor's degree *(for example: BA, AB, BS)*

☐ Master's degree *(for example: MA, MS, MEng, MEd, MSW, MBA)*

☐ Professional degree *(for example: MD, DDS, DVM, LLB, JD)*

☐ Doctorate degree *(for example: PhD, EdD)*

Major/Primary Field of Study

[   ]

Rate of pay per year	LCA Code	NAICS Code
[ ]	[ ]	[ ]

PART B.   Fee Exemption

In order for the Immigration and Naturalization Service to determine if you must pay the additional $1,000 fee, please answer all of the following questions:

Yes   No

1. ☐ ☐ Are you an institution of higher education as defined in the Higher Education Act of 1965, section 101(a), 20 U.S.C. section 1001 (a)?

2. ☐ ☐ Are you a nonprofit organization or entity related to or affiliated with an institution of higher education, as such institutions of higher education are defined in the Higher Education Act of 1965, section 101(a), 20 U.S.C. section 1001(a)?

3. ☐ ☐ Are you a nonprofit research organization or a governmental research organization, as defined in 8 CFR 214.2(h)(19)(iii)(C)?

4. ☐ ☐ Is this the second or subsequent request for an extension of stay that you have filed for this alien?

5. ☐ ☐ Is this an amended petition that does not contain any requests for extension of stay?

6. ☐ ☐ Are you filing this petition in order to correct a Service error?

7. ☐ ☐ Is the petitioner a primary or secondary education institution?

8. ☐ ☐ Is the petitioner a non-profit entity that engages in an established curriculum-related clinical training of students registered at such an institution?

If you answered **YES** to any of the sections above, you are **ONLY** required to submit the fee for your H-1B Form I-129 petition, which is $130.00.

PART C.   Numerical Limitation Exemption Information

Yes No

1. ☐ ☐ Are you an institution of higher education as defined in the Higher Education Act of 1965, section 101(a), 20 U.S.C. section 1001 (a)?

2. ☐ ☐ Are you a nonprofit organization or entity related to or affiliated with an institution of higher education, as such institutions of higher education are defined in the Higher Education Act of 1965, section 101(a), 20 U.S.C. section 1001(a)?

3. ☐ ☐ Are you a nonprofit research organization or a governmental research organization, as defined in 8 CFR 214.2(h)(19)(iii)(C)?

4. ☐ ☐ Is the beneficiary of this petition a J-1 nonimmigrant alien who received a waiver of the 2-year foreign residency requirement described in section 214 (l)(1)(B) of the Act?

5. ☐ ☐ Has the beneficiary of this petition been previously granted status as an H-1B nonimmigrant in the past 6 years and not left the U.S. for more than a year after attaining such status?

6. ☐ ☐ If the petition is to request a change of employer, did the beneficiary previously work as an H-1B for an institution of higher education, an entity related to or affiliated with an institution of higher education, or a nonprofit research organization or governmental research institution defined in questions 1, 2 and 3 of Part C of this form?

I certify under penalty of perjury, under the laws of the United States of America, that this attachment and the evidence submitted with it is true and correct. If filing this on behalf of an organization or entity, I certify that I am empowered to do so by that organization or entity. I authorize the release of any information from my records, or from the petitioning organization or entity's records, that the Immigration and Naturalization Service may need to determine eligibility for the exemption being sought.

Certification.

_____   _____
Signature   Print Name

_____   _____
Title   Date

U.S. Department of Justice
Immigration and Naturalization Service

OMB #1115-0054
Petition for Alien Relative

DO NOT WRITE IN THIS BLOCK - FOR EXAMINING OFFICE ONLY

A#	Action Stamp	Fee Stamp

Section of Law/Visa Category
- [ ] 201(b) Spouse - IR-1/CR-1
- [ ] 201(b) Child - IR-2/CR-2
- [ ] 201(b) Parent - IR-5
- [ ] 203(a)(1) Unm. S or D - F1-1
- [ ] 203(a)(2)(A)Spouse - F2-1
- [ ] 203(a)(2)(A) Child - F2-2
- [ ] 203(a)(2)(B) Unm. S or D - F2-4
- [ ] 203(a)(3) Married S or D - F3-1
- [ ] 203(a)(4) Brother/Sister - F4-1

Petition was filed on: _____ (priority date)
- [ ] Personal Interview
- [ ] Previously Forwarded
- [ ] Pet. [ ] Ben. " A" File Reviewed
- [ ] I-485 Filed Simultaneously
- [ ] Field Investigation
- [ ] 204(g) Resolved
- [ ] 203(a)(2)(A) Resolved
- [ ] 203(g) Resolved

Remarks:

A. Relationship   You are the petitioner; your relative is the beneficiary.

1. I am filing this petition for my:
- [ ] Husband/Wife
- [ ] Parent
- [ ] Brother/Sister
- [ ] Child

2. Are you related by adoption?
- [ ] Yes
- [ ] No

3. Did you gain permanent residence through adoption?
- [ ] Yes
- [ ] No

B. Information about you

1. Name (Family name in CAPS)   (First)   (Middle)

2. Address (Number and Street)   (Apt.No.)

(Town or City)   (State/Country)   (Zip/Postal Code)

3. Place of Birth (Town or City)   (State/Country)

4. Date of Birth (Month/Day/Year)

5. Gender
- [ ] Male
- [ ] Female

6. Marital Status
- [ ] Married
- [ ] Single
- [ ] Widowed
- [ ] Divorced

7. Other Names Used (including maiden name)

8. Date and Place of Present Marriage (if married)

9. Social Security Number (if any)   **10. Alien Registration Number**

11. Name(s) of Prior Husband(s)/Wive(s)   **12. Date(s) Marriage(s) Ended**

13. If you are a U.S. citizen, complete the following:
My citizenship was acquired through (check one):
- [ ] Birth in the U.S.
- [ ] Naturalization. Give certificate number and date and place of issuance.

- [ ] Parents. Have you obtained a certificate of citizenship in your own name?
    - [ ] Yes. Give certificate number, date and place of issuance.   [ ] No

14a. If you are a lawful permanent resident alien, complete the following: Date and place of admission for, or adjustment to, lawful permanent residence and class of admission.

14b. Did you gain permanent resident status through marriage to a United States citizen or lawful permanent resident?
- [ ] Yes
- [ ] No

C. Information about your relative

1. Name (Family name in CAPS)   (First)   (Middle)

2. Address (Number and Street)   (Apt. No.)

(Town or City)   (State/Country)   (Zip/Postal Code)

3. Place of Birth (Town or City)   (State/Country)

4. Date of Birth (Month/Day/Year)

5. Gender
- [ ] Male
- [ ] Female

6. Marital Status
- [ ] Married
- [ ] Single
- [ ] Widowed
- [ ] Divorced

7. Other Names Used (including maiden name)

8. Date and Place of Present Marriage (if married)

9. Social Security Number (if any)   **10. Alien Registration Number**

11. Name(s) of Prior Husband(s)/Wive(s)   **12. Date(s) Marriage(s) Ended**

13. Has your relative ever been in the U.S.?   [ ] Yes   [ ] No

14. If your relative is currently in the U.S., complete the following:
He or she arrived as a::
(visitor, student, stowaway, without inspection, etc.)

Arrival/Departure Record (I-94)   **Date arrived** (Month/Day/Year)

Date authorized stay expired, or will expire, as shown on Form I-94 or I-95

15. Name and address of present employer (if any)

Date this employment began (Month/Day/Year)

16. Has your relative ever been under immigration proceedings?
- [ ] No
- [ ] Yes   Where _____   When _____
- [ ] Removal
- [ ] Exclusion/Deportation
- [ ] Recission
- [ ] Judicial Proceedings

INITIAL RECEIPT   RESUBMITTED   RELOCATED: Rec'd _____   Sent _____   COMPLETED: Appv'd _____   Denied _____   Ret'd _____

Form I-130 (Rev. 06/05/02) Y

C. Information about your alien relative (continued)

17. List husband/wife and all children of your relative.

(Name)	(Relationship)	(Date of Birth)	(Country of Birth)

18. Address in the United States where your relative intends to live.

(Street Address)	(Town or City)	(State)

19. Your relative's address abroad. (Include street, city, province and country)

_____   Phone Number (if any)

20. If your relative's native alphabet is other than Roman letters, write his or her name and foreign address in the native alphabet.

(Name)   Address (Include street, city, province and country):

21. If filing for your husband/wife, give last address at which you lived together. (Include street, city, province, if any, and country):

	From: (Month) (Year)	To: (Month) (Year)

22. Complete the information below if your relative is in the United States and will apply for adjustment of status

Your relative is in the United States and will apply for adjustment of status to that of a lawful permanent resident at the office of the Immigration and Naturalization Service in _____. If your relative is not eligible for adjustment of status, he or she

(City)   (State)

will apply for a visa abroad at the American consular post in _____ _____

(City)   (Country)

NOTE: Designation of an American embassy or consulate outside the country of your relative's last residence does not guarantee acceptance for processing by that post. Acceptance is at the discretion of the designated embassy or consulate.

D. Other information

1. If separate petitions are also being submitted for other relatives, give names of each and relationship.

2. Have you ever filed a petition for this or any other alien before? ☐ Yes ☐ No

If "Yes," give name, place and date of filing and result.

WARNING: INS investigates claimed relationships and verifies the validity of documents. INS seeks criminal prosecutions when family relationships are falsified to obtain visas.

PENALTIES: By law, you may be imprisoned for not more than five years or fined $250,000, or both, for entering into a marriage contract for the purpose of evading any provision of the immigration laws. In addition, you may be fined up to $10,000 and imprisoned for up to five years, or both, for knowingly and willfully falsifying or concealing a material fact or using any false document in submitting this petition.

YOUR CERTIFICATION: I certify, under penalty of perjury under the laws of the United States of America, that the foregoing is true and correct. Furthermore, I authorize the release of any information from my records which the Immigration and Naturalization Service needs to determine eligibility for the benefit that I am seeking.

E. Signature of petitioner.

Date   Phone Number

F. Signature of person preparing this form, if other than the petitioner.

I declare that I prepared this document at the request of the person above and that it is based on all information of which I have any knowledge.

Print Name _____   Signature _____   Date _____

Address _____   G-28 ID or VOLAG Number, if any. _____

Department of Homeland Security
U.S. Citizenship and Immigration Services

OMB No. 1615-0013; Exp. 6/30/04

I-131, Application for Travel Document

DO NOT WRITE IN THIS BLOCK		FOR CIS USE ONLY *(except G-28 block below)*

Document Issued
- ☐ Reentry Permit
- ☐ Refugee Travel Document
- ☐ Single Advance Parole
- ☐ Multiple Advance Parole
  Valid to:_____

If Reentry Permit or Refugee Travel Document, mail to:
- ☐ Address in Part 1
- ☐ American embassy/consulate at:_____
- ☐ Overseas DHS office at:_____

Action Block

Receipt

☐ Document Hand Delivered

On _____ By _____

To be completed by Attorney/Representative, if any.

Attorney State License # _____

☐ Check box if G-28 is attached.

Part 1.   Information about you. *(Please type or print in black ink.)*

1. A #

2. Date of Birth *(mm/dd/yyyy)*

3. Class of Admission

4. Gender   Male ☐   Female ☐

5. Name *(Family name in captial letters)*   *(First)*   *(Middle)*

6. Address *(Number and Street)*   Apt. #

City   State or Province   Zip/Postal Code   Country

7. Country of Birth

8. Country of Citizenship

9. Social Security # *(if any)*

Part 2.   Application type *(check one).*

a. ☐ I am a permanent resident or conditional resident of the United States and I am applying for a reentry permit.

b. ☐ I now hold U.S. refugee or asylee status and I am applying for a refugee travel document.

c. ☐ I am a permanent resident as a direct result of refugee or asylee status and I am applying for a refugee travel document.

d. ☐ I am applying for an advance parole document to allow me to return to the United States after temporary foreign travel.

e. ☐ I am outside the United States and I am applying for an advance parole document.

f. ☐ I am applying for an advance parole document for a person who is outside the United States. *If you checked box "f", provide the following information about that person:*

1. Name *(Family name in captial letters)*   *(First)*   *(Middle)*

2. Date of Birth *(mm/dd/yyyy)*

3. Country of Birth

4. Country of Citizenship

5. Address *(Number and Street)*   Apt. #   Daytime Telephone # *(area/country code)*

City   State or Province   Zip/Postal Code   Country

INITIAL RECEIPT _____ RESUBMITTED _____ RELOCATED: Rec'd. _____ Sent _____ COMPLETED: Appv'd. _____ Denied _____ Ret'd. _____

Form I-131 (Rev. 09/19/03) N *Prior versions may be used until 12/31/03*

Part 3. Processing information.

1. Date of Intended Departure *(mm/dd/yyyy)*

2. Expected Length of Trip

3. Are you, or any person included in this application, now in exclusion, deportation, removal or recission proceedings? ☐ No ☐ Yes *(Name of DHS office)*:

If you are applying for an Advance Parole Document, skip to Part 7.

4. Have you ever before been issued a reentry permit or refugee travel *for the last document issued to you)*: ☐ No ☐ Yes *(Give the following information*

Date Issued *(mm/dd/yyyy)*: 　　　　　　　　Disposition *(attached, lost, etc.)*:

5. Where do you want this travel document sent? *(Check one)*

a. ☐ To the U.S. address shown in **Part 1** on the first page of this form.

b. ☐ To an American embassy or consulate at:　City: 　　　　　Country:

c. ☐ To a DHS office overseas at:　　City: 　　　　　Country:

d. If you checked "b" or "c", where should the notice to pick up the travel document be sent?

☐ To the address shown in **Part 2** on the first page of this form.

☐ To the address shown below:

Address *(Number and Street)*　　　　　Apt. #　　Daytime Telephone # *(area/country code)*

City　　　　　State or Province　　　　　Zip/Postal Code　　Country

Part 4. Information about your proposed travel.

Purpose of trip. *If you need more room, continue on a seperate sheet(s) of paper.*

List the countries you intend to visit.

Part 5. Complete only if applying for a reentry permit.

Since becoming a permanent resident of the United States (or during the past five years, whichever is less) how much total time have you spent outside the United States?

☐ less than six months ☐ two to three years
☐ six months to one year ☐ three to four years
☐ one to two years ☐ more than four years

Since you became a permanent resident of the United States, have you ever filed a federal income tax return as a nonresident, or failed to file a federal income tax return because you considered yourself to be a nonresident? *(If "Yes," give details on a seperate sheet(s) of paper.)* ☐ Yes ☐ No

Part 6. Complete only if applying for a refugee travel document.

1. Country from which you are a refugee or asylee:

If you answer "Yes" to any of the following questions, you must explain on a seperate sheet(s) of paper.

2. Do you plan to travel to the above named country? ☐ Yes ☐ No

3. Since you were accorded refugee/asylee status, have you ever:
a. returned to the above named country? ☐ Yes ☐ No
b. applied for and/or obtained a national passport, passport renewal or entry permit of that country? ☐ Yes ☐ No
c. applied for and/or received any benefit from such country (for example, health insurance benefits). ☐ Yes ☐ No

4. Since you were accorded refugee/asylee status, have you, by any legal procedure or voluntary act:
a. reacquired the nationality of the above named country? ☐ Yes ☐ No
b. acquired a new nationality? ☐ Yes ☐ No
c. been granted refugee or asylee status in any other country? ☐ Yes ☐ No

Part 7. Complete only if applying for advance parole.

On a separate sheet(s) of paper, please explain how you qualify for an advance parole document and what circumstances warrant issuance of advance parole. Include copies of any documents you wish considered. *(See instructions.)*

1. For how many trips do you intend to use this document? ☐ One trip ☐ More than one trip

2. If the person intended to receive an advance parole document is outside the United States, provide the location (city and country) of the American embassy or consulate or the DHS overseas office that you want us to notify.

City

Country

3. If the travel document will be delivered to an overseas office, where should the notice to pick up the document be sent:

☐ To the address shown in **Part 2** on the first page of this form.

☐ To the address shown below:

Address *(Number and Street)*

Apt. #

Daytime Telephone # *(area/country code)*

City

State or Province

Zip/Postal Code

Country

Part 8. Signature. *Read the information on penalties in the instructions before completing this section. If you are filing for a reentry permit or refugee travel document, you must be in the United States to file this application.*

I certify, under penalty of perjury under the laws of the United States of America, that this application and the evidence submitted with it are all true and correct. I authorize the release of any information from my records which the U.S. Citizenship and Immigration Services needs to determine eligibility for the benefit I am seeking.

Signature

Date *(mm/dd/yyyy)*

Daytime Telephone Number *(with area code)*

Please Note: If you do not completely fill out this form or fail to submit required documents listed in the instructions, you may not be found eligible for the requested document and this application may be denied.

Part 9. Signature of person preparing form, if other than the applicant. *(Sign below.)*

I declare that I prepared this application at the request of the applicant and it is based on all information of which I have knowledge.

Signature

Print or Type Your Name

Firm Name and Address

Daytime Telephone Number *(with area code)*

Fax Number *(if any)*

Date *(mm/dd/yyyy)*

U.S. Department of Justice
Immigration and Naturalization Service

Affidavit of Support

(Answer All Items: Fill in with Typewriter or Print in Block Letters in Ink.)

I, _____ residing at _____
(Name)   (Street and Number)

_____   _____   _____   _____
(City)   (State)   (Zip Code if in U.S.)   (Country)

BEING DULY SWORN DEPOSE AND SAY:

1. I was born on _____ at _____
(Date)   (City)   (Country)

   If you are **not** a native born United States citizen, answer the following as appropriate:

   a. If a United States citizen through naturalization, give certificate of naturalization number _____

   b. If a United States citizen through parent(s) or marriage, give citizenship certificate number _____

   c. If United States citizenship was derived by some other method, attach a statement of explanation.

   d. If a lawfully admitted permanent resident of the United States, give "A" number _____

2. That I am _____ years of age and have resided in the United States since (date) _____

3. That this affidavit is executed in behalf of the following person:

Name		Gender	Age
Citizen of (Country)	Marital Status	Relationship to Sponsor	
Presently resides at (Street and Number)	(City)	(State)	(Country)

Name of spouse and children accompanying or following to join person:

Spouse	Gender	Age	Child		Gender	Age
Child	Gender	Age	Child		Gender	Age
Child	Gender	Age	Child		Gender	Age

4. That this affidavit is made by me for the purpose of assuring the United States Government that the person(s) named in item 3 will not become a public charge in the United States.

5. That I am willing and able to receive, maintain and support the person(s) named in item 3. That I am ready and willing to deposit a bond, if necessary, to guarantee that such person(s) will not become a public charge during his or her stay in the United States, or to guarantee that the above named person(s) will maintain his or her nonimmigrant status, if admitted temporarily and will depart prior to the expiration of his or her authorized stay in the United States.

6. That I understand this affidavit will be binding upon me for a period of three (3) years after entry of the person(s) named in item 3 and that the information and documentation provided by me may be made available to the Secretary of Health and Human Services and the Secretary of Agriculture, who may make it available to a public assistance agency.

7. That I am employed as, or engaged in the business of _____ with _____
(Type of Business)   (Name of concern)

   at _____   _____   _____   _____
   (Street and Number)   (City)   (State)   (Zip Code)

   I derive an annual income of *(if self-employed, I have attached a copy of my last income tax return or report of commercial rating concern which I certify to be true and correct to the best of my knowledge and belief. See instructions for nature of evidence of net worth to be submitted.)* $ _____

   I have on deposit in savings banks in the United States $ _____

   I have other personal property, the reasonable value of which is $ _____

OVER

I have stocks and bonds with the following market value, as indicated on the attached list, which I certify to be true and correct to the best of my knowledge and belief. $ _____

I have life insurance in the sum of $ _____

With a cash surrender value of $ _____

I own real estate valued at $ _____

With mortgage(s) or other encumbrance(s) thereon amounting to $ _____

Which is located at _____

(Street and Number)   (City)   (State)   (Zip Code)

8. That the following persons are dependent upon me for support: *(Place an "x" in the appropriate column to indicate whether the person named is **wholly** or **partially** dependent upon you for support.)*

Name of Person	Wholly Dependent	Partially Dependent	Age	Relationship to Me

9. That I have previously submitted affidavit(s) of support for the following person(s). If none, state **"None."**

Name		Date submitted

10. That I have submitted visa petition(s) to the Immigration and Naturalization Service on behalf of the following person(s). If none, state none.

Name	Relationship	Date submitted

11. *(Complete this block only if the person named in the item 3 will be in the United States temporarily.)*
   That I ☐ intend ☐ do not intend, to make specific contributions to the support of the person named in item 3. *(If you check "intend," indicate the exact nature and duration of the contributions. For example, if you intend to furnish room and board, state for how long and, if money, state the amount in United States dollars and state whether it is to be given in a lump sum, weekly or monthly, or for how long.)*

_____

_____

Oath or Affirmation of Sponsor

I acknowledge at that I have read Part III of the Instructions, Sponsor and Alien Liability, and am aware of my responsibilities as an immigrant sponsor under the Social Security Act, as amended, and the Food Stamp Act, as amended.

I swear (affirm) that I know the contents of this affidavit signed by me and the statements are true and correct.

Signature of sponsor _____

Subscribed and sworn to (affirmed) before me this _____ **day of** _____ , _____

at _____ . **My commission expires on** _____

Signature of Officer Administering Oath _____ Title _____

If affidavit prepared by other than sponsor, please complete the following: I declare that this document was prepared by me at the request of the sponsor and is based on all information of which I have knowledge.

_____

(Signature)   **(Address)**   **(Date)**

Department of Homeland Security
U.S. Citizenship and Immigration Services

OMB No. 1615-0015; Exp. 8-31-04

I-140, Immigrant Petition for Alien Worker

START HERE - Please Type or Print in Black Ink.

FOR CIS USE ONLY

Returned	Receipt
Date	
Date	
Resubmitted	
Date	
Date	
Reloc Sent	
Date	
Date	
Reloc Rec'd	
Date	
Date	

Part 1. Information about the person or organization filing this petition.
If an individual is filing, use the top name line. Organizations should use the second line.

Family Name (Last Name)   Given Name (First Name)   Full Middle Name

Company or Organization Name

Address: (Street Number and Name)   Suite #

Attn:

City   State/Province

Country   Zip/Postal Code

IRS Tax #   Social Security # *(if any)*   E-Mail Address *(if any)*

Part 2. Petition type.

This petition is being filed for: *(Check one)*

a. ☐ An alien of extraordinary ability.
b. ☐ An outstanding professor or researcher.
c. ☐ A multinational executive or manager.
d. ☐ A member of the professions holding an advanced degree or an alien of exceptional ability (who is **NOT** seeking a National Interest Waiver).
e. ☐ A professional (at a minimum, possessing a bachelor's degree or a foreign degree equivalent to a U.S. bachelor's degree) or a skilled worker (requiring at least two years of specialized training or experience).
f. ☐ (Reserved.)
g. ☐ Any other worker (requiring less than two years of training or experience).
h. ☐ Soviet Scientist.
i. ☐ An alien applying for a National Interest Waiver (who **IS** a member of the professions holding an advanced degree or an alien of exceptional ability).

Classification:
☐ 203(b)(1)(A) Alien of Extraordinary Ability
☐ 203(b)(1)(B) Outstanding Professor or Researcher
☐ 203(b)(1)(C) Multi-National Executive or Manager
☐ 203(b)(2) Member of Professions w/Adv. Degree or Exceptional Ability
☐ 203(b)(3)(A)(i) Skilled Worker
☐ 203(b)(3)(A)(ii) Professional
☐ 203(b)(3)(A)(iii) Other Worker

Certification:
☐ National Interest Waiver (NIW)
☐ Schedule A, Group I
☐ Schedule A, Group II

Priority Date	Consulate

Concurrent Filing:
☐ **I-485 filed concurrently.**

Part 3. Information about the person you are filing for.

Family Name (Last Name)   Given Name (First Name)   Full Middle Name

Address: (Street Number and Name)   Apt. #

C/O: (In Care Of)

City   State/Province

Country   Zip/Postal Code   E-Mail Address *(if any)*

Daytime Phone # *(with area/country code)*   Date of Birth *(mm/dd/yyyy)*

City/Town/Village of Birth   State/Province of Birth   Country of Birth

Country of Nationality/Citizenship   A # *(if any)*   Social Security # *(if any)*

Remarks

Action Block

IF IN THE U.S.

Date of Arrival *(mm/dd/yyyy)*   I-94 # *(Arrival/Departure Document)*

Current Nonimmigrant Status   Date Status Expires *(mm/dd/yyyy)*

To Be Completed by
Attorney or Representative, if any.
☐ Fill in box if G-28 is attached to represent the applicant.

ATTY State License #

Form I-140 (Rev. 09/26/03)N (Prior versions may be used until 12/31/03)

Part 4. Processing Information.

1. Please complete the following for the person named in Part 3: *(Check one)*

☐ Alien will apply for a visa abroad at the American Embassy or Consulate at:

City	Foreign Country

☐ Alien is in the United States and will apply for adjustment of status to that of lawful permanent resident.

Alien's country of current residence or, if now in the U.S., last permanent residence abroad.

2. If you provided a U.S. address in Part 3, print the person's foreign address:

3. If the person's native alphabet is other than Roman letters, write the person's foreign name and address in the native alphabet:

4. Are any other petition(s) or application(s) being filed with this Form I-140?
☐ No   ☐ Yes-(check all that apply)   ☐ Form I-485   ☐ Form I-765
                                                  ☐ Form I-131   ☐ Other - attach explanation

5. Is the person you are filing for in removal proceedings?   ☐ No   ☐ Yes-attach an explanation

6. Has any immigrant visa petition ever been filed by or on behalf of this person?   ☐ No   ☐ Yes-attach an explanation

If you answered yes to any of these questions, please provide the case number, office location, date of decision and disposition of the decision on a separate sheet(s) of paper.

Part 5. Additional information about the petitioner.

1. Type of petitioner *(Check one)*.

☐ Employer   ☐ Self   ☐ Other (Explain, e.g., Permanent Resident, U.S. Citzen or any other person filing on behalf of the alien.)

2. If a company, give the following:

Type of Business	Date Established *(mm/dd/yyyy)*	Current Number of Employees

Gross Annual Income	Net Annual Income	NAICS Code

DOL/ETA Case Number

3. If an individual, give the following:

Occupation	Annual Income

Part 6. Basic information about the proposed employment.

1. Job Title

2. SOC Code

3. Nontechnical Description of Job

4. Address where the person will work if different from address in Part 1.

5. Is this a full-time position?
☐ Yes ☐ No

6. If the answer to Number 5 is "No," how many hours per week for the position?

7. Is this a permanent position?
☐ Yes ☐ No

8. Is this a new position?
☐ Yes ☐ No

9. Wages per week
$

Part 7. Information on spouse and all children of the person for whom you are filing.

List husband/wife and all children related to the individual for whom the petition is being filed. Provide an attachment of additional family members, if needed.

Name *(First/Middle/Last)*	Relationship	Date of Birth *(mm/dd/yyyy)*	Country of Birth

Part 8. Signature.
Read the information on penalties in the instructions before completing this section. If someone helped you prepare this petition, he or she must complete Part 9.

I certify, under penalty of perjury under the laws of the United States of America, that this petition and the evidence submitted with it are all true and correct. I authorize the U.S. Citizenship and Immigration Services to release to other government agencies any information from my CIS (or former INS) records, if the CIS determines that such action is necessary to determine eligibility for the benefit sought.

Petitioner's Signature

Daytime Phone Number *(Area/Country Code)*

E-mail Address

Print Name

Date *(mm/dd/yyyy)*

Please Note: *If you do not fully complete this form or fail to submit the required documents listed in the instructions, a final decision on your petition may be delayed or the petition may be denied.*

Part 9. Signature of person preparing form, if other than above.   *(Sign below)*

I declare that I prepared this petition at the request of the above person and it is based on all information of which I have knowledge.

Attorney or Representative: In the event of a Request for Evidence (RFE), may the BCIS contact you by Fax or E-mail? ☐ Yes   ☐ No

Signature

Print Name

Date *(mm/dd/yyyy)*

Firm Name and Address

Daytime Phone Number *(Area/Country Code)*

Fax Number *(Area/Country Code)*

E-mail Address

OMB No. 1115-0032

U.S. Department of Justice
Immigration and Naturalization Service

Application for Advance Permission to Return to Unrelinquished Domicile

(See instructions on reverse. Please typewrite or print plainly in ink.)

FEE STAMP

Alien Registration No.

Date

(1) I hereby apply for permission to return to the United States under the authority contained in Section 212(c) of the Immigration and Nationality Act.

MY NAME IS:	*(First)*	*(Middle)*	*(Last)*
DATE OF BIRTH: *(Month, day, year)*	PLACE OF BIRTH: *(City, province, country)*		I AM A CITIZEN OF: *(Country)*
PRESENT ADDRESS: *(Street and number, apt. no., city, state, country)*			

(2) I was lawfully admitted to the United States for permanent residence at:

PORT/INS OFFICE:	DATE: *(Month, day, year)*	NAME OF VESSEL OR OTHER MEANS OF CONVEYANCE:

(3) Since that admission I have departed from and reentered the United States as follows:

DEPARTED FROM THE UNITED STATES			RETURNED TO THE UNITED STATES			PURPOSE OF TRIP
Port	Date *(Month, day, year)*	Vessel or Other Means of Conveyance	Port	Date *(Month, day, year)*	Vessel or Other Means Conveyance	

(4) During the past seven years I have resided at the following places: *(List present address first)*

(Complete Address - Include Apt. No.)	From -	To- Present time

(5) During the past seven years I have been employed as follows: *(List present employment first)*

From -	To -	Employer's Name	Address	Occupation or Type of business

(6) My immediate family consists of the following persons:

Name	Relation	Date and Country of Birth	Citizen of	Present Address

(7) I _____ depart(ed) temporarily from the United States on or about _____ and will remain
   (Intend to or have)   *(Date)*

in _____ approximately _____ , for the purpose of
   (Country)   *(Length of Time)*

_____ ; and expect to apply for admission at _____
                                                              (Port)

RECEIVED	TRANS. IN	RET'D-TRANS. OUT	COMPLETED

Form I-191 (Rev. 11/23/01)Y

(8) I believe I may be inadmissible to the United States for the following reasons:

_____

_____

_____

_____

I understand that the information herein contained may be used in any criminal or civil proceedings, including removal, hereafter instituted against me.

I certify that the statements above are true and correct to the best of my knowledge and belief.

_____

(Signature of Applicant)

SIGNATURE OF PERSON PREPARING FORM, IF OTHER THAN APPLICANT
I declare that the document was prepared by me at the request of the applicant and is based on all information of which I have any knowledge.

(Signature)	*(Address)*	*(Date)*

Decision:	
☐ Application granted upon the following terms and conditions:	DATE OF ACTION
	DD
	DISTRICT

INSTRUCTIONS TO THE APPLICANT

READ INSTRUCTIONS CAREFULLY - FEE WILL NOT BE REFUNDED

(A) This form, when completely executed, should be submitted to the District Director of the Immigration and Naturalization Service (INS) office having jurisdiction over your place of permanent residence.

(B) A fee of $195.00 must be paid for filing this application. It cannot be refunded, regardless of the action taken on the application. DO NOT MAIL CASH. ALL FEES MUST BE SUBMITTED IN THE EXACT AMOUNT. Payment by check or money order must be drawn on a bank or other institution located in the United States and be payable in United States currency. If the applicant resides in Guam, check or money order must be payable to the "Treasurer Guam." If the Applicant resides in the Virgin Islands, check or money order must be payable to the "Commissioner of Finance of the Virgin Islands." All other applicants must make the check or money order payable to the "Immigration and Naturalization Service." When the check is drawn on account of a person other than the applicant, the name of the applicant must be entered on the face of the check. If application is submitted from outside the United States, remittance may be made by bank international money order or foreign draft drawn on a financial institution in the United States and payable to the Immigration and Naturalization Service in United States currency. Personal checks are accepted subject to collection. An uncollected check will render the application and any document issued pursuant thereto invalid. A charge of $30.00 will be imposed if a check in payment of a fee is not honored by the bank on which it is drawn.

(C) If the space provided in the form is insufficient to answer a question fully, you should attach a sheet(s) of paper containing your answer which should be numbered to correspond with the question.

(D) In Part (3), where absences have been numerous as a resident alien border crosser or as a seaman, it will be sufficient to give the approximate number of such absences and the years covered thereby.

(E) List specifically and in detail your reasons for possible inadmissibility. For example, if the application is made because the applicant may be inadmissible due to conviction of a crime, state in the application the designation of the crime, the date and place of its commission and of conviction therefor, and the sentence or other judgement of the court. In the case of disease, mental or physical defect or other disability, give exact description, duration thereof and date and place last treated.

(F) If applicant is mentally incompetent or is under 14 years of age, the application shall be executed by his parent or guardian.

Authority for collecting this information requested on this form is contained in 8 USC 1103(a). Submission of the information is voluntary. The principal purpose for which the information is solicited is for use by a District Director of the Immigration and Naturalization Service to determine whether the applicant is eligible for advance permission to return to an unrelinquished domicile pursuant to the provisions of section 212(c) of the Immigration and Nationality Act, 8 USC 1182(c). To elicit further information during the course of investigation, INS may as a matter of routine use, in order to carry out its function, disclose the information to other federal, state, local, and foreign law enforcement and regulatory agencies, the Department of Defense, including any component thereof (if the applicant has served, or is serving in the Armed Forces of the United States), the Department of State, Central Intelligence Agency, Interpol, and individuals and organizations. Failure to provide any or all of the solicited information may result in the denial of the application.

Reporting Burden. A person is not required to respond to a collection of information unless it displays a currently valid OMB control number. We try to create forms and instructions that are accurate, can be easily understood, and which impose the least possible burden on you to provide us with information. Often this is difficult because some immigration laws are very complex. Accordingly, the reporting burden for this collection of information is computed as follows: 1) learning about the law and form, and reading and understanding the form, 5 minutes; 2) completing the form, 5 minutes; 3) assembling and filing the form, 5 minutes, for an estimated average of 15 minutes per response. If you have comments regarding the accuracy of this estimate, or suggestions for making this form simpler, you can write to the Immigration and Naturalization Service, HQPDI, 425 I Street, N.W.; Room 4034, Washington, DC 20536, OMB No. 1115-0032. **Do not mail your completed application to this address.**

OMB No. 1115-0117

U.S. Department of Justice
Immigration and Naturalization Service

Petition for Amerasian, Widow(er), or Special Immigrant

START HERE - Please Type or Print

Part 1. Information about person or organization filing this petition.
(Individuals should use the top name line; organizations should use the second line.) If you are a self-petitioning spouse or child and do not want INS to send notices about this petition to your home, you may show an alternate mailing address here. If you are filing for yourself and do not want to use an alternate mailing address, skip to part 2.

Family Name	Given Name	Middle Initial

Company or Organization Name

Address - C/O

Street Number and Name		Apt. #
City	State or Province	
Country	Zip/Postal Code	

U.S. Social Security #	A #	IRS Tax # (if any)

Part 2. Classification Requested (check one):

a. ☐ Amerasian
b. ☐ Widow(er) of a U.S. citizen who died within the past two (2) years
c. ☐ Special Immigrant Juvenile
d. ☐ Special Immigrant Religious Worker
e. ☐ Special Immigrant based on employrnent with the Panama Canal Company, Canal Zone Government or U.S. Government in the Canal Zone
f. ☐ Special Immigrant Physician
g. ☐ Special Immigrant International Organization Employee or family member
h. ☐ Special Immigrant Armed Forces Member
i. ☐ Self-Petitioning Spouse of Abusive U.S. Citizen or Lawful Permanent Resident
j. ☐ Self-Petitioning Child of Abusive U.S. Citizen or Lawful Permanent Resident
k. ☐ Other, explain:

Part 3. Information about the person this petition is for.

Family Name	Given Name	Middle Initial

Address - C/O

Street Number and Name		Apt. #
City	State or Province	
Country	Zip/Postal Code	

Date of Birth (Month/Day/Year)	Country of Birth

U.S. Social Security #	A # (if any)

Marital Status: ☐ Single ☐ Married ☐ Divorced ☐ Widowed

Complete the items below if this person is in the United States:

Date of Arrival (Month/Day/Year)	I-94#
Current Nonimmigrant Status	Expires on (Month/Day/Year)

FOR INS USE ONLY

Returned	Receipt
Resubmitted	
Reloc Sent	
Reloc Rec'd	

☐ Petitioner/ Applicant Interviewed

☐ Benefitiary Interviewed

☐ I-485 Filed Concurrently
☐ Bene "A" File Reviewed

Classification

Consulate

Priority Date

Remarks:

Action Block

To Be Completed by Attorney or Representative, if any

☐ Fill in box if G-28 is attached to represent the applicant

VOLAG#

ATTY State License #

Continued on back.

Form I-360 (Rev. 09/11/00)Y Page 6

Part 4. Processing Information.

Below give to United States Consulate you want notified if this petition is approved and if any requested adjustment of status cannot be granted.

American Consulate: City	Country

If you gave a United States address in Part 3, print the person's foreign address below. If his/her native alphabet does not use Roman letters, print his/her name and foreign address in the native alphabet.

Name	Address

Sex of the person this petition is for.	☐ Male	☐ Female
Are you filing any other petitions or applications with this one?	☐ No	☐ Yes (How many? _____)
Is the person this petition is for in exclusion or deportation proceedings?	☐ No	☐ Yes (Explain an a separate sheet of paper)
Has the person this petition is for ever worked in the U.S. without permission?	☐ No	☐ Yes (Explain an a separate sheet of paper)
Is an appilication for adjustment of status attached to this petition?	☐ No	☐ Yes

Part 5. Complete only if filing for an Amerasian.

Section A. Information about the mother of the Amerasian

Family Name	Given Name	Middle Initial

Living? ☐ No (Give date of death _____)   ☐ Yes (complete address line below)   ☐ Unknown (attach a full explanation)
Address

Section B. Information about the father of the Amerasian: If possible, attach a notarized statement from the father regarding parentage. Explain on separate paper any question you cannot fully answer in the space provided on this form.

Family Name	Given Name	Middle Initial

Date of Birth (Month/Day/Year)	Country of Birth

Living? ☐ No (give date of death_____)   ☐ Yes (complete address line below)   ☐ Unknown (attach a full explanation)
Home Address

Home Phone #	Work Phone #

At the time the Amerasian was conceived:

☐ The father was in the military (indicate branch of service below - and give service number here): _____

   ☐ Army   ☐ Air Force   ☐ Navy   ☐ Marine Corps   ☐ Coast Guard

☐ The father was a civilian employed abroad. Attach a list of names and addresses of organizations which employed him at that time.
☐ The father was not in the military, and was not a civilian employed abroad. (Attach a full explanation of the circumstances.)

Part 6. Complete only if filing for a Special Immigrant Juvenile Court Dependent.

Section A. Information about the Juvenile

List any other names used.

Answer the following questions regarding the person this petition is for. If you answer "no," explain on a separate sheet of paper.

Is he or she still dependent upon the juvenile court or still legally committed to or under the custody of an agency or department of a state?	☐ No	☐ Yes
Does he/she continue to be eligible for long term foster care?	☐ No	☐ Yes

Continued on next page.

Part 7. Complete only if filing as a Widow/Widower, a Self-petitioning Spouse of an Abuser, or as a Self-petitioning Child of an Abuser.

Section A. Information about the U.S. citizen husband or wife who died or about the U.S. citizen or lawful permanent resident abuser.

Family Name	Given Name	Middle Initial

Date of Birth (Month/Day/Year)	Country of Birth	Date of Death (Month/Day/Year)

He or she is now, or was at time of death a (check one):

☐ U.S. citizen through Naturalization (Show A #) _____

☐ U.S. citizen born in the United States.

☐ U.S. citizen born abroad to U.S. citizen parents.

☐ U.S. lawful permanent resident (Show A #) _____

☐ Other, explain _____

Section B. Additional Information about you.

How many times have you been married?	How many times was the person in Section A married?	Give the date and place you and the person in Section A were married. (If you are a self-petitioning child, write: "N/A")

When did you live with the person named in Section A? From (Month/Year)_____ until (Month/Year) _____

If you are filing as a widow/widower, were you legally separated at the time of to U.S citizens's death?   ☐ No   ☐ Yes, (attach explanation).

Give the last address at which you lived together with the person named in Section A, and show the last date that you lived together with that person at that address:

If you we filing as a self-petitioning spouse, have any of your children filed separate self-petitions?   ☐ No   ☐ Yes (show child(ren)'s full names):

Part 8. Information about the spouse and children of the person this petition is for. A widow/widower or a self-petitioning spouse of an abusive citizen or lawful permanent resident should also list the children of the deceased spouse or of the abuser.

A. Family Name	Given Name	Middle Initial	Date of Birth (Month/Day/Year)
Country of Birth	Relationship ☐ Spouse ☐ Child		A #

B. Family Name	Given Name	Middle Initial	Date of Birth (Month/Day/Year)
Country of Birth	Relationship ☐ Child		A #

C. Family Name	Given Name	Middle Initial	Date of Birth (Month/Day/Year)
Country of Birth	Relationship ☐ Child		A #

D. Family Name	Given Name	Middle Initial	Date of Birth (Month/Day/Year)
Country of Birth	Relationship ☐ Child		A #

E. Family Name	Given Name	Middle Initial	Date of Birth (Month/Day/Year)
Country of Birth	Relationship ☐ Child		A #

F. Family Name	Given Name	Middle Initial	Date of Birth (Month/Day/Year)
Country of Birth	Relationship ☐ Child		A #

G. Family Name		Given Name	Middle Initial	Date of Birth (Month/Day/Year)
Country of Birth		Relationship ☐ Child		A#
H. Family Name		Given Name	Middle Initial	Date of Birth (Month/Day/Year)
Country of Birth		Relationship ☐ Child		A#

Part 9. Signature.

Read the information on penalties in the instructions before completing this part. If you are going to file this petition at an INS office in the United States, sign below. If you are going to file it at a U.S. consulate or INS office overseas, sign in front of a U.S. INS or consular official.

I certify, or, if outside the United States, I swear or affirm, under penalty of perjury under the laws of the United States of America, that this petition and the evidence submitted with it is all true and correct. If filing this on behalf at an organization, I certify that I am empowered to do so by that organization. I authorize the release of any information from my records, or from the petitioning organization's records, which the Immigration and Naturalization Service needs to determine eligibility for the benefit being sought.

Signature	Date

Signature of INS or Consular Official	Print Name	Date

Please Note: If you do not completely fill out this form or fail to submit required documents listed in the instructions, the person(s) filed for may not be found eligible for a requested benefit and it may have to be denied.

Part 10. Signature of person preparing form if other than above. (sign below)

I declare that I prepared this application at the request of the above person and it is based on all information of which I have knowledge.

Signature	Print Your Name	Date

Firm Name and Address		

U.S. Department of Justice
Immigration and Naturalization Service

Form I-485, Application to Register Permanent Resident or Adjust Status

---

START HERE - Please Type or Print

Part 1.   Information About You.

Family Name	Given Name	Middle Initial

Address - C/O

Street Number and Name	Apt. #

City

State	Zip Code

Date of Birth (month/day/year)	Country of Birth

Social Security #	A # (if any)

Date of Last Arrival (month/day/year)	I-94 #

Current INS Status	Expires on (month/day/year)

Part 2.   Application Type. *(check one)*

I am applying for an adjustment to permanent resident status because:

a. ☐ an immigrant petition giving me an immediately available immigrant visa number has been approved. (Attach a copy of the approval notice-- or a relative, special immigrant juvenile or special immigrant military visa petition filed with this application that will give you an immediately available visa number, if approved.)

b. ☐ my spouse or parent applied for adjustment of status or was granted lawful permanent residence in an immigrant visa category that allows derivative status for spouses and children.

c. ☐ I entered as a K-1 fiance(e) of a U.S. citizen whom I married within 90 days of entry, or I am the K-2 child of such a fiance(e). [Attach a copy of the fiance(e) petition approval notice and the marriage certificate.]

d. ☐ I was granted asylum or derivative asylum status as the spouse or child of a person granted asylum and am eligible for adjustment.

e. ☐ I am a native or citizen of Cuba admitted or paroled into the U.S. after January 1, 1959, and thereafter have been physically present in the U.S. for at least one year.

f. ☐ I am the husband, wife or minor unmarried child of a Cuban described in (e) and am residing with that person, and was admitted or paroled into the U.S. after January 1, 1959, and thereafter have been physically present in the U.S. for at least one year.

g. ☐ I have continuously resided in the U.S. since before January 1, 1972.

h. ☐ Other basis of eligibility. Explain. (If additional space is needed, use a separate piece of paper.)

I am already a permanent resident and am applying to have the date I was granted permanent residence adjusted to the date I originally arrived in the U.S. as a nonimmigrant or parolee, or as of May 2,1964, whichever date is later, and: *(Check one)*

i. ☐ I am a native or citizen of Cuba and meet the description in (e), above.

j. ☐ I am the husband, wife or minor unmarried child of a Cuban, and meet the description in (f), above.

FOR INS USE ONLY

Returned	Receipt
Resubmitted	
Reloc Sent	
Reloc Rec'd	
Applicant Interviewed	

Section of Law
☐ Sec. 209(b), INA
☐ Sec. 13, Act of 9/11/57
☐ Sec. 245, INA
☐ Sec. 249, INA
☐ Sec. 2 Act of 11/2/66
☐ Sec. 2 Act of 11/2/66
☐ Other _____

Country Chargeable

Eligibility Under Sec. 245
Approved Visa Petition
Dependent of Principal Alien
Special Immigrant
Other _____

Preference

Action Block

To be Completed by
Attorney or Representative, if any
☐ Fill in box if G-28 is attached to represent the applicant.
VOLAG #

ATTY State License #

Part 3. Processing Information.

A. City/Town/Village of Birth	Current Occupation
Your Mother's First Name	Your Father's First Name

Give your name exactly how it appears on your Arrival /Departure Record (Form I-94)

Place of Last Entry Into the U.S. (City/State)	In what status did you last enter? (*Visitor, student, exchange alien, crewman, temporary worker, without inspection, etc.*)
Were you inspected by a U.S. Immigration Officer? ☐ Yes ☐ No	
Nonimmigrant Visa Number	Consulate Where Visa Was Issued
Date Visa Was Issued (month/day/year) Sex: ☐ Male ☐ Female	Marital Status ☐ Married ☐ Single ☐ Divorced ☐ Widowed

Have you ever before applied for permanent resident status in the U.S.? ☐ No ☐ Yes If you checked "Yes," give date and place of filing and final disposition.

B. List your present husband/wife and all your sons and daughters. (If you have none, write "none." If additional space is needed, use a separate piece of paper.)

Family Name	Given Name	Middle Initial	Date of Birth (month/day/year)
Country of Birth	Relationship	A #	Applying with You? ☐ Yes ☐ No
Family Name	Given Name	Middle Initial	Date of Birth (month/day/year)
Country of Birth	Relationship	A #	Applying with You? ☐ Yes ☐ No
Family Name	Given Name	Middle Initial	Date of Birth (month/day/year)
Country of Birth	Relationship	A #	Applying with You? ☐ Yes ☐ No
Family Name	Given Name	Middle Initial	Date of Birth (month/day/year)
Country of Birth	Relationship	A #	Applying with You? ☐ Yes ☐ No
Family Name	Given Name	Middle Initial	Date of Birth (month/day/year)
Country of Birth	Relationship	A #	Applying with You? ☐ Yes ☐ No

C. List your present and past membership in or affiliation with every political organization, association, fund, foundation, party, club, society or similar group in the United States or in other places since your 16th birthday. Include any foreign military service in this part. If none, write "none." Include the name(s) of the organization(s), location(s), dates of membership from and to, and the nature of the organization (s). If additional space is needed, use a separate piece of paper.

_____

_____

_____

_____

_____

_____

Part 3. Processing Information. *(Continued)*

Please answer the following questions. (If your answer is **"Yes"** to any one of these questions, explain on a separate piece of paper. Answering **"Yes"** does not necessarily mean that you are not entitled to adjust your status or register for permanent residence.)

1. Have you ever, in or outside the U. S.:
   a. knowingly committed any crime of moral turpitude or a drug-related offense for which you have not been arrested? ☐ Yes ☐ No

   b. been arrested, cited, charged, indicted, fined or imprisoned for breaking or violating any law or ordinance, excluding traffic violations? ☐ Yes ☐ No

   c. been the beneficiary of a pardon, amnesty, rehabilitation decree, other act of clemency or similar action? ☐ Yes ☐ No

   d. exercised diplomatic immunity to avoid prosecution for a criminal offense in the U. S.? ☐ Yes ☐ No

2. Have you received public assistance in the U.S. from any source, including the U.S. government or any state, county, city or municipality (other than emergency medical treatment), or are you likely to receive public assistance in the future? ☐ Yes ☐ No

3. Have you ever:
   a. within the past ten years been a prostitute or procured anyone for prostitution, or intend to engage in such activities in the future? ☐ Yes ☐ No

   b. engaged in any unlawful commercialized vice, including, but not limited to, illegal gambling? ☐ Yes ☐ No

   c. knowingly encouraged, induced, assisted, abetted or aided any alien to try to enter the U.S. illegally? ☐ Yes ☐ No

   d. illicitly trafficked in any controlled substance, or knowingly assisted, abetted or colluded in the illicit trafficking of any controlled substance? ☐ Yes ☐ No

4. Have you ever engaged in, conspired to engage in, or do you intend to engage in, or have you ever solicited membership or funds for, or have you through any means ever assisted or provided any type of material support to, any person or organization that has ever engaged or conspired to engage, in sabotage, kidnapping, political assassination, hijacking or any other form of terrorist activity? ☐ Yes ☐ No

5. Do you intend to engage in the U.S. in:
   a. espionage? ☐ Yes ☐ No

   b. any activity a purpose of which is opposition to, or the control or overthrow of, the government of the United States, by force, violence or other unlawful means? ☐ Yes ☐ No

   c. any activity to violate or evade any law prohibiting the export from the United States of goods, technology or sensitive information? ☐ Yes ☐ No

6. Have you ever been a member of, or in any way affiliated with, the Communist Party or any other totalitarian party? ☐ Yes ☐ No

7. Did you, during the period from March 23, 1933 to May 8, 1945, in association with either the Nazi Government of Germany or any organization or government associated or allied with the Nazi Government of Germany, ever order, incite, assist or otherwise participate in the persecution of any person because of race, religion, national origin or political opinion? ☐ Yes ☐ No

8. Have you ever engaged in genocide, or otherwise ordered, incited, assisted or otherwise participated in the killing of any person because of race, religion, nationality, ethnic origin or political opinion? ☐ Yes ☐ No

9. Have you ever been deported from the U.S., or removed from the U.S. at government expense, excluded within the past year, or are you now in exclusion or deportation proceedings? ☐ Yes ☐ No

10. Are you under a final order of civil penalty for violating section 274C of the Immigration and Nationality Act for use of fradulent documents or have you, by fraud or willful misrepresentation of a material fact, ever sought to procure, or procured, a visa, other documentation, entry into the U.S. or any immigration benefit? ☐ Yes ☐ No

11. Have you ever left the U.S. to avoid being drafted into the U.S. Armed Forces? ☐ Yes ☐ No

12. Have you ever been a J nonimmigrant exchange visitor who was subject to the two-year foreign residence requirement and not yet complied with that requirement or obtained a waiver? ☐ Yes ☐ No

13. Are you now withholding custody of a U.S. citizen child outside the U.S. from a person granted custody of the child? ☐ Yes ☐ No

14. Do you plan to practice polygamy in the U.S.? ☐ Yes ☐ No

Continued on back

Form I-485 (Rev. 02/07/00)N Page 3

Part 4. Signature. *(Read the information on penalties in the instructions before completing this section. You must file this application while in the United States.)*

I certify, under penalty of perjury under the laws of the United States of America, that this application and the evidence submitted with it is all true and correct. I authorize the release of any information from my records which the INS needs to determine eligibility for the benefit I am seeking.

Selective Service Registration. The following applies to you if you are a man at least 18 years old, but not yet 26 years old, who is required to register with the Selective Service System: I understand that my filing this adjustment of status application with the Immigration and Naturalization Service authorizes the INS to provide certain registration information to the Selective Service System in accordance with the Military Selective Service Act. Upon INS acceptance of my application, I authorize INS to transmit to the Selective Service System my name, current address, Social Security number, date of birth and the date I filed the application for the purpose of recording my Selective Service registration as of the filing date. If, however, the INS does not accept my application, I further understand that, if so required, I am responsible for registering with the Selective Service by other means, provided I have not yet reached age 26.

Signature	*Print Your Name*	*Date*	*Daytime Phone Number*

Please Note: *If you do not completely fill out this form or fail to submit required documents listed in the instructions, you may not be found eligible for the requested benefit and this application may be denied.*

Part 5. Signature of Person Preparing Form, If Other Than Above. *(Sign Below)*

I declare that I prepared this application at the request of the above person and it is based on all information of which I have knowledge.

Signature	*Print Your Name*	*Date*	*Daytime Phone Number*

Firm Name
and Address

U.S. Department of Homeland Security
Bureau of Citizenship Immigration and Service

Supplement A to Form I-485
Adjustment of Status Under Section 245(i)

Only use this form if you are applying to adjust status to that of a lawful permanent resident under Section 245(i) of the Immigration and Nationality Act.

Part A.   Information about you.

BCIS Use Only

Last Name   First Name   Middle Name

Address: In Care Of

Street Number and Name   Apt. #

City   State   Zip Code

Alien Registration Number (A #) if any   Date of Birth *(mm/dd/yyyy)*

Country of Birth   Country of Citizenship/Nationality

Part B. Eligibility. *(Check the correct response.)*

1. **I am filing Supplement A to Form I-485 because:**

   a. ☐ I am the beneficiary of a visa petition filed on or before January 14, 1998.
   b. ☐ I am the beneficiary of a visa petition filed on or after January 15, 1998, and on or before April 30, 2001.
   c. ☐ I am the beneficiary of an application for a labor certification filed on or before January 14, 1998.
   d. ☐ I am the beneficiary of an application for a labor certification filed on or after January 15, 1998, and on or before April 30, 2001.

   If you checked box b or d on question one, you must submit evidence demonstrating that you were physically present in the United States on December 21, 2000.

2. **And I fall into one or more of these categories:** *(Check all that apply to you.)*

   a. ☐ I entered the United States as an alien crewman;
   b. ☐ I have accepted employment without authorization;
   c. ☐ I am in unlawful immigration status because I entered the United States without inspection or I remained in the United States past the expiration of the period of my lawful admission;
   d. ☐ I have failed (except through no fault of my own or for technical reasons) to maintain, continuously, lawful status;
   e. ☐ I was admitted to the United States in transit without a visa;
   f. ☐ I was admitted as a nonimmigrant visitor without a visa;
   g. ☐ I was admitted to the United States as a nonimmigrant in the S classification; or
   h. ☐ I am seeking employment-based adjustment of status and am not in lawful nonimmigrant status.

Part C. Additional eligibility information.

1. **Are you applying to adjust status based on any of the below reasons?**

   a. You were granted asylum in the United States;
   b. You have continuously resided in the United States since January 1, 1972;
   c. You entered as a K-1 fiance'(e) of a United States citizen;
   d. You have an approved Form I-360, Petition for Amerasian, Widow(er), or Special Immigrant, and are applying for adjustment as a special immigrant juvenile court dependent or a special immigrant who has served in the United States armed forces, or a battered spouse or child;
   e. You are a native or citizen of Cuba, or the spouse or child of such alien, who was not lawfully inspected or admitted to the United States;
   f. You are a special immigrant retired international organization employee or family member;
   g. You are a special immigrant physician;

h. You are a public interest parolee, who was denied refugee status, and are from the former Soviet Union, Vietnam, Laos or Cambodia (a "Lautenberg Parolee" under Public Law 101-167); or

i. You are eligible under the Immigration Nursing Relief Act.

☐ **NO.** I am not applying for adjustment of status for any of these reasons. *(Go to next question.)*

☐ **YES.** I am applying for adjustment of status for any one of these reasons. *(If you answered "YES", do not file this form.)*

Part C. Additional eligibility information *(Continued)*.

2. **Do any of the following conditions describe you?**

a. You are already a lawful permanent resident of the United States.

b. You have continuously maintained lawful immigration status in the United States since November 5, 1986.

c. You are applying to adjust status as the spouse or unmarried minor child of a United States citizen or the parent of a U.S. citizen child at least 21 years of age, and you were inspected and lawfully admitted to the United States.

☐ **NO.** None of these conditions describe me. *(Go to next question.)*

☐ **YES.** *If you answered "YES", do not file this form.*

Part D. Fees.

Aliens filing this form with Form I-485* need to pay the following fees:

$ 255 Fee required with Form I-485 and

$ 50 Fingerprint Service Fee. (Applicants younger than 14 or older than 79 years of age do not have to pay this fee.)

$ 1,000 Fee required with Supplement A to Form I-485

If you filed Form I-485 separately, attach a copy of your filing receipt and pay only the additional sum of $1,000.

There are two categories of applicants using this form who do not need to pay the $1,000 fee:

1. applicants under the age of 17 years; and

2. applicants who are an unmarried son or daughter of a legalized alien and less than 21 years of age or the spouse of a legalized alien, and have attached a copy of a receipt or an approval notice showing that a Form I-817, Application for Voluntary Departure under the Family Unity Program, has been properly filed.

Part E. Signature. *Read the information on penalties in the instructions before completing this section.*

I certify, under penalty of perjury under the laws of the United States of America, that this application and the evidence submitted with it is all true and correct. I authorize the release of any information from my records which the Bureau of Citizenship and Immigration Services needs to determine eligibility for the benefit being sought.

Signature	Print Name	Date

Part F. Signature of person preparing form, if other than above. *Read the information on penalties in the instructions before completing this section.*

I certify, under penalty of perjury under the laws of the United States of America, that I prepared this form at the request of the above person and that to the best of my knowledge the contents of this application are all true and corect.

Signature	Print Name	Date

Firm Name and Address	Daytime Phone Number *(Area Code and Number)*
	Fax Number *(Area Code and Number)*

U.S. Department of Homeland Security
Bureau of Citizenship and Immigration Services

OMB #1615-0026: Exp. 2/28/05

I-526, Immigrant Petition by Alien Entrepreneur

DO NOT WRITE IN THIS BLOCK - FOR BCIS USE ONLY (Except G-28 Block Below)

Classification	**Action Block**	Fee Receipt
Priority Date		**To be completed by Attorney or Representative, if any** ☐ G-28 is attached Attorney's State License No. _____

Remarks:

START HERE - Type or Print in Black Ink.

Part 1.   Information about you.

Family Name _____ Given Name _____ Middle Name _____

Address:
In care of _____

Number and Street _____ Apt. # ____

City _____ State or Province _____ Country _____ Zip/Postal Code ____

Date of Birth (mm/dd/yyyy) _____ Country of Birth _____ Social Security # (if any) _____ A # (if any) _____

If you are in the United States, provide the following information:
Date of Arrival (mm/dd/yyyy) _____ I-94 # _____

Current Nonimmigrant Status _____ Date Current Status Expires (mm/dd/yyyy) _____ Daytime Phone # with Area Code _____

Part 2.   Application type (Check one).

a. ☐ This petition is based on an investment in a commercial enterprise in a targeted employment area for which the required amount of capital invested has been adjusted downward.

b. ☐ This petition is based on an investment in a commercial enterprise in an area for which the required amount of capital invested has been adjusted upward.

c. ☐ This petition is based on an investment in a commercial enterprise that is not in either a targeted area or in an upward adjustment area.

Part 3.   Information about your investment.

Name of commercial enterprise in which funds are invested _____

Street Address _____

Phone # with Area Code _____ Business organized as (corporation, partnership, etc.) _____

Kind of business (e.g. furniture manfacturer) _____ Date established (mm/dd/yyyy) _____ IRS Tax # _____

RECEIVED: _____ RESUBMITTED: _____ RELOCATED: SENT _____ REC'D _____

Form I-526 (Rev. 05/09/03)N (Prior versions may be used until 09/30/03)

Part 3. Information about your investment. (continued)

Date of your initial investment (mm/dd/yyyy)	Amount of your initial investment $
Your total capital investment in the enterprise to date $	Percentage of the enterprise you own

If you are not the sole investor in the new commercial enterprise, list on separate paper the names of all other parties (natural and non-natural) who hold a percentage share of ownership of the new enterprise and indicate whether any of these parties is seeking classification as an alien entrepreneur. Include the name, percentage of ownership and whether or not the person is seeking classification under section 203(b)(5). **NOTE:** A "natural" party would be an individual person and a "non-natural" party would be an entity such as a corporation, consortium, investment group, partnership, etc.

If you indicated in **Part 2** that the enterprise is in a targeted employment area or in an upward adjustment area, name the county and state: County   State

Part 4. Additional information about the enterprise.

Type of Enterprise (check one):

☐ New commercial enterprise resulting from the creation of a new business.

☐ New commercial enterprise resulting from the purchase of an existing business.

☐ New commercial enterprise resulting from a capital investment in an existing business.

Composition of the Petitioner's Investment:

Total amount in U.S. bank account .... $

Total value of all assets purchased for use in the enterprise.. $

Total value of all property transferred from abroad to the new enterprise..................... $

Total of all debt financing... $

Total stock purchases... $

Other (explain on separate paper)... $

Total $

Income:

When you made the investment.......... Gross $ Net $

Now... Gross $ Net $

Net worth:

When you made investment................. Gross $ Now $

Part 5.   Employment creation information.

Number of full-time employees in the enterprise in U.S. (excluding you, your spouse, sons and daughters)

When you made your initial investment? [ ]   Now [ ]   Difference [ ]

How many of these new jobs were created by your investment? [ ]   How many additional new jobs will be created by your additional investment? [ ]

What is your position, office or title with the new commercial enterprise?

[ ]

Briefly describe your duties, activities and responsibilities.

[ ]

What is your salary? $ [ ]   What is the cost of your benefits? $ [ ]

Part 6.   Processing information.

Check One:

[ ] The person named in **Part 1** is now in the United States and an application to adjust status to permanent resident will be filed if this petition is approved.

[ ] If the petition is approved and the person named in **Part 1** wishes to apply for an immigrant visa abroad, complete the following for that person:

Country of nationality: [ ]

Country of current residence or, if now in the United States, last permanent residence abroad: [ ]

If you provided a United States address in **Part 1**, print the person's foreign address:

[ ]

If the person's native alphabet is other than Roman letters, write the foreign address in the native alphabet:

[ ]

Is a Form I-485, Application for Adjustment of Status, attached to this petition?   [ ] Yes   [ ] No

Are you in deportation or removal proceedings?   [ ] Yes (Explain on separate paper)   [ ] No

Have you ever worked in the United States without permission?   [ ] Yes (Explain on separate paper)   [ ] No

Part 7.   Signature.   *Read the information on penalties in the instrucitons before completing this section.*

I certify, under penalty of perjury under the laws of the United States of America, that this petition and the evidence submitted with it is all true and correct. I authorize the release of any information from my records which the Bureau of Citizenship and Immigration Services needs to determine eligibility for the benefit I am seeking.

Signature [ ]   Date [ ]

Please Note: If you do not completely fill out this form or fail to the submit the required documents listed in the instructions, you may not be found eligible for the immigration benefit you are seeking and this petition may be denied.

Part 8.   Signature of person preparing form, if other than above. (Sign below)

I declare that I prepared this application at the request of the above person and it is based on all information of which I have knowledge.

Signature [ ]   Print Your Name [ ]   Date [ ]

Firm Name [ ]   Daytime phone # with area code [(   ) -]

Address [ ]

U.S. Department of Justice
Immigration and Naturalization Service

OMB No. 1115-0093; Expires 7/31/04

Application to Extend/Change Nonimmigrant Status

START HERE - Please Type or Print.

FOR INS USE ONLY

Part 1.   Information about you.

Family Name		Given Name			Middle Initial

Address -
In care of -

Street Number and Name				Apt. #

City	State	Zip Code	Daytime Phone #

Country of Birth		Country of Citizenship

Date of Birth (MM/DD/YYYY)	Social Security # (if any)	A # (if any)

Date of Last Arrival Into the U.S.	I-94 #

Current Nonimmigrant Status	Expires on (MM/DD/YYYY)

Part 2.   Application type. *(See instructions for fee.)*

1. I am applying for: *(Check one.)*
   - a. ☐ An extension of stay in my current status.
   - b. ☐ A change of status. The new status I am requesting is: _____
   - c. ☐ Other: *(Describe grounds of eligibility.)* _____
2. Number of people included in this application: *(Check one.)*
   - a. ☐ I am the only applicant.
   - b. ☐ Members of my family are filing this application with me.
     The total number of people (including me) in the application is: _____
     (Complete the supplement for each co-applicant.)

Part 3.   Processing information.

1. I/We request that my/our current or requested status be extended until (MM/DD/YYYY): _____
2. Is this application based on an extension or change of status already granted to your spouse, child or parent?
   ☐ No ☐ Yes, Receipt # _____
3. Is this application based on a separate petition or application to give your spouse, child or parent an extension or change of status? ☐ No ☐ Yes, filed with this I-539.
   ☐ Yes, filed previously and pending with INS. INS receipt number: _____
4. If you answered "Yes" to Question 3, give the name of the petitioner or applicant:

   If the petition or application is pending with INS, also give the following information:

Office filed at _____ Filed on (MM/DD/YYYY) _____

Part 4.   Additional information.

1. For applicant #1, provide passport information:
   Country of Issuance | Valid to: (MM/DD/YYYY)
2. Foreign Address: Street Number and Name | Apt. #

City or Town	State or Province

Country	Zip/Postal Code

FOR INS USE ONLY

Returned	Receipt
Date	
Resubmitted	
Date	
Reloc Sent	
Date	
Reloc Rec'd	
Date	

☐ Applicant Interviewed on
_____
Date

☐ *Extension Granted to (Date):*
_____

Change of Status/Extension Granted
New Class: From *(Date)*: _____
_____   To *(Date)*: _____

If Denied:
☐ Still within period of stay
☐ S/D to: _____
☐ Place under docket control

Remarks:

Action Block

To be Completed by
Attorney or Representative, if any

☐ Fill in box if G-28 is attached to represent the applicant.

ATTY State License # _____

Form I-539 (Rev. 09/04/01)Y

Part 4. Additional information.

3. Answer the following questions. If you answer "Yes" to any question, explain on separate sheet of paper.	Yes	No
a. Are you, or any other person included on the application, an applicant for an immigrant visa?		
b. Has an immigrant petition ever been filed for you or for any other person included in this application?		
c. Has a Form I-485, Application to Register Permanent Residence or Adjust Status, ever been filed by you or by any other person included in this application?		
d. Have you, or any other person included in this application, ever been arrested or convicted of any criminal offense since last entering the U.S.?		
e. Have you, or any other person included in this application, done anything that violated the terms of the nonimmigrant status you now hold?		
f. Are you, or any other person included in this application, now in removal proceedings?		
g. Have you, or any other person included in this application, been employed in the U.S. since last admitted or granted an extension or change of status?		

- If you answered "Yes" to Question 3f, give the following information concerning the removal proceedings on the attached page entitled "**Part 4. Additional information. Page for answers to 3f and 3g.**" Include the name of the person in removal proceedings and information on jurisdiction, date proceedings began and status of proceedings.
- If you answered "No" to Question 3g, fully describe how you are supporting yourself on the attached page entitled "**Part 4. Additional information. Page for answers to 3f and 3g.**" Include the source, amount and basis for any income.
- If you answered "Yes" to Question 3g, fully describe the employment on the attached page entitled "**Part 4. Additional information. Page for answers to 3f and 3g.**" Include the name of the person employed, name and address of the employer, weekly income and whether the employment was specifically authorized by INS.

Part 5. Signature. (*Read the information on penalties in the instructions before completing this section. You must file this application while in the United States.*)

I certify, under penalty of perjury under the laws of the United States of America, that this application and the evidence submitted with it is all true and correct. I authorize the release of any information from my records which the Immigration and Naturalization Service needs to determine eligibility for the benefit I am seeking.

Signature	Print your Name	Date

Please note: *If you do not completely fill out this form, or fail to submit required documents listed in the instructions, you may not be found eligible for the requested benefit and this application will have to be denied.*

Part 6. Signature of person preparing form, if other than above. *(Sign below.)*

I declare that I prepared this application at the request of the above person and it is based on all information of which I have knowledge.

Signature	Print your Name	Date
Firm Name and Address	Daytime Phone Number *(Area Code and Number)*	
	Fax Number *(Area Code and Number)*	

(Please remember to enclose the mailing label with your application.)

Part 4. Additional information. Page for answers to 3f and 3g.

If you answered "Yes" to Question 3f in Part 4 on page 3 of this form, give the following information concerning the removal proceedings. Include the name of the person in removal proceedings and information on jurisdiction, date proceedings began and status of proceedings.

If you answered "No" to Question 3g in Part 4 on page 3 of this form, fully describe how you are supporting yourself. Include the source, amount and basis for any income.

If you answered "Yes" to Question 3g in Part 4 on page 3 of this form, fully describe the employment. Include the name of the person employed, name and address of the employer, weekly income and whether the employment was specifically authorized by INS.

Supplement -1
Attach to Form I-539 when more than one person is included in the petition or application.
(List each person separately. Do not include the person named in the form.)

Family Name	Given Name	Middle Name	Date of Birth (MM/DD/YYYY)
County of Birth	County of Citizenship	Social Security # (if any)	A # (if any)
Date of Arrival (MM/DD/YYYY)		I-94 #	
Current Nonimmigrant Status:		Expires On (MM/DD/YYYY)	
Country Where Passport Issued		Expiration Date (MM/DD/YYYY)	

Family Name	Given Name	Middle Name	Date of Birth (MM/DD/YYYY)
County of Birth	County of Citizenship	Social Security # (if any)	A # (if any)
Date of Arrival (MM/DD/YYYY)		I-94 #	
Current Nonimmigrant Status:		Expires On (MM/DD/YYYY)	
Country Where Passport Issued		Expiration Date (MM/DD/YYYY)	

Family Name	Given Name	Middle Name	Date of Birth (MM/DD/YYYY)
County of Birth	County of Citizenship	Social Security # (if any)	A # (if any)
Date of Arrival (MM/DD/YYYY)		I-94 #	
Current Nonimmigrant Status:		Expires On (MM/DD/YYYY)	
Country Where Passport Issued		Expiration Date (MM/DD/YYYY)	

Family Name	Given Name	Middle Name	Date of Birth (MM/DD/YYYY)
County of Birth	County of Citizenship	Social Security # (if any)	A # (if any)
Date of Arrival (MM/DD/YYYY)		I-94 #	
Current Nonimmigrant Status:		Expires On (MM/DD/YYYY)	
Country Where Passport Issued		Expiration Date (MM/DD/YYYY)	

Family Name	Given Name	Middle Name	Date of Birth (MM/DD/YYYY)
County of Birth	County of Citizenship	Social Security # (if any)	A # (if any)
Date of Arrival (MM/DD/YYYY)		I-94 #	
Current Nonimmigrant Status:		Expires On (MM/DD/YYYY)	
Country Where Passport Issued		Expiration Date (MM/DD/YYYY)	

If you need additional space, attach a separate sheet(s) of paper.
Place your name, A # if any, date of birth, form number and application date at the top of the sheet(s) of paper.

U.S. Department of Justice
Immigration and Naturalization Service

Supplement A to Form I-539
(Filing Instructions for V Nonimmigrant Status)

Additional Instructions to Form I-539 for V Nonimmigrant Status

What is the purpose of this form?

This form contains additional instructions for Form I-539, Application to Extend/Change Nonimmigrant Status, for aliens physically in the United States who are applying for V nonimmigrant status. **If you are not applying to obtain V nonimmigrant status, you do not need to use this form.** Aliens who are applying for V nonimmigrant status should complete Form I-539, and follow the instructions contained in Supplement A to Form I-539 as well as those contained in Form I-539.

Note: Aliens who are using this form in conjunction with the Form I-539 do not necessarily have to be in a valid nonimmigrant status to obtain V nonimmigrant status in the United States. See "Who is Eligible for V Nonimmigrant Status?" below.

Who is Eligible for V Nonimmigrant Status?

To be eligible for V nonimmigrant status, an alien must be the spouse or child of a lawful permanent resident and be the beneficiary of a properly filed Form I-130, Petition for Alien Relative, filed on or before December 21, 2000. In addition, the Form I-130 must have been filed three (3) or more years prior to the date of filing Supplement A to Form I-539, and be:

- Still pending; or

- Approved, and the alien beneficiary must either:

  (1) Waiting for an immigrant visa number to become available, or;

  (2) If the visa number is immediately available, the alien must have pending an application for adjustment of status or an application for an immigrant visa.

In addition, applicants must be admissible to the United States, except where the grounds of inadmissibility do not apply or have been waived. The grounds of inadmissibility that do not apply are INA sections:

- 212(a)(6)(A) -- Aliens present without admission or parole;

- 212(a)(7) -- Aliens without valid passports, visas, or other entry documents; and

- 212(a)(9)(B) -- Aliens who were unlawfully present for more than 180 days, then departed, and seek admission while barred from doing so.

Additional Instructions.

1. The applicant should check box "b" in part 2 of Form I-539, and indicate "V" in the provided space;

2. The applicant should use information from the qualifying Form I-130 for his or her response to Part 3, question 4 of Form I-539.

Additional Evidence Requirements.

In addition to the General Filing Instructions and Initial Evidence required by the instructions to Form I-539, the following requirements must be submitted:

1. Form I-693, Medical Examination of Aliens Seeking Adjustment of Status without vaccination supplement; and

2. Additional Initial Evidence. An alien applying for V nonimmigrant status with the Immigration and Naturalization Service (Service) should submit proof of filing of the immigrant petition that qualifies the alien for V status, and if necessary, proof of filing of the Form I-485, Application to Register Permanent Residence or Adjust Status. Proof of filing may be in the form of Form I-797, Notice of Action, which serves as a receipt or as a notice of approval, or a receipt for a filed Form I-130 or Form I-485, or notice of approval issued by a local district office. If the alien does not have such proof, the Service will review other forms of evidence, such as correspondence to or from the Service regarding a pending petition. If the alien does not have any of the above items, but believes he or she is eligibile for V nonimmigrant status, he or she should state where and when the petition was filed, the name and alien number of the petitioner, and the names of all beneficiaries.

Where to File.

Aliens filing for V nonimmigrant status should file at:

U.S. Immigration and Naturalization Service
P.O. Box 7216
Chicago, IL 60680 - 7216

Fee.

In addition to the application fee required for Form I-539, the applicants must remit the fingerprint service fee of $25.00, as required by 8 CFR 103.2(e)(4).

Privacy Act Notice.

We ask for the information on this form, and associated evidence, to determine if you have established eligibility for the immigration benefit for which you are filing. Our legal right to ask for this information is in 8 U.S.C. 1103. We may provide this information to other government agencies. Failure to provide this information, and any requested evidence, may delay a final decision or result in denial of your request.

Paperwork Reduction Act Notice.

An agency may not conduct or sponsor an information collection and a person is not required to respond to a collection of information unless it contains a currently valid OMB approval number. We try to create forms and instructions that are accurate, can be easily understood, and which impose the least possible burden on you to provide us with information. Often this is difficult because some immigration laws are very complex. The estimated average time to complete and file Form I-539, to which this form is a supplement is as follows: (1) 10 minutes to learn about the law and form; (2) 5 minutes to complete the form; (3) 15 minutes to assemble and file the application; for a total estimated average response of 30 minutes per application. If you have comments regarding the accuracy of this estimate, or suggestions for making this form simpler, you can write to the Immigration and Naturlization Service, HQPDI, 425 I Street, N.W., Room 4034, Washington, DC 20536; OMB No. 1115-0237. *(Do not mail your completed application to this address.)*

U.S. Department of Justice
Immigration and Naturalization Service

OMB No. 1115-0086

Application for Asylum and for Withholding of Removal

Start Here - Please Type or Print. USE BLACK INK. SEE THE SEPARATE INSTRUCTION PAMPHLET FOR INFORMATION ABOUT ELIGIBILITY AND HOW TO COMPLETE AND FILE THIS APPLICATION. (Note: There is NO filing fee for this application.)

Please check the box if you also want to apply for withholding of removal under the Convention Against Torture. ☐

PART A. I. INFORMATION ABOUT YOU

1. Alien Registration Number(s)(A#'s)(If any)	2. Social Security No. (If any)

3. Complete Last Name	4. First Name	5. Middle Name

6. What other names have you used? *(Include maiden name and aliases.)*

7. Residence in the U.S. C/O	Telephone Number
Street Number and Name	Apt. No.
City State	ZIP Code

8. Mailing Address in the U.S., if other than above	Telephone Number
Street Number and Name	Apt. No.
City State	ZIP Code

9. Sex ☐ Male ☐ Female	10. Marital Status: ☐ Single ☐ Married ☐ Divorced ☐ Widowed

11. Date of Birth *(Mo/Day/Yr)*	12. City and Country of Birth

13. Present Nationality *(Citizenship)*	14. Nationality at Birth	15. Race, Ethnic or Tribal Group	16. Religion

17. *Check the box, a through c that applies:*   a. ☐ I have never been in immigration court proceedings.
b. ☐ I am now in immigration court proceedings.   c. ☐ I am **not** now in immigration court proceedings, but I have been in the past.

18. *Complete 18 a through c.*
a. When did you last leave your country? *(Mo/Day/Yr)* _____   b. What is your current I-94 Number, if any? _____

c. Please list each entry to the U.S. beginning with your most recent entry.
List date *(Mo/Day/Yr)*, place, and your status for each entry. *(Attach additional sheets as needed.)*

Date _____	Place _____	Status _____	Date Status Expires _____
Date _____	Place _____	Status _____	
Date _____	Place _____	Status _____	
Date _____	Place _____	Status _____	

19. What country issued your last passport or travel document?	20. Passport # Travel Document #	21. Expiration Date *(Mo/Day/Yr)*

22. What is your native language?	23. Are you fluent in English? ☐ Yes ☐ No	24. What other languages do you speak fluently?

FOR EOIR USE ONLY	**FOR INS USE ONLY**
	Action: Interview Date: _____ **Decision:** __ Approval Date: _____ — Denial Date: _____ — Referral Date: _____ Asylum Officer ID# _____

Form I-589 (Rev. 10/18/01)N

PART A. II. INFORMATION ABOUT YOUR SPOUSE AND CHILDREN

Your Spouse. ☐ I am not married. (Skip to *Your Children*, below.)

1. Alien Registration Number (A#) *(If any)*	2. Passport/ID Card No. *(If any)*	3. Date of Birth *(Mo/Day/Yr)*	4. Social Security No. *(If any)*
5. Complete Last Name	6. First Name	7. Middle Name	8. Maiden Name

9. Date of Marriage *(Mo/Day/Yr)*	10. Place of Marriage	11. City and Country of Birth

12. Nationality *(Citizenship)*	13. Race, Ethnic or Tribal Group	14. Sex ☐ Male ☐ Female

15. Is this person in the U.S.? ☐ Yes *(Complete blocks 16 to 24.)* ☐ No *(Specify location)*

16. Place of last entry in the U.S.?	17. Date of last entry in the U.S. *(Mo/Day/Yr)*	18. I-94 No. *(If any)*	19. Status when last admitted *(Visa type, if any)*
20. What is your spouse's current status?	21. What is the expiration date of his/her authorized stay, if any? *(Mo/Day/Yr)*	22. Is your spouse in immigration court proceedings? ☐ Yes ☐ No	23. If previously in the U.S., date of previous arrival *(Mo/Day/Yr)*

24. If in the U.S., is your spouse to be included in this application? *(Check the appropriate box.)*

☐ Yes *(Attach one (1) photograph of your spouse in the upper right hand corner of page 9 on the extra copy of the application submitted for this person.)*

☐ No

Your Children. Please list **ALL** of your children, regardless of age, location, or marital status.

☐ I do not have any children. *(Skip to Part A. III., Information about Your Background.)*
☐ I do have children. Total number of children _____

(Use Supplement A Form I-589 or attach additional pages and documentation if you have more than four (4) children.)

1. Alien Registration Number (A#) *(If any)*	2. Passport/ID Card No. *(If any)*	3. Marital Status *(Married, Single, Divorced, Widowed)*	4. Social Security No. *(If any)*
5. Complete Last Name	6. First Name	7. Middle Name	8. Date of Birth *(Mo/Day/Yr)*

9. City and Country of Birth	10. Nationality *(Citizenship)*	11. Race, Ethnic or Tribal Group	12. Sex ☐ Male ☐ Female

13. Is this child in the U.S.? ☐ Yes *(Complete blocks 14 to 21.)* ☐ No *(Specify Location)*

14. Place of last entry in the U.S.?	15. Date of last entry in the U.S.? *(Mo/Day/Yr)*	16. I-94 No. *(If any)*	17. Status when last admitted *(Visa type, if any)*
18. What is your child's current status?	19. What is the expiration date of his/her authorized stay, if any?*(Mo/Day/Yr)*	20. Is your child in immigration court proceedings? ☐ Yes ☐ No	

21. If in the U.S., is this child to be included in this application? *(Check the appropriate box.)*

☐ Yes *(Attach one (1) photograph of your child in the upper right hand corner of page 9 on the extra copy of the application submitted for this person.)*

☐ No

PART A. II. INFORMATION ABOUT YOUR SPOUSE AND CHILDREN Continued

1. Alien Registration Number (A#) *(If any)*	2. Passport/IDCard No. *(If any)*	3. Marital Status *(Married, Single, Divorced, Widowed)*	4. Social Security No. *(If any)*
5. Complete Last Name	6. First Name	7. Middle Name	8. Date of Birth *(Mo/Day/Yr)*
9. City and Country of Birth	10. Nationality *(Citizenship)*	11. Race, Ethnic or Tribal Group	12. Sex ☐ Male ☐ Female

13. Is this child in the U.S.? ☐ Yes *(Complete blocks 14 to 21.)* ☐ No *(Specify Location)*

14. Place of last entry in the U.S.?	15. Date of last entry in the U.S. ? *(Mo/Day/Yr)*	16. I-94 No. *(If any)*	17. Status when last admitted *(Visa type, if any)*
18. What is your child's current status?	19. What is the expiration date of his/her authorized stay,*(if any)? (Mo/Day/Yr)*	20. Is your child in immigration court proceedings? ☐ Yes ☐ No	

21. If in the U.S., is this child to be included in this application? *(Check the appropriate box.)*

☐ Yes *(Attach one (1) photograph of your child in the upper right hand corner of page 9 on the extra copy of the application submitted for this person.)*

☐ No

1. Alien Registration Number (A#) *(If any)*	2. Passport/ID Card No.*(If any)*	3. Marital Status *(Married, Single, Divorced, Widowed)*	4. Social Security No. *(If any)*
5. Complete Last Name	6. First Name	7. Middle Name	8. Date of Birth *(Mo/Day/Yr)*
9. City and Country of Birth	10. Nationality *(Citizenship)*	11. Race, Ethnic or Tribal Group	12. Sex ☐ Male ☐ Female

13. Is this child in the U.S. ? ☐ Yes *(Complete blocks 14 to 21.)* ☐ No *(Specify Location)*

14. Place of last entry in the U.S.?	15. Date of last entry in the U.S.? *(Mo/Day/Yr)*	16. I-94 No. *(If any)*	17. Status when last admitted *(Visa type, if any)*
18. What is your child's current status?	19. What is the expiration date of his/her authorized stay, if any? *(Mo/Day/Yr)*	20. Is your child in immigration court proceedings? ☐ Yes ☐ No	

21. If in the U.S., is this child to be included in this application? *(Check the appropriate box.)*

☐ Yes *(Attach one (1) photograph of your child in the upper right hand corner of page 9 on the extra copy of the application submitted for this person.)*

☐ No

1. Alien Registration Number (A#) *(If any)*	2. Passport/ID Card No. *(If any)*	3. Marital Status *(Married, Single. Divorced, Widowed)*	4. Social Security No. *(If any)*
5. Complete Last Name	6. First Name	7. Middle Name	8. Date of Birth *(Mo/Day/Yr)*
9. City and Country of Birth	10. Nationality *(Citizenship)*	11. Race, Ethnic or Tribal Group	12. Sex ☐ Male ☐ Female

13. Is this child in the U.S.? ☐ Yes *(Complete blocks 14 to 21.)* ☐ No *(Specify Location)*

14. Place of last entry in the U.S.?	15. Date of last entry in the U.S.? *(Mo/Day/Yr)*	16. I-94 No. (If *any)*	17. Status when last admitted *(Visa type, if any)*
18. What is your child's current status?	19. What is the expiration date of his/her authorized stay, if any? *(Mo/Day/Yr)*	20. Is your child in immigration court proceedings? ☐ Yes ☐ No	

21. If in the U.S., is this child to be included in this application? *(Check the appropriate box.)*

☐ Yes *(Attach one (1) photograph of your child in the upper right hand corner of page 9 on the extra copy of the application submitted for this person.)*

☐ No

PART A. III.   INFORMATION ABOUT YOUR BACKGROUND

1. Please list your last address where you lived before coming to the U.S. If this is not the country where you fear persecution, also list the last address in the country where you fear persecution. *(List Address, City/Town, Department, Province, or State, and Country.) (Use Supplement B Form I-589 or additional sheets of paper if necessary.)*

Number and Street *(Provide if available)*	City/Town	Department, Province or State	Country	Dates From *(Mo/Yr)* To *(Mo/Yr)*	

2. Provide the following information about your residences during the last five years. List your present address first. *(Use Supplement Form B or additional sheets of paper if necessary.)*

Number and Street	City/Town	Department, Province or State	Country	Dates From *(Mo/Yr)* To *(Mo/Yr)*	

3. Provide the following information about your education, beginning with the most recent. *(Use Supplement B Form I-589 or additional sheets of paper if necessary.)*

Name of School	Type of School	Location (Address)	Attended From *(Mo/Yr)* To *(Mo/Yr)*	

4. Provide the following information about your employment during the last five years. List your present employment first. *(Use Supplement Form B or additional sheets of paper if necessary.)*

Name and Address of Employer	Your Occupation	Dates From *(Mo/Yr)* To *(Mo/Yr)*	

5. Provide the following information about your parents and siblings (brother and sisters). Check box if the person is deceased. *(Use Supplement B Form I-589 or additional sheets of paper if necessary.)*

Name	City/Town and Country of Birth	Current Location
Mother		☐ Deceased
Father		☐ Deceased
Siblings		☐ Deceased
		☐ Deceased

PART B. INFORMATION ABOUT YOUR APPLICATION

(Use Supplement B Form I-589 or attach additional sheets of paper as needed to complete your responses to the questions contained in PART B.)

When answering the following questions about your asylum or other protection claim (withholding of removal under 241(b)(3) of the Act or withholding of removal under the Convention Against Torture) you should provide a detailed and specific account of the basis of your claim to asylum or other protection. To the best of your ability, provide specific dates, places, and descriptions about each event or action described. You should attach documents evidencing the general conditions in the country from which you are seeking asylum or other protection and the specific facts on which you are relying to support your claim. If this documentation is unavailable or you are not providing this documentation with your application, please explain why in your responses to the following questions. Refer to Instructions, Part 1: Filing Instructions, Section II, "Basis of Eligibility," Parts A - D, Section V, "Completing the Form," Part B, and Section VII, "Additional Documents that You Should Submit" for more information on completing this section of the form.

1. Why are you applying for asylum or withholding of removal under section 241(b)(3) of the Act, or for withholding of removal under the Convention Against Torture? Check the appropriate box (es) below and then provide detailed answers to questions A and B below:

    I am seeking asylum or withholding of removal based on

    ☐ Race
    ☐ Religion
    ☐ Nationality
    ☐ Political opinion
    ☐ Membership in a particular social group
    ☐ Torture Convention

A. Have you, your family, or close friends or colleagues ever experienced harm or mistreatment or threats in the past by anyone?
    ☐ No ☐ Yes If your answer is "Yes," explain in detail:

    1) What happened;
    2) When the harm or mistreatment or threats occurred;
    3) Who caused the harm or mistreatment or threats; and
    4) Why you believe the harm or mistreatment or threats occurred.

B. Do you fear harm or mistreatment if you return to your home country?
    ☐ No ☐ Yes If your answer is "Yes," explain in detail:

    1) What harm or mistreatment you fear;
    2) Who you believe would harm or mistreat you; and
    3) Why you believe you would or could be harmed or mistreated.

PART B.   INFORMATION ABOUT YOUR APPLICATION Continued

2. Have you or your family members ever been accused, charged, arrested, detained, interrogated, convicted and sentenced, or imprisoned in any country other than the United States?

☐ No   ☐ Yes If "Yes," explain the circumstances and reasons for the action.

3. A. Have you or your family members ever belonged to or been associated with any organizations or groups in your home country, such as, but not limited to, a political party, student group, labor union, religious organization, military or paramilitary group, civil patrol, guerrilla organization, ethnic group, human rights group, or the press or media?

☐ No   ☐ Yes If "Yes," describe for each person the level of participation, any leadership or other positions held, and the length of time you or your family members were involved in each organization or activity.

B. Do you or your family members continue to participate in any way in these organizations or groups?

☐ No   ☐ Yes If "Yes," describe for each person, your or your family members' current level of participation, any leadership or other positions currently held, and the length of time you or your family members have been involved in each organization or group.

4. Are you afraid of being subjected to torture in your home country or any other country to which you may be returned?

☐ No   ☐ Yes If "Yes," explain why you are afraid and describe the nature of the torture you fear, by whom, and why it would be inflicted.

PART C. ADDITIONAL INFORMATION ABOUT YOUR APPLICATION

(Use Supplement B Form I-589 or attach additional sheets of paper as needed to complete your responses to the questions contained in Part C.)

1. Have you, your spouse, your child(ren), your parents, or your siblings ever applied to the United States Government for refugee status, asylum, or withholding of removal? ☐ No ☐ Yes

    If "Yes" explain the decision and what happened to any status you, your spouse, your child(ren), your parents, or your siblings received as a result of that decision. Please indicate whether or not you were included in a parent or spouse's application. If so, please include your parent or spouse's A- number in your response. If you have been denied asylum by an Immigration Judge or the Board of Immigration Appeals, please describe any change(s) in conditions in your country or your own personal circumstances since the date of the denial that may affect your eligibility for asylum.

2. A. After leaving the country from which you are claiming asylum, did you or your spouse or child(ren), who are now in the United States, travel through or reside in any other country before entering the United States? ☐ No ☐ Yes

    B. Have you, your spouse, your child(ren), or other family members such as your parents or siblings ever applied for or received any lawful status in any country other than the one from which you are now claiming asylum? ☐ No ☐ Yes

    If "Yes" to either or both questions (2A and/or 2B), provide for each person the following: the name of each country and the length of stay; the person's status while there; the reasons for leaving; whether the person is entitled to return for lawful residence purposes; and whether the person applied for refugee status or for asylum while there, and, if not, why he or she did not do so.

3. Have you, your spouse, or child(ren) ever ordered, incited, assisted, or otherwise participated in causing harm or suffering to any person because of his or her race, religion, nationality, membership in a particular social group or belief in a particular political opinion?

    ☐ No ☐ Yes If "Yes," describe in detail each such incident and your own or your spouse's or child(ren)'s involvement.

PART C. ADDITIONAL INFORMATION ABOUT YOUR APPLICATION Continued

4.   After you left the country where you were harmed or fear harm, did you return to that country?

☐ No   ☐ Yes If "Yes," describe in detail the circumstances of your visit (for example, the date(s) of the trip(s), the purpose(s) of the trip(s), and the length of time you remained in that country for the visit(s)).

5.   Are you filing the application more than one year after your last arrival in the United States?

☐ No   ☐ Yes If "Yes," explain why you did not file within the first year after you arrived. You should be prepared to explain at your interview or hearing why you did not file your asylum application within the first year after you arrived. For guidance in answering this question, see Instructions, Part 1: Filing Instructions, Section V. "Completing the Form," Part C.

6.   Have you or any member of your family included in the application ever committed any crime and/or been arrested, charged, convicted and sentenced for any crimes in the United States?

☐ No   ☐ Yes If "Yes," for each instance, specify in your response what occurred and the circumstances; dates; length of sentence received; location; the duration of the detention or imprisonment; the reason(s) for the detention or conviction; any formal charges that were lodged against you or your relatives included in your application; the reason(s) for release. Attach documents referring to these incidents, if they are available, or an explanation of why documents are not available.

OMB No. 1115-0086

PART D.   YOUR SIGNATURE

After reading the information regarding penalties in the instructions, complete and sign below. If someone helped you prepare this application, he or she must complete Part E.

I certify, under penalty of perjury under the laws of the United States of America, that this application and the evidence submitted with it are all true and correct. Title 18, United States Code, Section 1546, provides in part: "Whoever knowingly makes under oath, or as permitted under penalty of perjury under Section 1746 of Title 28, United States Code, knowingly subscribes as true, any false statement with respect to a material fact in any application, affidavit, or knowingly presents any such application, affidavit, or other document required by the immigration laws or regulations prescribed thereunder, or knowingly presents any such application, affidavit, or other document containing any such false statement or which fails to contain any reasonable basis in law or fact - shall be fined in accordance with this title or imprisoned not more than five years, or both." I authorize the release of any information from my record which the Immigration and Naturalization Service needs to determine eligibility for the benefit I am seeking.

Staple your photograph here or the photograph of the family member to be included on the extra copy of the application submitted for that person.

WARNING: Applicants who are in the United States illegally are subject to removal if their asylum or withholding claims are not granted by an Asylum Officer or an Immigration Judge. Any information provided in completing this application may be used as a basis for the institution of, or as evidence in, removal proceedings even if the application is later withdrawn. Applicants determined to have knowingly made a frivolous application for asylum will be permanently ineligible for any benefits under the Immigration and Nationality Act. See 208(d)(6) of the Act and 8 CFR 208.20.

Print Complete Name

Write your name in your native alphabet

Did your spouse, parent, or child(ren) assist you in completing this application?   ☐ No ☐ Yes *(If "Yes," list the name and relationship.)*

_____   _____   _____   _____
        (Name)   *(Relationship)*   *(Name)*   *(Relationship)*

Did someone other than your spouse, parent, or child(ren) prepare this application?   ☐ No ☐ Yes *(If "Yes," complete Part E)*

Asylum applicants may be represented by counsel. Have you been provided with a list of persons who may be available to assist you, at little or no cost, with your asylum claim?   ☐ No ☐ Yes

Signature of Applicant *(The person in Part A. 1.)*

[_____]   _____
       Sign your name so it all appears within the brackets   Date *(Mo/Day/Yr)*

PART E.   DECLARATION OF PERSON PREPARING FORM IF OTHER THAN APPLICANT, SPOUSE, PARENT OR CHILD

I declare that I have prepared this application at the request of the person named in Part D, that the responses provided are based on all information of which I have knowledge, or which was provided to me by the applicant and that the completed application was read to the applicant in his or her native language or a language he or she understands for verification before he or she signed the application in my presence. I am aware that the knowing placement of false information on the Form I-589 may also subject me to civil penalties under 8 U.S.C. 1324(c).

Signature of Preparer	Print Complete Name		
Daytime Telephone Number ( )	Address of Preparer: Street Number and Name		
Apt. No.	City	State	ZIP Code

PART F.   TO BE COMPLETED AT INTERVIEW OR HEARING

You will be asked to complete this Part when you appear before an Asylum Officer of the Immigration and Naturalization Service (INS), or an Immigration Judge of the Executive Office for Immigration Review (EOIR) for examination.

I swear (affirm) that I know the contents of this application that I am signing, including the attached documents and supplements, that they are all true to the best of my knowledge taking into account correction(s) numbered _____ to _____ that were made by me or at my request.

Signed and sworn to before me by the above named applicant on:

_____   _____
Signature of Applicant   Date *(Mo/Day/Yr)*

_____   _____
Write Your Name in Your Native Alphabet   Signature of Asylum Officer or Immigration Judge

Form I-589 (Rev. 10/18/01)N Page 9

A # *(If available)*	Date
Applicant's Name	Applicant's Signature

LIST ALL OF YOUR CHILDREN, REGARDLESS OF AGE OR MARITAL STATUS.

(Use this form and attach additional pages and documentation as needed to your application if you have more than four (4) children.)

1. Alien Registration Number (A#)*(If any)*	2. Passport/ID Card No. *(If any)*	3. Marital Status *(Married, Single, Divorced, Widowed)*	4. Social Security No. *(If any)*
5. Complete Last Name	6. First Name	7. Middle Name	8. Date of Birth *(Mo/Day/Yr)*
9. City and Country of Birth	10. Nationality *(Citizenship)*	11. Race, Ethnic or Tribal Group	12. Sex ☐ Male ☐ Female

13. Is this child in the U.S.? ☐ Yes *(Complete blocks 14 to 21.)* ☐ No *(Specify Location)*

14. Place of last entry in the U.S.?	15. Date of last entry in the U.S.? *(Mo/Day/Yr)*	16. I-94 No. *(If any)*	17. Status when last admitted *(Visa type, if any)*
18. What is your child's current status?	19. What is the expiration date of his/her authorized stay, if any? *(Mo/Day/Yr)*	20. Is your child in immigration court proceedings? ☐ Yes ☐ No	

21. If in the U.S., is this child to be included in this application? *(Check the appropriate box.)*
☐ Yes *(Attach one (1) photograph of your child in the upper right hand corner of page 9 on the extra copy of the application submitted for this person.)*
☐ No

1. Alien Registration Number (A#)*(If any)*	2. Passport/ID Card No. *(If any)*	3. Marital Status *(Married, Single, Divorced, Widowed)*	4. Social Security No. *(If any)*
5. Complete Last Name	6. First Name	7. Middle Name	8. Date of Birth *(Mo/Day/Yr)*
9. City and Country of Birth	10. Nationality *(Citizenship)*	11. Race, Ethnic or Tribal Group	12. Sex ☐ Male ☐ Female

13. Is this child in the U.S.? ☐ Yes *(Complete blocks 14 to 21.)* ☐ No *(Specify Location)*

14. Place of last entry in the U.S.?	15. Date of last entry in the U.S.? *(Mo/Day/Yr)*	16. I-94 No. *(If any)*	17. Status when last admitted *(Visa type, if any)*
18. What is your child's current status?	19. What is the expiration date of his/her authorized stay, if any? *(Mo/Day/Yr)*	20. Is your child in immigration court proceedings? ☐ Yes ☐ No	

21. If in the U.S., is this child to be included in this application? *(Check the appropriate box.)*
☐ Yes *(Attach one (1) photograph of your child in the upper right hand corner of page 9 on the extra copy of the application submitted for this person.)*
☐ No

OMB No. 1115-0086

ADDITIONAL INFORMATION ABOUT YOUR CLAIM TO ASYLUM.

A # *(If available)*	Date
Applicant's Name	Applicant's Signature

Use this as a continuation page for any information requested. Please copy and complete as needed.

PART _____

QUESTION _____

U.S. Department of Justice
Immigration and Naturalization Service

OMB No. 1115-0057

Registration for Classification as Refugee

Type or print the following information. *(Read instructions on reverse)*

A File No.: _____

1. Name: _____ *(First)* _____ *(Middle)* _____ *(Last)*

2. Present address:

3. Date of birth: *(Month/Day/Year)*	Place of birth *(City or Town)*	*(Province)*	*(Country)*	Present nationality:

4. Country from which I fled or was displaced: _____ On or about *(Month/Day/Year)*: _____

5. Reasons *(State in detail)*:

_____

_____

_____

_____

_____

_____

_____

_____

6. My present immigration status in _____ *(country in which residing)* is: _____

Evidence of my immigration status is: _____

(Describe)

7. Name of spouse:	8. Present address of spouse *(if different)*:	9. Nationality of spouse:

10. My spouse ☐ will ☐ will not accompany me to the United States.

11. Name of child (ren)	Date of birth	Place of birth	Present address *(if different)*
⌐			
⌐			
⌐			
⌐			
⌐			

Place a mark (x) in front of name of each child who will accompany you to the United States.

12. Schooling or education

Name and location of school	Type	Dates attended	Title of degree or diploma

13. Military service

Country	Branch and organization	Dates	Serial No.	Rank attained

Form I-590 (Rev. 04/12/2000) Y Page 1

14. Political, professional or social organizations of which I am now or have been a member or with which I am now or have been affiliated since my 16th birthday (If you have never been a member of any organization, state **"None."**)

_____

_____

_____

15. I [ ] have [ ] have not been charged with a violation of law. (If you have ever been charged with a violation of law, give date, place and nature of each charge and the final result.) _____

_____

_____

16. I [ ] have [ ] have not been in the United States. (If you have ever been in the United States, show the dates of entry and departure and the purpose of your entry (visitor, permanent resident, student, seaman, etc.).

_____ File or Alien Registration Number: _____

17. I have the following close relatives in the United States:

Name	Relationship	Present address

18. I am being sponsored by (Name and address of United States sponsor):

Date:	Signature of registrant:

DO NOT WRITE BELOW THIS LINE

I,_____, do swear (affirm) that I know the contents of this registration subscribed by me including the attached documents, that the same are true to the best of my knowledge, and that corrections numbered (   ) to (   ) were made by me or at my request, and that this registration was signed by me with my full, true name:

(Complete and true signature of registrant)

Subscribed and sworn to before me by the above-named registrant at_____ on_____

(Month/Day/Year)

(Signature and title of officer)

INTERVIEW	APPROVED	
DATE	DATE	
AT		
_____	_____	
Immigration Officer	Officer in Charge	

INSTRUCTIONS

This form should be executed, signed and submitted to the Officer in Charge of the nearest overseas office of the United States Immigration and Naturalization Service. When your name has been reached as a registrant you will be furnished additional instructions.

Registration - A separate Registration Form must be executed by each registrant and submitted in one copy. A Registration Form in behalf of a child under 14 years of age shall be executed by the parent of guardian.

Public reporting burden for this collection of information is estimated to average 35 minutes per response. If you have comments regarding the accuracy of this estimate or suggestions for simplifying this form, you can write to the U.S. Department of Justice, Immigration and Naturalization Service, 425 I Street, N.W.; Room 4034, Washington, D.C. 20536, OMB No. 1115-0057.

OMB No. 1115-0049

Petition to Classify Orphan as an Immediate Relative

[Section 101 (b)(1)(F) of the Immigration and Nationality Act, as amended.]

U.S. Department of Justice
Immigration and Naturalization Service

Please do not write in this block.

TO THE SECRETARY OF STATE;

The petition was filed by:

☐ Married petitioner   ☐ Unmarried petitioner

The petition is approved for orphan:

☐ Adopted abroad   ☐ Coming to U.S. for adoption. Preadoption requirements have been met.

Remarks:

Fee Stamp

File number

DATE OF ACTION

DD

DISTRICT

Please type or print legibly in ink. Use a separate petition for each child.

Petition is being made to classify the named orphan as an immediate relative.

BLOCK I - Information about prospective

1. My name is: (Last)   (First)   (Middle)

2. Other names used (including maiden name if appropriate):

3. I reside in the U.S.   (C/O if appropriate)   (Apt. No.)

    (Number and street)   (Town or city)   (State)   (Zip Code)

4. Address abroad (if any)(Number and street)   (Apt. No.)

    (Town or city)   (Province)   (Country)

5. I was born on: (Month)   (Day)   (Year)

    In: (Town or City)   (State or Province)   (Country)

6. My phone number is: (Include Area Code)

7. My marital status is:
   ☐ Married
   ☐ Widowed
   ☐ Divorced
   ☐ Single
     ☐ I have never been married.
     ☐ I have been previously married _____ time(s).

8. If you are now married, give the following information:

Date and place of present marriage

Name of present spouse (include maiden name of wife)

Date of birth of spouse   Place of birth of spouse

Number of prior marriages of spouse

My spouse resides ☐ With me   ☐ Apart from me
                           (provide address below)

(Apt. No.)   (No. and street)   (City)   (State)   (Country)

9. I am a citizen of the United States through:
   ☐ Birth   ☐ Parents   ☐ Naturalization

If acquired through naturalization, give name under which naturalized, number of naturalization certificate, and date and place of naturalization:

If not, submit evidence of citizenship. See Instruction 2.a(2).

If acquired through parentage, have you obtained a certificate in your own name based on that acquisition?
   ☐ No   ☐ Yes

Have you or any person through whom you claimed citizenship ever lost United States citizenship?
   ☐ No   ☐ Yes (If yes, attach detailed explanation.)

Continue on reverse.

Received	Trans. In	Ret'd Trans. Out	Completed

Form I-600 (Rev. 11/28/01)Y Page 1

BLOCK II - Information about orphan beneficiary

10. Name at birth   (First)   (Middle)   (Last)

11. Name at present   (First)   (Middle)   (Last)

12. Any other names by which orphan is or was known.

13. Sex   ☐ Male   14. Date of birth (Month/Day/Year)
       ☐ Female

15. Place of birth   (City)   (State or Province)   (Country)

16. The beneficiary is an orphan because (check One)
    ☐ He/she has no parents.
    ☐ He/she has only one parent who is the sole or surviving

17. If the orphan has only one parent, answer the following
   a. State what has become of the other parent:

   b. Is the remaining parent capable of providing for the orphan's support?   ☐ Yes   ☐ No
   c. Has the remaining parent, in writing, irrevocably released orphan for emigration and adoption? ☐ Yes   ☐ No

18. Has the orphan been adopted abroad by the petitioner and jointly or the unmarried petitioner?   ☐ Yes   ☐ No

     If yes, did the petitioner and spouse or unmarried petitioner personally see and observe the child prior to or during the adoption proceedings?   ☐ Yes   ☐ No

     Date of adoption

     Place of adoption

19. If either answer in question 18 is "No", answer the following:
   a. Do petitioner and spouse jointly or does the unmarried intend to adopt the orphan in the United States?
                    ☐ Yes   ☐ No
   b. Have the preadoption requirements, if any, of the orphan's proposed state of residence been met?
                    ☐ Yes   ☐ No
   c. If b. is answered "No", will they be met later?   ☐ Yes   ☐ No

20. To petitioner's knowledge, does the orphan have any physical or affliction?   ☐ Yes   ☐ No
     If "Yes", name the affliction.

21. Who has legal custody of the child?

22. Name of child welfare agency, if any, assisting in this case:

23. Name of attorney abroad, if any, representing petitioner in this
     Address of above.

24. Address in the United States where orphan will reside.

25. Present address of orphan.

25. If orphan is residing in an institution, give full name of institution.

26. If orphan is not residing in an institution, give full name of person whom orphan is residing.

27. Give any additional information necessary to locate orphan such as name of district, section, zone or locality in which orphan resides.

28. Location of American Consulate where application for visa will be made.
     (City in Foreign Country)   (Foreign Country)

Certification of prospective petitioner
I certify under penalty of perjury under the laws of the United States of America that the foregoing is true and correct and that I will care for an orphan/orphans properly if admitted to the United States.

(Signature of Prospective Petitioner)

Executed on (Date)

Certification of married prospective petitioner's spouse
I certify under penalty of perjury under the laws of the United States of America that the foregoing is true and correct and that my spouse and I will care for an orphan/orphans properly if admitted to the United States.

(Signature of Prospective Petitioner)

Executed on (Date)

Signature of person preparing form, if other than petitioner
I declare that this document was prepared by me at the request of the prospective petitioner and is based on all information of which I have any knowledge.

(Signature)

Address

Executed on (Date)

OMB No. 1115-0049

U.S. Department of Justice
Immigration and Naturalization Service

Application for Advance Processing of Orphan Petition [8CFR 204.1(b)(3)]

Please do not write in this block.

It has been determined that the
☐ Married   ☐ Unmarried

Fee Stamp

There
☐ are   ☐ are not
preadoptive requirements in the state of the child's
proposed residence.

The following is a description of the preadoption requirements, if
any, of the state of the child's proposed residence:

DATE OF FAVORABLE
DETERMINATION

DD

DISTRICT

The preadoption requirements, if any,
☐ have been met.   ☐ have not been met.

File number of petitioner, if applicable

Please type or print legibly in ink.

Application is made by the named prospective petitioner for advance processing of an orphan petition.

BLOCK I - Information about prospective petitioner

1. My name is: (Last)   (First)   (Middle)

2. Other names used (including maiden name if appropriate):

3. I reside in the U.S. at: (C/O if appropriate)   (Apt. No.)

   (Number and street)   (Town or city)   (State)   (ZIP Code)

4. Address abroad (if any):   (Number and street)   (Apt. No.)

   (Town or city)   (Province)   (Country)

5. I was born on: (Month)   (Day)   (Year)

   In: (Town or City)   (State or Province)   (Country)

6. My phone number is: (Include Area Code)

7. My marital status is:
   ☐ Married
   ☐ Widowed
   ☐ Divorced
   ☐ Single
      ☐ I have never been married.
      ☐ I have been previously married _____ time(s).

8. If you are now married, give the following information:
   Date and place of present marriage

   Name of present spouse (include maiden name of wife)

   Date of birth of spouse   Place of birth of spouse

   Number of prior marriages of spouse

   My spouse resides ☐ With me   ☐ Apart from me
                                 (provide address below)
   (Apt. No.)   (No. and street)   (City)   (State)   (Country)

9. I am a citizen of the United States through:
   ☐ Birth   ☐ Parents   ☐ Naturalization
   If acquired through naturalization, give name under which
   naturalized, number of naturalization certificate, and date and
   place of naturalization.

   If not, submit evidence of citizenship. See Instruction 2.a(2).
   If acquired through parentage, have you obtained a certificate
   in your own name based on that acquisition?
   ☐ No   ☐ Yes
   Have you or any person through whom you claimed citizenship
   ever lost United States citizenship?
   ☐ No   ☐ Yes (If yes, attach detailed explanation.)

Continue on reverse.

Received	Trans. In	Ret'd Trans. Out	Completed

Form I-600A (Rev. 12/04/01)Y Page 1

BLOCK II - General information

10. Name and address of organization or individual assisting you in locating or identifying an orphan

   (Name)

   _____

   (Address)

11. Do you plan to travel abroad to locate or adopt a child?
   ☐ Yes ☐ No

12. Does your spouse, if any, plan to travel abroad to locate or adopt a child?
   ☐ Yes ☐ No

13. If the answer to question 11 or 12 is "yes," give the following information:

   a. Your date of intended departure _____

   b. Your spouse's date of intended departure _____

   c. City, province _____

14. Will the child come to the United States for adoption after compliance with the preadoption requirements, if any, of the state of proposed residence?
   ☐ Yes ☐ No

15. If the answer to question 14 is "no," will the child be adopted abroad after having been personally seen and observed by you and your spouse, if married?
   ☐ Yes ☐ No

16. Where do you wish to file your orphan petition?

   The service office located at

   _____

   The American Embassy or Consulate at

   _____

17. Do you plan to adopt more than one child?
   ☐ Yes ☐ No

   If "Yes", how many children do you plan to adopt?

Certification of prospective petitioner

I certify, under penalty of perjury under the laws of the United States of America, that the foregoing is true and correct and that I will care for an orphan/orphans properly if admitted to the United States.

(Signature of Prospective Petitioner)

Executed on (Date)

Certification of married prospective petitioner's spouse

I certify, under penalty of perjury under the laws of the United States of America, that the foregoing is true and correct and that my spouse and I will care for an orphan/orphans properly if admitted to the United States.

(Signature of Prospective Petitioner)

Executed on (Date)

Signature of person preparing form, if other than petitioner

I declare that this document was prepared by me at the request of the prospective petitioner and is based on all information of which I have any knowledge.

(Signature)

Address

Executed on (Date)

Application for Waiver of Ground of Excludability

U. S. Department of Justice
Immigration and Naturalization Service

DO NOT WRITE IN THIS BLOCK

Fee Stamp

☐ 212 (a) (1)   ☐ 212 (a) (10)
☐ 212 (a) (3)   ☐ 212 (a) (12)
☐ 212 (a) (6)   ☐ 212 (a) (19)
☐ 212 (a) (9)   ☐ 212 (a) (23)

A. Information about applicant

1. Family Name (Surname In CAPS)   (First)   (Middle)

2. Address (Number and Street)   (Apartment Number)

3. (Town or City)   (State/Country)   (Zip/Postal Code)

4. Date of Birth *(Month/Day/Year)*   5. INS File Number
   A-

6. City of Birth   7. Country of Birth

8. Date of Visa Application   9. Visa Applied for at:

10. Applicant was declared inadmissible to the United States for the following reasons: (List acts, convictions, or physical or mental conditions. If applicant has active or suspected tuberculosis, page 2 of this fom must be fully completed.)

11. Applicant was previously in the United States, as follows:
   City and State   From (Date)   To (Date)   INS Status

12. Applicant's Social Security Number (if any)

B. Information about relative, through whom applicant claims eligibility for a waiver

1. Family Name (Surname in CAPS)   (First)   (Middle)

2. Address (Number and Street)   (Apartment Number)

3. (Town or City)   (State/Country)   (Zip/Postal Code)

4. Relationship to applicant   5. INS Status

C. Information about applicant's other relatives in the U.S.
(List only U.S. citizens and permanent residents)

1. Family Name (Surname in CAPS)   (First)   (Middle)

2. Address (Number and Street)   (Apartment Number)

3. (Town or City)   (State/Country)   (Zip/Postal Code)

4. Relationship to applicant   5. INS Status

1. Family Name (Surname in CAPS)   (First)   (Middle)

2. Address (Number and Street)   (Apartment Number)

3. (Town or City)   (State/Country)   (Zip/Postal Code)

4. Relationship to applicant   5. INS Status

1. Family Name (Surname in CAPS)   (First)   (Middle)

2. Address (Number and Street)   (Apartment Number)

3. (Town or City)   (State/Country)   (Zip/Postal Code)

4. Relationship to applicant   5. INS Status

Signature (of applicant or petitioning relative)

Relationship to applicant   Date

Signature (of person preparing application, if not the applicant or petitioning relative). I declare that this document was prepared by me at the request of the applicant or petitioning relative, and is based on all information of which I have any knowledge.

Signature

Address   Date

FOR INS USE ONLY. DO NOT WRITE IN THIS AREA.	Initial receipt	Resubmitted	Relocated		Completed		
			Received	Sent	Approved	Denied	Returned

Form I-601 (Rev. 01/16/02)Y

To be Completed for Applicants with
Active Tuberculosis or Suspected Tuberculosis

A. Statement by Applicant

Upon admission to the United States I will:

1. Go directly to the physician or health facility named in Section B;

2. Present all X-rays used in the visa medical examination to substantiate diagnosis;

3. Submit to such examinations, treatment, isolation and medical regimen as may be required; and

4. Remain under the prescribed treatment or observation whether on inpatient or outpatient basis, until discharged.

_____
Signature of Applicant

_____
Date

B. Statement by Physician or Health Facility

(May be executed by a private physician, health department, other public or private health facility or military hospital.)

I agree to supply any treatment or observation necessary for the proper management of the alien's tuberculosis condition.

I agree to submit Form CDC 75.18, "Report on Alien with Tuberculosis Waiver," to the health officer named in Section D:

1. Within 30 days of the alien's reporting for care, indicating presumptive diagnosis, test results and plans for future care of the alien; or

2. 30 days after receiving Form CDC 75.18, if the alien has not reported.

Satisfactory financial arrangements have been made. (This statement does not relieve the alien from submitting evidence, as required by consul, to establish that the alien is not likely to become a public charge.)

I represent (enter an "X" in the appropriate box and give the complete name and address of the facility below.)

☐ 1. Local Health Department
☐ 2. Other Public or Private Facility
☐ 3. Private Practice
☐ 4. Military Hospital

_____
Name of Facility (please type or print)

_____
Address (Number and Street)   **(Apartment Number)**

_____
City, State and Zip Code

_____
Signature of Physician   **Date**

C. Applicant's Sponsor in the U.S.

Arrange for medical care of the applicant and have the physician complete Section B.

If medical care will be provided by a physician who checked box 2 or 3, in Section B, have Section D completed by the local or State Health Officer who has jurisdiction in the U.S. area where the applicant plans to reside.

If medical care will be provided by a physician who checked box 4, in Section B, forward this form directly to the military facility at the address provided in Section B.

Address in the U.S. where the alien plans to reside.

_____
Address (Number and Street)   (Apartment Number)

_____
City, State and Zip Code

D. Endorsement of Local or State Health Officer

Endorsement signifies recognition of the physician or facility for the purpose of providing care for tuberculosis. If the facility or physician who signed his or her name in Section B is not in your health jurisdiction and not familiar to you, you may want to contact the health officer responsible for the jurisdiction of the facility or physician prior to endorsing.

_____
Endorsed by: Signature of Health Officer

_____
Date

Enter below the name and address of the Local Health Department where the "Notice of Arrival of Alien with Tuberculosis Waiver" should be sent when the alien arrives in the U.S.

_____
Official Name of Department

_____
Address (Number and Street)   (Apartment Number)

_____
City, State and Zip Code

If further assistance is needed, contact the INS office with jurisdiction over the intended place of U.S. residence of the applicant.

Application for Waiver of Ground of Excludability

U. S. Department of Justice
Immigration and Naturalization Service

DO NOT WRITE IN THIS BLOCK

☐ 212 (a) (1)   ☐ 212 (a) (10)   Fee Stamp
☐ 212 (a) (3)   ☐ 212 (a) (12)
☐ 212 (a) (6)   ☐ 212 (a) (19)
☐ 212 (a) (9)   ☐ 212 (a) (23)

A. Information about applicant

1. Family Name (Surname In CAPS)   (First)   (Middle)

2. Address (Number and Street)   (Apartment Number)

3. (Town or City)   (State/Country)   (Zip/Postal Code)

4. Date of Birth *(Month/Day/Year)*   5. INS File Number
A-

6. City of Birth   7. Country of Birth

8. Date of Visa Application   9. Visa Applied for at:

10. Applicant was declared inadmissible to the United States for the following reasons: (List acts, convictions, or physical or mental conditions. If applicant has active or suspected tuberculosis, page 2 of this form must be fully completed.)

11. Applicant was previously in the United States, as follows:
City and State   From (Date)   To (Date)   INS Status

12. Applicant's Social Security Number (if any)

B. Information about relative, through whom applicant claims eligibility for a waiver

1. Family Name (Surname in CAPS)   (First)   (Middle)

2. Address (Number and Street)   (Apartment Number)

3. (Town or City)   (State/Country)   (Zip/Postal Code)

4. Relationship to applicant   5. INS Status

C. Information about applicant's other relatives in the U.S.
(List only U.S. citizens and permanent residents)

1. Family Name (Surname in CAPS)   (First)   (Middle)

2. Address (Number and Street)   (Apartment Number)

3. (Town or City)   (State/Country)   (Zip/Postal Code)

4. Relationship to applicant   5. INS Status

1. Family Name (Surname in CAPS)   (First)   (Middle)

2. Address (Number and Street)   (Apartment Number)

3. (Town or City)   (State/Country)   (Zip/Postal Code)

4. Relationship to applicant   5. INS Status

1. Family Name (Surname in CAPS)   (First)   (Middle)

2. Address (Number and Street)   (Apartment Number)

3. (Town or City)   (State/Country)   (Zip/Postal Code)

4. Relationship to applicant   5. INS Status

INS Use Only: Additional Information and Instructions

Signature and Title of Requesting Officer

Address   Date

This office will maintain only a folder relating to the applicant pursuant to A.M. 2712.01

AGENCY COPY

Application for Waiver of the Foreign Residence Requirement of Section 212(e) of the Immigration and Nationality Act, as amended

U. S. Department of Justice
Immigration and Naturalization Service

This application must be typewritten or printed legibly in black ink with block letters.

Fee Stamp

1. Name (Last in CAPS)	First	Middle	If you are a married woman, give your maiden

2. Mailing Address _(Apt. No.)_ _(Number and Street)_ _(Town or City)_ _(State or Province)_ _(Country)_ _(Zip Code, if in U.S.)_

Present or last U.S. residence _(Number and Street)_ _(City)_ _(State)_ _(ZIP Code)_

3. Date of Birth	Country of Birth	Country of Nationality	Country of Last Foreign Residence

Alien Registration Number, If Known

4. I believe I am subject to the foreign residence requirements because: (Check appropriate box(es))

A. ☐ I participated in an exchange program which was financed by an agency of the U.S. Government or the government of the country of my nationality or last foreign residence for the purpose of promoting international educational, and cultural exchange.

B. ☐ An agency of the Government of the U.S. or the government of the country of my nationality or last foreign residence gave me a grant (such as a Fullbright grant), stipend or allowance for the purpose of participation in an exchange program. Name of U.S. Government agency or foreign country

_____ .

C. ☐ I became an exchange visitor after the Secretary of State designated the country of my nationality or last foreign residence as clearly requiring the services of persons with my specialized knowledge or skill.

D. ☐ I entered the United States as, or my status was changed to that of, an exchange visitor on or after January 10, 1977 to participate in graduate medical education or training.

5. I am applying for waiver of the foreign residence requirement on the ground that: (Check appropriate box(es))

A. ☐ My departure from the United States would impose exceptional hardship on my United States citizen or lawful permanent resident spouse or child.

B. ☐ I cannot return to the country of my nationality or last foreign residence because I would be subject to persecution on account of race, religion or political opinion.

IMPORTANT: If you have checked "A" under number 5, you must attach to this application a statement dated and signed by you giving a _detailed explanation_ of the basis for your belief that compliance by you with the two-year foreign residence requirement of Section 212(e) of the Immigration and Nationality Act, as amended, would impose exceptional hardship on your spouse or child who is a citizen of the United States or a lawful permanent resident thereof. Without such statement your application is incomplete. You must include in the statement all pertinent information concerning the income and savings of yourself and your spouse. There should also be attached such documentary evidence as may be available to support the allegations of hardship.

If you have checked "B" under number 5, you must attach a statement dated and signed by you setting forth in detail the reason(s) you believe that you cannot return to the country of your nationality or last foreign residence because you would be subject to persecution on account of race, religion or political opinion. There should also be attached such documentary evidence as may be available to support the allegations of persecution.

6. If married, check appropriate box(es): (See Instruction No. 4)

A. ☐ My spouse is included in this application. B. ☐ My spouse is filing a separate application for waiver.

RECEIVED	TRANS. IN	RET'D TRANS. OUT	COMPLETED

7. List all program numbers and names of *all* program sponsors.

8. Major field of activity (*Check one*)

☐ (1) Agriculture   ☐ (4) Engineering   ☐ (7) Natural And Physical Sciences

☐ (2) Business Administration   ☐ (5) Humanities   ☐ (8) Social Sciences

☐ (3) Education   ☐ (6) Medicine   ☐ (9) Other

9. Occupation

10. Date and port of last arrival in the United States as participant in a designated exchange program.

---

11. If you are now abroad, give date of departure from U.S.

12. Number of prior marriages of applicant _____

If married, number of prior marriages of applicant's spouse _____

13. Name of spouse	Date and Country of birth	Nationality	Country of last foreign residence
14. Names of children	Date and Country of birth	Nationality	Country of last foreign residence

---

15. If you checked "A" under number 5 on page 1 of this form, furnish the following information concerning your spouse or one of your children who is a citizen of the United States and who you believe would suffer exceptional hardship if you resided outside the United States for 2 years following your departure from this country.

If United States citizenship of spouse or child was acquired through naturalization, give the following:

Name of United States citizen spouse or child:

United States citizenship of spouse or child was acquired through (*check one*)

☐ Birth in the United States   ☐ Naturalization   ☐ Parent(s)

Number of naturalization certificate	Date of naturalization	Place of naturalization

If United States citizenship of spouse or child was acquired through parent(s), has spouse or child obtained a certificate of citizenship? _____

If so, give number of certificate _____ If not, submit evidence in accordance with instruction 6(a) (2).

---

16. If you checked "A" under number 5 on page 1 of this form, and you do not have a spouse or child who is a citizen of the United States, furnish the following information concerning your spouse or one of your children who is a lawful permanent resident of the United States and who you believe would suffer exceptional hardship if you resided outside the United States for two years following your departure from this country.

Name of lawful resident alien spouse or child:	Alien Registration Number

Date, place and means of admission for lawful permanent residence:

I certify under penalty of perjury under the laws of the United States of America that the foregoing is true and correct.

Executed on _____ _____ _____
       (Date)   *(Place)*   *(Signature of applicant)*

Signature of person preparing form, if other than applicant: I declare that this document was prepared by me at the request of the applicant and is based on all information of which I have any knowledge:

_____
(Signature)

_____ _____ _____
(Address of person preparing form, if other than applicant)   *(Date)*   *(Occupation)*

OMB No. 1115-0121

Refugee/Asylee Relative Petition

START HERE - Please Type or Print

Part 1. Information about you.

Family Name	Given Name	Middle Name

Address - C/O

Street Number and Name		Apt.

City	State or Province

Country	ZIP/Postal Code	Sex: a. ☐ Male b. ☐ Female

Date of Birth *(Month/Day/Year)*	Country of Birth

A#	Social Security #

Other names used *(including maiden name)*

Present Status: *(check one)*
a. ☐ Refugee ☐ Lawful Permanent Resident based on previous Refugee status
b ☐ Asylee ☐ Lawful Permanent Resident based on previous Asylee status

Date *(Month/Day/Year)* and Place Refugee or Asylee status was granted:

If granted Refugee status, Date *(Month/Day/Year)* and Place Admitted to the United States:

If Married, Date *(Month/Day/Year)* and Place of Present Marriage:

If Previously Married, Name(s) of Prior Spouse(s):

Date(s) Previous Marriage(s) Ended: *(Month/Day/Year)*

Part 2. Information about the relationship.

The alien relative is my:
a. ☐ Spouse
b. ☐ Unmarried child under 21 years of age

Number of relatives I am filing for: _____ (_____ of _____)

Part 3. Information about your alien relative. *(If you are petitioning for more than one family member you must complete and file a separate Form I-730 for each additional family member.)*

Family Name	Given Name	Middle Name

Address - C/O

Street Number and Name	Apt #

FOR INS USE ONLY

Returned	Receipt
Submitted	
Reloc Sent	
Reloc Rec'd	

☐ Petitioner Interviewed

☐ Beneficiary Interviewed

Consulate

Sections of Law
☐ 207 (c) (2) Spouse
☐ 207 (c) (2) Child
☐ 208 (b) (3) Spouse
☐ 208 (b) (3) Child

Remarks

Action Block

To Be Completed by Attorney or Representative, If any

☐ Fill in box if G-28 is attached to represent the applicant

Volag #

Atty State License #

Form I-730 (Rev. 09/18/00) Y

Part 3. Information about your alien relative.   *Continue*

City	State or Providence

Country	ZIP/Postal Code	Sex: a. ☐ Male b. ☐ Female

Date of Birth *(Month/Day/Year)*	Country of Birth

Alien # *(If any)*	Social Security # *(If Any)*

Other name(s) used *(including maiden name)*

If Married, Date *(Month/Day/Year)* and Place of Present Marriage:

If Previously Married, Name(s) of Prior Spouse(s):

Date(s) Previous Marriage(s) Ended: *(Month/Day/Year)*

Part 4.   Processing Information.

A. Check One: a. ☐ The person named in Part 3 is now in the United States.

b. ☐ The person named in Part 3 is now outside the United States. (Please indicate the location of the American Consulate or Embassy where your relative will apply for a visa.)

American Consulate/Embassy at: _____

City and Country

B. Is the person named in Part 3 in exclusion, deportation, or removal proceedings in the United States?

a. ☐ No

b. ☐ Yes (Please explain on a separate paper.)

Part 5. Signature.   *Read the information on penalties in the instructions before completing this section and sign below. If someone helped you to prepare this petition, he or she must complete Part 6.*

I certify or, if outside the United States, I swear or affirm, under penalty of perjury under the laws of the United States of America, that this petition and the evidence submitted with it, is all true and correct. I authorize the release of any information from my record which the Immigration and Naturalization Service needs to determine eligibility for the benefit I am seeking.

Signature	Print Name	Date	Daytime Telephone #
			( )

Please Note: *If you do not completely fill out this form, or fail to submit the required documents listed in the instructions, your relative may not be found eligible for the requested benefit and this petition may be denied.*

Part 6. Signature of person preparing form if other than Petitioner above. *(Sign Below)*

I declare that I prepared this petition at the request of the above person and it is based on all of the information of which I have knowledge.

Signature	Print Name	Date	Daytime Telephone #
			( )

*Firm Name
and Address*

OMB No. 1115-0145

Petition to Remove the Conditions on Residence

START HERE - Please Type or Print

FOR INS USE ONLY

Part 1. Information about you.

Family Name	Given Name	Middle Initial

Address - C/O:

Street Number and Name		Apt. #

City	State or Province

Country	ZIP/Postal Code

Date of Birth (month/day/year)	Country of Birth

Social Security # (if any)	A#

Conditional residence expires on (month/day/year)

Mailing address if different from address listed above:

Street Number and Name	Apt. #

City	State or Province

Country	ZIP/Postal Code

Returned

Resubmitted

Reloc Sent

Reloc Rec'd

☐ Applicant Interviewed

Receipt

Part 2. Basis for petition *(check one).*

a. ☐ My conditional residence is based on my marriage to a U.S. citizen or permanent resident, and we are filing this petition together.

b. ☐ I am a child who entered as a conditional permanent resident and I am unable to be included in a Joint Petition to Remove the Conditional Basis of Alien's Permanent Residence (Form 1-751) filed by my parent(s).

My conditional residence is based on my marriage to a U.S. citizen or permanent resident, but I am unable to file a joint petition and I request a waiver because: (check one)

c. ☐ My spouse is deceased.

d. ☐ I entered into the marriage in good faith, but the marriage was terminated through divorce/annulment.

e. ☐ I am a conditional resident spouse who entered into the marriage in good faith, or I am a conditional resident child, who has been battered or subjected to extreme cruelty by my citizen or permanent resident spouse or parent.

f. ☐ The termination of my status and removal from the United States would result in an extreme hardship.

Remark

Action

Part 3. Additional information about you.

Other Names Used *(including maiden name)*:	Telephone #

Date of Marriage	Place of Marriage

If your spouse is deceased, give the date of death. (month/day/year)

- Are you in removal or deportation proceedings?   ☐ Yes ☐ No

- Was a fee paid to anyone other than an attorney in connection with this petition?   ☐ Yes ☐ No

To Be Completed by Attorney or Representative, if any

☐ Fill in box if G-28 is attached to represent the applicant

VOLAG#

ATTY State License #

Continued on back.

Part 3. Additional information about you. (continued)

- Since becoming a conditional resident, have you ever been arrested, cited, charged, indicted, convicted, fined or imprisoned for breaking or violating any law or ordinance (excluding traffic regulations), or committed any crime for which you were not arrested? ☐ Yes ☐ No

- If you are married, is this a different marriage than the one through which conditional residence status was obtained? ☐ Yes ☐ No

- Have you resided at any other address since you became a permanent resident? *(If yes, attach a list of all addresses and dates.)* ☐ Yes ☐ No

- Is your spouse currently serving with or employed by the U.S. government and serving outside the United States? ☐ Yes ☐ No

Part 4. Information about the spouse or parent through whom you gained your conditional residence.

Family Name	Given Name	Middle Initial	Phone Number

Address

Date of Birth (month/day/year)	Social Security # (if any)	A#

Part 5. Information about your children. *List all your children. Attach another sheet(s) if necessary.*

Name	Date of Birth (month/day/year)	If in U.S., give A number, current immigration status and U.S. address.	Living with you?
1.			☐ Yes ☐ No
2.			☐ Yes ☐ No
3.			☐ Yes ☐ No
4.			☐ Yes ☐ No

Part 6. Signature. *Read the information on penalties in the instructions before completing this section. If you checked block " a" in Part 2, your spouse must also sign below.*

I certify, under penalty of perjury under the laws of the United States of America, that this petition and the evidence submitted with it is all true and correct. If conditional residence was based on a marriage, I further certify that the marriage was entered into in accordance with the laws of the place where the marriage took place and was not for the purpose of procuring an immigration benefit. I also authorize the release of any information from my records that the Immigration and Naturalization Service needs to determine eligibility for the benefit sought.

Signature	Print Name	Date
Signature of Spouse	Print Name	Date

Please note: If you do not completely fill out this form or fail to submit any required documents listed in the instructions, you cannot be found eligible for the requested benefit and this petition may be denied.

Part 7. Signature of person preparing form, if other than above.

I declare that I prepared this petition at the request of the above person and it is based on all information of which I have knowledge.

Signature	Print Name	Date

Firm Name and Address

U.S. Department of Justice
Immigration and Naturalization Service

OMB No. 1115-0163; Expires 04/30/05
Application for Employment Authorization

Do Not Write in This Block.

Remarks	Action Stamp	Fee Stamp
A#		
Applicant is filing under §274a.12 _____		

☐ Application Approved. Employment Authorized / Extended (Circle One)   until _____ (Date).
_____ (Date).

Subject to the following conditions: _____

☐ Application Denied.
  ☐ Failed to establish eligibility under 8 CFR 274a.12 (a) or (c).
  ☐ Failed to establish economic necessity as required in 8 CFR 274a.12(c)(14), (18) and 8 CFR 214.2(f)

I am applying for:
  ☐ Permission to accept employment.
  ☐ Replacement (of lost employment authorization document).
  ☐ Renewal of my permission to accept employment (attach previous employment authorization document).

1. Name (Family Name in CAPS)   (First)   (Middle)

2. Other Names Used (Include Maiden Name)

3. Address in the United States (Number and Street)   (Apt. Number)

(Town or City)   (State/Country)   (ZIP Code)

4. Country of Citizenship/Nationality

5. Place of Birth (Town or City)   (State/Province)   (Country)

6. Date of Birth   7. Sex   ☐ Male   ☐ Female

8. Marital Status   ☐ Married   ☐ Single   ☐ Widowed   ☐ Divorced

9. Social Security Number (Include all Numbers you have ever used) (if any)

10. Alien Registration Number (A-Number) or I-94 Number (if any)

11. Have you ever before applied for employment authorization from INS?
  ☐ Yes (If yes, complete below)   ☐ No
  Which INS Office?   Date(s)

  Results (Granted or Denied - attach all documentation)

12. Date of Last Entry into the U.S. (Month/Day/Year)

13. Place of Last Entry into the U.S.

14. Manner of Last Entry (Visitor, Student, etc.)

15. Current Immigration Status (Visitor, Student, etc.)

16. Go to Part 2 of the Instructions, Eligibility Categories. In the space below, place the letter and number of the category you selected from the instructions (For example, (a)(8), (c)(17)(iii), etc.).

Eligibility under 8 CFR 274a.12

(   ) (   ) (   )

Certification.

Your Certification: I certify, under penalty of perjury under the laws of the United States of America, that the foregoing is true and correct. Furthermore, I authorize the release of any information which the Immigration and Naturalization Service needs to determine eligibility for the benefit I am seeking. I have read the Instructions in Part 2 and have identified the appropriate eligibility category in Block 16.

Signature   Telephone Number   Date

Signature of Person Preparing Form, If Other Than Above: I declare that this document was prepared by me at the request of the applicant and is based on all information of which I have any knowledge.

Print Name   Address   Signature   Date

	Initial Receipt	Resubmitted	Relocated		Completed		
			Rec'd	Sent	Approved	Denied	Returned

Form I-765 (Rev. 5/09/02)Y

U.S. Department of Justice
Immigration and Naturalization Service

OMB No. 1115-0166

Application for Family Unity Benefits

Print or type information requested. Use BLACK ink. Use CAPITAL

FOR INS USE ONLY

Part 1. Information about you. (Person requesting Family Unity benefits.)

Family Name (Last Name)

Given Name (First Name)

Full Middle Name

INS A #

Social Security #

Date of Birth (Month/Day/Year)

Country of Birth

Country of Citizenship

Sex
☐ Male
☐ Female

Home Address:
Street Number and Name (include apartment number)

City

State

Zip

Daytime Phone (Area Code and Number)

Mailing Address: (if different from home address)
Street Number and Name/P.O. Box Number

Care Of (for use if you do not have your own mailing address)

City

State

Zip Code

Part 2. Basis for my application.

1. **If you are applying for family unity benefits, select one and place a check in the box describing your relationship to a legalized alien or an alien who is eligible or applied for adjustment of status pursuant to the LIFE Act.**

A. ☐ I am the spouse of an alien who was legalized under section 245A of the INA and we have been married since at least May 5, 1988.

B. ☐ I am the spouse of an alien who was legalized as a Special Agricultural Worker under section 210 of the INA and we have been married since at least December 1, 1988.

C. ☐ As of May 5, 1988, I was the unmarried child under the age of 21 of an alien who was legalized under 245A of the INA. I am currently the child, son, or daughter of the same parent. That parent is currently either a legalized alien or a naturalized U.S. citizen who was a legalized alien on or before May 5, 1988, and who maintained such status until his or her naturalization.

D. ☐ As of December 1, 1988, I was the unmarried child under the age of 21 of an alien who was legalized as a Special Agricultural Worker under section 210 of the INA. I am currently the child, son, or daughter of the same parent. That parent is either a legalized alien or a naturalized U.S. citizen who was a legalized alien on or before December 1, 1988, and who maintained such status until his or her naturalization.

E. ☐ I am the spouse of a legalized alien who adjusted under section 202 of the Immigration Reform and Control Act of 1986 (Cuban/Haitian Adjustment) and we have been married since at least May 5, 1988.

F. ☐ As of May 5, 1988, I was the unmarried child under the age of 21 of a legalized alien who adjusted under section 202 of the Immigration Reform and Control Act of 1986 (Cuban/Haitian Adjustment). I am currently the child, son, or daughter of the same parent. That parent is either a legalized alien or a naturalized U.S. citizen who was a legalized alien on or before May 5, 1988, and who maintained such status until his or her naturalization.

Form I-817 (Rev. 01/27/02)N

G. ☐ I am the spouse of an alien who is eligible for adjustment pursuant to section 1104(b) of Pub. L. 106-553, the **LIFE** Act.
I entered the United States before December 1, 1988, and was in the United States on that date.

H. ☐ I am the unmarried child of an alien who is eligible for adjustment pursuant to section 1104(b) of Pub. L. 106-553, the **LIFE** Act. I entered the United States before December 1, 1988, and was in the United States on that date.

2. Select one and place a check in the box. I am requesting:

A. ☐ initial family unity benefits under section 301 of the IMMACT 90.

B. ☐ an extension of family unity benefits under section 301 of IMMACT 90.

C. ☐ initial family unity benefits under section 1504 of Public Law 106-554, the LIFE Act as amended.

Part 3. Additional Information. (Information about you, the applicant for Family Unity benefits.)

If you need additional space to answer 1 through 5, attach a separate sheet of paper

1. At the time of your last entry into the United States, you:

a. ☐ were inspected and admitted   ☐ were inspected and paroled   ☐ entered without inspection

b.

Date of last arrival (Month/Day/Year)	I-94, Arrival/Departure Document #	Current or most recent immigration status	Date status expires (Month/Day/Year)	Date continuous U.S. residence began (Month/Day/Year)

2. Give the U.S. address where you lived on May 5, 1988 (Sec. 245A/Cuban Haitian Adjustment) or December 1, 1988 (Sec. 210).

Street Number and Name (include apartment number)

City	State	Zip Code

3. Have you ever applied before for the Family Unity Program?   ☐ Yes   ☐ No
If "Yes," provide the following information:

Name under which you applied	City and State where application was filed

Date filed (Month/Day/Year)	INS A#	INS action taken on application
		☐ Approved ☐ Denied

4. If separate applications for the Family Unity Program are being submitted at this time for other relatives, give the following information.

Family Name (Last Name)	Given Name (First Name)	Relationship	INS A #

5. List all other names you have used (including maiden name)

Part 3. Additional Information (continuation). (Information about you, the applicant for Family Unity benefits)

If you need additional space to answer 1 through 5, attach a separate sheet of paper

6. Do you have or have you ever you had:

   a. a communicable disease of public health significance (including chancroid, gonorrhea, granuloma inguinale, human immunodeficiency virus (HIV) infection, infectious leprosy, lymphogranuloma venereum, infectious stage syphilis, and active tuberculosis)?   ☐ Yes ☐ No

   b. a physical or mental disorder and behavior associated with the disorder which has posed or may pose a threat to the property, safety or welfare of yourself or others?   ☐ Yes ☐ No

7. Have you ever:

   a. knowingly committed a crime for which you have not been arrested?   ☐ Yes ☐ No

   b. been convicted of a felony or three (3) or more misdemeanors in the United States?   ☐ Yes ☐ No

   c. been convicted of two (2) or more offenses for which the aggregate sentences were five (5) or more years of confinement?   ☐ Yes ☐ No

   d. been arrested, cited, charged, indicted, fined, or imprisoned for breaking or violating any law or ordinance, excluding traffic violations?   ☐ Yes ☐ No

   e. been the beneficiary of a pardon, amnesty, rehabilitation decree, other act of clemency or similar action?   ☐ Yes ☐ No

   f. illicitly trafficked in any controlled substance or knowingly assisted, abetted or colluded with others in the illicit trafficking of any controlled substance?   ☐ Yes ☐ No

   g. committed a criminal offense in the United States and asserted immunity from prosecution?   ☐ Yes ☐ No

8. Have you, at any time within the past three (3) years, engaged in the non-medical use of any drug listed in section 202 of the Controlled Substances Act (including, but not limited to, sedative, hypnotic, or anxiolytic substances[tranquilizers], amphetamines, cannabinoids, cocaine, hallucinogens, opioids, phencyclidine [PCP], and related substances)?   ☐ Yes ☐ No

9. Have you, at any time within the past two (2) years, engaged in the use of any psychoactive substance not listed in section 202 of the Controlled Substance Act (including, but not limited to alcohol and inhalants) which resulted in behavior that has posed a threat to the property, safety or welfare of yourself or others or which behavior is likely to recur or to lead to other harmful behavior?   ☐ Yes ☐ No

10. Have you ever committed an act of juvenile delinquency which if committed by an adult would be classified as follows: [If you are a LIFE Act applicant skip this question]

    a. a felony crime of violence that has an element the use or attempted use of physical force against another?   ☐ Yes ☐ No

    b. a felony offense that by its nature involves a substantial risk that physical force against another may be used in the course of committing the offense?   ☐ Yes ☐ No

11. Do you intend to engage solely, principally, or incidentally in prostitution in the United States, or are you now or have you within the past 10 years, engaged in, procured, or received income from prostitution?   ☐ Yes ☐ No

12. Have you been or do you intend to be involved in any commercial vice?   ☐ Yes ☐ No

13. Have you ever practiced or do you intend to practice polygamy?   ☐ Yes ☐ No

14. Are you under a final order of civil penalty for violating section 274C of the Immigration and Nationality Act for use of fraudulent documents, or have you, by fraud or willful misrepresentation of a material fact, ever sought to procure, or procured, a visa, other documentation, entry into the United States, or any immigration benefit?   ☐ Yes ☐ No

15. Have you ever falsely represented yourself to be a citizen of the United States for any purpose or benefit under the Immigration and Nationality Act or any Federal or State law?   ☐ Yes ☐ No

16. Are you a former citizen of the United States who renounced your United States citizenship for the purpose of avoiding taxation by the United States?   ☐ Yes ☐ No

17. Have you ever been an F-1 nonimmigrant student who violated status by attending a public elementary or secondary school in violation of immigration law?   ☐ Yes ☐ No

18. Have you ever failed or refused to attend or remain in attendance at a hearing to determine your admissibility to or deportability from the United States?   ☐ Yes ☐ No

19. Have you ever been identified by INS as having obtained transportation to the United States without the consent of the owner, charterer, master or person in charge of the vessel or aircraft through concealment on board, such vessel or aircraft on which you arrived?   ☐ Yes ☐ No

If you need additional space to answer 1 through 5, attach a separate sheet of paper

20. Have you been ordered deported, excluded, or removed from the United States? ☐ Yes ☐ No

21. Have you ever departed the United States after having been unlawfully present for 180 days but less than 365 days? ☐ Yes ☐ No

22. Have you ever departed the United States after having been unlawfully present for 365 days or longer? ☐ Yes ☐ No

23. Have you ever knowingly encouraged, induced, assisted, abetted, or aided, anyone to enter the United States in violation of the law? ☐ Yes ☐ No

24. Were you a guardian required to accompany an individual certified as helpless who was found to be inadmissible to the United States? ☐ Yes ☐ No

25. Have you detained, retained, or withheld the custody of a U.S citizen child outside the United States from a person granted custody of such child by a U.S. court order? ☐ Yes ☐ No

26. Have you ever engaged in, conspired to engage in, or do you intend to engage solely, principally, or incidentally in:

    a. any activity to violate any U. S. law relating to espionage or sabotage? ☐ Yes ☐ No

    b. any activity to violate or evade any law prohibiting the export from the United States of goods, technology, or sensitive information? ☐ Yes ☐ No

    c. any other activity the purpose of which is in opposition to, or the control of, or overthrow of the government of the United States, by force, violence, or other unlawful means? ☐ Yes ☐ No

    d. any other unlawful activity? ☐ Yes ☐ No

27. Have you:

    a. ever engaged in, conspired to engage in or do you intend to engage in a terrorist activity? ☐ Yes ☐ No

    b. ever incited terrorist activity with intent to cause death or serious bodily harm? ☐ Yes ☐ No

    c. ever been a representative of a terrorist organization or a member of an organization which you knew or or should have known is a terrorist organization? ☐ Yes ☐ No

28. Have you ever engaged in or do you intend to engage in any activity in the United States that would have potentially serious adverse foreign policy consequences for the United States? ☐ Yes ☐ No

29. Have you:

    a. ever been or are you now a member of the Communist or other totalitarian party? ☐ Yes ☐ No

    b. ever engaged in genocide, or ordered, incited, assisted or otherwise participated in the persecution of any person because of race, religion, national origin, membership in a particular social group, or political opinion? ☐ Yes ☐ No

30. During the periods of March 23, 1933 to May 8, 1945, in association with either the Nazi Government of Germany or any organization or government associated or allied with the Nazi Government of Germany, did you ever order, incite, assist or otherwise participate in the persecution of any person because of race, religion, national origin, or political opinion? ☐ Yes ☐ No

31. Have you ever left the United States to avoid being drafted into the U.S. Armed Forces? ☐ Yes ☐ No

32. Have you received public assistance from any source, including the U.S. government or any state, county, city, or other municipality; or are you likely to request public assistance in the future? ☐ Yes ☐ No

33. Have you ever been a J nonimmigrant exchange visitor who was subject to the two-year foreign residence requirement and not yet complied with the requirement? ☐ Yes ☐ No

34. Have you ever voted in violation of any Federal, State, or local constitutional provision, statute, ordinance, or regulation? ☐ Yes ☐ No

If you answered "Yes" to any of the above questions, provide a full explanation on a separate sheet of paper.

Part 4. Information about legalized alien or an alien who is eligible for adjustment pursuant to section 1104(b) of Pub. L. 106-553, the LIFE Act.

1. Provide the following information about the legalized alien through whom you are claiming your eligibility.

Family Name (Last Name)	Given Name (First Name)	Full Middle Name

INS A #	Class of Admission	Social Security #	Date of Birth (Month/Day/Year)	Sex
				☐ Male ☐ Female

Part 4. Information about legalized alien or an alien who is eligible for adjustment pursuant to section 1104(b) of Pub. L. 106-553, the LIFE Act (continuation).

Home Address: Street Number and Name (include apartment number)

City	State	Zip Code	Daytime Phone (Area Code and Number)

2. List all other names used (including maiden name)

Part 5. Complete only if legalized alien is your spouse or if your spouse is an alien who is eligible for adjustment pursuant to section 1104(b) of Pub. L. 106-553, the LIFE Act .

1. Provide the following information about you and your spouse.

Number of times you have been married	Number of times your spouse has been married

2. Provide the following information about your current marriage:

Date of Marriage (Month/Day/Year)	Place of Marriage (City and State or Country)

Type of Ceremony: ☐ Religious ☐ Civil ☐ None   We are: ☐ Living together ☐ Not living together

Part 6. Complete only if you are the child of a legalized alien or the child of an alien who is eligible for adjustment pursuant to section 1104(b) of Pub. L. 106-553, the LIFE Act.

1. If the legalized alien is your parent or if your parent is an alien who is eligible for adjustment pursuant to section 1104(b) of Pub. L. 106-553, the LIFE Act; please indicate how that parent is related to you:

☐ biological mother.

☐ biological father who was married to my mother when I was born.

☐ biological father who was not married to my mother when I was born.

☐ stepparent based on marriage to my parent which occurred before my 18th birthday.

☐ adoptive parent and

    a. the adoption occurred before my 16th birthday.   ☐ Yes ☐ No

    b. my adoptive parent had legal custody of me for at least two years prior to May 5, 1988 or December 1, 1988, as appropriate.   ☐ Yes ☐ No

    c. I lived with my adoptive parent for at least two years prior to May 5, 1988 or December 1, 1988, as appropriate.   ☐ Yes ☐ No

☐ parent based on circumstances not described above. (Explain in detail on a separate sheet of paper.)

2. Give the following information about your present marital status:

    ☐ Single   ☐ Married   ☐ Divorced   ☐ Widowed

3. Give the following information if you are married, divorced or widowed:

Date of Marriage (Month/Day/Year)	Place of Marriage (City and State or Country)

If Divorced or Widowed, Date Marriage Ended (Month/Day/Year)	Place Marriage Ended (City and State or Country)

Type of Ceremony: ☐ Religious ☐ Civil ☐ None   We are: ☐ Living together ☐ Not living together

Part 7. Your signature.

I certify, under penalty of perjury under the laws of the United States, that this application and the evidence submitted with it is all true and correct.
I authorize the release of any information from my records which INS needs to determine eligibility for the benefit I am seeking.

Applicant's Signature	Date (Month/Day/Year)

Signature of Parent or Legal Guardian (If filed in behalf of a child under age 14)	Date (Month/Day/Year)

Part 8. Signature of person preparing form, if other than above.

I declare that I prepared this application at the request of the above person and it is based on all information of which I have knowledge.

Preparer's Printed Name	Preparer's Signature

Preparer's Address	Date (Month/Day/Year)

Name of Business/Organization (if applicable)	Daytime Phone (Area Code and Number)

MAKE SURE YOUR APPLICATION PACKAGE IS COMPLETE BEFORE FILING.
REFER TO THE LAST PAGE OF THE INSTRUCTIONS FOR AN APPLICATION CHECKLIST.

OMB No. 1115-0170

Application for Temporary Protected Status

START HERE - Please Type or Print

Part 1. Type of application *(check one)*

1. ☐ This is my first application to register for Temporary Protected Status.
2. ☐ This is my application for annual registration/re-registration. I have previously been granted Temporary Protected Status. I have maintained and continue to maintain the conditions of eligibility for Temporary Protected Status.

Part 2. Information about you

Family Name	First	Middle Initial

U.S. Mailing Address - Care of

Street Number and Name	Apt. #

Town/City	County

State	Zip Code

Place of Birth (Town or City)	(State/Country)

Country of Residence	Country of Citizenship

Date of Birth *(month/day/year)*	Gender ☐ Male ☐ Female

Marital Status ☐ Single ☐ Divorced ☐ Married ☐ Widowed	Other Names Used *(including maiden name)*

Date of entry into the U.S.	Place of entry into the U.S.

Manner of Arrival *(Visitor, student, stowaway, without inspection, etc.)*

Arrival/Departure Record (I-94) Number	Date authorized stay expired/or will expire, as shown on Form I-94 or I-95

Your current immigration status
In status (state nonimmigrant classification, e.g. F-1, etc.)

Out of status *(state nonimmigrant violation, e.g,. overstay student, EWI etc.)*

Alien Registration Number *(If any)*	Social Security Number (if any)

Are you now or have you ever been under immigration proceedings?
☐ Yes   ☐ No   Where _____   When _____
☐ Exclusion   ☐ Removal/Deportation   ☐ Recission   ☐ Judicial Proceedings

Part 3. Information about your spouse and children *(if any)*

Last Name of Spouse	First	Middle Initial

Address (Street Number and Name)	Apt #

Town/City	State

Country	Zip/Postal Code

Continued on next page.

FOR INS USE ONLY

Remarks

Action Stamp

Fee Stamp

Case ID#:

A#:

To Be Completed by
Attomey or Representatlve, if any
Fill in box if G-28 is attached to represent the applicant

VOLAG#

ATTY State License #

Form I-821 (Rev. 04/15/02)Y

Part 3.   Information about your spouse and children (continued)

Date of Birth	Date and Place of Present Marriage
Name of Prior Husbands/Wives	Date(s) Marriage(s) Ended

List the names, ages and current residence of any children

Name - (Last)	(First)	Middle Initial	Date of Birth	Residence

Part 4.   Eligibility standards.

1.   **Fill in the necessary information:**

I am a national of, or an alien having no nationality who last habitually resided in the foreign state _____

and I entered the United States on _____ , and I have resided in the United States since that time.

If any of the statements below apply to you, indicate which one(s) by numbered reference on the line below (for example "2 k") and include a full explanation on a separate sheets(s) of paper. If you were ever arrested, you should provide the disposition (outcome) of the arrest (for example, "case dismissed") from the appropriate authority.

_____

PLEASE NOTE: If you placed any of the following numbered references on the line above, you may be eligible for a waiver of the grounds described in the statements: 2e; 2f; 2g; 2h; 2i; 2j; 2k; 2l; 2m; 2n or 2o. The I-601 or I-724 are INS forms used to request a waiver. These forms are available at local INS offices or by calling the INS toll-free forms line at 1-800-870-3676.

2.   To be eligible for Temporary Protected Status, you must be admissible as an immigrant to the United States, with certain exceptions. Do any of the following apply to you?

a.   have you been convicted of any felony or two or more misdemeanors committed in the United States;

b.   (i) have you ordered, incited, assisted, or otherwise participated in the persecution of any person on account of race, religion, nationality, membership in a particular social group or political opinion;

(ii) have you been convicted by a final judgment of a particularly serious crime, constituting a danger to the community of the United States (an alien convicted of an aggravated felony is considered to have committed a particularly serious crime);

(iii) have you committed a serious nonpolitical crime outside of the United States prior to your arrival in the United States; or

(iv) have you engaged in or are you still engaged in activities that could be reasonable grounds for concluding that you are a danger to the security of the United States;

Continued on next page.

c.   (i) have you been convicted of, or have you committed acts which constitute the essential elements of a crime (other than a purely political offense) or a violation of or a conspiracy to violate any law relating to a controlled substance as defined in Section 102 of the Controlled Substance Act;

(ii) have you been convicted of two or more offenses (other than purely political offenses) for which the aggregate sentences to confinement actually imposed were five years or more;

(iii) have you trafficked in or do you continue to traffic in any controlled substance or are or have been a knowing assister, abettor, conspirator, or colluder with others in the illicit trafficking of any controlled substance;

(iv) have you engaged or do you continue to engage solely, principally, or incidentally in any activity related to espionage or sabotage or violate any law involving the export of goods, technology, or sensitive information, any other unlawful activity, or any activity the purpose of which is in opposition, or the control, or overthrow of the government of the United States;

(v) have you engaged in or do you continue to engage in terrorist activities;

(vi) have you engaged in or do you continue to engage or plan to engage in activities in the United States that would have potentially serious adverse foreign policy consequences for the United States;

(vii) have you been or do you continue to be a member of the Communist or other totalitarian party, except when membership was involuntary; and

(viii) have you participated in Nazi persecution or genocide;

d.   have you been arrested, cited, charged, indicted, fined, or imprisoned for breaking or violating any law or ordinance, excluding traffic violations, or been the beneficiary of a pardon, amnesty, rehabilitation decree, other act of clemency or similar action;

e.   have you committed a serious criminal offense in the United States and asserted immunity from prosecution;

f.   have you within the past ten years engaged in prostitution or procurement of prostitution or do you continue to engage in prostitution or procurement of prostitution;

g.   have you been or do you intend to be involved in any other commercial vice;

h   have you been excluded and deported from the United States within the past year, or have you been deported or removed from the United States at government expense within the last five years (20 years if you have been convicted of an aggravated felony);

i.   have you ever assisted any other person to enter the United States in violation of the law;

j.   (i) do you have a communicable disease of public health significance,

(ii) do you have or have you had a physical or mental disorder and behavior (or a history of behavior that is likely to recur) associated with the disorder which has posed or may pose a threat to the property, safety or welfare of yourself or others;

(iii) are you now or have you been a drug abuser or drug addict;

k.   have you entered the United States as a stowaway;

l.   are you subject to a final order for violation of section 274C (producing and/or using false documentation to unlawfully satisfy a requirement of the Immigration and Nationality Act);

m   do you practice polygamy;

n.   were you the guardian of, and did you accompany another alien who was ordered excluded and deported (or removed) from the United States;

o.   have you detained, retained, or withheld the custody of a child, having a lawful claim to United States citizenship, outside the United States from a United States citizen granted custody?

Certification on next page.

Part 5.   Your certification

Your certification: I certify, under penalty of perjury under the laws of the United States of America, that the foregoing is true and correct. Copies of documents submitted are exact photocopies of unaltered original documents and I understand that I may be required to submit original documents to INS at a later date. Furthermore, I authorize the release of any information from my records which the Immigration and Naturalization Service needs to determine eligibility for the benefit that I am seeking.

Signature: _____   Date: _____   Telephone No.: _____

Signature of person preparing form, if other than above:

I declare that I prepared this document at the request of the person above and that it is based on all information of which I have any knowledge.

Print Name: _____   Signature: _____   Date: _____

Address: _____

Part 6.   Checklist

☐ Did you answer each question?
☐ Did you sign the Form I-821 application?
☐ If you are a first time TPS applicant, did you submit the required
   application and fingerprinting fees?
☐ Did you submit the necessary documents and photos, if so required?
☐ Did you also submit the Form I-765 and fee, if required to pay the fee?

Have you submitted:

☐ the filing fee for this application or a written request for a waiver of the filing fee (see instructions, item 12)?

☐ supporting evidence to prove identity, nationality, date of entry and residence?

☐ other required supporting documents (photos, etc.) for each application?

Do you need additional information?:

It is not possible to cover all the conditions for eligibility or to give instructions for every situation. If you have carefully read all the instructions and still have questions, please contact your nearest INS office. It Is recommended that you keep a copy of this application and supporting documents for your records. For additional information, call our National Customer Service Center toll-free number at 1-800-375-5283 or visit the INS internet web site at www.ins.usdoj.gov.

OMB No. 1615-0045; Exp.12/31/05

I-829, Petition by Entrepreneur to Remove Conditions

START HERE - Please Type or Print

DO NOT WRITE IN THIS BLOCK - FOR BCIS USE ONLY (Except G-28 Block Below)

☐ Applicant Interviewed	Action	Fee Receipt
		To be completed by Attorney or Representative, if any ☐ G-28 is attached Attorney's State License No. _____

Remarks:

START HERE - Type or Print in Black Ink.

Part 1.   Information about you.

A # (if any) [ ]   Form I-526 Receipt Number [ ]

Family Name [ ]   Given Name [ ]   Middle Name [ ]

Address:
In care of [ ]

Number and Street [ ]   Apt. # [ ]

City [ ]   State or Province [ ]

Country [ ]   Zip/Postal Code [ ]   Daytime Phone # [ ]

Date of Birth (mm/dd/yyyy) [ ]   Country of Birth [ ]   Social Security # (if any) [ ]

Since becoming a conditional permanent resident, have you ever been arrested, cited, charged, indicted, convicted, fined or imprisoned for breaking or violating any law or ordinance (excluding traffic regulations), or committed any crime for which you were not arrested?
☐ Yes   ☐ No   (If yes, explain on separate sheet(s) of paper, including disposition, if any.)

Part 2. Basis for petition.   (Check one)

a. ☐ My conditional permanent residence is based on an investment in a commercial enterprise.
b. ☐ I am a conditional permanent resident spouse or child of an entrepreneur, and I am unable to be included in a Petition by Entrepreneur to Remove Conditions (Form I-829) filed by my conditional resident spouse or parent.
c. ☐ I am a conditional permanent resident spouse or child of an entrepreneur who is deceased.

Part 3. Information about your husband or wife.

Family Name [ ]   Given Name [ ]   Middle Name [ ]

Gender ☐ Male   ☐ Female   Date of Birth (mm/dd/yyyy) [ ]   Date of Marriage (mm/ddy/yyyy) [ ]

Other names used (including maiden name or aliases) [ ]

A# (If any) [ ]   Current Immigration Status [ ]   Is your current immigration status based on the petitioner's current status?   ☐ Yes   ☐ No

RECEIVED: _____ RESUBMITTED:_____ RELOCATED: SENT _____ REC'D _____

Form I-829 (Rev. 05/12/03)N (Prior versions may be used until 09/30/03)

Part 4. Children. *(List all your children. Attach another sheet(s), if necessary.)*

Family Name		Given Name		Middle Name	
A# (if any)	Current Immigration Status		Date of Birth (mm/dd/yyyy)		Living with you? ☐ Yes ☐ No

Family Name		Given Name		Middle Name	
A# (if any)	Current Immigration Status		Date of Birth (mm/dd/yyyy)		Living with you? ☐ Yes ☐ No

Family Name		Given Name		Middle Name	
A# (if any)	Current Immigration Status		Date of Birth (mm/dd/yyyy)		Living with you? ☐ Yes ☐ No

Family Name		Given Name		Middle Name	
A# (if any)	Current Immigration Status		Date of Birth (mm/dd/yyyy)		Living with you? ☐ Yes ☐ No

Family Name		Given Name		Middle Name	
A# (if any)	Current Immigration Status		Date of Birth (mm/dd/yyyy)		Living with you? ☐ Yes ☐ No

Family Name		Given Name		Middle Name	
A# (if any)	Current Immigration Status		Date of Birth (mm/dd/yyyy)		Living with you? ☐ Yes ☐ No

Part 5. Information about your commercial enterprise.

Type of Enterprise *(Check one)*:

☐ New commercial enterprise resulting from the creation of a new business.

☐ New commercial enterprise resulting from the reorganization of an existing business.

☐ New commercial enterprise resulting from a capital investment in an existing business.

Kind of Business *(Be as specific as possible):*

Date Business Established (mm/dd/yyyy)　　　　　Amount of Initial Investment

Date of Initial Investment (mm/dd/yyyy)　　　　　% of Enterprise You Own

Number of full-time employees in enterprise in United States (excluding you, your spouse, sons and daughters):

At the time of your initial investment:　　　　Presently:　　　　Difference:

How many of these new jobs were created by your investment?

Part 5. Information about your commercial enterprise (continued).

Subsequent Investment in the Enterprise:

Date of Investment	Amount of Investment	Type of Investment

Provide the gross and net incomes generated annually by the commercial enterprise since your initial investment. Include all income generated up to date during the present year.

Year	Gross Income	Net Income

Has your commercial enterprise filed for bankruptcy, ceased business operations, or have any changes in its business organization or ownership occurred since the date of your initial investment? ☐ Yes (Explain on separate sheet) ☐ No

Has your commercial enterprise sold any corporate assets, shares, property, or had any capital withdrawn since the date of your initial investment? ☐ Yes (Explain on separate sheet) ☐ No

Part 6. Signature. (Read the information on penalties in the instructions before completing this section.)

I certify, under penalty of perjury under the laws of the United States of America, that this petition and the evidence submitted with it is all true and correct. I further certify that the investment was made in accordance with the laws of the United States and was not for the purpose of evading United States immigration laws. I also authorize the release of any information from my records which the Bureau of Citizenship and Immigration Services needs to determine eligibility for the benefit being sought.

Signature of Applicant	Print Name	Date

Please note: If you do not completely fill out this form or fail to submit any required documents listed in the instructions, you cannot be found eligible for the requested benefit and this petition may be denied.

Part 6. Signature of person preparing form, if other than above.

I declare that I prepared this petition at the request of the above person and it is based on all information of which I have knowledge.

Signature	Print Name	Date

Firm Name and Address

U.S. Department of Justice
Immigration and Naturalization Service

Affidavit of Support Under Section 213A of the Act

START HERE - Please Type or Print

Part 1.   Information on Sponsor (You)

Last Name	First Name	Middle Name

Mailing Address *(Street Number and Name)*	Apt/Suite Number

City	State or Province

Country	ZIP/Postal Code	Telephone Number

Place of Residence if different from above *(Street Number and Name)*	Apt/Suite Number

FOR AGENCY USE ONLY

City	State or Province

This Affidavit | Receipt

[ ] Meets

Country	ZIP/Postal Code	Telephone Number

[ ] Does not
meet

Requirements of
Section 213A

Date of Birth *(Month, Day, Year)*	Place of Birth *(City, State, Country)*	Are you a U.S. Citizen? ☐ Yes ☐ No

Social Security Number	A-Number *(If any)*

Part 2.   Basis for Filing Affidavit of Support

I am filing this affidavit of support because *(check one)*:

a. ☐ I filed/am filing the alien relative petition.

b. ☐ I filed/am filing an alien worker petition on behalf of the intending

immigrant, who is related to me as my _____.
(relationship)

Officer or I.J.
Signature

c. ☐ I have ownership interest of at least 5% _____.
(name of entity which filed visa petition)

which filed an alien worker petition on behalf of the intending

Location

immigrant, who is related to me as my _____
(relationship)

Date

d. ☐ I am a joint sponsor willing to accept the legal obligations with any other sponsor(s).

Part 3.   Information on the Immigrant(s) You Are Sponsoring

Last Name	First Name	Middle Name

Date of Birth *(Month, Day, Year)*	Sex ☐ Male ☐ Female	Social Security Number *(If any)*

Country of Citizenship	A-Number *(If any)*

Current Address *(Street Number and Name)*	Apt/Suite Number	City

State/Province	Country	ZIP/Postal Code	Telephone Number

List any spouse and/or children immigrating with the immigrant named above in this Part: *(Use additional sheet of paper if necessary.)*

Name	Relationship to Sponsored Immigrant			Date of Birth			A-Number *(If any)*	Social Security *(If any)*
	Spouse	Son	Daughter	Mo.	Day	Yr.		

Form I-864 (Rev. 11/05/01)Y

Part 4.   Eligibility to Sponsor

To be a sponsor you must be a U.S. citizen or national or a lawful permanent resident. If you are not the petitioning relative, you must provide proof of status. To prove status, U.S. citizens or nationals must attach a copy of a document proving status, such as a U.S. passport, birth certificate, or certificate of naturalization, and lawful permanent residents must attach a copy of both sides of their Permanent Resident Card (Form I-551).

The determination of your eligibility to sponsor an immigrant will be based on an evaluation of your demonstrated ability to maintain an annual income at or above 125 percent of the Federal poverty line (100 percent if you are a petitioner sponsoring your spouse or child and you are on active duty in the U.S. Armed Forces). The assessment of your ability to maintain an adequate income will include your current employment, household size, and household income as shown on the Federal income tax returns for the 3 most recent tax years. Assets that are readily converted to cash and that can be made available for the support of sponsored immigrants if necessary, including any such assets of the immigrant(s) you are sponsoring, may also be considered.

The greatest weight in determining eligibility will be placed on current employment and household income. If a petitioner is unable to demonstrate ability to meet the stated income and asset requirements, a joint sponsor who *can* meet the income and asset requirements is needed. Failure to provide adequate evidence of income and/or assets or an affidavit of support completed by a joint sponsor will result in denial of the immigrant's application for an immigrant visa or adjustment to permanent resident status.

A. Sponsor's Employment

I am: 1. ☐ Employed by _____ *(Provide evidence of employment)*

Annual salary _____ or hourly wage $ _____ *(for _____ hours per week)*

2. ☐ Self employed _____ *(Name of business)*

Nature of employment or business _____

3. ☐ Unemployed or retired since _____

B. Sponsor's Household Size   **Number**

1. Number of persons (related to you by birth, marriage, or adoption) living in your residence, including yourself *(Do NOT include persons being sponsored in this affidavit.)*   _____

2. Number of immigrants being sponsored in this affidavit *(Include all persons in Part 3.)*   _____

3. Number of immigrants **NOT** living in your household whom you are obligated to support under a previously signed Form I-864.   _____

4. Number of persons who are otherwise dependent on you, as claimed in your tax return for the most recent tax year.   _____

5. Total household size. *(Add lines 1 through 4.)*   **Total**   _____

List persons below who are included in lines 1 or 3 for whom you previously have submitted INS Form I-864, *if your support obligation has not terminated.*

(If additional space is needed, use additional paper)

Name	A-Number	Date Affidavit of Support Signed	Relationship

C. Sponsor's Annual Household Income

Enter total unadjusted income from your Federal income tax return for the most recent tax year below. If you last filed a joint income tax return but are using only your *own* income to qualify, list total earnings from your W-2 Forms, or, *if* necessary to reach the required income for your household size, include income from other sources listed on your tax return. If your *individual* income does not meet the income requirement for your household size, you may also list total income for anyone related to you by birth, marriage, or adoption currently living with you in your residence if they have lived in your residence for the previous 6 months, or any person shown as a dependent on your Federal income tax return for the most recent tax year, even if not living in the household. For their income to be considered, household members or dependents must be willing to make their income available for support of the sponsored immigrant(s) and to complete and sign Form I-864A, Contract Between Sponsor and Household Member. A sponsored immigrant/household member only need complete Form I-864A if his or her income will be used to determine your ability to support a spouse and/or children immigrating with him or her.

You must attach evidence of current employment and copies of income tax returns as filed with the IRS for the most recent 3 tax years for yourself and all persons whose income is listed below. See "Required Evidence " in Instructions. Income from all 3 years will be considered in determining your ability to support the immigrant(s) you are sponsoring.

☐ I filed a single/separate tax return for the most recent tax year.

☐ I filed a joint return for the most recent tax year which includes only my own income.

☐ I filed a joint return for the most recent tax year which includes income for my spouse and myself.

    ☐ I am submitting documentation of my individual income (Forms W-2 and 1099).

    ☐ I am qualifying using my spouse's income; my spouse is submitting a Form I-864A.

Indicate most recent tax year

_____
(tax year)

Sponsor's individual income $ _____

or

Sponsor and spouse's combined income $ _____
(If spouse's income is to be considered, spouse must submit Form I-864A.)

Income of other qualifying persons.
(List names; include spouse if applicable. Each person must complete Form I-864A.)

_____ $ _____

_____ $ _____

_____ $ _____

Total Household Income $ _____

Explain on separate sheet of paper if you or any of the above listed individuals were not required to file Federal income tax returns for the most recent 3 years, or if other explanation of income, employment, or evidence is necessary.

D. Determination of Eligibility Based on Income

1. ☐ I am subject to the 125 percent of poverty line requirement for sponsors.

    ☐ I am subject to the 100 percent of poverty line requirement for sponsors on active duty in the U.S. Armed Forces sponsoring their spouse or child.

2. Sponsor's total household size, from Part 4.B., line 5 _____.

3. Minimum income requirement from the Poverty Guidelines chart for the year of _____ is $ _____
    for this household size.   *(year)*

If you are currently employed and your household income for your household size is equal to or greater than the applicable poverty line requirement (from line D.3.), you do not need to list assets (Parts 4.E. and 5) or have a joint sponsor (Part 6) unless you are requested to do so by a Consular or Immigration Officer. You may skip to Part 7, Use of the Affidavit of Support to Overcome Public Charge Ground of Admissibility. **Otherwise, you should continue with Part 4.E.**

E. Sponsor's Assets and Liabilities

Your assets and those of your qualifying household members and dependents may be used to demonstrate ability to maintain an income at or above 125 percent (or 100 percent, if applicable) of the poverty line *if* they are available for the support of the sponsored immigrant(s) and can readily be converted into cash within 1 year. The household member, other than the immigrant(s) you are sponsoring, must complete and sign Form I-864A, Contract Between Sponsor and Household Member. List the cash value of each asset *after* any debts or liens are subtracted. Supporting evidence must be attached to establish location, ownership, date of acquisition, and value of each asset listed, including any liens and liabilities related to each asset listed. See "Evidence of Assets" in Instructions.

Type of Asset	Cash Value of Assets *(Subtract any debts)*
Savings deposits	$
Stocks, bonds, certificates of deposit	$
Life insurance cash value	$
Real estate	$
Other *(specify)*	$
Total Cash Value of Assets	$ _____

Part 5.   Immigrant's Assets and Offsetting Liabilities

The sponsored immigrant's assets may also be used in support of your ability to maintain income at or above 125 percent of the poverty line *if* the assets are or will be available in the United States for the support of the sponsored immigrant(s) and can readily be converted into cash within 1 year.

The sponsored immigrant should provide information on his or her assets in a format similar to part 4.E. above. Supporting evidence must be attached to establish location, ownership, and value of each asset listed, including any liens and liabilities for each asset listed. See "Evidence of Assets" in Instructions.

Part 6.   Joint Sponsors

If household income and assets do not meet the appropriate poverty line for your household size, a joint sponsor is required. There may be more than one joint sponsor, but each joint sponsor must individually meet the 125 percent of poverty line requirement based on his or her household income and/or assets, including any assets of the sponsored immigrant. By submitting a separate Affidavit of Support under Section 213A of the Act (Form I-864), a joint sponsor accepts joint responsibility with the petitioner for the sponsored immigrant(s) until they become U.S. citizens, can be credited with 40 quarters of work, leave the United States permanently, or die.

Part 7.   Use of the Affidavit of Support to Overcome Public Charge Ground of Inadmissibility

Section 212(a)(4)(C) of the Immigration and Nationality Act provides that an alien seeking permanent residence as an immediate relative (including an orphan), as a family-sponsored immigrant, or as an alien who will accompany or follow to join another alien is considered to be likely to become a public charge and is inadmissible to the United States unless a sponsor submits a legally enforceable affidavit of support on behalf of the alien. Section 212(a)(4)(D) imposes the same requirement on an employment-based immigrant, and those aliens who accompany or follow to join the employment- based immigrant, if the employment-based immigrant will be employed by a relative, or by a firm in which a relative owns a significant interest. Separate affidavits of support are required for family members at the time they immigrate if they are not included on this affidavit of support or do not apply for an immigrant visa or adjustment of status within 6 months of the date this affidavit of support is originally signed. The sponsor must provide the sponsored immigrant(s) whatever support is necessary to maintain them at an income that is at least 125 percent of the Federal poverty guidelines.

> *I submit this affidavit of support in consideration of the sponsored immigrant(s) not being found inadmissible to the United States under section 212(a)(4)(C) (or 212(a)(4)(D) for an employment-based immigrant) and to enable the sponsored immigrant(s) to overcome this ground of inadmissibility. I agree to provide the sponsored immigrant(s) whatever support is necessary to maintain the sponsored immigrant(s) at an income that is at least 125 percent of the Federal poverty guidelines. I understand that my obligation will continue until my death or the sponsored immigrant(s) have become U.S. citizens, can be credited with 40 quarters of work, depart the United States permanently, or die.*

Part 7.   Use of the Affidavit of Support to Overcome Public Charge Grounds   *(Continued)*

Notice of Change of Address.

Sponsors are required to provide written notice of any change of address within 30 days of the change in address until the sponsored immigrant(s) have become U.S. citizens, can be credited with 40 quarters of work, depart the United States permanently, or die. To comply with this requirement, the sponsor must complete INS Form I-865. Failure to give this notice may subject the sponsor to the civil penalty established under section 213A(d)(2) which ranges from $250 to $2,000, unless the failure to report occurred with the knowledge that the sponsored immigrant(s) had received means-tested public benefits, in which case the penalty ranges from $2,000 to $5,000.

> *If my address changes for any reason before my obligations under this affidavit of support terminate, I will complete and file INS Form I-865, Sponsor's Notice of Change of Address, within 30 days of the change of address. I understand that failure to give this notice may subject me to civil penalties.*

Means-tested Public Benefit Prohibitions and Exceptions.

Under section 403(a) of Public Law 104-193 (Welfare Reform Act), aliens lawfully admitted for permanent residence in the United States, with certain exceptions, are ineligible for most Federally-funded means-tested public benefits during their first 5 years in the United States. This provision does not apply to public benefits specified in section 403(c) of the Welfare Reform Act or to State public benefits, including emergency Medicaid; short-term, non-cash emergency relief; services provided under the National School Lunch and Child Nutrition Acts; immunizations and testing and treatment for communicable diseases; student assistance under the Higher Education Act and the Public Health Service Act; certain forms of foster-care or adoption assistance under the Social Security Act; Head Start programs; means-tested programs under the Elementary and Secondary Education Act; and Job Training Partnership Act programs.

Consideration of Sponsor's Income in Determining Eligibility for Benefits.

If a permanent resident alien is no longer statutorily barred from a Federally-funded means-tested public benefit program and applies for such a benefit, the income and resources of the sponsor and the sponsor's spouse will be considered (or deemed) to be the income and resources of the sponsored immigrant in determining the immigrant's eligibility for Federal means-tested public benefits. Any State or local government may also choose to consider (or deem) the income and resources of the sponsor and the sponsor's spouse to be the income and resources of the immigrant for the purposes of determining eligibility for their means-tested public benefits. The attribution of the income and resources of the sponsor and the sponsor's spouse to the immigrant will continue until the immigrant becomes a U.S. citizen or has worked or can be credited with 40 qualifying quarters of work, provided that the immigrant or the worker crediting the quarters to the immigrant has not received any Federal means-tested public benefit during any creditable quarter for any period after December 31, 1996.

> *I understand that, under section 213A of the Immigration and Nationality Act (the Act), as amended, this affidavit of support constitutes a contract between me and the U.S. Government. This contract is designed to protect the United States Government, and State and local government agencies or private entities that provide means-tested public benefits, from having to pay benefits to or on behalf of the sponsored immigrant(s), for as long as I am obligated to support them under this affidavit of support. I understand that the sponsored immigrants, or any Federal, State, local, or private entity that pays any means-tested benefit to or on behalf of the sponsored immigrant(s), are entitled to sue me if I fail to meet my obligations under this affidavit of support, as defined by section 213A and INS regulations.*

Civil Action to Enforce.

If the immigrant on whose behalf this affidavit of support is executed receives any Federal, State, or local means-tested public benefit before this obligation terminates, the Federal, State, or local agency or private entity may request reimbursement from the sponsor who signed this affidavit. If the sponsor fails to honor the request for reimbursement, the agency may sue the sponsor in any U.S. District Court or any State court with jurisdiction of civil actions for breach of contract. INS will provide names, addresses, and Social Security account numbers of sponsors to benefit-providing agencies for this purpose. Sponsors may also be liable for paying the costs of collection, including legal fees.

Part 7. Use of the Affidavit of Support to Overcome Public Charge Grounds *(Continued)*

I acknowledge that section 213A(a)(1)(B) of the Act grants the sponsored immigrant(s) and any Federal, State, local, or private agency that pays any means-tested public benefit to or on behalf of the sponsored immigrant(s) standing to sue me for failing to meet my obligations under this affidavit of support. I agree to submit to the personal jurisdiction of any court of the United States or of any State, territory, or possession of the United States if the court has subject matter jurisdiction of a civil lawsuit to enforce this affidavit of support. I agree that no lawsuit to enforce this affidavit of support shall be barred by any statute of limitations that might otherwise apply, so long as the plaintiff initiates the civil lawsuit no later than ten (10) years after the date on which a sponsored immigrant last received any means-tested public benefits.

Collection of Judgment.

I acknowledge that a plaintiff may seek specific performance of my support obligation. Furthermore, any money judgment against me based on this affidavit of support may be collected through the use of a judgment lien under 28 U.S.C 3201, a writ of execution under 28 U.S.C 3203, a judicial installment payment order under 28 U.S.C 3204, garnishment under 28 U.S.C 3205, or through the use of any corresponding remedy under State law. I may also be held liable for costs of collection, including attorney fees.

Concluding Provisions.

I, _____ , *certify under penalty of perjury under the laws of the United States that:*

     (a) I know the contents of this affidavit of support signed by me;

     (b) All the statements in this affidavit of support are true and correct,

     (c) I make this affidavit of support for the consideration stated in Part 7, freely, and without any mental reservation or purpose of evasion;

     (d) Income tax returns submitted in support of this affidavit are true copies of the returns filed with the Internal Revenue Service; and

     (e) Any other evidence submitted is true and correct.

_____   _____
(Sponsor's Signature)   *(Date)*

Subscribed and sworn to (or affirmed) before me this

_____ day of _____ , _____

                           (Month)   *(Year)*

at _____ .

My commission expires on _____ .

_____
(Signature of Notary Public or Officer Administering Oath)

_____
(Title)

Part 8. If someone other than the sponsor prepared this affidavit of support, that person must complete the following:

I certify under penalty of perjury under the laws of the United States that I prepared this affidavit of support at the sponsor's request, and that this affidavit of support is based on all information of which I have knowledge.

Signature	Print Your Name	Date	Daytime Telephone Number

Firm Name and Address

OMB No. 1115-0214

Contract Between Sponsor and Household Member

Sponsor's Name *(Last, First, Middle)*	Social Security Number	A-Number (If any)

General Filing Instruction

Form I-864A, Contract Between Sponsor and Household Member, is an attachment to Form I-864, Affidavit of Support Under Section 213A of the Immigration and Nationality Act (the Act). The sponsor enters the information above, complete Part 2 of this form, and signs in Part 5. The household member completes Parts 1 and 3 of this form and signs in Part 6. A household member who is also the sponsored immigrant completes Parts 1 and 4 (instead of Part 3) of this form and signs i Part 6. The Privacy Act Notice and information on penalties for misrepresentation or fraud are included on the instructions to Form I-864.

The signatures on the I-864A must be notarized by a notary public or signed before an immigration or consular officer. A separate form must be used for each household member whose income and/or assets are being used to qualify. This blank form may be photocopied for that purpose. A sponsored immigrant who qualifies as a household member is only required to complete this form if he or she has one or more family members immigrating with him or her and is making his or her *income* available for their support. Sponsored immigrants who are using their *assets* to qualify are not required to complete this form. This completed form is submitted with Form I-864 by the sponsored immigrant with an application for an immigrant visa or adjustment of status.

Purpose

This contract is intended to benefit the sponsored immigrant(s) and any agency of the Federal Government, any agency of a State or local government, or any private entity to which the sponsor has an obligation under the affidavit of support to reimburse for benefits granted to the sponsored immigrant, and these parties will have the right to enforce this contract in ar court with appropriate jurisdiction. Under Section 213A of Act, this contract must be completed and signed by the sponsor and any household member, including the sponsor's spouse, whose income is included as household income by a person sponsoring one or more immigrants. The contract must also be completed if a sponsor is relying on the assets of a househo member who is not the sponsored immigrant to meet the income requirements. If the sponsored immigrant is a household member immigrating with a spouse or children, and is using his or her income to assist the sponsor in meeting the income requirement, he or she must complete and sign this contract as a "sponsored immigrant/household member."

By signing this form, a household member, who is not a sponsored immigrant, agrees to make his or her income and/or assets available to the sponsor to help support the immigrant(s) for whom the sponsor has filed an affidavit of support and to be responsible, along with the sponsor, to pay any debt incurred by the sponsor under the affidavit of support. A sponsored immigrant/household member who signs this contract agrees to make his or her income available to the sponsor to help support any spouse or children immigrating with him or her and to be responsible, along with the sponsor, to pay any debt incurred by the sponsor under the affidavit of support. The obligations of the household member and the sponsored immigrant/household member under this contract terminate when the obligations of the sponsor under the affidavit of support terminate. For additional information see section 213A of the Act, part 213a of title 8 of the Code of Federal Regulations, and Form I-864, Affidavit of Support Under Section 213A of the Act.

Definitions:

1) An "affidavit of support" refers to Form I-864, Affidavit of Support Under Section 213A of the Act, which is complete and filed by the sponsor.

2) A "sponsor" is a person, either the petitioning relative, the relative with a significant ownership interest in the petitionin entity, or another person accepting joint and several liability with the sponsor, who completes and files the Affidavit of Support under Section 213A of the Act on behalf of a sponsored immigrant.

3) A "household member" is any person (a) sharing a residence with the sponsor for at least the last 6 months who is related to the sponsor by birth, marriage, or adoption, *or* (b) whom the sponsor has lawfully claimed as a dependent or the sponsor's most recent federal income tax return even if that person does not live at the same residence as the sponsor, *and* whose income and/or assets will be used to demonstrate the sponsor's ability to maintain the sponsored immigrant(s) at an annual income at the level specified in section 213A(f)(1)(E) or 213A(f)(3) of the Act.

4) A "sponsored immigrant" is a person listed on this form on whose behalf an affidavit of support will be completed and filed.

5) A "sponsored immigrant/household member" is a sponsored immigrant who is also a household member.

Part 1. Information on Sponsor's Household Member or Sponsored Immigrant/Household Member

Last Name	First Name	Middle Name

Date of Birth *(Month, Day, Year)*	Social Security Number *(Mandatory for non-citizens; voluntary for U.S. citizens)*	A-Number *(If any)*

Address *(Street Number and Name)* Apt Number	City	State/Province	ZIP/Postal Code

Telephone Number ( )	Relationship to Sponsor: I am: ☐ The sponsor's household member. *(Complete Part 3.)* ☐ The sponsored immigrant/household member. *(Complete Part*	Length of residence with sponsor _____ years, _____ months)

Part 2. Sponsor's Promise

I, THE SPONSOR, _____ , in consideration of the household member's promise to support the
(Print name of sponsor)

sponsored immigrant(s) and to be jointly and severally liable for any obligations I incur under the affidavit of support,

promise to complete and file an affidavit of support on behalf of the following_____ sponsored immigrant(s):
(Indicate number)

Name of Sponsored Immigrant *(First, Middle, Last)*	Date of Birth *(Month, Day, Year)*	Social Security Number *(If any)*	A-Number *(If any)*
_____	_____	_____	_____
_____	_____	_____	_____
_____	_____	_____	_____
_____	_____	_____	_____
_____	_____	_____	_____
_____	_____	_____	_____

Part 3. Household Member's Promise

I, THE HOUSEHOLD _____ , in consideration of the sponsor's
(Print name of household member)

promise to complete and file the affidavit of support on behalf of the sponsored immigrant(s):

1) Promise to provide any and all financial support necessary to assist the sponsor in maintaining the sponsored immigrant(s) at or above the minimum income provided for in section 213A(a)(1)(A) of the Act (not less than 125 percent of the Federal Poverty Guidelines) during the period in which the affidavit of support is enforceable;

2) Agree to be jointly and severally liable for payment of any and all obligations owed by the sponsor under the affidavit of support to the sponsored immigrant(s), to any agency of the Federal Government, to any agency of a state or local government, or to any private entity;

3) Agree to submit to the personal jurisdiction of any court of the United States or of any state, territory, or possession of the United States if the court has subject matter jurisdiction of a civil lawsuit to enforce this contract or the affidavit of support; and

4) Certify under penalty of perjury under the laws of the United States that all the information provided on this form is true and correct to the best of my knowledge and belief and that the income tax returns I submitted in support of the sponsor affidavit are true copies of the returns filed with the Internal Revenue Service.

Part 4. Sponsored Immigrant/Household Member's Promise

I, THE SPONSORED IMMIGRANT/HOUSEHOLD _____
(Print name o f sponsored immigrant)

in consideration of the sponsor's promise to complete and file the affidavit of support on behalf of the sponsored immigrant(s) accompanying me:

1) Promise to provide any and all financial support necessary to assist the sponsor in maintaining any sponsored immigrant(s) immigrating with me at or above the minimum income provided for in section 213A(a)(1)(A) of the Act (not less than 125 percent of the Federal Poverty Guidelines) during the period in which the affidavit of support is enforceable;

2) Agree to be jointly and severally liable for payment of any and all obligations owed by the sponsor under the affidavit of support to any sponsored immigrant(s) immigrating with me, to any agency of the Federal Government, to any agency of a state or local government, or to any private entity;

3) Agree to submit to the personal jurisdiction of any court of the United States or of any state, territory, or possession of the United States if the court has subject matter jurisdiction of a civil lawsuit to enforce this contract or the affidavit of support; and

4) Certify under penalty of perjury under the laws of the United States that all the information provided on this form is tru and correct to the best of my knowledge and belief and that the income tax returns I submitted in support of the sponsor's affidavit of support are true copies of the returns filed with the Internal Revenue Service.

Part 5. Sponsor's Signature

_____   Date: _____
Sponsor's Signature

Subscribed and sworn to *(or affirmed)* before me this_____ day of _____ , _____
                                                       (Month)   *(Year)*

at _____ . My commission expires on_____ .

_____   _____
Signature of Notary Public or Officer Administering Oath   *Title*

Part 6. Household Member's or Sponsored Immigrant/Household Member's Signature

_____   Date: _____
Household Member's or Sponsored Immigrant/Household Member's Signature

Subscribed and sworn to *(or affirmed)* before me this_____ day of _____ , _____
                                                       (Month)   *(Year)*

at _____ . My commission expires on_____ .

_____   _____
Signature of Notary Public or Officer Administering Oath   *Title*

2003 Poverty Guidelines*
Minimum Income Requirement For Use in Completing Form I-864

For the 48 Contiguous States, the District of Columbia, Puerto Rico, the U.S. Virgin Islands, and Guam:

Sponsor's Household Size	100% of Poverty Line For sponsors on active duty in the U.S. Armed Forces who are petitioning for their spouse or child.	125% of Poverty Line For all other sponsors
2	$12,120	$15,150
3	15,260	19,075
4	18,400	23,000
5	21,540	26,925
6	24,680	30,850
7	27,820	34,775
8	30,960	38,700
	Add $3,140 for each additional person.	Add $3,925 for each additional person.

Sponsor's Household Size	For Alaska		For Hawaii	
	100% of Poverty Line For sponsors on active duty in the U.S. Armed Forces who are petitioning for their spouse or child	125% of Poverty Line For all other sponsors	100% of Poverty Line For sponsors on active duty in the U.S. Armed Forces who are petitioning for their spouse or child	125% of Poverty Line For all other sponsors
2	$15,140	$18,925	$13,940	$17,425
3	19,070	23,837	17,550	21,937
4	23,000	28,750	21,160	26,450
5	26,930	33,662	24,770	30,962
6	30,860	38,575	28,380	35,475
7	34,790	43,487	31,990	39,987
8	38,720	48,400	35,600	44,500
	Add $3,930 for each additional person.	Add $4,912 for each additional person.	Add $3,610 for each additional person.	Add $4,512 for each additional person.

Means-tested Public Benefits

Federal Means-tested Public Benefits. To date, Federal agencies administering benefit programs have determined that Federal means-tested public benefits include Food Stamps, Medicaid, Supplemental Security Income (SSI), Temporary Assistance for Needy Families (TANF), and the State Child Health Insurance Program (SCHIP).

State Means-tested Public Benefits. Each State will determine which, if any, of its public benefits are means-tested. If a State determines that it has programs which meet this definition, it is encouraged to provide notice to the public on which programs are included. Check with the State public assistance office to determine which, if any, State assistance programs have been determined to be State means-tested public benefits.

Programs Not Included: The following Federal and State programs are *not* included as means-tested benefits: emergency Medicaid; short-term, non-cash emergency relief; services provided under the National School Lunch and Child Nutrition Acts; immunizations and testing and treatment for communicable diseases; student assistance under the Higher Education Act and the Public Health Service Act; certain forms of foster-care or adoption assistance under the Social Security Act; Head Start Programs; means-tested programs under the Elementary and Secondary Education Act; and Job Training Partnership Act programs.

* These poverty guidelines remain in effect for use with the Form I-864 Affidavit of Support from April 1, 2003 until new poverty guidelines go into effect in the Spring of 2004.

OMB No. 1115-0215

Sponsor's Notice of Change of Address

START HERE - Please Type or Print   Answer all Questions

Part 1.   Information about Sponsor

Last Name	First Name	Middle Name

Date of Birth *(Month, Day, Year)*	Place of Birth *(City, State, Country)*

A-Number *(If any)*	Social Security Number

My **New** Mailing Address *(Street Number and Name)*	Apt/Suite Number	**FOR AGENCY USE ONLY**
		Receipt

City	State or Province

Country	ZIP/Postal Code	Telephone Number

My **New** Place of Residence if different from above *(Street Number and Name)*	Apt/Suite Number

City	State or Province

Country	ZIP/Postal Code	Telephone Number

Effective Date of Change of Address

Part 2.   Sponsor's Signature

I certify under penalty of perjury under the laws of the United States of America that all information on this notice is true and correct.

Signature	Date	Daytime Telephone

Part 3.   Signature of person preparing notice if other than sponsor

I declare I prepared this application at the request of the above person and it is based on information of which I have knowledge.

Signature	Date	Daytime Telephone

Last Name *(Print)*	First name	Middle Initial

Firm Name and Address   *(Print)*

Public Reporting Burden

Paperwork Reduction Act Notice. Under the Paperwork Reduction Act, a person is not required to respond to a collection of information unless it displays a currently valid OMB control number. We try to create forms and instructions that are accurate, can be easily understood, and which impose the least possible burden on you to provide us with information. Often this is difficult because some immigration laws are very complex. The estimated average time to complete and file this form is 15 minutes. If you have comments regarding the accuracy of this estimate, or suggestions for making this form simpler, you can write to the Immigration and Naturalization Service, HQPDI, 425 I Street, N.W., Room 4034, Washington, DC 20536, OMB No.1115-0215. **DO NOT MAIL THIS FORM TO THIS ADDRESS.**

U.S. Department of Justice
Immigration and Naturalization Service

Application for Suspension of Deportation or Special Rule Cancellation of Removal (Pursuant to Section 203 of Public Law 105-100 (NACARA))

START HERE - Please Type or Print. If any question does not apply to you, write "None" or "N/A" in the appropriate space.

Part 1. Background information about YOU

Alien Registration Number(s), if any (List every "A-number" you have been given)

Family Name/Names	Given Name	Middle Initial

What other names have you used? (Include maiden name and aliases)

Address - Street Number and Name (or PO Box)   Apt #

City	State	Zip Code

Date of Birth (month/day/year)   Place of Birth (City or Town and Country)

Social Security #   Gender   ☐ Male   ☐ Female

Present Nationality (Citizenship)   Home Phone #
(   )   -

Part 2. Application type (check all that are applicable to you)

I am eligible to apply for suspension of deportation or special rule cancellation of removal under the Nicaraguan Adjustment and Central American Relief Act (NACARA) because I have not been convicted of an aggravated felony and:

☐ a) I am a national of El Salvador who first entered the United States on or before September 19, 1990, or a national of Guatemala who first entered the United States on or before October 1, 1990. I also registered for benefits under the settlement agreement in *American Baptist Churches v. Thornburgh (ABC)*, 760 F.Supp.796 (N.D.Cal. 1991), either directly or, if Salvadoran, by applying for Temporary Protected Status (TPS), and I have not been apprehended at time of entry after December 19, 1990.

☐ b) I am a national of Guatemala or El Salvador who filed an application for asylum on or before April 1, 1990.

☐ c) I entered the United States on or before December 31, 1990; filed an application for asylum on or before December 31, 1991; and at the time of filing was a national of the Soviet Union (USSR), Russia, any republic of the former Soviet Union, Latvia, Estonia, Lithuania, Poland, Czechoslovakia, Romania, Hungary, Bulgaria, Albania, East Germany, Yugoslavia, or any state of the former Yugoslavia.

☐ d) I am the spouse, child (unmarried and under 21 years of age), unmarried son or unmarried daughter of someone who has already applied for, or is presently filing with me for suspension of deportation or special rule cancellation of removal under NACARA. If I am an unmarried son or unmarried daughter, I entered the United States on or before October 1, 1990, or my parent was granted suspension of deportation or special rule cancellation of removal when I was less than 21 years of age. Attach proof of relationship and provide the following information about that spouse or parent:

Name:
A-number(s):
The person who has applied for special rule cancellation of removal or suspension of deportation is your: ☐ Spouse   ☐ Parent
Your spouse or parent applied with: ☐ INS   ☐ EOIR (Executive Office for Immigration Review)

FOR INS USE ONLY

Returned	Receipt
Resubmitted	
Reloc. Sent	
Reloc. Received	

Decision

☐ Suspension of Deportation or Special Rule Cancellation of Removal and adjustment of status granted

☐ Referred to Immigration Judge in accordance with 8 CFR Section

_____
(Adjudicating Officer's Signature)

_____   _____
(Date of Action)   (Office Location)

EOIR Actions

Attorney or Representative, if any
☐ Check box if G-28 is attached.
VOLAG#
Atty. State License #

Form I-881 (Rev. 09/28/00)Y

Part 3. Information about your presence in the United States

1. Provide information about the places where you have resided in the United States during the last ten years:*(List PRESENT ADDRESS FIRST and work back in time. List only places where you resided 60 days or more. Attach additional sheets of paper as needed.)*

Street and Number	Apt. Or Room #	City or Town	State	ZIP Code	Resided From: (Month/Year)	Resided To: (Month/Year)
						Present

2. Provide information about your first entry into the United States

Name used when first entered the United States: *(FamilyName, First, Middle)*	Place of first entry into the United States: *(City and State)*
Your status when you first entered the United States:	Date of first entry into the United States: *(Month/Day/Year)*	Period for which admitted:*(Month/Day/Year)* From: To:
If you changed nonimmigrant status after entry, list status you changed to:	Date you changed status: *(Month/Day/Year)*	Last Extension of Stay expired on: *(Month/Day/Year)*

3. Provide information about any departure from and return to the United States you have made since your first entry: *(Please list all departures, including brief ones. Attach additional sheets of paper as needed.)*

If you have not departed the United States since your first date of entry, please mark an X in this box: ☐

Port of Departure: *(Place or Port, City, State)*	Departure Date: *(Month/Day/Year)*	Purpose of Travel:	Destination:
Port of Return: *(Place or Port, City, State)*	Return Date: *(Month/Day/Year)*	Status at Entry:	Inspected and Admitted ☐ Yes ☐ No
Port of Departure:*(Place or Port, City, State)*	Departure Date: *(Month/Dqy/Year)*	Purpose of Travel:	Destination:
Port of Return: *(Place or Port, City, State)*	Return Date: *(Month/Day/Year)*	Status at Entry:	Inspected and Admitted? ☐ Yes ☐ No

4. Have you ever:

    a) been ordered deported or removed?   ☐ Yes ☐ No

    b) departed the United States under an order of deportation or removal?   ☐ Yes ☐ No

    c) overstayed a grant of voluntary departure from an Immigration Judge or INS?   ☐ Yes ☐ No

    d) departed the United States pursuant to a grant of voluntary departure?   ☐ Yes ☐ No

    e) failed to appear for deportation or removal?   ☐ Yes ☐ No

If you responded "Yes" to any of the above, please indicate the name and Alien Registration # you were using at that time, along with the date you left the United States, if applicable: _____

If you are unsure about any of your answers to questions 4(a)-(e) above, please indicate which question(s) and explain why you are unsure about the response(s) you have given: *(Attach additional sheets of paper as needed.)*

Part 4. Information about your financial status and employment

1. Provide information about the places where you have been employed for the last ten years: *(List PRESENT EMPLOYMENT FIRST and work back in time. Include all employment, even if less than full-time. If you did the same type of work for three or more employers during any six-month period and you do not know the names and addresses of those employers, you may state "multiple employers," indicate the city or region where you did the work, list the type of work you did, and estimate your earnings during that period. Any periods of unemployment, unpaid work (as a homemaker or intern, for example), or school attendance should be specified. Attach additional sheets of paper as needed.)*

Full Name and Address of Employer or School: *(If self-employed, give name and address of business.)*	Earnings per Week *(approximate)*	Type Of Work Performed:	Employed From:*(Month/ Year)*	Employed To: *(Month/Year)*
_____				Present
_____				
_____				
_____				
_____				
_____				
_____				

2. Provide information about your assets in the United States and other countries, including those held jointly with your spouse, if you are married, or with others. Do not include the value of clothing and household necessities. If married, provide information about your spouse's assets that he or she does not hold jointly with you:

Self *(Including assets jointly owned with Spouse or others)*		Spouse	
Cash, Checking or Savings Accounts:	$	Cash, Checking or Savings Accounts:	$
Motor Vehicle(s): *(Minus any amount owed)*	$	Motor Vehicle(s): *(Minus any amount owed)*	$
Real Estate: *(Minus any amount owed)*	$	Real Estate: *(Minus any amount owed)*	$
Other: *(Describe below, e.g., stocks, bonds)*	$	Other: *(Describe below, e.g., stocks, bonds)*	$
Total:	$	**Total:**	$

3. Have you filed a federal income tax return while in the United States? ☐Yes ☐ No If "Yes," indicate the years you filed and attach evidence that you filed the returns. If you did not file a tax return during any particular year(s), please explain why you did not file. *(Attach additional sheets of paper as needed):*

Part 5. Information about your marital status and spouse

Marital status: ☐ Married ☐ Single *(If single, skip this Part and go to Part 6)* ☐ Divorce ☐ Separated ☐ Widower

1. Information about Spouse:

Name: *(Family Name(s), First, Middle)*	Date of Marriage: *(Month/Day/Year)*	Place of Marriage: *(City and Country)*
Place of Birth: *(City and Country)*	Date of Birth: *(Month/Day/Year)*	Citizenship:

Your spouse currently resides at:
(Indicate "with me" if spouse resides with you)

Number and Street Apt. # City or Town State/Country Zip Code

If presently residing in the United States, your spouse's present status is: ☐ U.S. Citizen ☐ Lawful Permanent Resident ☐ Asylee ☐ Asylum Applicant ☐ Other *(Please describe):*

His/her alien registration number(s) is *(List all A#s your spouse has been given): A #*

Your spouse ☐ is ☐ is not employed. If employed, please give salary and the name and address of the place(s) of employment:

Full Name and Address of Employer:	Earnings Per Week:	Type of Work:	Employed from: *(Month/Day/Year)*	Employed to: *(Month/Day/Year)*

2. Information about Previous Spouse(s):

I ☐ have ☐ have not been previously married: *(If previously married, list the names of each prior spouse, the dates on each marriage began and ended, the place where the marriage ended, and describe how each marriage ended. Attach additional sheets of paper as needed.)*

Name of Prior Spouse: *(FamilyName(s), First, Middle Initial)*	Date married: *(Month/Day/Year)*	Date marriage ended *(Month/Day/Year)*	Place marriage ended: *(City and Country)*	Manner in which marriage was terminated or ended *(i.e. death of spouse, divorce):*

3. Have you been ordered by any court, or are you otherwise under any legal obligation to provide child support and/or spousal maintenance? ☐ Yes ☐ No If "Yes," on a separate piece of paper please explain what type of obligation you have, to whom it is owed, and whether you are fulfilling that obligation.

Part 6. Information about your child/children
1. Do you have children? ☐ Yes ☐ No *(If "No," then skip this Part and go to Part 7)*
2. Please list all your children below, regardless of their age, giving the requested information about each of them. *(In the Address box, indicate "with me" if child currently resides with you, or list Number and Street, City, and State or Country of residence. Attach additional sheets of paper as needed.)*

Name of Child: *(Family Name(s), First, Middle)*	A-Number:	Place of Birth:	Date of Birth:	Immigration Status:
1)				
Current Address:			Citizenship:	
2)				
Current Address:			Citizenship:	
3)				
Current Address:			Citizenship:	
4)				
Current Address:			Citizenship:	

Part 7. Information about your parent/parents

You do not need to provide information about your parents' assets and earnings unless you believe that your removal would result in extreme hardship to your parent or parents.

Name of Parent: *(Family Name(s), First, Middle)*	A-Number:	Place of Birth: *(City and Country)*	Date of Birth: *(Month/Day/Year)*	Immigration Status:
Father:				
Current Address: *(Number and Street, City, State or Country)*			Citizenship:	
Estimated total assets: $		Weekly earnings: $		
Mother:				
Current Address:			Citizenship:	
Estimated total assets: $		Weekly earnings: $		

Part 8. Miscellaneous information

Please respond to the following questions. If you answer "Yes" to any of these questions, please provide an explanation of your answer on an attached sheet of paper.

1. Have you ever (either in the United States or in a foreign country) been arrested, summoned into court as a defendant, convicted, fined, imprisoned, placed on probation, or forfeited collateral for an act involving a felony, misdemeanor, or breach of any public law or ordinance (including, but not limited to, driving violations involving alcohol)? ☐ Yes ☐ No
(If you answered "Yes," your explanation should include a brief description of each offense, including the name and location of the offense, date of conviction, any penalty imposed, any sentence imposed and the time actually served.)

2. Have you ever been:		
☐ Yes	☐ No	A habitual drunkard?
☐ Yes	☐ No	One who has derived income principally from illegal gambling?
☐ Yes	☐ No	One who has given false testimony for the purpose of obtaining immigration benefits?
☐ Yes	☐ No	One who has engaged in prostitution or unlawful commercialized vice?
☐ Yes	☐ No	Involved in a serious criminal offense and asserted immunity from prosecution?
☐ Yes	☐ No	One who has aided and/or abetted another to enter the United States illegally?
☐ Yes	☐ No	A trafficker of a controlled substance, or one who knowingly assisted, abetted, conspired, or colluded with others in any such trafficking (not including a single offense of simple possession of 30 grams or less of marijuana)?
☐ Yes	☐ No	A practicing polygamist?
☐ Yes	☐ No	Admitted into the United States as a crewman after June 30, 1964?
☐ Yes	☐ No	Admitted into the United States as, or after arrival acquired the status of, an exchange visitor?
☐ Yes	☐ No	Inadmissible or deportable on security related grounds under sections 212(a)(3) or 237(a)(4) (for cancellation applicants), or under pre-IIRIRA section 241(a)(4) (for suspension applicants) of the Immigration and Nationality Act (INA)?
☐ Yes	☐ No	One who has ordered, incited, assisted, or otherwise participated in the persecution of an individual on account of his or her race, religion, nationality, membership in a particular social group, or political opinion?
☐ Yes	☐ No	A person previously granted relief under section 212(c) or 244(a) (suspension of deportation) of the INA or whose removal has previously been canceled under section 240A (cancellation of removal) of the INA?

Part 9. Information about hardship you and/or your family will face if you are deported or removed from the United States

Please answer the following questions by checking "Yes," "No" or "Not Applicable" in the boxes provided. Where required, please provide an explanation of your answer on an attached sheet of paper. You should reference the number of each question for which you are providing an explanation. Your responses in this Part should be about you and/or your qualifying family member(s), except for your response to question 11. A qualifying family member is a parent, spouse, or child who is a United States citizen (USC) or lawful permanent resident (LPR) of the United States. When providing responses about a family member, please provide the family member's name and his or her relationship to you. **Please attach any documents you have to support the responses you give below.** *(See the Instructions for types of documents that you may wish to submit. Please provide explanations to your answers below on an attached sheet of paper.)*

IMPORTANT: *If you meet the eligibility requirements for NACARA suspension of deportation or special rule cancellation of removal listed in (a) or (b), under **Part 2, Application type** on Page 1 of this form and you complete this form, you will be presumed to meet the extreme hardship requirement, unless evidence in the record establishes that neither you nor your qualified relative are likely to experience extreme hardship if you are deported or removed from the United States. If you qualify for a presumption of extreme hardship, you do not need to submit documents that support your answers below regarding your claim to extreme hardship, **but you need to provide explanations to your answers below.***

1. ☐ Yes ☐ No☐ Not applicable - If you have (USC/LPR) children, do your children speak, read, and write English?

2. ☐ Yes ☐ No☐ Not applicable - If you have (USC/LPR) children, do your children speak, read and write the native language of the country you would be returned to if deported or removed?

3. ☐ Yes ☐ No - Do you or any of your qualified family members suffer or have suffered any illness, health problem, or disability that required medical attention? If yes, please provide information about the health problem, the name of the qualified family member who suffers from it, and any care the person receives in the United States that would not be available in the country to which you would be deported or removed.

4. ☐ Yes ☐ No - Would you be able to obtain employment in the country to which you would be deported or removed? If yes, explain the type of employment you would be able to obtain. If no, explain why you would be unable to find employment.

5. ☐ Yes ☐ No ☐ Not applicable - If you or a qualified family member are currently pursuing educational opportunities in the United States, would you or the qualified family member continue to pursue the educational opportunities if deported or removed from the United States? If no, explain why not.

6. ☐ Yes ☐ No ☐ Not applicable - If you are deported or removed from the United States, would all qualified family member(s) accompany you? If no, list which qualified family member(s) would not accompany you. Also, explain why the qualified family member(s) would not accompany you and how that affects you and your family member(s).

7. ☐ Yes ☐ No - Would you or qualified members of your family experience any emotional or psychological impact if you were deported or removed from the United States? If yes, please explain.

8. ☐ Yes ☐ No - Would the current conditions in the country to which you would be deported or removed cause you or qualified family members extreme hardship if you were returned? If yes, please explain.

9. ☐ Yes ☐ No - Do you presently have any other way, besides this application for suspension of deportation or special cancellation of removal, to adjust status to that of a permanent resident in the United States? If yes, please explain.

10. ☐ Yes ☐ No ☐ Not applicable - If you belong to any civic, political, religious, community, or social organization, association, foundation, club, or similar group or participate in volunteer activities, would your separation from these community ties and activities affect you if you are deported or removed from the United States? If yes, please explain.

11. ☐ Yes ☐ No - Is there any other type of hardship that you or your family would face if you are deported or removed from the United States? Include any hardship to your non USC/LPR children, spouse or parents and any hardship to brothers, sisters, grandparents or other extended family members. If yes, please explain.

Part 10. Signature

After reading the information on penalties in the instructions, complete and sign below. If someone helped you prepare this application, he or she must complete **Part II.**

I certify, under penalty of perjury under the laws of the United States of America, that this application and the evidence submitted with it is all true and correct. Title 18, United States Code, Section 1546, provides in part: "Whoever knowingly makes under oath, or as permitted under penalty of perjury under Section 1746 of Title 28, United States Code, knowingly subscribes as true, any false statement with respect to a material fact in any application, affidavit, or other document required by the immigration laws or regulations prescribed thereunder, or knowingly presents any such application, affidavit, or other document containing any such false information or which fails to contain any reasonable basis in law or fact--shall be fined in accordance with this title or imprisoned not more than five years, or both."

Staple your

photographs

here

I authorize the release of any information from my record which the Immigration and Naturalization Service needs to determine eligibility for the benefit I am seeking.

WARNING: Applicants who are in the United States illegally are subject to deportation or removal if their applications are not granted by an asylum officer or an Immigration Judge. Any information provided in completing this application may be used as a basis for the institution of, or as evidence in, deportation or removal proceedings, even if the application is later withdrawn.

Signature of Applicant:	Date: _____
	(Month/Day/Year)
Print Name:	Write your name in your native alphabet:

Part 11. Signature of person preparing form, if other than above *(Read the following information and sign below.)*

I declare that I have prepared this application at the request of the person named in Part 10, that the responses provided are based on all information of which I have knowledge, or which was provided to me by the applicant, and that the completed application was read to the applicant in a language the applicant speaks fluently for verification before he or she signed the application in my presence. I am aware that the knowing placement of false information on the Form I-881 may subject me to civil penalties under 8 U.S.C. 1324 (c).

| Signature of Preparer: | Print Name: | Date: *(Month/Day/Year)* |
| Daytime Telephone #: ( ) | Address of Preparer: *(Street # and Name, City or Town, State, Zip Code)* | |

Part 12. To be completed at interview or hearing

You will be asked to complete this Part when you before an Asylum Officer of the Immigration and Naturalization Service (INS), or an Immigration Judge of the Executive Office for Immigration Review (EOIR) for examination.

I swear (affirm) that I know the contents of this application that I am signing, including the attached documents and supplements, that they are ☐ all true or ☐ not all true to the best of my knowledge and that the corrections numbered _____ to _____ were made by me or at my request.

Signed and sworn to before me by the above-named applicant on:

| _____ | _____ |
| Signature of Applicant | Date *(Month/Day/Year)* |

| _____ | _____ |
| Write your Name in your Native Alphabet | Signature of Asylum Officer or Immigration Judge |

Use this blank sheet to supplement any information requested. Please copy and submit as needed.

A # _____ Print Name _____

Signature of Applicant: _____ Date: _____

Part _____

Question _____

A # _____ Print Name _____

Signature of Applicant: _____ Date: _____

Part _____

Question _____

A # _____ Print Name _____

Signature of Applicant: _____ Date: _____

Part _____

Question _____

A # _____ Print Name _____

Signature of Applicant: _____ Date: _____

Part _____

Question _____

U. S. IMMIGRATION & NATURALIZATION SERVICE

COLOR PHOTOGRAPH SPECIFICATIONS

IDEAL PHOTOGRAPH

◄

IMAGE MUST FIT INSIDE THIS BOX ►

THE PICTURE AT LEFT IS IDEAL SIZE, COLOR, BACKGROUND, AND POSE. THE IMAGE SHOULD BE 3OMM (1 3/16IN) FROM THE HAIR TO JUST BELOW THE CHIN, AND 26MM (1 IN) FROM LEFT CHEEK TO RIGHT EAR. THE IMAGE MUST FIT IN THE BOX AT RIGHT.

THE PHOTOGRAPH

* THE OVERALL SIZE OF THE PICTURE, INCLUDING THE BACKGROUND, MUST BE AT LEAST 40MM (1 9/16 INCHES) IN HEIGHT BY 35MM (1 3/8IN) IN WIDTH.

* PHOTOS MUST BE FREE OF SHADOWS AND CONTAIN NO MARKS, SPLOTCHES, OR DISCOLORATIONS.

* PHOTOS SHOULD BE HIGH QUALITY, WITH GOOD BACK LIGHTING OR WRAP AROUND LIGHTING, AND MUST HAVE A WHITE OR OFF-WHITE BACKGROUND.

* PHOTOS MUST BE A GLOSSY OR MATTE FINISH AND UN-RETOUCHED.

* POLAROID FILM HYBRID #5 IS ACCEPTABLE; HOWEVER SX-70 TYPE FILM OR ANY OTHER INSTANT PROCESSING TYPE FILM IS UNACCEPTABLE. NON-PEEL APART FILMS ARE EASILY RECOGNIZED BECAUSE THE BACK OF THE FILM IS BLACK. ACCEPTABLE INSTANT COLOR FILM HAS A GRAY-TONED BACKING.

THE IMAGE OF THE PERSON

* THE DIMENSIONS OF THE IMAGE SHOULD BE 30MM (1 3/16 INCHES) FROM THE HAIR TO THE NECK JUST BELOW THE CHIN, AND 26MM (1 INCH) FROM THE RIGHT EAR TO THE LEFT CHEEK. IMAGE CANNOT EXCEED 32MM BY 28MM (1 1/4IN X 1 1/16IN).

* IF THE IMAGE AREA ON THE PHOTOGRAPH IS TOO LARGE OR TOO SMALL, THE PHOTO CANNOT BE USED.

* PHOTOGRAPHS MUST SHOW THE ENTIRE FACE OF THE PERSON IN A 3/4 VIEW SHOWING THE RIGHT EAR AND LEFT EYE.

* FACIAL FEATURES **MUST BE IDENTIFIABLE.**

* CONTRAST BETWEEN THE IMAGE AND BACKGROUND IS ESSENTIAL. PHOTOS FOR VERY LIGHT SKINNED PEOPLE SHOULD BE SLIGHTLY UNDER-EXPOSED. PHOTOS FOR VERY DARK SKINNED PEOPLE SHOULD BE SLIGHTLY OVER-EXPOSED.

SAMPLES OF UNACCEPTABLE PHOTOGRAPHS

INCORRECT POSE

IMAGE TOO LARGE

IMAGE TOO SMALL

IMAGE TOO DARK UNDER-EXPOSED

IMAGE TOO LIGHT

DARK BACKGROUND

OVER-EXPOSED

SHADOWS ON PIC

Immigration & Naturalization Service
Form M-378 (6-92)

U.S. Department of Justice
Immigration and Naturalization Service

OMB No. 1115-0009

Application for Naturalization

Print clearly or type your answers using CAPITAL letters. Failure to print clearly may delay your application. Use black or blue ink.

Part 1. Your Name *(The Person Applying for Naturalization)*

Write your INS "A"- number here:

A __ __ __ __ __ __ __ __ __

A. Your current legal name.

Family Name *(Last Name)*

Given Name *(First Name)*

Full Middle Name *(If applicable)*

FOR INS USE ONLY

Bar Code	Date Stamp

Remarks

B. Your name **exactly** as it appears on your Permanent Resident Card.

Family Name *(Last Name)*

Given Name *(First Name)*

Full Middle Name *(If applicable)*

C. If you have ever used other names, provide them below.

Family Name *(Last Name)*	Given Name *(First Name)*	Middle Name

D. Name change *(optional)*

Please read the Instructions before you decide whether to change your name.

1. Would you like to legally change your name? ☐ Yes ☐ No
2. If "Yes," print the new name you would like to use. Do not use initials or abbreviations when writing your new name.

Family Name *(Last Name)*

Given Name *(First Name)*

Full Middle Name

Action

Part 2. Information About Your Eligibility *(Check Only One)*

I am at least 18 years old **AND**

A. ☐ I have been a Lawful Permanent Resident of the United States for at least 5 years.

B. ☐ I have been a Lawful Permanent Resident of the United States for at least 3 years, AND I have been married to and living with the same U.S. citizen for the last 3 years, AND my spouse has been a U.S. citizen for the last 3 years.

C. ☐ I am applying on the basis of qualifying military service.

D. ☐ Other *(Please explain)* _____

Form N-400 (Rev. 07/23/02)

Write your INS "A"- number here:

A __ __ __ __ __ __ __ __ __ __

A. Social Security Number

___ ___ ___ - ___ ___ - ___ ___ ___ ___

B. Date of Birth *(Month/Day/Year)*

__ __ / __ __ / __ __ __ __

C. Date You Became a Permanent Resident *(Month/Day/Year)*

__ __ / __ __ / __ __ __ __

D. Country of Birth

E. Country of Nationality

F. Are either of your parents U.S. citizens? *(if yes, see Instructions)* ☐ Yes ☐ No

G. What is your current marital status? ☐ Single, Never Married ☐ Married ☐ Divorced ☐ Widowed

☐ Marriage Annulled or Other *(Explain)* _____

H. Are you requesting a waiver of the English and/or U.S. History and Government requirements based on a disability or impairment and attaching a Form N-648 with your application? ☐ Yes ☐ No

I. Are you requesting an accommodation to the naturalization process because of a disability or impairment? *(See Instructions for some examples of accommodations.)* ☐ Yes ☐ No

If you answered "Yes", check the box below that applies:

☐ I am deaf or hearing impaired and need a sign language interpreter who uses the following language: _____

☐ I use a wheelchair.

☐ I am blind or sight impaired.

☐ I will need another type of accommodation. Please explain: _____

_____

_____

A. Home Address - Street Number and Name *(Do NOT write a P.O. Box in this space)*

Apartment Number

City	County	State	ZIP Code	Country

B. Care of

Mailing Address - Street Number and Name *(If different from home address)*

Apartment Number

City	State	ZIP Code	Country

C. Daytime Phone Number *(If any)*

( )

Evening Phone Number *(If any)*

( )

E-mail Address *(If any)*

Part 5. Information for Criminal Records Search

Note: The categories below are those required by the FBI. See Instructions for more information.

A. Gender

☐ Male   ☐ Female

B. Height

Feet	Inches

C. Weight

Pounds

D. Are you Hispanic or Latino?   ☐ Yes   ☐ No

E. Race *(Select one or more.)*

☐ White   ☐ Asian   ☐ Black or African American   ☐ American Indian or Alaskan Native   ☐ Native Hawaiian or Other Pacific Islander

F. Hair color

☐ Black   ☐ Brown   ☐ Blonde   ☐ Gray   ☐ White   ☐ Red   ☐ Sandy   ☐ Bald (No Hair)

G. Eye color

☐ Brown   ☐ Blue   ☐ Green   ☐ Hazel   ☐ Gray   ☐ Black   ☐ Pink   ☐ Maroon   ☐ Other

Part 6. Information About Your Residence and Employment

A. Where have you lived during the last 5 years? Begin with where you live now and then list every place you lived for the last 5 years. If you need more space, use a separate sheet of paper.

Street Number and Name, Apartment Number, City, State, Zip Code and Country	Dates *(Month/Year)*	
	From	To
Current Home Address - Same as Part 4.A	_ _ / _ _ _ _	Present
	_ _ / _ _ _ _	_ _ / _ _ _ _
	_ _ / _ _ _ _	_ _ / _ _ _ _
	_ _ / _ _ _ _	_ _ / _ _ _ _
	_ _ / _ _ _ _	_ _ / _ _ _ _

B. Where have you worked (or, if you were a student, what schools did you attend) during the last 5 years? Include military service. Begin with your current or latest employer and then list every place you have worked or studied for the last 5 years. If you need more space, use a separate sheet of paper.

Employer or School Name	Employer or School Address *(Street, City and State)*	Dates *(Month/Year)*		Your Occupation
		From	To	
		_ _ / _ _ _ _	_ _ / _ _ _ _	
		_ _ / _ _ _ _	_ _ / _ _ _ _	
		_ _ / _ _ _ _	_ _ / _ _ _ _	
		_ _ / _ _ _ _	_ _ / _ _ _ _	
		_ _ / _ _ _ _	_ _ / _ _ _ _	

Part 7. Time Outside the United States
(Including Trips to Canada, Mexico, and the Caribbean Islands)

Write your INS "A"- number here:

A __ __ __ __ __ __ __ __ __

A. How many total days did you spend outside of the United States during the past 5 years? [____] days

B. How many trips of 24 hours or more have you taken outside of the United States during the past 5 years? [____] trips

C. List below all the trips of 24 hours or more that you have taken outside of the United States since becoming a Lawful Permanent Resident. Begin with your most recent trip. If you need more space, use a separate sheet of paper.

Date You Left the United States (Month/Day/Year)	Date You Returned to the United States (Month/Day/Year)	Did Trip Last 6 Months or More?	Countries to Which You Traveled	Total Days Out of the United States
__ __ / __ __ / __ __ __ __	__ __ / __ __ / __ __ __ __	☐ Yes ☐ No		
__ __ / __ __ / __ __ __ __	__ __ / __ __ / __ __ __ __	☐ Yes ☐ No		
__ __ / __ __ / __ __ __ __	__ __ / __ __ / __ __ __ __	☐ Yes ☐ No		
__ __ / __ __ / __ __ __ __	__ __ / __ __ / __ __ __ __	☐ Yes ☐ No		
__ __ / __ __ / __ __ __ __	__ __ / __ __ / __ __ __ __	☐ Yes ☐ No		
__ __ / __ __ / __ __ __ __	__ __ / __ __ / __ __ __ __	☐ Yes ☐ No		
__ __ / __ __ / __ __ __ __	__ __ / __ __ / __ __ __ __	☐ Yes ☐ No		
__ __ / __ __ / __ __ __ __	__ __ / __ __ / __ __ __ __	☐ Yes ☐ No		
__ __ / __ __ / __ __ __ __	__ __ / __ __ / __ __ __ __	☐ Yes ☐ No		
__ __ / __ __ / __ __ __ __	__ __ / __ __ / __ __ __ __	☐ Yes ☐ No		

Part 8. Information About Your Marital History

A. How many times have you been married (including annulled marriages)? [____] If you have NEVER been married, go to Part 9.

B. If you are now married, give the following information about your spouse:

1. Spouse's Family Name (Last Name)   Given Name (First Name)   Full Middle Name (If applicable)

2. Date of Birth (Month/Day/Year)   3. Date of Marriage (Month/Day/Year)   4. Spouse's Social Security Number

__ __ / __ __ / __ __ __ __   __ __ / __ __ / __ __ __ __   __ __ __ - __ __ - __ __ __ __

5. Home Address - Street Number and Name   Apartment Number

City   State   ZIP Code

Write your INS "A"- number here:

A _ _ _ _ _ _ _ _ _ _ _

C. Is your spouse a U.S. citizen?   ☐ Yes   ☐ No

D. If your spouse is a U.S. citizen, give the following information:

   1. When did your spouse become a U.S. citizen?   ☐ At Birth   ☐ Other

   If "Other," give the following information:

   2. Date your spouse became a U.S. citizen

   `_ _/_ _/_ _ _ _`

   3. Place your spouse became a U.S. citizen *(Please see Instructions)*

   City and State

E. If your spouse is NOT a U.S. citizen, give the following information :

   1. Spouse's Country of Citizenship

   2. Spouse's INS "A"- Number *(If applicable)*

   A _ _ _ _ _ _ _ _ _ _

   3. Spouse's Immigration Status

   ☐ Lawful Permanent Resident   ☐ Other _____

F. If you were married before, provide the following information about your prior spouse. If you have more than one previous marriage, use a separate sheet of paper to provide the information requested in questions 1-5 below.

   1. Prior Spouse's Family Name *(Last Name)*   Given Name *(First Name)*   Full Middle Name *(If applicable)*

   2. Prior Spouse's Immigration Status

   ☐ U.S. Citizen

   ☐ Lawful Permanent Resident

   ☐ Other _____

   3. Date of Marriage *(Month/Day/Year)*

   `_ _/_ _/_ _ _ _`

   4. Date Marriage Ended *(Month/Day/Year)*

   `_ _/_ _/_ _ _ _`

   5. How Marriage Ended

   ☐ Divorce   ☐ Spouse Died   ☐ Other _____

G. How many times has your current spouse been married (including annulled marriages)? ☐

   If your spouse has EVER been married before, give the following information about **your spouse's** prior marriage.
   If your spouse has more than one previous marriage, use a separate sheet of paper to provide the information requested in questions 1 - 5 below.

   1. Prior Spouse's Family Name *(Last Name)*   Given Name *(First Name)*   Full Middle Name *(If applicable)*

   2. Prior Spouse's Immigration Status

   ☐ U.S. Citizen

   ☐ Lawful Permanent Resident

   ☐ Other _____

   3. Date of Marriage *(Month/Day/Year)*

   `_ _/_ _/_ _ _ _`

   4. Date Marriage Ended *(Month/Day/Year)*

   `_ _/_ _/_ _ _ _`

   5. How Marriage Ended

   ☐ Divorce   ☐ Spouse Died   ☐ Other _____

A. How many sons and daughters have you had? For more information on which sons and daughters you should include and how to complete this section, see the Instructions.

B. Provide the following information about all of your sons and daughters. If you need more space, use a separate sheet of paper.

Full Name of Son or Daughter	Date of Birth (Month/Day/Year)	INS "A"- number (if child has one)	Country of Birth	Current Address (Street, City, State & Country)
	__ __ / __ / __ __ __ __	A __ __ __ __ __ __ __ __ __		
	__ __ / __ / __ __ __ __	A __ __ __ __ __ __ __ __ __		
	__ __ / __ / __ __ __ __	A __ __ __ __ __ __ __ __ __		
	__ __ / __ / __ __ __ __	A __ __ __ __ __ __ __ __ __		
	__ __ / __ / __ __ __ __	A __ __ __ __ __ __ __ __ __		
	__ __ / __ / __ __ __ __	A __ __ __ __ __ __ __ __ __		
	__ __ / __ / __ __ __ __	A __ __ __ __ __ __ __ __ __		
	__ __ / __ / __ __ __ __	A __ __ __ __ __ __ __ __ __		

Part 10. Additional Questions

Please answer questions 1 through 14. If you answer "Yes" to any of these questions, include a written explanation with this form. Your written explanation should (1) explain why your answer was "Yes," and (2) provide any additional information that helps to explain your answer.

A. General Questions

1. Have you **EVER** claimed to be a U.S. citizen *(in writing or any other way)*? ☐ Yes ☐ No

2. Have you **EVER** registered to vote in any Federal, state, or local election in the United States? ☐ Yes ☐ No

3. Have you **EVER** voted in any Federal, state, or local election in the United States? ☐ Yes ☐ No

4. Since becoming a Lawful Permanent Resident, have you **EVER** failed to file a required Federal, state, or local tax return? ☐ Yes ☐ No

5. Do you owe any Federal, state, or local taxes that are overdue? ☐ Yes ☐ No

6. Do you have any title of nobility in any foreign country? ☐ Yes ☐ No

7. Have you ever been declared legally incompetent or been confined to a mental institution within the last 5 years? ☐ Yes ☐ No

B. Affiliations

8. a. Have you **EVER** been a member of or associated with any organization, association, fund, foundation, party, club, society, or similar group in the United States or in any other place? ☐ Yes ☐ No

   b. If you answered "Yes," list the name of each group below. If you need more space, attach the names of the other group(s) on a separate sheet of paper.

Name of Group	Name of Group
1.	6.
2.	7.
3.	8.
4.	9.
5.	10.

9. Have you **EVER** been a member of or in any way associated *(either directly or indirectly)* with:

   a. The Communist Party? ☐ Yes ☐ No

   b. Any other totalitarian party? ☐ Yes ☐ No

   c. A terrorist organization? ☐ Yes ☐ No

10. Have you **EVER** advocated *(either directly or indirectly)* the overthrow of any government by force or violence? ☐ Yes ☐ No

11. Have you **EVER** persecuted *(either directly or indirectly)* any person because of race, religion, national origin, membership in a particular social group, or political opinion? ☐ Yes ☐ No

12. Between March 23, 1933, and May 8, 1945, did you work for or associate in any way *(either directly or indirectly)* with:

   a. The Nazi government of Germany? ☐ Yes ☐ No

   b. Any government in any area (1) occupied by, (2) allied with, or (3) established with the help of the Nazi government of Germany? ☐ Yes ☐ No

   c. Any German, Nazi, or S.S. military unit, paramilitary unit, self-defense unit, vigilante unit, citizen unit, police unit, government agency or office, extermination camp, concentration camp, prisoner of war camp, prison, labor camp, or transit camp? ☐ Yes ☐ No

C. Continuous Residence

Since becoming a Lawful Permanent Resident of the United States:

13. Have you **EVER** called yourself a "nonresident" on a Federal, state, or local tax return? ☐ Yes ☐ No

14. Have you **EVER** failed to file a Federal, state, or local tax return because you considered yourself to be a "nonresident"? ☐ Yes ☐ No

Write your INS "A"- number here:

A __ __ __ __ __ __ __ __ __ __

D. Good Moral Character

For the purposes of this application, you must answer "Yes" to the following questions, if applicable, even if your records were sealed or otherwise cleared or if anyone, including a judge, law enforcement officer, or attorney, told you that you no longer have a record.

15. Have you **EVER** committed a crime or offense for which you were NOT arrested? ☐ Yes ☐ No

16. Have you **EVER** been arrested, cited, or detained by any law enforcement officer (including INS and military officers) for any reason? ☐ Yes ☐ No

17. Have you **EVER** been charged with committing any crime or offense? ☐ Yes ☐ No

18. Have you **EVER** been convicted of a crime or offense? ☐ Yes ☐ No

19. Have you **EVER** been placed in an alternative sentencing or a rehabilitative program (for example: diversion, deferred prosecution, withheld adjudication, deferred adjudication)? ☐ Yes ☐ No

20. Have you **EVER** received a suspended sentence, been placed on probation, or been paroled? ☐ Yes ☐ No

21. Have you **EVER** been in jail or prison? ☐ Yes ☐ No

If you answered "Yes" to any of questions 15 through 21, complete the following table. If you need more space, use a separate sheet of paper to give the same information.

Why were you arrested, cited, detained, or charged?	Date arrested, cited, detained, or charged *(Month/Day/Year)*	Where were you arrested, cited, detained or charged? *(City, State, Country)*	Outcome or disposition of the arrest, citation, detention or charge *(No charges filed, charges dismissed, jail, probation, etc.)*

Answer questions 22 through 33. If you answer "Yes" to any of these questions, attach (1) your written explanation why your answer was "Yes," and (2) any additional information or documentation that helps explain your answer.

22. Have you **EVER**:

    a. been a habitual drunkard? ☐ Yes ☐ No

    b. been a prostitute, or procured anyone for prostitution? ☐ Yes ☐ No

    c. sold or smuggled controlled substances, illegal drugs or narcotics? ☐ Yes ☐ No

    d. been married to more than one person at the same time? ☐ Yes ☐ No

    e. helped anyone enter or try to enter the United States illegally? ☐ Yes ☐ No

    f. gambled illegally or received income from illegal gambling? ☐ Yes ☐ No

    g. failed to support your dependents or to pay alimony? ☐ Yes ☐ No

23. Have you **EVER** given false or misleading information to any U.S. government official while applying for any immigration benefit or to prevent deportation, exclusion, or removal? ☐ Yes ☐ No

24. Have you **EVER** lied to any U.S. government official to gain entry or admission into the United States? ☐ Yes ☐ No

E. Removal, Exclusion, and Deportation Proceedings

25. Are removal, exclusion, rescission or deportation proceedings pending against you? ☐ Yes ☐ No

26. Have you **EVER** been removed, excluded, or deported from the United States? ☐ Yes ☐ No

27. Have you **EVER** been ordered to be removed, excluded, or deported from the United States? ☐ Yes ☐ No

28. Have you **EVER** applied for any kind of relief from removal, exclusion, or deportation? ☐ Yes ☐ No

F. Military Service

29. Have you **EVER** served in the U.S. Armed Forces? ☐ Yes ☐ No

30. Have you **EVER** left the United States to avoid being drafted into the U.S. Armed Forces? ☐ Yes ☐ No

31. Have you **EVER** applied for any kind of exemption from military service in the U.S. Armed Forces? ☐ Yes ☐ No

32. Have you **EVER** deserted from the U.S. Armed Forces? ☐ Yes ☐ No

G. Selective Service Registration

33. Are you a male who lived in the United States at any time between your 18th and 26th birthdays
in any status except as a lawful nonimmigrant? ☐ Yes ☐ No

If you answered "NO", go on to question 34.

If you answered "YES", provide the information below.

If you answered "YES", but you did NOT register with the Selective Service System and are still under 26 years of age, you
must register before you apply for naturalization, so that you can complete the information below:

Date Registered (Month/Day/Year) [_____] Selective Service Number [_ _ / _ _ _ _ _ _ _ /_]

If you answered "YES", but you did NOT register with the Selective Service and you are now 26 years old or older, attach a
statement explaining why you did not register.

H. Oath Requirements *(See Part 14 for the text of the oath)*

Answer questions 34 through 39. If you answer "No" to any of these questions, attach (1) your written explanation why the answer was
"No" and (2) any additional information or documentation that helps to explain your answer.

34. Do you support the Constitution and form of government of the United States? ☐ Yes ☐ No

35. Do you understand the full Oath of Allegiance to the United States? ☐ Yes ☐ No

36. Are you willing to take the full Oath of Allegiance to the United States? ☐ Yes ☐ No

37. If the law requires it, are you willing to bear arms on behalf of the United States? ☐ Yes ☐ No

38. If the law requires it, are you willing to perform noncombatant services in the U.S. Armed Forces? ☐ Yes ☐ No

39. If the law requires it, are you willing to perform work of national importance under civilian
direction? ☐ Yes ☐ No

Part 11. Your Signature

Write your INS "A"- number here:

A _ _ _ _ _ _ _ _ _ _

I certify, under penalty of perjury under the laws of the United States of America, that this application, and the evidence submitted with it, are all true and correct. I authorize the release of any information which INS needs to determine my eligibility for naturalization.

Your Signature

Date *(Month/Day/Year)*

_ _ / _ _ / _ _ _ _

Part 12. Signature of Person Who Prepared This Application for You *(if applicable)*

I declare under penalty of perjury that I prepared this application at the request of the above person. The answers provided are based on information of which I have personal knowledge and/or were provided to me by the above named person in response to the *exact questions* contained on this form.

Preparer's Printed Name

Preparer's Signature

Date *(Month/Day/Year)*

_ _ / _ _ / _ _ _ _

Preparer's Firm or Organization Name *(If applicable)*

Preparer's Daytime Phone Number

( )

Preparer's Address - Street Number and Name

City

State

ZIP Code

Do Not Complete Parts 13 and 14 Until an INS Officer Instructs You To Do So

Part 13. Signature at Interview

I swear (affirm) and certify under penalty of perjury under the laws of the United States of America that I know that the contents of this application for naturalization subscribed by me, including corrections numbered 1 through _____ and the evidence submitted by me numbered pages 1 through _____ , are true and correct to the best of my knowledge and belief.

Subscribed to and sworn to (affirmed) before me

Officer's Printed Name or Stamp

Date *(Month/Day/Year)*

Complete Signature of Applicant

Officer's Signature

Part 14. Oath of Allegiance

If your application is approved, you will be scheduled for a public oath ceremony at which time you will be required to take the following oath of allegiance immediately prior to becoming a naturalized citizen. By signing , you acknowledge your willingness and ability to take this oath:

I hereby declare, on oath, that I absolutely and entirely renounce and abjure all allegiance and fidelity to any foreign prince, potentate, state, or sovereignty, of whom or which which I have heretofore been a subject or citizen;

that I will support and defend the Constitution and laws of the United States of America against all enemies, foreign and domestic;
that I will bear true faith and allegiance to the same;
that I will bear arms on behalf of the United States when required by the law;
that I will perform noncombatant service in the Armed Forces of the United States when required by the law;
that I will perform work of national importance under civilian direction when required by the law; and
that I take this obligation freely, without any mental reservation or purpose of evasion; so help me God.

Printed Name of Applicant

Complete Signature of Applicant

U.S. Department of Justice
Immigration and Naturalization Service

Application for Replacement
Naturalization/Citizenship Document

START HERE - Please type or print

Part 1. Information about you.

Family Name	Given Name	Middle Name

Address - In care of:

Street # and Name		Apt #

City or town	State or Province

Country	Zip or Postal Code

Date of Birth *(Month/Day/Year)*	Country of Birth

Certificate #	A #

Part 2. Type of application.

1. I hereby apply for: (check one)

a. ☐ a new Certificate of Citizenship
b. ☐ a new Certificate of Naturalization
c. ☐ a new Certificate of Repatriation
d. ☐ a new Declaration of Intention
e. ☐ a special Certificate of Naturalization to obtain recognition of my U.S. citizenship by a foreign country

2. Basis for application: (If you checked other than "e" in Part 1, check one)

a. ☐ my certificate is/was lost, stolen or destroyed (attach a copy of the certificate if you have one). Explain when, where and how.

_____

_____

b. ☐ my certificate is mutilated (attach the certificate)
c. ☐ my name has been changed (attach the certificate)
d. ☐ my certificate or declaration is incorrect (attach the documents)

Part 3. Processing information.

SEX ☐ Male ☐ Female	Height	Marital Status	☐ Single ☐ Married	☐ Widowed ☐ Divorced

My last certificate or declaration of Intention was issued to me by:

INS Office or Name of court	Date *(Month/Day/Year)*

Name in which the document was issued:

_____

Other names I have used (if none, so indicate):

_____

Since becoming a citizen, have you lost your citizenship in any manner?

☐ No   ☐ Yes (attach an explanation)

Part 4. Complete if applying for a new document because of name change.

Name changed to present name by: (check one)

☐ Marriage or Divorce on (month/day/year) _____ (attach a copy of marriage or divorce certificate)

☐ Court Decree (month/day/year) _____ (attach a copy of the court decree)

FOR INS USE ONLY

Returned	Receipt
Resubmitted	
Reloc Sent	
Reloc Rec'd	

☐ Applicant Interviewed

☐ Declaration of Intention verified by _____

☐ Citizenship verified by _____

Remarks

Action Block

To Be Completed by
***Attorney or Representative*, if any**
☐ Fill in box if G-28 is attached to represent the applicant

VOLAG#

ATTY State License #

Part 5. Complete if applying to correct your document.

If you are applying for a new certificate or declaration of intention because your current one is incorrect, explain why it is incorrect and attach copies of the documents supporting your request.

_____

_____

_____

_____

Part 6. Complete if applying for a special certificate of recognition as a citizen of the U.S. by the Government of the foreign country.

Name of Foreign Country _____

Information about official of the country who has requested this certificate (if known)

Name	Official Title

Government Agency _____

Address: Street # and Name		Room #
City	State Province	
Country		Zip Postal Code

Part 7. Signature. _Read the information on penalties in the instructions before completing this part. If you are going to file this application at an INS office in the U.S., sign below. If you are going to file it at a U.S. INS office overseas, sign in front of a U.S. INS or Consular Official._

I certify, or if outside the United States, I swear or affirm, under penalty of perjury under the laws of the United States of America, that this application and the evidence submitted with it is all true and correct. I authorize the release of any information from my records which the Immigration and Naturalization Service needs to determine eligibility for the benefit I am seeking.

Signature	Date

Signature of INS or Consular Official	Print Name	Date

Please Note: _If you do not completely fill out this form, or fail to submit required documents listed in the instructions, you may not be found eligible for a certificate and this application may be denied._

Part 8. Signature of person preparing form, if other than above. (sign below)

I declare that I prepared this application at the request of the above person and it is based on all information of which I have knowledge.

Signature	Print Your Name	Date

Firm Name and Address

OMB NO. 1115-0018; Expires 7/31/05

U.S. Department of Justice
Immigration and Naturalization Service

Application for Citizenship

Print clearly or type your answers using CAPITAL letters. Failure to print clearly may delay your application. Use black or blue Ink.

Part 1. Information About You *(Provide information about yourself, if you are a person applying for the Certificate of Citizenship. If you are a U.S. citizen parent applying for a Certificate of Citizenship for your minor child, **provide information about your child**).*

If Your Child has an INS "A" Number, Write it Here:

A_____ - _____ - _____

A. Current legal name

Family Name *(Last Name)*

Given Name *(First Name)*   Full Middle Name *(If Applicable)*

B. Name <u>exactly</u> as it appears on your Permanent Resident Card *(If Applicable).*

Family Name *(Last Name)*

Given Name *(First Name)*   Full Middle Name *(If Applicable)*

C. Other names used since birth

Family Name *(Last Name)*	Given Name *(First Name)*	Middle Name *(If Applicable)*

D. Social Security Number *(If Applicable)*

E. Date of Birth *(Month/Day/Year)*

F. Country of Birth

G. Country of Prior Nationality

H. Gender

Male ☐   Female ☐

I. Height

FOR INS USE ONLY

Bar Code	Date Stamp

Remarks

Action

Part 2. Information About Your Eligibility *(Check only one).*

A. I am claiming United States citizenship through:

☐ A United States citizen father or a United States citizen mother.

☐ Both United States citizen parents.

☐ A United States citizen adoptive parent(s).

☐ An alien parent(s) who naturalized.

B. ☐ **I am a United States citizen parent applying for a certificate of citizenship on behalf of my minor (under 18 years) BIOLOGICAL child.**

C. ☐ **I am a United States citizen parent applying for a certificate of citizenship on behalf of my minor (less than 18 years) ADOPTED child.**

D. ☐ **Other** *(Please explain fully)* _____

_____

_____

Additional Information About You *(Provide additional information about yourself, if you are the person applying for the Certificate of Citizenship. If you are a U.S. citizen parent applying for a Certificate of Citizenship for your minor child, **provide the additional information about your minor child**).*

A. **Home Address** - Street Number and Name *(Do NOT Write a P.O. Box in This Space)*   Apartment Number

City	County	State	Country	Zip Code

B. **Mailing Address** - Street Number and Name *(If Different From Home Address)*   Apartment Number

City	County	State or Province	Country	Zip Code

C. **Daytime Phone Number** *(If Any)*   Evening Phone Number *(If Any)*   E-Mail Address *(If Any)*

( )   ( )

D. **Marital Status**

☐ Single, Never Married   ☐ Married   ☐ Divorced   ☐ Widowed

☐ Marriage Annulled or Other *(Explain)* _____

E. **Information about entry into the United States and current immigration status**

1. I arrived in the following manner:

   Port of Entry *(City/State)*   Date of Entry *(Month/Day/Year)*

   _____   ____ / ____ / ____

   Exact Name Used at Time of Entry:

   _____

2. I used the following travel document to enter:

   ☐ Passport

   Passport Number   Country Issuing Passport   Date Passport Issued *(Month/Day/Year)*

   _____   _____   ____ / ____ / ____

   ☐ Other *(Please Specify Name of Document and Dates of Issuance)* _____

3. I entered as:

   ☐ An immigrant (lawful permanent resident) using an immigrant visa

   ☐ A nonimmigrant

   ☐ A refugee

   ☐ Other *(Explain)*

4. I obtained lawful permanent resident status through adjustment of status *(If Applicable)*:

   Date You Became a Permanent Resident *(Month/Day/Year)*   INS Office Where Granted Adjustment of Status

   _____   _____

F. **Have you previously applied for a certificate of citizenship or United States passport?**   ☐ No   ☐ Yes *(Attach Explanation)*

G. **Were you adopted?** ☐ No   ☐ Yes *(Please complete the following information)*:

Date of Adoption *(Month/Day/Year)*

Place of Final Adoption *(City/State or Country)*

Date Legal Custody Began *(Month/Day/Year)*

Date Physical Custody Began *(Month/Day/Year)*

H. **Did you have to be re-adopted in the United States?**   ☐ No   ☐ Yes *(Please complete the following information):*

Date of Final Adoption *(Month/Day/Year)*

Place of Final Adoption *(City/State)*

Date Legal Custody Began *(Month/Day/Year)*

Date Physical Custody Began *(Month/Day/Year)*

I. **Were your parents married to each other when you were born (or adopted)?**   ☐ No   ☐ Yes

J. **Have you been absent from the United States since you first arrived?**   ☐ No   ☐ Yes

(Only for persons born before October 10, 1952 who are claiming United States citizenship at time of birth, otherwise, please do not complete this section.)

If yes, please complete the following information about all absences, beginning with your most recent trip. If you need more space, use a separate sheet of paper.

Date You Left the United States *(Month/Day/Year)*	Date You Returned to the United States *(Month/Day/Year)*	Place of Entry Upon Return to United States

Part 4. Information About United States Citizen Father (or Adoptive Father) - *(Complete this section if you are claiming citizenship through a United States citizen father. If you are a United States citizen father applying for a Certificate of Citizenship on behalf of your minor biological or adopted child, provide information about YOURSELF below).*

A. **Current legal name of United States citizen father.**

Family Name *(Last Name)*

Given Name *(First Name)*

Full Middle Name *(If Applicable)*

B. **Date of Birth** *(Month/Day/Year)*   C. **Country of Birth**

D. **Home Address** - Street Number and Name

Apartment Number

City

County

State or Province

Country

Zip Code

Part 4. **Information About United States Citizen Father (or Adoptive Father)** - *(Complete this section if you are claiming citizenship through a United States citizen father. If you are a United States citizen father applying for a Certificate of Citizenship on behalf of your minor biological or adopted child, provide information about YOURSELF below).* **Continued**

F. **United States citizen by:**

☐ Birth in the United States

☐ Naturalization

Date of Naturalization *(Month/Day/Year)*

Place of Naturalization *(Name of Court & City/State or INS Office Location)*

Certificate of Naturalization Number

Former "A" Number *(If Known)*

☐ Through birth abroad to United States citizen parent(s)

☐ Acquired after birth through naturalization of alien parent(s)

G. **Has your father ever lost United States citizenship or taken any action that would cause loss of United States citizenship?**

☐ No   ☐ Yes *(Please Provide Full Explanation)*

H. **Dates of Residence and/or Physical Presence in the United States** *(Complete this only if you are an applicant claiming United States citizenship at time of birth abroad)*

Provide the dates your U.S. citizen father resided in or was physically present in the United States. If you need more space, use a separate sheet of paper.

From *(Month/Day/Year)*	**To** *(Month/Day/Year)*

H. **Marital History**

1. How many times has your U.S. citizen father been married (including annulled marriages)?

2. Information about U.S. citizen father's **current spouse:**

Family Name *(Last Name)*

Given Name *(First Name)*

Full Middle Name *(If Applicable)*

Date of Birth *(Month/Day/Year)*

Country of Birth

Country of Nationality

Home Address - Street Number and Name

Apartment Number

City

County

State or Province

Country

Zip Code

Date of Marriage *(Month/Day/Year)*

Place of Marriage *(City/State or Country)*

Spouse's Immigration Status:

☐ United States Citizen   ☐ Lawful Permanent Resident   ☐ Other *(Explain)*

3. Is your U.S. citizen father's current spouse also your mother?   ☐ No   ☐ Yes

Part 5. Information About Your United States Citizen Mother (or Adoptive Mother) - *(Complete this section if you are claiming citizenship through a United States citizen mother (or adoptive mother). If you are a United States citizen mother applying for a Certificate of Citizenship on behalf of your minor biological or adopted child, provide information about YOURSELF below).*

A. **Current legal name of United States citizen mother.**

Family Name *(Last Name)*

Given Name *(First Name)*

Full Middle Name *(If Applicable)*

B. **Date of Birth (Month/Day/Year)**

C. **Country of Birth**

D. **Country of Nationality**

E. **Home Address - Street Number and Name (If Deceased, so State & Enter Date of Death)**

Apartment Number

City

County

State or Province

Country

Zip Code

F. **United States citizen by:**

☐ Birth in the United States

☐ Naturalization

Date of Naturalization *(Month/Day/Year)*

Place of Naturalization *(Name of Court & City/State or INS Office Location)*

Certificate of Naturalization Number

Former "A" Number *(If Known)*

☐ Through birth abroad to United States citizen parent(s)

☐ Acquired after birth through naturalization of alien parent(s)

G. **Has your mother ever lost United States citizenship or taken any action that would cause loss of United States citizenship?**

☐ No   ☐ Yes *(Please Provide Full Explanation)*

H. **Dates of Residence and/or Physical Presence in the United States** *(Complete this only if you are an applicant claiming United States citizenship at time of birth abroad)*

Provide the dates your U.S. citizen mother resided in or was physically present in the United States. If you need more space, use a separate sheet of paper.

From *(Month/Day/Year)*	To *(Month/Day/Year)*

I. **Marital History**

1. How many times has your U.S. citizen mother been married (including annulled marriages)?

2. Information about U.S. citizen mother's **current spouse:**

Family Name *(Last Name)*

Given Name *(First Name)*

Full Middle Name *(If Applicable)*

Date of Birth *(Month/Day/Year)*

Country of Birth

Country of Nationality

Part 5. **Information About Your United States Citizen Mother (or Adoptive Mother)** - *(Complete this section if you are claiming citizenship through a United States citizen mother (or adoptive mother). If you are a United States citizen mother applying for a Certificate of Citizenship on behalf of your minor biological or adopted child, provide information about YOURSELF below).* - **Continued**

Home Address - Street Number and Name

Apartment Number

City	County	State or Province	Country	Zip Code

Date of Marriage *(Month/Day/Year)*

Place of Marriage *(City/State or Country)*

Spouse's Immigration Status:

☐ United States Citizen ☐ Lawful Permanent Resident ☐ Other *(Explain)* _____

3. Is your U.S. citizen mother's current spouse also your father? ☐ No ☐ Yes

Part 6. **Information About Military Service of United States Citizen Parent(s)** - *(Complete this only if you are an applicant claiming United States citizenship at time of birth abroad)*

Has your United States citizen parent(s) served in the armed forces? ☐ No ☐ Yes

☐ United States Citizen Father ☐ United States Citizen Mother

Dates of Service *(Month/Day/Year to Month/Day/Year)* If time of service fulfills any of required physical presence, submit evidence of service.

TO

Discharge ☐ Honorable ☐ Other than Honorable ☐ Dishonorable

Part 7. Signature.

I certify, under penalty of perjury under the laws of the United States, that this application, and the evidence submitted with it, is all true and correct. I authorize the release of any information from my records, or my minor child's records, that the INS needs to determine eligibility for the benefit I am seeking.

Applicant's Signature

Print Name

Date *(Month/Day/Year)*

Part 8. Signature of Person Preparing This Form If Other Than Applicant

I declare that I prepared this application at the request of the above person. The answers provided are based on information of which I have personal knowledge and/or were provided to me by the above-named person in response to the questions contained on this form.

Preparer's Printed Name

Preparer's Signature

Name of Business/Organization *(If Applicable)*

Preparer's Daytime Phone Number

Date *(Month/Day/Year)*

Preparer's Address - Street Number and Name

City	County	State	Zip Code

DO NOT COMPLETE THE FOLLOWING PARTS UNLESS INS OFFICER INSTRUCTS YOU TO DO SO AT THE INTERVIEW

Part 8. Affidavit

I, the (applicant, parent, or legal guardian) _____ do swear or affirm, under penalty of perjury laws of the United States, that I know and understand the contents of this application signed by me, and the attached supplementary pages number (   ) to (   ) inclusive, that the same are true and correct to the best of my knowledge, and that corrections number (   ) to (   ) were made by me or at my request.

Signature of parent, guardian, or applicant

Date *(Month/Day/Year)*

Subscribed and sworn or affirmed before me upon examination of the applicant (parent, guardian) on _____ at
_____ .

Signature of Interviewing Officer

Title

Part 9. Officer Report and Recommendation on Application for Certificate of Citizenship

On the basis of the documents, records, and the testimony of persons examined, and the identification upon personal appearance of the underage beneficiary, I find that all the facts and conclusions set forth under oath in this application are _____ true and correct; that the applicant did _____ derive or acquire United States citizenship on _____ *(month/day/year)*, through *(mark "X" in appropriate section of law or, if section of law not reflected, insert applicable section of law in "Other" block)*: **section 301 of the INA___** ; **section 309 of the INA** ; **section 320 of the INA _____** ; **section 321 of the INA _____** ; **Other** _____

and that (s)he _____ *(has/has not)* been expatriated since that time, I recommend that this application be ———————— *(granted or denied)* and that _____ *(A or AA)* Certificate of Citizenship _____ be issued in the name of _____ .

District Adjudication Officer's Name and Title

District Adjudication Officer's Signature

I do _____ concur in recommendation of the application.

Date: _____
(Month/Day/Year)

District Director or Officer-in-Charge Signature

U.S. Department of Justice
Immigration and Naturalization Service

Application for Transmission of Citizenship Through a Grandparent

Part A. INSTRUCTIONS

This is a supplement for Forms N-600 and N-643. Attach the completed supplement *(Printed or typed in black or blue ink)* to your Form N-600 or Form 643 and take or mail the application to the appropriate INS office in the United States. *(See reverse for more instructions)*

Part B. INFORMATION ABOUT CHILD *(PRINT OR TYPE)*

Last Name	First Name	Middle Name	Date of Birth *(Month/Day/Year)*

As a United States citizen parent, I am applying for a certificate of citizenship for my child through his or her *(check appropriate box)*

☐ Grandfather   ☐ Grandmother

Part C. INFORMATION ABOUT GRANDFATHER *(PRINT OR TYPE)*

Grandfather's Last Name	First Name	Middle Name	Date of Birth *(Month/Day/Year)*

Place of Birth *(City/State/Country)*	He currently resides at *(Street Address/City/State/Country) (If Deceased, So State)*

He became a citizen of the United States by: ☐ Birth ☐ Naturalization ☐ Derivation On *(Month/Day/Year):* _____

In the *(Name of Court, City, State)* _____ , Certificate of Naturalization Number: _____

Or through his parent(s), and ☐ was ☐ was not issued a Certificate of Citizenship. If issued provide Number A or AA

_____ . His former Alien Registration Number was _____ . He ☐ has ☐ has not

lost United States citizenship. *(If citizenship lost, attach full explanation)* He resided in the United States from *(Year)* _____

to *(Year)* _____ ; from *(Year)* _____ to *(Year)* _____ ; from *(Year)* _____ to *(Year)* _____ .

Part D. INFORMATION ABOUT GRANDMOTHER *(PRINT OR TYPE)*

Grandmother's Last Name	First Name	Middle Name	Date of Birth *(Month/Day/Year)*

Place of Birth *(City/State/Country)*	She currently resides at *(Street Address/City/State/Country) (If Deceased, So State)*

She became a citizen of the United States ☐ Birth ☐ Naturalization ☐ Derivation On *(Month/Day/Year):* _____

In the *(Name of Court, City, State)* _____ , Certificate of Naturalization Number: _____

Or through her parent(s), and ☐ was ☐ was not issued a Certificate of Citizenship. If issued provide Number A or AA

_____ . Her former Alien Registration Number was _____ . She ☐ has ☐ has not

lost United States citizenship. *(If citizenship lost, attach full explanation)* She resided in the United States from *(Year)* _____

to *(Year)* _____ ; from *(Year)* _____ to *(Year)* _____ ; from *(Year)* _____ to *(Year)* _____ .

My child's grandparents were married to each other on _____ at _____
_____*(Month/Day/Year)*_____   _____*(City/State/County/Country)*_____

I certify, under penalty of perjury under the laws of the United States of America, that this application, and the evidence submitted with it, are all true and correct. I authorize the release of any information from my records which the Immigration and Naturalization Service needs to determine eligibility for the benefit I am seeking.

Signature	Print Your Name	Date

U.S. Department of Homeland Security
Bureau of Citizenship and Immigration Services

Application for Citizenship and Issuance of Certificate under Section 322

Print clearly or type your answers using CAPITAL letters. Failure to print clearly may delay your application. Use black or blue Ink.

Part 1. Information About Your Child *(Provide information about the child on whose behalf this application for citizenship and a Certificate of Citizenship is being filed.)*

A. Current legal name.

Family Name *(Last Name)*

Given Name *(First Name)*   Full Middle Name *(If Applicable)*

B. Name exactly as it appears on your Permanent Resident Card (If Applicable).

Family Name *(Last Name)*

Given Name *(First Name)*   Full Middle Name *(If Applicable)*

C. Other names used since birth.

Family Name *(Last Name)*	Given Name *(First Name)*	Middle Name *(If Applicable)*

D. Social Security Number *(If Applicable)*   **E. Date of Birth** *(Month/Day/Year)*

F. Country of Birth   **G. Country of Nationality**

H. Gender   **I. Height**
Male ☐   Female ☐

If Your Child has an "A" Number, Write it Here:

A_____ - _____ - _____

FOR BCIS USE ONLY

Bar Code	Date Stamp

Remarks

Action

Part 2. Information About the Child's Eligibility *(Check only one).*

This application is being filed on my behalf based on the fact that:

A. ☐ I am a BIOLOGICAL child (under 18 years) of a United States citizen parent who is applying for citizenship on my behalf.

B. ☐ I am an ADOPTED child (under 18 years) of a United States citizen parent who is applying for citizenship on my behalf.

C. ☐ I am a child (under 18 years) of a United States citizen parent who died during the five years preceding the filing of this application. A United States citizen grandparent or a United States citizen legal guardian is applying for citizenship on my behalf.

Part 3. Additional Information About the Child *(Provide information about the child on whose behalf this application for citizenship and a Certificate of Citizenship is being filed.)*

A. Home Address - Street Number and Name *(Do NOT Write a P.O. Box in This Space)*   Apartment Number

City   County

State or Province   Country   Zip Code

B. **Mailing Address** - Street Number and Name *(If Different From Home Address)* | Apartment Number

City | County | State or Province | Country | Zip Code

C. **Daytime Phone Number** *(If Any)* | Evening Phone Number *(If Any)* | E-Mail Address *(If Any)*

D. **Marital Status**

- [ ] Single, Never Married
- [ ] Married
- [ ] Divorced
- [ ] Widowed
- [ ] Marriage Annulled or Other *(Explain)* _____

E. **Information about entry into the United States and current immigration status**
*(Do **not** complete this section. The Adjudicator will complete it with you during the interview.)*

I arrived in the following manner:

Port of Entry *(City/State)* | Date of Entry *(Month/Day/Year)* | Current Immigration Status

Exact Name Used at Time of Entry:

F. **Do you know of any prior application for a certificate of citizenship or United States passport for this child?** [ ] No [ ] Yes

G. **Was the child adopted?** [ ] No [ ] Yes *(Please complete the following information):*

Date of Adoption *(Month/Day/Year)* | Date Legal Custody Began *(Month/Day/Year)* | Date Physical Custody Began *(Month/Day/Year)*

H. **Were the child's parents married to each other when the child was born (or adopted)?** [ ] No [ ] Yes

Part 4. Information About the child's U.S. Citizen Father or Mother (or Adoptive Father or Mother) - *(If you are a United States citizen father or mother applying for citizenship and a Certificate of Citizenship on behalf of your eligible child, provide information about YOURSELF below). If you are a U.S. citizen grandparent or legal guardian, provide information about the child's U.S. citizen PARENT in the sections noted.*

A. **Current legal name of United States citizen father or mother.**

Family Name *(Last Name)* | Given Name *(First Name)* | Full Middle Name *(If Applicable)*

B. **Date of Birth** *(Month/Day/Year)* | **C.** **Country of Birth**

D. **Home Address** - Street Number and Name | Apartment Number

City | County | State or Province | Country | Zip Code

Part 4. Information About the Child's U.S. Citizen Father or Mother (or Adoptive Father or Mother) - *(If you are a United States citizen father or mother applying for citizenship and a Certificate on behalf of your eligible child, provide information about YOURSELF below). If you are a U.S. citizen grandparent or legal guardian, provide information about the child's U.S. citizen PARENT in the sections noted.* **(Continued)**

E. United States citizen by:

☐ Birth in the United States

☐ Naturalization

Date of Naturalization *(Month/Day/Year)*

Place of Naturalization *(Name of Court & City/State or INS Office Location)*

Certificate of Naturalization Number

Former "A" Number *(If Known)*

☐ Through birth abroad to United States citizen parent(s)

☐ Acquired after birth through naturalization of alien parent(s)

F. Has the U.S. citizen father or mother ever lost United States citizenship or taken any action that would cause loss of United States citizenship?

☐ No   ☐ Yes *(Please Provide Full Explanation)*

G. Dates of Residence and/or Physical Presence in the United States

Provide the dates the U.S. citizen father or mother resided in or was physically present in the United States. If you need more space, use a separate sheet of paper.

From *(Month/Day/Year)*	**To** *(Month/Day/Year)*

H. Marital History

1. How many times has the U.S. citizen father or mother been married (including annulled marriages)?

2. Information about the U.S. citizen father or mother's **current spouse:**

Family Name *(Last Name)*

Given Name *(First Name)*

Full Middle Name *(If Applicable)*

Date of Birth *(Month/Day/Year)*

Country of Birth

Country of Nationality

Home Address - Street Number and Name

Apartment Number

City   County   State or Province   Country   Zip Code

Date of Marriage *(Month/Day/Year)*

Place of Marriage *(City/State or Country)*

Spouse's Immigration Status:

☐ United States Citizen   ☐ Lawful Permanent Resident   ☐ Other *(Explain)*

3. Is the person listed in question 2 above also your parent (biological or adoptive)?   ☐ No   ☐ Yes

Part 5. Information About the U.S. Citizen Grandfather or Grandmother - *(Complete this section **ONLY** if you are a U.S. citizen parent (or adoptive parent) grandparent or legal guardian applying for a Certificate of Citizenship for your biological or adopted child and the citizen parent **HAS NOT** been been physically present in the United States for 5 years, 2 years of which were after the age of 14. The information provided here should describe, the U.S. citizen grandfather or U.S. grandmother of the minor child.)*

A. **Current legal name of United States citizen grandfather or grandmother.**

Family Name *(Last Name)*

Given Name *(First Name)*

Full Middle Name *(If Applicable)*

B. **Date of Birth** *(Month/Day/Year)*

C. **Country of Birth**

D. **Home Address** - Street Number and Name

Apartment Number

City

County

State or Province

Country

Zip Code

E. **United States citizen by:**

☐ Birth in the United States

☐ Naturalization

Date of Naturalization *(Month/Day/Year)*

Place of Naturalization *(Name of Court & City/State or INS Office Location)*

Certificate of Naturalization Number

Former "A" Number *(If Known)*

☐ Through birth abroad to United States citizen parent(s)

☐ Acquired after birth through naturalization of alien parent(s)

F. **Has your father or mother *(your child's grandfather or grandmother)* ever lost United States citizenship or taken any action that would cause loss of United States citizenship?**

☐ No   ☐ Yes *(Please Provide Full Explanation)* _____

_____

_____

G. **Dates of Residence and/or Physical Presence in the United States**

Provide the dates that your U.S. citizen father or mother *(your child's grandfather or grandmother)* lived in the United States. If you need more space, use a separate sheet of paper.

From (Month/Day/Year)	**To** (Month/Day/Year)

Part 6. Legal Guardian *(Complete this part only for applications filed by a legal guardian in lieu of a deceased United States citizen parent.)*

A. **Current legal name of United States citizen Legal Guardian.**

Family Name *(Last Name)*

Given Name *(First Name)*

Full Middle Name *(If Applicable)*

B. **Date of Birth** *(Month/Day/Year)*

C. **Country of Birth**

D. **Home Address** - Street Number and Name

Apartment Number

City

County

State or Province

Country

Zip Code

E. **United States citizen by:**

☐ Birth in the United States

☐ Naturalization

Date of Naturalization *(Month/Day/Year)*

Place of Naturalization *(Name of Court & City/State or INS Office Location)*

Certificate of Naturalization Number

Former "A" Number *(If Known)*

☐ Through birth abroad to United States citizen parent(s)

☐ Acquired after birth through naturalization of alien parent(s)

F. **Date of Legal Guardianship**

G. **Name of Authority that Granted Legal Guardianship**

H. **Address of Authority that Granted Legal Guardianship**

Part 7. Your Signature

I certify, under penalty of perjury under the laws of the United States, that this application, and the evidence submitted with it, is all true and correct. I authorize the release of any information from my records that the BCIS needs to determine eligibility for the benefit I am seeking.

Applicant's Signature

Print Name

Date *(Month/Day/Year)*

Part 8. Signature of Person Preparing This Form If Other Than Above

I declare that I prepared this application at the request of the above person. The answers provided are based on information of which I have personal knowledge and/or were provided to me by the above-named person in response to the questions contained on this form.

Part 8. Signature of Person Preparing This Form If Other Than Above - *Continued*

Preparer's Printed Name

Preparer's Signature

Name of Business/Organization *(If Applicable)*

Preparer's Daytime Phone Number

Date *(Month/Day/Year)*

Preparer's Address - Street Number and Name

City

County

State

Zip Code

DO NOT COMPLETE THE FOLLOWING PARTS UNLESS BCIS OFFICER INSTRUCTS YOU TO DO SO AT THE INTERVIEW

Part 9. Affidavit

I, the parent/grandparent/legal guardian, _____ do swear or affirm, under penalty of perjury laws of the United States, that I know and understand the contents of this application signed by me, and the attached supplementary pages number (   ) to (   ) inclusive, that the same are true and correct to the best of my knowledge, and that corrections number (   ) to (   ) were made by me or at my request.

Signature of U.S. citizen parent/grandparent/legal guardian

Date *(Month/Day/Year)*

Subscribed and sworn or affirmed before me upon examination of the applicant and U.S. citizen parent/grandparent/legal guardian on _____ at _____ .

Signature of Interviewing Officer

Title

Part 10. Officer Report and Recommendation

On the basis of the documents, records, and the testimony of persons examined, and the identification upon personal appearance of the underage beneficiary, I find that all the facts and conclusions set forth under oath in this application are _____ true and correct; that the applicant is eligible to be naturalized on _____ *(month/day/year)*, through **section 322 of the INA** _____ ; **section 322 of the INA (grandparent residence)** _____ **section 322 of the INA (grandparent or legal guardian application)** _____ .

and I recommend that this application be _____ *(granted or denied)* and that a Certificate of Citizenship be issued in the name of _____ .

District Adjudications Officer's Name and Title

District Adjudications Officer's Signature

I do _____ concur in recommendation of the application.

Date: _____
(Month/Day/Year)

District Director or Officer-in-Charge Signature:

Part I. THIS SECTION TO BE COMPLETED BY APPLICANT (please print or type information)

Last Name	First Name	Middle Name	Alien Number
Address			Social Security Number
City		State	ZIP Code
Telephone Number		Date of Birth	Gender

I, _____ , authorize _____
    (Applicant's Name)   *(Licensed medical doctor, doctor of osteopathy, or clinical psychologist)*

to release all relevant physical and mental health information related to my medical status to the INS for the purpose of applying for an exception from the English language and U.S. civics testing requirements for naturalization. I certify under penalty of perjury, pursuant to Title 28 U.S.C. Section 1746, that the information on the form and any evidence submitted with it are all true and correct. I am aware that the knowing placement of false information on the Form N-648 and related documents may also subject me to civil penalties under 8 U.S.C. 1324c.

Signature _____ Date_____

Part II. THIS SECTION TO BE COMPLETED BY A LICENSED MEDICAL DOCTOR, DOCTOR OF OSTEOPATHY, OR LICENSED CLINICAL PSYCHOLOGIST (see Instructions)

Purpose of this Form: The individual named above is applying to become a United States citizen. Applicants for naturalization are required to learn and/or demonstrate knowledge of the English language, including an ability to read, write, and speak words in ordinary usage in the English language, as well as knowledge and understanding of the fundamentals of the history, and of the principles and form of government of the United States. Individuals who are unable, because of a disability, to learn and/or demostrate this required knowledge may apply for a waiver. The purpose of this form is to help determine whether your patient is eligible for this waiver.

Definition of Disability: An individual is eligible for this waiver if he or she is *unable* to learn and/or demonstrate knowledge of English and/or U.S. history and civics because of a physical or mental impairment (or combination of impairments). These impairments must result from anatomical, physiological, or psychological abnormalities, which can be shown by medically acceptable clinical and laboratory diagnostic techniques. The impairment(s) must result in functioning so impaired as to render an individual *unable* to demonstrate the *required* knowledge.

NOTE: This *definition of disability* is *different* from the definition used by the Social Security Administration, Department of Veterans Affairs, or worker's compensation programs. If your responses do not address the applicant's disability for the purposes of naturalization, we will require the applicant to submit a revised or second form with the appropriate information.

*Provide **all** of the following required information, using common terminology that a person without medical training can understand, with no abbreviations. Type or print clearly. Illegible and incomplete forms will be returned. If you need additional space to provide your answers, attach additional pages.*

NATURE AND DURATION OF IMPAIRMENT(S)

1.   (a) Based on your examination of the applicant, the applicant's symptoms, previous medical records, clinical findings, or tests, does the applicant have any impairment(s) that affect his or her ability to learn and/or demonstrate knowledge?

     ☐ Yes   ☐ No   **Note:** If *you answer "No", applicant is ineligible for a waiver; please continue with Part II. 6.*

  (b) Has the applicant's impairment(s) lasted or do you expect it to last 12 months or longer?

     ☐ Yes   ☐ No   **Note:** If *you answer "No", applicant is ineligible for a waiver; please continue with Part II. 6.*

  (c) Is the applicant's impairment(s) the direct effect of the illegal use of drugs?

     ☐ Yes   ☐ No   **Note:** If *you answer "Yes", applicant is ineligible for a waiver; please continue with Part II. 6.*

Applicant Name	Alien Registration Number
	A-

DIAGNOSIS OF IMPAIRMENT(S)

2. (a) Provide your clinical diagnosis of the applicant's impairment(s) *and* describe the impairment(s) in terms a person without medical training can understand *(see Instructions for examples)*.

(b) Provide the relevant DSM-IV code(s) for each mental impairment that you described above. If a DSM-IV code does not exist, write "N/A."

CONNECTION BETWEEN IMPAIRMENT(S) AND INABILITY TO LEARN/DEMONSTRATE KNOWLEDGE

The law requires that applicants for citizenship demonstrate (1) an understanding of the English language, including the *ability* to read, and speak simple words and phrases in ordinary usage; and (2) a knowledge and understanding of the fundamentals of U.S. history and civics. An applicant's *difficulty* in fulfiling the requirements is not sufficient to support a waiver. In addition, *illiteracy* in the applicant's native language is *not* sufficient, by itself, to support a finding of inability to learn and/or demonstrate knowledge.

3. Based on your examination of the applicant, provide *detailed* information on the connection between the impairment(s) and the applicant's inability to learn and/or demonstrate knowledge of English and/or U.S. history and civics *(see Instructions for examples)*.

Note: *This description should address the severity of the effects of the impairment(s) including the specific limitations that affect the applicant's ability to learn and/or demonstrate knowledge.*

Applicant Name	Alien Registration Number A-

PROFESSIONAL CERTIFIED OPINION

The law requires that in order to be eligible for the disability exception, the applicant must be *unable* to fulfill the requirements for English proficiency and/or knowledge of U.S. history and civics. An applicant's *difficulty* in fulfilling the requirements is not sufficient to support a waiver. In addition, *illiteracy* in the applicant's native language is *not* sufficient, by itself, to support a finding of inability to learn and/or demonstrate knowledge.

4. English Requirement

(a) In your professional opinion, has the impairment(s) described above affected the applicant's functioning to such a degree that he or she *is unable* to learn and/or demonstrate an ability to speak, read, or write English?

☐ Yes   ☐ No

(b) If *Yes*, which of the following is the applicant unable to learn and/or demonstrate? *(Check all that apply)*

☐ Speaking   ☐ Reading   ☐ Writing

5. U.S. History and Civics Requirement

In your professional opinion, has the impairment(s) described above affected the applicant's functioning to such a degree that he or she is *unable* to learn and/or demonstrate knowledge of U.S. history and civics, even in a language the applicant understands?

☐ Yes   ☐ No

BACKGROUND INFORMATION

6. Date of your most recent examination of the applicant (mm/dd/yyyy), _____

7. Is this your first examination of the individual?

☐ Yes   If *Yes*, from whom does the applicant usually receive medical care (i.e., name of doctor/clinic; if the applicant does not have an ongoing source of medical care, please write "N/A")

_____

_____

☐ No   If *No*, for how long and for what conditions have you been treating the applicant? (If the conditions are the same as in Part II. 2, specify the length of time and write "Conditions -- Same as Part II. 2")

_____

_____

8. What is the nature of your medical practice? (e.g., family/general practice, internal medicine, psychiatry, cardiology)

_____

I certify, under penalty of perjury under the laws of the United States of America, that the information on the form and any evidence submitted with it are all true and correct. Upon consent of the applicant, I agree to release this applicant's relevant medical records upon request from the U.S. Immigration and Naturalization Service. I am aware that the knowing placement of false information on the Form N-648 and related documents may also subject me to criminal penalites under Title 18, U.S.C. 1546 and civil penalties under 8 U.S.C. Section 1324c.

Signature _____ **Date** _____

Type or print the following information:

Last Name	First Name	Middle Name
Business Address	City, State, ZIP Code	Telephone
License Number		Licensing State

Index

A

G

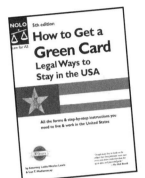
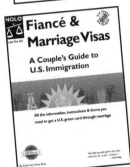
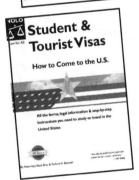

Remember:

Little publishers have big ears.
We really listen to you.

Take 2 Minutes & Give Us Your 2 cents

Your comments make a big difference in the development and revision of Nolo books and software. Please take a few minutes and register your Nolo product—and your comments—with us. Not only will your input make a difference, you'll receive special offers available only to registered owners of Nolo products on our newest books and software. Register now by:

PHONE
1-800-728-3555

FAX
1-800-645-0895

EMAIL
cs@nolo.com

or **MAIL** us
this registration card

fold here

Registration Card

NAME _____ DATE _____

ADDRESS _____

_____

CITY _____ STATE _____ ZIP _____

PHONE _____ E-MAIL _____

WHERE DID YOU HEAR ABOUT THIS PRODUCT? _____

WHERE DID YOU PURCHASE THIS PRODUCT? _____

DID YOU CONSULT A LAWYER? (PLEASE CIRCLE ONE)   YES   NO   NOT APPLICABLE

DID YOU FIND THIS BOOK HELPFUL?   (VERY)   5   4   3   2   1   (NOT AT ALL)

COMMENTS _____

_____

_____

WAS IT EASY TO USE?   (VERY EASY)   5   4   3   2   1   (VERY DIFFICULT)

We occasionally make our mailing list available to carefully selected companies whose products may be of interest to you.

❑ If you do not wish to receive mailings from these companies, please check this box.

❑ You can quote me in future Nolo promotional materials.
Daytime phone number _____.

IMEZ 11.0

Nolo in the NEWS

"Nolo helps lay people perform legal tasks without the aid—or fees—of lawyers."

—USA TODAY

Nolo books are ..."*written in plain language, free of legal mumbo jumbo, and spiced with witty personal observations.*"

—ASSOCIATED PRESS

"*...Nolo publications...guide people simply through the how, when, where and why of law.*"

—WASHINGTON POST

"*Increasingly, people who are not lawyers are performing tasks usually regarded as legal work... And consumers, using books like Nolo's, do routine legal work themselves.*"

—NEW YORK TIMES

"*...All of [Nolo's] books are easy-to-understand, are updated regularly, provide pull-out forms...and are often quite moving in their sense of compassion for the struggles of the lay reader.*"

—SAN FRANCISCO CHRONICLE

- - - - - - - - - - - - - - - - - - - fold here -

Place
stamp here

Nolo
950 Parker Street
Berkeley, CA 94710-9867

Attn: IMEZ 11.0